Studies in Economic Ethics and Philosophy

Series Editor
Peter Koslowski

Editorial Board
F. Neil Brady
James M. Buchanan
Richard De George
Jon Elster
Amitai Etzioni
Gérard Gäfgen
Serge-Christophe Kolm
Michael S. McPherson
Yuichi Shionoya
Philippe Van Parijs

Springer
*Berlin
Heidelberg
New York
Barcelona
Hong Kong
London
Milan
Paris
Singapore
Tokyo*

Peter Koslowski (Ed.)

The Theory of Capitalism in the German Economic Tradition

Historism, Ordo-Liberalism,
Critical Theory, Solidarism

With 2 Tables

Springer

Prof. Dr. Dr. h.c. Peter Koslowski
Centre for Ethical Economy and Business Culture
The Hannover Institute of Philosophical Research
Gerberstr. 26
D-30169 Hannover
Germany
E-mail: P. Koslowski@fiph.uni-hannover.de

Printed with the support of the Fritz Thyssen Stiftung Köln

ISBN 3-540-66674-5 Springer-Verlag Berlin Heidelberg New York

Cataloging-in-Publication Data applied for
Die Deutsche Bibliothek – CIP-Einheitsaufnahme
The theory of capitalism in the German economic tradition: historism, ordo-liberalism, critical theory, solidarism / Peter Koslowski (ed.). – Berlin; Heidelberg; New York; Barcelona; Hong Kong; London; Milan; Paris; Singapore; Tokyo: Springer, 2000
(Studies in economic ethics and philosophy)
ISBN 3-540-66674-5

This work is subject to copyright. All rights are reserved, whether the whole or part of the material is concerned, specifically the rights of translation, reprinting, reuse of illustrations, recitation, broadcasting, reproduction on microfilm or in any other way, and storage in data banks. Duplication of this publication or parts thereof is permitted only under the provisions of the German Copyright Law of September 9, 1965, in its current version, and permission for use must always be obtained from Springer-Verlag. Violations are liable for prosecution under the German Copyright Law.

© Springer-Verlag Berlin · Heidelberg 2000
Printed in Germany

The use of general descriptive names, registered names, trademarks, etc. in this publication does not imply, even in the absence of a specific statement, that such names are exempt from the relevant protective laws and regulations and therefore free for general use.

Hardcover Design: Erich Kirchner, Heidelberg

SPIN 10749038   42/2202-5 4 3 2 1 0 – Printed on acid-free paper

Preface

The theory of capitalism and of the economic order is the central topic of the German economic tradition in the 20th century. Capitalism has not only been the topic for Marxist economics and for the Frankfurt School but also for the Historical School and for the postmarxist theory of capitalism in Ordo- and Neo-Liberalism as well as in Solidarism. The question of the foundations of the economic order of the market economy and of capitalism as well as the problem whether a third path between capitalism and socialism is possible occupied this tradition from the Historical School to Ordo-Liberalism and the theory of the social market economy.

The theory of capitalism and of the social market economy as well as the critique and reform developed in this theoretical tradition is important for the theory of economic systems as well as for today's problems of the economic order. Its relevance for the present world economy is visible in the discussions whether there exist different models of capitalism and whether they can be described as the Anglo-American and as the Rhenish model of capitalism influenced by the thought of the German economic tradition. Michel Albert, the author of this classification, gave the key-word in his book *Capitalism against Capitalism*. The papers of this book can help to clarify this debate by giving a first hand introduction to some of the main economic thinkers of capitalism.

With this third volume, the project "Economics and Ethics in the Historical School. Achievements and Present Relevance" completes its series of books on the Historical School of Economics. The first two volumes are *The Theory of Ethical Economy in the Historical School. Wilhelm Roscher, Lorenz von Stein, Gustav Schmoller, Wilhelm Dilthey and Contemporary Theory* (1995, reprinted 1997) and *Methodology of the Social Sciences, Ethics, and Economics in the Newer Historical School. From Max Weber and Rickert to Sombart and Rothacker* (1997). They are complemented by the book *Modern Economic Ethics and Business Ethics* (1999), a comparative study of contemporary approaches to economic ethics and business ethics in Germany and Europe on the one hand and the United States on the other hand. All the three volumes mentioned have been published in the

PREFACE

series "Studies in Economic Ethics and Philosophy", Berlin, New York, Tokyo (Springer-Verlag), and edited by Peter Koslowski.

The project "Economics and Ethics in the Historical School. Achievements and Present Relevance" is organised by the Centre for Ethical Economy and Business Culture - Centrum für Ethische Ökonomie und Wirtschaftskultur, The Hannover Institute of Philosophical Research - Forschungsinstitut für Philosophie Hannover, Hannover, Germany, and supported by the Fritz Thyssen Stiftung Köln, Germany.

With this completion of the studies on the Historical School of Economics and of the German economic tradition, the project will be extended to "The Historical School. Economic Ethics, Theory of History, Law, and Political Science in the German Human Sciences Tradition". The project will widen its scope in the years 2000 and 2001 by the philosophy and theory of history, by the theory of law, and by the theory of politics and the state.

The volume at hand publishes the proceedings of the conference "Economic Ethics and the Theory of Capitalism in the German Tradition of Economics: Historism, Ordo-Liberalism, Critical Theory, Solidarism", held at Marienrode near Hannover, Germany, on 29 October to 1 November 1997. The conference formed the "Fifth Annual SEEP-Conference on Economic Ethics and Philosophy 1997".

A special word of gratitude is due the Fritz Thyssen Stiftung whose financial support made the conference and the printing of this book possible.

Hannover, October 1999   Peter Koslowski

Contents

Preface V

Part One

Theory of Capitalism, Historism, and Economics in Joseph Schumpeter, Emil Lederer, and Franz Oppenheimer

Chapter 1

Joseph Schumpeter and the German Historical School
YUICHI SHIONOYA 3

Discussion Summary 24

Chapter 2

Emil Lederer (1882-1939): Economical and Sociological Analyst and Critic of Capitalist Development
HARALD HAGEMANN 26

Discussion Summary 52

Chapter 3

Franz Oppenheimer's Theory of Capitalism and of a Third Path
DIETER HASELBACH 54

CONTENTS

Discussion Summary 87

Part Two

The Theory of Capitalism, the Historical School, and the Theory of the Social Market Economy in Ordo-Liberalism and Neo-Liberalism: Walter Eucken, Alfred Müller-Armack, Franz Böhm, Friedrich Hayek

Chapter 4

Walter Eucken (1891-1950) and the Historical School
HELGE PEUKERT 93

Discussion Summary 146

Chapter 5

Franz Böhm and the Theory of the Private Law Society
KNUT WOLFGANG NÖRR 148

Discussion Summary 189

Chapter 6

Alfred Müller-Armack - Economic Policy Maker and Sociologist of Religion
CHRISTIAN WATRIN 192

Discussion Summary 221

CONTENTS

Chapter 7

The Market Economy and the State. Hayekian and Ordoliberal Conceptions
MANFRED E. STREIT and MICHAEL WOHLGEMUTH 224

Discussion Summary 270

Part Three

The Critique of Capitalism in Hilferding and in the Frankfurt School

Chapter 8

Rudolf Hilferding's Theory of Finance Capitalism and Today's World Financial Markets
JONAS ZONINSEIN 275

Discussion Summary 305

Chapter 9

The Early Frankfurt School Critique of Capitalism: Critical Theory Between Pollock's "State Capitalism" and the Critique of Instrumental Reason
HARRY F. DAHMS 309

Discussion Summary 362

CONTENTS

Part Four

The Theory and Critique of Capitalism and Economic Ethics in Solidarism (Christian Social Thought): Heinrich Pesch and Gustav Gundlach

Chapter 10

Solidarism, Capitalism, and Economic Ethics in Heinrich Pesch
PETER KOSLOWSKI 371

Discussion Summary 395

Chapter 11

Theory and Critique of Capitalism in Gustav Gundlach
ANTON RAUSCHER 397

Discussion Summary 413

Part Five

Historism in Other Schools of Economics

Chapter 12

Intensive and Extensive Mobilisation in the Japanese Economy:
An Interpretation of Japanese Capitalism in Historical Perspective
KIICHIRO YAGI 419

Discussion Summary 447

CONTENTS

Chapter 13

The Historical School in Sweden: A Sketch
HANS DE GEER 449

Discussion Summary 462

Part Six

Historism in Economic Law

Chapter 14

Jurisprudence, History, National Economics After 1850
SIBYLLE HOFER 467

Discussion Summary 504

Part Seven

Historism, Relativism, and the Critique of Historicism

Chapter 15

Karl Popper's Critique of Historicism, the Historical School, and the Contemporary Debate
ADAM J. CHMIELEWSKI 509

Discussion Summary 532

CONTENTS

Chapter 16

Does Historism Mean Relativism? Remarks on the Debate on Historism in the German Political Economy of the Late 19th Century
ANNETTE WITTKAU-HORGBY 534

Discussion Summary 558

List of Authors and Discussants 561

Index of Names 563

Part One

Theory of Capitalism, Historism, and Economics in Joseph Schumpeter, Emil Lederer and Franz Oppenheimer

Chapter 1

Joseph Schumpeter and the German Historical School

YUICHI SHIONOYA

I. Introduction
II. Overview on Schumpeter's Work
III. Historical and Ethical Approach
IV. Apparatus of Economic Sociology
V. Conclusion

I. Introduction

This paper discusses the relationship between Joseph Schumpeter and the German Historical School with regard to the theory and methodology of economics. Schumpeter was influenced by the approach of the German Historical School, especially that of the younger Historical School led by Gustav von Schmoller. The Historical School, however, was not the sole source of influence on Schumpeter's thought; Léon Walras and Karl Marx influenced him to a greater extent. Thus, the historical economics, neo-classical economics, and Marxian economics were the intellectual field to which Schumpeter was positively committed. From this heterogeneous complex he developed his own system of social science.[1]

Schumpeter formulated the essence of historical economics into a workable form, introducing also the insight of neo-classical and Marxian economics. As he was working on it, he had to compete against John Maynard Keynes in explaining fluctuations and development of a capitalist economy,

---

1 SHIONOYA (1997b).

the urgent issue of the time. In fact, Schumpeter failed to immediately affect the course of events in theory and policy. The Keynesian Revolution and the subsequent Age of Keynes in the mid-20th century retarded the acceptance and spread of Schumpeter's thought that would convey the legacy of German economics.

After the 1980s, however, the growing interest among economists in the long-term development of capitalism has stimulated an attention to historism, institutionalism, and evolutionism through a reappraisal of Schumpeter's work. His rich vision in the long-term and wide-ranging perspective has certainly given a stimulus to broadening the scope of economics.

In order to discuss the relationship between Schumpeter and the German Historical School, the present paper focuses on how Schumpeter reconstructed the research programme of German historical economics from a methodological point of view, and how he developed his own system for a substantive analysis of the transformation of a capitalist economy. In my view, the Historical School tried to address the problems of the evolution of institutions through the historical and ethical methods. Their scope and methods of economics differed from those of classical and neo-classical economics, which were concerned with the problems of the determination of equilibrium prices and the abstract and value-free methods. Schumpeter was an important mediator who would bequeath the legacy of the Historical School to the future generations. The key words of this paper are institution, evolution, history, and ethics.

II. Overview on Schumpeter's Work

Before discussing Schumpeter's response to the Historical School, it is useful to give a bird's-eye view on his work. At the University of Vienna Schumpeter studied law, history and economics and made his debut as an *enfant terrible* in the field of abstract economic theory. Although his major teachers were Eugen von Böhm-Bawerk and the Friedrich von Wieser, major figures of the Austrian School, he was not accepted among Austrian School because he was critical of its essentialism and psychologism.

In 1908, he published *Das Wesen und der Hauptinhalt der theoretischen Nationalökonomie*, which was the recapitulation of neo-classical economics on the lines of the general equilibrium theory of Léon Walras. The book was a methodological work that aimed to make a contribution to the solution of the *Methodenstreit* between Carl Menger and Gustav von Schmoller. Schumpeter ingeniously adapted the philosophy of science of Ernst Mach to economics and developed the economic methodology of instrumentalism, the view that theories are not descriptions but instruments for deriving useful results and are neither true nor false.[2] According to this methodology, it is of no use to quarrel about the superiority of historical and theoretical methods because they are designed for different purposes. Schumpeter's methodological work can be compared to that of Max Weber, who was also devoted to the solution of the conflict between theory and history at the time.[3]

In 1912, Schumpeter published *Theorie der wirtschaftlichen Entwicklung*, which was a unique attempt to establish a dynamic economic theory on the basis of neo-classical static theory. Static theory had explored the logic of economic behaviour that formulated the most pervasive adaptive forces of an economy in response to changes in exogenous factors, and had been applied to the circular flow and the steady process of economic growth. In contrast, Schumpeter's economic dynamics or theory of economic development was concerned with destruction of the circular flow by the introduction of innovation that includes new products, new techniques, new markets, new sources of supply and new forms of organisation. He defined economic development by reference to innovation (the cause of development), entrepreneurs (the carriers of development), and bank credit (the means of development). He emphasised the role of entrepreneurs because he sought an endogenous explanation of economic changes originating from an economic system itself rather than emerging from external disturbances.

When Schumpeter explained the nature of his theory of economic development, he referred to two great figures, Léon Walras and Karl Marx, to whom he had been indebted.[4] According to him, the former provided "a pure logic of the interdependence between economic quantities" and the latter "a vision of economic evolution as a distinct process generated by the economic system itself." Schumpeter's basic idea of evolutionary economic

---

2 SHIONOYA (1990a).
3 SCHIONOYA (1991, 1996).
4 SCHUMPETER (1937).

changes is that both a cause of changes in economic system and a response mechanism to changes are endogenous; thus he regarded entrepreneurial innovation as the cause of economic development and formulated the phenomenon of business cycles as the process spreading and absorbing the impact of innovation through the response mechanism of an economy.

It is important to observe that Schumpeter's entrepreneur is a special kind of a leader in the economic domain. The leader as the carrier of innovations in a particular area of social life is in marked contrast to the majority of people who only take adaptive or routine actions. Schumpeter believed that such a contrast exists not only in economy but also in science, the arts, politics, and so on. He based the statics-dynamics dichotomy in various aspects of social life on the dichotomy of human types, i.e., the static and the dynamic man. In Chapter 7 of the first edition of *Theorie der wirtschaftlichen Entwicklung*, that was omitted from the subsequent editions, he gave a sketch of developments of a society as a whole in terms of the interrelations between the different areas of social life, that are characterised by different logic of statics and dynamics. This idea eventually led to his conception of universal social science.[5]

He noted that the concepts of statics and dynamics were introduced into economics, not from mechanics but from zoology via Henri de Blainville, Auguste Comte and John Stuart Mill, and that the idea of evolution depended on a zoological analogy, for a mechanical analogy does not apply to the development of an economy and society from within.[6] He meant, for instance, that if a study of the organs of a dog were compared to statics, research on how dogs have come to exist at all in terms of concepts such as selection, mutation or evolution would be rooted in dynamics.[7]

After the publication of *Entwicklung*, Schumpeter soon shifted his interest to economic sociology and developed a theory of social classes that would serve as the link between the concept of leadership in various areas of social life, on the one hand, and the overall concept of civilisation or the *Zeitgeist*, on the other.[8] In other words, social classes mediated the interrelationships between the economic and non-economic areas. This idea was a simplified and strategic version of the general interdependence between

---

5   SHIONOYA (1990b).
6   SCHUMPETER (1934, p. xi).
7   SCHUMPETER (1939, Vol. 1, pp. 36-37).
8   SCHUMPETER (1927).

different areas of social life and shaped the skeleton of his economic sociology that was later developed in *Capitalism, Socialism and Democracy* (1942). In this book he presented his famous thesis on the demise of capitalism as the result of its success: according to him, the very success of capitalist economy will produce non-economic factors that are inconsistent with it; these factors will, in turn, worsen the economic performance of capitalism. This successful book was a synthesis of his work in economic sociology based on the research programme of the German Historical School.

Before this book, Schumpeter published *Business Cycles* (1939), in two massive volumes, with the subtitle "A Theoretical, Historical and Statistical Analysis of the Capitalist Process". This book was intended as an expansion and elaboration of the theory of economic development in historical and statistical context, and Schumpeter meant the book as a genuine product of historical economics. Thus he wrote:

> Since what we are trying to understand is economic change in historic time, there is little exaggeration in saying that the ultimate goal is simply a reasoned (=conceptually clarified) history, not of crises only, nor of cycles or waves, but of the economic process in all its aspects and bearings to which theory merely supplies some tools and schemata, and statistics merely part of material. It is obvious that only detailed historic knowledge can definitively answer most of the questions of individual causation and mechanism and that without it the study of time series must remain inconclusive, and theoretical analysis empty.[9]

This remark manifests the essential spirit of the German Historical School. His comment concerning the goal of his research - "filling the bloodless theoretical schemata and statistical contour lines with live fact"[10] - is also the aspiration of that school. These remarks can be compared to what Schmoller wrote for a summary of the bearings of the historical research in economics:

> Historical research has created the conceptions of the historical development of nation, of man, and of economic institutions. It has properly brought economic research into contact with morals, law, the state, and the causes of cultural development in general. It has

---

9 SCHUMPETER (1939, Vol. 1, p. 220).
10 SCHUMPETER (1939, Vol. 1, p. 222).

shown how to inquire into collective phenomena in addition to the conclusions starting from individuals and their self-interest. It has shown how to do a proper synthesis in addition to an analysis. It has given, for the first time, a proper complement to an isolating abstraction by showing how to regard the results of the abstraction as part of a coherent whole. Thus what used to be faded abstraction and dead schema has recovered blood and life.[11]

Business Cycles was not a success because it did not appeal to economists who had been seriously infected with the Keynesian Revolution.

Schumpeter's another *tour de force* was *History of Economic Analysis* (1954), which demonstrated that he was perhaps the last of the great polymaths. This work was not a hobby of the social scientist; there was a deeper reason for his interest in the history of economics.[12] For him, the development of an economy and society, on the one hand, and the development of science and thought, on the other, are two aspects of the same evolutionary process. Corresponding to three branches of social studies, economic statics, economic dynamics and economic sociology, he worked on the philosophy of science (the methodology for the rules of scientific procedure), the history of science (the development of scientific apparatus) and the sociology of science (the nature of scientific activity carried out in social circumstance). These two sets of work and their relationships constitute Schumpeter's universal social science, which was a substitute for Marx's economic interpretation of history concerning the relationships between the substructure and the superstructure of a society. Schumpeter's two-structure approach to mind and society did not extend beyond comparing chronologically the long waves of economic activity with those of scientific economics.

---

11 SCHMOLLER (1911, pp. 464-465).
12 SHIONOYA (1997a).

III. Historical and Ethical Approach

In his early work on the economic doctrines and methods, Schumpeter summarised six basic viewpoints of the German Historical School:[13] (1) a belief in the unity of social life and the inseparable relationship among its components, (2) a concern for development, (3) an organic and holistic point of view, (4) a recognition of the plurality of human motives, (5) an interest in concrete, individual relationships rather than the general nature of events, and (6) historical relativity. This is an excellent analysis of the scope and methods of the Historical School.

The greatest significance of the historical method for Schumpeter was the recognition that historical materials reflect the development phenomenon and indicate the relationship between economic and non-economic facts, thus suggesting how the disciplines of the social sciences should interact. He later observed: "The historical report cannot be purely economic but must inevitably reflect also 'institutional' facts that are not purely economic: therefore it affords the best method for understanding how economic and non-economic facts are related to one another and how the various social sciences should be related to one another."[14] This recognition of the unity of social life and development, a combination of (1) and (2) above, was the essence of the German Historical School, as Schumpeter understood it. Historical research is important not so much in informing us of detailed knowledge about a certain time and place as in providing us with an understanding of the way in which a society as a whole actually changes over time.

While viewpoints (1) and (2) relate to the scope of the subject matters of the Historical School, (3), (4), (5), and (6) concern its methods. Schumpeter admitted a scientific value in the claims of (3) and (4), which are distinct from the assumptions of neo-classical economics, those of methodological individualism and utility maximisation. Rejecting the assumptions of the rational maximising behaviour of autonomous individuals, Schmoller held that customs, laws, and morals constitute the institutional framework of a society and that the plural values, especially ethical ones, are formed by

---

13 SCHUMPETER (1914, pp. 110-113).
14 SCHUMPETER (1954, p. 13).

institutions. Schumpeter advocated that these claims could be developed in the economic sociology of institutions.

Schumpeter did not show much interest in viewpoints (5), the issue of individuality versus generality, and (6), the issue of relativity versus the universality of social knowledge. Although the position of historism used to be bound up with an interest in individuality and relativity, Schumpeter argued, this should not deny the possibility of general and universal knowledge. Max Weber's methodological work, consisting of "understanding" (*Verstehen*) and "ideal types," was a solution to the problems concerning viewpoints (5) and (6).

Since, according to Schumpeter, the Historical School as a genuine school emerged at Schmoller,[15] it is convenient for us to identify the Historical School with Schmoller insofar as we are concerned with the relationship between Schumpeter and the Historical School. Indeed the Historical School before Schmoller generally emphasised the importance of historical research in reconstructing economics, but it was Schmoller who explicitly combined history and ethics. In fact, Schmoller called his school "historico-ethical."[16]

The weight of the challenge of Schmoller's historical-ethical approach is illustrated by two controversies created by two aspects of that approach: the *Methodenstreit* between Schmoller and Menger and the *Werturteilstreit* between Schmoller and Weber. Although it is often asserted that Schmoller lost in both battlefields, the assertion is not necessarily fair in view of the simple fact that both theory and history are necessary and that values cannot be maintained by science. Schumpeter's famous 1926 essay on Schmoller examined the historical and ethical aspects of Schmoller's approach and suggested the possibility of a new, productive interpretation.[17]

Schumpeter interpreted Schmoller's research programme as the prototype of economic sociology and characterised its goal as a "unified sociology or social science as the mentally ('theoretically') worked out universal history."[18] But he did not accept Schmoller's research programme as it stood. He critically reconstructed it from the viewpoint of integrating his-

---

15 SCHUMPETER (1954, p. 809).
16 SHIONOYA (1995).
17 SCHUMPETER (1926).
18 SCHUMPETER (1926, p. 382).

tory and theory. Let me examine Schumpeter's position on the two aspects of Schmoller's research programme: historical and ethical.

Schumpeter accepted Schmoller's belief in the importance of the historical perspective, but he emphasised the need to construct a theory rather than to be content with the mere collection, classification, summarisation, and *ad hoc* explanation of data. For Schumpeter, economic sociology was essentially characterised by the continual interaction between history and theory. He wanted to put a brake on what might have appeared to be an endless process of data collection in Schmoller's research programme, a bottomless pit into which historical economists were liable to fall. To do so, he had to resort to a methodological perspective.

Schumpeter's methodology was instrumetalism, that had been developed in his first book *Das Wesen*. For him, economic sociology was part of theory in that it is a sort of generalised economic history with a focus on institutions. This is what he often meant by "reasoned history." Therefore economic sociology is subject to instrumentalist methodology. This standpoint served as a basic test for Schmoller's research programme.

In later years, in recalling the *Methodenstreit*, Schmoller seemed to have reached the same conclusion as Schumpeter:

> Today this controversy [between history and theory] has retreated into the background, owing to the recognition that each researcher may naturally use either more induction or more deduction or both methods, depending on the personal quality and nature of the inquiry, problems and questions to be dealt with, a narrower or broader scope of study, and whether the project is a study of unsettled questions or a description of settled ones; and owing to the recognition that in general it is not possible to speak of the superiority of one method over another.[19]

This is indeed a remarkable statement compared with his observations during the *Methodenstreit*, but there still remains an important difference between Schmoller and Schumpeter. For Schmoller, a theory is no more than a summary or generalisation of empirical data, and deductive theorising for complex social phenomena is possible only after a sufficient amount of inductive work has been accumulated.

Schumpeter's instrumentalism, in contrast, asserts that assumptions or hypotheses are arbitrary creations of human mind and need not be justified

---

19 SCHMOLLER (1911, p. 479).

by facts. Theories deduced from assumptions are not descriptive statements but instruments for understanding and explaining facts. Instrumentalism facilitates deductive attempts even when empirical data are not sufficient according to the Schmollerian standard. A theory is useful not only as a device for collecting, classifying, and systematising a given body of observable facts but also as a guide for exploring, predicting, and discovering facts undetected thus far. Therefore a theoretical formulation is rather essential for achieving Schmoller's historically oriented research programme.

Then, the ethical aspect of Schmoller's programme needs a more sophisticated analysis than a mere dichotomy between facts and values. It is a mistake to reject Schmoller's ethical approach by referring to the stereotyped notion of value-free science.

Schmoller's view of economic institutions or organisations was that they are not only natural and technical but also spiritual and ethical. He believed that the historical evolution of institutions should be the theme of economics and focused on customs, laws and morals as the social determinants of institutions. He described:

> Economic behaviour and economic institutions should not be derived only from value phenomena or something like instinct but, following the unity of today's human sciences, from psychological power in general, from sentiment and instinct, from ethical ideas, and economic behaviour should be grasped in the framework of morals, customs, and law.[20]

Schmoller's treatment of ethical factors in economics was sufficiently careful to support the total structure of his thought. Before considering Schumpeter's argument, we summarise the characteristics of Schmoller's ethical approach.[21]

First, by ethics Schmoller did not mean his subjective moral judgements but objective moral beliefs in the sense of historical facts. For him ethical values were empirical materials in the historical research of institutional changes because these values are more or less embodied in institutions. Schmoller argued:

> As ethics becomes more and more empirical so that it describes ethical duty, virtue, and good in the form of historical development

---

20 SCHMOLLER (1911, p. 448).
21 SHIONOYA (1995, pp. 71-77).

rather than teaching norms, the elements of beliefs and their function in ethics naturally decline. Thus ethics resembles social science or what we call today sociology.[22]

We can call these ethical values factual values.

Second, in dealing with factual values, Schmoller wanted to discuss universally valid values that were concerned with the total interests of a society and shared by all of its members, in opposition to partial values advocated by political parties and social classes. He believed in the trend toward the empirical unification of ethical systems and wrote:

> One might dispute many individual points, the derivation of ethical truth, and the scientific construction of an ethical system, but on the most important value judgements, good and cultivated people of the same nation in the same cultural age tend to agree more and more.[23]

Third, Schmoller asserted that the ethical approach not only aims at the recognition of moral facts but is also framed in a teleological form. If a society can be regarded as a unified entity with its own objectives - in other words, if holism can be assumed -, teleological inquiry is possible. Because ethical values are to govern a society as a whole, teleology is effective in the study of institutional organisations that embody ethics. For Schmoller, the major component of teleology was the principle of justice. He argued:

> The economic organisation of a nation is not a natural product as was thought for a long time, but mainly a product of current ethical views about what is right and just in relation to different social classes.[24]

Moreover, it is important to realise that for Schmoller teleology was used as a heuristic device that supplements an empirical inquiry when empirical knowledge is insufficient. Thus, he maintained:

> Teleological investigation is the most important method because it grasps the totality of phenomena, whose inner causal relations are not yet known, as if the whole has a meaning. It is similar to a systematic investigation insofar as the latter approach systematises and grasps the total of phenomena or truth consistently.[25]

---

22 SCHMOLLER (1911, p. 438).
23 SCHMOLLER (1911, pp. 494-495).
24 SCHMOLLER (1874/1890, pp. 55-56).
25 SCHMOLLER (1911, p. 437).

Although Schumpeter's essay on Schmoller has often been discussed in relation to Schumpeter's demand for the formulation of historical approach, little attention has been given to the ethical part of Schumpeter's essay, which seems to shed new light on his ideas on norms.

Schumpeter was right in viewing that Schmoller dealt with policy and institutions without advocating a particular partisan position, without defending the existing social order, and without indicating his own preference. Schumpeter was interested to see how it was possible to propose universally valid ethical values. He found the diminishing conflicts of interest in the context of the trend of rationalisation in capitalism:

> Rationalisation, equalisation, mechanisation, and democratisation, all of which constitute an aspect of the nature of capitalist civilisation, facilitate the unity of aspirations all the more. In the rationalised world of capitalism, political parties lose their sacred banners.[26]

By the development of science and realistic policies, conflicts based on ideological illusion will be reduced. Just as rationalism expels ideology from science, it excludes ideology from society. "The time will come, when social preferences are unified so that in every given situation the choice of goals is made possible by means of science".[27] I would call this the essential trend of history.

According to Schumpeter, Schmoller thought that, based on the essential trend of history, the unity of policy objectives will be realised so that certain ethical values be embodied in institutions. When Schumpeter discussed the transformation of a capitalist system, he utilised the notions of the *Zeitgeist*, ethical values, and the ways of thinking, embedded in the institutions of capitalism, as the crucial factors to be dealt with by the apparatus of his economic sociology.

The basic scheme of Schmoller's evolutionary economics was presented in the form of a stage theory of development. Developments in stages from village economy to city economy to territorial economy to national economy were designed in terms of the regional community as the carrier of social policy in a wide sense that worked to control the free play of firms in markets. The stage scheme was concerned with the evolution of institutions brought about by the interactions between ethics and economy, between

---

26 SCHUMPETER (1926, p. 350).
27 SCHUMPETER (1926, p. 351).

spiritual-social and natural-technical factors. This is to be compared to Marx's schema of economic interpretation of history, consisting of the interactions between the superstructure and substructure of a society, and Schumpeter's schema of economic sociology, consisting of the interaction between the economic and non-economic areas.

IV. Apparatus of Economic Sociology

In *Capitalism, Socialism and Democracy*, Schumpeter presented his famous thesis on the demise of capitalism in consequence of its success. Although this book might appear to be a paradoxical and eccentric impromptu, it was a serious work of economic sociology and its scientific components were structured in many years of Schumpeter's academic life.

In fact, no book has been misinterpreted and misunderstood than this. *Foreign Affairs* in the 75th Anniversary issue selects some sixty volumes as the "Significant Books of the Last 75 Years." Francis Fukuyama's comment on *Capitalism, Socialism and Democracy* is representative of the general misunderstanding: "Schumpeter's work stands as one of the most brilliantly wrong-headed books of the century in its central prediction that socialism would ultimately replace capitalism because of the latter's insuperable cultural contradictions."[28]

If Schumpeter had in fact predicted unconditionally the arrival of socialism, it would be natural to say that he was wrong, in view of the fact that present-day capitalism is far from dying and moving to socialism; on the contrary, socialism has collapsed and is moving to capitalism. But he did not make such a prediction. In order to remove such a misunderstanding, a few methodological notes should be presented.

First, by socialism Schumpeter did not mean the development-oriented system actually adopted by dictatorship in less developed countries. He believed that as capitalism grows and matures, it must change itself in the historical process. Socialism is, as it were, the highest stage of capitalism. The readers of Schumpeter should not confuse the two understandings of socialism. Moreover, as he consistently asserted that the premature sociali-

---

28 *Foreign Affairs*, September-October 1997, p. 214.

sation of countries would result in economic failure and political oppression, the breakdown of the socialist countries in the contemporary world rather demonstrates the truth of his thesis.

Second, Schumpeter did not contend that capitalism would automatically bring about a socialist system; rather, if the tendency inherent in capitalism should fully work itself out, socialism would be feasible. Even when it is feasible, it can be realised only by political choice, not spontaneously. If political choice in a large scale is directed to the resurgence of capitalism, the tendencies toward socialism can be reversed.

Schumpeter replied to the charge that his argument was defeatist:

> The report that a given ship is sinking is not defeatist. Only the spirit in which this report is received can be defeatist: The crew can sit down and drink. But it can also rush to the pumps. If the men merely deny the report though it be carefully substantiated, then they are escapists.[29]

The quest for a small government that started with the Thatcher-Reagan revolution in the 1980s has become quite common in most of the advanced capitalist countries today. The leading idea, attaching importance to the market principle, advocates the abolition of government regulations, the restructuring of the welfare state, and the improvement of efficiency in government administration.

Indeed, in the 1920s and 1930s, the capitalist countries suffered from two evils of capitalism, depressions and distributive inequality, and faced at the same time ideological challenge from communism. But they got rid of the crisis owing to the Keynesian full employment policy and the Beveridgian social security system. The continuous intervention of governments into markets before long had to affect the functions of a capitalist system adversely, because capitalism under social policy was more and more approaching socialism. Schumpeter continued to give warning against this situation, calling it "capitalism in the oxygen tent" or "capitalism in fetters." The current attempts of reform in the advanced capitalist countries are nothing but what Schumpeter called the rush to the pumps to save a ship. The real process of institutional changes must be a zigzag around the

---

29 SCHUMPETER (1950a, p. xi).

essential trend of history, and Schumpeter said about this process: "a century is a 'short run'."[30]

Third, Schumpeter's argument does not depend on the value judgements that socialism is desirable. In terms of ideology he had a negative attitude toward socialism, but in terms of science he submitted a hypothesis on the trend of economic system toward socialism. After World War I, he joined the Socialisation Commission of Germany and the cabinet of Austria, though he was not a socialist. Asked about the motive, he is remembered to have said that "If somebody wants to commit suicide, it is a good thing if a doctor is present."

So much for the methodological notes. Schumpeter summarised the lines of reasoning as follows:[31] (1) as innovations are organised, automated, and routinized, economic development becomes the task of experts in government bureaucracy, so that the function of entrepreneurs tends to become obsolete and their social status is lost; (2) owing to the development of rational habits of mind, the pre-capitalist elements that supported the working of capitalism with regard to moral, disciplinary, habitual, and institutional aspects are destroyed; (3) the development of capitalism has created a political system of democracy that is interventionist in the interest of workers and an intellectual class that is hostile to capitalism; (4) the value scheme of capitalist society, with wealth as the standard of success, loses its hold, and there is an increased preference for equality, social security, government regulation, and leisure time.

Most readers of *Capitalism, Socialism and Democracy* are fascinated by his pens and liable to overlook the framework of economic sociology in that book. According to my reconstruction of the materials he left, the apparatus of Schumpeter's economic sociology consists of a set of submodels: (1) general theory of innovation, (2) theory of social classes, (3) theory of social values or social leadership, (4) theory of *Zeitgeist* or ideology, and (5) interactions between economic and non-economic areas.

Schumpeter maintained that there are a limited number of people in various areas of social life, who are able to destroy existing orders through the introduction of innovations and thereby succeed in creating the current of the time, in contrast to the majority of people who stick to adaptive and customary types of behaviour. Those innovative people are called leaders or

---

30 SCHUMPETER (1950a, p. 163).
31 SCHUMPETER (1950b, pp. 446-456).

innovators. Entrepreneurs are innovators in the economic area. Based on the dichotomy of human types, Schumpeter distinguished between statics and dynamics in various areas of social life.

Such leaders in various areas, each in his own way, ascend the upper rank of society and form a set of social classes. Schumpeter's theory of social classes sums up the performance of various social areas and thus serves as a conceptual pivot for a universal social science. It was presented as a theoretical scaffold for his move from economics to sociology. His major points were as follows: Entrepreneurs can stand on the top of not only the economic but also the social pyramid and exert influence on the spirit, culture, and politics of the time. However, there are leaders other than entrepreneurs; the social pyramid is not solely composed of economic material. The social pyramid is not single-peaked but consists of old and new strata involving a historical time lag.

Theory of social classes is closely related to two fundamental concepts: social values (or social leadership) and the *Zeitgeist*. Each social area has a social function (i.e., economic, ideological, military, and political) to undertake the specific tasks of a society imposed by the environment, and to contribute to the formation of social classes. Social functions attributed to individual social classes do not have equal rank. A hierarchy of classes, constituting the social order, is explained by the relative importance of social functions that determines social values or social leadership.

The superstructure is established as consciousness, culture, and institutional framework, which are peculiarly related to the class endowed with social leadership in view of its contribution to social values. Schumpeter's concept of the *Zeitgeist* or ideology can be used to symbolically denote the superstructure of a society. It is an analysis of the culture, ways of thinking, and value schemes of the time and corresponds to Schmoller's conception of ethics that was concerned with factual values rather than normative prescriptions.

Because in age of capitalism, the economic area has the greatest social function and determines the principle ideas of the society, it is natural from the standpoint of scientific strategy that Schumpeter focused on economic sociology that is concerned with the interactions between the economy and surrounding institutions. In this picture of the society, the concept of social classes is pivotal, mediating the interactions between economic machinery endowed with social leadership, on the one hand, and the non-economic, institutional superstructure, on the other. This approach is compared to

Marx's economic interpretation of history that is concerned with the relationship between the substructure and the superstructure of a society.

Based on the apparatus of economic sociology, Schumpeter's thesis of the demise of capitalism is derived as a result of historically specific interactions between economic machinery and the superstructure. The essence of the thesis lies, in my view, in the conflicting relationships between entrepreneurs and the bourgeois class, between anti-rationalistic entrepreneurship and rationalistic bourgeois mentality. The bourgeois class is the sum of the business class and the capitalist class. Entrepreneurs do not constitute a class, but successful entrepreneurs, irrespective of their origins, enter the bourgeois class together with their family. The ideology of the bourgeois class is rationalism, as is the civilisation of capitalism. In contrast, Schumpeter persistently argued, the ideology of entrepreneurs is anti-rationalistic and anti-hedonistic. The rationalistic ideology emanating from the bourgeois class affects adversely the hotbed of entrepreneurship. In this manner, the economic world loses the only source of romance and heroism that survived in the form of entrepreneurship even in the unromantic and unheroic civilisation of capitalism.

Thus, Schumpeter wrote:

> The capitalist process rationalizes behavior and ideas and by so doing chases from our minds, along with metaphysical belief, mystic and romantic ideas of all sorts... Also, capitalist civilization is rationalistic 'and anti-heroic'. The two go together of course. Success in industry and commerce requires a lot of stamina, yet industrial and commercial activity is essentially unheroic in the knight's sense... and the ideology that glorifies the idea of fighting for fighting's sake and of victory for victory's sake understandably withers in the office among all the columns of figures.[32]

It is my interpretation that, in the general term, Schumpeter's thesis should be read with reference to the sociological framework of social leadership versus the *Zeitgeist*. In the ideological context, the thesis is interpreted as the antinomy between heroism and rationalism. It is interesting to see that, in the last analysis, Schumpeter's economic sociology is reduced to a sort of Hegelian idealism. This point might be illustrated by Samuelson's memoir of a Harvard seminar:[33] Wassily Leontief dextrously summarised

---

32 SCHUMPETER (1950a, pp. 127-128).
33 SAMUELSON (1981, p. 8).

the discussions of Paul Sweezy and Schumpeter on the fate of capitalism to the effect that, according to Sweezy based on Marx, capitalism is dying of a malignant cancer, while, according to Schumpeter, it is dying of a psychosomatic ailment. The causal relationships between the superstructure and the substructure are just the opposite in the diagnosis of Marx and Schumpeter. Was Marx inverted who had inverted Hegel?

V. Conclusion

From the foregoing discussions we can summarise the relationship between Schumpeter and the Historical School in four major points.

(1) *Instrumentalism*. Schumpeter's contribution to the *Methodenstreit* was a formulation of instrumentalist methodology for economics. Although Max Weber's methodological work on the ideal type has exclusively been referred to as the solution to the debate, Schumpeter's work on instrumentalism is no less important. It is rather striking to see the similarity of their methodology. It is also illuminating to compare the two approaches with reference to their different origins, Neo-Kantian and Machian philosophy of science.

(2) *Historism*. Schumpeter accepted the idea of historism from the Historical School and interpreted it as the combined claim of development and the unity of social life as the subject matters of historical research. According to him, only from the viewpoint of development historical facts reveal the interdependence and unity of social life. He emphasised the need for the integration of theory and history. For Schumpeter, economic sociology rather than historiography was the discipline of historism. Reasoned history (i.e., theoretically worked out history) was his substitute for monographic history. Schumpeter's case for economic sociology was supported methodologically by instrumetalism.

(3) *Evolutionism*. Schumpeter's evolutionary science in terms of the relationship between the economic and non-economic areas was animated by Schmoller's dichotomy between ethics and economy as well as Marx's dichotomy between the superstructure and the substructure. Schumpeter's theory of economic development was not fully evolutionary because it was confined to the economic area. Schumpeter's approach to economic sociol-

ogy is to be compared to those of Schmoller, Marx, Comte, Weber, and Pareto, who had more or less broad views of society integrating economics and sociology.

(4) *Institutionalism.* Schumpeter defined economic sociology as the analysis of economic institutions and accepted Schmoller's research programme with the evolution of institutions as the subject matters. Schmoller, as the defender of the "historico-ethical" approach, insisted that three kinds of norms (custom, law, and moral) are embedded in economic and social institutions and developed the stage theory of evolution in terms of the interactions between spiritual-ethical and physical-technical factors. Schumpeter's thesis on the fall of capitalism that was derived from the apparatus of economic sociology can be interpreted as a version of the Schmollerian analysis of the interaction between ethics and economy. Schumpeter's work on the spiritual-ethical aspect of institutions is compared to Weber's work on the Protestant ethic and the spirit of capitalism.

Lastly, the character of *Capitalism, Socialism and Democracy*, the product from Schumpeter's apparatus of economic sociology, must be identified. The inclusion of ethics, spirits, value schemes is crucial, but the treatment of these elements differs from an ordinary method of ethical and ideological prescription. They are embedded in institutions; thus they are the objects of science and analysed as the factual values. To analyse the consistency or inconsistency between value schemes and economic machinery and to argue the evolution of institutions from this standpoint is the basic task of economic sociology. This is the prominent feature of discourses in the tradition of the German Historical School.

References

SAMUELSON, P. A.: "Schumpeter's Capitalism, Socialism and Democracy", in: A. HEERTJE (Ed.): *Schumpeter's Vision: Capitalism, Socialism and Democracy after 40 Years*, New York (Praeger) 1981, pp. 1-21.
SCHMOLLER, G. VON: "Die sociale Frage und der preussische Staat", *Preussische Jahrbuch*, 33 (1874). (Reprinted in *Zur Social- und Gewerbepolitik der Gegenwart*, Leipzig (Duncker & Humblot) 1890, pp. 37-63).

SCHMOLLER, G. VON: *Grundriss der allgemeinen Volkswirtschaftslehre*, Leipzig (Duncker & Humblot) Vol. 1, 1901.

SCHMOLLER, G. VON: "Volkswirtschaft, Volkswirtschaftslehre und Methode", in: *Handwörterbuch der Staatswissenschaften*, Jena (Verlag von Gustav Fischer), 3rd ed., Vol. 8, 1911, pp. 426-501.

SCHUMPETER, J. A.: *Epochen der Dogmen- und Methodengeschichte*, Tübingen (J. C. B. Mohr) 1914.

SCHUMPETER, J. A.: "Gustav v. Schmoller und die Probleme von heute", *Schmollers Jahrbuch*, 50 (1926), pp. 337-388.

SCHUMPETER, J. A.: "Die sozialen Klassen in ethnisch homogenen Milieu", *Archiv für Sozialwissenschaft und Sozialpolitik*, 57 (1927), pp. 1-67.

SCHUMPETER, J. A.: "Preface to the Japanese Edition of *Theorie der wirtschaftlichen Entwicklung*", Tokyo (Iwanami Shoten) 1937. (Reprinted in R. V. CLEMENCE (Ed.): *Essays of J. A. Schumpeter*, Cambridge, MA (Addison-Wesley Press) 1951, pp. 158-163.)

SCHUMPETER, J. A.: *The Theory of Economic Development*, Cambridge, MA (Harvard University Press) 1934.

SCHUMPETER, J. A.: *Business Cycles*, New York (McGraw-Hill) 1939.

SCHUMPETER, J. A. (1950a): *Capitalism, Socialism and Democracy*, New York (Harper & Brothers) 3rd ed. 1950.

SCHUMPETER, J. A. (1950b): "March into Socialism", *American Economic Review*, 40 (1950), pp. 415-425.

SCHUMPETER, J. A.: *History of Economic Analysis*, New York (Oxford University Press) 1954.

SHIONOYA, Y. (1990a): "Instrumentalism in Schumpeter's Economic Methodology", *History of Political Economy*, 22 (1990), pp. 187-222.

SHIONOYA, Y. (1990b): "The Origin of the Schumpeterian Research Programme: A Chapter Omitted from Schumpeter's *Theory of Economic Development*", *Journal of Institutional and Theoretical Economics*, 146 (1990), pp. 314-327.

SHIONOYA, Y.: "Schumpeter on Schmoller and Weber: A Methodology of Economic Sociology", *History of Political Economy*, 23 (1991), pp. 193-219.

SHIONOYA, Y.: "Methodological Appraisal of Schmoller's Research Program", in: P. KOSLOWSKI (Ed.): *The Theory of Ethical Economy in the Historical School*, Berlin (Springer-Verlag) 1995, pp. 57-78.

SHIONOYA, Y.: "Getting Back Max Weber from Sociology to Economics", in: H. RIETER (Ed.): *Studien zur Entwicklung der ökonomischen Theorie XV*, Berlin (Duncker & Humblot) 1996, pp. 47-66.

SHIONOYA, Y. (1997a): "Reflections on Schumpeter's *History of Economic Analysis* in Light of His Universal Social Science", in: J. P. HENDERSON (Ed.): *The State of the History of Economics*, London (Routledge) 1997, pp. 81-104.

JOSEPH SCHUMPETER AND THE GERMAN HISTORICAL SCHOOL

SHIONOYA, Y. (1997b): *Schumpeter and the Idea of Social Science: A Metatheoretical Study*, Cambridge (Cambridge University Press) 1997.

Discussion Summary

Johan Tralau

Paper discussed:
Yuichi Shionoya: Joseph Schumpeter and the German Historical School

The discussion first concerned Schumpeter's theory of the innovator. Could the political and economic liberalisation in the 1970s and 80s be described as innovation, and Reagan and Thatcher thus as innovators in the Schumpeterian sense (Zoninsein)? Schumpeter gives no real definition of the political innovator; yet if one applies the term to the present world, one can surely see the trends towards liberalisation in that manner (Shionoya). Schumpeter spoke of political innovators in 1942. However, one must not forget that Müller-Armack worked out the same theory independently of Schumpeter (Wohlgemuth, Haselbach).

The focus then shifted toward Schumpeter's prophecy of the inevitable transformation from capitalism to socialism. This diagnosis has been repeated by György Soros. Was the Schumpeterian conception influenced by Hegel (Chmielewski)? This was clearly not the case (Shionoya). The pathology of capitalism was now mentioned. Which diagnosis did Schumpeter give, and which were the reasons for it (Koslowski)? Schumpeter's diagnosis concerned the automatisation of innovations, the anti-rationalist decline, and the genesis of interventionist and anti-materialist ideas. The cause of social metamorphosis was hence, according to Schumpeter, to be found in the superstructure of society, not in its basis (Shionoya). What, then, is rationalism? Does it primarily concern economics, or the Enlightenment in general (Koslowski)? Rationalism in capitalism must be approached as a fairly broad concept. (Shionoya). Since every thinker is a product of his time, one must ask what role the development in Eastern Europe played for Schumpeter. In classical economics, as in Marx, the cause of economic development is located in the economy itself; here, however, they and Schumpeter part company. What did he mean, then, by eth-

DISCUSSION SUMMARY

ics, and what was his opinion on utilitarianism (RAUSCHER)? Schumpeter did not propose a prescriptive ethics, but rather wished to discuss factual values and ways of thinking. He rejected utilitarianism as a "pagan philosophy" (SHIONOYA). Could not Schumpeter's thinking be regarded as a kind of refined utilitarianism (CHMIELEWSKI)? Schumpeter's very point was to challenge the conception of equilibrium, and thus utilitarianism. The term "anti-rationalistic" captures only half of Schumpeter. However, Schumpeter must be considered to be a hedonist (HASELBACH). Schumpeter's statement that innovations can be planned by the state seems to be inconsistent with his own early writings, and is most probably wrong anyway (WOHLGEMUTH). The size of the firms is not important, be they small or national; rather, the entrepreneurship plays the leading role (SHIONOYA). The cause of failure in the socialist economies was primarily economic misery, and not changes in the intellectual climate (RAUSCHER). In the economic system itself, this most certainly was the case (SHIONOYA). Did instrumentalism save Schmoller's thinking, or is it inconsistent (YAGI)? One difference betwixt Schmoller and Schumpeter was that the latter wished to put an end to the endless collection of data, which according to him blurred rather than improved historical and social research (SHIONOYA).

The question was raised whether there is a theoretical core in Schumpeter's work as regards the entrepreneur. The Schumpeterian prophecy of the movement from capitalism to socialism is not deterministic; alternatives such as the Catholic social theory, to which the conception of a society of entrepreneurs was added, were discussed by Schumpeter as late as at the end of the 1940s (DAHMS). Hereafter, the notion of innovation was discussed. Could the transformation of social values become the basis of a new agenda (ZONINSEIN)? When innovations shift from the economic to other spheres, they also leave Schumpeter's own sphere of interest (DAHMS).

Chapter 2

Emil Lederer (1882-1939): Economical and Sociological Analyst and Critic of Capitalist Development

HARALD HAGEMANN

I. Academic Career
II. The Analysis of the New Middle Classes
III. Technological Progress and Unemployment
IV. Crisis, Unemployment and the Wage Question
V. Editing Economic Journals: From the *Archiv für Sozialwissenschaft und Sozialpolitik* to *Social Research*
VI. The University in Exile and the State of the Masses

I. Academic Career

Emil Lederer was born in the Bohemian town of Pilsen on July 22, 1882. After finishing the German gymnasium with first-class honours in July 1901 he began to study law and economics at the University of Vienna, where Eugen von Böhm-Bawerk, Carl Menger, Eugen von Philippovich and Friedrich von Wieser were among his major teachers and Joseph A. Schumpeter and the Austromarxists Otto Bauer, Rudolf Hilferding and Otto Neurath were his fellow students. In summer 1903 he also studied in Berlin for one semester where he attended the major lecture on economics given by Gustav Schmoller. But the economic thinking of Lederer, who remained a life-long 'liberal socialist' was formed by his Vienna teachers, among whom Philippovich, who was one of the leading socialists of the chair, had perhaps the greatest influence. His very first scientific publication (1906) documents Lederer's early intensive study of Marx' *Capital*. Although he was strongly influenced by Marx' philosophy of history (without its Hegelian flavour), by Marx' analysis of accumulation and technical progress and by Hilferding's book on *Finance Capital*, Lederer never became an orthodox Marxist.

After receiving his first doctoral degree in law at the University of Vienna, Lederer worked as the Secretary of the Chamber of Commerce in Lower Austria from 1906 to 1910. In 1907 he converted from the mosaic to the Protestant belief and married Emy Seidler, the daughter of a Hungarian industrialist whose sister was a close friend of Georg Lukacs. Lederer thus developed intensive contacts with top-calibre intellectuals from Budapest of whom the economic journalist Albert Bela Halasi became his closest friend and the leading sociologist Karl Mannheim a life-long friend and later colleague at the University of Heidelberg. During his practical experience Lederer recognized the growing importance of the *Angestellten* in the development of industrial economies. His analysis of the role of white-collar workers formed the basis of his academic career. Within a year Lederer obtained a second doctoral degree, now in economics in July 1911 with the thesis *Die Pensionsversicherung der Privatangestellten* from the University of Munich, where Lujo Brentano was his supervisor, and his habilitation at the philosophical faculty of the University of Heidelberg in February 1912. Alfred Weber and Eberhard Gothein, the holders of the two chairs in economics were the referees of his habilitation thesis on *The Problem of the Modern Salaried Employee: Its Theoretical and Statistical Basis* ([1912] 1937) which can be considered as "the first comprehensive analysis of the working conditions and political attitudes of salaried employees" (Dickler 1987, p. 157). Lederer continued this kind of socioeconomic analysis in his later work on the "new middle classes". After becoming secretary to the editors of the *Archiv für Sozialwissenschaft und Sozialpolitik* in January 1911 he had already started to write a regular chronicle on sociopolitical developments in Germany and Austria. Having been a *Privatdozent* for more than six years Lederer became an extraordinary Associate Professor only in 1918, shortly before the end of the First World War. The new Weimar Republic then offered new career prospects. When in 1920 the third regular Professorship in economics was founded within the Philosophical Faculty Lederer became a regular Associate Professor for Social Policy. In connection with an offer from the University of Leipzig, which he rejected, Lederer became Full Professor in August 1922. In April 1923 he succeeded Gothein on the chair of economics and public finance and got permission for a two-years leave to accept the offer for a Guest Professorship at the Imperial University in Tokyo.

Together with Alfred Weber, the younger brother of Max Weber, who was the founding director of the *Institute for Social and State Sciences* (InSoSta)[1], Lederer played the key role in economics and social sciences in Heidelberg during the Weimar Republic. Both, Weber and Lederer, represented the essential characteristics of the Institute, i.e. unity of the social sciences. Lederer served as Professor in Heidelberg until 1931. In 1929 he rejected the offer to succeed Franz Oppenheimer on the chair for economic theory and sociology at the Goethe University in Frankfurt, but in 1931 he accepted the call from the University of Berlin to succeed Heinrich Herkner on the chair which formerly had been held by Gustav Schmoller. But the Berlin episode was not a lucky and only a short one. The attempt to appoint Schumpeter to a chair was blocked by the majority of the faculty[2], and after only three semesters the Nazis' rise to power forced Lederer to emigrate in April 1933. At the invitation of Alvin Johnson Lederer became the founding Dean of the new 'University in Exile'[3], the Graduate Faculty of Political and Social Sciences at the New School for Social Research in New York, where he stayed as Professor of Economics until his early death. Lederer died of thrombosis in New York at May 29, 1939.

II. The Analysis of the New Middle Classes

The theme of the salaried employee in modern society was one of the central topics in Lederer's scientific life-work. Like many social scientists of his generation who had socialist convictions he grew up with the Marxian view that the number of manual workers increases both absolutely and relatively with progressive capitalist development. Lederer saw rather early that this view which originally had developed out of Marx's analysis of British industry in the mid-nineteenth century, particularly Marx's experience with

---

1   On the history of the InSoSta between 1918 and 1958 see BLOMERT/ESSLINGER/GIOVANNINI (1997).
2   See STOLPER (1994, pp. 311-2).
3   For a detailed history of the University in Exile see KROHN (1993).

the English textile industry, was at odds with the rapid growth of the salaried employees since the 1890s which had changed the structure of modern capitalist society considerably. Lederer not only recognised as one of the first social scientists the international tendency that the proportion of manual workers, contrary to their growth in earlier stages, had begun to decline relatively to the group of salaried employees in the period of high capitalism, but also that this group with their diverging behaviour patterns, states of consciousness and traditions had formed their own independent trade union organisations and thereby shifted the social stratification. With his early analysis of the role of white-collar workers in the modern economy Lederer was the first to call attention to the problem of this special group of employees, their working conditions and political attitudes, and became the forerunner of many in that field, not least his own students, including Fritz Croner and his assistant in Berlin Hans Speier who also belonged to the Mayflower generation of New School professors and continued to work in this field.[4]

The separation of the employees into the two groups of workers and salaried employees and the analysis of its sociopolitical implications was the prime movement of Lederer's sociological studies. His analysis is characterised by the permanent confrontation of existing theories, particularly the Marxian theory of classes with her prediction of a growing polarisation process which makes white collar workers members of the proletariat, and his strong belief in the evolution of society through enlightenment which later was shaken to a certain degree by the successes of the Nazis. This twofold intention comes out most clearly in the analysis of the role of the new middle classes carried through jointly with Jacob Marschak.[5] Whereas the few members of the "old" middle classes had widely been regarded as members of the bourgeoisie, the exact position of the increasing number of persons who belonged to the "new" middle classes became an issue of heavy controversies. Lederer and Marschak made a major attempt to come to a differentiated view by a thorough study of the complexities of the social position of this group which not only considered the mere economic facts

---

4 SPEIER (1979) also edited the collection of essays by Lederer which paid primary attention to these changes in the structure of the capitalist society with their implications on the sociological basis of economic and political theories.
5 See LEDERER/MARSCHAK (1926, 1927).

but also the social self-interpretation of this group which in modern language is called "collective mentalities".

Lederer and Marschak started with the confrontation of the optimistic or harmonic view, which sees the new middle classes playing the role of a mediator between capital and labour whose function it is to reduce the fragility of the social system and to act as a lubricant for the unity of the social classes, with the opposite Marxian view which recognises an aggravation of the class struggle in capitalism as necessary and inevitable and consequently perceives the new middle class as "*Stehkragenproletariat*" (stand-up collar proletariat). Lederer and Marschak made a careful attempt first to clarify the exact position of the very heterogenous groups of the new middle classes comprising various subgroups of private salaried employees and civil servants. They came to the result that the aggregate of these various subgroups cannot be reduced to a common technical or economic function, but is only given by a joint social position of being "between the classes", that is the new middle classes form an unity only by a negative criterion with regard to the other classes.[6] Nevertheless, the authors came to the clear conclusion that if sometimes an aggregation into any social class should occur, only the organisations of the working class come into question. This development is enforced by the behaviour of the employers' organisations which makes a "position between the classes" impossible and the contrast employer versus employee more and more sweeping. The authors saw the main reason for this development in the fact that the economic collapse at the end of the First World War with its destruction of the traditional social order had widely eliminated the economic differences within the new middle classes. This homogenisation process had also considerably reduced the barriers on the side of the white collar workers to co-operate with the trade union movement. Lederer and Marschak, who shared the belief that the new middle classes were critical for a greater stability of the democracy, followed the political purpose to attract the salaried employees to the trade union movement and to progressive political action. This was based on an analysis which came to the final conclusion "that the idea of social harmony is a literary idea"[7] which was not realised because the social stratification of the population into classes had considerably progressed compared to pre-war times.

---

6 See LEDERER/MARSCHAK (1926, pp. 123-4).
7 *Ibid.*, p. 141.

The sociological as well as economic studies of Lederer show his deep interest and attachment for the analysis of the transformation of a political system under the influence of socioeconomical changes. This is best demonstrated in his country studies, of which the analysis of the Japanese society and economy in transition stands out. In this work, which was written together with his first wife Emy Seidler (Lederer/Lederer 1929), the conflict between traditional structures and the sudden introduction of modern production methods, for military and imperial purposes under prevention of their consequences for private consumption and social relationships, was carefully analysed. It shows a deep historical knowledge and a great awareness for the problems of a foreign culture. The book not only had a greater impact in Japan, but also in the United States where a revised and completed edition was published (Lederer/Lederer 1937). The analysis of the growth process of the Japanese economy in the inter-war period, with its export-led strategy combined with a policy of import substitution, a high degree of governmental regulation and in the interest of military armament with its promotion of heavy industries, is not only a fine piece of interdisciplinary scholarship in the social sciences, but became also of greater interest for the general public with the growing awareness of Japanese imperialism in the late 1930s.

III. Technological Progress and Unemployment

Hans Staudinger, Lederer's close friend who had made his Ph.D. with Alfred Weber in Heidelberg in 1913 and was a later long-time dean at the Graduate Faculty of the New School from 1941-1943 and 1950-1959, posthumously called Lederer a *"sozialpolitischen Sozialisten"* (Staudinger 1982, p. 13). From his early engagement in the German and Austrian Commissions on Socialization until the end of his life the fight against unemployment had highest priority for Lederer. Naturally this became a key issue when high unemployment in the late 1920s and the strong increase in the wake of the Great Depression placed the unemployment problem into the centre of economic and political debates. Looking into Lederer's list of publications, the year 1927 can be identified as a turning-point at which a shift from sociological themes and studies on countries in the Far East to the analysis of the consequences of technological change and business-cycle problems occurred. For Lederer the real threat for society and the Weimar Republic resulted from rising mass unemployment and the consequential tendency to a destabilisation of the democratic institutions. This caused him to participate in the controversial debates on the displacement and compensation effects of new technologies and on the wage-employment relationship.

Rapid labour saving technical progress was regarded by Lederer as a decisive factor in explaining the severity of unemployment. Lederer, who was passionately committed to democracy and social justice, was a dispassionate analyst of the causes and effects of technical progress. Lederer published numerous articles and two monographs on this issue, of which *Technical Progress and Unemployment. An enquiry into the obstacles to economic expansion* (Lederer 1938), a study issued by the International Labour Office in Geneva, is a widely extended version of his earlier German monograph on technical progress and unemployment (Lederer 1931). His analysis of the complex technological change, capital accumulation and unemployment is an important aspect of the thesis that the key themes of Lederer's scientific interest had not been altered due to emigration.

Lederer had observed that the great wave of rationalisation in Germany in the mid- and late 1920s led to great displacements which were not compensated because the speed of innovations had slowed down. In the second as well as in the first edition of his book Lederer was aware that the compensation process is not an automatic one. Whereas the subtitle with its emphasis on "obstacles" indicates continuity, the greater emphasis on the aspects of technical progress which promote economic growth in the second edition demonstrates evolution in Lederer's thought.[8] In his analysis of the employment consequences of technological change Lederer combines central elements of the Marxian theory of accumulation with Schumpeterian ideas of innovation and credit in long-run development. Like Schumpeter, Lederer held the view that capitalist economies normally are in a dynamic disequilibrium. He recognised technological unemployment as an essentially

---

[8] This is also clearly visible in LEDERER (1935) where the author discusses the development of new industries arising out of spontaneous innovations which are of particular importance to overcome the depression. For a thorough discussion of the influence of emigration on Lederer's economic writings see ESSLINGER (1993).

dynamic and not static phenomenon. This is clearly seen by Marschak who in his obituary on Lederer as an economist emphasised the following fact: "He knew that his was a time of transition and disequilibrium. He foresaw - earlier than most of his contemporaries - that economic theory will become an analysis of transition and disequilibrium, and that instead of relying placidly on the blind forces of the market men will have to learn how to master them" (Marschak 1941, p. 79). For Lederer capitalist dynamics was not only "development" but also "destruction". Nevertheless he always had a differentiated view, that is the progressive nature of technical progress was never denied. For example, in the preface to *Technischer Fortschritt und Arbeitslosigkeit* Lederer, on the one side, discusses the devastating consequences technical progress *can* involve which makes the social curbing of technical development a vital question of European nations, and, on the other side, he pronounces that, nevertheless, technical development offers tremendous possibilities of most rapid expansion of production and increasing employment with growing real incomes of the masses.[9]

Lederer described the process of labour displacement by technical progress and the requirements for compensation on the basis of a twosectoral model in which the economy consists of a so-called *static* sector, comprising a large number of small industries and firms which grow in conformity with the (natural) rate of population growth, and a *dynamic* sector comprising only one industry with large firms which produce capital goods. Whereas the small firms in the static sector producing both capital goods and consumption goods realise normal profits, the large firms in the dynamic sector, by introducing highly mechanised new production methods, are capable to realize above normal rates of return on investment, particularly in times of booms. The fact that the dynamic firms thus are able to renumerate capital at a higher rate than the firms in the static sector causes a diversion of capital from the static to the dynamic sector of the economy. This process undermines the ability of the society to achieve the macroeconomic goal of full employment since it implies that on top of the direct displacement of workers due to the introduction of labour-saving innovations in the dynamic sector there is an indirect displacement effect due to the lowering capacity of the static sector to absorb the displaced workers and/or the growing labour supply. In contrast to the members of the Kiel

---

9   See LEDERER (1931b, V-VI).

School, like Alfred Kähler,[10] Lowe and Neisser, Lederer therefore was more critical of the basic compensation argument which had been deployed first by Ricardo in his analysis of the machinery problem, namely that a process of additional capital accumulation is a necessary condition for a successful compensation process. Lederer emphasised "that capital formation on its own does not guarantee growth in the number of jobs. If the speed of the increase in the organic composition becomes so fast that despite the capital accumulation the demand for workers falls permanently behind the supply of workers, then unemployment becomes *structural*."[11]

The core of Lederer's dynamic concept of structural unemployment states that enlarged investment is not sufficient to compensate the displacement of workers by rationalisation investment. The similarity of Lederer's argument with Marx's 'general law of capitalist accumulation' is clear. The accelerated introduction of new machinery into the industries and firms of the dynamic sector goes along with an accelerated accumulation of 'constant' capital, that is an increase in the organic composition of capital. Notice that, in contrast to the business-cycle theories of Mises and Hayek, Lederer does not refer to the banks as the real 'villains' of the piece who arbitrarily lower the money rate of interest and lend more credit than is justified by the amount of savings in the economy.[12] The basic factor identi-

---

10 Surprisingly Kähler's important study on the displacement of workers by machinery which is based on a very advanced embryo of input-output analysis (KAEHLER 1933), is not discussed at all in the second edition by Lederer. Kähler is also absent from the list of six colleagues mentioned in the preface (LEDERER 1938) who gave valuable comments on the draft manuscript, although Kähler was a colleague of Lederer at the New School and continued to write on the problem of technological unemployment.

11 LEDERER (1931b, p. 72 n; my italic).

12 Interestingly Kaldor, who carried through his vehement attack against Lederer (1931b) from the basis of the static neo-classical theory of income distribution and therefore came to the conclusion that "monopolistic interference with the price system, either from the side of capital or from the side of labour", and not technical progress, was responsible for causing unemployment, also identified credit expansion, initiated by a labour-saving invention which raises the equilibrium rate of interest above the level of existing money-rates, as the cause of an excess of investments over savings and thereby "as the *cause* of the 'unemployment of a later period'" (KALDOR 1932, p. 195). In doing this Kaldor explicitly referred to Hayek's monetary theory of the business cycle.

fied to cause the disequilibrium is the technically determined drive of the large firms to realise economies of scale which leads to disequilibrium and a growing tendency to concentration and cartelization.[13]

This tendency has also implications for income distribution which is changed in favour of the capitalists. Monopolistic market structures prevent prices from falling in proportion or faster than money wages. The decreasing purchasing power of wage earners causes a lack of demand for consumer goods which indirectly reduces the demand for capital goods and thus leads to excess capacity in the industries producing capital goods. Instead of a movement along a balanced growth path the economy ends up in relative stagnation[14], that is a slowdown of the growth process which is caused by the introduction of new labour-saving methods of production associated with an accelerated speed of accumulation of constant capital in the dynamic sector and a diversion of capital from the static sector of the economy. Technological unemployment exists unless product innovations open up new market possibilities and stimulate labour-absorbing investment. Lederer explained the depth and duration of the Great Depression in the 1930s with the simultaneousness of a faster speed in the rationalisation process and a slowdown in the growth of market-enhancing innovations.

---

13 The process of cartelization played already a major part in Lederer's theory of business cycles and crises. See, for example, LEDERER (1925).

14 For a detailed analysis and elaboration of Lederer's theory of structural unemployment see the contributions of DICKLER who has the merit of preventing the ideas of a heterodox Austrian economist from fully sinking into oblivion. Whereas GOURVITCH (1940, pp. 134-142) had discussed Lederer's analyses of technical progress and unemployment as an outstanding modern contribution, they were almost forgotten when, against the background of rising unemployment and the microelectronics revolution the spectre of technological unemployment entered centre stage again in the mid 1970s. DICKLER (1981) is a valuable postscript on the relevance of Lederer's contribution for modern economic analysis. He also stresses the usefulness of Lederer's classification of technical progress as an element of an analysis of long waves (DICKLER 1983) and explores to integrate Lederer's stagnation theorem, which underlines the importance of the structural composition of investment, into modern models of aggregate demand/aggregate supply and non-linear models of the business cycle (DICKLER 1996).

Finally I want to make some reflections on Lederer's concept and definition of *technological unemployment*. Lederer identifies as technological unemployment that part of unemployment which, caused by technical progress, is neither compensated by the indirect effects of technical progress over a certain period of time nor by the autonomous spontaneous development within the economic system. Thus technological unemployment can only occur when the speed of technical progress is higher than "normal".[15] According to this definition the unemployment we have experienced in Germany and other European countries since the mid 1970s is not technological unemployment because there was a remarkable slowdown in productivity growth compared to the two decades before. Unemployment arose because the slowdown in economic growth was stronger than the reduced speed of technical progress, measured by the rate of productivity growth. This points to a lacuna in Lederer's definition of technological unemployment, which should be modified and expanded to comprise also those cases where unemployment is not the result of a faster speed of technical progress but of a weakening of the endogenous compensation effects.[16]

IV. Crisis, Unemployment and the Wage Question

As a consequence of the outbreak of the Great Depression and after Brüning's assumption of office as the Reichskanzler in 1930, the wage-employment debate, which was already going on in Germany in the late 1920s, intensified dramatically, now focusing primarily on the employment effects of wage cuts. Lederer, like Marschak and economists from the Kiel Institute of World Economics, such as Gerhard Colm, Adolf Löwe and Hans Neisser, played a very active role in that debate. In 1975 Georges Garvy (1913-87), who had been a young student of Lederer in Berlin 1931-33 and now was Vice President of the Federal Reserve Bank of New York, published an article 'Keynes and the Economic Activists of Pre-Hitler Germany' (Garvy 1975) in a leading American journal which was not only

---

15 See LEDERER (1938, ch. II).
16 For a detailed discussion of the indirect compensation effects of technological change see HAGEMANN (1995).

widely read but also led to controversial debates which have continued ever since.[17] Garvy evaluated the work of those German economists who in the contemporary debate opposed the view that wage cuts were a successful remedy for fighting unemployment and advocated public work programmes. Among the economists whose contributions are favourably discussed only Lederer, Löwe and Werner Sombart were holders of chairs in economics. Furthermore, Wilhelm Lautenbach, Ernst Wagemann, Wladimir Woytinsky and a group of young economists, including Colm, Marschak, Neisser, Fritz Baade and Ludwig Erhard are explicitly mentioned. Thus the group of Lederer and his friends had a great weight. They all argued strongly against a deflationary wage policy as the central element of a crisis management strategy. Their social-democratic convictions and their closeness to the trade unions were no barrier to them in warning - as Keynes did in the contemporary British debate - against the exaggerations of the purchasing power theory. Nevertheless there were some internal differences. Colm and Neisser, for example, were more critical of the purchasing power argument than Lederer and Marschak.[18]

Lederer wrote many papers where he argued against a general wage reduction as an adequate means for employment creation in the crisis. His small booklet *Wirkungen des Lohnabbaus*, published at the end of 1931, can be seen as a synthesis of his ideas on this issue. It concludes with the often-quoted pungent statement: "The primitive conception that, when*ever* unemployment exists, one could always restore equilibrium by a reduction in wages belongs into the junk-room of theory" (Lederer 1931d, p. 32). Like his associate in a similar study a year before (Marschak 1930) Lederer took a differentiated view concerning the employment consequences of higher or lower wages. For example, he argued against the solicitors of a primitive

---

17 Whereas Bombach et al. shared Garvy's view that the "reformers" or "activists" among the German economists who had developed policy conclusions similar to Keynes can be regarded as "pre-Keynesians", and accordingly used the translation of Garvy's paper as the introductory text of their documentation (BOMBACH 1976), Patinkin summarily dismissed the German economists from his considerations when he analysed possible anticipators of Keynes's *General Theory* (PATINKIN 1982).

18 For a detailed comparison of the common ground and the differences between the members of the Kiel-Heidelberg group and the comparison with Keynes see HAGEMANN (1999).

purchasing power theory who did not recognise that wage reductions often lead to shifts in purchasing power and not to absolute losses (*ibid.*, p. 3). Naturally, the discussion of technological progress as a possible cause of unemployment plays a major role, this time with particular emphasis on the effects of wages. Lederer argues strongly against the orthodox argument according to which there is only one reason for persistent unemployment, namely that real wages are too high and too inflexible downwards which leads to capital shortage unemployment in the medium run and technological unemployment in the long run. Lederer, on the other hand, emphasised that the introduction of basic new technologies, like mechanical looms in the 19th century, which displaced workers on a large scale and rather suddenly, cannot be prevented by a policy of lowering wages. "One cannot blame the wage level as the decisive reason for unemployment which had been caused by technological progress (even if only temporary), no more than for unemployment in a "normal" economic crisis. Neither can one cure these cases of unemployment by a forced reduction of wages. ... The great technical innovations have not come into being under the pressure of an excessive wage level due to the bargaining power of the trade unions" (*ibid.*, p. 13-14). Half a century later Wassily Leontief, who had been a member of the Kiel Institute of World Economics in the years 1927-28 and 1931-32 and knew the old debates very well, argued in a similar way in a famous paper in the *Scientific American*:" A drastic general wage cut might temporarily arrest the adoption of labour-saving technology, even though dirt-cheap labour could not compete in many operations with very powerful or very sophisticated machines. The old trend would be bound to resume, however, unless special barriers were erected against labour-saving devices" (Leontief 1985, p. 369). Lederer saw the reason for technological unemployment in the slow speed of the compensation process.

Two further causes of the high unemployment recognised by Lederer are worth mentioning. Like Colm, Lederer emphasised the drastic increase in the risk premium after the electoral success of the Nazi Party in the September elections 1930 which led to a strong capital flight. Thus there were political factors of the movement of the interest rate which were strictly contradictory to the economic requirements in the crisis. Lederer saw a vicious circle at work. Mass unemployment brought about a strengthening of the Nazi party which led to capital flight and higher interest rates and thus contributed to an increase of unemployment for a greater part. In that situation wage cuts could neither be legitimated nor would they help to reduce unemployment. On the contrary, politically imposed wage cuts would lead to social disruptions and thereby to an increase in the risk premium and to a further increase in unemployment.[19]

It was Löwe who in the contemporary debate saw a successful remedy of the crisis in a massive reduction of the cartel rent in the monopolised industries which had helped to stabilise the sectoral disproportionalities of the First World War. In particular he insisted first on realising the conditions of a market economy before advocating wage reductions on the basis of that economy's logic.[20] The argument of international competitiveness, which is normally used to claim for wage reductions, thus got a different thrust. The cartel problem was one of Lederer's old central topics, and it is therefore not surprising to see him joining forces with Löwe in the wage debate during the Brüning era. In particular he emphasised the strong underutilization of production capacities as the consequence of the fetters of the cartels which constitutes a decisive difference to crises in earlier phases of capitalism when fixed costs played a minor role and the more inefficient firms were eliminated. Due to this fixed-cost element monopolies cause dangerous consequences in the crisis.[21] Like Löwe, who had pointed out that the crisis had lost its capitalist sense in the age of cartels and monopolies, Lederer denied that wage cuts would help to solve the problem of oversized basic industries: "Should a lowering of wages cure the nonsense of a wrong allocation of production?" (*ibid.*, p. 30). The simple orthodox causal nexus, according to which wage cuts imply higher profits and are thus a condition for an increase in investment and the employment level, is fragile at a decisive moment - precisely in the depression. In a time when the degree of capacity utilization of existing machines is very low and debts with the banks are very high, there is considerable danger that the entrepreneurs will use their higher profits due to the lowering of wages for repayment of debts instead of the financing of new investment. Thus there is the threat of an aggravation of the deflationary process and the extent of the crisis which has transformed capital shortage into capital abundance. This danger of '*self-aggravation* of depression', which was conjured up by Le-

---

19 See LEDERER (1931d, pp. 4 and 31-32).
20 See for example LOEWE (1930).
21 See LEDERER (1931d, pp. 17-18 and 28-30).

derer (*ibid.*, p. 23) was also for Neisser a decisive argument against wage cuts as a means to fight against the crisis.[22]

The discussion on Garvy's article also revealed some diverging views among Lederer's friends on the importance of his contributions to the contemporary German debate. Marschak criticised that Garvy did not pay enough attention to Lederer and emphasized "Lederer's powerful and original anti-deflationary stand in Bruening's critical period of high unemployment ... The main idea, that public works would not be inflationary as long as there was much unused production capacity was mainly due to Lederer"[23]. Staudinger, on the other hand, thought that Marschak exaggerated Lederer's role.[24] Whereas Staudinger was right concerning a general assessment, nevertheless Marschak's claim was correct with regard to the specific issue being addressed, namely the problem of a tremendous underutilization of production capacities in cartelized industries during the Great Depression.

The perception that the pricing mechanism in a monopolised economy was no longer in force is a major reason why Lederer advocated national economic planning. His conviction that a mixed economy, that is a combination of a market economy with elements of economic planning based on a democratic decision process, is the best way to overcome the world-wide depression[25], however, had been inspired far earlier by Walther Rathenau, the architect of German economic mobilisation in the First World War who was killed by nationalist terrorists in 1922. This conviction also underlined his engaged work in the two socialisation commissions of the young Republics of Germany and Austria between December 1918 and 1920.[26]

---

22 See, for example, NEISSER (1930).
23 Jacob Marschak, letter to Hans Speier, April 14, 1977, Speier papers, State University of New York at Albany.
24 See SPEIER (1979, 289 n. 28) and ESSLINGER (1997, p. 121).
25 See, for example, LEDERER (1931c).
26 For an early analysis of the problems of socialisation see LEDERER (1919). On Lederer's theory of socialisation and his leading role in the socialisation commissions in Germany and Austria during the period 1918-20 see HEIMANN (1941, pp. 93-100). KOENKE (1990) compares Lederer's view with those of Heimann and Lowe, and sees all three social democratic "reform economists" having made important early contributions to the concept of social market economy who, in stressing the theoretical necessity of the market economy from the

Lederer saw in socialisation and economic planning basically a means of organising the productive factors of an economy in a more efficient way, that is he favoured a kind of socialisation in which some principles of economic behaviour were safeguarded. This would be in the interest of the workers and the modern salaried employees. These convictions also formed the basis of his involvement in the supervisory board of the research unit on economic and social policy which was jointly run by the trade unions and the Social Democratic Party. Lederer was the Vice Chairman and intellectual leader of this board which was founded in mid-1929 and played an important role in the shaping of economic policy ideas among the democratic left. The chairman of the board was the trade unionist Fritz Tarnow who, together with Woytinsky and Baade, co-authored the famous public works programme which the German trade unions launched in the winter 1931-32.

V. Editing Economic Journals: From the *Archiv für Sozialwissenschaft und Sozialpolitik* to *Social Research*

Lederer played an important role in the advancement of socio-economic thinking as a supervisor of doctoral theses and as an editor of economic journals. He supported the brightest minds among the young economists with great engagement and enthusiasm. His most outstanding student was Jacob Marschak (1898-1977) who wrote his dissertation on the quantity equation (1922) and his habilitation on the elasticity on demand (1930) with Lederer as the key referee.[27] Among his doctoral students we find Arthur Feiler (1923), who later became Professor at the New School, Carlo Mierendorff (1923), one of the most promising young politicians of the Social Democratic Party who was put into a concentration camp by the Nazis for many years and died during an air-raid on Berlin in 1943, and Alfred Sohn-Rethel (1928), an economic philosopher in the tradition of Marx and analyst of the economic basis of fascism who later got a kind of cult status during

---

viewpoint of the interests of the working class, smoothed the way for the later integration of the trade unions and the social democracy into the system of the market economy after the Second World War.

27 On Marschak see HAGEMANN (1997).

the student movement in Germany.[28] Lederer attracted many former Russian Menshevists like Marschak, Mark Mitnitzky (1930) and the political economist Paul Baran (1932) who became Lederer's only and most prominent PhD student for the short time he spent in Berlin.

Lederer came to Heidelberg in 1910 with the recommendation of Böhm-Bawerk and on the initiative of Edgar Jaffé (1866-1921), who in 1904 had habilitated in Heidelberg. In the same year Jaffé and his wife Else had bought the journal *Archiv für soziale Gesetzgebung und Statistik* from the social democrat Heinrich Braun who had founded the journal as a forum for the analysis of the state of society, in particular the labour question. There had never been any doubt that the special topical perspective of the *Archiv* was to analyse the impact of the (r)evolutionary changes in capitalism on the situation of the labouring classes. But Braun as well as all his successors always emphasised and managed to execute the non-partisan and scholarly character of the journal. Among the eminent authors who contributed important papers in the years of Braun's editorship from 1888 to 1903 had been Werner Sombart, Michail Tugan-Baranowsky as well as Sidney and Beatrice Webb. But after the acquisition of the journal by Jaffé it became Germany's most important learned journal in the social sciences for the next three decades. Since 1904 Jaffé edited the journal in co-operation with Sombart and Max Weber who in the following year published his classical study on 'The Protestant Ethic and the "Spirit" of Capitalism' in the journal. Although already in 1910 Jaffé moved to the University of Munich where Max Weber also became Professor in the last year of his life (1919-20), the *Archiv für Sozialwissenschaft und Sozialpolitik*[29], as it was called since 1904, was a genuine Heidelberg journal. The interdisciplinary character and the emphasis on the unity of the social sciences was an essential characteristics, like in the InSoSta whose members published regularly in the *Archiv*.

Emil Lederer not only contributed many of his own papers to the journal, but played a key role in the editorship of the *Archiv*. Having been secretary to the editors since 1911, he became *Schriftleiter* (general secretary) in 1918 and from 1922 onwards the managing editor, with the two new associate editors Joseph Schumpeter and Alfred Weber. During that period

---

28 For a full list of the Heidelberg years see ESSLINGER (1997, pp. 145-6).
29 All volumes of the *Archiv* were reprinted by Johnson Publishers, New York and London 1971.

the *Archiv* reached a quality and reputation which was never regained by any other German journal after 1933. Among the many outstanding papers still cited in the literature we find Nikolai Kondratieff's article on 'The long waves in economic life' (1926), which made his statistical investigations known to the Western world, and Wassily Leontief's Ph.D. thesis on 'The Economy as a Circular Flow' which he had finished at the University of Berlin under the supervision of Sombart and Ladislaus von Bortkiewicz. In this work which was translated into English only in 1991 and which "sounds the first note of the ouverture to his *Ring* of Input-Output" (Samuelson 1991, p. 177) analysis for which he received the Nobel prize in economics in 1973, Leontief described the way the economic system moves towards equilibrium over a period of time.

The *Archiv* came to be known as the "Lederer-Archiv". Although many papers were published by authors who were critics of the capitalist system, like Eduard Heimann, Karl Polanyi, Marschak or Lederer himself, or by members of the Frankfurt Institute for Social Research, like Herbert Marcuse, Otto Kirchheimer, Felix Weil or Karl August Wittfogel, the characteristic openness of the editorial policy can be seen from the treatment of members from the Austrian School. Starting with the publication of two articles on the demand for labour by Richard Schüller, a former student of Carl Menger, in 1911 the *Archiv* in Lederer's period always had been a forum for the ideas of the economists from Vienna to which it was probably more open than most other German journals. Whereas Hayek published a paper on the problem of interest theory in 1927, Ludwig von Mises published not less than ten papers in the period 1913-1929, among them the famous article which launched the socialist calculation debate (Mises 1920). Lederer shared Max Weber's view that scientific statements can and should claim validity among scientists with diverging *Weltanschauungen*.[30] However, he perceived clearer than Weber that the sciences, and particularly the social sciences, depended on the basic conditions of freedom and democracy. Since the destruction of the latter would endanger the (social) sciences, the scientists themselves have to defend the values of a free society, a position he advocated even more vehemently after emigration.

---

30 These principles were formulated in a famous paper by Max Weber on the "objectivity" of judgements in the social sciences at the beginning of his period as a (co-)editor of the *Archiv*, See WEBER (1904).

The *Archiv* also published articles which were pathbreaking for the development of new disciplines like Political Science and Political Sociology. This was for a greater part related with the defence of the new democratic republic which had been established after the end of the First World War. For example, Hans Kelsen, who was one of the architects of the constitution of the new Austrian Republic published an elaborate paper on the essence and value of democracy (Kelsen 1920). Some years later Marschak wrote a long two-part study in which he gave an early analysis of the character of Italian Fascists which revealed their despotic opportunism. Nevertheless, the liberal editorial policy of Emil Lederer allowed Robert Michels, a former socialist who had converted to Italian Fascism, to regularly contribute papers until 1932.

The *Archiv* published more outstanding papers within a year than many other journals within a decade. For example, if we take 1927 as a normal year within the Weimar period, the journal published contributions by Lederer, Schumpeter, Haberler, Hayek, Oppenheimer, Pigou and Röpke as well as articles by the sociologists Mannheim, Michels and Tönnies. And it was the *Archiv* which in 1933 after the Nazis' rise to power as the only one of the learned journals in economics had to terminate publication whereas most other scholarly journals had to substitute editors to survive, with Spiethoff who stayed as the editor of *Schmollers Jahrbuch* as a notable exception.[31]

Less than a year later, in February 1934, the first issue of *Social Research*, an international quarterly of political and social science, was published. For many good reasons this new journal which was published by the Graduate Faculty of the New School for Social Research can be regarded as the legitimate successor of the *Archiv*. *Social Research* served as an adjunct of the General Seminar of the Graduate Faculty in which the interdisciplinary atmosphere of Heidelberg's InSoSta and the Kiel group was kept alive and continued. It also reflected the collective spirit of the continental scholars who now had to adjust to a new environment. The General Seminar and the journal served as a forum for a cross-fertilization of cultures which gave an impetus for the genesis of many new ideas. For a greater part attention

---

31 With the *Archiv* coming to an end, the Vienna-based *Zeitschrift für Nationalökonomie* was the most important scholarly journal in the German language area until 1938 when Oskar Morgenstern, who had been managing editor since 1930 emigrated after the *Anschluss*. See HAGEMANN (1991, pp. 46-48).

was focused to the analysis and solution of the major political, social and economic problems of the 1930s from a more international perspective. Lederer, the co-director of the InSoSta and the managing editor of the *Archiv*, became the founding dean of the Graduate Faculty and the editor of *Social Research* who himself contributed the opening article to the first issue. Of the authors who contributed to the last two volumes of the *Archiv*, besides Lederer we also find Colm, Mitnitzky, Neisser and the sociologists Albert Salomon and Hans Speier among the authors of the first volume of *Social Research*. Contrary to today where it is mainly a forum for the social sciences, in the 1930s the themes of the journal were largely determined by the economists. The journal had an unexpected success. In 1939, the year of Lederer's death, *Social Research* not only had more than 800 subscribers, but also had a greater impact on public debates.

VI. The University in Exile and the State of the Masses

Naturally, the emigré economists, sociologists and political scientists at the New School dedicated a greater part of their scientific work to the analysis of national socialism and fascism.[32] Many articles on this issue were published in *Social Research*, starting with a paper by Borgese on the intellectual origins of fascism in the very first volume. Some projects deserve special attention. In Heimann's studies, which culminated in the book *Communism, Fascism or Democracy?* (1938), some important historical shortcomings of the socialist movement are pointed out which the author makes partly responsible for the rise of fascism, like the neglect of the role of the middle classes whose irrational rebellion against the dynamics of modern developments contributed to the victory of the Nazis. In the joint project of the members of the Graduate Faculty, *War in our time* (Speier/Kaehler 1939) the illusionary character of Chamberlain's statement "Peace in our time" at the Munich conference on the Nazi occupation of Czech territory is revealed. The authors convincingly challenged the view that the Munich agreement had safeguarded the peace in Europe. On the contrary, they showed that the 'not-yet war' situation had escalated. In

---

32 For greater details see KROHN (1993, pp. 129-139).

spring 1939 the first complete and unabridged English translation of Hitler's *Mein Kampf* was edited at the New School and published in New York, in which the most aggressive passages which were missing in the former version, officially authorised by the Nazi government, were put in italics. This was the last project in which Colm was involved before he went to Washington. In the context of the publication of Hitler's book Staudinger was stimulated to write *The Inner Nazi. A Critical Analysis of Mein Kampf*, in which the exiled Weimar civil servant analysed how far the Nazi ideology had permeated the German society and asked for the conditions of a successful building up of a democratic society in postwar Germany.[33]

Colm had already published an early paper on the role of the masses (Colm 1924) which in the late 1930s also became a central topic of Lederer's research. His book *State of the Masses. The Threat of the Classless Society* (Lederer 1940), edited posthumously by Hans Speier, is the outcome of his studies and Lederer's last major work in which he came back to his earlier analysis of the role of the middle classes. Lederer's analysis has several similarities with Colm's study, for example concerning the impact of the masses and the role of the leader in their steering and control. On the other hand, Colm sees a typical characteristics of the masses in their homogeneity which closes his mind to the insights of social stratification analysis. Lederer, who in his earlier work had emphasised the social stratification of the population into classes, meanwhile had made the experience that in Europe degraded and disoriented parts of the middle classes became a breeding place of fascism whereas the United States were an essentially capitalistic country which did not pervert to fascism. This learning process caused a significant shift of emphasis in Lederer's analysis. He now points out the destructive dynamics which can be caused by mass movements. Contrary to his earlier emphasis on class-consciousness, revolutionary changes and socialisation, the experience with fascism led Lederer to see in a differentiated social stratification not only the driving force for socio-economic changes but also the guarantee for the survival and evolution of a free democratic society. He now regarded the ideal of a classless society as a Marxian myth and suggested to give up the old socialist idea of the historical role of the proletariat. Although Lederer's study gives the impression of an unfinished work which partly lacks precision, his clear insights into

---

[33] Whereas the manuscript was finished in 1941, the book was only published posthumously (STAUDINGER 1981).

the weaknesses of the democracy which did not use its power monopoly and into the destructive dynamics of mass movements formed the basis for later analyses of the origins of totalitarianism, like that of Hannah Arendt.

According to Schumpeter, Lederer was "the leading academic socialist in the 1920s" (Schumpeter 1954, p. 854n). In that decade he wrote his advanced economics textbook on the foundations of economic theory, first published in 1922 and in the revised third edition *Aufriss der ökonomischen Theorie* published in 1931. In this work Lederer (1931a) gave an authoritative exposition and critique of those two traditions in which he was socialised as an economist: the marginal utility theory and the labour theory of value. He criticised the latter because of its neglect of effective demand failures caused by changes in consumer preferences. On the other hand, he agreed with the Marxists in not believing in unchangeable economic laws which in the long run are stronger than power, as it had been stressed by his teacher Böhm-Bawerk. Lederer can be seen as a representative of a dualistic objective and subjective value theory who was aiming at a synthesis of the psychological theory of the Austrian school and the objective theory of Karl Marx. Due to his academic training in Vienna he never lost his critical stance against Marxian economics and was alienated by the attempts of the German labour movement to find in its tradition of orthodox Marxist theory the modern tools it needed for a concrete vision of economic planning and a successful fight against hyperinflation after the First World War or a concept against unemployment some years later. However, he never forgot the sociological, historical and political conditions that are underlying all economics. His sense for these issues was sharpened by the fact that his life and academic career took place in four different political cultures: from the old Danube Monarchy, via Wilhelminic Germany and the Weimar Republic, to the United States of America in the phase of the depression and the New Deal Policy. Lederer's analysis got its strength from this interdisciplinary approach in combination with a great social engagement and the open-mindedness of a non-partisan procedure. This also holds for his economic theory which lacks the precision of modern mathematical theorising but is characterised by brilliant intuition and a clear vision of those factors which are important for the long-run development of the capitalist system. With Schumpeter, who, "in his economic theory,...was Lederer's 'master'"[34], he shared the view that emphasis in economic theory should be put on the

---

34 Jacob Marschak, letter to Hans Speier, April 14, 1977.

analysis of the short-run and particularly the long-run dynamics of the economy. Lederer saw rather early the importance of increasing returns to scale in production and their negative implications concerning the simple application of the principle of marginal productivity. In general, the interaction between dynamic changes and imperfect competition plays a most fruitful role in Lederer's analysis. This holds for his business-cycle theory, where increasing returns build a starting-point, as well as for his analysis of the employment consequences of technological change or of changes in income distribution. Since his student days in Vienna Lederer knew that economics means exact and strong thinking. However, the recognition of important dynamic changes includes factors which fall into the fields of sociology, political science, history, psychology or engineering science. "Their inclusion makes economics less "exact" but possibly that much truer, and is necessary to raise economics from the status of hypothetical deductions to a description of economic life, that is to say, to make it again a social science."[35] Consequently Lederer called himself a *Sozialökonom*, and it is in this area, social economics, that he made some of his strongest contributions, like his early and pioneering analysis of the role of the modern salaried employees.

References

BOMBACH, G. et al. (Eds.): *Der Keynesianismus II. Die beschäftigungspolitische Diskussion vor Keynes in Deutschland*, Berlin/Heidelberg/New York (Springer) 1976.

COLM, G.: "Die Masse. Ein Beitrag zur Systematik der Gruppen", *Archiv für Sozialwissenschaft und Sozialpolitik*, 52 (1924), pp. 680-694.

DICKLER, R. A: "Emil Lederer und die moderne Theorie des wirtschaftlichen Wachstums", Postscript to: E. LEDERER: *Technischer Fortschritt und Arbeitslosigkeit. Eine Untersuchung der Hindernisse des ökonomischen Wachstums, New Edition*, Frankfurt/M. (Europäische Verlagsanstalt) 1981, pp. 265-327.

---

35 KAEHLER (1941, pp. 86-87).

EMIL LEDERER: ECONOMICAL AND SOCIOLOGICAL ANALYST

DICKLER, R. A.: "Lederers Theorie der strukturellen Arbeitslosigkeit und lange Wellen", in: H. HAGEMANN, P. KALMBACH (Eds.): *Technischer Fortschritt und Arbeitslosigkeit*, Frankfurt/M. and New York (Campus) 1983, pp. 186-203.

DICKLER, R. A.: "Emil Lederer (1882-1939)", in: J. EATWELL, M. MILGATE, P. NEWMAN (Eds.): *The New Palgrave. A Dictionary of Economics*, Vol. 3, London (Macmillan) 1987, pp. 157-158.

DICKLER, R. A.: "Das Lederer Stagnationstheorem: Anhaltspunkte zur Weiterführung?", *Discussion Paper 127*, Department of Economics, University of Hohenheim, Stuttgart 1996.

ESSLINGER, H. U.: "The Impact of Emigration on Emil Lederer's Work on Economics", *History of Economic Ideas*, 1 (1993), pp. 111-140.

ESSLINGER, H. U.: "Interdisziplinarität. Zu Emil Lederer's Wissenschaftsverständnis am InSoSta", in: R. BLOMERT, H. U. ESSLINGER, N. GIOVANNINI (Eds.): *Heidelberger Sozial- und Staatswissenschaften. Das Institut für Sozial- und Staatswissenschaften zwischen 1918 und 1958*, Marburg (Metropolis) 1997, pp. 117-158.

FACTOR, R. A.: *Guide to the Archiv für Sozialwissenschaft und Sozialpolitik Group, 1904-1933. A History and Comprehensive Bibliography*, New York (Greenwood Press) 1988.

GARVY, G.: "Keynes and the Economic Activists of Pre-Hitler Germany", *Journal of Political Economy*, 83 (1975), pp. 391-405.

GOURVITCH, A.: *Survey of Economic Theory on Technological Change and Employment*, Philadelphia 1940, Reprint New York (Augustus M. Kelley) 1966.

HAGEMANN, H.: "Learned Journals and the Professionalization of Economics: The German Language Area", *Economic Notes*, 20 (1991), pp. 33-57.

HAGEMANN, H.: "Technological Unemployment", in: P. ARESTIS, M. MARSHALL (Eds.): *The Political Economy of Full Employment*, Aldershot (Edward Elgar) 1995, pp. 36-53.

HAGEMANN, H.: "Jacob Marschak (1898-1977)", in: R. BLOMERT, H. U. ESSLINGER, N. GIOVANNINI (Eds.): *Heidelberger Sozial- und Staatswissenschaften. Das Institut für Sozial- und Staatswissenschaften zwischen 1918 und 1958*, Marburg (Metropolis) 1997, pp. 211-244.

HAGEMANN, H.: "The Analysis of Wages and Unemployment Revisited: Keynes and Economic 'Activists' of Pre-Hitler Germany", in: L. PASINETTI, B. SCHEFOLD (Eds.): *The Impact of Keynes on Economics in the 20th Century*, Cheltenham (Edward Elgar) 1999, pp. 117-130.

HAYEK, F. A.: "Zur Problemstellung der Zinstheorie", *Archiv für Sozialwissenschaft und Sozialpolitik*, 58 (1927), pp. 517-532.

HEIMANN, E.: *Communism, Fascism or Democracy*, New York 1938.

HEIMANN, E., KÄHLER, A., MARSCHAK, J.: "Emil Lederer, 1882-1939. II. The Economist", *Social Research*, 8 (1941), pp. 79-105.

KAEHLER, A.: *Die Theorie der Arbeiterfreisetzung durch die Maschine*, Greifswald (Julius Abel) 1933.

KALDOR, N.: "A Case against Technical Progress?", *Economica*, 12 (1932), pp. 180-196.

KELSEN, H.: "Vom Wesen und Wert der Demokratie", *Archiv für Sozialwissenschaft und Sozialpolitik*, 47 (1920), pp. 50-85.

KÖNKE, G.: "Planwirtschaft oder Marktwirtschaft? Ordnungspolitische Vorstellungen sozialdemokratischer National-Ökonomen in der Weimarer Republik", *Vierteljahresschrift für Sozial- und Wirtschaftsgeschichte*, 77 (1990), pp. 457-487.

KROHN, C. D.: *Intellectuals in Exile. Refugee Scholars and the New School for Social Research*, Amherst (University of Massachusetts Press) 1993. Original: *Wissenschaft im Exil. Deutsche Sozial- und Wirtschaftswissenschaftler in den USA und die New School for Social Research*, Frankfurt/M. (Campus) 1987.

LASKER, B., SALOMON, A., STAUDINGER, H.: "Emil Lederer, 1882-1939. I The Sociologist", *Social Research*, 7 (1940), pp. 337-358.

LEDERER, E.: "Beiträge zur Kritik des Marxschen Systems", *Zeitschrift für Volkswirtschaft, Sozialpolitik und Verwaltung*, 15 (1906), pp. 307-324.

LEDERER, E.: *The Problem of the Modern Salaried Employee: Its Theoretical and Statistical Basis*, New York 1937, Original: *Die Privatangestellten in der modernen Wirtschaftsentwicklung*, Tübingen (J.C.B. Mohr) 1912.

LEDERER, E.: "Probleme der Sozialisierung", *Schriften des Vereins für Sozialpolitik*, Vol. 159, Munich (Duncker & Humblot) 1919, pp. 99-116.

LEDERER, E.: "Konjunktur und Krisen", *Grundriss der Sozialökonomik*, Abt. IV, Part I, Tübingen (J.C.B. Mohr) 1925, pp. 354-413.

LEDERER, E. (1931a): *Aufriss der ökonomischen Theorie*, Tübingen (J.C.B. Mohr) 3d edition 1931.

LEDERER, E. (1931b): *Technischer Fortschritt und Arbeitslosigkeit*, Tübingen (J.C.B. Mohr) 1931.

LEDERER, E. (1931c): *Wege aus der Krise*, Tübingen (J.C.B. Mohr) 1931.

LEDERER, E. (1931d): *Wirkungen des Lohnabbaus*, Tübingen (J.C.B. Mohr) 1931.

LEDERER, E.: "The Problem of Development and Growth in the Economic System", *Social Research*, 2 (1935), pp. 20-38.

LEDERER, E.: *Technical Progress and Unemployment. An Enquiry into the Obstacles to Economic Expansion*, Geneva (International Labour Office) 1938.

LEDERER, E.: *State of the Masses. The Threat of the Classless Society*, New York (W.W. Norton & Co) 1940.

LEDERER, E., LEDERER-SEIDLER, E.: *Japan-Europa. Wandlungen im Fernen Osten*, Frankfurt/M. (Frankfurter Societäts-Druckerei) 1929.

LEDERER, E., LEDERER-SEIDLER, E.: *Japan in Transition*, New Haven (Yale University Press) 1938.

EMIL LEDERER: ECONOMICAL AND SOCIOLOGICAL ANALYST

LEDERER, E., MARSCHAK, J.: "Der neue Mittelstand", in: *Grundriss der Sozialökonomik*, Abt. IX, Part I, Tübingen (J.C.B. Mohr) 1926, pp. 120-141.

LEDERER, E., MARSCHAK, J.: "Die Klassen auf dem Arbeitsmarkt und ihre Organisationen", in: *Grundriss der Sozialökonomik*, Sect. IX, Part II, Tübingen (J.C.B. Mohr) 1927, pp. 106-258.

LEONTIEF, W.: "The distribution of work and income", *Scientific American*, September 1982. Reprinted in: W. LEONTIEF: *Input-Output Economics*, New York and Oxford (Oxford University Press) 2nd edition 1985, pp. 363-378.

LÖWE, A.: "Lohnabbau als Mittel der Krisenbekämpfung?" *Neue Blätter für den Sozialismus*, 1 (1930), pp. 289-295.

MARSCHAK, J.: "Der korporative und der hierarchische Gedanke im Fascismus", *Archiv für Sozialwissenschaft und Sozialpolitik*, 52 (1924), pp. 695-728 and 53 (1925), pp. 81-140.

MARSCHAK, J.: *Die Lohndiskussion*, Tübingen (J.C.B. Mohr) 1930.

MISES, L. v.: "Die Wirtschaftsrechnung im sozialistischen Gemeinwesen", *Archiv für Sozialwissenschaft und Sozialpolitik*, 47 (1920), pp. 86-121.

NEISSER, H.: "Lohnsenkung als Heilmittel gegen Arbeitslosigkeit?", *Magazin der Wirtschaft*, 1930, pp. 1301-1306.

PATINKIN, D.: *Anticipations of the General Theory? And other Essays on Keynes*, Chicago (Chicago University Press) 1982.

SAMUELSON, P. A.: "Leontief's 'The Economy as a Circular Flow': An Introduction", *Structural Change and Economic Dynamics*, 2 (1991), pp. 177-179.

SCHUMPETER, J. A.: *History of Economic Analysis*, London (George Allen & Unwin) 1954.

SPEIER, H.: "Emil Lederer: Leben und Werk", in E. LEDERER: *Kapitalismus, Klassenstruktur und Probleme der Demokratie in Deutschland 1910-1940. Selected Essays*, Göttingen (Vandenhoeck & Ruprecht) 1979, pp. 253-272.

SPEIER, H., KAEHLER, A. (Eds.): *War in Our Time*, New York 1939.

STAUDINGER, H.: *The Inner Nazi. A Critical Analysis of Mein Kampf*, edited and introduced by P. M. Rutkoff and W. B. Scott, Baton Rouge (Louisiana State University Press) 1981.

STAUDINGER, H.: *Wirtschaftspolitik im Weimarer Staat. Lebenserinnerungen eines politischen Beamten im Reich und in Preußen 1889 bis 1934*, edited and introduced by H. Schulze, Bonn (Verlag Neue Gesellschaft) 1982.

STOLPER, W. F.: *Joseph Alois Schumpeter. The Public Life of a Private Man*, Princeton (University Press) 1994.

WEBER, M.: "Die 'Objektivität' sozialwissenschaftlicher und sozialpolitischer Erkenntnis", *Archiv für Sozialwissenschaft und Sozialpolitik*, 19 (1904), pp. 22-87.

Discussion Summary

Johan Tralau

Paper discussed:
HARALD HAGEMANN: Emil Lederer (1882-1939): Economical and Sociological Analyst and Critic of Capitalist Development

At the beginning of the discussion, it was asked to which extent Lederer's thinking was a product of his own time (ZONINSEIN). Lederer certainly did not agree with Weber on the value of "value-free" science. Lederer's own model is not very convincing, however. The influence of the spirit of the times and the Weimar Republic was great, hence the emphasis on the problems of cartelisation and under-consumption (HAGEMANN).

The discussion then turned to cartelisation, and the question how it was supposed to solve the problem of under-consumption. This is not clear, and rather dubious as a part of a political programme (KOSLOWSKI). Whereas Gustav Gundlach considered cartelisation to be the greater problem, Lederer quite evidently thought it was a solution, a lesser evil (RAUSCHER). Economists certainly were in favour of cartelisation in the Weimar Republic. This positive evaluation of cartelisation can be explained historically, yet one fails to see how it actually could solve any problems (KOSLOWSKI). In a market where no perfect competition prevails, cartelisation may evidently be the lesser evil (RAUSCHER). However, one must consider the impact of cartelisation on the entire economy, not just on one sector of the market, as was the case in some analyses (HAGEMANN). Moreover, the negative effects which cartelisation may have can be seen in Poland, where the coal industry has control over the state; hence it is possible for it to dump coal in other countries, yet sell to Polish consumers at extremely high a price (CHMIELEWSKI). The cartelisation in the Weimar Republic was possible due to the international isolation of Germany; thus, there was no

DISCUSSION SUMMARY

free market. In a society with more of a free market, the conditions are completely different (KOSLOWSKI).

The present globalisation of economies shows that the scheme of supply and demand is wrong. Therefore, one must think critically as regards to its over-simplification (ZONINSEIN). This is not necessarily the case, since employment effects vary in different sectors of the economy (HAGEMANN). That is, however, not an economic problem for the capitalist order, but rather a political and social one (ZONINSEIN). The discussion then focused on Lederer's contact with Japan. Arisawa, an influential pupil of Lederer's, was mentioned, as well as his teachings on technological change. Lederer's book on Japan has never been translated into Japanese (HAGEMANN, YAGI).

The discussion then concerned Lederer's critique of mass democracy. It seems to be analogous to the earlier and contemporary social psychology. What was, then, the more precise content of Lederer's theory regarding the state of the masses (WOHLGEMUTH)? In his analysis, the link to white-collar workers played the most important role. According to Lederer, the cause of the crisis connected to the masses was the erosion of the middle classes. As we can see today as well, this development destabilises society (HAGEMANN). In the present research on the period, the historical perspective has been neglected; it is important to note that also people from the left and liberals were fascinated by National Socialism. The totalitarian movement must be considered in its epoch (HASELBACH). The discussion finally concerned the historical rise of the group of white-collar workers. What was the reason for the tremendous growth of bureaucracy? It would be a tautology to try and explain it by the multiplication of the bureaucratic personnel (KOSLOWSKI). As the group of white-collar workers grew, distribution problems arose, problems which could be solved only by means of the expansion of the number of bureaucrats (HAGEMANN).

Chapter 3

Franz Oppenheimer's Theory of Capitalism and of a Third Path

DIETER HASELBACH

I. Introduction
II. Biographical Sketch
III. Two Strands of Economic Liberalism
IV. Oppenheimer's Work
V. Oppenheimer's Role in Weimar
VI. Post-war Reception of Oppenheimer

I. Introduction

Two motives[1] can be cited for the inclusion of Franz Oppenheimer in a conference exploring the influence of the Historical School on German social and economic thought. The first is Oppenheimer's role in the inter-war economic discussions and his influences on the key players of post-war economics and economic policy in Germany. The second is the widely held belief that Oppenheimer is one of the intellectual forefathers of the West German economic concept of the Social Market Economy that was so successful in the 1950s and 1960s.

Yet, both these views are not without problems. First, Oppenheimer never showed any sympathy for the positions of the Historical School. His work does not contain any more than a conventional classical-minded criti-

---

[1] I want to thank Helen Kelly-Holmes for her help in making my English sound more English, and I want to thank the participants of the SEEP in Hildesheim for their criticism in an interesting discussion of this paper.

cism of this School. Oppenheimer was in opposition to the School that so clearly represented the main stream of economic debate during most of his life-time. It comes as no surprise that Oppenheimer was considered an outsider to the discipline. But it was not only his leaning toward a classical mode of economic theorising that made him an outsider. In the core of his works there are some deeply held beliefs that did not even appear plausible to those of his contemporaries sympathetic toward his methodological approach.[2] The fact that Oppenheimer was an outsider became even more obvious after his death, and when an open discussion of economic theory and practice was possible again after 1945. He was considered worthy of some scholarly attention mainly in debates at the fringes of scholarship, or which were - as will be shown - more the outcome of political and ideological motivations than of a renewed interest in his theoretical position.

What was Oppenheimer's position with regard to the Historical School? It can be summarised as follows: Oppenheimer was a rationalist and a supporter of a strictly deductive theory. He supported a transformation of history into a deductive science, from the art of narration. This was a concept alien to all methodological beliefs in the Historical School. If one does find a positive reference to the Historical School in Oppenheimer's writing, its context is always - so to speak - an embracing of the enemy, in order to incorporate their work into the great rationalist vision of a positivistic synthesis of sciences.

But was Oppenheimer, then, a beacon of neo-classical economical thought in an ocean of historical economy? Again, the answer can be rather straightforward. Oppenheimer did not get involved in the newly emerging themes and discussions of the marginalists. His field was clearly confined to the classical political economy, and again he was out of tune with the contemporary scholarly debate. He was not only an outsider to the outmoded fashion of economics, but was also an outsider to what emerged as the new orthodoxy, as the successor to the Historical School.

In an unpublished manuscript, most likely written after Oppenheimer had escaped from Nazi Germany in 1938, he distanced himself from both the Historical School and marginalist economics in clear words. The quota-

---

2 Cf. H. D. KURZ: "Franz Oppenheimer und das Problem der 'Bodensperrung'", in: V. CASPARI, B. SCHEFOLD (Eds): *Franz Oppenheimer und Adolph Lowe: Zwei Wirtschaftswissenschaftler der Frankfurter Universität*, Marburg (Metropolis) 1996, pp. 65-120.

tion below also shows that Oppenheimer liked the rhetoric of the class struggle, this without ever having been a follower of a Marxist notion of class. In this text, Oppenheimer argues that after the Marxist attack on bourgeois economy in the mid 19th century, there was a need for a new political economy:

> The ruling class was in dire need of an entirely new science of political economy suited to being taught without disgrace, from the academic chairs, and, if not so at least, innocuous to capitalist domination.
> The bourgeoisie, becoming more and more feudalised, confided the difficult task in the first instance to the old, "traditionalist" or "romanticist" enemies of liberalism. The 'historical school of economics,' through a full generation, ruled with an iron rod all universities of the civilised world, assigning each vacated chair to its devotees. In the long run, however, it proved impossible to convince the world, that history of economy is economic theory. The time of the subjectivists had come. They meanwhile had worked out a very intricate and elaborate theory with all the externals of, not only serious, but even strictly rigorous science, up to a superabundant wealth of algebraic formulas and illustrating graphs, a truly imposing window dressing. This so splendidly rigged up doctrine was, if not outright apologetic, in any event harmless, viewed from the standpoint of capitalist interests. Thus the crown of officialdom passed from the completely exploded Historical School to this new subjectivist sect of "Marginalists," as they usually are called.
> This monopoly was bound to fall just as that of the predecessor. It rested on the identical sleight of hand that the Historical School had executed: The marginalists teach psychology, and a rather questionable one, pretending to teach economic theory.[3]

Of course, even an answer in the negative, to the question of connections between Oppenheimer and the Historical School, needs a more elaborate argument. In this article, I want to stress three points. First, Oppenheimer represents an undercurrent of economic thought that accompanies the development of liberal capitalism. Rightly, Oppenheimer's theory has

---

[3] F. OPPENHEIMER: *The Austrian School of Marginal Utility and Value*, Typoscript, 113 pages, not dated, pp. 2/3 (held in the Central Zionist Archives in the Oppenheimer papers (A161, Box 40). Further references to the collection Oppenheimer papers are referenced as CZA, Box number).

been included among theories of a third path that avoids the extremisms both of the political left and right. In exactly this role Oppenheimer has been claimed by Ludwig Erhard as a forefather of West Germany's Social Market Economy. Erhard considered Oppenheimer's economic policy as a newer application of a third path. Using Oppenheimer's work as a starting point, I want to come to a sharper definition of 'third-path-theories' in this paper.

Second, Oppenheimer is in one respect a unique theorist in the development of social science in Germany. He was one of the last scholars who managed to bridge the widening gap between sociology as a soft social science and economy as an increasingly mathematically oriented, and model-building exercise, framing itself in terms of exact science. Oppenheimer, stemming this tide that separated the two former parts of *Staatswissenschaft*, was capable of introducing into economics, some insights that helped understanding of the various crises that accompanied, and still accompany, the process of modernisation. In addition, as one of the very few academically established scholars in classical economics, his seminar in Frankfurt attracted much of the soon to be influential new generation of neo-classical economic thinkers, and the best representatives of post-orthodox, ethical socialism. I shall argue that his role as the, so to speak, school-head of new economic thought in Germany came upon Oppenheimer by default, and that his influence on his disciples was limited, to say the least.

Third, the often argued connection of his theory to the success story of post-war West German economic reconstruction, the 'Social Market Economy,' deserves special discussion. Over the last few years, with a renewed interest in the life and work of Oppenheimer, quite a few scholarly works have been written that stress this point in particular. In discussing this literature, I want to argue that besides all personal relations of Oppenheimer and key players of the post-war period, intellectual connections between Oppenheimer's approach and the Social Market Economy remain rather weak.

Arguments surrounding the foundation and development of the Social Market Economy are highly charged in the German political and historic debate, as this doctrine and practice represent nothing less than the founding myth of the West German state, and explain much of the country's still largely 'post'-national identity. While this point cannot be fully argued in this paper[4], it makes clear why the discussion of Oppenheimer and his contribution to the Social Market Economy receives so much scholarly attention.

I want to proceed as follows. I would like to start with a brief biographical outline (II) Then I want to suggest a distinction between two strands of liberalism relevant to the discussion of Oppenheimer, ordoliberalism, and the Social Market Economy, which will facilitate a definition of a third path as an economic strategy (III) Then, I want to give an account of Oppenheimer's theory in some detail (IV) and discuss, why he did not have substantial influence on his students (V) Oppenheimer will be portrayed as a scholar, obsessed with one single, in my opinion, flawed idea on how to fundamentally reform capitalism. In the final chapter, I want to point out, why I consider it unsound to propose a strong intellectual connection between Oppenheimer and the Social Market Economy, and for what reasons, counterfactually, this proposition remains prominent anyway.

II. Biographical Sketch

Franz Oppenheimer was born in 1864 into a liberal Jewish family in Berlin.[5] Although he was more interested in the Humanities, he was forced to study medicine, as this was a profession open to Germans of Jewish faith without foreseeable institutional discrimination. Some years of practice in a proletarian neighbourhood of Berlin gave Oppenheimer, so he claimed, insights into the 'social question.' A period spent as general practitioner in

---

4   I have given fuller account of this problem in two articles. "'Soziale Marktwirtschaft' als Gründungsmythos. Zur Identitätsbildung im Nachkriegsdeutschland", in: C. MAYER-ISWANDY (Ed.): *Zwischen Traum und Trauma - Die Nation. Transatlantische Perspektiven zur Geschichte eines Problems*, Tübingen (Stauffenburg) 1994, pp. 255-266; "Nation, Gott und Markt. Mythos und gesellschaftliche Integration bei Alfred Müller-Armack", in: M. Th GREVEN, P. KÜHLER, M. SCHMITZ (Eds): *Politikwissenschaft als Kritische Theorie. Festschrift für Kurt Lenk*, Baden-Baden (Nomos) 1994, pp. 215-230.
5   For this and the following part cf. Oppenheimer's autobiography (F. OPPENHEIMER: *Erlebtes, Erstrebtes, Erreichtes. Lebenserinnerungen*, Düsseldorf (Melzer) 1964), first published in 1931.

rural north-eastern Germany provided even more impressive insights into the living conditions of rural workers. In the 1890s, Oppenheimer gave up the medical profession, and made his living as a journalist and as an activist in a number of groups and initiatives working on non-Marxist ways of overcoming capitalism. These groups may be best described in today's terms as New Social Movements, their class background was mainly bourgeois and petit bourgeois, the political passions were not revolutionary, but aimed at a fundamental reform of capitalism. Of particular importance to the groups in which Oppenheimer was particularly engaged, were Henry George's *new physiocratic theory*, the idea of a *co-operative economy,* and the striving for an *ethical reform* of society.

Different from today's New Social Movements that are backed by a structurally growing social basis in contemporary society, the groups Oppenheimer was involved in were on the defensive, both in political and economic terms. Small scale businesses, and economically dependent academic professions viewed themselves as losers in the structural changes that accompanied the build-up of corporate capitalism. The political mood of these groups in Germany at the turn of the century was an odd mixture of anti-capitalism, nationalism, and radical libertarianism. They were liberal at heart, but they did not believe in liberalism's capacity to hold out against power, the power of the old elite and the powers of big business. Power was considered by many of them as the main obstacle to their social and economic success. This liberalism was well rooted in the British and European tradition of individualism, anti-statist sentiments; it was a political world view that was both market-minded and concerned about civil liberties and did not see any contradiction or conflict between those goals.

Oppenheimer, as a part of this world of middle class beliefs, considered co-operatives to be the key to social reform. In this orientation, he found himself in sympathy with a wide range of German, and indeed European, middle class activists, including early Zionists, on whom he exercised some influence: Oppenheimer was chosen by Theodor Herzl as his principle economic advisor. Independent from Oppenheimer, but very much in tune with the time, Herzl had drafted the idea of a co-operative Jewish state, that was to be established by way of founding co-operative agrarian settlements. Herzl was attracted by Oppenheimer's like-mindedness, and hoped to exploit his economic expertise for the Zionist cause.[6] Although Oppenheimer, particularly in the years before the First World War, devoted much of his time to the Zionist movement[7], for him, Zionism was rather a means than an end of his political ambitions. Although he was for some decades, as he had put it, in the role of the 'leading economist of the Zionist movement'[8], he was more interested in co-operative settlements themselves (the agrarian settlement co-operative[9]) than in the Jewish homeland. Although Oppenheimer was strongly opposed to the sharp nationalistic turn Zionism took after the end of the First World War, he nevertheless remained in close contact with the Zionist movement until the 1930s, and served in numerous official positions within the organisation.

In 1909, after many years of independent studies and numerous publications in the field of political economy[10], Oppenheimer became a *Privatdoz-*

---

6 The letters exchanged between Herzl and Oppenheimer are printed in: T. HERZL, F. OPPENHEIMER: "Briefwechsel", *Bulletin für die Mitglieder der Gesellschaft der Freunde des Leo Baeck Institute*, 7 (1964), pp. 21-55. Cf. also B. VOGT: "Die Utopie als Tatsache? Judentum und Europa bei Franz Oppenheimer", *Menora. Jahrbuch für deutsch-jüdische Geschichte* (1994), pp. 123-142.

7 This is illustrated by the letters, exchanged between the Zionist central office in Cologne and Oppenheimer in the year before First World War, documented in CZA 10-12.

8 OPPENHEIMER, *Erlebtes, op.cit.*, p. 212.

9 With support and financial help of international Zionist organisations, Oppenheimer funded a settlement co-operative in Palestine. The settlement was economically successful, and still exists as a Kibbutz in Israel. Yet, after the first few years, the settlement did not follow Oppenheimer's prescriptions any more, but followed a trend toward collective, rather than co-operative settlement approaches within Zionism. Cf. H. BARKAI: "Oppenheimer and the Zionist Resettlement of Palestine: The Genossenschaft versus the Collective Settlement", in: V. CASPARI/B. SCHEFOLD (Eds.): *Franz Oppenheimer und Adolph Lowe: Zwei Wirtschaftswissenschaftler der Frankfurter Universität*, Marburg (Metropolis) 1996, pp. 17-64.

10 A Bibliography of Oppenheimer's works has been published by FELICIA FUSS ("A Bibliography of Franz Oppenheimer, 1864-1943", *The American Journal of Economics and Sociology*, 6 (1946/47, No. 1), pp. 95-112 and 7 (1947/48, No. 1), pp. 107-117), B. VOGT (*Franz Oppenheimer. Wissenschaft und Ethik der*

ent in Berlin; his habilitation (postdoctoral thesis) was supported by Germany's most reputable economists Adolph Wagner and Gustav Schmoller, the latter being the head of the younger Historical School. Taking up his duties as *Privatdozent* (private lecturer), Oppenheimer was a stunning success; his lectures were social events in a wider intellectual community and attracted crowds that filled the largest lecture hall at the Humboldt University. Oppenheimer was equally successful as a writer. He wrote quickly, easily, profusely, and in a style without any scholarly heavy-handedness. Accordingly, he was an asset for both publishers and journals and received numerous invitations for—usually well paid—contributions or book contracts over the years. Yet, until 1918, Oppenheimer was blocked from becoming a university professor, on account of his being a Jew. Only after the War was this practical veto on Jewish scholars overcome[11]. In 1918, Oppenheimer accepted an offer by the newly founded Goethe University of Frankfurt to become the holder of the first chair in a German university in the new discipline of sociology.[12]

Yet, the circumstances of Oppenheimer's appointment in Frankfurt[13] give evidence that his was not the glamorous career it seemed to be at first sight. The chair that Oppenheimer came to occupy was endowed by the Frankfurt businessman and patrician Consul Karl Kotzenberg. The endowment, probably not Kotzenberg's contribution alone but topped up by other Frankfurt area supporters of Oppenheimer[14], was made on the condition that Oppenheimer would be the first holder of the chair.[15] Yet, the faculty

---

sozialen Marktwirtschaft (Studien zur Geistesgeschichte 22), Bodenheim (Philo) 1997) has found some writings that had been overseen by Fuss.

11 Oppenheimer's academic fate parallels that of the prominent sociologist Georg Simmel who got his first appointment in 1914 at the age of 56 at the University of Strassburg. Many such examples of institutionalized ethnic discrimination occurred in Wilhelmian Germany.

12 The president of the German Sociological Association, Ferdinand Tönnies recognised on a short undated note on a business card to Oppenheimer, this first chair in sociology (CZA, 73).

13 Cf. Paul Kluke's history of the Frankfurt University (*Die Stiftungsuniversität Frankfurt am Main 1914-1932*, Frankfurt 1972).

14 Letter Oppenheimer to Kotzenberg, 7 January, 1918, typescript (CZA, 71).

15 A first contact between Oppenheimer and Kotzenberg is documented in letters as early as 1915: Kotzenberg had organised a twelve part lecture series of Oppenheimer in Franfurt (cf. CZA, 69).

in Frankfurt was rather hostile to Oppenheimer. While the endowment was being negotiated, Kotzenberg wrote to Oppenheimer, warning that his name should under no condition be disclosed before the deal was made, 'because you have only adversaries in the faculty, something which you should in fact take as a compliment.'[16] The faculty later openly opposed the appointment of Oppenheimer. In a symbolically belligerent, but, in practice, conciliatory move, they put his name only in second place on the short list, behind the positivistic social philosopher and sociologist Paul Barth. In the negotiations with Oppenheimer over the terms and conditions of employment, it again became clear that he had no support among his colleagues— they initially opposed Oppenheimer's wish to extend his teaching responsibilities from sociology to include theoretical economics (*theoretische Nationalökonomie*) and they obstructed his wish to build up a library for his line of research; this meant that more endowment money, originally meant to pay Oppenheimer's salary, had to be chipped in.

After Oppenheimer had taken up his duties, relations with the faculty did not improve much - he remained an outsider during his Frankfurt years. The Frankfurt employment, that he had started with some enthusiasm, soon became a half exile. At the earliest possible occasion, in 1929, Oppenheimer chose to become an emeritus professor, and he moved from Frankfurt back to the Berlin area, where he took up residence on one of the agrarian settlements that had been started with the help of the Prussian government following his advice.

After the Nazis had taken power, Oppenheimer, who had seen no contradiction between his Jewish ancestry and being a German patriot, and who could not imagine being in personal danger in Germany, tried to stay in the country. In 1938, after the state initiated pogroms had peaked in the so called *Kristallnacht*, the situation became unbearable and Oppenheimer was forced into emigration. After a short stay in Japan, Oppenheimer had to

---

16 Letter Kotzenberg to Oppenheimer, 2 February 1918, typescript (CZA, 71). The context was a meeting of Kotzenberg with the mayor of Frankfurt, who served on the University Committee: '*In Ihrer Angelegenheit habe ich bereits Schritte getan, die Sache steht aber noch aus; jedenfalls steht aber der Oberbürgermeister als Vorsitzender des Kuratoriums meinem Wunsche sympathisch gegenüber, nur sagt auch er, dass wir uns sehr hüten müssen, vorläufig Ihren Namen zu nennen, da Sie an der Fakultät eigentlich nur Widersacher haben, was ja für Sie höchstens ein Kompliment ist.*'

leave here too - he became an unwanted person after the Berlin-Tokyo axis was created. Oppenheimer and his youngest daughter Renate went on to Singapore and awaited the papers that would allow Renate to accompany her father to the US. Eventually, Oppenheimer and Renate settled in Los Angeles. Oppenheimer, now well into his seventies, used his migration years to translate much of his work into English, and to write new abbreviated versions of his main books in the new language. Most of it remained unpublished,[17] as he did not find a publisher who was interested in the writings of a German émigré at the margins of his discipline, set in an awkward English, and resonating times and concerns that seemed obsolete since the onset of the new World War. Only in a group of Neo-Physiocrats did Oppenheimer find some allies for his ideas. With like-minded people, he co-founded *The American Journal of Economics and Sociology*. The journal was originally sectarian, leaning toward Henry George and the Single Tax Movement[18]. It was here that Oppenheimer published his last articles, attempts to contribute to a post-war order, by exploiting the same ideas that had been to the fore of this thought since he had started publishing more than fifty years earlier.

Oppenheimer died in Los Angeles in 1943.[19]

The short years in Los Angeles did not facilitate a wider interest in the works of Oppenheimer in the English-speaking world. With the singular exception of his book *The State*, he is still almost unknown both in North America and in Britain. This book was translated into English in 1922[20], and has been republished several times since.[21] Oppenheimer's sociological scheme for mankind's early history was the object of some discussion in the

---

17 The typoscripts of these translations are collected with the Oppenheimer papers in Jerusalem (CZA).
18 Since then the journal has grown in reputation. It is now an established and intellectually widely accepted journal with a soft libertarian orientation.
19 EDUARD HEIMANN wrote an obituary in The American Journal of Sociology ("In Memoriam Franz Oppenheimer, 1863-1943", *American Journal of Sociology*, 49 (1943), p. 225).
20 *The State. Its History and Development Viewed Sociologically*. Authorized translation by John M. Gitterman, New York (Huebsch) 1922.
21 Cf. for example an edition Montreal (Black Rose Books) 1975. In 1972, another edition was published in the series: 'Right Wing Individualist Tradition in America.'

fields of early history and anthropology[22]. Since, Oppenheimer's name has only appeared peripherally in standard textbooks on the history of sociology which discuss his contributions to a general sociology of history, but not his economic doctrines[23]. Judgements as to where to locate Oppenheimer in the politico-intellectual landscape, have proven conspicuously insecure. Oppenheimer has been accorded some recognition in anarchist and libertarian discourses. It would be an exaggeration to claim that Oppenheimer's work is, or has ever been, really known in the English speaking world.

III. Two Strands of Economic Liberalism

What was Oppenheimer's contribution to the social sciences? Oppenheimer's work tried to re-write liberal economic theory with a distinctively anti-capitalist stance, albeit by reinvigorating the liberal utopia, and by reinterpreting the notion of capitalism. This theoretical approach can be characterised as a theory of a third path between capitalism and communism

After the death of Engels, and with no political praxis in government, Marxism had become increasingly dogmatic, and had lost touch with reality. It was Eduard Bernstein's mission to overhaul the doctrines of Marxism completely, and to propose streamlining the political praxis of Social Democracy. Since then, the dualism of *orthodoxy* and *revisionism* impregnates theoretical and programmatic debates in socialism.

In order to locate the work of Oppenheimer within the history of liberal economic thought, I want to suggest a parallel distinction for liberalism. There is classical liberal thought. It was partly evolving into a hardened dogmatic stance, the orthodoxy of Manchester liberalism, a degeneration of theory into an interest position. What then could liberal revisionism be? In one respect, the case of liberalism fundamentally differs from Marxism. In the 19th century, liberalism already reflected praxis, reflected policy, while

---

22 Cf. LOWIE, R.: *The Origin of the State*, New York (Russel & Russel) 1927 and MACLEOD, W. CH.: *The Origin of the State*, Philadelphia 1924.

23 Cf. among others: SOROKIN, P. A.: *Contemporary Sociological Theories*, New York 1928, pp. 483-487, and BECKER, H. and BARNES, H. E.: *Social Thought from Lore to Science*, 3 vols., 3rd ed., Gloucester, Mass. 1978, pp. 721-730.

Marxism did not. Social Democratic revisionism had to bring theory up to the level of an achievable political praxis. In contrast, liberal revisionism had to tackle the question of why liberal praxis had failed, why liberalism had not delivered on its political promises. The question for liberal revisionism was thus, why liberalism, as a practical policy, had not succeeded in harmonising and ordering the economic and social world through the invisible hand of the market forces, but had, instead, brought about new social divisions and political turmoil, the Social Question. Why was there not economic and political harmony in market societies rather than the lingering threat of an anti-capitalist, which was also: an anti-liberal, revolution?

In principle, two answers to the problem are possible. One would tackle shortcomings in liberal theory, either with the effect at scaling down the pretensions of liberalism, or to improve its praxis. The other would be to blame reality, in order to keep up the fullest belief in the promises of liberal theory. I suggest calling the first strategy *liberal revisionism*, and such liberal revisionism has become the mainstream of liberal economic thought since the turn of the century. In Germany, for example, the ordoliberal school was, and claimed to be, revisionist[24] in exactly this sense, and so was the school founded in England by Keynes.

For the second strategy of explaining the gap between liberal promise and actually existing capitalism, and for suggesting a strategy on how to overcome it, a name has to be coined. One could call it 'orthodoxy *aprés la lettre.*' Or, with a bit of irony, and if the term would not be in use elsewhere: 'neo-classical economics.' For the catchingness of the term, rather than for historical precision, I want to call this approach *messianic liberalism*, and by doing so, I do not want to suggest that what has just been labelled liberal revisionism would always be free of messianic traits[25].

In its explanatory strategy and in its policy suggestions, messianic liberalism differs radically from liberal revisionism. Revisionism is a disenchanted liberalism. For the most part, it has been cleared of the belief in a

---

24 Cf. Alexander Rüstow's famous speech at the *Verein für Sozialpolitik* in 1932 (reprinted: RÜSTOW, A.: *Rede und Antwort*, Ludwigsburg 1963, pp. 249-258).
25 The terminology has been inspired by A. RÜSTOW: *Das Versagen des Wirtschaftsliberalismus als religionsgeschichtliches Problem*, Istanbul 1945. In this book, he convincingly traces Deistic motives back to the very beginnings of liberal thought.

pre-stabilised harmony of societies organised around markets. Revisionists suggest a more sober approach and less utopian foresight than their classical precursors. Economic theory in liberal revisionism is not meant to sketch out heaven on earth, but it should serve as a tool for politics, an assistant in engineering, or steering, the economy on a path that - for the good of the people - remains within the realm of market regulations. Whether there are some overstretched pretensions in this aim, may remain undiscussed here. For revisionists, markets are historical institutions, man-made, necessitating a lot of upkeep and constant repair work. In admitting to the historical nature of economic institutions, revisionists pay some credit to the Historical School.

Liberal believers, in contrast, have not given up the theoretical Deism in liberal theory. For them, the explanatory strategy of theory, the purpose of theory, is to strengthen the position of a radical application of the market, even against the evidence of market failure. Messianic liberals use their theoretical efforts for explaining the sins that have to be overcome on the road to liberal resurrection. Liberal theology shares its hope for resurrection with other eschatological theories.

In a different, and maybe more familiar terminological distinction, one could call the liberal revisionists proponents of a reflexive modernity, and the believers in the messianic message modernists, as yet unaffected by reflexivity. But, for the distinction that I have in mind here, this terminological juxtaposition of modernism and reflexive modernism, or modernism and post-modernism, has a severe disadvantage: It obfuscates the fact that these discussions are much older than the recent, and now fashionable, invention of a post-, or reflexive, modernity. I would argue that reflexivity has been a trait inherent to modern thought since its beginnings. Ordoliberalism is a good example. Its revisionist scepticism against an unreflected modernity can be traced back to the eminent Catholic thinkers George Sorel, and in Germany Carl Schmitt, and I would suggest that the political economy of fascism and ordoliberalism share, to some extent, a common outlook on the political and economic problems of the times, they are both children of the troubled inter-war period in Europe[26]. - Yet, I do not draw this connection to a defamatory end, but to understand intellectual life at a

---

26 Cf. the first chapter of my book: *Autoritärer Liberalismus und Soziale Marktwirtschaft. Gesellschaft und Politik im Ordoliberalismus*, Baden-Baden (Nomos) 1991.

time when fascism was not equalled with evil, but seen as a valid attempt to save societies which were in the grip of a deep structural, both political and economic crises, from worse fates.

Oppenheimer's work can be seen as a prime example of messianic liberalism. But the phenomenon is more widespread. Messianic liberalism is the most important economic motive in third-path-scenarios. Where third paths explore economic territory, they search for political options beyond the apparently inescapable alternatives of capitalism and socialism. Third paths aim at market economy without capitalism, without concentration of power, without monopolies, without a Social Question. As they oppose capitalism - that is actually existing liberalism - they oppose socialism, because if market co-ordination is possible without the disadvantages of capitalism, any attempt at socialist policies loses its rationale. As market oriented anti-capitalists, proponents of a third path often oppose the social welfare state. It is perceived as a first step on the slippery slope down into the abyss of collectivism, and it would prove unnecessary if the proposed policies of the protagonists of a third path were to be realised.

As a political metaphor, the third path claims a larger field than just economics. Third path took on the meaning of to bridge the gap, or find an alternative approach beyond the dualism of modernity and tradition, of liberal democracy and authoritarian rule, of rationalism and *Heimat*. In the German political discourse for the larger part of our century, the metaphor of a third path proved so popular that it was exploited by a wide array of political movements or political attempts. Namely, protagonists of West Germany's Social Market Economy claimed, in a rather blurred notion, that their political programme represented a third path, avoiding the pitfalls of both the radicalisms of left and right, of unadulterated liberalism and of a planned economy. This was a late, and convoluted use of the metaphor. Before 1948, Germany, as a land in the centre of Europe, had had a wider use for this metaphor. Since then, the growing consensus on the western orientation of West Germany, strongly facilitated by the dichotomous situation of the Cold War that would not allow for positions in between, has gradually diminished the use of this metaphor in the political mainstream. Third path theories were pushed to the fringes of the political spectre. But in Oppenheimer's time, of course, the metaphor was still centre stage.

Economically, third path theories typically bank on the institution of small private property, or on co-operative forms of market economy. If one is to translate third paths into economic interest positions in actually existing market economies, then they represent, to a large extent, the less dynamic, traditional, only nominally independent economic players, that is small proprietors, small shop holders, crafts people, the weaker of the professions, in a word: minor bourgeois. If they organise as social movements, third path movements are individualistic, populist, more often oriented to the political Right than to the Left. Yet, lines of influence and cross-influence run between mainstream liberalism, the labour movement and the third path theories.

Economic programmes of third paths are founded on messianic liberalism. In this respect, Franz Oppenheimer is - for his generation - the arch-theorist of a third path. And he shares one more characteristic with other third-path-theories: the theoretical single-mindedness, his *idée fixe*, the strong tendency in his theory to explain every phenomenon, and every strategy from one single point.

IV. Oppenheimer's Work

Oppenheimer has often been called an eclectic writer, and in fact he himself did not claim originality for much of his writing, but underlined that he was deeply indebted to many economic and sociological theorists. For this reason, it appears appropriate to explain the main theoretical thrust of Oppenheimer's work by referring to three 19th century writers, each of them sharing with Oppenheimer the fate of intellectual outsider. Given restrictions of space, and in the attempt to condense a life-work into its main ideas, the following claims to be nothing more than an ideal typical construct of Oppenheimer's theory.

The first in the line of influences important to Oppenheimer was *Eugen Dühring*[27], a Berlin Social Democrat who is better known as the target of Frederick Engels' *Anti-Dühring* than as a scholar with a substantial contribution to the theory and strategy of the labour movement. Yet he was an

---

27 Cf. D. DOWE and K. TENFELDE: "Zur Rezeption Eugen Dührings in der deutschen Arbeiterbewegung in den 1870er Jahren", in: *Wissenschaftlicher Sozialismus und Arbeiterbewegung* (Schriften aus dem Karl-Marx-Haus 24), Trier 1980, pp. 25-58.

important player in the intellectual debates of the social democratic movement of the time, with a substantial number of followers inside and outside the party. This is illustrated by the fact that he was considered worthy of such a vigorous attack by Engels. As in the case of Oppenheimer, Dühring's analysis can be characterised by reference to messianic liberalism and to a third path of economic policy. The question motivating Dühring's theoretical thought was why the 'invisible hand' did not do its job? Dühring conceived a phenomenon which he called the 'original violence' (ursprüngliche Gewalt) embedded in the social structure. The shortcomings of actual liberalism as opposed to the liberal promise were blamed on this 'original violence.' In turn, if it was possible to overcome, or to counterbalance, 'original violence', the 'invisible hand' would become uncuffed. Dühring intended to find a force countering 'original violence,' and he found it in the trade unions. Their force was needed to help build a society of 'mutual reciprocity (*gleiche Gegenseitigkeit*)' in the face of 'original violence.' Considering later developments in social democratic theory and policy this early attempt to reconcile economic liberalism with the trade union movement proves more valid than Engels could admit in his polemic. Dühring's ideas some years later gained prominence in Eduard Bernstein's 'revisionist' works. As with Oppenheimer, Bernstein was strongly influenced by Dühring, however, not so much by his messianic liberalism as by the Kantian understanding of law that he found in Dühring.[28] There were, no doubt, numerous flaws in Dühring's theory. In particular, his inability to concretise what original violence in historic terms means is obvious. In addition, severe personality flaws, not least of which was his vigorous anti-Semitism, proved an enormous obstacle to a positive reception of Dühring in the social democracy.[29]

---

28 Cf. GUSTAFSSON, B.: *Marxismus und Revisionismus. Eduard Bernsteins Kritik des Marxismus und ihre ideengeschichtlichen Voraussetzungen*, 1st part, Frankfurt 1972.
29 In his memoirs, Oppenheimer regrets Dühring's Antisemitism, and the fact that he never able to meet Dühring in person, but nonetheless claims for himself the distinction of being 'the only academic expert' who 'in principle accepted and further developed his theory' (OPPENHEIMER: *Erlebtes, op.cit.*, p. 155).

DIETER HASELBACH

The second name to mention here is the legal scholar and sociologist *Ludwig Gumplowicz*[30]. By origin a Jew from Krakow, an activist in the Polish nationalist liberation struggle against the empire, and later a teacher of constitutional law in Graz, Austria, he developed a theory which gave the concept of original violence some historical foundation. Gumplowicz's main theoretical contribution to the young discipline of sociology was his 'sociological theory of the state.' He viewed any statehood as the result of a foregoing conquest of outside invaders; thus for him any given state was founded on, what Dühring would have called, 'original violence.' Furthermore, Gumplowicz interpreted all stratification within states as fallout from this initial violence that had led to the foundation of the state. Implicitly, Gumplowicz's theory operated on the assumption that social relations of a pre-statehood stage were free from violence, free from oppression, and that they were harmonious in nature. So, besides the seemingly naturalistic and positivistic facade of Gumplowicz's theory, it was connected both to the biblical notion of original sin, and to the liberal notion of a society coordinating naturally to the end of realising the common good.

Gumplowicz was not a messianic liberal, he valued liberalism in general as not more than a harmonistic illusion in a world trapped in an endless cycles of statehood, that was for him conquest and violence. The crucial problem in incorporating Gumplowicz's concretisation of 'original violence' into the perspective of messianic liberalism, became a question of how to regain the advantages of the common good *after* conquest. How was it possible to overcome the lasting effects of 'original violence,' of the state. Just as in the case of Dühring, this came to be Oppenheimer's principle question, yet he tried to find a different way of tackling it.

A third dimension has to come into play at this point. Neither Dühring nor Gumplowicz thought about the problem of violence and society as an economic problem. Gumplowicz had framed violence in terms of a sociological theory of universal history, and Dühring, in his theoretical world, could explain all concrete economic problems with a simple reference to this 'original violence,' a magical black box from which all theoretical explanation sprang.

It was the utopian writer *Theodor Hertzka* who gave Oppenheimer the idea for the last piece to a theoretical body which was the core of his messi-

---

30 Cf. G. MOZETIČ (1985): "Ein unzeitgemäßer Soziologe: Ludwig Gumplowicz", *Kölner Zeitschrift für Soziologie und Sozialpsychologie*, 37 (1985), pp. 621-47.

anic liberalism. Hertzka wrote in a neophysiocratic tradition[31], and blamed rent, the institution of the private ownership of land, for the uneven distribution of wealth and the uneven power structure in capitalist societies. Hertzka was a messianic liberal himself: his idea was that if all lands were publicly owned, there would be no rent. Then the 'invisible hand' could direct the economy appropriately and transform capitalism into a good society. But Hertzka also had a detailed plan for how to achieve the good society in practice. He wanted to occupy 'a no-man's land' in Africa, and set up a 'free land colony' there, forbidding any private ownership of land. By sheer force of competition, this colony would gradually turn the world into a liberal paradise. Hertzka collected money for this plan from amongst admirers in Germany, and equipped an expedition to the promised land. Trouble arose as soon as the hypothesis of the existence of 'no man's land' was put to a test: English colonial officials refused entry into Uganda, and the would-be settlers, and saviours of the world, had to return to Germany.

The main influences on Oppenheimer's approach are now assembled. Oppenheimer shared Dühring's belief that the social question was not to be blamed on the market, but on original violence. He shared Gumplowicz's belief that this original violence was to be traced back to the conquests precipitating the emergence of states. He shared Hertzka's belief that private ownership of land was the economic manifestation of original violence, and that, in economic terms, rent was the main problem of distorting market economy into capitalism. Yet, Oppenheimer criticised Hertzka for his utopian plans for setting up paradise in 'no man's land.' It was Oppenheimer's aim to find a practical, not utopian, solution to break the political blockade of land, a class monopoly originating from the first conquest. A solution was only practical, if it targeted the blockade, where it had its impact, in Europe, at home. Oppenheimer's first economic publication was a polemical booklet against Hertzka. The title was *Free Land in Germany*.[32]

Oppenheimer believed that once land was not privately owned, and was open to free agrarian settlement, an economic situation would emerge com-

---

31 The best known representitive of this approach in North America was Henry George. An unpublished Oppenheimer manuscript covers the intellectual history of the neo-physiocratic land reform movement: 'Land Reform,' an undated typescript translated by W. F. Roberts, 1944. Both the University of California at Berkeley and the Central Zionist Archives in Jerusalem possess copies.

32 F. OPPENHEIMER: *Freiland in Deutschland*, Berlin 1895.

parable to frontier societies, even in densely populated Europe. Everybody would have the choice of either becoming a settler on his own land or working as a wage earner. Surplus labour would dry up, the bargaining power of those still employed would rise, wages would move upwards toward a non-exploitative level. The Social Question would disappear. So too would business cycles, indeed any economic volatility, which Oppenheimer interpreted as an outcome of exploitation and under-consumption.

Oppenheimer blamed Hertzka for one faulty deduction that had misdirected his attempts toward creating 'free land' in Africa rather than in Europe. Hertzka was convinced that any attempt to build a 'free land' settlement in a densely-populated area would have the immediate effect of raising real estate prices in the vicinity. This in turn would strangle any attempts to expand the 'free land,' which in turn would limit the economic impact of such liberated areas to the immediate vicinity. Oppenheimer, not very convincingly, took the opposite position, and claimed that rent in the vicinity of such a 'free land' settlement would fall rather than rise, as the attractiveness of the free land would be much higher than of the surrounding area. Thus, once a nucleus of a sufficiently large 'free land' was established, that would allow anyone to settle there who wanted to do so, its expansion was possible without limits, as the land around it would fall into possession of the settlement at ever falling prices. Oppenheimer saw no obstacles for the growth of this liberated area, and thus no limits to the predicted socio-economic implications deriving from its existence.

In his memoirs in 1931, Oppenheimer remembered as the turning point of his life the moment when he found this criticism of Hertzka:

> And then, like a flash, it came to me, in an unforgettable night in late 1893, the discovery that decided over my life and my striving; the moment of "divine calling." From that moment, I was "obsessed," in the true meaning of the word. A thought of most enormous consequence had taken possession of me. From that moment on, I did not any more belong to myself, to my little empirical person, but to the great cause.[33]

---

[33] 'Und da kam mir in einer unvergeßlichen Nacht Ende 1893 die blitzartige Erkenntnis, die über mein Leben und Streben entschied, sozusagen der Augenblick der 'Gnadenwahl.' Von da an war ich im wörtlichsten Sinne des Wortes 'besessen'; ein Gedanke von ungeheuerster Tragweite hatte von mir Besitz ergriffen;

FRANZ OPPENHEIMER'S THEORY OF CAPITALISM

From then on, Oppenheimer's work was shaped by this 'great cause,' indeed, it had only one theme, and that was to realise 'free land' in Germany. All his publications were devoted to the realisation of nuclei of a liberated liberal society on 'free land colonies,' from the *Siedlungsgenossenschaft* of 1896[34], where he developed a practical plan of the foundation of settlement co-operatives, or 'free land colonies,' and the historical and theoretical work *Großgrundeigentum und soziale Frage* (Large landed property and the social question) of 1898[35], to the over 4,000 pages *magnum opus System der Soziologie*[36], published in the 1920s and 1930.

The 'great cause' also determined Oppenheimer's practical and political work. He did not hesitate to invest all his private means into realising his settlement plans. Furthermore, he tried to convince the government of the day, under every regime until 1933, to donate this initial piece of land and the resources to realise settlement co-operatives. He attempted to influence legislation for his cause, and he tried - albeit not very successfully - to build up a network of disciples in political parties and in public administration.

Indeed, Oppenheimer was 'obsessed' by an *idée fixe*, by a single cause which, he hoped, would bring an end to the distortion of a market economy towards 'capitalism.' He saw contemporary society suffering the remains of 'original violence,' as manifested in the *Bodensperre*, a class monopoly on the ownership of, and control over, land. And he was convinced that the foundation of settlement co-operatives would provide a quick remedy to this

---

ich gehörte nicht mehr mir, meiner kleinen empirischen Person, sondern fortan nur noch der Sache.' (OPPENHEIMER: *Erlebtes, op.cit.*, p. 41/2).

34 F. OPPENHEIMER: *Die Siedlungsgenossenschaft. Versuch einer positiven Überwindung des Kommunismus durch Lösung des Genossenschaftsproblems und der Agrarfrage*, Berlin 1896. The subtitle reads in English: Attempt at positively overcoming communism, by solving the problem of co-operatives and the agrarian question.

35 F. OPPENHEIMER: *Großgrundeigentum und soziale Frage. Versuch einer neuen Grundlegung der Gesellschaftswissenschaft*, Berlin 1898, now reprinted in F. OPPENHEIMER: *Gesammelte Schriften*, vol. 1, Berlin (Akademie) 1996, pp. 1-280.

36 F. OPPENHEIMER: *System der Soziologie*, 8 vols., 2nd ed., Stuttgart (Gustav Fischer) 1965. The first edition, published from 1922 to 1935, was destroyed by order of the Nazi government.

last remnant of a culture based on violence, so that liberal society could develop freely.

In the foreword to the last volume of *System der Soziologie*, Oppenheimer summarised his view on the path of world history as a whole, a passage that shows the deep passion that drove Oppenheimer's theoretical and political engagement. These words are Oppenheimer's intellectual legacy, and they can be read as the manifestation of his deeply religious philosophy of history:

> "World history" is nothing but the process of a "distraction" of natural equilibrium (the "consensus") of human society. An infectant has entered from outside the great supraorganism of society. The supraorganism tries to neutralise or to expel it. ... The history of the states is the course of a disease and its healing. This is its "meaning" and its "value result." The categories of history shall vanish as they emerged, what shall remain are the eternal categories that history had covered up and distorted: community with its law of equality and liberty.[37]

I do not want to go into the economic specificities of Oppenheimer's ideas. They are documented in detail in some recent works[38] on Oppen-

---

37 *"Die 'Weltgeschichte' ist nichts anderes als der Ablauf einer 'Störung' des natürlichen Gleichgewichts (des 'Consensus') der menschlichen Gesellschaft. Ein Fremdkörper ist von außen her eingedrungen: der große Supraorganismus sucht ihn zu neutralisieren oder auszustoßen. ... Die Staatengeschichte ist der Verlauf einer Krankheit und ihrer Heilung. Das ist ihr 'Sinn' und ihr 'Wertergebnis'. Die historischen Kategorien werden verschwinden, wie sie entstanden sind, aber bleiben werden die von ihnen überdeckten und verzerrten ewigen Kategorien: die Gemeinschaft mit ihrem Recht der Gleichheit und der Freiheit."* (F. OPPENHEIMER: "System", *ibid.*, vol. IV, part 3, p. XI).

38 Cf. B. VOGT: *Oppenheimer*, *op.cit.*; W. KRUCK: *Franz Oppenheimer - Vordenker der Sozialen Marktwirtschaft und Selbsthilfegesellschaft*, Berlin (Berlin Verlag) 1997; the articles on Oppenheimer in V. CASPARI, B. SCHEFOLD (Eds.): *Franz Oppenheimer und Adolph Lowe: Zwei Wirtschaftswissenschaftler der Frankfurter Universität*, Marburg (Metropolis) 1996; D. HASELBACH: *Franz Oppenheimer. Soziologie, Geschichtsphilosophie und Politik des "liberalen Sozialismus"*, Opladen (Leske & Budrich) 1985, D. HASELBACH: "Franz Oppenheimer's Contribution to the Theory of Co-operation", forthcoming in: *Communal Societies. The Journal of the Communal Studies Association*.

heimer. Oppenheimer's economic ideas had already met with profound criticism from some of his contemporaries[39].

Certainly, both the weakness and the strength of Oppenheimer lie with his *idée fixe*. It forced Oppenheimer to explore a wide body of knowledge, it forced him, in particular, to withstand the trend in the social sciences towards ever increasing specialisation and the creation of separate sub-disciplines and bodies of knowledge. Oppenheimer, matched only by his contemporary Alois Schumpeter, bridged the widening gap between economics and sociology with a work that is, even today, still an insightful representation of social science in the inter-war period. Yet, as was his *idée fixe*, so was the organising vision of his life-work, that of a unified, positive, strictly deductive system of science, already antiquated when Oppenheimer started to publish it.

As a political economist and social scientist, Oppenheimer was a singular phenomenon in Germany. He opposed not only the Historical School, because they contradicted his belief in the soundness of classical economic thought, he also opposed neo-classical thought, because he considered their calculations of marginal utility mere psychology, and a distortion from the real problems as they were raised in classical political economy. In the end, Oppenheimer came to oppose almost any other theory, when it would not fit into his masterplan of a 'liberal socialism,' a reform of society organised around settlement co-operatives. During his academic life, Oppenheimer was belligerent and engaged in quite a few intellectual controversies. In all these controversies, the point of dissent can be pinned down to his adversaries not sharing in his belief of an imminent liberal paradise, not sharing in his position firmly rooted in messianic liberalism. It is for this reason that the strongest impact Oppenheimer's writings enjoyed in political economy was that in textbooks on the history of economic doctrines. Oppenheimer's work was never really relevant in the ongoing discussions of the discipline, he was never really taken seriously. The same can be said about his contributions to sociology, yet to a lesser degree. Through Oppenheimer, Gumplowicz's conflict theory of the state was saved from obscurity and had a bit of an after-life in Alexander Rüstow's grandiose epos of the Cold War

---

39 Cf. KURZ: *Oppenheimer, op.cit.*

Ortsbestimmung der Gegenwart[40] and in Gottfried Salomon-Delatour's *Moderne Staatslehren*[41].

V. Oppenheimer's Role in Weimar

Oppenheimer's role in the social sciences in the inter-war period, as an academic teacher and in the politics of the profession, reflects his position as an intellectual outsider. In sociology, he was one of the founding members of the German Sociological Association, and attended most of their conventions, often as a speaker. But he never, however, held an institutional post in the association, nor did he influence its policies significantly. His writings did not represent any of the main intellectual strands in the discipline.

In economics, the picture is much the same. Oppenheimer was of course read, and, as just mentioned, he engaged in quite a number of controversies with colleagues over aspects of his work, or criticism of his work. But he was strangely out of tune with the main debates, and this limited the appreciation of his works in the profession.

Yet, Oppenheimer did have an important role as a university teacher. When he took his chair in Frankfurt, the economic discipline in Germany was still widely dominated by the younger Historical School. As a political economist in the classical tradition, Oppenheimer was an exception, and it was for this reason that his seminar attracted a wide array of students who were interested in theoretical alternatives to the main stream. It was for that reason that many of those who were later to become leading economists, both in scholarship and in politics, appeared among the students of Oppenheimer. In most cases, this does not mean that these students followed Oppenheimer in his messianic liberal beliefs. But Oppenheimer was famous for his intellectual tolerance. He did not expect his students to follow his beliefs, but he hoped to convince them of the correctness of his deductions,

---

40 3 Vols., Erlenbach-Zürich (Rentsch) 1950-7. An abbreviated English translation was published as: *Freedom and Domination: a Historical Critique of Civilization*, Princeton (Princeton University Press) 1980.
41 Neuwied (Luchterhand) 1965.

unsuccessfully, for the most part. Oppenheimer's role in teaching was that of an intellectual catalyst in the time of reorientation for the economic discipline in Germany.

Just a few names ought to be mentioned here. Adolph Lowe (Adolph Löwe before emigration) was particularly close to Oppenheimer, he corresponded regularly with his teacher, and was well acquainted with the Oppenheimer family. Yet, when Lowe was accepted for a chair in economics in Frankfurt, some years after Oppenheimer had left, he found some resentment among his colleagues, as they suspected him of being a follower of Oppenheimer, and he was accepted only upon clarification that, intellectually, he had nothing to do with his teacher.[42] This illustrates the point that, while Oppenheimer's seminar was an exciting intellectual market place, for the students it was a risk to have too close a relationship with their 'teacher,' as this was considered harmful for their further professional development. Gottfried Salomon,[43] not an economist but a sociologist and social philosopher, was closer to Oppenheimer. He was assistant with him in Frankfurt, but with his own profile and field of scholarship he was never identified with Oppenheimer's *idée fixe*. Salomon's intellectual roots can be found in Georg Simmel as much as in Oppenheimer's sociology.

As long as the disputes were rationalistic and argumentative, Oppenheimer's scholarly tolerance was legendary. His seminar brought together liberals like Joachim Tiburtius with Marxists, such as Fritz Sternberg, featured students of almost any political conviction. Eduard Heimann was also among those who had studied with Oppenheimer. But when Heimann inquired with Oppenheimer in 1921 whether he was willing to support his habilitation at the Frankfurt faculty[44], despite all scholarly differences between them, he got an answer that shows a different image of Oppenheimer as academic teacher: He accused Heimann of a gross intellectual misrepresentation, when he had attempted to criticise Oppenheimer's work, not

---

[42] Cf. A. LOWE: "Rückblick auf meine verkürzte Mitgliedschaft in der fünften Fakultät", B. SCHEFOLD (Ed.): *Wirtschafts- und Sozialwissenschaftler in Frankfurt am Main. Erinnerungen an die Wirtschafts- und Sozialwissenschaftliche Fakultät und an die Anfänge des Fachbereichs Wirtschaftswissenschaften der Johann Wolfgang Goethe-Universität*, Marburg 1989, pp. 93-95.

[43] After the Second World War, Salomon added his French resistance name: Gottfried Salomon-Delatour.

[44] Letter Heimann to Oppenheimer, 23 January 1921, handwritten (CZA, 74).

intellectually, but in disparaging remarks about Oppenheimer's deepest intellectual convictions, an offence against the honour almost inexcusable for a man of Oppenheimer's generation:

> ... you have grossly lacked in acting with the respect that I am entitled to, both as a man so much older and as a scholar. Even worse, if you don't know of it! When we last talked—since then I avoided to meet you—I mentioned some matter, it might have been my socio-economic understanding of history. You answered most brusquely: "Just leave this alone, I can't bear to hear it any more". ... the tone and the mental attitude toward a man who was to you a devoted teacher was, to say the least, inappropriate to the highest degree.... It is my duty toward the colleagues in the faculty, not to hide my opinion on you, as a scholar as well as on your character.[45]

This row was settled eventually, by a further exchange of letters, and after a personal conversation between the two men. Oppenheimer agreed not to get involved in the habilitation application - it eventually failed in any case, for different reasons.

The quarrel with Heimann hints at the tragic side of Oppenheimer's role as a university teacher. He was a man of deep convictions, and a scholar who believed he had at hand a solution for all social and economic woes. Oppenheimer expected his students, and everyone else, to share his convictions, and to become disciples, to bring the message to the world. This was exactly what did not happen. The letters Oppenheimer exchanged with many of his students and former students, feature a somewhat a-symmetrical mode of communication: Oppenheimer expected an enthusiasm

---

45 *"Sie haben mir gegenüber den Respekt, den ich als so viel älterer Mann und Gelehrter zu fordern berechtigt bin, gröblich verletzt. Wenn Sie davon nichts wissen, um so schlimmer! Bei unserer letzten Unterredung - ich habe es seitdem vermieden, mit Ihnen zusammenzutreffen - sprach ich Ihnen von irgend etwas, ich glaube von der sozial-ökonomischen Geschichtsauffassung. Darauf erwiderten Sie in brüskestem Tone: 'Lassen Sie doch das, ich kann es schon nicht mehr hören'. ... der Ton und die ganze seeliche (sic!) Einstellung gegnüber (sic!) dem Manne, der Ihnen doch ein hingebungsvoller Lehrer gewesen war, ist, sehr gelinde ausgedrückt, im höchsten Masse unangemessen gewesen. ... Es ist meine Pflicht, meinen Collegen in der Fakultät gegenüber mit meiner Ansicht über Ihre Person als Gelehrter und Charakter nicht hinter dem Berge zu halten."* (Letter Oppenheimer to Heimann, 25 January 1921, carbon copy of typescript, CZA, 74.)

that they would try to avoid showing. Whatever the substantive points in their criticism of Oppenheimer, his convictions were not to be argued with. From this perspective, Heimann's misbehaviour may have been no more than an unfortunate slip of the tongue.

A few further names of students in Oppenheimer's seminar should be mentioned here. There were the economists Hans Peter, and Fritz Neumark, there was the philosopher Julius Kraft, later editor of the international positivistic journal *Ratio*. Of course, Ludwig Erhard, later minister of economics and chancellor of West Germany, was also one of Oppenheimer's many dissertation candidates, but he did not leave much of a mark in the inner circles of Oppenheimer's students. In his Frankfurt seminar, Oppenheimer taught quite a few of the economic theorists who later made significant contributions to the discipline. Core members of the Institute for World Economics in Kiel, and later of the New School of Social Research in New York, knew each other from Oppenheimer's seminar in Frankfurt.

One group of Oppenheimer's students deserves a closer look, as they were disciples of his 'liberal socialism.' Oppenheimer was claimed as a principal economic theorist by a small but active group of ethical socialists, centred around the autocratic liberal philosopher Leonard Nelson. Nelson was a Neo-Kantian, deeply influenced by the 1848 philosopher Jacob Friedrich Fries. Fries' main idea was that ethics could find an empirical foundation in a deep rooted ethical feeling, and that this feeling could be uncovered in any individual. This became the doctrine of Nelson and of his group, the *Internationaler Jugendbund* (IJB, later *Internationaler Sozialistischer Kampfbund*, ISK[46]). Oppenheimer accepted this doctrine as an ethical foundation for his 'liberal socialism,' and in turn Nelson and his group adopted Oppenheimer's economic programme as their party doctrine. Nelson and Oppenheimer not only co-operated politically and intellectually, they also swapped advanced students on a regular basis between Frankfurt

---

46 Cf. W. LINK: "Die Geschichte der Internationalen Jugend-Bundes (IJB) und des Internationalen Sozialistischen Kampf-Bundes (ISK). Ein Beitrag zur Geschichte der Arbeiterbewegung in der Weimarer Republik und im Dritten Reich", in: W. ABENDROTH (Ed.): *Marburger Abhandlungen zur politischen Wissenschaft*, vol. 1, Meisenheim am Glan (Anton Hain) 1964; and K.-H. KLÄR: "Zwei Nelson-Bünde. Internationaler Jugend-Bund (IJB) und Internationaler Sozialistischer Kampfbund (ISK) im Lichte neuer Quellen", *Internationale Wissenschaftliche Korrespondenz zur Geschichte der Arbeiterbewegung*, 18 (1982), pp. 310-60.

and Göttingen. For these students, most of what has been said above has to be modified: they were true in their belief in Oppenheimer's prescription of economic and social reform. Only later, after Nelson's death, and against the impact of the world economic crisis, the group's programmatic orientation changed to a more main-stream social democratic approach to economic policy.

Except for this group, there was no organised support for Oppenheimer and his plans to overcome capitalism. He had a few disciples everywhere, friends in public administration, in centre and left leaning political parties, among journalists, and in commerce and industry, yet no influential organised support devoted to his ideas. With these contacts, though, he managed now and again, to start some settlements somewhere, at least to prove that his was a suitable method of agrarian 'colonisation,' in competition with other methods of 'internal colonisation' on former landed estates, mainly in Eastern Prussia. In the late 1920s and early 1930s, he even got financial support from the Prussian Ministry of Agriculture to run some agrarian settlement co-operatives on estates near Berlin. Yet, before the enterprises were properly established, the Nazis took power in Germany, closed the co-operatives, and Oppenheimer once again did not have the chance to prove his point in practice. Oppenheimer did not give up, and tried after 1933 to found new agrarian settlements in France, the further fate of which is not known.[47] Oppenheimer was the prophet who remained unheard in his own land - he never really got close to achieving his goal of breaking the 'blockade of land' with the means of his settlement co-operative.[48]

---

[47] These French settlements are mentioned in some letters to Oppenheimer at the occasion of his 70th birthday in 1934 (cf. CZA, 76).

[48] One rather sad and ironic document has to be reported here. Erich Preiser, one of the Frankfurt students of Oppenheimer, wrote to Oppenheimer on his 70th birthday, claiming that it would be the Nazis to put in practice Oppenheimer's plans. The point that Oppenheimer's settlements near Berlin had been closed by the Nazi administration seems to have been lost on Preiser: *"Sie feiern Ihren siebzigsten Geburtstag im Ausland, wenn auch nicht im Exil. Sie feiern ihn in einer Zeit, in der man sich anschickt Gedanken zu verwirklichen, die - sieht man aufs Ganze - in der Richtung dessen liegen, was Sie zu Ihrer Lebensaufgabe gemacht haben: in der Richtung des dritten Weges zwischen Kapitalismus und Marxismus. Alles ist noch in den Anfängen, aber niemand kann daran zweifeln, dass wenn überhaupt jemals so jetzt die Aufgabe gelöst wird. Ich wenigstens habe aller Zuversicht und bin darum mit Überzeugung Mitglied der SA. ... Es*

VI. Post-war Reception of Oppenheimer

As a university teacher, Oppenheimer got in the position of a catalyst of the reorientation of economics after the end of the Historical School. He was not successful with his own programme of 'liberal socialism,', and he was considered by contemporaries as an economic sectarian, and not as the saviour of the liberal world, as he perceived himself. On the basis of this finding, one could close the books on Oppenheimer, and include him in the archives of the discipline, as one of the late Wilhelminian intellectuals who wanted to cure the world, and, for the better or the worse, did not succeed. Yet Oppenheimer's thought lives on, in the claim that he was one of the precursors of the Social Market Economy of today's Germany.

Judging from Oppenheimer's theory, there is not much grounding for any such claim. Intellectually, the closest ally of Oppenheimer's liberal socialism would be anarchism, which itself is a theory deeply rooted in messianic liberalism. Yet, claims on Oppenheimer have been laid from positions outside liberal anarchism as well. First the IJB/ISK, which had been active in resistance and exile during the Nazi years, and had eventually entered, as a still largely intact group, the Social Democratic Party, claimed the succession to 'liberal socialism,' although the group had abandoned Oppenheimer's position in the 1930s. Second, Ludwig Erhard, on the other side of the political spectre claimed to realise Oppenheimer's master plan, altered only in the methods of implication, but not in the goals, that he still shared with Oppenheimer. Thus, Oppenheimer became a target for competing intellectual histories in West Germany. And competition, as the German proverb goes, raises the level of business.

Ludwig Erhard had often claimed that the economic position he took as West Germany's minister of economics was an application of what he had learned, as a doctoral student, from Oppenheimer. Yet, the literature for the most part dismissed Erhard's conviction that the 'Social Market Economy' was in fact the realisation of Oppenheimer's liberal socialism[49]. And, in-

---

ist wahrhaft tragisch - hier passt das Wort einmal -, daß gerade Sie, hochverehrter Herr Professor, am Aufbau nicht teilnehmen dürfen." (Letter Preiser to Oppenheimer in Paris, 25 March 1934, typescript, CZA, 75).

49 Cf. Erhard's speech at a memorial for Oppenheimer on his centenary in Berlin in 1964: L. ERHARD: *Wirken und Reden*, Ludwigsburg 1966, pp. 365-73.

deed, Erhard's claim seems to rest on very shaky grounds, if one is to look into the context of both his writings and his policies. But, as Horst Friedrich Wünsche has argued recently, this does not rule out that Erhard himself was personally convinced of such a connection between his own final goals and Oppenheimer's. As Wünsche, one of the most knowledgeable contemporary Erhard scholars, argues, it was Erhard's aspiration to realise Oppenheimer's ideal not with the methods his teacher had thought were indispensable, but by using the means of the state to transform capitalism into a true market economy.

'In Erhard's Social Market Economy the state is given a function for the "society of free and equal people." This way, Erhard solves a question that has not been satisfactorily answered by Oppenheimer'.[50]

It is hard to argue how Erhard may have viewed himself and how he framed his own motives, many of his writings are not very focused theoretically. As for Wünsche's point, I would argue that by getting the state into responsibility for ordering or steering the market, Erhard shifts, as for the theoretical foundation of his policy, from messianic liberalism to revisionist liberalism, in other words, from Oppenheimer to Walter Eucken and Wilhelm Röpke.

If one applies a very general notion of intellectual influence, one could make the point that Oppenheimer as a liberal teacher of political economy from the 1890s to the inter-war period had an influence on liberal thought since then. Yet, if one compares the doctrines of German ordoliberalism, as it became influential in West Germany's Social Market Economy, and Oppenheimer's messianic liberalism, those influences are rather blurred, to say the least. It all comes down to a shared appreciation of the power of markets as institutions central to running modern societies on a large scale. While Oppenheimer thought that markets would still have their day in the future, once power relations in society were eliminated, the ordoliberals had

---

50 *'Erhards Soziale Marktwirtschaft weist dem Staat ... eine Funktion in einer "Gesellschaft der Freien und Gleichen" zu und löst damit eine von Oppenheimer nicht befriedigend beantwortete Frage'* [The inner quote is an often used phrase of Oppenheimer]. (H. F. WÜNSCHE: "Der Einfluß Oppenheimers auf Erhard und dessen Konzeption von der Sozialen Marktwirtschaft", in: V. CASPARI, B. SCHEFOLD (Eds.): *Franz Oppenheimer und Adolph Lowe: Zwei Wirtschaftswissenschaftler der Frankfurter Universität*, Marburg (Metropolis) 1996, pp. 144-145).

the opposite conviction, that markets would need to be framed in a state administered framework, politics of order (*Ordnungspolitik*), as without such order, markets were in danger of destroying with their dynamics the very preconditions they needed for survival, both economically and culturally. The very idea that markets would need to be limited by an institutional framework is alien to Oppenheimer's system of liberal socialism[51]. With his opposition to any power and domination in society, Oppenheimer, the utopian, has nothing in common with the ruler of the day. Oppenheimer has to be remembered as an outsider, who opposed rationally and emotionally any form of oppression. He did this against the background of a teleological interpretation of liberalism, a tale of sin and resurrection. In this eschatological structure, Oppenheimer's theory is obsolete, and it was already during his life-time. The discourse of modernity, even then, was more self-critical, more reflexive, more post-modern, than many want to know nowadays.

As for the theory of liberalism, Oppenheimer's work reminds us that a liberal economy in a world of perpetual political domination, is only a half-baked liberalism. And this applies, even if such half-baked liberalism were the best that can be achieved for the time being.

---

[51] In this point, the otherwise informative book of Bernhard Vogt on Franz Oppenheimer is flawed. (VOGT: *Oppenheimer*, *op.cit.*). Anthony Nicholls also tries to make the point that there was an influence of Oppenheimer on Ludwig Erhard and the Social Market Economy, but he did not bother to actually read Oppenheimer, and presents a greatly distorted picture of him (A. J. NICHOLLS: *Freedom with Responsibility. The Social Market Economy in Germany, 1918-1963*, Oxford (Clarendon) 1994, p. 74). Kruck's book on Oppenheimer (*op.cit.*) does not add anything significant to the debate, except for repeating, with great conviction, the claim that Oppenheimer was, indeed, a precursor to the Social Market Economy.

DIETER HASELBACH

References

['CZA' refers to the Oppenheimer papers in the Central Zionist Archive in Jerusalem]

BARKAI, H.: "Oppenheimer and the Zionist Resettlement of Palestine: The Genossenschaft versus the Collective Settlement", in: V. CASPARI, B. SCHEFOLD (Eds.): *Franz Oppenheimer und Adolph Lowe: Zwei Wirtschaftswissenschaftler der Frankfurter Universität*, Marburg (Metropolis) 1996, pp. 17-64.

BECKER, H., BARNES, H. E.: *Social Thought from Lore to Science*, 3 vols., 3rd ed., Gloucester, Mass. 1978.

CASPARI, V., SCHEFOLD, B. (Eds.): *Franz Oppenheimer und Adolph Lowe: Zwei Wirtschaftswissenschaftler der Frankfurter Universität*, Marburg (Metropolis) 1996.

DOWE, D., TENFELDE, K.: "Zur Rezeption Eugen Dührings in der deutschen Arbeiterbewegung in den 1870er Jahren", in: *Wissenschaftlicher Sozialismus und Arbeiterbewegung* (Schriften aus dem Karl-Marx-Haus 24), Trier 1980, pp. 25-58.

ERHARD, L.: *Wirken und Reden*, Ludwigsburg 1966.

FUSS, F.: "A Bibliography of Franz Oppenheimer, 1864-1943", *The American Journal of Economics and Sociology*, 6 (1946/47, No. 1), pp. 95-112 and 7 (1947/48, No. 1), pp. 107-117.

GUSTAFSSON, B.: *Marxismus und Revisionismus. Eduard Bernsteins Kritik des Marxismus und ihre ideengeschichtlichen Voraussetzungen*, 1st part, Frankfurt 1972.

HASELBACH, D.: *Franz Oppenheimer. Soziologie, Geschichtsphilosophie und Politik des "liberalen Sozialismus"*, Opladen (Leske & Budrich) 1985.

HASELBACH, D.: *Autoritärer Liberalismus und Soziale Marktwirtschaft. Gesellschaft und Politik im Ordoliberalismus*, Baden-Baden (Nomos) 1991.

HASELBACH, D. (1994a): "Nation, Gott und Markt. Mythos und gesellschaftliche Integration bei Alfred Müller-Armack", in: M. TH. GREVEN, P. KÜHLER, M. SCHMITZ (Eds.): *Politikwissenschaft als Kritische Theorie. Festschrift für Kurt Lenk*, Baden-Baden (Nomos) 1994, pp. 215-230.

HASELBACH, D. (1994b): "'Soziale Marktwirtschaft' als Gründungsmythos. Zur Identitätsbildung im Nachkriegsdeutschland", in: C. MAYER-ISWANDY (Ed.): *Zwischen Traum und Trauma - Die Nation. Transatlantische Perspektiven zur Geschichte eines Problems*, Tübingen (Stauffenburg) 1994, pp. 255-266.

HASELBACH, D.: "Franz Oppenheimer's Contribution to the Theory of Cooperation", *Communal Societies. The Journal of the Communal Studies Association* (forthcoming).

FRANZ OPPENHEIMER'S THEORY OF CAPITALISM

HEIMANN, E.: "In Memoriam Franz Oppenheimer, 1863-1943", *American Journal of Sociology* 49 (1943), p. 225.

HERZL, T., F. OPPENHEIMER: "Briefwechsel", *Bulletin für die Mitglieder der Gesellschaft der Freunde des Leo Baeck Institute*, 7 (1964), pp. 21-55.

KLÄR, K.-H.: "Zwei Nelson-Bünde. Internationaler Jugend-Bund (IJB) und Internationaler Sozialistischer Kampfbund (ISK) im Lichte neuer Quellen", *Internationale Wissenschaftliche Korrespondenz zur Geschichte der Arbeiterbewegung*, 18 (1982), pp. 310-60.

KLUKE, P.: *Die Stiftungsuniversität Frankfurt am Main 1914-1932*, Frankfurt 1972.

KURZ, H. D.: "Franz Oppenheimer und das Problem der 'Bodensperrung'", in: V. CASPARI, B. SCHEFOLD (Eds.): *Franz Oppenheimer und Adolph Lowe: Zwei Wirtschaftswissenschaftler der Frankfurter Universität*, Marburg (Metropolis) 1996, pp. 65-120.

LINK, W.: "Die Geschichte der Internationalen Jugend-Bundes (IJB) und des Internationalen Sozialistischen Kampf-Bundes (ISK). Ein Beitrag zur Geschichte der Arbeiterbewegung in der Weimarer Republik und im Dritten Reich", in: W. ABENDROTH (Ed.): *Marburger Abhandlungen zur politischen Wissenschaft*, vol. 1, Meisenheim am Glan (Anton Hain) 1964.

LOWE, A.: "Rückblick auf meine verkürzte Mitgliedschaft in der fünften Fakultät", in: B. SCHEFOLD (Ed.): *Wirtschafts- und Sozialwissenschaftler in Frankfurt am Main. Erinnerungen an die Wirtschafts- und Sozialwissenschaftliche Fakultät und an die Anfänge des Fachbereichs Wirtschaftsiwssenschaften der Johann Wolfgang Goethe-Universität*, Marburg 1989, pp. 93-95.

LOWIE, R.: *The Origin of the State*, New York (Russel & Russel) 1927.

MACLEOD, W. CH.: *The Origin of the State*, Philadelphia 1924.

MOZETIČ, G.: "Ein unzeitgemäßer Soziologe: Ludwig Gumplowicz", *Kölner Zeitschrift für Soziologie und Sozialpsychologie*, 37 (1985), pp. 621-47.

NICHOLLS, A.J.: *Freedom with Responsibility. The Social Market Economy in Germany, 1918-1963*, Oxford (Clarendon) 1994.

OPPENHEIMER, F.: *Freiland in Deutschland*, Berlin 1895.

OPPENHEIMER, F.: *Die Siedlungsgenossenschaft. Versuch einer positiven Überwindung des Kommunismus durch Lösung des Genossenschaftsproblems und der Agrarfrage*, Berlin 1896.

OPPENHEIMER, F.: *Großgrundeigentum und soziale Frage. Versuch einer neuen Grundlegung der Gesellschaftswissenschaft*, Berlin 1898.

OPPENHEIMER, F.: *The State. Its History and Development Viewed Sociologically*. Authorized translation by John M. Gitterman, New York (Huebsch) 1922.

OPPENHEIMER, F.: *The Austrian School of Marginal Utility and Value*, Typoscript, 113 pages, unpublished, not dated [ca. 1942] (CZA, 40).

OPPENHEIMER, F.: *Land Reform*, translated by W.F. Roberts, unpublished, 1944 (copies in CZA and in the Archives of the University of California at Berkeley).

OPPENHEIMER, F.: *Erlebtes, Erstrebtes, Erreichtes. Lebenserinnerungen*, Düsseldorf (Melzer) 1964.
OPPENHEIMER, F.: *System der Soziologie*, 8 vols., 2nd ed., Stuttgart (G. Fischer) 1965.
OPPENHEIMER, F.: *The State*, with an introduction by C. HAMILTON, Montreal (Black Rose Books) 1975.
OPPENHEIMER, F.: *Gesammelte Schriften*, 2 vols., Berlin (Akademie) 1996.
RÜSTOW, A.: *Das Versagen des Wirtschaftsliberalismus als religionsgeschichtliches Problem* (Istanbuler Schriften 12), Istanbul 1945.
RÜSTOW, A.: *Ortsbestimmung der Gegenwart*, 3 vols., Erlenbach-Zürich (Rentsch) 1950-7.
RÜSTOW, A.: *Rede und Antwort*, Ludwigsburg 1963.
RÜSTOW, A.: *Freedom and Domination: A Historical Critique of Civilization*, Princeton (Princeton University Press) 1980.
SALOMON-DELATOUR, G.: *Moderne Staatslehren*, Neuwied (Luchterhand) 1965.
SOROKIN, P. A.: *Contemporary Sociological Theories*, New York 1928.
VOGT, B.: "Die Utopie als Tatsache? Judentum und Europa bei Franz Oppenheimer", *Menora. Jahrbuch für deutsch-jüdische Geschichte* (1994), pp. 123-142.
VOGT, B.: *Franz Oppenheimer. Wissenschaft und Ethik der sozialen Marktwirtschaft* (Studien zur Geistesgeschichte 22), Bodenheim (Philo) 1997.
WÜNSCHE, H. F.: "Der Einfluß Oppenheimers auf Erhard und dessen Konzeption von der Sozialen Marktwirtschaft", in: V. CASPARI, B. SCHEFOLD (Eds.): *Franz Oppenheimer und Adolph Lowe: Zwei Wirtschaftswissenschaftler der Frankfurter Universität*, Marburg (Metropolis) 1996, pp. 141-162.

Discussion Summary

ELKE SCHWINGER

Paper discussed:
DIETER HASELBACH: Franz Oppenheimer's Theory of Capitalism and of a Third Path

The main topic of the discussion was Haselbach's description of Oppenheimer as an outsider and a singular phenomenon in his time because of his idea of a "social liberalism". In the core of his thinking, i.e. a sort of "messianic liberalism", there is an "idée fixe" the "Bodensperre", which means a closure of land. There is also a lack of recognition by the contemporary Austrian historical school especially by his own disciples, caused by Oppenheimers obsession to prove his theory (HASELBACH). HAGEMANN's argument of a theoretical relationship to the works of Erich Preiser and his question about the link to the *American Journal of Economics and Sociology*, a journal founded by H. Georg, seems to be overvalued (HASELBACH): Oppenheimer published only two essays there.

Against HASELBACH it was argued that the idea of "Third Path" should also be interpreted more as a social praxis than as an ideology or a theoretical project. There can be seen a network of thinkers and practically involved persons, who are all interested to finding an answer to the basic question: How to balance the social and economic problems of the capitalistic system in a way different from the American way. In this European discussion there could not be a clear-cut distinction between the influence of one or the other (PEUKERT). Oppenheimer clearly belonged to this network of influences and relationships and he participated in these discussions. But especially to the topic of the landrent-discussion other theorists, like Rüstow and Tillich, were more important than Oppenheimer (HASELBACH). The topic he was interested in was the internal colonisation of Germany, a political phenomenon of domination. Also Schumpeter's dynamic concept of capitalism (RAUSCHER) cannot be connected with Oppenheimer's ideas, because Oppenheimer usually did not think in such historical terms like

DISCUSSION SUMMARY

"evolutionäre" or "stationäre Gesellschaft". This two theorists were not on friendly terms, as demonstrated in a theoretical controversy in 1920 (HASELBACH).

The question of Oppenheimer's connection to the biblical debate of interest in particular of landrent (RAUSCHER) as an elementary part of his investigations, has also to be answered negative: Oppenheimer used biblical motives only to underline his point. He used for example the typical topic of the prohibition of interest, but he wasn't a believer in a restricted sense of the biblical debate: He was an economic liberal in the most restricted sense and nothing else (HASELBACH).

The discussion of Oppenheimer's influences on the German practical politics after the World War II was concentrated around the question, whether Ludwig Erhard could be seen really as a disciple of Oppenheimer or whether Erhard stressed the influence of his teacher only in a rhetorical way. And the question was, whether there is a definite line to be drawn from Oppenheimer's ideas to the development of the idea of the social market economy. KOSLOWSKI argued, that the social market economy represented a third path between Manchester liberalism and historical marxism. The German roots of the social market theory can be found in the pre-nazi German thinking. Erhard and other politicians wanted to use this tradition for the project of rebuilding Germany after World War II. The idea of the Third Path seems to be very influential on the concept of social market economy in two respects. First, because it belongs to a long tradition, which is sceptical of free trade. And second, for Germany as one of the second powers in the international relations other interests have more importance than for the first powers like America. In this sense Oppenheimer's idea was useful for German politics to find a way, which did not follow the Anglo-American type of liberalism and could be different from the East-European type of socialism. So it can be said, that there are alternative ways to discuss Oppenheimer's influence: On the one hand by the question of theoretical validity and on the other hand by the question of forming practical politics (KOSLOWSKI). For HASELBACH it is clear that Erhard was convinced in what he said. But Erhard was ideologically bound to a special ideological picture of the political world, in which Germany was the centre between the eastern and the western world. It is possible to link this metaphor of the centre to the metaphor of Third Path because it was in a technical sense a way to avoid the existing forms and problems of capitalism and socialism as realised in the other countries (HASELBACH). This metaphor is

DISCUSSION SUMMARY

a way of mythological self-description, which was typical for practical politics in the time after the second world war (KOSLOWSKI). But in HASELBACH's interpretation, Oppenheimer was thinking only in terms of the classical political economy. Actual politics after World War II has nothing to do with Oppenheimer's basic idea: The strategy of post-war economic policies was to overcome shortcomings of liberalism by framing them within political institutions. On the contrary, Oppenheimer did not see much need for a framing of markets by order, but he supported in a classical manner the liberation of markets from all limitations. Oppenheimer's frame of reference would also be ill described in the geographical, east-west-centre, metaphor. For this reason, Erhard's description as a disciple of Oppenheimer has merely a psychological value as a self-perception (HASELBACH).

Part Two

The Theory of Capitalism, the Historical School, and the Theory of the Social Market Economy in Ordo-Liberalism and Neo-Liberalism: Walter Eucken, Alfred Müller-Armack, Franz Böhm, Friedrich Hayek

Chapter 4

Walter Eucken (1891-1950) and the Historical School

HELGE PEUKERT

I. Introduction
II. The Emergence of Eucken's Research Programme
III. The Second Debate on Method: Eucken's Great Antinomy and the Critique of the Historical School
IV. History and Theory in the Analysis of Economic Reality
V. Economic Policy in the Service of ORDO
VI. The Relevance of Eucken and the Historical School at the Turn of the Century

I. Introduction[1]

In the following, two visions (Heilbroner and Milberg 1995) of science, economy and society, will be compared. First, Eucken's concept of ordered competition and secondly the institutional approach of the historical school (HS). For reasons of space and the high quality of the existing secondary literature we shall neither give an overview of the ordoliberal or historical school(s) as such, their impact on economic policy and their precise history of thought background or specific embeddedness in German history and policy, nor shall we describe in detail all aspects of Eucken's work (see the bibliography and references in Walter Eucken Institut (Ed.) 1992, pp. 125-137). Instead, we shall follow Eucken's main contributions in a more

---

1 This reserach was supported by a Feodor-Lynen grant by the Alexander von Humboldt foundation.

chronological order and confront them with the programme of the HS in terms of method, 'theory,' and social and economic policy implications.

The mainstream interpretation of their relationship can be summarised as follows (it is often hidden, but it is in a relativistic version nowadays almost canonical, e.g. Lutz 1968, Holzwarth 1985, pp. 15ff., Lenel 1989a, p. 294, Jöhr 1965, p. 570 and Eucken 1952, pp. 85-96, slightly different Hutchison 1984, pp. 21-22): The HS was a non-theoretical, social-philosophical, romantic, and universalistic movement stemming from the retarded nation building process in Germany. It prevented the emergence of economic theory proper and was therefore theoretically responsible for the German hyperinflation (and indirectly for what followed after 1933). After a struggle of escape from the HS, Eucken (like Menger before him in the first debate on method) paved the way towards 'theory' after 1923. The HS ended in a dead end.

From the background of training and sympathies leaning in the HS's direction, though with an appreciation of its limitations, the relationship between Eucken and the HS is much more complicated. A first question is: What is the common denominator of the HS, is it a coherent school at all? For simplicity we can only state that the older HS had major shortcomings (arguments are delivered in Peukert 1997a). Roscher (see 1886-1894) and Hildebrand are essentially eclectic and Knies presupposes a counterfactual popular spirit (*Volksgeist*). An alternative theoretical approach was not developed before Schmoller, who is considered as the main representative of the (younger) HS. According to Schumpeter (1954, pp. 811-813), the HS is characterised by a fight for social reform, scepticism against theoretical generalisations, a critique of the method of isolation, the concentration on institutional and cultural factors and a preference for monographic-historical research methods. Amid disagreement the core of the HS and American ("old") institutionalism entails the following elements: "(1) group behaviour, not price, should be central in economic thinking; (2) more attention should be given to uniformities of custom, habit and law as modes of organising economic life; (3) individuals are influenced by motives that cannot be quantitatively measured; (4) economic behaviour is constantly changing; therefore, economic generalisations should specify limits of culture and time to which they apply; (5) it is the task of the economist to study the sources of the conflict of interests in the existing social structure as an integral factor rather than a something diverging from a hypothetical norm" (Atkins 1932, p. 111).

WALTER EUCKEN AND THE HISTORICAL SCHOOL

To demarcate the difference between economic schools in general, a polar "pointed abstraction" (Eucken should be mentioned. Modern economic theory follows a different conception of what things make up the world. It is the implicit ontology of formalism, "characterised by a sharp distinction between two aspects of reality, the empirical and the logical (or mathematical or rational). In its logical aspect reality is orderly, systematic, and general, while in its empirical aspect it is haphazard and particular. The logical aspect of reality is what makes it knowable, intelligible, explainable. ... [Scientists] must penetrate into experience to locate the underlying logical order that produces surface regularity, and must replace the vague entities of sense with clear and distinct logical ideas ... [They are] the knowable part of reality and mathematics is the instrument for studying it" (Diesing 1972, pp. 125-126 and 130). Formalists develop the idea of relatively closed systems in which balanced internal exchanges of components, a set of identifiable elements and relations occur, mathematics being the language of science and "nature". Seen from the formalist's point of view, empiricism is the non-scientific opposite, concentrated on the surface appearances of things and missing the underlying logic. Prime examples given are the HS and institutionalism.

"Empiricists" argue that many kinds of order cannot be put in numbers (legal codes, ceremonies, economic styles etc., see McCloskey 1985). Their opposite ontology can be called the holist standpoint (Diesing 1972, ch. 10; Kapp 1961). It "includes the belief that human systems tend to develop a characteristic wholeness or integrity. They are not simply a loose collection of traits or wants or reflexes or variables of any sort ... they have a unity that manifests itself in nearly every part" (Diesing 1972, p. 137). Their variation is not merely a problem of measurement and correlation in a natural science manner. This is also Schmoller's basic principle. "The leading idea of our political economy is that the economic life of mankind is carried out by political and social institutions. Every institution keeps its unity by its territorial borders, technique, and the like but in the first place by its spiritual unity, by the socialisation of the participants ... Their most perceptible symptoms are custom, law, morals and religion" (1978b, pp. 760-761; all German translations by us). The adequate method to analyse them is the method of "understanding" (field work, participant observation, interpretation of documents, monographs etc., see Gadamer 1986). The ensuing theories are furthermore concatenated (relatively independent, loosely linked parts and not deductions from a few basic postulates, see Kaplan 1964) with little deduction and no mathematical logic. "Empirical" meaning is necessarily close to ordinary experience because their definitions have vague meaning. Instead of "rigour" and "precision" they are closer to "observations" and "examples", often including emotive and subjective elements which are often dialectic. E.g. this means that society and economy are characterised by basic polarities like culture and personality (normative rules vs. "autonomous will" and creativity), unity and diversity, consensus and conflict. They exhibit not quantitative, but qualitative *Gestalt* switches, e.g. from feudalism to capitalism. Through the lenses of a holist, the formal ontology is guilty of atomism, irrelevance etc.

In our view these are the two great, equally valid but irreconcilable ontologies in the social sciences, especially in economics (a further breakdown is possible, e.g. in terms of Rutherford's rationality versus rule following, evolution versus design, efficiency versus reform dichotomies, see Rutherford 1996). Both give different answers to different questions and lead to different views of how things are. All debates on method can be understood as a clash of these two ontological perspectives. Our predilection for the holist ontology is due to our respect for human beings who should not be treated as passive things and reduced to a set of variables.

II. The Emergence of Eucken's Research Programme

Walter Eucken was born in 1891 in Jena (see the biographical reports in Lenel 1989a, 1989b and 1990, Lutz 1961, Molsberger 1987, Welter 1965, Götz 1990, Jöhr 1965, and their references). His father was the philosopher and Nobel laureate in literature, Rudolf Eucken (1922) who read Aristotle with both his sons which provided them a humanist background which is typical for the representatives of the HS (see e.g. Roscher 1908 and Schmoller and their aristocratic policy model). In addition, his influence consisted less of a neo-Kantian research strategy but rather in his insistence on (a) that a human life needs a focused concentration on principles, (b) that science should never lose contact with the real world (the primacy of practical philosophy), (c) a life philosophical attitude of free will, (d) a non-individualistic citizen and common good perspective, and (e) that a basic cultural change was needed in times of decay.

WALTER EUCKEN AND THE HISTORICAL SCHOOL

It is worth mentioning that W. Eucken considered studying history but finally decided to study economics (in Kiel, Bonn and Jena). Welter (1965, p. 558) notes that this difficult decision was of great significance. In Bonn he was first influenced by the theoretically oriented Dietzel (see e.g. Eucken 1968, pp. 29 and 99; and 1947, p. 84, fn. 2), but then he became assistant of H. Schumacher who belonged to the younger HS (Wendt 1956). Eucken followed him from Bonn to Berlin and Schumacher supervised his dissertation (1914) and habilitation (1921a). "This starting point of his scientific activities was without doubt essential for his later life-work" (Lutz 1961, p.353). The cross-fertilisation between the theoretical, historical, liberal and interventionist camps was by no means unusual at that time (Herbst 1965, Seligman 1925, and Senn 1993). Grossekettler's genealogical table of ordo-liberalism (see Grossekettler 1994, p. 11 and 1987b, p. 61) is but a first approximation. It should be expanded to include Lachmann who studied under Sombart, Weber's influence on Mises, and Knight's conversation with the HS (see the details in Boyd 1997) all of which depict an even more dense communication and influence network, not to speak of the influence of Spann's universalism, Wagemann's empirical business cycle studies, Gottl-Ottlilienfeld's life philosophy, Oppenheimer's sociology (see Haselbach 1985) and liberal socialism (see Jöhr 1965, p. 569; for the description of the diversity in the social-political school see Schmidt 1997). There are two ways by which historical and institutional thought reached the ordo-liberals. "(1) There is a direct way via Knies' student, Schmoller, and his students, Schumacher and Oppenheimer. The latter two supervised Eucken's, Welter's and Erhard's dissertation theses. Two of Schmoller's other disciples, namely Sombart and Max Weber, considerably influenced Müller-Armack at the same time. (2) There is an indirect way via Knies' disciple, Ely, to the American Institutionalists, and from there mainly via Commons to the Older Chicago School, and finally from that school via Simons and Lippmann to Eucken" (Grossekettler 1994, p. 12, and Grossekettler 1987a and 1987b for the details).

Eucken's dissertation and habilitation are usually described as written mainly in the tradition of the HS (Lenel 1990, p. 15). A closer look reveals that this statement can be qualified. *Die Verbandsbildung in der Seeschiffahrt* (1914) already entailed his research question: the problems of cartels and the emergence of economic power and abolishing competition by associations. His aim is "to detect the essential in the current of fleeting appearances" (1914, p. VII). This is a typical formulation which can be found as well in his later "post-historical" writings. He distinguished technical (e.g. the emergence of mass production) and historical economic changes (1968, p. 54), like the development of an internationally integrated market. He explained in detail how competition had been suppressed (price, quality etc.), the difficulties in forming cartels over time (different price structures, number of cartel members etc.), their policy against outsiders, the differences between a cartelized and a "free market" (1914, pp. 180ff.) etc. Although he mentions the fact that cartels lead to a stabilised capacity utilisation, he underlines the fact of increasing prices and discusses countermeasures of the state. The government should not be a competitor itself, *"but should strengthen private competitive forces against the cartels"* (1914, p. 285). Finally he concludes that "after the emergence of a cartelizable object and the intensification of competition *the emergence of associations* [*Verbände*] become a necessity" (1914, p. 291). Referring to the pro-cartel literature of his time (Kleinwächter, Pohle, Liefmann) his absolutely neutral and extremely detailed and informed description, with an excellent feeling for economic policy considerations, can almost be interpreted as a dissenting statement. At least it raises an important issue: what is better in general, free trade (with prices going down to production and transport costs, p. 180) or monopolising associations (with a stabilisation of output)?

His habilitation *Die Stickstoffversorgung der Welt* (1921a) on the world supply of nitrogen is an empirical monograph exclusively about the specialities and changing conditions of supply and demand in a very peculiar market. No theoretical or policy questions are raised at all. Both books can be described as "historical-empirical" but they do not really belong to the HS because the HS's underlying and more or less optimistic theory about the necessity of social associations, the positive role of the state and law in fostering market institutions and the usefulness of partial restrictions of competition (Schmoller 1892) is completely missing. Both books concentrate on the development of technology and markets (e.g. Schmoller 1978b, p. 748 can be read as a critique of Eucken in this respect).

The canonical version interprets Eucken's *Kritische Betrachtungen zum deutschen Geldproblem* (1923) as the first explicit critique of the blind empiricism of the HS carrying a high responsibility for the German hyperinflation in the 1920s (Miksch 1950, p. 282; see the description of the social and economic history of the Weimar republic, which is essential to understand Eucken, in Stolper et al. 1964, part 4). In fact, the influence of the HS in academia was going downhill for some time (Wagner 1950, p. 172) and it is open to doubt if the HS influenced the practical policy of the *Reichsbank* and the *Reichsregierung*. They seem to have been much more influenced by the explanations of the old banking school à la Fullarton (1844) and Tooke (1844) and their theory of internal money creation and the unproblematic view of bills of exchange. It is a certain contradiction to state (a) that the HS had no theory at all and yet on the other hand (b) that it had the wrong theory (i.e. a more or less naive version of the balance of payments theory). Practically, the theoretical debate was dominated by the contributions of I. Fisher, Wicksell, Cassel, Hahn, Mises, Wagemann, Menger, and Schumpeter (see the references in Ehrlicher 1965, and the excellent description of the debate in the 1920s in Palyi 1925).

Eucken – who does not mention the shortcomings of the HS once in his book – states that the balance of payments theory (*Zahlungsbilanztheorie*) belongs to a group of theories which try to explain inflation from real sector influences (like Tooke). Very roughly, these theories stated that the passivity of the balance of payments, due to the payment obligations after the Versailles peace treaty, led to an outflow of paper money. So the price for foreign currencies and the prices of imported goods (as well as the discounting of commodity bills) increased. Therefore, the German price level rose and caused a deficit in the budget which raised inflation. The remedies are lower interest rates and an increase in exports or a decrease in imports. According to Eucken, Knapp (who has to be considered as a representative of an institutional theory of money and who influenced Helfferich) asks the fundamental qualitative question of the legal conditions for (fiat) money but Knapp did *not* explicitly consider the problem of the determination of the price level or supported the inflationists theoretically. Only indirectly did he support a real sphere determination of the price level (Eucken 1923, p. 10) although it is hard to see a necessary link between an institutional qualitative theory of money and a real sphere explanation of the price level.

Like Bonn, Mises, Pohle, and Hahn, Eucken fosters an explanation of inflation as a monetary phenomenon (see the precise but analytically weak reconstruction in Folz 1970 and the survey in Meyer 1961). It is caused by budget deficits and an artificially low interest rate by the central bank, an approach which holds for the circumstances of that period (Giersch 1956) and resembles the theoretical discourse of the last decades (Friedman 1959, and Mishkin 1995, part VI). Eucken does not consider credit money of the banks and explains the foreign value of currency by the classical purchasing power parity theory (Eucken 1925a and 1925b; see the critical discussion in

Isard 1995). Until his last publications (e.g. 1952, pp. 74-76) he supported the quantity theory of money. The general aversion against the quantity theory was an international phenomenon caused by the defeat of bimetallism. It says that the money supply times velocity of circulation equals the price level times the volume of output. An increase in the money supply increases the price level if the volume of output and the velocity are considered constant. Is this a theoretical transgression, away from the empiricism of the HS? We do not think so because Schmoller did not criticise the quantity theory in general (he supported the use of such theoretical tools). He states that it should not be misused as a simplifying formula which reduces complex interrelationships (Schmoller 1978, p. 118). Eucken agreed, the quantity theory should not be misunderstood as a causal theory. In addition, he underlines that the four variables themselves are influenced by many forces and that expectations play an important role (Eucken 1926, pp. 307-309). Eucken does not start with an abstract theory, but with an empirical critique of balance of payments theory and its inner contradictions. Then, based on statistics and logical conclusions, and taking the quantity theory as background, he develops his non-formal inflation explanation which includes the policy recommendations of a balanced budget (if possible) and an adequate interest rate, embedded in the specific historical context of the German economy in 1923.

His book therefore is a prime example of Schmoller's (1883) mysterious claim of the combination of induction and deduction. It culminates in a long-run vista which is typical for a holist or *staatswissenschaftliche* perspective: the state is under the pressure of interest groups and therefore will not restrict the money supply as necessary. The solution would be a strict return to the pure gold standard to limit the power of the state (1923, pp. 79-81; unfortunately we have to leave out his capital theory, for an overview see Fehl 1989 and his proposals concerning the business cycle 1933, see Eucken 1929 and 1933). Compared with the HS, a difference in policy considerations but not in method/ontology emerges here. It conveys "his insistence on grounding theory in reality observable every day" (Yeager 1994, p. 72); or in his own words: "to acquire results which are logically conclusive and near to realistic" (1937, p. 231).

Eucken wrote on the structural changes of the state and the crisis of capitalism (1932) in a universal history perspective. The text is often seen as the founding manifesto of the ordo-liberal movement (Dürr 1954, pp. 8ff.). He criticised the view that the entrepreneurs lost their alertness - even in the monopolised or cartelized part of the economy, like the chemical industry, technical innovations occur. Many inventions only wait to be realised as new combinations in the Schumpeterian sense. He describes "capitalism" (a notion of the *Begriffsnationalökonomie*) in the perspective of Schumpeter's model of creative destruction. But also a non-dynamic, stable, and less mobile capitalism is considered possible (1932, pp. 299-301 and 314-315).

Then a developmental pattern of state, economy, and society is presented which resembles a stage theory: in the mercantile system the sovereign created markets and infrastructure to support his power and left the rest of the economy alone. Then after the liberal, the economic state as a distinct phase emerged. First – in the Bismarck era – interventionism was *à la raison d'état*, but when Bismarck left, a new quality of interventionism was reached. State and economy changed roles in terms of the power relationship. The state became the powerless servant of interest groups, "the economic policy of the state and the representation of the interests of entrepreneurs merge into a compact unity" (1932, p. 304). This sounds like leftist state monopoly capitalism but Eucken quickly changes the perspective. In an Ortega Y Gasset like manner the masses are put on the stage, quite untypical in a liberal framework (see Dörge 1959, pp. 89-92). Their anti-capitalistic attitude is explained by a substitution process. Religion vanished and the ensuing vacuum was filled by a belief in a total, all-encompassing state (1932, p. 306). The democratisation of the party system enabled the masses to transform the new aspirations in interventionist activities to influence economic policy, e.g. price controls for housing rents. Referring to C. Schmitt, the power of the state vanishes, it has "absolutely no unifying thought and will" (1932, p. 307) any more. The state almost becomes a "real entity" when he states "but when the state recognises ... if he finds the power" (1932, p. 318) – but who are the real actors of his state? Eucken is very sceptical vis-à-vis democracy and universal suffrage. In a 'world-historical perspective' he summarises: "In the final instance it was and is the masses under whose increasing pressure during the third phase the historical structure of the state had been destroyed and the economic state had been erected ... *whereby the social and the structure of the state decay*" (1932, p. 312). Eucken comes very close to Aristotle's conservative vista (shared by Roscher in 1918 and conflicting with his social concern). But what is Eucken's practical alternative to the ancient city state?

III. The Second Debate on Method: Eucken's Great Antinomy and the Critique of the Historical School

In 1934, Eucken introduced his methodological approach (1954, pp. 1-51) which was only slightly elaborated upon in further studies (1971, 1938, 1940, 1965, pp. 1-68 etc.). The main objective was a critique of the empiricism of the HS, secondarily a critique of rationalism (classical economics). It demarcates a sharp break with the HS although he tries to transcend the antinomy between empiricism and rationalism (Wagner 1950, doubts that Eucken achieved this aim). The importance of his (methodological) break with the HS is highlighted by the fact, that in the first common positive statement about the new research agenda with Böhm and Grossmann-Doerth in 1936, in an introduction to the series *Ordnung der Wirtschaft,* the main arguments are developed in opposition to the HS. The starting point is the observation that law and economics - which should closely move together - lost their practical leading function in public discourse ("Führerstelle im öffentlichen Leben", 1971, p. 87). Like the HS they hold that the neighbouring science of economics is law (among others) and not mathematics (or econometrics , see Büchner 1954, p. 78). Interdisciplinary research has to serve a public function with a universal historical perspective (Böhm and Grossmann-Doerth became law professors in Freiburg, when Eucken taught there, see Böhm 1957).

Economic theory has to advise (economic) policy, this is one of the main reasons why Schmoller co-founded the *Verein für Socialpolitik* in 1872 (Lindenlaub 1967) and purported what the authors describe as a "moral and political science" (1971, p. 92). But the historical law school in the tradition of Savigny and the HS in economics were both under the damaging influence of historism as a scientific attitude with relativism and fatalism as its main negative ingredients. That is why they rejected basic decisions and decided economic policy questions opportunistically from case to case. Law and economies were interpreted as natural and spontaneous expressions of the history of people/nations, e.g. cartels were accepted as an inevitable fact by the German *Reichsgericht* in 1897. But scientists in their role as *clerks* (J. Benda) need "the central point, the idea of law to tackle the shaping of things ... the strength of science to be a power of life" (1971, pp. 89, 91 and 92). Scientific reasoning leads to the idea of an "economic constitution as a political general decision on the order of the national economic life ...

the order of law as an order of the economy" (1971, p. 96). In the centre of this order is free competition (*freier Wettbewerb*,1971, p. 96), which later on became Eucken's market form of full competition (*vollständige Konkurrenz*).

In pointed abstraction their argument is that there is objective knowledge about society, mainly economic in character, which can be got by using the right method and that this knowledge is based on few principles which have to be implemented, even if usually naive people think differently or do not understand it (like Erhard's non-democratic currency reform and price liberalisation in 1948, see Richter (Ed.) 1979, and Klump 1997, Erhard 1962, p. 8; compare the predictive power of Eucken and Meyer 1948, but see also Wünsche 1997; for the interventionist mainstream opinion at this time see Hutchison 1979, pp. 435-440; in how far Eucken's message was implemented in 1947ff. is discussed by Oberender 1989).

We may leave open whether Eucken's reconstruction of historism (1938) is adequate (see Heussi 1932 for the different currents in historism). His attack on Schmoller as a relativist claims that he is responsible for unsystematic thinking ("*punktuelles Denken*", 1938, p. 69) and that German economists lost the ability "to see single economic questions as partial questions of the total economic constitution" and made an organised "state order of the economy" impossible (1938, pp. 79 and 81). In a reply, Laum argued that Schmoller was not a relativist and believed in the 'absolute value of social justice' (whatever this meant in detail). It was exactly the HS, "which pleads for the primacy of the political against the economical, i.e. the integration of economic life in the order of law set up by the state" (1938, p. 91). Eucken's apt reply (1940) put Schmoller in social-philosophical perspective. Around 1840 a cultural switch from the idealist, literary-philosophical orientation, to modern realism happened in Germany, with Schmoller (influenced by Darwin and Spencer) on the modernist's side. He purported a social-utilitarian moral philosophy with the idea of progress and development at its core, only secondarily mixed with Heglian idealism and Christian beliefs. Eucken doubts the moral betterment of man due to education (the *Reichskristallnacht* was just over when he wrote his reply). The vital and elementary drive for power which plays a central role in Eucken's thinking cannot be eradicated. In fact, Schmoller simply presupposes the idea of progress. The incompatible muddle of idealism and realism in Schmoller may even be worse than Eucken described it (Peukert 1997a, ch. III.1. and Raab 1934), but it is independent of his economic theory and policy. Eucken with his more negative ontology (and the simple decree that a power drive exists) calls for an "ideal" state/society as well.

But how should "the total connection" ("*der Gesammtzusammenhang*", 1940, p. 492) be analysed, what is Eucken's new method to solve the "great antinomy"? He makes a clear distinction between everyday and scientific knowledge in terms of radicalism of questioning, inter-relatedness of facts etc. (1954, pp.1-5). In practice, rationalism and empirism prevail in science (1954, p. 6), a difference that dominates methodological debates since Bacon and Descartes. Although the rationalist starts with some observations, after having found some generalities, he immediately uses abstract thinking to deduce objective knowledge like Walras or in Ricardo's and Menger's value theories which finally only entail hypothetical judgements (if - then). Empiricists like Roscher and Schmoller start with the recognition of concrete facts as well. Schmoller "is sceptical where longer chains of reasoning and hypothetical judgements are concerned ... Schmoller's Grundriss is a mosaic of individual investigations" (1954, p. 9). It should be mentioned that Schmoller had no coherent methodology (1883). In his books and articles sometimes induction precedes deduction, sometimes induction is considered more important than deduction, sometimes induction and deduction change dialectically, sometimes deduction is the crowning end of inductive reasoning (Peukert 1997a, pp. 68ff.). It is very questionable, if it makes sense to put Menger and Ricardo into the same category, because Menger - influenced by historism (like Schmoller and Eucken) - tried to solve the antinomy with an Aristotelian strategy (Alter 1990), while Ricardo tried to argue in a formal mathematical way.

The problem with Eucken's reasoning is that it is somewhat superficial and below the usual demarcation lines of methodological discourse. He never defines what the process of abstract reasoning really means, how it proceeds and what its standards of validity are. Empiricism, Husserl's phenomenology, the use of mathematics, logical positivism, rationalism in the strict Cartesian sense, Kant's method, Menger's Aristotelism, were in the air at his time. Eucken's methodological way of thinking rests on an unsound basis, because he held, in Gadamer's terms (1986), a "naive methodology." For example, in his text on historism he declares, that it is easy to check the validity of Marxian value theory. Like every theory it lies in its capacity to explain reality. According to theory, land (which is not produced by labour) should have no value, but a price is often paid for it - thus Marxian value theory is disproved by the facts (1938, p. 75). Statements like this can be called Eucken's methodological fallacy of misplaced concreteness. He does not take into consideration the problems raised in the Popper (whose main book on method was published before Eucken's book), Kuhn, and Feyerabend debate (the non-refutability of theories by single observations etc., see Lakatos and Musgrave (Eds.) 1970). Even Friedman's ad hoc/prediction ("down to the facts") approach (1953a) consciously excludes the question if theories with predictive power can be verified or are objectively right or wrong.

Eucken's critique of the economics of notions (*Begriffsnationalökonomie*, i.e. Spann, and Sombart) which starts with definitions (universalism, capitalism) instead of facts (1954, pp. 11ff.) is correct as such but does not consider the difference between the method of research and the method of presentation. Before Ricardo started writing he had an understanding of the main mechanisms of the economy. Theories usually evolve in a complex context of observations, maps of thought, theoretical discussions in the professions, specific problems (unemployment, encroached liberty), general cultural background and value commitments with inductive and deductive chains of reasoning going back and forth (Polanyi 1958; Weippert 1941/42 criticises that Eucken accepts only one type of theory). The final presentation has a composition of its own (the complex view how research works is admirably exemplified in A. Smith's text on astronomy, see Smith 1982). Eucken supports a naive *carte blanche* theory: only recognition of facts are acceptable (1954, p. 13f.). The interrelation of prices as the major general problem is presented as plainly obvious (1954, 17ff. and 1965, pp. 1ff., e.g. he talks about "five questions which sprout out of our nearest surroundings", 1954, p. 5), as well as the non-existence of a general theory of business cycles (1954, p. 18)! His theoretical-methodological prescriptions are of little help; for example: 'these hypothetical conditions are more removed from reality as it is adequate for our aim of knowledge" (1954, p. 21). But who knows precisely if they are, what is the objective measure to distinguish between artificial and real constructs (1954, p. 22), does the homo oeconomicus belong to his category of artificiality or not (1954, p. 23)?

One distinguishing feature of Eucken is his negation of trade-offs, e.g. between liberty and social justice, and between realism of assumptions and rigor of the result. In our view a formalist ontology leads to evident results but the cost is somewhat unrealistic assumptions. This holds for general price theory, monetary theory, the theory of international trade etc. which

Eucken praises (1954, pp. 35-36). But he does not buy their necessarily unrealistic assumptions. This is a contradiction which Eucken tries to overcome by sticking to the hyper-paradox: "The stronger the individuality is emphasised in the historical constellation, the more evident becomes the lasting and constant in history" (1940, p. 487). Like Menger (Schmoller was never really interested in methodological questions) Eucken tried to solve the antinomies in an open-minded, honest and sincere way - he failed but he caused a high-level debate, necessarily without results (e.g. Lenel 1989b, pp. 15-18, Albert 1985, Kloten 1955, Machlup 1961) because he tried to unify the formalist and the holist ontology.

Eucken tried to reconcile rationalism and historical diversity, watertight economic analysis and realism - the everyday mind as a starting point but which has to be surmounted. On the one hand the one great problem of economics emerges naturally from everyday experience (*"Alltagserfahrung"*, 1965, p. 7), on the other hand the natural order (the *Wettbewerbsordnung*) had been delivered by the classical economists (1965, p. 25). According to Eucken they have been too one-sided and abstract, not analysing monopoly as a fact of real economic life. Is it also true for A. Smith? It can be argued that he was not abstract enough, because he could not objectively and exactly prove that markets without barriers to entry work well without state intervention (assuming a propensity to monopolise) and that full competition is better than (temporary) oligopoly or monopoly in a macroeconomic, dynamic, non-determinate perspective (the Schumpeterian challenge, compare Eucken 1932, 297-301). To "prove" existence, stability and Pareto optimality ("efficiency") very severe and necessarily unrealistic assumptions are necessary (nicely discussed in Koopmans' early 1957 essays, and stated e.g. in Varian 1994). Eucken asks for an objective and logic analysis. So a Hayekian 'pattern prediction' is not enough and is in itself inconsistent: if all knowledge is bound to time and space, how can Hayek formulate his very general statements about spontaneous orders, social policy etc.?

Eucken assumes that there are two ideal types of knowledge: Firstly, a structural and abstract "concept knowledge" and secondly, a time and space dependent, disaggregated, "bounded knowledge". He is sceptical of mathematics (1965, p. 34, and see his letter to Röpke in Röpke 1960/61, p. 5) and abstract models but he refers to their theoretical results (Stackelberg 1942, pp. 270-271, and Peter's criticism in 1951/52). This is Eucken's particular antinomy (Jöhr 1965, p. 577).

WALTER EUCKEN AND THE HISTORICAL SCHOOL

His rejection of economic styles of Hildebrand, Schmoller, Spiethoff, and Sombart should be mentioned before we see how he tries to solve his antinomy (for the dichotomous categories see Sombart 1930, pp. 206-207 and Spiethoff 1932, pp. 76-77). He criticises their evolutionary (*"gradlinig herausentwickelt"*, 1965, p. 44), unilateral (no involutions, 1965, p. 46), generalising (e.g. the difference between the guilds in the north and south in Italy is neglected, 1965, p. 49) real type method. Furthermore, they use abstract notions like capitalism or city economy (1965, p. 58). His critical remarks already imply his own theory (different market forms are realised in a Weberian type city economy, so it must be a wrong concept). Eucken presupposes that there is only one natural basic question and natural level of abstraction in economics (Weisser 1965, p. 271). The stage theories (some like Rüstow's are still in circulation) in Thucydides, Plato, Aristotle, Smith, List et al. can be read in a naive (as real types) or sophisticated version. They can be read as a Kantian clue (*Leitfaden*), making sense of history from specific perspectives like Schmoller's increasingly complex social institutions or Spiethoff and Sombart who are dealing with the abrupt transition from feudalism to capitalism in Germany, from community to society (*Gemeinschaft* to *Gesellschaft*). Eucken's oeuvre itself was centered around the big antithesis of his days: capitalism (exchange economy) versus socialism (centrally administered economy). In fact, he never really talks about Sombart's concept of "capitalism" (see Brocke 1987).

An organic-evolutionary viewpoint is not necessarily connected with stages as the proponents of the younger stage theories demonstrated (e.g. Gerloff and Mitscherlich, see the references in Schachtschabel 1943 and Peters 1987). Stage theories are much less monolithic than Eucken seems to assume. An example is Spiethoff's bizarre incorporation of a concept of a timeless economy (1932, p. 52-53) which is an adaptation of Wieser (1924, p. 2). But most interesting is the fact that Eucken's morphology incorporates most elements of the Spiethoff and Sombart dichotomies so that Stackelberg describes him as a "perfecter and fulfiller" (1942, p. 256) of their endeavour. In fact, like the formalists Eucken differentiates the empirical and the logical but he tries to do so without mathematics.

HELGE PEUKERT

IV. History and Theory in the Analysis of Economic Reality

This is the subtitle of Eucken's "Foundations", first published in 1940 (Eucken 1951a, translated by T. W. Hutchison). It can only be mentioned in passing that behind the apparently abstract (methodological) debate lay his struggle against totalitarianism (Röpke 1959). It secures him an everlasting place in the pantheon of humanism. (Some days after he finished the book the German army invaded Poland.) "The period of national socialism became the great challenge of Eucken's life. At the *Erfurter Rektorentag* in 1933 he tried to persuade the German universities to stand up against Hitler and failed. He continued his struggle at Freiburg as Martin Heidegger attempted to establish the *Führerprinzip* at the university. In 1936 he delivered the lecture, *Kampf der Wissenschaft*, against Nazi ideology. He collaborated with the Bekennende Kirche and other dissident groups" (Oswalt-Eucken 1994, p. 38; Blumenberg-Lampe 1973; and Johnson 1989a).

The skeleton of his 1940 book can be summarised in a few words (cf. Lutz 1940): 1. "The actions of any director of an economic structure or unit are always based on an economic plan" (1951a, pp. 117-118). 2. Two pure elemental forms exist, "the *centrally directed economy*, in which there is no exchange, and the type of system we call the *exchange economy*" (1951a, p. 118). 3. The first has two forms: the simple centrally directed economy or independent economy (like an autonomous peasant household) and the much larger centrally administered economy (like the early Egyptian or Inca empires), which can be subdivided in: (1) the totally centralised economy characterised by the prohibition of all exchange, (2) the centrally directed economy with free exchange of consumers' goods, and (3) with consumers' choice. Exchange economies differ according to the planner's taking the price as a datum or not, differentiable in 25 forms of markets (competition, partial oligopoly, partial monopoly, and monopoly, as forms of supply or demand) which may be open or closed (see 1951a, p. 158).

Equally important for real economies are the types of monetary systems: "(a) Money often originates, with some commodity being used as money ... (b) Money may come into existence as a return for the provision of a good or service ... (c) Our third monetary system is one under which the granter of credit creates money" (1951a, pp. 165,167, and169, in italics; for reasons of space we cannot discuss them further). In addition, five sets of economic data (the needs to be satisfied, natural resources, labour, the stock of previously produced goods, technical knowledge, and the legal and social organisation) and three empirical rules (Gossen's first law – compare the critique in Stackelberg 1942, p. 262, the law of diminishing marginal returns, and the increase of productivity by the lengthening of the period of gestation) plus the fact of risk and uncertainty must be taken into consideration by any planner and economist (Eucken is fully aware of the problems of limited knowledge). Finally, he mentions (1951a, pp. 274ff.) some human constants (humans always follow the economic principle, the level of needs is alterable or it is approximately stable over shorter or longer periods, the plan is for the long term or for the short, and the head (of a firm) is "*either* aiming at maximum net receipts for himself, *or* at the optimum output for those working with him or whom he is supplying" (1951a, p. 288).

This summary gives the impression of a relatively old-fashioned, somewhat tepid, at least not ingenious book. In fact, Eucken's achievement does not stand out in most summaries. The flavour of novelty and originality only becomes evident in reading the book page by page (even the excellent English translation sometimes misses the essential little differences, e.g. "optimum output" in the last citation reads in German "*möglichst gute Versorgung*", 1965, p. 217, which sounds much less neo-classical).

Eucken insists his theory is based on completely new grounds, but the co-ordination of plans as a starting point was already emphasised by K. F. Maier (1935, p. 67, see also Veit 1980, Eucken 1951a, p. 130). The market forms were developed by Stackelberg (1940), Böhm-Bawerk (1900-1902) and E. Schneider (1938) and emphasised by W. Neuling (1939). Much of the data and empirical rules find a correspondence in the Spiethoff and Sombart dichotomies. The first similarity between Sombart and Eucken consists in the fact that Eucken develops his distinctions mainly as dichotomies. Eucken's exchange versus administered economy distinction shows up in Spiethoff's IV. 12-15 and in Sombart's B.I.-B.VI. categories. Like Eucken, they consider markets as the distinguishing feature of exchange economies. Spiethoff's natural and technical conditions (Sombart's category C.) are discussed by Eucken under the rubric of needs, labour, technical resources, and technical knowledge (for a more extended comparison see Möller 1940). But Sombart's subdivision of techniques is more complex than Eucken's whose market forms and monetary systems are much more refined. In so far both approaches could be regarded as complementary.

A crucial point is the "spirit" category, put at the top in Sombart's (A. *Geist*) and Spiethoff's (I. *Wirtschaftsgeist*) classification, underlining their holist, historical and institutional creed. Specific and historically changing ways of thinking, like Weber's spirit of capitalism or Sombart's (A.3.) solidarism versus individualism, are the overarching main characteristics of structurally different economies. They are holistically characterised in all its parts and aspects by this spirit (*Wirtschaftsgesinnung*) and the ensuing social and legal order. Here a marked difference becomes obvious: Eucken starts bottom-up with the precise analysis of market forms at the centre (but implying "ontologically" that markets as such are in the centre; "capitalism", which defined as an exchange economy already implies this viewpoint) and then looks at the surrounding data, social order, and mind sets to demarcate the historically specific totality.

The HS and institutionalism start the other way round, so that markets are "merely" a set of institutionalised rules and have no logic of their own. Competition has no inherent tendencies other than those implanted in the specific working rules of society, "an artificial arrangement supported by the moral, economic, and physical sanctions of collective action" (Commons 1934, p. 713; Ramstad 1990, Schmoller 1978a, pp. 5-9). For Schmoller, the great economic miracle is not the autonomous interplay of market forces but the co-operation of human beings in social institutions (which he calls *Organe*) with common values, language etc. (1978a, 748-749). He develops a modern socialisation theorem including Smith's sympathy concept (1978a, pp. 10-17). He holds a dialectical homo duplex model, i.e. man is driven by rivalry (an individualistic tendency) and by the need for social acceptance (the socialising tendency, see 1978a, pp. 28-35). Likewise in all "organs" and institutions, double impulses are at work. Insurances have "a pure private law, egoistic and a humane public welfare component; for the business man the first, for the social thinker the second, is more attractive" (1978b, p. 398; Schmoller's exact chain of reasoning including his subjective-institutional value theory is developed in Peukert 1997a). Schmoller would have been very sceptical about the long-run workability of a completely individualistic shareholder-value society.

Eucken tries to integrate different viewpoints: on the one hand market and administered forms have an inner logic, once established. "At first we are free, but then we are servants" (Goethe, in Eucken 1968, p. 222). He does not share the neo-classical, cliometric, game theoretical, and (naive version of) transaction cost analysis view of man and social and economic development of man as an individualised brute U-maximiser and history as a one-way road to reduce transaction costs (Borchardt 1977). In major regards, Eucken argues against their specific concept of universal maximisation and rationality. Although individuals behave according to Gossen's first law and (their subjective understanding of) the economic principle, he states that the planner of a (totally) centralised economy may act to satisfy the needs of the population as best as possible (this and Eucken's understanding of the role of the state is opposite to public choice assumptions). In market forms, except full competition, the planner may maximise net receipts (the shareholder value philosophy) or pay high productivity oriented wages (a social market policy) and deliver more goods than the Cournot point would suggest. For Eucken, this behaviour is not irrational, but corresponds to a specific value commitment outside the confines of economic reasoning. In his framework, needs can be approximately stable. This violates the essential non-satiability assumption of convex indifference curves. In addition, the planning horizon may be short or long.

Maybe the most important similarity consists in his assumption that the "data", like the social and legal forms, cannot be integrated in the core as technical development is integrated in recent growth theories, i.e. analysable by strict logical analysis. But at the same time it is fundamental to understand a real economic setting (1951a, p. 186). "Data ... are those facts which determine the nature of the economic world without themselves being economic facts. On coming up against these data theoretical explanation has to break off. The task of theory is to follow out the necessary relationships as far as the particular set of data, and in the other direction to show how the course of economic events depends on the data. Economic theory cannot show how these data come to exist" (1951a, p. 213). He rejects both economic imperialism (a Gary S. Becker type analysis, Eucken mentions Ricardo's economising determination of the size of the population, 1951a, p. 217), economists ignorance (not relevant or accessible for economic analysis, contra Leipold 1989, p. 129 and Heuss 1989, p. 24) and interdisciplinary separation, i.e. that the data should be analysed by sociologists. This view is explicitly rejected. "(T)he task of obtaining the data cannot be left to sociology or history, which are not fitted for carrying it out" (1951a, p. 342, fn. 52).

Eucken's strong claim is that "*an almost unlimited variety of actual economic systems can be made up out of a limited number of basic pure forms* ... to discover all those ideal types of economic forms out of which actual economic systems present and past have been, and are, composed" (1951a, p. 109). He pretends to have found them by direct observation (1951a, pp. 106-109). They are objectively given, like the chemical elements. It is questionable if hunter and gatherer societies (mentioned e.g. in 1951a, p. 210, 1968, p. 20 and 1947, p. 35) which make up 99% of the time man had lived on earth can be analysed by his dichotomies regarding their spontaneous mode of (re)production beyond exchange and administration (Lee 1984, Peukert 1993; if the HS is much better in this respect is open to doubt, see Peukert 1997c). But it has to be mentioned that Eucken's use and knowledge of more recent economic history is impressive.

Are his (market) forms real or ideal types? "These types do not purport to be pictures of actual economic life, that is, they are not real types ..., but purely ideal types each representing one single aspect of a group of cases. That does not mean that they are "Utopian", as Max Weber mistakenly called them" (1951a, p. 173). But when they are ideal types how can they be the strict measure for economic policy proposals (Kapp 1953)? A first interpretation could be that the behaviour of firms in a specific market form is behaviourally clearly determined, e.g. monopolies realise Cournot's maximum point (1951a, p. 200) *or* this is only on average / potentially / typically the case (1953, p. 14). On the other hand, the types can be understood in the sense of his example of the cotton spinning and weaving mill "T" (1951a, p. 107): for the sale of spinning products, the firm participates in a cartel agreement, for woven goods competition prevails. The factory belonged to an exchange economy in general. From a more disaggregated viewpoint it was active in two different ideal type forms. In so far his types are real and ideal at the same time as in his example of the Bobbio cloisters. "The prevailing features of Bobbio were those of a centrally directed economy. They predominated, but not exclusively. They were supplemented by elements of an exchange economy ... Its whole economic structure was a complex of structural elements" (1951a, p. 112). So Bobbio (like most real economic units according to Eucken) had a mixed economy but it was predominantly centrally administered. But then why should mixed economies not be integrated as specifically structured theoretical ideal types in theory and practice (as Kröll 1952 and Kloten 1955 suggest)?

This raises an interesting question: How does he conclude which system dominates? By analysing the *Sinnzusammenhang* (1965, p. 128, translated as interrelated purposes in 1951a, p. 179) of the monk community, by different turnovers, by the differing number of transactions or how else? Here is the *hermeneutic surplus* in Eucken's approach. The elementary forms are the starting point, the individuality of real economies is due to the fact that "in economic life, both past and present, the different forms ... are blended together in great variety" (1951a, p. 156). The combination of these manifold pure forms into a meaningful structure cannot be done in a formal way and he never gives any methodological device how to do it; but Eucken's practice corresponds to a method of understanding which in fact cannot be described in an abstract way (although Sombart in 1930 and some others tried hard).

As a result, the difference to the HS narrows considerably. But when Eucken states "'exchange economy' is simply a pure elemental form (just as is that of the centrally directed economy), which is to be found at all periods of human history ... by abstracting their significant characteristics" (1951a, p. 129) the HS might wonder if e.g. a middle-age guild system or even his description of the exchange economy in Bobbio (where long-term customary contracts prevailed) can be described adequately with Eucken's distinctions. Aren't the essential peculiarities of these systems lost and only much later reintroduced by the data-analysis? On the other hand it can be argued that the market forms, devoid of ideological connotations (like the Inca religion, justifying stratification) enable a sober look at the facts (the Incas accumulating rents by exploiting the subjugated on their monopoly markets). No general conclusion seems reasonable (but our analysis of the classical Greek economic system might have gained by the inclusion of his market forms, see Peukert 1995).

It is important to keep Eucken's understanding and definition of full competition in mind. Competition is *not* defined by an absolutely elastic demand curve, homogenous products or an infinite number of firms. Eucken criticises abstract models and unrealistic general equilibrium equations (see his comment on Ricardo and Cassel, 1951a, p. 196). Competition means only that prices are taken as given in the plan of the economic agent. Homogeneity, the number of firms, immediate reactions, strictly rational agents, perfect knowledge or the fact that the economic agent's activity objectively more or less influences prices, quantities etc. is not important. Eucken's competition is not a night watchman competition (Lutz): firms may innovate, differentiate their product, advertise etc. (contra Stackelberg 1942, p. 266 who in general reads Eucken in the tradition of formal theory and therefore sometimes misses the mark; see Eucken's obituary in 1948d). The broadness of his analysis may be illustrated by the following example.

"Wine and beer being substitutes, does the brewery possess a monopoly? It does *not*, if in fixing its prices it makes them wholly dependent on wine prices ... taking the latter as a planning datum ... the brewery does have a monopoly if a sufficient range of prices exists for it to be possible to pursue a price policy for beer ... It may happen that of two firms in objectively the same situation one will act competitively and the other monopolistically ... If ... a strong movement of custom away from his hotel sets in he would be compelled by the facts to return to the path of his predecessor" (1951a, p. 142 and 144). Eucken's view of the economy - implicit in his many examples which have to be left out here - is non-deterministic. The data and risk/uncertainty are always changing the situation, thus nice maximisation under constraints is not possible. Economic agents make plans with limited knowledge, e.g. about the real demand curves and cross-price elasticity. They have a certain margin of freedom; the manager of one hotel in town is a price taker, another one is not – yet both can survive.

His economic world is populated by individuals as they were described by Shackle and the subjectivists in the Austrian tradition (Kirzner and Lachmann 1986, Boettke and Prychitko 1994): economic agents live in an uncertain world where prices have to be interpreted and surprises exist - like the potential entry of a competitor on an open monopoly market (1951a, p. 153-154), not to mention the constant fluctuation in prices (1951a, p. 200). "There is generally a greater or lesser degree of uncertainty. Expectations are only partially realised. It is because of the imperfection of expectations that the risk element makes itself felt" (1951a, p. 193). Eucken's subjectivism is also a methodological and pedagogical device. His introduction of the data and the empirical rules in an administered economy is argued from the perspective of everyday man. The validity of his argument consists in the synchronisation with our daily life experiences. In so far, he follows Husserl's philosophical turn (e.g. 1951a, p. 304), but not further (Holzwarth 1985, pp. 89ff. and Herrmann-Pillath's very interesting reinterpretation, e.g. in 1987 and 1994, do not really convince. Taking for granted a 'regional ontology' defined by scarcity and plans we see no evidence at all why we should end up with his market forms).

To determine if the real market form is competitive or monopolistic, the scientist has to study two things because formal and generalised criteria like the number of firms are rejected by Eucken (and which will cause major problems for a legal anti-trust policy). First, the subjective plan of the economic agent (compare Schmoller 1978b, pp. 52-53) has to be found out, which is an empirical-hermeneutic endeavour rightly in the tradition of the HS and Austrianism. Secondly, one has to check the precise historical-economic setting in which the firm operates in a qualitative and sometimes statistical way (compare Schmoller 1978b, p. 47, who lays less stress on the price taking criterion).

What Eucken does on a micro level, is what Schmoller had done with his monographs on a macro-level. Arguing against Chamberlain and Robinson, Eucken notes: "From the formal mathematical point of view monopoly is a limiting case of competition, or competition a limiting case of monopoly. *In the actual world monopoly is something quite different from competition*" (1951a, p. 145). But Eucken has a relativity problem here. He accepts the fact of monopoly margins, but the notion sufficient range and minor range cannot be clearly defined (except if the latter is zero). We could conceive of a continuum or many intermediate cases instead of two polar cases (a game Stackelberg plays in his review, see 1942, pp. 272ff.; the theoretical debate on Eucken's price theory is summarised in Steinbrück 1951, Brandt 1984, pp. 97-122, and Heuss 1980, pp. 679-683). Eucken argues that the demarcation cannot be done by formal reasoning but only in taking qualitatively the interplay of plans, specific situations and the broader environment using hermeneutic insight, statistical evidence and historical single case details with their political, social and cultural implications in a holist way into consideration.

A chapter has the title "Interdependence in the different types of economic systems" (1951a, pp. 206ff.). It is surprising that up until now neither Eucken nor any disciple has used his tool-box to analyse and describe a whole economy in all the rich dimensions pointed out by him. A substitute for a general equilibrium theory is also missing. "Because the sets of conditions in particular economic systems or particular forms of market or of monetary system, are never the same, the theoretical results of the analysis of a single type can never be directly taken over as propositions about interrelationships in other types of system" (1951a, p. 212). Adherents of the HS would wholeheartedly agree, but Eucken's analysis implies that an economy composed of markets with full competition are more or less stable. Exchange "systems are regulated by the well-known mechanism of competitive price formation, and under them there is a tendency for complete equilibrium to be brought about" (1951a, p. 262, see also 1953, pp. 9 and 15). But Eucken never demonstrates that the price adaptations necessarily move in the right direction and lead to an equilibrium (in his case of a stable level of needs an increase in wages may lead to a decrease in the labour supply and vice versa). Even more so when he criticises functional comparative statics as too abstract and supports what the Austrians call causal-genetic analysis (Mayer 1932), i.e. to concentrate on the adaptive processes in real time and space, so that price and quantity movements "depend(s) on the direction and extent of the changes as well as on the frictions that occur" (1951a, p. 255).

"It is in the interest of economic pressure groups to confuse the distinction between competition and monopoly. The effects of monopolies are shown to be harmless and the special problems of economic constitutional law which the existence of such powerful private bodies creates, are concealed ... Great differences remain. In the one case a single will and a single plan decides to the exclusion of all others, in the other case *all* the households and firms decide. The distribution of power is quite different in the two cases ... In the former case there is no free consumer's choice or free choice of occupation, as there is in the latter. Men live in two quite different economic worlds" (1951a, pp. 146 and 212). Eucken's main target is to minimise power in politics and *abolish* it in the economy (1951a, pp. 263ff.), probably motivated by his experiences in the Weimar republic. Power begins where the price as a datum for the firm ends, i.e. with monopolies and oligopolies (he never discusses oligopolistic strategies like the Cournot, Stackelberg, Bowley and Bertrand or Edgeworth solutions, see Ott 1970, pp. 209ff. and Scherer 1970, ch. 5).

Schmoller develops an elementary model of market interaction in his *Grundriss* (1978b, § 172ff., see Peukert 1997a, pp. 106ff.) which is the basis for his historical method and his economic policy of stabilising institutions, i.e. "an approach as a piece" and not the simple support of ad hoc experimentation which Eucken criticises so much. Schmoller does not assume transaction cost free markets with an abstract auctioneer, and he is not a "value essentialist". Specific prices are given, haggling and bargaining (*Marktfeilschen*) sets in. Actors are not really sure about the bid and ask prices. They make unsecure forecasts on supply and demand (curves), the spot prices need interpretation and a general but time and space bound qualitative, hermeneutic knowledge is essential. "Actors have to know the extension of the market and its relations ... the manner of its provisioning (if it happens once a year or without interruption)... they must know where and at what time the main part of supply is concentrated, e.g. in specific storehouses, special auctions; they have to know the interplay of different markets" (1978b, p. 117).

This is still compatible with Eucken II (see below). But for Eucken full competition is the standard case, for Schmoller (and for e.g. Williamson, see 1985, pp. 52 and 61ff.) it is the bilateral monopoly. "The actions on the market are not the result of a formal calculation based on the magnitudes of supply and demand, but of the psychic interaction of a number of people, *usually of two groups of people* ... relevant are the motives of buyers and sellers, their knowledge, and power relations, according to the conditions and market institutions and regulations ... the complex interplay of social relations" (1978b, p. 118; italics added). In bilateral monopoly both sides can pursue the strategy of quantity adaptation, one can pursue a price dominance and the other a quantity adaptation strategy, or one can try an options fixing strategy (quantity and price), setting the other at the exploitation point (Stigler 1966, Schumann 1992, p. 301 and the references and discussion in Peukert 1997a, appendix 2). Only the two less realistic options fixing and the quantity adaptation strategy of both sides can be analysed in a formal way. That is why Schmoller was in favour of a historical research method. Usually the result of transactions depends on knowledge, material reserves, financial capacity, the level of information, education, motives and the capacity to withhold ("*Geschäftsdringlichkeit*"; for an analysis of the price determined by the second best real alternative in this tradition see Stützel 1972). Taken all these elements together, diverging power positions are established, including price setting behaviour. Full competition understood as equality of power is but a special – and in Schmoller's time an improbable - case. Eucken argues that bilateral monopolies (and oligopolies, see Weippert 1958 for an intricate analysis of Schmoller's opinion on oligopolies) are unstable and lead to group anarchy (see e.g. Eucken 1968, pp. 46, 147, 171, 215-217, and 240). Schmoller argues that this is correct in a strictly formal economic perspective but that we inevitably live in a time of concentrated markets because enterprises realise a bunch of economies of scale or scope (Chandler 1977, Monopolkommission 1978 and 1986) in the age of mass production. What we need is a social logic to stabilise markets, i.e. collective bargaining. Now price determination becomes a sociohistorical process of rational arguments in a situation of a more or less undistorted discourse (Habermas 1981).

The discussants consider "the production costs, the proper average profits, the repercussions of prices on the in- or decrease of business ... in the case of wages the standard of living, its betterment or deterioration will be discussed, comparisons with analogous social strata will be drawn"

(Schmoller 1978b, p. 125; for his analysis of the team-production process on the firm level, including many recently rediscovered insights of the new institutional economists, see Schneider 1993). The function of the state is to establish an order (general education, the freedom of strike etc.) to make the opposing market sides more equal and then let collective and cooperative bargaining do its job in the regulation of the market process. Here the function of the state should be minimised, defining the rules and making it a trust creating win-win game (Albrecht 1959 may be the best reference, stressing Schmoller's idea of subsidiarity). The result is "collective action in control, liberation and expansion of individual action" (Commons 1931, p. 651) – the idea of the social market economy in the perspective of the HS. But Schmoller exaggerated somewhat when he supported the idea of "good cartels" in Germany (for the dismal facts see Kröll 1958).

Eucken was a radical. He argued from the other side of the spectrum. In the next chapter we will see how economic policy should be designed to institutionalise a fully competitive market economy. Only an economy dominated by full competition solves the "great task(s) of the present age ... to find an effective and lasting system, which does justice to the dignity of man, for this new industrialised economy with its far-reaching division of labour" (1951a, p. 314) which Eucken takes as unavoidable and given. In modern times, "(t)he economic system has to be consciously shaped" (1951a, p. 314). He continues "the detailed problems of economic policy, ... trade policy, credit, monopoly, or tax policy, or of company or bankruptcy law, are part of the great problem of how the whole economy, ... and its rules, are to be shaped" (1951a, p. 314). He vigorously rejects the view that in societies with a high division of labour, "that although a legal system had to be established and build up, an efficient "natural" economic system would develop spontaneously" (1951a, p. 315). This is against a Hayekian view. The differences between Eucken and Hayek are differences of substance and not in degree (contra Holzwarth 1985, pp. 112ff.). Eucken's approach is in accordance with that of institutionalised markets in the tradition of the HS.

Eucken's ultimate claim is holistic and ontological. It resembles a naturalistic fallacy and may be a value fundamentalism. He compares his approach with the value systems of classical Greek philosophy and those of the middle ages. "'Order' has still another meaning: as order which corresponds to the essence of man and the order of things ... it signifies the meaningful combination of the manifold to a whole ... *The* unity is searched for – and different from the existing order – which is in accordance with reason or the nature of man and the things" (1965, p. 239; this part is missing in the edition of the English translation, it is included in the sixth German edition and in 1990, pp. 372-380). For Eucken, ORDO is INRI from a political economy viewpoint, full competition the cornerstone in methodological, ethical, moral and social respects (no rent appropriation is possible which would require redistribution).

V. Economic Policy in the Service of ORDO

Eucken died on March 20, 1950, after 23 years at Freiburg university. He had almost finished his *Principles of Economic Policy* (1968, edited by his wife and K. P. Hensel; there is no English translation; see also Eucken 1947, 1948a and 1949). They give a concise survey of the economic policy of the last (two) centuries and try to formulate a practical and possible economic policy in accordance with his theoretical foundations and which should not only be relevant for the reconstruction of Germany after the war (Wallich 1950). In the centre of his second main book are the constitutive and regulative principles. In the following we will neither streamline nor harmonise Eucken's ideas with the prevailing economic (e.g. anti-trust) policy or theories. A non-attenuated description should highlight "the will which is behind the words" (Edith Eucken in Eucken 1968, p. VI) to render possible an adequate comparison with the HS.

In part one, Eucken sets the stage in a universal history perspective, always keeping the interdependence of orders (economic, historical and social-philosophical) in mind. The first book or part starts with the two great revolutions in politics (the French revolution) and economics. Industrialisation, modern technique and mass production are our unromantic destiny in a world populated – at his time - by 2.3 billion people (1968, p. 184). Mass agglomerations in big towns, and secular ideologies are further consequences. The question is: How can the necessarily complex co-ordination of millions of interdependent plans be organised (if at all)?

The second part discusses two answers: the policy of laissez-faire (1800-1914) and the following policies of experiments which are central planning, full employment policies – Rathenau, Keynes, the middle way of partial nationalisation and the arbitration of interest groups (see the recent comparison in Tuchtfeldt 1989). In rejecting pre-Hayekian laissez-faire he does not choose the easy way (like most Austrians in the Mises-Hayek tradition) by arguing that monopolies were only the final result of unnecessary state interference (prohibitive tariffs etc.). Instead, like A. Smith, he assumes a drive to power (leading to cartelization, monopolisation etc.) to abolish competition as an ubiquitous phenomenon of socio-economic life. They have to be controlled because competition and the freedom of contract can abolish themselves. Eucken argues in a constructivist way. "The development of economic orders should not be left to themselves ... There is a universal "propensity to build up monopolies" – *a fact which has to be accounted for in any economic policy*" (1968, p. 55 and 31). Monopolies lead at best to "semi-equilibria." They produce less consumption goods and even if they invest profits to innovate it is forced saving (1952, p. 14) and misallocation and it contradicts a liberal constitution. The policies of the middle way lead to inefficiency, bureaucracy and they have an inherent tendency to monopolies or a fully administered economy (Mises domino theory, see 1968, pp. 35-36). "Today we know that Laissez-faire and full competition should not be confused. Instead Laissez-faire leads very often to market forms different from full competition" (1968, p. 191).

His discussion of centrally administered economies (1968, pp. 58-139), the problem of pricing, the consequences of full employment, inflationary pressures, how central plans are formulated, the situation of the consumer etc. is astonishingly precise, "modern", and full of insight and good intuition (see also Eucken 1948c and for a comparison see the references of the 'breakdown discussion' in Peukert 1997b, which has not produced much better explanations; see the recognition of Eucken's analysis of centrally planned economies in Klaus 1995 and Gutmann 1990).

Part three deals with freedom and order(ing), the problem of power (dependence on the state, collectives including trade unions, monopolised other sides of the market, see also 1952, pp. 27-40), the social question, the interdependence of orders and historical determinism (see also 1952 pp. 41-55). The latter is rejected. Hegel (for affinities between Eucken's and Hegel's view of the state see Friedrich 1963, p. 208), Marx but also modern positivist economic thinking (1968, p. 209) all assume a historical determinism often depending on mere phantom notions like "capitalism" or technological determinism. But substitution, the extension of relevant markets, an increased adaptability of production, the necessary distinction between the enterprise as a legal unit and the real production units, work against necessary monopolisation. Especially interesting is his remark, that the technical development itself depends on the market forms. This can be called the thesis of technical indeterminateness or malleabilty (see also Eucken 1950).

As in his investigations, Eucken emphatically states: "Economic policy has to realise the free, natural, godwilled order" (1968, p. 176) which is full competition. "Inner stability is always given in full competition because it has a mechanic which leads to the equilibrium of the economic process due to the guiding system of prices and therefore ensures stability of the economic order" (1968, p. 198). With this statement Eucken refers to the results of strict formal models (see e.g. his references on pages 34, 98 and 245) which he otherwise criticises as too abstract (1968, p. 248). But even worse: formal model building has demonstrated that Eucken's presumed result are at best exceptional (see the discussion and references in Boyer 1997) and the theory of the second best suggests (Lipsey and Lancaster 1956) that to counteract the violation of one precondition of full competition we may approach the situation of full competition better if we violate further preconditions (antidote principle).

But Eucken has another much less questionable description of the usefulness of full competition, so that we can distinguish Eucken I and Eucken II. "The market form of full competition surrenders each one to the control of the market, deprives him of power, forces him to increase his work, necessitates constant adaptations and by the means of bancruptcy has unpleasant means of coercion" (1968, p. 237). These are – the HS would point out: institutional/behavioural – arguments which are 'concrete' and 'real' and do not need any unrealistic assumptions, proofs etc. The only assumption is that prices measure scarcity. But the HS would hasten to add that he cannot show that an overall equilibrium including the labour market will necessarily develop and make social and business cycle policy obsolete (1968, pp. 308-324).

The constitutive and regulative principles in part four (1968, pp. 254-304) are the best known part of Eucken, although usually in a reduced version (Weber 1992). For Eucken the decision is the centrally administered, group dominated or fully competitive economy (which is more than a loosely defined 'functioning price system'). "Instead a positive economic constitutional policy is necessary which aims at developing the market form of full competition and thereby fulfils the basic principle ... That is the strategical point" (1968, p. 255). The function of all principles is to secure full competition, "the establishment of a functioning price system of full competition" (1968, p. 254). Otherwise Eucken's peculiar arguments and claims lose their inner logic and consistency (see also Böhm 1950, pp. XXXII-XXIII).

The first principle is the primacy of the monetary order (Voeller 1985, critical Streissler et al. 1976), i.e. the stability of the value of currency. The reason for this monetarist viewpoint is that the cost accounting of firms and the measurement of scarcity is impeded because prices have differing stickiness. Even if they do not, the debts of firms are artificially reduced as well as savings. But today the state is under the pressure of interest groups thus an inflationary policy is likely and economic agents have no firm prices as planning data. Contradicting Gestrich (compare Eucken 1944) the creation of money by the central bank (open market policy, discount window, reserve requirements) and commercial banks (money multiplier) destabilises the economy. His concern is not how innovations are fuelled as best as possible with bank credits (Schumpeter 1934) but how a decentralised and power minimising full competition economy can be secured. At the same time he is sceptical about the state administration, so rules should be implemented. Instead of the gold standard (see 1924 and 1969, p. 169) he now proposes to consider the Graham plan (Graham 1937; compare the criticism of Friedman 1953b), where a bundle of commodities functions as gold and as an automatic stabiliser so that the value of money depends on the scarcity of the bundle. Moreover, Eucken proposes that banks should have a 100% reserve requirement according to the Chicago plan (Simons 1948) so that they cannot create money either (see the references in Meijer 1994, p. 33, and Issing 1989).

The second principle is the creation of open markets which has to complement full competition. Closed supply and/or demand markets and competition can exist at the same time (1968, p. 265), but they make monopolisation easier and the competitive system does not "fully" function (Eucken has no general abstract analytical tool to describe this in more detail). The closing can be carried out by the state (import restrictions, prohibitive tariffs, foreign trade monopolies etc.) or by private power groups. "What does freedom of trade mean when a rolling mill cannot be established because the existing syndicate prevents it with open economic hostilities? Every type of "competition of impediment", i.e. closures, loyalty rebates, exclusive contracts, and aggressive low prices against outsiders with the aim to deter or destroy must be forbidden" (1968, p. 267). Eucken's definition of closed markets goes very far, including the private and the state sector. "Investment prohibitions, cultivation restrictions, building prohibitions, closures for immigration and emigration, hindrance of the free choice of a profession, licence systems with requirements for trade, craft, and industry, ... and the prohibition to run different businesses at the same time" (1968, p. 265) belong to this category as well as trade mark laws, the resale price maintenance and suggestive advertisement (1969, p. 269). Eucken is very radical in his definition but on the other hand he accepts that e.g. tariffs are in principle compatible with full competition (1968, p. 267).

He is most unorthodox and radical when he discusses modern patent law, which might have to be abolished completely and substituted by an adequate license fee and supplemented by contract coercion to break the patent monopoly. Schmoller would underline the politically conscious development of Eucken's "data" which makes competition possible. Competition "flourishes only in public, excluding fraud and violence, under the social ordering of the markets, the organisation of measures, weights and currency. A control which checks persons and commodities ... In a market we will never encounter only egoistic drives or the profit motive; social "instincts", and respect, customs and orders have to restrict them and the more so the more the transacting people differ" (1978b, p. 21).

Private property is not introduced by referring to natural rights considerations (1968, p. 290) but in relation to the power problem. It is only acceptable and functions in a social positive way when it operates on fully competitive markets, otherwise it is anti-social (Eucken 1953, p. 19). Eucken (unlike e.g. Rüstow) does not pose the problem of different initial endowments and injustices in the laws of descent. The freedom of contract is necessary and dangerous at the same time as a means to abolish competition and enabling the exercise of power (the single day-labourer versus a monopsony of a landed proprietor). "Freedom of contract should also only be accepted in the *economic process* where full competition exists" (1968, p. 279). Schmoller stresses a double tendency in modern economies. On the one hand, private property becomes more important but at the same time the increasing number of economic actors increases the importance of a dense network of laws and other integrating institutions, i.e. a mutual enhancement of both takes place (1978a, p. 425, the example of contract law is developed in 1978b, pp. 17-18).

Like A. Smith, Eucken is very radical and conservative where the liability law is concerned, and severely criticises limited liability (see Ott 1977, Rittstieg 1975, part 6, and Mestmäcker 1958). It fosters concentration, destroys the symmetrical principle of rewards and punishments and the principle of prudence in investment decisions and opens the door to fraudulent manipulations like bankruptcy. Corporate law, which had a positive function in the last century in the collection of savings for railroads via stocks, nowadays is primarily an economic means to dominate the market. For Eucken, the Berle and Means view of the functionaries as a new class is correct. His proposal is that the majority stockholders should be fully liable. This does not preclude take-overs, but the firm which takes over is fully liable. In joint stock companies with dispersed stocks the managers of the board of directors should be fully liable. "Liability is not only a precondition of the economic order of competition but in general for a society in which freedom and self-determination prevail" (1968, p. 285). Finally, he underlines the importance of the constancy of the data so that the difference between planning data *ex post* and *ex ante* are reduced to a manageable level in an uncertain world. All these principles are interrelated and mutually necessary as principles of the economy on a constitutional level (1968, pp. 289-291).

The second set of principles deals with domains where full competition cannot be realised or where competition exhibits consequences which need correction, e.g. the distribution of income. Eucken is in favour of progressive taxation. The aim is not to reduce savings but rather because without progressive taxes, luxury products are produced too early while urgent needs at the bottom of society are still unfulfilled (Böhm-Bawerk's argument). Although taxing should not go so far as to impede investment (his extreme example operates with a marginal tax of 90%, see 1968, p. 301) this widely opens the door for social and tax policy (compare Eucken 1948b and 1952, pp. 56-68 and Gröner 1989) in principle, but leaves open the degree of taxation (consider e.g. Laffer-curve type of arguments). Here the criticism of ordo-liberalism as an "end-state liberalism" where it is difficult to see any theoretical stopping point sets in (Barry 1989a; Wiseman 1989b). Another principle is the correction of abnormal supply reactions mentioned above, e.g. workers increase the supply when the wage is reduced. In this case only, minimum wages may be necessary (1968, p. 304).

The next principle is the correction of external effects which is discussed in ecological terms. In Eucken's view ad hoc measures, indifference and laissez-faire are wrong in this respect. State intervention is necessary because the destruction of nature does not enter the cost accounting of firms, so the markets - even if fully competitive (what sometimes might reduce destruction, see 1968, p. 302) - cannot solve this problem. The ecological problem is a constitutive, necessary and complementary part of his basic principles of a free society (Oswalt-Eucken 1994, p. 43). Although Eucken did not consider the ecological problem as a major one he is much ahead of his time (and if we look at the discussions from Rio to Kyoto maybe our own). "The economic system works very well but it does not consider the repercussions which the realisation of individual plans exert on the aggregate of the social data ... An example is the destruction of forests in North America which leads to a deterioration of the soil and climate and to the development of prairies ... Or let us consider the health injuries which are often caused by the chemical industry and their waste water" (1968, p. 302).

A question can be posed here: if the Austrian government puts a high import tariff on timber from Canada, to compensate the irresponsible clear-cutting which allows extremely low prices (every year in Canada 1 million m2 are deforested), does this policy refer to Eucken's regulative principle or does it violate the open market rule? As cited, a social aspect is included in this principle due to the conflict between the individual accounting and the common social interest (1968, p. 302). Therefore, Eucken accepts a regulation of "the work of women and children, regulations on the length of the working day, protection against accidents and by the means of industrial inspection a protection of workers" (1968, p. 303). The same question as above (which principle is touched?) can be raised. At least, it is fully compatible with Schmoller's social policy proposals. We can also ask, if Eucken would have been against an insurance model concerning health, retirement and illness. The question in principle is not identical with the discussion of the adequate level of coverage - here Eucken and Schmoller might not agree.

The most radical and consequential regulative principle is monopoly control by an autonomous agency to correct market power and to prevent the necessarily ensuing anarchy of groups (Ottel 1951 is sceptical about this assertion, Bombach 1990, p. 55 on his underestimation of unstable solutions). "Monopoly control should be exerted by a public monopoly control agency. To make it independent of the dangerous influences of the interest groups, it should be an independent agency which is only subject to law. It must not be a division of the Department of Commerce ... The monopoly agency has the duty to dissolve monopolies as much as possible and to control those which cannot be dissolved" (1968, p. 294). He rejects the nationalisation of monopolies as a fusion of economic and political power. Many if not most monopolies will disappear naturally (or by the demonopolization policies) if the other principles are realised and commercial, trade and tax policy and law will not support monopolies any more (as it did and does in the US where isolated antitrust policy necessarily failed but is nevertheless important, see Scherer 1992).

If monopolies are defined by the subjective plan it seems reasonable to control the natural monopolies continuously like the revenue-office. The agency would get immense power so that Eucken proposes an external abuse criteria penalising "closures, rebates, price differentiation (including dumping), aggressive prices and other symptoms" (1968, p. 295; see the details in Alsmöller 1982, pp. 80-89) to create "as if" competitive behaviour of the firms (*wettbewerbsanalog*). Therefore the agency has to estimate full competitive prices and quantities and enforce them if necessary. If marginal costs are above average costs the intersection of average costs and the demand curve should be chosen. But this presupposes much (interventionist) power and the nice world of geometric pictures and immense knowledge of them in non-existing full competitive equilibria (see the general discussion of the knowledge problem involved here in Streit and Wegner 1987). Even more, the agency fixing the prices should include a natural rate of rationalisation. He rejects Miksch's (1949) "*gebundene Konkurrenz*" ("bounded competition", see 1968, p. 298). Many oligopolies will disappear and those remaining will be deterred to behave like oligopolies because, if they do, the agency will intervene (see Lenel's sceptical remarks in 1990, pp. 31-33). Would this agency be a mammoth bureaucracy? Eucken assures no (1968, p. 299), but many critics thought so (the German antitrust debate on this cannot be resumed here, see Bartling 1980, Cox et al. 1981). At any rate the (commercial, patent, tax, joint stock) law should be designed to deprive big economic units of power (1947, p. 78; see the intricate discussion of problems of an anti-monopoly policy in Lenel 1975a).

In the final part Eucken asks what the driving forces will be to realise his programme of securing ordered competition which ideally combines self- and common interests without interfering in its process by an efficient and powerful constitutional state beyond the interest groups. They should be dissolved or limited as much as possible. One force could be the churches

(1968, pp. 347ff.) and their subsidiary principle, but he rejects their idea of a limited interest rate. The second force is science, not only economics. But a wrong positivist bias (1968, p. 340, we leave open if this really grasps Weber's point of view, see Tenbruck 1959), specialisation together with fragmentism, historism and relativism (Spengler, Mach, Pareto) impede its really designing, normative practical function (Hoppmann 1995, p. 16). Opportunism reigns instead. Schmoller too held a normative concept of science searching for objective truth but being able to make practical proposals (Schmoller 1881).

"In the striving to not make economic policy judgements, science accepted goals which are set by the state and politically powerful groups. It evaded the problem of political order; but it did not avoid the dependence on the political interests of the day" (1968, p. 342). Therefore he sceptically resumes, it lacks "in all countries a leading stratum which understood what the economic order really is: not only an order of the economy but also a necessary precondition of an order of society as a great antitype" (1968, p. 371; see the critique in Herrmann 1952). Beckerath wonders if Eucken's leading and directing function is incompatible with parliamentary democracy (1953, p. 296; see the extensive discussion in Fischer 1990, Strubl 1954 and Runge 1971). Eucken calls it a dilemma that there is no (liberal ordo) state imaginable without some power (1952, p. 38, and 1968, p. 175). Schmoller dealt with the same problem. He did not hold an idealist or contractual theory but a superimposition/dominance theory of the state (1978a, p. 17 and 1978b, pp. 58, 462, 635 and 641). But in his monographs Schmoller tried to show that markets can be the result of the prudent policy of the rulers. In this respect, his great hope was the Prussian monarchs and the(ir) education of the bureaucracy. Even Eucken stated "(h)ere he [Gestrich] was able to see, what independent civil servants are able to do vis-à-vis interest groups" (1944, p. VI).

VI. The Relevance of Eucken and the Historical School at the Turn of the Century

The HS and Eucken are both a reaction to the great transformation (Polanyi 1978; Baum 1996), i.e. industrialisation and marketization. They try 'to make capitalism good' (Commons). For both, the reference unit is a strong nation state. Both diverge from neo-classical economics as they are not primarily equilibrium oriented, they take system changes and not only incremental changes into consideration, they do not see economics as a technical subject, they do consider exploitation, they do not see the government as a mere sum of interest groups, do not take monopoly as a minor deviation, and do not take the viewpoint of individual preferences, and do not regard the market as the solution to all problems (Sherman 1987, pp. 5-7). Eucken opposes the Atkins criteria (mentioned at the beginning of this paper) 1 and 4 and supports criteria 2,3, and 5. Both try to integrate theoretical and historical research. Like Veblen, the Ordo movement tries to liberate exchange economies from their feudalist elements. They do not assume a Chicago type tight prior equilibrium or a Hayekian steadily innovating economy. Instead things can go wrong in exchange economies which need constructivist intervention guided by an underlying practical philosophy in the Christian and Kantian humanist tradition. "The greatest moral progress of man is based on the fact that the individual is regarded as the highest value, as a value in itself, beyond all economic values so that certain actions do not appear as purchasable or payable" (Schmoller 1978b, p. 111). For both, ethics, history and theory form a unity, taking into account the cultural and ethical dimension of the economy and the methodological and epistemological problems of the discipline (although methodologically they failed). They are both typical offsprings of a continental European and especially German speaking background in that they rejected an untempered capitalism without checks and balances. Economics was a social science for them, interdisciplinary in the sense of the "*gesamte Staatswissenschaft*".

However, the HS was more collective oriented. The fact that man lives in social groups is missing in Eucken. The backbone of any economy are legal institutions for the HS; in Eucken's view economics has "to put the process of price formation in the centre of analysis" (1947, p. 43). So Eucken provides a theory of elementary economic forms, while the HS provides concepts for the systematic interplay of the "data", missing in Eucken. He thought that "economic policy could of its own accord check the development of monopoly" (1952, p. 93-94; the German original reads "verhindern" which means prevent, see 1951b, p. 70). The HS was sceptical about this optimism and fostered mutual arbitration and countervailing power. The weak point in Eucken is his referring to equilibrium without "proving" it, which would make social policy on a larger scale unnecessary.

The weak point in Schmoller is his enthusiasm for all kinds of "organs", including cartels etc. So Eucken with his insistence on the monopoly and power problem is strong where the HS is weak and the HS with its insistence on social policy issues is strong where Eucken is weak. The *Modell Deutschland*, the social market economy now under attack was in a certain sense a productive and contradictory synthesis of both (what Müller-Armack in 1976 called a compromise of styles, a *Stilkompromiß*). Both believed in a state above the interest groups. Eucken and the HS also share a common fate: representatives of the HS are crowded out of the economic profession despite growing interest (Priddat 1995, Penz and Wilkop (Eds.) 1996, Schellschmidt 1997 etc.) and appealing examples of the applicability of the economic style concept (Schefold 1994 and 1995).

Some claim that Eucken's economic policy had been realised in Germany after the war (Jöhr 1965, p. 583) and in fact a certain renaissance of "ordo" (Issing (Ed.), 1981, Streissler and Watrin (Eds.) 1980, Tuchtfeldt (Ed.) 1973) especially after his 100th birthday at 17.1.1991 took place. A special volume of *Ordo* (1989) and of the *Journal of Economic Studies* (1994), and several books (e.g. Peacock and Willgerodt (Eds.) 1989a and 1989b and Walter Eucken Institut (Ed.) 1992) were published. But national economic and antitrust policy and theory (Lenel 1975b, Möschel 1992, and Grossekettler 1994) have not taken up Eucken's decentralisation and anti-power approach (Kleinewefers 1988, p. 10), internationally it remained almost unknown (but see Zweig 1980). Eucken's chair in Freiburg remained empty for some time (Woll 1989, pp. 87-88), Eastern Europeans reject his radicalism (Klaus 1995). Even the Kronberger Kreis considers his strict anti-power commitment as counterproductive in the age of globalization and open markets (Engels 1991, contra Hansen 1991). At best Eucken is interpreted from a Hayekian or Schumpeterian angle (Streit 1995, Woll 1989, Schlecht 1996 and many others). As we have seen for Eucken antitrust policy is an important element and economic order cannot be left to an evolutionary process.

His vision has been lost in the East-West confrontation after the war (Blum 1969). This is not to say that a social market economy as a mixed economy had not been realised in Germany, but it intermingled with a quasi Schmollerian social and economic policy (arbitration, "welfare state") in the tradition of the HS, with the influence of sociological neoliberalism like Müller-Armack's (growth plus redistribution, see for the different concepts Becker 1965) and surely the vested interests (Kloten 1997). After the war

Eucken worked out detailed and radical antimonopolistic economic policy proposals, hitherto almost (but see Eucken 1961 and 1951/52) unpublished (they are in the Eucken archive in Frankfurt).

Only Eucken's grandson, Walter Oswalt, follows his tradition. He proposes to abolish big firms by means of a conglomeration tax, full liability etc. to enforce a maximum size of firms (Oswalt 1996a and 1996b and our critical comments in Peukert 1996). From a basic democratic and ecological viewpoint like Oswalt's, Eucken's "small is beautiful" (Schumacher 1989) approach is very appealing, because ecological policy is an integral component of his programme (in terms of liability law, certificates, administrative law of order etc., see Gerken and Renner 1996, pp. 58-60). Eucken's vision of ordered competition (full competition, a commodity reserve currency etc., which might limit Wall Street supremacy, see Henwood 1997) tries to tame the dragon. Eucken never talked about economic growth as a target. As mentioned, in an earlier article (1932, pp. 300-301) he distinguished between two types of "capitalism": a dynamic and a more static one. An Eucken economy would probably grow less fast or not at all, innovations (or their rate and speed) would probably be implemented more slowly. But the question is if both is good as such (this is the latent assumption of a Hayekian worldview) and the costs in terms of power should not be overlooked (Dugger 1989).

The general claim that Eucken's conception is blind for innovative, necessary part-time monopolies (e.g. Arndt 1994) does not hold in an Eucken II perspective. Schumpeter competition may occur in an Eucken economy but anti-monopoly abuse control, full liability, a different monetary order, and the reform of the patent law etc. would very quickly allow imitators to follow so that the innovative/monopoly market resembles more a competitive market and the innovations may have a different character (many small, no or few big innovations). A market theory taking Eucken's frame of reference as a starting point does not seem impossible. But nobody really "tried" (*pace* Franz Böhm, who was a lawyer). The problems of the monopoly agency could be eased by introducing maximum size rules (H. C. Simons' plan). Combined with a severe tax in the law of descent, profit shares of the employed (which were considered positively by Eucken) etc. we would live in a different economic universe, maybe less stressful (Reheis 1996) and resource-consuming than today. "'(C)omplete' Competition was not in the first instance used as an indicator of efficiency. It was rather circumscribing the ideal of a consumer-oriented economy in which the social and political problem of economic power is solved" (Streit and Wohlgemuth 1997, p. 15). The joy of life would consist in living in a more egalitarian, power reducing, decentralised, vitally satisfying, ecologically sound society in which "being" would be more important than "having" (*Ersatz* consumption of material goods). A society which deserves the characterisation being in "ordo".

The neoliberal policy and practice of globalization with the whole world as one liberalised, deregulated and privatised market (Martin and Schumann 1997) with its polarisation of incomes, almost complete deregulation of the financial markets which become the arbiters of national economic policies, the emergence of the working poor in the West, the importance of the global players and their power to generate huge subsidy donations, would not find the acclaim of either Eucken or the HS. The 100 biggest TNC realise 2/3 of the world trade, not to mention the big international mutual trusts, pension and hedge funds enforcing a rude shareholder value philosophy or what Eucken called the short term maximum net receipts type. It drives the nation states in a tax reducing competition and minimisation of tax payments by transfer pricing, endangering the sovereignty of the nation states and often put the squeeze on communities by threatening with exodus to produce in countries with child labour, no protection of the work force, massive degradation of the environment etc.

The social messages of the HS and Eucken's power problem are not less important in the age of globalization (as the light liberals like Engels 1991 suggest) but even more so than some decades ago. Eucken's dictum that the state is powerless today and at the mercy of vested interests and that unrestricted laissez-faire capitalism is dangerous for the survival of a democratic society is more true than ever (see also Soros 1996). In principle globalization is not different from the process of the nationalisation of the economies in the last centuries, it only occurs on another level. So the old battles have to be fought again in a European/world context with Europe being the world's biggest domestic market, able to suggest/enforce rules on a European and international level to regain the primacy of politics. The HS would underline the necessity of international social (child labour, working conditions etc.) and ecological standards which might be enforced by the WTO, a reorganisation of labour unions on a European level, a tax reform taxing energy and relieving labour, and maybe a luxury tax (on private jets etc. because of impossibility to tax capital gains higher in Europe than abroad and to let the winners participate in necessary state finance). In Schmoller's understanding the "Euro" adventure can be understood as the attempt to institutionalise new "organs" in a broader context as a necessary means to political integration.

In addition, in Eucken's perspective a common European tax system closing the loop-holes would be necessary to enforce his progressive tax and could take into consideration his ecological insights. A common economic policy stopping the ruinous competition of governments to attract investments is also necessary. He might have proposed his profit-sharing idea and strongly support a stable European currency. But he would have asked, where the automatic stabilisers are and if the stabilisation of exchange rates is possible without a commodity reserve system or something similar. As a second best solution he may have supported a Tobin-tax (see Haq et al. (eds.) 1996) to control unproductive speculation which makes exchange rates much more volatile than necessary and severely limits the freedom to act of governments (Eichengreen et al. 1995). Eucken would vigorously raise the monopoly and power problem (some TNC having a higher turnover than the GDP of some European countries). For Eucken, this would include reform of the (European) liability and patent law which supports bigness and concentration. Neither a debate considering the possibilities of full competition in a European context took place, nor has the interdependence of orders been taken seriously (industrial policy); external effects are accentuated ("liberalisation" of the long distance truck traffic, deregulation in air traffic and its exemption from the gasoline tax).

Economic development is not a deterministic, natural process, determined by "technical necessities", "economic logic", or "economic progress". This was Eucken's and the HS's insight. Laissez-faire can abolish liberty and democracy. This was the lesson especially Eucken learnt in the 1930s. More than half a century later the question is: will we take up the gauntlet or not? The study of the HS and ordo-liberalism may be a source of inspiration in the tradition of an enlightened (and why not maybe old fashioned) European humanism.

WALTER EUCKEN AND THE HISTORICAL SCHOOL

References

ALBERT, H.: "Grundprobleme rationaler Ordnungspolitik", in: H. MILDE, H. G. MONISSEN (Eds.): *Rationale Wirtschaftspolitik in komplexen Gesellschaften*, Stuttgart (Kohlhammer) 1985, pp. 53-63.

ALSMÖLLER, H.: *Wettbewerbspolitische Ziele und kooperationstheoretische Hypothesen im Wandel der Zeit*, Tübingen (Mohr) 1982.

ALTER, M.: *Carl Menger and the Origins of Austrian Economics*, Boulder (Westview Press) 1990.

ARNDT, H.: *Lehrbuch der Wirtschaftsentwicklung*, Berlin (Duncker und Humblot) 1994.

ATKINS, B.: "Discussion", *American Economic Review Supplement*, 22 (1932), pp. 111-112.

BARRY, N. P.: "Political and Economic Thought of German Neo-Liberals", in: A. PEACOCK, H. WILLGERODT (Eds.): *German Neoliberals and the Social Market Economy*, New York (St. Martin's Press) 1989, pp. 105-124.

BARTLING, H.: *Leitbilder der Wettbewerbspolitik*, München (Verlag Franz Vahlen) 1980.

BAUM, G.: *Karl Polanyi on Ethics and Economics*, Montreal (Mc Gill-Queen's University Press) 1996.

BECKER, H. P.: *Die soziale Frage im Neoliberalismus*, Löwen (F.H. Kerle Verlag) 1965.

BECKERATH, E.: "Walter Euckens Grundsätze der Wirtschaftspolitik", *Ordo*, 5 (1953), pp. 289-297.

BINSWANGER, H. C.: "Kommentar zu W. Oswalt", *Kontraste*, 95 (1996), pp. 8-10.

BLUM, R.: *Soziale Marktwirtschaft*, Tübingen (J.C.B. Mohr) 1969.

BLUMENBERG-LAMPE, C.: *Das wirtschaftspolitische Programm des 'Freiburger Kreises'*, Berlin (Duncker und Humblot) 1973.

BÖHM, F.: "Die Idee des Ordo im Denken Walter Euckens", *Ordo*, 3 (1950), pp. XV-LXIV.

BÖHM, F.: "Die Forschungs- und Lehrgemeinschaft zwischen Juristen und Volkswirten an der Universität Freiburg", in: H. J. WOLFF (Ed.): *Aus der Geschichte der Rechts- und Staatswissenschaften zu Freiburg i. Br.*, Freiburg (E. Albert Universitätsbuchhandlung) 1957, pp. 95-113.

BÖHM-BAWERK, E.: *Capital und Capitalzins*, Innsbruck (Wagner) 1900-1902.

BOETTKE, P. J., PRYCHITKO, D. L. (Eds.): *The Market Process – Essays in Contemporary Austrian Economics*, Aldershot (Edward Elgar) 1994.

BOMBACH, G.: "Walter Euckens "Grundlagen der Nationalökonomie"", in: G. BOMBACH et al.: *Vademecum zu einem Wegbereiter der modernen Theorie in Deutschland*, Düsseldorf (Verlag Wirtschaft und Finanzen) 1990, pp. 37-62.

BORCHARDT, K.: "'Der Property Rights-Ansatz' in der Wirtschaftswissenschaft", in: J. KOCKA (Ed.): *Theorien in der Praxis des Historikers*, Göttingen (Vandenhoeck und Ruprecht) 1977, pp. 140-160.

BOYD, R.: "Introduction", in: F. H. KNIGHT: *The Ethics of Competition*, New Brunswick (Transaction Publishers) 1997, pp. VII-XXXII.

BOYER, R.: "The Variety and Unequal Performance of Really Existing Markets: Farewell to Doctor Pangloss?", in: J. R. HOLLINGSWORTH, R. BOYER (Eds.): *Contemporary Capitalism*, Cambridge (University Press) 1997, pp. 55-93.

BRANDT, K.: "Das neoklassische Marktmodell und die Wettbewerbstheorie", *Jahrbücher für Nationalökonomie und Statistik*, 199 (1984), pp. 97-122.

BROCKE, B. (Ed.): *Sombarts "Moderner Kapitalismus"*, München (DTV) 1987.

BÜCHNER, R.: "Walter Euckens Grundsätze der Wirtschaftspolitik (Review)", *Journal of Institutional and Theoretical Economics*, 110 (1954), pp. 72-79.

CHANDLER, A. D.: *The Visible Hand*, Cambridge (Harvard University Press) 1977.

COMMONS, J. R.: "Institutional Economics", *American Economic Review*, 21 (1931), pp. 648-657.

COMMONS, J. R.: *Institutional Economics*, New York (Macmillan) 1934.

COX, H. et al. (Eds.): *Handbuch des Wettbewerbs*, München (Verlag Franz Vahlen) 1981.

DIESING, P.: *Patterns of Discovery in the Social Sciences*, London (Routledge) 1972.

DÖRGE, F.-W.: "Menschenbild und Institution in der Idee des Wirtschaftsliberalismus", *Hamburger Jahrbuch für Wirtschafts- und Gesellschaftspolitik*, 4 (1959), pp. 82-99.

DUGGER, W. M.: *Corporate Hegemony*, Greenwood (Grennwood Press) 1989.

DÜRR, E.-W.: *Wesen und Ziele des Ordoliberalismus*, Winterthur (P.G. Keller) 1954.

EHRLICHER, W.: "Geldtheorie", in: E. BECKERATH (Ed.): *Handwörterbuch der Sozialwissenschaften*, Vol. 4, Stuttgart (Fischer) 1965, p. 231-258.

EICHENGREEN, B. et al.: "Two Cases for Sand in the Wheels of International Finance", *Economic Journal*, 105 (1995), pp. 162-172.

ENGELS, W.: "Freiburger Imperativ", *Wirtschaftswoche*, 18.1.1991, p. 110.

ERHARD, L.: *Deutsche Wirtschaftspolitik*, Düsseldorf (Econ) 1962.

EUCKEN, R.: *Der Sinn des Lebens*, Leipzig (Quelle und Meyer) 1922.

EUCKEN, W.: *Die Verbandsbildung in der Seeschiffahrt*, München (Duncker und Humblot) 1914.

EUCKEN, W. (1921a): *Die Stickstoffversorgung der Welt*, Stuttgart (Deutsche Verlags-Anstalt) 1921.

WALTER EUCKEN AND THE HISTORICAL SCHOOL

EUCKEN, W. (1921b): "Zur Würdigung St. Simons", *Schmollers Jahrbuch*, 45 (1921), pp. 115-130.

EUCKEN, W.: *Kritische Betrachtungen zum deutschen Geldproblem*, Jena (Gustav Fischer) 1923.

EUCKEN, W. (1925a): *Das internationale Währungsproblem*, Berlin (Gersbach und Sohn) 1925.

EUCKEN, W. (1925b): "Das Übertragungsproblem", *Jahrbücher für Nationalökonomie und Statistik*, 68 (1925), pp. 145-164.

EUCKEN, W.: "Die Ursachen der potenzierten Wirkung des vermehrten Geldumlaufs auf das Preisniveau", *Jahrbücher für Nationalökonomie und Statistik*, 70 (1926), pp. 289-309.

EUCKEN, W.: "Kredit und Konjunktur", in: F. BOESE (Ed.): *Wandlungen des Kapitalismus*, München (Duncker und Humblot) 1929, pp. 287-305 and 386-391.

EUCKEN, W.: "Staatliche Strukturwandlungen und die Krisis des Kapitalismus", *Weltwirtschaftliches Archiv*, 36 (1932), pp. 297-321.

EUCKEN, W.: "Walter Eucken", in: *Festschrift für A. Spiethoff - Der Stand und die nächste Zukunft der Konjunkturforschung*, München (Duncker und Humblot) 1933, pp. 74-78.

EUCKEN, W.: "Die Leistung der deutschen Volkswirtschaftslehre (Review)", *Jahrbuch für Nationalökonomie und Statistik*, 146 (1937), pp. 225-231.

EUCKEN, W.: "Die Überwindung des Historismus", *Schmollers Jahrbuch*, 62 (1938), pp. 63-86.

EUCKEN, W.: "Wissenschaft im Stile Schmollers", *Weltwirtschaftliches Archiv*, 52 (1940), pp. 468-506.

EUCKEN, W. "Vorwort", in: H. GESTRICH: *Kredit und Sparen*, Jena (Gustav Fischer) 1944, pp. V-XI.

EUCKEN, W.: *Nationalökonomie - Wozu?*, Godesberg (Verlag Helmut Küpper) 1947.

EUCKEN, W. (1948a): "Das ordnungspolitische Problem", *Ordo*, 1 (1948), pp. 56-90.

EUCKEN, W. (1948b): "Die soziale Frage", in: E. SALIN (Ed.): *Synopsis*, Heidelberg (Verlag Lambert Schneider) 1948, pp. 113-131.

EUCKEN, W. (1948c): "On the Theory of the Centrally Administered Economy", *Economica*, 15 (1948), pp. 79-100 and 173-193.

EUCKEN, W. (1948d): "Obituary - Heinrich von Stackelberg", *Economic Journal*, 58 (1948), pp. 132-135.

EUCKEN, W.: "Die Wettbewerbsordnung und ihre Verwirklichung", *Ordo*, 2 (1949), pp. 1-99.

EUCKEN, W.: "Technik, Konzentration und Ordnung der Wirtschaft", *Ordo*, 3 (1950), pp. 3-17.

EUCKEN, W. (1951a): *The Foundations of Economics*, Chicago (Chicago Press) 1951.
EUCKEN, W. (1951b): *Unser Zeitalter der Mißerfolge*, Tübingen (J.C.B. Mohr) 1951.
EUCKEN, W.: "Konzernentflechtung und Kartellauflösung", *Wirtschaft und Wettbewerb*, 1/2 (1951/52), p. 35.
EUCKEN, W.: *This Unsuccesful Age or the Pains of Economic Progress*, New York (Oxford University Press) 1952.
EUCKEN, W.: *Wettbewerb, Monopol und Unternehmer*, Bad Nauheim (Vita Verlag) 1953.
EUCKEN, W.: *Kapitaltheoretische Untersuchungen*, Tübingen (J.C.B. Mohr) 1954.
EUCKEN, W.: "Bemerkungen zur Währungsfrage", in: H. MÖLLER (Ed.): *Zur Vorgeschichte der deutschen Mark*, Tübingen (J.C.B. Mohr) 1961, pp. 202-211.
EUCKEN, W.: *Die Grundlagen der Nationalökonomie*, Berlin (Springer Verlag) 1965.
EUCKEN, W.: *Grundsätze der Wirtschaftspolitik*, Tübingen (J.C.B. Mohr) 1968.
EUCKEN, W. et al.: "Unsere Aufgabe", in: F. A. LUTZ: *Politische Überzeugungen und nationalökonomische Theorie*, Tübingen (J.C.B. Mohr) 1971, pp. 87-97.
EUCKEN, W., MEYER, F. W.: "The Economic Situation in Germany", *The Annals of the American Academy of Political and Social Science* (Philadelphia), 260 (1948), pp. 53-62.
FEHL, U.: "Zu Walter Euckens kapitaltheoretischen Überlegungen", *Ordo*, 40 (1989), pp. 71-83.
FISCHER, T.: *Staat, Recht und Verfassung im Denken von Walter Eucken*, Frankfurt (Peter Lang) 1990.
FOLZ, W. J.: *Das geldtheoretische und geldpolitische Werk Walter Euckens*, Berlin (Duncker und Humblot) 1970.
FRIEDMAN, M. (1953a): "The Methodology of Positive Economics", in: M. FRIEDMAN: *Essays in Positive Economics*, Chicago (University of Chicago Press) 1953, pp. 3-43.
FRIEDMAN, M.: "Geldangebot, Preis- und Produktionsänderungen", *Ordo*, 11 (1959), pp. 193-216.
FRIEDMAN, M. (1953b): "Commodity-reserve Currency", in: M. FRIEDMAN: *Essays in Positive Economics*, Chicago (University of Chicago Press) 1953, pp. 204-250.
FRIEDRICH; C. J.: "Das Denken des Neoliberalismus", in C. J. FRIEDRICH: *Zur Theorie und Politik der Verfassungsordnung*, Heidelberg (Quelle und Meyer) 1963, pp. 205-218.
GADAMER, H.-G.: *Wahrheit und Methode*, Tübingen (Mohr) 1986.
GERKEN, L., RENNER, A.: "Der Wettbewerb der Ordnungen als Entdeckungsverfahren für eine nachhaltige Entwicklung", in: L. GERKEN (Ed.): *Ordnungspoli-*

tische Grundfragen einer Politik der Nachhaltigkeit, Baden-Baden (Nomos) 1996, pp. 51-102.
GIERSCH, H.: "Inflation", in: E. BECKERATH et al. (Eds.): *Handwörterbuch der Sozialwissenschaften*, Vol. 5, Stuttgart (Fischer) 1956, pp. 281-293.
GÖTZ, H. H.: "Walter Eucken", in: *Orientierungen zur Wirtschafts- und Gesellschaftspolitik*, 46 (1990), pp. 73-76.
GRAHAM, B.: *Storage and Stability*, New York (Mc Graw-Hill) 1937.
GRÖNER, H.: "Gerechtigkeitsvorstellungen bei W. Eucken und K. P. Hensel", in: G. GUTMANN et al. (Eds.): *Ethik und Ordnungsfragen der Wirtschaft*, Baden-Baden (Nomos Verlag) 1989, pp. 309-321.
GROSSEKETTLER, H. G. (1987a): *Der Beitrag der Freiburger Schule zur Theorie der Gestaltung von Wirtschaftssystemen*, Münster (Volkswirtschaftliche Diskussionsbeiträge Nr. 90, Universität Münster) 1987.
GROSSEKETTLER, H. G. (1987b): "On Designing an Economic Order: The Contribution of the Frieburg School", in: D. A. WALKER (Ed.): *Perspectives on the History of Economic Thought II*, Aldershot (Edward Elgar), 1987, pp. 38-84.
GROSSEKETTLER, H. G.: "On Designing an Institutional Infrastructure for Economies: The Freiburg Legacy After 50 Years", *Journal of Economic Studies*, 21 (1994), pp. 9-24.
GUTMANN, G.: "Euckens konstituierende Prinzipien der Wirtschaftspolitik und der ordnungspolitische Wandel in den Ländern Osteuropas", in: FORSCHUNGSSTELLE ZUM VERGLEICH WIRTSCHAFTLICHER LENKUNGSSYSTEME (Ed.): *Zur Transformation von Wirtschaftssystemen*, Marburg (Universität Marburg) 1990, pp. 61-69.
HABERMAS, J.: *Theorie des kommunikativen Handelns*, 2 Vols., Frankfurt (Suhrkamp) 1981.
HANSEN, K.: "Zur Aktualität des 'Freiburger Imperativs'", *Wirtschaft und Wettbewerb,* 41 (1991), pp. 287-290.
HASELBACH, D.: *Franz Oppenheimer*, Opladen (Leske Verlag) 1985.
HAQ, M. U. et al. (Eds.): *The Tobin Tax*, New York (Oxford University Press) 1996.
HEILBRONER, R., MILBERG, W.: *The Crisis of Vision in Modern Economic Thought*, New York (Cambridge University Press) 1995.
HENWOOD, D.: *Wall Street*, New York (Verso) 1997.
HERBST, J.: *The German Historical School in American Scholarship*, Ithaca (Cornell University Press) 1975.
HERRMANN, W.: 'Grundsätze der Wirtschaftspolitik (Review)", *Zeitschift für handelswissenschaftliche Forschung*, 4 (1952), pp. 420-427.
HERRMANN-PILLATH, C.: "Kritischer Rationalismus, Strukturalismus und die methodologischen Prinzipien von Eucken/Hensel", in: FORSCHUNGSSTELLE ZUM

VERGLEICH WIRTSCHAFTLICHER LENKUNGSSYSTEME (Ed.): *Ordnungstheorie*, Marburg (Universität Marburg) 1987, pp. 32-73.
HERRMANN-PILLATH, C.: "Methodological Aspects of Eucken's Work", *Journal of Economic Studies*, 21 (1994), pp. 46-60.
HEUSS, E.: "Artikel Wettbewerb", in: W. ALBERS et al. (Eds.): *Handwörterbuch der Wirtschaftswissenschaft*, Vol. 8, Stuttgart (Fischer) 1988, pp. 679-697.
HEUSSI, K.: *Die Krisis des Historismus*, Tübingen (Mohr) 1932.
HOLZWARTH, F.: *Ordnung der Wirtschaft durch Wettbewerb*, Freiburg (Rudolf Haufe Verlag) 1985.
HOPPMANN, E.: *Walter Eucken – Heute*, Baden-Baden (Nomos Verlag) 1995.
HUTCHISON, T. W.: "Notes on the Effects of Economic Ideas on Policy: the Example of the German Social Market Economy", *Journal of Institutional and Theoretical Economics*, 135 (1979), pp. 426-441.
HUTCHISON, T. W.: "Institutionalist Economics Old and New", *Journal of Institutional and Theoretical Economics*, 140 (1984), pp. 20-29.
ISARD, P.: *Exchange Rate Economics*, Cambridge (Cambridge University Press) 1995.
ISSING, O. (Ed.): *Zukunftsprobleme der sozialen Marktwirtschaft*, Berlin (J.C.B. Mohr) 1981.
ISSING, O.: "Vom Primat der Währungspolitik", *Ordo,* 40 (1989), pp. 351-361.
JOHNSON, D.: "Exiles and Half-exiles", in: A. PEACOCK, H. WILLGERODT (Eds.): *German Neo-Liberals and the Social Market Economy*, New York (St. Martin's Press) 1989, pp. 40-68.
JÖHR, W. A.: "Walter Eucken", in: H. C. RECKTENWALD (Ed.): *Lebensbilder großer Nationalökonomen*, Köln (Kiepenheuer und Witsch) 1965, pp. 569-583.
KAPLAN, A.: *The Conduct of Inquiry*, San Francisco (Chandler) 1964.
KAPP, K. W.: *Toward a Science of Man in Society*, The Hague (Martinus Nijhoff) 1961.
KAPP, K. W.: "Eucken's Posthumous Work on Economic Policy", *Kyklos,* 6 (1953), pp. 165-169.
KIRZNER, I., LACHMANN, L. M. (Eds.): *Subjectivism, Intelligibility and Economic Understanding*, New York (New York University Press) 1986.
KLAUS, V.: "Walter Eucken und die Transformationsprozesse der Gegenwart", in: R. BAADER, (Ed.): *Wider die Wohlfahrtsdiktatur*, Gräfelfing (Ingo Resch) 1995, pp. 57-66.
KLEINEWEFERS, H.: *Grundzüge einer verallgemeinerten Wirtschaftsordnungstheorie*, Tübingen (J.C.B. Mohr) 1988.
KLOTEN, N.: "Was zu bedenken ist", in: N. KLOTEN et al.: *Die Umsetzung wirtschaftspolitischer Grundkonzeptionen in die kontinentaleuropäische Praxis des 19. und 20. Jahrhunderts*, Part 1, Berlin (Duncker und Humblot) 1997, pp. 161-170.

KLOTEN, N.: "Zur Typenlehre der Wirtschafts- und Gesellschaftsordnungen", *Ordo,* 7 (1955), pp. 123-143.

KLUMP, R.: "Wege zur Sozialen Marktwirtschaft", in: N. KLOTEN et al.: *Die Umsetzung wirtschaftspolitischer Grundkonzeptionen in die kontinentaleuropäische Praxis des 19. und 20. Jahrhunderts,* Part 1, Berlin (Duncker und Humblot) 1997, pp. 130-160.

KOOPMANS, T. C.: *Three Essays on the State of Economic Science,* New York (McGraw-Hill) 1957.

KRÖLL, M.: "Die Wirtschaftstypologien Euckens und Ritschls", *Journal of Institutional and Theoretical Economics,* 208 (1952), pp. 470-494.

LAKATOS, I., MUSGRAVE, A. (Eds.): *Criticism and the Growth of Knowledge,* Cambridge (Cambridge University Press) 1970.

LAUM, B.: "Entgegnung zu Euckens Aufsatz", *Schmollers Jahrbuch,* 62 (1938), pp. 87-92.

LEE, R. B.: *The !Dobe Kung,* New York (Holt) 1984.

LENEL, H. O. (1975a): "Vollständiger und freier Wettbewerb als Leitbild für die Wettbewerbspolitik gegenüber mächtigen Unternehmen", in: H. SAUERMANN, E.-J. MESTMÄCKER (Eds.): *Wirtschaftsordnung und Staatsverfassung,* Tübingen (J.C.B. Mohr) 1975, pp. 317-340.

LENEL, H. O. (1975b): "Walter Euckens ordnungspolitische Konzeption, die wirtschaftspolitische Lehre in der Bundesrepublik und die Wettbewerbstheorie von heute", *Ordo,* 26 (1975), pp. 22-78.

LENEL, H. O. (1989a): "Walter Eucken", in: J. STARBATTY (Ed.): *Klassiker des ökonomischen Denkens,* München (C.H. Beck) 1989, pp. 293-311.

LENEL, H. O. (1989b): "Walter Euckens "Grundlagen der NationalökonomieÔ", *Ordo,* 40 (1989), pp. 3-20.

LENEL, H. O.: "Walter Eucken", in: G. BOMBACH et al.: *Vademecum zu einem Wegbereiter der modernen Theorie in Deutschland,* Düsseldorf (Verlag Wirtschaft und Finanzen) 1990, pp. 15-35.

LINDENLAUB, D.: *Richtungskämpfe im Verein für Sozialpolitik,* Wiesbaden (Steiner) 1967.

LIPSEY, R. G., LANCASTER, K.: "The general Theory of Second Best", *Review of Economic Studies,* 24 (1956), pp. 11-32.

LUTZ, F. A.: "Die Grundlagen der Nationalökonomie (Review)", *American Economic Review,* 30 (1940), pp. 587-588.

LUTZ, F. A.: "Walter Eucken", in: E. BECKERATH et al. (Eds.): *Handwörterbuch der Sozialwissenschaften,* Vol. 3, Stuttgart (J.C.B. Mohr) 1961, pp. 353-356.

MACHLUP, F.: "Idealtypus, Wirklichkeit und Konstruktion", *Ordo,* 12 (1961), pp. 21-57.

MARTIN, H.-P., SCHUMANN, H.: *Die Globalisierungsfalle,* Hamburg (Rowohlt) 1997.

MAYER, H.: "Der Erkenntniswert der funktionellen Preistheorien", in: H. MAYER et al. (Eds.): *Die Wirtschaftstheorie der Gegenwart*, Vol. 2, Wien (Springer) 1932.
MCCLOSKEY, D. N.: *The Rhetoric of Economics*, Madison (University of Wisconsin Press) 1985.
MEIJER, G.: "Walter Eucken's Contribution to Economics in an International Perspective", *Journal of Economic Studies*, 21 (1994), pp. 25-37.
MESTMÄCKER, E.-J.: *Verwaltung, Konzerngewalt und Rechte der Aktionäre*, Karlsruhe (C.F. Müller) 1958.
MEYER, F. W.: "Wechselkurse", in: E. BECKERATH et al. (Eds.): *Handwörterbuch der Sozialwissenschaften*, Vol. 11, Stuttgart (J.C.B. Mohr) 1961, pp. 571-585.
MIKSCH, L.: "Walter Eucken", *Kyklos*, 4 (1950), pp. 279-290.
MIKSCH, L.: "Die Wirtschaftspolitik des Als-Ob", *Journal of Institutional and Theoretical Economics*, 105 (1949), pp. 310-338.
MISHKIN, F. S.: *Money, Banking and Financial Markets*, New York (Harper Collins) 1995.
MÖLLER, H.: "Wirtschaftsordnung, Wirtschaftssystem und Wirtschaftsstil", *Schmollers Jahrbuch*, 64 (1940), pp. 75- 98.
MOLSBERGER, J.: "Eucken, Walter", in: J. EATWELL et al. (Eds.): *The New Palgrave*, Vol. 2, New York (Stockton Press) 1987, pp. 195-196.
MÖSCHEL, W.: "Wettbewerbspolitik vor neuen Herausforderungen", in: WALTER EUCKEN INSTITUT (Ed.): *Ordnung in Freiheit*, Tübingen (J.C.B. Mohr) 1992, pp. 61-78.
MONOPOLKOMMISSION (Ed.): *Fortschreitende Konzentration bei Großunternehmen*, Baden-Baden (Nomos) 1978.
MONOPOLKOMMISSION (Ed.): *Gesamtwirtschaftliche Chancen und Risiken wachsender Unternehmensgrößen*, Baden-Baden (Nomos) 1986.
MÜLLER-ARMACK, A.: *Wirtschaftsordnung und Wirtschaftspolitik*, Bern (Paul Haupt) 1976.
NAWROTH, E. E.: *Die Sozial- und Wirtschaftsphilosophie des Neoliberalismus*, Heidelberg (F.H. Kerle Verlag) 1961.
NAWROTH, E. E.: *Die wirtschaftspolitischen Ordnungsvorstellungen des Neoliberalismus*, Köln (Carl Heymanns Verlag) 1962.
NEULING, W.: "Wettbewerb, Monopol und Befehl in der heutigen Wirtschaft", *Journal of Institutional and Theoretical Economics*, 8 (1939), pp. 279-319.
OBERENDER, P.: "Der Einfluß ordnungstheoretischer Prinzipien Walter Eucken's auf die deutsche Wirtschaftspolitik nach dem Zweiten Weltkrieg", *Ordo*, 40 (1989), pp. 321-350.
OSWALT, W. (1996a): "Chancen für den radikalen Liberalismus", *Kontraste*, 95 (1996), pp. 11-14.
OSWALT, W. (1996b): "Machtfreie Marktwirtschaft", *Kommune* 13 (1996), pp. 50-58.

WALTER EUCKEN AND THE HISTORICAL SCHOOL

OSWALT-EUCKEN, I.: "Freedom and Economic Power: Neglected Aspects of Walter Eucken's work", *Journal of Economic Studies*, 21 (1994), pp. 38-45.
OTT, A.: *Grundzüge der Preistheorie*, Göttingen (Vandenhoeck und Ruprecht) 1970.
OTT, C.: *Recht und Realität der Unternehmenskorporation*, Tübingen (Mohr) 1977.
OTTEL, F.: "Wirtschaftspolitische Mißerfolge und Ordo", *Jahrbücher für Nationalökonomie und Statistik*, 163 (1951), pp.382-398.
PALYI, M.: "Ungelöste Fragen der Geldtheorie", in: M. J. BONN, M. PALYI (Eds.): *Die Wirtschaftswissenschaften nach dem Kriege*, 2. Vol., München (Duncker und Humblot) 1925, pp. 455-517.
PEACOCK, A., WILLGERODT, H. (Eds.) (1989a): *German Neo-Liberals and the Social Market Economy*, New York (St. Martin's Press) 1989.
PEACOCK, A., WILLGERODT, H. (Eds.) (1989b): *Germany's Social Market Economy: Origins and Evolution*, New York (St. Martin's Press) 1989.
PENZ, R., WILKOP, H. (Eds.): *Zeit der Institutionen*, Marburg (Metropolis) 1996.
PETER, H.: "Die Grundlagen der Nationalökonomie (Review)", *Finanzarchiv*, 8 (1940/41), pp. 158-171.
PETER, H.: "Grundsätze der Wirtschaftspolitik (Review)", *Finanzarchiv*, 13 (1951/52), pp. 729-733.
PETERS, H.-R.: *Einführung in die Theorie der Wirtschaftssysteme*, München (Oldenbourgh) 1987.
PEUKERT, H.: *Das sozialökonomische Werk Wilhelm Röpkes*, Frankfurt (Peter Lang) 1992.
PEUKERT, H.: *Wirtschaftssystem und -stil der Wildbeuter und früher Landwirtschaftsgesellschaften*, Frankfurt (Schriftenreihe des Projekts "Wirtschaftssysteme im historischen Vergleich", Nr. 5) 1993.
PEUKERT, H. *Das klassische griechische Wirtschaftssystem und der Wirtschaftsstil unter besonderer Berücksichtigung des Geld- und Bankwesens*, Frankfurt (Schriftenreihe des Projekts "Wirtschaftssysteme im historischen Vergleich", Nr. 7) 1995.
PEUKERT, H.: "Kommentar zu W. Oswalt: Machtfreie Marktwirtschaft", *Kontraste*, 94 (1996), pp. 33-37.
PEUKERT, H. (1997a): *Das Handlungsparadigma in der Nationalökonomie*, Marburg (Metropolis) 1997.
PEUKERT, H. (1997b): "Zur Transformationsdebatte von Wirtschaftssystemen am Beispiel Lettlands", in: G. WEGNER, J. WIELAND (Eds.): *Formale und informale Institutionen*, Marburg (Metropolis) 1997, 25 pp. In print.
PEUKERT, H. (1997c): "K. Bücher on Early Societies", in: J. BACKHAUS (Ed.): *Karl Bücher*, 1997, 25 pp. In print.
POLANYI, K.: *The Great Transformation*, Frankfurt (Suhrkamp) 1978.
POLANYI, M.: *Personal Knowledge*, London (Routledge) 1958.
PRIDDAT, B.P.: *Die andere Ökonomie*, Marburg (Metropolis) 1995.

RAAB, F.: *Die Fortschrittsidee bei Gustav Schmoller*, Freiburg (Kehrer) 1934.
RAMSTAD, Y.: "The Institutionalism of John R. Commons", in: W. J. SAMUELS (Ed.): *Research in the History of Economic Thought and Methodology*, Greenwich (Jai Press), Vol. 8, 1990, pp. 53-104.
REHEIS, F.: *Die Kreativität der Langsamkeit*, Darmstadt (Wissenschaftliche Buchgesellschaft) 1996.
RICHTER, R. (Ed.): "Symposium 'Currency and Economic Reform – West Germany After World War II'", *Journal of Institutional and Theoretical Economics*, 135 (1979), pp. 297-532.
RITTSTIEG, H.: *Eigentum als Verfassungsproblem*, Darmstadt (Wissenschaftliche Buchgesellschaft) 1975.
RÖPKE, W.: "Blätter der Erinnerung an Walter Eucken", *Ordo*, 12 (1960/61), pp. 3-19.
RÖPKE, W.: "Walter Eucken", in: W. RÖPKE: *Gegen die Brandung*, Erlenbach-Zürich (Eugen Rentsch) 1959, pp. 374-379.
ROSCHER, W.: *Politik*, Stuttgart (Cotta) 1908.
ROSCHER, W.: *System der Volkswirtschaft*, Stuttgart (Cotta) 1886-1894.
RUNGE, U.: *Antinomien des Freiheitsbegriffs im Rechtsbild des Ordoliberalismus*, Tübingen (J.C.B. Mohr) 1971.
RUTHERFORD, M.: *Institutions in Economics*, Cambridge (Cambridge University Press) 1996.
SCHACHTSCHABEL, H. G.: "Zur Genealogie der Wirtschaftsstile", *Schmollers Jahrbuch*, 67 (1943), pp. 65-88.
SCHEFOLD, B.: *Wirtschaftsstile*, 2 Vols., Frankfurt (Fischer) 1994 and 1995.
SCHELLSCHMIDT, H.: *Ökonomische Institutionenanalyse und Sozialpolitik*, Marburg (Metropolis) 1997.
SCHERER, F. M.: "Antitrust: Ideology or Economics?", *Critical Review*, 5 (1992), pp. 497-511.
SCHERER, F. M.: *Industrial Market Structure and Economic Performance*, Chicago (Rand McNally College Publishing Company) 1970.
SCHLECHT, O.: "Der Wettbewerb braucht Pionierunternehmer", *Orientierungen zur Wirtschafts- und Gesellschaftspolitik*, 70 (1996), pp. 2-6.
SCHMIDT, K.-H.: "Gustav Schmoller und die Entwicklung einer sozialpolitischen Schule in Deutschland", in: N. KLOTEN et al.: *Die Umsetzung wirtschaftspolitischer Grundkonzeptionen in die kontinentaleuropäische Praxis des 19. und 20. Jahrhunderts*, Part 1, Berlin (Duncker und Humblot) 1997, pp. 43-79.
SCHMIDTCHEN, D.: "German "Ordnungspolitik" as Institutional Choice", *Journal of Institutional and Theoretical Economics*, 140 (1984), pp. 54-70.
SCHMOLLER, G.: "Über Zweck und Ziele des Jahrbuchs", *Schmollers Jahrbuch*, 5 (1881), pp. 1-18.

SCHMOLLER, G.: "Zur Methodologie der Staats- und Sozial-Wissenschaften", *Schmollers Jahrbuch*, 7 (1883), pp. 239-258.
SCHMOLLER, G.: *Die preussische Seidenindustrie im 18. Jahrhundert und ihre Begründung durch Friedrich den Großen*, Berlin (Parey) 1892.
SCHMOLLER, G.: *Grundriß der Allgemeinen Volkswirtschaftslehre*, 2 Vols., Berlin (Duncker und Humblot) 1978a and 1978b.
SCHNEIDER, D.: "Schmoller und die Lehre von der Unternehmensverfassung von der Betriebswirtschaftslehre", in: J. BACKHAUS (Ed.): *Gustav von Schmoller und die Probleme von heute*, Berlin (Duncker und Humblot) 1993, pp. 243-259.
SCHNEIDER, E.: "Zur Konkurrenz und Preisbildung auf vollkommenen und unvollkommenen Märkten", *Weltwirtschaftliches Archiv*, 48 (1938), pp. 399-419.
SCHUMACHER, E. F.: *Small is Beautiful*, New York (Harper Perennial) 1989.
SCHUMANN, J.: *Grundzüge der mikroökonomischen Theorie*, Berlin (Springer) 1992.
SCHUMPETER, J. A.: *History of Economic Analysis*, New York (Oxford University Press) 1954.
SCHUMPETER, J. A.: *The Theory of Economic Development*, Cambridge (Cambridge University Press) 1934.
SELIGMAN, E. R. A.: "Die Sozialökonomie in den Vereinigten Staaten", in: M. J. BONN, M. PALYI (Eds.): *Die Wirtschaftswissenschaften nach dem Kriege*, 2. Vol., München (Duncker und Humblot) 1925, pp. 59-78.
SENN, P. R.: "Gustav Schmoller auf englisch: Welche Spuren hat er hinterlassen", in: J. BACKHAUS (Ed.): *Gustav Schmoller und die Probleme von heute*, Berlin (Duncker und Humblot) 1993, pp. 27-79.
SHERMAN, H. J.: *Foundations of Radical Political Economy*, Armonk (M.E. Sharpe) 1987.
SIMONS, H. C.: *Economic Policy for a Free Society*, Chicago (University of Chicago Press) 1948.
SMITH, A.: "The Principles Which Lead and Direct Philosophical Enquiries, Illustrated by the History of Astronomy", in: A. SMITH: *Essays on Philosophy*, Hildesheim (Georg Ohms Verlag) 1982, pp. 1-93.
SOMBART, W.: *Die drei Nationalökonomien*, München (Duncker und Humblot) 1930.
SOROS, G.: "Can Europe Work?", *Foreign Affairs*, 75 (1996), pp. 8-14.
SPIETHOFF, A.: "Die Allgemeine Volkswirtschaftslehre als geschichtliche Theorie", *Schmollers Jahrbuch*, 56 (1932), pp. 51-84.
STACKELBERG, H.: *Marktform und Gleichgewicht*, Wien (Springer) 1934.
STACKELBERG, H.: "Die Grundlagen der Nationalökonomie", *Weltwirtschaftliches Archiv*, 51 (1940), pp. 245-286.
STEINBRÜCK, K.: *Vom unvollkommenen Markt zur heterogenen Konkurrenz*, Frankfurt (Knapp) 1951.
STIGLER, G. J.: *The Theory of Price*, New York (Macmillan), 1966.

STOLPER, G. et al.: *Deutsche Wirtschaft seit 1870*, Tübingen (J.C.B. Mohr) 1966.
STREISSLER, E. et al. (Eds.): *Zur Relativierung des Zieles der Geldwertstabilität*, Göttingen (Schwartz) 1976.
STREISSLER, E., WATRIN, CH. (Eds.): *Zur Theorie marktwirtschaftlicher Ordnungen*, Tübingen (Mohr) 1980.
STREIT, M. E., WOHLGEMUTH, M.: *The Market Economy and the State*, Mimeo 1997.
STREIT, M. E., WEGNER, G.: "Wissensmangel, Wissenserwerb und Wettbewerbsfolgen", *Ordo,* 40 (1989), pp. 183-200.
STREIT, M. E.: *Freiburger Beiträge zur Ordnungsökonomik*, Tübingen (J.C.B. Mohr) 1995.
STRUBL, G.: *Die Staatsauffassung des Neoliberalismus*, Tübingen (Repro) 1954.
STÜTZEL, W.: *Preis, Wert und Macht*, Aalen (Scientia-Verlag) 1972.
TENBRUCK, F. H.: "Die Genesis der Methodologie Max Webers", *Kölner Zeitschrift für Soziologie und Sozialpsychologie*, 11 (1959), pp. 573-630.
TUCHTFELDT, E. (Ed.): *Soziale Marktwirtschaft im Wandel*, Freiburg (Rombach) 1973.
TUCHTFELDT; E.: *Das 20. Jahrhundert als Zeitalter der Experimente*, Bern (Volkswirtschaftliches Institut, Universität Bern) 1989.
VARIAN, H.R.: *Mikroökonomie*, München (Oldenbourgh) 1994.
VEIT, R.: "Karl Friedrich Maier als Mikro-Ökonom", *Ordo*, 31 (1980), pp. 229-234.
VLEUGELS, W.: "Die Grundlagen der Nationalökonomie (Review)", *Jahrbücher für Nationalökonomie und Statistik*, 152 (1940), pp. 497-525.
VOELLER, J.: *Euckens "Primat der Währungspolitik" als ordnungspolitisches Problem*, Karlsruhe (Institut für Wirtschaftstheorie) 1985.
WAGNER, V. F.: "Walter Eucken", *Schweizerische Zeitschrift für Volkswirtschaft und Statistik*, 86 (1950), pp. 172-174.
WALLICH, H. C.: *Mainsprings of the German Revival*, New Haven (Yale University Press) 1955.
WALTER EUCKEN INSTITUT (Ed.): *Ordnung in Freiheit*, Tübingen (J.C.B. Mohr) 1992.
WEBER, R. L.: "Walter Eucken und der Wandel von Wirtschaftssystemen", *Wirtschaftswissenschaftliches Studium*, 21 (1992), pp. 579-583.
WEIPPERT, G. "Die wirtschaftstheoretische und wirtschaftspolitische Bedeutung der Kartelldebatte auf der Tagung des Vereins für Socialpolitik im Jahre 1905", *Jahrbuch für Sozialwissenschaft*, 50 (1958), pp. 125-183.
WEIPPERT, G.: "Walter Euckens Grundlagen der Nationalökonomie", *Journal of Institutional and Theoretical Economics*, 102 (1941/42), pp. 1-58 and 271-337.
WEISSER, G.: "Wirtschaftstypen", in: E. BECKERATH et al. (Eds.): *Handwörterbuch der Sozialwissenschaften*, Vol. 12, Stuttgart (Fischer) 1965, pp. 269-280.

WALTER EUCKEN AND THE HISTORICAL SCHOOL

WELTER, E.: "Walter Eucken", in: H. C. RECKTENWALD (Ed.): *Lebensbilder großer Nationalökonomen*, Köln (Kiepenheuer und Witsch) 1965, pp. 559-569.

WENDT, S.: "Schumacher, Hermann", in: E. BECKERATH et al. (Eds.): *Handwörterbuch der Sozialwissenschaften*, Vol. 9, Stuttgart (Fischer) 1956, pp. 150-151.

WIESER, F.: *Theorie der gesellschaftlichen Wirtschaft*, Tübingen (Mohr) 1924.

WISEMAN, J.: "Social Policy and the Social Market Economy", in: A. PEACOCK, H. WILLGERODT (Eds.): *Germany's Social Market Economy: Origins and Evolution*, New York (St. Martin's Press) 1989, pp. 160-178.

WOLL, A.: "Freiheit durch Ordnung", *Ordo*, 40 (1989), pp. 87-97.

WÜNSCHE, H. F.: "Erhards soziale Marktwirtschaft: von Eucken programmemiert, von Müller-Armack inspiriert?', in: LUDWIG-ERHARD-STIFTUNG (Ed.): *Soziale Marktwirtschaft als historische Weichenstellung*, Bonn (ST Verlag) 1997, pp. 131-169.

YEAGER, L.: "Eucken on Capital and Interest", *Journal of Economic Studies*, 21 (1994), pp. 61-75.

ZWEIG, K.: *The Origins of the German Social Market Economy*, London (Adam Smith Institute) 1980.

Discussion Summary

Johan Tralau

Paper discussed:
Helge Peukert: Walter Eucken (1891 - 1950) and the Historical School

The claim that Eucken was more and more influenced by the Austrian School is most startling, and would, were it correct, most indubitably show an inconsistency in Eucken's thinking. Hayek, for instance, rejected Saint-Simon and Comte (Wohlgemuth). Indeed, the connection must be seen as surprising. As to the view that producers should not influence prices, one must ask oneself what Eucken really meant by the term "monopoly". There seem to be contradictions in his own programme. Here, it may be useful to distinguish between Eucken as a politician and Eucken as an economist. It is not surprising that Eucken advocated different policies in his different roles. Furthermore, Hayek's theory can be criticised as regards its internal consistency, too. The characterisation of knowledge as time- and space-bound would seem to contradict the theory of the spontaneous order, since the latter claims to be valid quite independently of time and space (Peukert).

At this point, the historical context of Eucken's work was discussed. Eucken, like Carl Schmitt, poses a theoretical problem. As society is secularised, it is imperative that a total state should be established as a substitute for it. How can, then, a state be strong enough to implement its policies, thus making a leap from quantity to quality and ensuring social order? (Haselbach) The analogy Schmitt-Eucken is incorrect. Eucken must be understood in a completely different context: he is concerned about the legitimacy of the state based on Christian belief. This implies that certain principles must not and cannot be violated by the state or politicians, be it Bismarck or be it Schmitt (Peukert). The question of Friedrich Lutz's influence on Eucken was raised. It was also noted that Eucken in an article in 1940 pointed to the danger of the approach of the Historical School.

DISCUSSION SUMMARY

According to Eucken, it could lead to Social Darwinism. Here, surely, he alludes to National Socialism; his writings about the repression of the Bartholomew Night also clearly allegorically criticise the so-called "Reichskristallnacht" of November 9th, 1938 (HAGEMANN). Lutz's influence on Eucken must not be underestimated (PEUKERT).

The discussion of the connection between National Socialism and the Historical School was then continued. The one intrinsic affinity that is to be found is the nationalist emphasis on the spirit of the people. Yet the particularism of the Historical School encumbered its becoming racist, and thus pseudo-universalistic. It would, therefore, be unjust to judge the entire Historical School in that manner. The question is, however, fairly difficult. On the one hand, the Historical School in general rejected National Socialism, but on the other hand, Mussolini was greeted in Schmoller's Yearbook. The definition of the people, the "Volk", differed: for the Historical School the important point was the language and the culture, not race or blood (KOSLOWSKI). It is of utmost importance that the historical context should be taken into consideration. After all, Hitler was named Man of the Year by *Time Magazine* in 1940. The crisis of 1929 certainly had a great impact on the economists. The longing for community was very strong during the period, and most certainly played a leading role in the development leading to the National Socialist political take-over in 1933 (RAUSCHER).

Chapter 5

Franz Böhm and the Theory of the Private Law Society

KNUT WOLFGANG NÖRR

I. The Background: Cartelization of German Industry Since Late 19th Century
II. Weimar Regulations and Debates
III. Böhm's Monograph of 1933 on Competition and Monopolies
IV. Böhm's Article of 1966 on Private Law Society: Some Critical Remarks
V. On the Fragmentary Character of the Concept of Private Law Society
VI. Extracts From Franz Böhm: "Private Law Society and Market Economy" (1966)

I. The Background: Cartelization of German Industry Since Late 19th Century

When Franz Böhm wrote the article on private law society and market economy in 1966, he had already reflected on matters of law and economy for no less than forty years. During the late 1920s he had served as an official in the Ministry of Economics of the Weimar Republic, and here he met with the dubiosities of the type of an economy that we may call organised economy, an economy which has prevailed in Germany since the ill-famous protectionist turn of economic policy in 1878/79, a turn, again, that was approved of not only by industrialists and big landowners but also by the school or at least the majority among economists and jurists (remember the debates within the Verein für Socialpolitik/Association for the Promotion of

FRANZ BÖHM AND THE THEORY OF PRIVATE LAW SOCIETY

Social Policy). The experience that Böhm gained serving the Ministry of Economics, above all in regard to the cartelization of German industry, continued to be the incitement of his scholarly work from the Weimar Republic through the Nazi period until the Federal Republic. In a way, we may call the experience of the twenties the background radiation of his whole thinking and writing including his contributions to the debates in the Bundestag, whose member he was from 1953 to 1965 after joining the Christian Democrats. Thus we should take a look at the state of affairs in the period before 1933, especially in regard to the cartel movement, from a conceptual as well as a political point of view, in order to understand the contextual background of the concept of private law society.

Among all the practices entailing restraint of competition, the cartel attracted the most attention in public opinion, politics, and the relevant disciplines. This attention was by no means uncritical but did not lead to efficient control or even a ban on cartels. Quite the contrary, it produced stocks of justifications and thus actually consolidated the cartel. The stocks laid in around the turn of the century lasted for many decades until the end of the Weimar Republic, and even in the early days of the Federal Republic of Germany the opponents of the prohibition of cartels tried to make use of it.

I would like to specify four items out of this stock of justifications. The first justification of the cartel was supplied by the theory of history - one is tempted to say metaphysics of history - of the Historical School. This metaphysics expressed itself in the well-known theories of stages which go back to the great Scottish thinkers of the 18th century, such as Lord Kames and Adam Smith. These theories would have been harmless with respect to our topic had they not taken on evolutionist and deterministic traits.

Development, the step from one stage to the next, was not just a temporal process but was turned into a self-supporting law. An inevitable nomology established itself beside mere chronology, and the age-old distinction between causality and finality was revoked in favour of a linearist philosophy of history. Now, in light of these theories, organised economy was on a higher stage than the economy of the free market and of free competition. If one looked at them in principle, free competition on the one hand and organised competition on the other did not belong to the same stage but to two different stages of development, and according to the law of history, the organised form ranked higher because it was the more recent one.

Jurists were deeply impressed with this kind of reasoning. This became particularly obvious at the Juristentage (conventions of lawyers) which were concerned with the cartel problem in 1902 and 1904 and then again in 1928, during the Weimar period. At these conventions, it was argued that a process of transition towards a new economic period took place, and on the threshold of it there were the cartels.

The cartel movement embodied all the attributes which guaranteed that the historical course of the economic stages was a purposeful process: cartels were not arbitrary but historically necessary forms of development; they coincided with the great tendencies of the economic order; and they represented a progressive stage in national economy, progress which would inevitably lead to a more highly organised form of national economy. Therefore, cartels could not be banned because the transition towards a higher economic stage could not be halted nor prohibited.

A second justification of the cartel idea lay in collectivism, a sociocultural way of looking at things which forced classical individualism more and more to the defensive. Above all, cartels were put on the same level with co-operative societies, i.e., collective institutions whose economic and social legitimacy was beyond dispute. Otto v. Gierke provided the legal theory for the co-operative idea as a form of collectivism.

As early as 1890, the Reichsgericht (the supreme court in the German Empire and in the Weimar Republic) ruled that tradesmen were permitted to regulate the market by means of "self-help on a co-operative basis". The court repeated this rule in the famous decision of 1897 on the Saxon Woodpulp Producers' Association, the leading case in cartel law defining the practice of the Reichsgericht for the next generation. For this decision, the judges had consulted the writings of political economists, since legal authors had until then paid hardly any attention to the cartel problem. To my knowledge, there was no other ruling during the Reichsgericht's seventy years of history which relied as heavily on economics as did the cartel decision.

This brief affair with political economy did not do the legal development any good; at any rate this is today's judgement, because freedom of trade and of competition were not accepted as goods to be protected by the rules of private law. The consequence was that the courts prohibited cartels and cartel practices only if they infringed upon the good morals clause (of the Civil Code or the Unfair Competition Act), which means however, that the judges forged a sword which turned out to be almost blunt.

The collectivist tendency, as described, overlapped with the idea of organisation. In the decades around 1900, organisation was one of the great catchwords of public opinion. The idea connected with it was that behind the wide variety of organisations and associations in politics, society, and economy, a uniform principle revealed itself. Then, co-operative societies and cartels were only exemplifications of a new phenomenon, and this phenomenon was certified as having a higher morality.

At the conventions of lawyers, it was said that every organisation and every methodicalness in economic life must be promoted, since they were beneficial reactions against the ravages of hyperindividualism. For Gustav Schmoller, the head of the Historical School, the cartels were psychologically and morally significant because they came into being through co-operative contract, through subordination, through insight into what is necessary, and through the victory of common interests over stubbornness and short-sighted egoism. Thus, cartels represented moral progress as well, and so gave the theory of economic stages mentioned above its ethical orientation in addition to its evolutionist character.

For the third justifying factor we need to remind ourselves that the development of the cartels took place during a period of awareness of power and power politics by the state. When the cartel problem was discussed, the role of cartels as an instrument of the national ambition for power was brought up again and again. The arguments were that the state needed a strong national economy which, for its part, could not do without cartels. The cartels testified to a new mercantilism. Without them, the state would not be able to extend its economic sphere of power.

In the international competition for the world market, the cartels acted as industrial fighting organisations against foreign competitors and against the transatlantic trusts in particular; repression of the cartels confined to Germany would be unthinkable. The cartels were a factor in international politics, and they sprang from the same roots as protectionism, colonial policy, naval policy, and the other off-springs of modern imperialism. Thus, in the process of assessing the cartels, the law found itself captivated by Realpolitik along the lines of Bismarck, but there were hardly any jurists who would have opposed this kind of political realism.

Finally, the cartel idea benefited from the fact that it unfolded during a period for which we have to diagnose a decline of the idea of law, a de-legalising, as it were, of whatever was measured by the standards of the law. The ideology of power politics and Realpolitik just mentioned was one aspect of this decline. Another one was the spirit of utilitarianism pushing forward and revealing itself through its emphasis on expediency and interest; Rudolf v. Jhering tried to supply the appropriate theory to this kind of legal realism.

As a result, the benefit of the cartels for the state, for the national economy and for the large groups of interested parties was the prime concern, and the infringement of rights of all those who had had unfavourable experiences with the cartels was only of secondary importance. Legal principles such as freedom of contract or freedom of competition were not on the agenda of the cartel debate at the conventions of lawyers; they were even pushed aside as being inopportune. The courts also used the standard of good morals to weigh up interests against each other, thereby relativizing all legal principles and dissolving them into a casuistic proportionalism. However, some people did raise their voices and warned of displacing the idea of law by the ideology of purpose and interests, but they did not meet with any response, and all objections were in vain.

II. Weimar Regulations and Debates

Thus, it is obvious that we must not confine ourselves to the economic perspective if we want to give an historical explanation of why Germany became the land of the cartels. We also need to stick to this (if the expression is allowed) trans-economic way of explanation when we turn now to the Weimar Republic.

Statistically, the significance of the cartels fluctuated during the individual economic phases which alternated rapidly between 1918 and 1933, but the cartel idea itself never suffered a loss. Quite the reverse: in the beginning of the Republic, it received a boost. The stock of justifications mentioned earlier was now extended even further.

The revolution of 1918 had been a socialist one but its intention was by no means to implement the entire socialist programme as it unfolded in the 19th century. Among other things, one shrank from abolishing private ownership of the means of production; instead, ownership was to be incorporated into an organisation consisting of self-governing bodies which were politically controlled. This economic-political construction was labelled "*Gemeinwirtschaft*" (collective or publicly controlled economy).

FRANZ BÖHM AND THE THEORY OF PRIVATE LAW SOCIETY

The transformation of private economy into Gemeinwirtschaft presupposed the formation of cartels. If the companies did not voluntarily merge into cartels the government could force them to do so; that is, it could establish compulsory cartels. Thus, cartels were the core and the basis of these politically planned constructions. In light of our stock of justifications, the point is that the transformation of private economy into Gemeinwirtschaft was viewed as a matter of constitutional law, as well.

This has to do, of course, with the socialist doctrine that the political and the economic constitution are inseparable. Accordingly, the Weimar Constitutional Charter of 1919 contained an article which established Gemeinwirtschaft as an alternative to private economy. Thus, within the framework of collective economy, the formation of cartels was substantiated by the Constitution. This amounts to a constitutionalization, so to speak, of the cartel, a process, of course, also to the benefit and justification of private cartels outside collective economy.

If we look at the cartel from the perspective of the categories of our legal system, we can observe that the localization of the cartel within civil law was performed before the First World War; we have mentioned the certainly meagre control of the cartels by the standard of good morals, which belongs to the field of civil law. We see now that beside civil law, constitutional law became another category for the legal assessment of cartels. One might also speak of different layers of regulations which were relevant to the cartels. During the Weimar period, a third layer was added, namely, cartel law in the strict sense of the word.

A statute concerning cartels had already been called for before the war, and the demand was repeated several times after 1918, but the Federal Ministry of Economics did not comply since it preferred informal control by means of "confident co-operation" between the bureaucracy and the cartellized industry. Numerous arguments were presented against restricting the formation of cartels. There was the quite popular argument of the singularization of the cartels, since abuse of economic power was not their exclusive domain but could also be encountered in the capital accumulations of the big stock corporations and affiliated companies.

The argument of protection of small business was popular as well, since restrictions on the cartels would foster the growth of the big companies and trusts. However, these arguments did not help any more when, in the second half of 1923, the Republic was in a dangerous crisis of domestic policy brought about by hyperinflation, the occupation of the Ruhr district, and other incidents. The final impulse came from the practice of the cartels to pass the risk of currency depreciation on to the buyers so that the burden fell at the end on the consumers.

The Cartel Ordinance, enacted by the Stresemann administration in November 1923, had a "normative heading", so to speak, i.e., the heading already contained a topic and programme: "Ordinance against the Abuse of Economic Power". The aim, then, was not to prohibit cartels but to prevent cartels from abusing their economic position. The standard was put forward by an objective criterion: endangering the national economy or public welfare. Such an endangerment could also consist of cartel measures "unreasonably" infringing, as the wording run, upon the economic freedom of the individual. For the first time, the text of a law mentioned freedom in connection with restraint of trade and considered it, to a certain degree, worth protecting. Admittedly, this aspect of freedom had to put up with many other points of view as we can learn from the press release that accompanied the Cartel Ordinance, where, again, the cartels' justification came clearly to the fore.

The press release read mainly as follows (allow of some omissions):

> The Ordinance against the Abuse of Economic Power must be seen in the overall context of measures taken by the Government of the Reich in order to increase production, free the economy from unproductive constraints, and remove unhealthy constraints on free competition.
> The policy of the cartels and conventions in regard to production and prices has for many months now been subject to violent attacks from among the group of consumers as well as by certain segments of the manufacturers. The Government saw itself as responsible for examining whether the complaints which had been raised were justified and, giving first consideration to general economic factors, for taking measures based solely on objective standards. It is indisputable that the devaluation of German currency and the conditions of production and marketing which resulted from it has frequently led to deplorable abuses within the organisations of manufacturers. Due to the increasing gravity of the economic situation since the summer of this year, because of which the prices of certain German products have also been pushed beyond their limits in comparison with the international market, there is a general interest in restoring a truly free market and thus in most emphatically combating artificial restraints on production, excessive "risk premiums", and methods of price

> fixing which are not justified by actual production costs, as well as in forcing the groups engaged in production and trade to re-establish their frequently mislaid sense of responsibility towards the public interest.
>
> The Government believes, however, that in order to reach this goal, to which it decidedly aspires, it must not follow the course of completely destroying the cartels, as is demanded by some. These radical plans must by necessity misunderstand the important function for the national economy which responsible oganizations of manufacturers seem destined to fulfill precisely in the actual economic crisis. If the present Ordinance is intended as offering an instrument for rigorously combating the damaging outgrowths of cartelization, then on the other hand, by cleaning up these organisations it seeks to enable them to support the initiation of fair business policies, the propagation of rational methods of production, and the standardization of price calculations. Finally, one cannot overlook the fact that a complete destruction of the cartels would not in the least encourage the free market in the long run, but on the contrary in the ensuing process of reorganisation would only put a great number of healthy middle-sized or small firms at the mercy of the financial superiority of large concerns.
>
> The present ordinance entrusts the Reich Minister of Economics and a Cartel Court still to be created with carrying out the national cartel policy.

The Cartel Ordinance, however, did not put an end to cartel criticism. The power exerted by the cartels had always been met with critical attention. What was disturbing about this power was that it came from private bodies but radiated into the public sphere. Public power over public matters, i.e., government, was accepted, as was private power in the private sphere (the small and medium sized dimensions of power in social and economic life), but not private power transcending the private sphere and spreading out into the public. Criticism remained reserved as long as the individual or the sum of the individuals, however large it may be, fell victim to private power. However, criticism grew enormously when it became clear that the state itself was endangered by private power.

This cartel criticism, prompted by worry about the state, could be found in the literature of the Weimar Republic even before the great state crisis broke out, but it came to be sharply formulated in the beginning of the thirties. Among economists reference should be made to Moritz Julius Bonn,

Walter Eucken, and, to a certain extent, Götz Briefs, as well as Alexander Rüstow, who coined the often quoted phrase of the state falling prey to the big crowds of interested groups. Among jurists - and here the name appears again which we are dealing with - it was Franz Böhm who was worried about the problem of private power as it was exerted by cartels and monopolies and who ventured to radically rethink, even to revolutionize, the legal views concerning the cartels.

III. Böhm's Monograph of 1933 on Competition and Monopolies

It was characteristic of Böhm that he no longer followed the Historical School but leaned to the international mainstream of economic theory. In his great monograph of 1933 on competition and monopolies - which can be read as the declaration of independence of the idea of competition - he wrote that he wanted to turn to the classical economic philosophy, but to do this as a jurist, and that, therefore, his task was to translate this classical edifice of teachings from the language of political economy into the language of legal science. But what was Böhm's view of this process of translation, and which legal conclusions did he draw from it?

First, he adopted the idea of "prestabilized harmony" which, of course, is a refined version of the aim of increasing the national product, and thereby justified the economy of free competition based on performance, in contrast to market arrangements and market regulation. Then, the task of law - and that means here, private law - is to ensure the prerequisites and the undisturbed course of competition based on performance.

Second, Böhm pointed out, against the opponents of the free market economy, that competition does not generate an anarchic and chaotic labyrinth but an order in its own right. For the jurist, however, order means legal rules and regulations. If the phenomenon concerned is the economic order, and if this order does not hang in the air but materialises within the borders of a political unit, then one is not mistaken to look at the conceptions of politics and public law and to import from them the concept of the constitution, in other words, to speak of a state's economic order as its economic constitution.

FRANZ BÖHM AND THE THEORY OF PRIVATE LAW SOCIETY

The concept of economic constitution had already been in use but had until then been reserved for the organised economy as we came across it in the form of the Gemeinwirtschaft. Böhm applied it now to the counterorder, so to speak, of the free market economy.

Third, Böhm adopted the economic way of thinking in models also for the person who participates in the competition and acts on the market. This shows that he pursued a methodological and psychological individualism (not identical with individualism in terms of general or legal philosophy, though).

From these premises he unfolded a consistent theory of competition from the viewpoint of law, a theory which overcame the cartel centred way of thinking and, explicitly as well as implicitly, pushed aside the old justifications. From these premises he also conceived competition as an institution, in the sense that institutions needed a fundamental decision in politics and law in order to come into existence. Competition was to be the very essence of economy and not merely an instrument to control abuses that counted among the attributes of organised economy.

But now, when the idea of competition came to the fore, what would be, in turn, the justification for that? What legitimates competition and the fight against monopolies? To answer this question, Böhm recurred to the notion of Gemeinschaft (community). Discussing the traditional distinction between public and private law as it was drawn by the Roman jurist Ulpianus - *publicum ius est quod ad statum rei Romanae spectat, privatum quod ad singulorum utilitatem* - Böhm explained that competition as an institution would belong to neither one. For competition means a kind of economic co-operation but a co-operation free from dominance and subordination and therefore outside the sphere of the state; on the other hand, competition does not envisage the interest of the individual but through increasing the social dividend serves the common weal, the weal of the community. There is, says Böhm, not only the state here and the individual there but also the community as an organisation based on co-operation of individuals and rejecting dominance and any authoritative kind of planning.

In the Weimar period, of course, the term Gemeinschaft easily flowed from the lips and we have to be careful whenever we try to find out which concept of community the writer had in mind. In the case of Böhm we are not able to give an answer; his concept of community remained vague and indistinct and he did not explain what the values and institutions were that would fill in the concept. It seems that he considered it a half political, half sociological category but more precise information we cannot gain from the text.

IV. Böhm's Article of 1966 on Private Law Society: Some Critical Remarks

Apparently, Böhm himself was not wholly content with the appeal to community; at any rate, after 1945 he did not return to it but began to look for another substratum of competition and the market. This time he tried to develop a new concept by presenting the idea of private law society. The term appeared for the first time in an article of 1951 on worker's co-determination but it was not before 1966 that he entered into details and explained the reasons of the concept. Let us try to find out what his understanding of the matter has been (quotations are from the select English translation, edited by Alan Peacock and Hans Willgerodt, with some minor additions).

Böhm concluded from a historical event, the French Revolution, that the individual had not been emancipated from society, rather society had changed and was transformed from a feudal society of privileges into a private law society based on co-ordination of free and equal members of society. (We will leave the question open whether Böhm's remarks were historically correct or not.) Faced with the state's power human and constitutional rights had been developed in favour of the individual. But alongside the classical understanding of constitutional rights a new understanding emerged rooted in the societal membership of the individual. Böhm did not deny the immediate confrontation between the individual and the state, but more important was the indirect confrontation through the medium of society whose member the individual was. In this way the individual was bound to his state through the medium of the private law society, said Böhm:

> In a word, anyone who in the structure of the modern, post-revolutionary, democratic industrial nation perceives only the state on the one hand and the individual on the other, overlooks an important element of modern constitutional reality. The legal reality is that the individual, given the constitutional scheme upon which all

modern constitutional states are based, is bound to his state through the medium of the private law society.

Now, this medium was no innocent aggregate of singles but represented some kind of entity or organism or substance or whatever you like. Therefore the emphasis that it was the private law society which was assigned to the state, and not an accumulation of millions of unconnected individuals; after discussing intermediate social authorities such as political parties Böhm pointed out:

> The main point, however, is that since the abolition of the feudal society, the private law society has been embodied in the state but not as an accumulation of millions of unconnected individuals.

Therefore the Hegelian jawbreaker that the co-ordination of the society's members would constitute a *"verobjektivierte Besonderheit wechselseitiger Abhängigkeit"* (untranslatable). In this way we can see how the points of departure were interchanged by Böhm, and how society ranked first being, as it were, the vanishing point from which our thoughts would descend to the parts and particles, the individuals. The individuals perform certain functions, e.g. they enter into contracts, in order to keep society alive, in the same way as their actions keep market economy in motion. This functionality meant co-ordination and subordination at the same time: co-ordination as far as the mutually interdependent actions of the individuals are concerned, subordination, however, in the individual's relation to society and the market. The individual would have to accept and follow the "musical score", to use Böhm's appropriate metaphor, which governs the realm of the market and the realm of society. The musical score distributes roles among the individuals, the role of the consumer, the role of the producer, the role of the investor. For the sake of these roles, for the sake of the market and private law society autonomy was granted the individual. Thus autonomy depended on his status as a social citizen, on his *"gesellschaftliches Bürgerrecht"*, to quote Böhm literally:

> Over and above all this, the private law order delegates to all persons who move within its jurisdiction, an extremely extensive freedom of movement, a competence for planning and existence in relation to their fellow men, a status within the private law society which is by no means simply a gift of nature - a dowry of natural talents and will-power - but a social civic right. Not a natural faculty but a social permission.

Beyond performance according to the score there was no private autonomy, no legitimacy of economic acting or non-acting. *Extra ecclesiam nulla salus*. As a result, and to sum up, whoever will rely on Böhm's private law society should take his concept into account which was of an institutional or mediatizing or sociological kind, and did not, as one would perhaps expect, liberate the individual from objectivations whatever their names would have been.

V. On the Fragmentary Character of the Concept of Private Law Society

I should add, however, that Böhm's article, and therefore his concept of private law society, remained fragmentary. Thus we would look in vain for answers to certain questions. Most important in this regard was the constitutional question. When Böhm used the metaphor of the musical score which controls the conduct of the members of the private law society as well as of the state authorities, i.e. the conduct of the governed as well as of the governors, he emphasised a mandate given to government that entails the creation of a regulative framework which would guarantee the functioning of the free market system. This mandate emanated from the constitution but it is not clear if Böhm was dealing with constitution in terms of a political-programmatic concept or rather of a legal concept aiming at the concrete constitution of the state in which he lived, therefore the Basic Law of the Federal Republic (enacted in 1949). In the former case he might , of course, feel free to postulate a constitution which would provide the score he had in mind to promote and secure the private law society and market economy. But when it comes to interpreting the Basic Law it would not be easy to discover Böhm's mandate in its text, nor was our Constitutional Court ever inclined to read the text along the lines of Böhm's conception. On the contrary, if we may point out just one significant detail in this connection, Böhm had emphasised, this time following "classic" liberal lines, as a precondition of legitimate legislation the generality of law whereas the Federal Constitutional Court has discarded the principle of generality as an essential of the concept of law and legislation, for which it was greatly applauded by the main stream of both politicians and constitutional lawyers.

VI. Extracts from Franz Böhm: "Private Law Society and Market Economy" (1966)[1]

Rule of Law in a Market Economy[2]

The lawyer knows what private law is. The economist knows what the market economy is. But what is the private law society? The term is not commonly used in academic circles. Neither jurisprudence nor economics nor sociology use it. Yet one of the great objectives of the French Revolution was to transform the pre-revolutionary society into a private law society. Oddly enough, however, this objective was never positively defined: rather people spoke in terms of the elimination of class rights and class distinctions. They mentioned by name that society which they wanted to abolish but did not comment on the society which was to be established in place of the old society.

Development of the Private Law Society

The historically famous deed of the revolutionaries consisted in their violent uprising against a social order the institutions of which were felt to be an affront to human rights, justice and liberty. They also translated into reality the idea that in society everyone should have the same rights and status, namely the status of a person under private law. The pioneers of the revolution did not give any thought as o how the relations between these free and independent members of society should be regulated. Nor did they need to, for the rules which are supposed to prevail in a society of free subjects under private law based on co-ordination of a society of equals, had long been in existence. The form of society had already been handed down from antiquity and had enjoyed conventional or statutory validity since the emergence of the nations of the Western world; the rules of such societies had been cultivated, explained and further developed by whole generations of sagacious and distinguished legal scholars and judges. In short, the best

---

1 translated in: ALAN PEACOCK, H. WILLGERODT (Eds.): *Germany's Social Market Economy: Origins and Evolution*, London (Macmillan) 1989, pp. 46-67. Footnotes: K. W. N.

2 Translated from the original article which was published in 1966 in the *Ordo* yearbook, vol. 17. It was originally entitled "Private Law Society and the Market Economy".

thing that a revolution can produce, namely a good system of relations between free people, had already been long since achieved; the only thing still remaining to be done was to free private law from its Cinderella existence. To put this in political terms, private law had to be freed from its 'wretched and exploited state', elevated to a social system[3] and entrusted with the control of a society of free and independently-acting individuals and of the companies and corporations of private law established by them on a voluntary basis. The notion to do this and set it going was a new, great and bold political idea.

The conception which forms the basis of the private law system itself and which accounts for its ability to organise a society of free people to guide their co-operation into channels that are calculable and rationally justifiable, is another matter altogether. The instigators of that revolution which was later called the `bourgeois revolution` were entirely innocent of this conception. They were confident that the system of private law was an efficient one, whereby they could probably rely chiefly upon the successes achieved by private law in all periods, so long as there was no need to cope with the tasks of a social system. Within the context of differently constituted and overlapping social systems, private law merely had to regulate intercourse between such persons as happened to encounter one another on the basis of equality of rights and who wished to undertake something of mutual advantage which, exceptionally, was not prohibited or reserved for someone 'by virtue of rank'.

The decision to abolish all class prerogatives and privileges was justified by the maxim: henceforth in the field of society there shall be only one single legal status for all and only a single competent authority governing human plans and action, namely private autonomy. The administration of justice[4] would be totally free from all powers of domination and representation. This postulate that all members of society should have the same status is, of course, not a private law concept but a political one under constitutional law.

The most important thing is to understand how state and society work hand-in-hand. It must first be established that in both the pre-revolutionary and post-revolutionary eras there has always been, at least, a conventionally regulated relationship between state and society. In this context, state means

---

3   *Gesellschaftsordnung.*
4   read: This authority.

the social organism which administers and exercises political powers of control and society means everything else happening in a nation. This socially-regulated relationship shows a very specific and constant structure throughout the centuries, both before and after the 'great revolution'.

First, there is the fundamental notion that the administration of the means of control is a function which serves exclusively the protection and preservation of society. It must, however, have a special body responsible for it because society (the nation in its entirety) does not have the capacity to act. The state or, expressed in archaic terms the King, in order to attend to his duties for the welfare of society, must claim dominance over the members of society. Dominance is, however, vested in him in feudal tenure by the society which is devoid of the capacity to act. This is a somewhat singular relationship which in England, for the sake of practical clarity, was envisaged as an agreement on the basis of immemorial title. The state, so opinion had it, should confine itself to the necessary display of majesty and not be lured by the intoxication of ruling by, for instance, interfering with the everyday issues of society. The attempt was made to safeguard this principle in such a way that the functions assigned to monarchs were itemised and enumerated; everything else was the domain of society.

This principle which determined the scope of authority - namely, that which is not of the state by virtue of the constitution is of society, had determined the relationship between state and society in all Western European countries from the early Middle Ages until the present day. The exceptions are, of course, those countries in which a distinction between state and society is no longer acknowledged at all but in which the jurisdiction of the state has been extended to include the power to control, by means of government plans, all issues of society which can be controlled by any sovereign means. This type of state, however, was not in existence before 1914.

Also characteristic of the concept of the dual relationship between state and society was the idea that the observance of the bounds of competence on the part of political administration which is, after all, so much more strongly armoured than society, must be safeguarded by conceding to representatives of society effective powers of co-determination in ruling the state. For example, the estates of the realm would have the right to grant supply and to participate in legislation; the sovereign would have to exercise his powers in accordance with the laws of the land. In the event of contravention of these rights the King's counsellors should be held responsible, that is to say, should be arraigned before the courts by the estates.

This peculiar combination of state and society has been given the technical term 'constitutional'[5]. The earliest and most vehement constitutional battles were fought over this constitutional principle of power exercised in accordance with the law. The disagreements were particularly fierce when the state was still represented by the King and the representatives of society were interested not only in the compliance with the constitutional limits on the part of the King but also with maintaining their rights of co-determination.

So far, for reasons of simplification and illustration, state and society have been referred to as if they were willing members of an association[6]. That this applies to the state is undisputed; the state is a body equipped with institutions which, with the help of those institutions, can form and effect its will; can the same also be said of `society`? Can the term `society` mean something different to the lawyer from a mere word which is used to mean the general body of all citizens or inhabitants of a state?

Society, the State and the Individual

In the past, lawyers have never accepted `society` as a legal term in the sense in which it is used when the state is contrasted with society. There is no such thing as a `society` which, vis-à-vis the state, might be a body responsible for[7] constitutionally protected rights and powers. Such rights are assigned only to the individual members of society in so far as they are legal entities. For this reason, there has been no mention of a legally guaranteed sphere of responsibility[8] of society, but only of human rights or constitutional rights of the individual. The constitutional position of the individual vis-à-vis the representatives of executive power[9] is indeed the only thing that the practised legal eye is able to perceive for only legal subjects can be holders of legal positions and of rights. 'Society', however, is not a legal subject. It possesses no institutions which might be able to form a common will. Indeed, apart from the state, it does not even have an administrative apparatus of its own which might be able to procure for it some function within the framework of safeguarding of interests vis-à-vis the

---

5 "*rechtsstaatlich*".
6 *personifiziert*.
7 read: a subject of.
8 read: competences.
9 *Staatsgewalt*.

state. In consequence, when the lawyer thinks of the constitutional state, the picture flashes before his mind's eye: the individual and his state. The idea of society and its state does not convey any real thought to him.

This is not only the case with lawyers. The entire area which was inspired by the slogans of human rights thought of the tense relationship between the state and the individual. Even the opponents of the French Revolution took up this antithesis and imputed to the spirit of the Enlightenment that, as a result of the destruction of medieval society, man had been torn out of all his traditional and familiar social moulds and dragged, as it were, naked as a helpless and trembling creature, directly before the pitiless countenance of the colossal monster - the Leviathan of the 'state'. Thereby, all the topsoil had been scraped out of the earth of the nations. The hierarchically structured society which had once been so familiar had been robbed of its native character and, at the same time, the state had also been transformed into an impersonal mechanical skeleton. The world has been hearing such accusations as these for seven to eight generations from conservative, socialist, middle-class[10] and clerical quarters.

Nevertheless, the assumption that the French Revolution emancipated the individual from society is based on a fallacy. I do not wish to dispute here whether there were political and philosophical movements which wanted something of this nature. Rather I should like to establish, purely factually, that the French Revolution from the constitutional point of view, did not emancipate the individual from society, rather it left him in society. The only thing that happened was that the society was transformed from a feudal society of privileges, which amongst other things also possessed a private law, into a pure private law society. A private law society, however, is by no means merely a coexistence of unconnected individuals but is a plurality of people who are subject to a uniform order, indeed, to be more precise, a legal order. The private law order draws up rules to which the members of society are subjected when they enter into agreements with one another, acquire goods and titles from one another, co-operate with one another or exchange services on the basis of agreements, or else act, plan or are inactive outside all contractual relationships. Over and above all this, it delegates[11] to all persons who move within its jurisdiction, an extremely extensive freedom of movement, a competence for planning and existence

---

10 *Mittelständisch.*
11 *teilt zu.*

in relation to their fellow men, a status within the private law society which is by no means simply a gift of nature - a dowry of natural talents and will-power - but a social civic right[12].

In a word, anyone who in the structure of the modern, post-revolutionary, democratic industrial nation perceives only the state on the one hand and the individual on the other, overlooks an important element of modern constitutional reality. The legal reality is that the individual, given the constitutional scheme upon which all modern constitutional states are based, is bound to his state through the medium of the private law society.

It is true, of course, that the individual is confronted with the modern state without the intercession of so-called intermediate social authorities. He can create such intermediate authorities by means of private law contracts or by joining already created organisations with membership sanctioned by private law. Yet he must obtain these facilities by using his private autonomy; he will not come upon them, for instance, as a constituent of the political constitution. This applies even to political parties without which the citizen cannot accomplish much in a free state if he wishes to avail himself of his political franchise. They are also private clubs, created by the members of the private law society by virtue of their private autonomy with the aid of resources which private law makes available but they are not constituents of the political constitution. The main point, however, is that since the abolition of the feudal society, the private law society has been embodied in the[13] state but not as an accumulation of millions of unconnected individuals.

Society, then, is held together by an effective private law system but it does not possess any institutions of any kind nor has it any capacity to act either *vis-à-vis* its own members or outside forces, or for that matter its own state. It must now be asked how it is possible to visualise, legally or sociologically, the embedding of this private law society in the overall community[14] comprising state and society and interlocking with the state. What is the legal relation between the private law society and independent private law subjects?

---

12 *gesellschaftliches Bürgerrecht*. Böhm continues: "Not a natural faculty but a social permission".
13 *zugeordnet dem*.
14 *Gemeinwesen*.

FRANZ BÖHM AND THE THEORY OF PRIVATE LAW SOCIETY

It would be easy to be misled in answering these questions if the realities of formulating positive law were not considered. It can be observed from events in the past how the private law system gained and kept its authority - who interpreted the law, decided disputes and enforced obedience to decisions - and the methods of doing so. There will be registers and records of the private law system and information on those who provided the diverse auxiliary services. These cannot be provided without political authority, however, on which a developed and dynamic private law practice depends. Consideration of laws and legal and commercial reality indicates that the state as possessor of the machinery of political power comes to the aid of this mute corporeal private law society. A private law society cannot function without authority[15], even if it does have to assert itself against external or internal dangers. It requires a support, which it cannot produce from within its own resources, in order to function at all. This support, however, while admittedly only subsidiary, is nevertheless by nature invested with authority. Similarly, functions which are of no other use than to promote social functions such as the sovereign right to regulate the coinage, the right to stipulate weights and measures to regulate port traffic, trade fairs and markets, are among the oldest prerogatives of monarchs.

This view of the state is related to the fact that people were not merely prepared to invest the state with its essential, pompously resplendent, sovereign and ceremonial duties but also with lowly services of the night-watchman to the private law society. They saw in the devoted and intelligent performance of the night-watchman's services the essential and most important purpose of the state.

This conception might be outlined roughly as follows: the private law society complements[16] the functions of the sovereign body even if only to a modest extent and even if merely to allow natural development of their activities, so that the private law system can co-ordinate the plans of all its members in line with the system. To maintain its life blood it needs an armed night-watchman. It should be noted, however, that the plans of its members are guided by private law silently, automatically and with an amazing minimum of resistance caused by friction and disobedience.

The *modus operandi* of the private law system is characterised by the fact that people are not supplied with a prescription of the behaviour ex-

---

15 *Obrigkeit.*
16 read: requires assistance by.

pected of them *vis-à-vis* innumerable known and unknown members of society with equal rights. Rather it is left to their discretion. Moreover, people are expected to guess and find out for themselves the attitude that is in each case correct or expedient, that is to say they individually adjust, as it were, to the constellation of the outside world by taking their bearings from the social data known to them.

The need for each individual to bring his individual planning and attitude into line with the plans of others and with the social data, is given by the social situation itself. Anyone who moves among persons of equal rights and is dependent upon his peers, has to adapt to society. Here coercion derives from the situation, not from political authority. Anyone who lives within a community[17] has the right to plan and act independently, so long as he takes into account the rights and reactions of fellow men. Equal freedom of all others imposes an inherent limit upon the freedom of each and everyone and to this extent implies a kind of coercion for each and every free person concerned.

It may be argued, of course, that this system amounts to nothing more than a lottery, equally intolerable from the point of view of ethics, justice and social solidarity. Before passing such a harsh judgement, however, it should be borne in mind that the reactions of others in society are an extremely important source of information to any one individual wishing to undertake certain actions. Initially he will be in the dark, in a vast thicket of social data with only a very few of which he is familiar. The signals denoting success or failure which he receives suddenly bring some light into this darkness - now, at least, he knows how his fellow men have reacted. He will try to draw conclusions from these answers and adjust his future behaviour accordingly.

The coercion indicated by the signals is clear enough but must be distinguished from all legal and imperative coercion by the fact that the legal freedom of the person facing censure by others is not infringed upon. Whether one prefers to be pulled out by fate[18] or by public prosecutors, judges, police officials, ministerial and party officials, that is to say, by fellow men who dress up in the finery of authoritarian power, is a matter of taste.

---

17 *Gesellschaft von Menschen.*
18 i.e. by his failure.

FRANZ BÖHM AND THE THEORY OF PRIVATE LAW SOCIETY

The compulsion which takes place in a co-ordinated system is also to be distinguished from mandatory and imperative coercion. The member of society who is induced, as a result of his own failure, to change his attitude does not have a certain specific behaviour prescribed for him which he is to adopt henceforth in place of his former behaviour.

Signalling Systems in a Society

Yet this presupposes that social co-operation, based upon co-ordination between autonomous but not self-sufficient individuals, has a signalling system. The individuals making their own plans must be able to gather information about the planning, attitude and reaction of their fellow men and also about a series of other social data from outside which is as reliable and timely as possible. They do not want to be forced to make continuous and rapid adjustments to their plans as such adjustment may require costly investigations.

It was a discovery of vital importance when it was realised that such signalling systems do exist, that they have been cut and polished into shape by the instinctively intelligent everyday behaviour of innumerable generations of individuals in the course of history, more or less without the help of conscious human understanding. The most important of these signalling systems are language, private law, and market prices.

Even the internal structure of individual crystals within the general crystal of the private law system is so suited to excite admiration that many lawyers, as if blinded by the aesthetic magic of such a degree of logical unity, have not noticed at all how extremely effective the private law system is as an instrument of social control[19]. By laying down the rules which are compatible with the co-operation and coexistence of persons of equal rights responsible for their own conscious planning, the private law system simultaneously also influences imperceptibly, yet very effectively, the selection of individual plans, their content and their accommodation to the plans of others. Private law also is a social creation which, although composed and thought up by the people, once it is there, composes and thinks for everyone just as a language does.

Finally, as far as the last and most recent of these signalling systems, the market price system, is concerned, it is of all the signalling systems produced by society the most mechanical or exact. It is a system, which pre-

---

19 here and in the following control = *Lenkung, Steuerung*.

supposes a whole series of further social creations: first and foremost a highly developed civil law order; second, money; and third, an unusual degree of mobility of, and information about, social events.

Yet if the controlling force of market prices does not consist in bringing the partial plans of the autonomous participants into line with an overall plan and with a national result which is known and desired in advance, of what does it consist? The answer is as follows: the controlling force of the signals consists in the fact that they co-ordinate the partial plans of all participants on the basis of decisions which are made by these participants. Such co-ordination would include the mutually acceptable bargains, valid as exchange agreements in private law, which are agreed each day and in every instance of a movement of goods from one person to another.

What this means is that when the sale and delivery of goods takes place, the agreement of everyone involved in the transaction between the buyer and the seller legitimises the transaction. All persons participating in the movement of goods between persons indicate by the voluntary conclusions of agreements that they regard the transaction concerned as being in their interest. For each buyer the commodity is worth the money, for each seller the money received is worth parting with the commodity. In this respect, therefore, a given flow of goods has been moved via chains of voluntarily-concluded mutually-beneficial agreements through the transmission of information on demand requirements. This balancing of interests, which is in each case bilateral, is linked indirectly through the co-ordinating force of a private law transaction, namely by the contractual exchange agreement or the reciprocal obligation, the classic manifestation of which is the purchase. The exchange agreement and its fulfilment is the characteristic mode of co-operation between independent traders with equal rights. In this respect, therefore, the private law system is very decisively involved in controlling free market processes.

If prices are supposed to control the production plans of businesses which specialise in the regular production of specific goods, then prices which must be individually negotiated with each new transaction will prove less useful indicators. Preferable by far would be a method whereby when the agreements are being concluded, the negotiation of prices could be dispensed with and the sale offer could be based upon a price which was the same for all buyers and which, at the same time, tended to be adopted as the offer price by all competing sellers. Such a price would not have to be calculated at the desk on the basis of some statistical procedure or other; it would be a price which would be levelled out through careful observation of the market and of the customer reaction. There would be what might be called a power struggle but it would be a power struggle which ends with a decision which takes into account the interests of all customers and all suppliers of goods, a decision upon which no participant has any ascertainable influence. For any individual good at any time this process would produce a nearly uniform price, the level of which would depend on what a knowledgeable buyer and a knowledgeable seller would have in mind, bearing in mind relative scarcity. These are the so-called marginal buyer and marginal producer.

The marginal buyer and the marginal seller are not imaginary, fictitious persons, but real flesh-and-blood participants in any traded good. Put another way, their valuations of the goods to be exchanged, that is, the commodity on the one hand and the money on the other, are least determined by social interdependence. It may be said, therefore, that their valuations alone are influenced by the availability of purchasing power determined by a given distribution of national income and monetary policy and of the scarcity of the good concerned which, in turn, results from the composition of the overall quantity of goods supplied. In this way, the dependence of the individual member of society on all other members of society and on the functioning of a social system based on co-ordination (which is the mark of any society in which division of labour operates) becomes most evident. At the same time, no one individual is specifically dependent on particular individuals, social groups or classes. It is the arrangement by which the existence of the freedom of the individual is limited only by the equal freedom of all others or, to put it differently, it is the arrangement which occurs when there is an `association` in which the free development of each is the condition for the free development of all[20].

The General Will and the Free Market Economy

It is important to realise here that the functioning of the free market system presupposes the existence of a private law society. All members of society must enjoy the status of private autonomy, no member must be restricted and none may have more powers than those vested by private

---

20 Böhm's footnote: "This quotation from the Communist manifesto could serve as leading principle for private law society and its market economy".

autonomy. In associating[21] with one another, all members are restricted to resting content with the facilities provided by private law for the purpose of reaching their aims and purposes, which means that private autonomy must not include the power to command or tax another person. All decisions which require the use of force for their realisation and which must be vested with general liability[22] should require *volonté générale*. The only holders of *volonté générale*, however, should be the state or the local authorities.

The tasks which must be reserved for the *volonté générale* in a market economy include anything connected with the realisation of free market conditions. However great the scope given to the private autonomy of those engaged in economic activity in a market economy, it is nevertheless an established fact that even in the market economy, the function of laying down the ground rules covering private, autonomous plans cannot be the responsibility of the individual.

There has never been any difference of opinion over this thesis as far as the system of private law is concerned; private law plays a very active part in making the free market function. Establishing norms of private law is a legislative act. Whether this act is carried out by statute law or common law[23] is immaterial. Common law provisions also are normative provisions which are entitled to have binding force and to which the members of the legal community owe obedience whether or not they agree with the content and worth of the provision concerned. Yet, as already explained, private autonomy contains no title of private jurisdiction over those who do not consent to a contract or other transaction. The power to establish generally binding norms is essentially a political power which extends further than the autonomy authorised to a legal person responsible only to himself for his actions. Whoever lays claim to such authority assumes responsibility for interference in the sphere of others. The exercising of such authority must therefore be determined by rules other than those covering sole responsibility for one's own actions in which any inclusion of third parties is admissible only in so far as the legal agreement of these third parties is obtained.

The same thesis also applies, however, to those constituent parts of the free market system which do not have the character of legal provisions. In particular two important provisions apply.

---

21 *Verkehr*.
22 *Allgemeinverbindlichkeit*.
23 read: consuetudinary law.

FRANZ BÖHM AND THE THEORY OF PRIVATE LAW SOCIETY

First there is the sum total of all those measures which must be taken if bilaterally negotiated prices are to be successfully replaced by market prices, the level of which is the result of the social process of continuous equalisation and adaptation through arbitrage described by marginal utility theory. These measures include, for example, all efforts on the part of a government aimed at increasing road safety, improving the intelligibility of the economic process as well as the quality and universal character of news, freedom of movement and the movement of all those involved in economic activity. Above all, measures such as those aimed at protecting freedom of speech, of scientific work and of discussion are included.

The second provision consists of eliminating or minimising the influence exerted upon the price-fixing process by personal or other unilateral or disproportionate pressures whether these concern individuals or are limited to groups within society. This includes, in particular, the measures of a legislative or administrative nature which aim at influencing the market form, that is, creating favourable conditions for the emergence of effective competition. This entails counteracting the formation of monopolies and, if effective competition cannot be achieved, impairing the emergence of unilateral monopolies by promoting the effectiveness of other controls and countervailing actions. This would be in keeping with the maxim: a partial monopoly is better than a monopoly, a bilateral monopoly is better than a unilateral one, an oligopoly is better than a monopoly or partial monopoly and a partial oligopoly is better than a partial monopoly.

Furthermore, contained within the framework of regulating and controlling measures is the provision for a stable currency, which is indeed of central importance because price stability determines the aptitude of market prices to guide the production process in an economically correct way and to secure prices against speculative disturbances.

The idea of transforming the multi-tier society[24] into a private law society consisting of equally free people with equal rights aims at nothing less than a society in which the subjection of man to man and the exploitation of man by man must be stopped. This essay is not concerned with the question as to whether this idea was reasoned out thoroughly enough and whether and to what extent it has been realised. In the context of these reflections, it is sufficient for the present to realise that a start had to be made on bringing about equality by eliminating inequalities in the law. To this end it

---

24 add: of the pre-revolutionary era.

was necessary for all legal positions which owed their existence to the violent process of imposition to be cast aside.

The most important of these objectionable legal positions were the feudal sovereign rights (represented by the serfdom of the farming population) and the trade and industrial privileges. The latter were, historically, a phenomenon that appeared much later and they served the purpose of integrating into the two-tier society a group of individuals who were outside the feudal nexus. The abolition of serfdom was bound to be achieved at the expense of the ruling class[25] and signified their complete downfall. The abolition of trade and industrial privileges, on the other hand, did not directly affect the feudal hegemony because there was no legally-based state of dependence in the relationship between the feudal aristocracy and the free (privileged) traders.

By contrast, any award of privileges creates a legal relationship between the possessor of privileges and the executive power[26]. The abolition of the system of privileges meant, therefore, that a quite specific executive function and a quite specific sovereign prerogative had to be removed from the power of the executive. The right to act as an entrepreneur had also to be made a constituent part of private autonomy, that is, it required recognition of the competence of the private citizen to conduct his own economic affairs. In future, any intervention by the executive power in the plans and action of a trader would, under constitutional law, have the character of an encroachment on the freedom of the individual which is guaranteed under private law. The state executive was then required to obtain specific authorisation in the form of a genuine legal statute of general validity, that is, one that did not apply to the individual case alone. In the course of the constitutional[27] distribution of planning authority between the executive and a member of society, the decision as to the establishment of a commercial enterprise and the content of its programme of activity should lie with the private citizen[28] and not with the executive. In the event that state action is necessary to correct the private plans of the entrepreneurs, then the state should on no account be allowed to confer privileges as such a measure

---

25 *Herrenschicht*.
26 see 7.
27 see 3.
28 *Privatrechtssubjekt*.

would be compromised by the fact that it had been made to serve the end of preserving the feudal society and its hierarchical origins.

It must be kept in mind that the abolition of trade privileges had originally been made necessary by the plan to abolish feudal society, even before economic policy considerations were added. Before these economic policy matters gained ground, there were probably no clear views as to the extent to which governmental power should be used to control economic activity. People had certain ideas as to which means the government should not be allowed to use for this purpose and which purposes should not be permitted to be pursued by state intervention in the economic process. Only when philosophical and scientific investigations tackled the question as to what actually happens in a market economy in those areas in which government control is laid aside, did it come about that, for reasons relating to economic policy and theory, the stipulation was made that the government should refrain as far as possible from any intervention. Government should restrict itself to defining and maintaining the regulative framework[29] and also to the role of arbitrator; in other words, the influence of government on the system should be neutral in its effect.

The scientific insights which led to such a postulate were, of course, most warmly welcomed by those generations which had in mind a free society of autonomous citizens protected from oppression and pillage, for they now justified, from the point of view of practicality also, the great objectives of the revolution which envisaged three things:

(a) the establishment of private law society;

(b) the transfer of executive power to the members of the private law society in their entirety;

(c) a drastic easing of the burden of tasks imposed upon the executive power.

The restriction of government tasks makes it possible for the people to exercise their sovereignty effectively and to control the government appointed by parliament so efficiently that no new pressure groups[30] would be formed within the governmental controlling organisations[31]. These organisations[32] would not be in a position, by virtue of their indispensability as

---

29 *Ordnungsrahmen.*
30 *neue Machtgruppen.*
31 *Herrschaftsorganisationen.*
32 = 28.

specialists, to withdraw from any controlling influence which governed subjects try to exert.

Character of the New Society

Within society itself no power groups should be formed which would make it possible for others, individually or as groups, to be subjugated and exploited. The populace should be protected against this danger by the system of price competition, by the absence of social privileges and by the need to ensure a fair system by which services or assets could be subject to voluntary exchange agreements to ensure equivalent payment. Likewise, the formation of particular positions of power within the sphere of the state should not be possible. Protection against this danger should be provided by the development of democratic controls, universal suffrage, the accountability of the government to parliament and, above all, by limitation of the functions of government and their restriction to the development and maintenance of the regulative framework. It was a well-devised plan encompassing the whole society, the state and the interlocking of both. No one predicted that this concept, at the time when it emerged and matured in the seventeenth and eighteenth centuries, would be criticised at a later date by those who also aspired to a society free of suppression and exploitation 'in which the free development of each is the condition for the free development of all'. The later critics thought that such a society was a cunning system of suppression in the service of a new class of exploiters.

This view, which was expressed in the first half of the nineteenth century, was followed by some bitterly critical analysis later in the century. The phenomenon which came in for the greatest criticism was the plutocratic character of the new society. The distinction between ruling caste and *villeins* peculiar to the feudal system was replaced by the distinction between poor and rich. In particular, the distinction was between that class of society whose only source of income is the sale of their labour and the class which can also obtain income by making some of their capital available for the production process for reward (interest on capital). (Ultimately, they made such a large income that they were no longer dependent upon their physical labour.) The advocates of the free market system were fully aware of this peculiarity from the outset. No one, however, could have accurately predicted its social implications, the way in which it would appear historically following the establishment of the private law society, the accompanying state system and the consequences for the social climate.

FRANZ BÖHM AND THE THEORY OF PRIVATE LAW SOCIETY

If this wealthy class had appeared merely as a class of rentiers which consumed its income from capital at leisure or even formed new additional useful wealth from the non-consumed surpluses, then the social, political and moral reaction might perhaps have been restricted to annoyance at the inequality of the free market distribution of income and wealth. It is, however, characteristic of the free market society that not only is the satisfaction of consumer needs well above the average for the members of the wealthy class but also they are offered totally different possibilities of productive activity within society.

The socially most important task which appeals to the zest for enterprise of intelligent, daring people gifted with a combination of imagination and organisational talent, is that of combining their own and other people's capital with their own and other people's working capacity to produce an operational success. Therefore, the task of an entrepreneur also presupposes, unless concerns of a really modest scale are involved, the possession of substantial capital. In the private law society anyone who is dependent upon the capital and services of other people in order to achieve any private autonomous plans, must conclude exchange contracts against payment which make him the creditor in respect of the demands for his output and the debtor in respect of the obligation to pay for inputs. As a debtor he is obliged, by virtue of the system of private law, to meet punctually the wage claims of his workers, the claims of his suppliers and the interest claims of his investors. He will usually have to meet deadlines for these claims far ahead of the time when he first receives income from the sale of the goods he produces and entirely irrespective of whether his entrepreneurial activity yields profits or results in losses. For this reason, anyone who wishes to run an enterprise has no chance of finding workers, suppliers and creditors unless he is backed by adequate capital which the workers, suppliers and creditors assume will offer them an adequate security for payment of wages, supplies and interest even if the enterprise is unsuccessful.

Those members of the wealthy class who are actively engaged as entrepreneurs no doubt deserve a better social image than the pure rentiers who live on their interest and may, even with very luxurious consumption patterns, still have difficulty in avoiding becoming even richer. Anyone actively engaged as an entrepreneur devotes himself, at his own risk, to the most important social function there is within a free market system. Over and above this, in so far as he invests his own capital and labour in his own enterprise, he waives any actionable interest claim for making available parts of his private assets. Indeed, he even waives the claim to redemption of his own invested capital and also any actionable claim to salary for his labour input.

Therefore, instead of investing his assets in another person's enterprise (and receiving interest on his investment) and making his entrepreneurial skills and working capacity available to another person's enterprise in return for a large salary, the independent entrepreneur makes all these sacrifices *au fonds perdu*, in order to gain the satisfaction of being actively engaged as an entrepreneur. His source of income is then only business profit, that is to say the annual surplus of the returns over the costs, in the event that such a surplus is made. Over and above the shown profit he can also, quite legally, make withdrawals from the business capital for private consumption purposes but he then renders himself accountable under civil law to his creditors and may even be in violation of the law if he jeopardises claims of his creditors by such conduct. The same applies if his enterprise should incur losses. As soon as the repayment of his liabilities is jeopardised, he must promptly declare himself bankrupt in accordance with the provisions of the law or set in motion judicial proceedings in order to avert bankruptcy. In any event, the entrepreneur must always fully satisfy his creditors, even if his enterprise is working at a loss. If he becomes insolvent or refuses to pay, the company's creditors have the right to claim the entire private assets of the entrepreneur (including his house and personal belongings), for the purpose of settling their accounts.

It must be admitted that operating as an independent entrepreneur is socially by far the most meritorious occupation to which individuals of great wealth can devote themselves. It is an occupation which is suited to legitimising socially the possession of great wealth and justifying socially, rationally, and morally, a social system which permits and even promotes great differences of wealth and income. In any case, experience has shown that the members of the propertied class crowd in large numbers into the entrepreneurial profession and that those who do not do so are demonstrably eager to invest large sums of capital and, indeed, also of their income. Certainly, they act in this way partly because they expect material profit and partly because it is a most satisfying application of their resources and talents. It is a fact that no single system in recorded history has managed, with anything like the same degree of success as the private law society (with the economic system accompanying it), to induce the wealthy classes to participate in the production process and to invest almost their entire wealth in it -

the feudal lords loathed and despised trade and production. Even the authors of the Communist manifesto have stressed the totally unpredictable extent to which the system of co-ordination has managed to unleash productive energies.

Criticisms of the New Society
Nevertheless, the charges preferred against the plutocratic character of free market income distribution have been directed primarily against the entrepreneurs, not against the wealthy annuity-consumers. This may be because they are the activist-élite, representative of the entire propertied class. The chief reason, however, is probably because of the rival interests of wage-earner and entrepreneur. The interest of the entrepreneur is in as high a business profit as possible and this is synonymous with the payment of as low wages as possible. Moreover, the entrepreneurs are the representatives of the propertied class who face the workers in the firm as superiors by private agreement and in the labour market as buyers, equipped with the power of disposition over jobs. They are, therefore, in a particularly strong negotiating position.

In the judgement of this critique, the 'bourgeois' revolution is not a liberation movement but a new means of oppression. An antiquated veteran exploiting class was succeeded by a modern class of exploiters, whose members camouflaged themselves as private individuals and disguised their workers as contracting parties. In reality, they were only distinguished from slave-owners by the fact that they did not have to buy their slaves and were therefore not interested in maintaining their working capacity. The techniques of exploitation and oppression were merely changed and refined in the most subtle of ways.

The advocates of the market economy view the problem presented by the danger of exploitation in a different light. In their view there may indeed be a possibility that entrepreneurs will exploit the workers by paying too low wages. This possibility does not exist as a general rule, however, but only under certain preconditions which are known and can be described. In so far as the occurrence of one or other of these preconditions can be deliberately brought about by the entrepreneurs, there are possibilities of self-help for the workers and also possibilities for the legislator, the government or the courts. Employers can be prevented from exploiting workers and, in the event that they have done so, they can be made to abandon their practices. In so far as exploitation has been made possible by the presence of social or political or natural factors which can only be settled by the joint efforts of society, by acts of legislation or administration or, if necessary, by means of agreements with other states, then the attempt must be made to remedy those situations which promote exploitation.

This constitutes one of the most urgent problems facing society and the state. It has long since been identified and attempts have been made to deal with it; the extent to which it has been solved is open to question. It may be said that today the danger no longer has anything like the same degree of pressing urgency, that in many cases even the reverse danger has come into view, namely the danger that the national growth rate is being reduced by excessive wage levels, that is, by wages which lie above the scarcity wage. The assumption that the problem of removing the danger of exploitation for all practical purposes is soluble, may be based upon careful reflection and borne out by the historical course of development. The situation in a private law society, which is combined with a democratically structured constitutional state, favours the realisation of a social structure which makes the attempt by social groups to exploit other social groups a more and more hopeless undertaking. It is one which is even more dangerous for the originators and lends great encouragement to the tendencies, in state and society, not to tolerate attempts at exploitation.

An examination of the points at which, within the overall system, symptoms of failure and erroneous development currently appear will indicate that they are not so much in the sphere of society as near the boundary position between society and state.

Rousseau considered the division of labour to be no longer reversible. He was therefore preoccupied with the question of how man can free himself from subjection to the authorities without relinquishing the functions devolving upon the authorities in the interest of the governed. He answered this question in a way which at first strikes the reader, who is thinking of its practical side, as a philosophical trick. Expressed in simple terms the solution reads as follows: if people wish to be freed from subjection to human authorities, then the governed subjects must take command of the government and perform the functions of the authorities themselves. They must themselves become rulers, yet at the same time also remain governed subjects and as such submit voluntarily to the decisions and resolutions which they have made in their capacity as holders of government authority.

Rousseau was, of course, fully aware that the attempt to make the *volonté générale* an historical reality can only succeed if one unalterable requirement is met, namely the close-knit small[33] society and equally close-knit small state. The division of labour, however, not only makes the state essential but at the same time also causes the state functions to become more and more complicated. Jean-Jacques Rousseau had to, and did in fact, demand that the division of labour was not to be continued any further. Indeed, if at all possible, it was to retreat to an earlier stage of development. In this respect Rousseau called for the ascetic society, which was again a decidedly pedagogic concept. Herein lies the specifically politico-social importance of his now famous watchword: back to nature!

Although Rousseau's ideas were logically cogent, they were simply unattainable. It was a romantic, very conservative illusion, not just in Rousseau's times but even in very much earlier stages of historical development. Yet, if these preconditions were unattainable, then that meant the death warrant for the idea of the sovereignty of the people. The ethical aspect of the concept had no chance of becoming a reality.

An Alternative Society

At this point, however, an unforeseen ray of hope appeared. Other contemporary thinkers put forward the possibility of an `open` society[34] which would not be an ascetic society. It would allow the further division of labour but the range of government activity would be restricted. In this society, the individual plans of members of society would be controlled with the help of an automatically functioning co-ordination system. This would relieve the state of the task of central economic control and would restrict it to the task of defining the structural framework[35] which would preserve and enforce observance of the control laws. Moreover, the role of the state in the overall enforcement of this system would be so constituted that it would severely limit political discretion. If a political decision was taken to adopt such a system, then the rules would be laid down as to: (i) the task of the legislator, (ii) the role and duties of the government and (iii) the principles by which the courts would interpret the law.

This system is based upon an instrumental and procedural `score` of a predominantly standard[36] character which has been worked out to the last

---

33 Übersehbar.
34 *Möglichkeit, den Staat übersehbar zu machen.*
35 *Rahmenordnung.*
36 normative.

detail. The margin of discretion given to the autonomous members of society is limited by the peculiarity of their co-ordinated actions and by the consequent special feature of objective mutual interdependence. The margin of discretion given to persons with political authority is limited by the compulsion to submit to the mechanism of control which is laid down as in a musical score, as a modest - I should like to say both socially and politically harmless - minimum. This minimum, though it leaves many options open to the creative imagination which conforms to the system, nevertheless severely restricts the possibilities of ignoring the score and acting in a manner which does not conform to the system by setting the furies of economic and political disaster on the heels of the sinners.

In this system the governed are not only presented with the possibility of understanding political events to some extent, but the system itself also provides them with a rule book, so that they are placed in a position by which they can keep a critical eye on legislation, the measures taken by the government and the administration of justice in the courts.

In this way and within the scope of the possibilities offered, the governed members of the nation are given a real chance to assert sovereignty and exercise it to all practical purposes. Sovereignty is, of course, confined to electing deputies, who for their part exercise legislative authority co-operatively and appoint and control the government or at least the head of government. There is a risk, of course, that the appointed delegates of the people might disregard the popular will and form an independent *volonté professionelle* in place of the *volonté générale*. This risk is limited by the constitution which lays down the authority of each estate[37] so that the demands on the virtue of the governed, the *esprit de corps*[38], are relatively more modest than with Jean-Jacques Rousseau.

Difficulties may arise, however, when the popular will is expressed through elections and through public opinion. What the people expect from the government may diverge from what the constitution regards as the task of the government, at least in the economic sphere and within the scope of the free market system.

The constitutionally determined mandate to legislator and government in this respect is to create, preserve and manage that regulative framework which guarantees the functioning of the free market as an allocative de-

---

37 read: which necessitates certain rules and coercions.
38 *Gemeingeist*.

vice[39]. The decision as to the success or failure of all those involved in the economic process within the private sector, as to the nature and level of their incomes and thereby their production and consumption plans is therefore already taken care of through the market mechanism. The task of government consists merely in creating the conditions enabling this control mechanism to operate in accordance with the constitution. Accordance with the constitutional mandate is desired not only for itself, it is also in the interests of all citizens of the state that the government adheres strictly to this mandate. This interest exists as long as the free market system is adhered to. The only rational alternative would be an interest in abolishing the system. By contrast, the interest in damaging the system by conduct that is contrary to the 'core' is irrational and can be rationally justified, at best, as the strategy of revolution.

Problem of Pressure Groups

Empirically, of course, matters are such that in any system which is dependent upon the organising force of rules, it is possible for any participant and for any group of participants to obtain benefits by violating the rules. This occurs at the expense of other participants or groups of participants. In the market economy, also, it is possible to make a source of income out of cheating. For example, participants or groups of participants may try to cheat even in the sphere of the private law society. They do so on their own initiative, that is by deliberately abusing their private autonomy, whether in the disreputable form of unfair competition, usury and fraud or in the more honest but more harmful form of attempting to monopolise markets, for instance, by forming cartels.

Much more effective, however, is the attempt by groups of participants to recall the fact that their members are indeed voters with a share in the sovereignty of the people and to bring these qualities of their contributors to bear in the sphere of the state and politics. In this case, the individual does not expose himself to the odium of cheating but demands are made of the legislator or the government to elevate cheating to a legislative or governmental programme. Whoever acts as sovereign lives, as it were, in the blameless pastoral innocence where protective duties, tax privileges, direct subsidies, price supports, initial support for establishing monopoly or `orderly markets` can be demanded; it is even possible that social and po-

---

39 *des marktwirtschaftlichen Lenkungsmechanismus.*

litical reputations could be enhanced. This involves an influence, pursued in contest with rival pressure groups and exerted in superior style, on the formation of the *volonté générale* and in favour of groups of people engaged in economic activity who have organised themselves to promote a particular interest (*volonté particulaire*). It is the state itself which is to be enjoined to override the rules of the prevailing order in favour of one group and at the expense of other groups of citizens.

In the context of this study it is nevertheless important to realise that people engaged in economic activity whose interests coincide (workers and employers engaged in agriculture, industry, banking, handicrafts, small industrial firms, one-man businesses, *et cetera*) may be brought together while still safeguarding their own legitimate and obvious interests. Each of these interests, however, may be promoted by non-neutral political intervention in the market price mechanism, even if this would be to the detriment of other interests and almost always to the disadvantage of the regulative and controlling force of the prevailing constitutional system. Even though there is certainly no effective means of preventing political self-destruction, it is nevertheless the mark of a good system that it strengthens those trends in society and state that preserve the system while discouraging those trends that are disturbing to the system. Inherent in pressure group activity, however, is the tendency to push the politics of their state and the system of their state and society in a direction that contradicts the constitutional mandate of the state and is detrimental to the regulative instructions demanded by the political and social constitution.

This being so and given that neither voluntary democratic action nor the right of individuals to join pressure groups may be infringed upon, the only way that remains is to ward off the recognised dangers by means of appropriate attempts to mobilise defence mechanisms.

All sorts of political prejudices stand in the way of this precept. In particular, in the German tradition of thought, the participation of forces which are guided by principles and not interests, by the staging of political and social struggles, meets with resistance, derision and disdain. Every democratic politician or statesman knows and calculates that, no matter how he decides between conflicting forces, he must be prepared for certain disadvantages in the next election. Hence, he will be inclined to take decisions in such a way that those groups who are more important to the government camp are satisfied while dissatisfaction is confined to groups which are not so important for the elections. Yet how is this success to be achieved if bearings are taken from so-called regulative principles, that is, regulative principles from which every pressure group throughout the entire jurisdiction of the state hopes to be exempted? The very idea that the dogmatists might be able to push themselves more into the foreground of political activity drives any political pragmatist to angry despair. What can you do with people in politics who evidently do not appreciate that elections are there to be won? Conversely the pragmatists, even very successful ones, do not have any proper perception of the consequences of the disintegration of a system. They over-estimate the tenacity of political and social systems and assume that the system can assimilate any amounts of wrong decisions without detrimental consequences. The pragmatists not only ignore warnings but react to them with remarkable irritation.

It has already been mentioned that the government also is constantly faced with a considerable temptation to meet the contradictory demands of many pressure groups. By simultaneously taking into account group interests that oppose each other a government would not make itself as unpopular as it would if it adhered to principles. Thus it is not only the pressure groups that scratch each others' backs but also the pressure groups in association with the government.

It is certainly no exaggeration to describe these directly opposite events which tend to occur as a danger to the social system. The fact that this tendency is, as it were, in the nature of things makes it a weakness of the system which must be taken seriously.

In these circumstances, it is the duty of the scientist to draw the attention of the public to the danger. Unfortunately, it is precisely in the area of science that ideological views are held which encourage the actual trends towards a falsification of the system. This is not the case so much in research findings as in speculative hypotheses about historical and sociological forces or about the presumed interdependencies of different variables; these hypotheses often have no link with reality.

There is, for instance, much talk of 'intermediary powers' by which are meant these very pressure groups. If, by this expression, the intention is to delineate those functions which the associations claim for themselves, irrespective of the structure of the system which they also recognise, then no objection need be raised. A great deal more, however, is read into this term both by pressure groups and representatives of some scientific schools. They state that, thanks to the ministrations of mysterious forces which mould history of which they themselves are a part, the groups have managed to work their way out of the civil law substructure of society into the dignitaries' club of political functionaries. Some sort of sociological force is supposed to be at work. Anyone who has just emerged 'sociologically' need no longer be concerned about legal credentials. One further datum will ensure this, namely that of 'normative forces of actual events'[40].

Importance of Private Law

Indeed to this very day, happily, this involves nothing more than a matter of words which are devoid of any clear legal significance. No one as yet has been able to state clearly the distinction between the normative force of *de facto* occurrences and the exact and proven legal phenomena of negative prescription, forfeiture of right, usucaption or the formation of the common law[41]. The necessity for that distinction which is already discernible is, of course, not mentioned in public discussion. It would appear that what matters is the norm-creating force of very long periods of time during which a previously non-existent right has been claimed or alternatively, an existing right has not been exercised or action has been taken in accordance with a non-valid rule or contrary to a valid rule. By contrast, the `normative force of actual events', does not need the lapse of time. The remedial force of time is replaced by the remedial force of the will of whoever guides events and the strength of his social influence. It is the resistance-crushing radiation of the victorious cause to which homage is paid by the dogma of the 'normative force of actual events'.

In this respect there is an affinity linking this dogma with another legal phenomenon, namely the tenet that a successful revolution nullifies existing law and creates new law.

It is intended, so it would appear, to apply this tenet to actual minor rebellions and 'structural changes', which constantly occur in the core of society. As soon as matters are so arranged that some sufficiently influential group or other has managed to produce a *fait accompli* which, for the time being, can no longer be undermined, then the thunderer Zeus is supposed to appear in the clouds forthwith, if at all possible without observing a decent interval of any kind, to declare solemnly the *fait accompli* as lawful. The pressure group managers like to hear that. This is how the dogma of the

---

40 *"normative Kraft des Faktischen"*.
41 see 21.

'normative force of actual events' is often understood and not only by interested groups.

In legal practice, it would seem that the dogma of the 'normative force of actual events' has as yet achieved little importance. Its fateful importance lies in its psychological effect. Anyone who moves in practical political circles knows how great is the impression which the slogan of the 'normative force of the actual events' makes on the behaviour of those involved in the economic process and frequently on the behaviour of politicians. It fosters the inclination to have central control and saps the will to defend the rule of law and its institutions[42].

In this respect, therefore, signs of deformity clearly manifest themselves in our society. The task of removing this deformity lies before us. It is not Capuchin sermons that are needed but the practical act of putting one's shoulder to the wheel.

The author of this paper whose concern is primarily with legal and legal-political matters, feels that action is now needed. It will be necessary to pay attention first, in the area of jurisprudence, to the danger of neglecting the system of private law[43]. Above all, the belief in the 'normative force of actual events' should be replaced by understanding how standards[44] should govern events.

Further References for Publications in English

BÖHM, FRANZ: "Democracy and Economic power", in: INSTITUT FÜR AUSLÄNDISCHES UND INTERNATIONALES WIRTSCHAFTSRECHT AN DER JOHANN-WOLFGANG-GOETHE-UNIVERSITÄT FRANKFURT AM MAIN/INSTITUTE FOR INTERNATIONAL AND FOREIGN TRADE LAW OF THE GEORGETOWN UNIVERSITY LAW CENTER WASHINGTON D.C. (Ed.): *Kartelle und Monopole im modernen Recht*, Band I, Karlsruhe (C.F. Müller) 1961, pp. 25-45.

---

42 *Verteidigung der Ordnungskraft geltender Ordnungseinrichtungen.*
43 *Gefahr einer Systemverwahrlosung.*
44 norm.

BÖHM, FRANZ: "Private Law Society and the Market Economy", in: A. PEACOCK, H. WILLGERODT (Eds.): *Germany's Social Market Economy, Origins and Evolution*, London (Macmillan) 1989, pp. 46-67.

NÖRR, KNUT WOLFGANG: "Law and Market Organisation: the Historical Experience in Germany From 1900 to the Law Against Restraints of Competition (1957)", *Journal of Institutional and Theoretical Economics*, 151 (1995), pp. 5-20.

NÖRR, KNUT WOLFGANG: "On the Concept of the 'Economic Constitution' and the Importance of Franz Böhm from the Viewpoint of Legal History", *European Journal of Law and Economics,* 3 (1996), pp. 345-356.

TUMLIR, JAN: "Franz Böhm and the Development of Economic-constitutional Analysis", in: A. PEACOCK, H. WILLGERODT (Eds.): *German Neo-Liberals and the Social Market Economy*, London (Macmillan) 1989, pp. 125-141.

Discussion Summary

MICHAEL WOHLGEMUTH

Paper discussed:
KNUT WOLFGANG NÖRR: Franz Böhm and the Theory of the Private Law Society

Franz Böhm's vigorous condemnation of cartels was the first major subject for discussion. It was pointed out that Böhm had somewhat exaggerated his account of the position of major members of the Historical School when he accused them of advocating the building and maintenance of cartels as such. Schmoller, for example, did not unconditionally favour all kinds of cartels. He draws important distinctions depending on whether a cartel is obliged to accept new members or acts like a closed shop; another important distinction would be if cartels are self-regulated or the object of state regulation of decision processes and areas of legitimate collusion. In addition, there may be good reasons to regard cartels as (a) beneficent in some areas (like, e.g., the standardisation of technical norms), (b) "second best" alternatives to mergers (which ought to be regarded much stronger means to restrain competition) or (c) effective arrangements in order to avoid forms of "ruinous competition" such as could be observed during the 1920s or as can be theoretically deduced from a model consisting of an oligopoly of medium-sized firms competing with undifferentiated products (PEUKERT). In addition it was argued that certain forms of "supply-chain-management" could be justified, if they take the form of a cartelization between many (small-scale) suppliers vis- -vis one (large-scale) buyer. One might, e.g., think of "collusive" price-arrangements between the suppliers of Volkswagen, thus creating a countervailing power against a mighty oligopsonist. In fact, such cartels are now being legally accepted within the United Kingdom (KOSLOWSKI). In view of the Japanese economy some experiences of successful rationalisation might also be related to particular forms co-operative or cartelistic behaviour of firms. Also, the Japanese experience suggests that cartels made possible the standardisation of industrial norms

DISCUSSION SUMMARY

which, in turn, allowed for the realisation of economies of scale (YAGI). A similar argument can be put forward for the (so far rather successful) case of investment planning in South Korea (PEUKERT).

The theoretical content and distinguishing traits of the "Private Law Society" were the next focus of the discussion. It was stressed that Böhm's essay on the Privatrechtsgesellschaft (1966) represents a rather rough fragment, a provocative collection of ideas and historical examples rather than a rigorous theoretical system. Also, one can hardly find explicit references that would allow to identify deep intellectual roots within a particular tradition of German legal philosophy (as, e.g. that of Savigny or von Jhering). Hence, the Private Law Society as a collection of socio-economic principles and ideas is a rather innovative concept peculiar to Böhm. At best, some stronger influence of Friedrich A. von Hayek's work *The Constitution of Liberty* can be clearly identified (WOHLGEMUTH, NÖRR). Which particular concept of freedom Böhm seemed to apply was another subject of inquiry (SCHWINGER). It turned out that Böhm can be argued neither to adhere to a (e.g. Hobbesian) utilitarian concept nor to support collectivist ideals (Rousseau). Böhm's rejection of a French-style social romanticism and inclination towards a rather Lockeian understanding of freedom and the rule of law is most clearly stated in Böhm's essay on the rule of law and the modern welfare state (1953), where also the influence of Hayek is most obvious (WOHLGEMUTH).

Still within Böhm's theoretical framework connections to the Hegelian and also to the classical liberal distinction between state and society were debated (KOSLOWSKI, WOHLGEMUTH, NÖRR). Böhm was found to be very much in line with those who demand a rather strict separation between the responsibilities of "society" and "the state". Society consists of private actors who co-ordinate their actions according to voluntary agreements within the abstract rules of private law; the state is represented by society's agents who would above all have the obligation to enforce the rules of the law and act as arbiters. Thus "the state" would be reduced to the role of being "servant" to the private law society. It was further proposed that Böhm used such a conception of state and society not only as a normative concept but also as a reference scheme in order to describe phenomena that in modern social theories described as the mutual interpenetration of state and society. It was argued that the more the state permeates private (market-) co-ordination by ways of intervention, the more political decision makers are in danger of being captured by powerful interest groups thus creating what

DISCUSSION SUMMARY

Böhm called the "wild refeudalisation of society". This idea which is today used by such different scholars as Public-Choice economists, but also, e.g., Böckenförde or Habermas was argued to be a "modern" and lasting contribution of Böhm (WOHLGEMUTH). Such similarities, however, were also regarded to be highly superficial - more fundamental differences within the respective social philosophies being far more dominant (NÖRR). Concerning Böckenförde's lines of thought it was argued that he, contrary to Böhm, has his intellectual roots in Carl Schmitt, but also in Lorenz von Stein. Consequently, Böckenförde would rather stress the malaise of the state being captured by rich and powerful parts of society, whereas Böhm would lay the stress on the dangers of state interventionism (KOSLOWSKI). Finally, the very idea that state enforcement must always be present in order to enforce private contracts was questioned by ways of pointing to the existence and growth of international trade within what may be called the "international private law society". It is here that rules of a spontaneous order have developed that belong to a "new lex mercatoria" (law of merchants) which has been privately established and still today can be privately enforced (KOSLOWSKI, NÖRR).

Böhm's rather dualistic view of an individualistic (private law-) society on the one hand and the organisation of the state on the other was argued to be inadequate for integrating organisational forms like business corporations, churches, trade unions or political parties (YAGI, KOSLOWSKI). It was conceded that particularities which might require a special legal treatment of special forms of a "legal entity" ("juristische Person") were not sufficiently discussed by Böhm within his fragment-like presentation of Private Law Society (NÖRR).

Chapter 6

Alfred Müller-Armack - Economic Policy Maker and Sociologist of Religion

CHRISTIAN WATRIN

I. Brief Biography
II. Works on Economic Policy
   1. Early Contributions to Economic Policy and to the Theory of State Intervention
   2. National Socialism and Müller-Armack's Retreat into the Sociology of Economics
   3. The Program of the Social Market Economy
III. Müller-Armack's Religious and Socio-cultural Work

I. Brief Biography

Alfred Müller-Armack was born in Essen in 1901, the son of an industrial manager at Krupps. After completing his primary and secondary education, he studied economics, sociology and philosophy at the Universities of Gießen, Freiburg, Munich and Cologne. In 1923 he was granted a doctorate by the Economic and Social Sciences Faculty of the re-founded University of Cologne for his work, "Das Krisenproblem in der theoretischen Sozialökonomik" ("The Crisis Problem in Theoretical Social Economy"). Two and a half years later, he qualified as a lecturer of the same faculty with his thesis "Ökonomische Theorie der Konjunkturpolitik - Versuch einer Neubegründung der absoluten Überproduktionslehre" (Economic Theory of the Trade Cycle Policy - An Attempt to Re-establish the Absolute Doctrine of Overproduction). From 1926 to 1938 Müller-Armack was a non-established lecturer and, then, professor (from 1934) on of the Cologne faculty. In 1939, he was appointed as an established professor and one year later as be a full professor and chair of economic policy at the Münster University. In 1941, together with Ernst Hellmut Vits, he founded the "Forschungsstelle für Allgemeine und Textile Marktwirtschaft" (Research Institute for General and Textile Market Economy) in that city.

Shortly after the conclusion of W.W.II, Müller-Armack came forward with proposals for the reform of the centrally-planned economic system from the National Socialist period. In his book entitled "Wirtschaftslenkung und Marktwirschaft" ("Planned Economy and Market Economy"), which appeared in 1946, he developed a policy program for founding a "Social Market Economy" - a concept which has had a lasting influence on German economic policy. He was a member of discussion groups founded by Walter Eucken, Gerhard Weisser and Hermann Höpker-Aschoff for debating ways out of the deep economic collapse of the post-war years. In 1947 he took part in the famous conference of German university professors in Rothenburg-ob-der-Tauber, at which a program for the reconstruction of the German economy was adopted. In 1948 he was one of the founding members of the Scientific Advisory Board to the Federal Ministry of Economics. Besides that he was one of the first ten German members admitted to the Mont-Pelerin Society - an international organisation of liberal (in the classical sense) economists and social philosophers that was founded in Switzerland by Friedrich A. von Hayek and Wilhelm Röpke in 1947.

In 1950 Müller-Armack was elected to a chair of the Department of Economic Policy of the Faculty of Economic and Social Sciences at the University of Cologne. At the same time the faculty commissioned him to give lectures on the sociology of culture. Together with Franz Greiß he founded Cologne University's Institute for Economic Policy in 1951/52.

In 1952 Ludwig Erhard appointed him to be Head of the Central Policy Unit at the Federal Economic Ministry. Up to 1958 he combined this activity with the performance of his duties as full professor in Cologne. In his capacity as Head of the Central Policy Unit, Müller-Armack was involved with all aspects of German, European and international economic policy during the reconstruction phase of the German economy and the re-establishment of the German economic order, based on the principles of the Social Market Economy. To name but a few of the aspects he dealt with, the liberalisation of foreign commerce and the first steps towards free world trade, the convertibility of the German Mark, the consultations over the

EEC Treaty signed in Rome in 1957 and the shaping of business cycles policy should be mentioned.

With his appointment as Under-Secretary of State for European Affairs (1958), Müller-Armack was immersed in the problems of the construction of the European Economic Community in its early years. He served many times as the German representative to the EEC Council of Ministers. Following his proposal the EEC Committee on Business Cycle Policy was created, which he headed from 1960 until 1963. He participated in many important international conferences occupying positions of great responsibility. After the collapse of negotiations over the entry of Great Britain into the EEC - a step which Müller-Armack emphatically supported - he submitted his resignation from the post of Under-Secretary and returned to the University of Cologne.

Even after his resignation Müller-Armack still served in numerous public offices and performed tasks in the private sector of the economy. For example, he became the Federal Government's Coal Commissioner and a member of the Management Board of the European Bank im Luxemburg. Apart from that, he was a member and also Chairman of the Rheinstahl AG Supervisory Board. He also became the president of the Ludwig-Erhard-Foundation. Throughout his life, Müller-Armack was awarded with numerous public and academic honours.[1] He died in Cologne in 1978.

---

1 See the following Festschriften: GREIß, F., MEYER, F. W. (Eds.): *Gesellschaft und Kultur. Festgabe für Alfred Müller-Armack*, Berlin 1961; MEYER, F. W. and WILLGERODT, H. (Eds.): *Beiträge zur Ordnung von Wirtschaft und Gesellschaft. Festgabe für Alfred Müller-Armack. Institut für Wirtschaftspolitik an der Universität zu Köln*, 1966; WATRIN, CHR. and WILLGERODT, H. (Eds.): *Widersprüche der Kapitalismuskritik. Festschrift zum 75. Geburtstag von Alfred Müller-Armack*, Bern und Stuttgart 1976 and the degree of a doctor honoris causa from the Economic Faculty at the University of Vienna, Austria.

II. Works on Economic Policy

1. Early Contributions to Economic Policy and to the Theory of State Intervention

A great part of Müller-Armack's scholarly work concentrates on basic questions of economic policy and the policy of regulating a market economy, but also covers numerous unpublished memoranda concerning current problems of economic policy.[2] His post-doctoral thesis necessary for his appointment as a lecturer and his first scientific publications[3] deal with the building of theoretical foundations for economic policy. He thoroughly studied the theories of the trade cycle, which developed during the twenties, and programs to fight them. He developed an economic political concept, which he called an "adjustment method". In this context he rejected, on the one hand, the approaches being taken in those days, which sought the elimination of cyclical fluctuations by fixing prices[4]. On the other hand, he opposed the idea that the unimpeded flexibility of wages and prices would best be able to contribute to the recovery of economic activity. The action proposed by him was intended to be a sort of middle ground between the alternatives mentioned. He aspired to control and dampen cyclical variations in economic activity in such a manner that "false moves" and "overcapitalisation" could be avoided and that (through a trade-cycle policy) fluctuations should not be done away with, but probably smoothed out. Towards the end of the book he wrote: "Even if economic crises are characteristics of Capitalism, it would be wrong, all the same, to consider this malady to be untreatable. We note tendencies towards containing the destructive forces, not only in the area of organisation but also in the areas of

---

2 Regarding the latter, see the section "Grundlegende Entwürfe" in: MÜLLER-ARMACK, A.: *Wirtschaftsordnung und Wirtschaftspolitik*, pp. 419-469.

3 MÜLLER-ARMACK, A.: *Ökonomische Theorie der Konjunkturpolitik*. Kölner Wirtschafts- und Sozialwissenschaftliche Studien, Vol. 1, Leipzig 1926; MÜLLER-ARMACK, A.: "Formen der Kreditexpansion und der Kreditpolitik", in: *Die Kreditwirtschaft*, Leipzig 1927; MÜLLER-ARMACK, A.: "Konjunkturforschung und Konjunkturpolitik", in: *Handwörterbuch der Staatswissenschaft*, 4th edition, supplementary vol. Jena 1929, pp. 645-677.

4 For this, see STARBATTY, J.: "Werk und Wirken Alfred Müller-Armacks (1901-1978)", in: *Fragen der Freiheit*, Book 135 (November/December 1978), p. 78.

supply and demand".[5] He worked on this task - the containment of the destructive forces of business cycles - all his life both as an academic economist and as a practitioner of economic policy.

Müller-Armack's concept may be interpreted as a very early version of what was later to become the doctrine of smoothing the dynamic economic process, particularly after W.W.II. Later, admittedly, Müller-Armack was opposed to the full-employment policy inspired by Keynes, even though his thinking was marked by the conviction that trade-cycle policy should be a constant task even in a free-market society, since failures of co-ordination cannot be excluded in principle. Like Schumpeter, he held the view that the expansion of credit that accompanies an economic boom, and which could be affected by banks through an act of credit creation independent of previous savings, was always in danger of causing a misallocation of productive factors. Misapplied investments, though, are the germs spawning later setbacks and contractions in the economy.[6,7] On this account Müller-Armack had already demanded in the thirties that a restrictive credit policy, which brings the potential of banks to create credit under control, should be used as early as possible during the beginning of the upswing and not in the later phase of the boom.[8]

Towards the end of the twenties, the study of trade cycles also meant at the same time a dispute with the Marxian crisis theory and its critique of capitalism. The attack of the Marxists gave rise to an extensive research into capitalism and its institutions. Seen from the standpoint of present-day macro-economics, based on a small number of economic aggregates, and

---

5   MÜLLER-ARMACK, A.: *Wirtschaftslenkung und Marktwirtschaft*, Hamburg 2nd ed. 1948, pp. 35-39.
6   SCHUMPETER, J. A.: *Theorie der wirtschaftlichen Entwicklung*, Berlin 5th ed. 1952, pp. 107-110.
7   MÜLLER-ARMACK, A.: "Konjunkturforschung und Konjunkturpolitik". - ALBERT WISSLER gave an evaluation of this article, which according to him, was still worth reading. See his article in: *Fünfundzwanzigjähriges Jubiläum einer Arbeit über empirische Konjunkturforschung*. On Alfred Müller-Armack's article "Konjunkturforschung und Konjunkturpolitik" 1929, see in: *Vierteljahresheft zur Konjunkturpolitik*, 1954, p. 170ff.
8   See the Foreword of the editors (ERNST DÜRR, HARRIET HOFFMANN, EGON TUCHTFELD, CHRISTIAN WATRIN) to Alfred Müller-Armack's *Ausgewälte Werke, Genealogie der Sozialen Marktwirtschaft, Frühschriften und weiterführende Konzepte*, Bern and Stuttgart 2nd revised edition 1981, pp. 8 seq.

highly-formalised models, access to the older debates can scarcely be found. The elder investigations into capitalism gets its stimulus from traditional ways of thinking, first developed by Marx and elaborated further by Schumpeter in his theory of economic development "to unveil the laws of motion of modern society".[9] Marx's notion, which also plays a prominent part in the German historical school and in the sociology of Comte, is formulated as the *historical* theory of capitalism, in which four stages of economic development (feudalism, capitalism, socialism and full communism) follow each other in inevitable succession.

Later, Schumpeter tried in his contributions to the theory of the dynamic economy[10] to integrate ideas of economic development into economic thinking. Müller-Armack, however, wanted to formulate a general theory, above all in his "Entwicklungsgesetze des Kapitalismus" ("Laws of Capitalist Development") (1932)[11], which was intended to encompass the "entire social economic process". This has been considered to be thoroughly progressive thinking, when evolutionary ideas have been introduced into economic reasoning during recent decades. Müller-Armack's concepts, though, differed considerably from Schumpeter's views. Schumpeter expounded his dynamic evolutionary theory of the so-called capitalistic economic process, above all in 1942, in a manner based on the traditional philosophy of history and transformed Marx's teaching, in which the "anarchical system of competition"[12] inevitably leads to crisis, into the prediction that "[C]apitalism becomes the victim of its own success"[13]. Contrary to this hypothesis Müller-Armack claims that capitalism is an *'open system'*, whose future development *cannot be anticipated*, and is, therefore, *unpredictable*.

---

9 MARX, K.: *Das Kapital. Kritik der politischen Ökonomie*, (Dietz-Verlag) 1957, p. 16.
10 SCHUMPETER, J. A.: *Theorie der wirtschaftlichen Entwicklung. Eine Untersuchung über Unternehmergewinn, Kapital, Kredit, Zins und den Konjunkturzyklus*, Berlin 1st ed. 1911; 5th ed. 1926.
11 MÜLLER-ARMACK, A.: *Entwicklungsgesetze des Kapitalismus. Ökonomische, geschichtstheoretische und soziologische Studien zur modernen Wirtschaftsverfassung*, Berlin 1932, p. 8.
12 MARX, K.: *Das Kapital*, Vol. I, p. 467.
13 SCHUMPETER, J. A.: *Kapitalismus, Sozialismus und Demokratie*, München 2nd revised edition 1950, pp. 103 seq., pp. 252 seq. The English edition of this work appeared in 1942.

In this view lay, firstly, a rejection of the historical-philosophical speculation of Marxist provenance. Secondly, it made goal-oriented actions among men for the purpose of influencing and controlling social, and economic developments meaningful, thus contrasting the historical-deterministic Marxist teachings. In doing so, it inevitably gives attention to the problems associated with market co-ordination and steering. Thirdly, it allocated a central place to ethically-directed reasoning. Seen from this perspective, politics and economic policy could no longer be seen as the fulfilment of an incorrectable historic process[14] - only to be followed, but not changed. According to Müller-Armack, everybody taking part in economic life carries responsibility for his or her actions and decisions. Consequently, questions of ethics and justice lay both at the level of shaping the rules of the game and in the area of individual conduct under these rules. From this follows that questions of ethics and morals should also be the subject of the social and economic sciences.[15]

The construction of a theory of an open dynamic process is the dominant theme of Müller-Armack's early writings.[16] If modern capitalism were to be regarded as a system, in which "economic dynamics becomes the structural principle", then *the trade cycle can be seen as a partial phenomenon of such a general process of evolution where the future is unknown.*

At the same time Müller-Armack also believed that his theory was capable of explaining the roots and causes of the intervening state and the ac-

---

14 A similar position is found with Karl R. Popper, who - coming from scientific-theoretical positions - emphasised in the closing chapter of his critique of Marxism precisely the ethical dimension of an "open" (in the sense of not being historically determined) "society". See POPPER, K. R.: *The Open Society and its Enemies*, Vol. 2, in German translation under the title of *Falsche Propheten. Hegel, Marx und die Folgen*, Bern 1958, pp. 243 seq.
15 The utilitarian-orientated welfare economics reduces economic-ethical questions to positions of marked egalitarianism, especially in their older contributions (Abba P. Lerner, Jan Tinbergen); but in more days time there is a keener expert interest in questions of economic ethics in a much broader sense to be observed in German-speaking areas. See, for instance, the anthology by ENDERLE, G. (Ed.): *Ethik und Wirtschaftswissenschaft (Schriften des Vereins für Socialpolitik, Gesellschaft für Wirtschafts- und Sozialwissenschaften, N. F. Vol. 147)*, Berlin 1985.
16 See MÜLLER-ARMACK, A.: *Entwicklungsgesetze des Kapitalismus*; MÜLLER-ARMACK, A. : *Konjunkturforschung und Konjunkturpolitik*.

tions of special interest groups. His ideas though - unlike the present-day contributions to political economy and to the theory of constitutional economics - did not go in the direction of penetrating other disciplines with the economic paradigm. Instead he had a general social theory in mind, which combined isolated subjects such as political science, sociology and economics with one another.

Müller-Armack argued that modern society could not be explained by Marxist theory, which maintained that the formation of classes is both a consequence of the appropriation of the means of production by the so-called capitalists, as well as a result of the simultaneous separation of the workers from their means of production. Müller-Armack instead contended that the alleged "original accumulation" could not be proven historically and that within the entrepreneurial and capitalist groups - as opposed to the feudal society with its rule that one could never leave the social class into which he or she was born - no personal continuity can be observed. Like Schumpeter[17], he claimed that the Marxist explanation based on the power theory of classes and the ownership of the means of production by the capitalist class was inadequate to explain the structure of modern society. Instead of this, it was necessary to understand that the ascent - and also the descent - of entrepreneurs in modern society stemmed from their functions or malfunctions, respectively, in a dynamic economic system.[18] In a dynamic economy, which was no longer following the rules of feudalism, social advancement depended on one's competitive ability and market performance. Hence, exclusive and closed social units or groups like the nobility were no longer able to survive dominate as they had in the 'Old Society'. Further, the rules of a dynamic market system stipulated that those reaching entrepreneurial positions did not show any recognisable homogeneity neither according to their economic position nor to their social origins.[19] The entrepreneurial social strata of a modern society would not be propped up by any direct power. "It is guaranteed much more by its discharge of economic functions. The market mechanism objectively decides

---

17 SCHUMPETER, J. A.: "Unternehmerfunktion und Arbeiterinteresse", in: SCHUMPETER, J. A.: *Aufsätze zur Wirtschaftspolitik*, Tübingen 1985, pp. 160 seq.
18 See on this MÜLLER-ARMACK, A.: *Entwicklungsgesetze des Kapitalismus*, p. 57 and p. 200.
19 *Idem*, p. 200.

on its rise and fall".[20] The closeness of these ideas to the descriptions of globalisation today is considerable.

In Müller-Armack's opinion, it would be wrong to see in this development the fulfilment of the classical liberal idea of a peaceful society, in which the mutual interest in the furtherance of one's wealth dominates all other political problems. The belief in a society, free of force and coercion, in which rational management of the common interest takes the place of the political struggle, ignores the "essence of politics". It maintains that men, because of the constraints they face everywhere - (one could simplify this by saying: because of the scarcity of resources) - are permanently confronted with the need "for the artificial regulation of human relations". In this regard, however, a universal settlement is unachievable that would be valid at all times, for instance, in the world of a classless society or a peaceful exchange economy. Consequently, no more than a "provisional historical solution"[21] was available. The political sphere, therefore, is - alongside the economic - simply an unavoidable aspect of human existence.

It is from this position that the "interventionist party-state"[22], which arose in the twenties in Germany, should be understood. Its distinguishing mark was not only the wide expansion of its activities since the end of laissez-faire, but simultaneously the regimentation of (economic) society that, from the liberal point of view, lay far outside the State's legitimate powers. In the twenties, political parties, interest groups, cartels and trusts arose, which tried to make themselves politically useful to the State, thereby controlling the political process.[23] This course of events describes the new

---

20 *Idem*, p. 200.
21 *Idem*, p. 197. In recent days FRANCIS FUKUYAMA (*The End of History and the Last Man*, New York 1992) has undertaken the attempt to revive the Hegelian-Marxist concept of a final stage of development in society by maintaining that two institutions won a conclusive victory with the fall of Socialism, namely democracy and the market economy. The development of society is supposed to have reached (with these two institutions) its more-or-less final and highest stage - not unlike the Marxist idea of the classless society. This position is only tenable, if one really generously ignores the constant threats, to which the central institutions of a free society are exposed.
22 MÜLLER-ARMACK, A.: *Entwicklungsgesetze des Kapitalismus*, p. 196.
23 For the significance of the separation of State and Society for the constitution of a liberal polity in modern times, see BÖCKENFÖRDE, E.-W. (Ed.): *Staat und Gesellschaft*, Darmstadt 1976.

reality of the interventionist State, in which *the liberal constitutional separation of State and Society* was no longer a central principle of social order. Consequently, the new system of partisan politics should be made the subject of further economic-political research.

The problems sketched out here are just as real today as they were in Müller-Armack's early days. Political science has taken them on board, mainly within the framework of interest-group theory, while in economic theorising the New Political Economy and the theory of public goods focus on the same phenomenon. A thorough-going political-constitutional solution that society comes under the control of the State by means of an unrestrained collective interventionism, and the "utilisation of the state power by particularist interests", requires the development of a new theory of economic order.

2. National Socialism and Müller-Armack's Retreat into the Sociology of Economics

The occupation of state power by the National Socialist German Workers' Party (NSDAP) even meant for Müller-Armack a serious turning point in his life. In the initial phase of the NS-regime he nursed hopes that it could promote a political recovery. He was not an exceptional case considering the susceptibility of wide circles, which hailed the totalitarian spirit of the age and refuted liberalism. It is possible that Müller-Armack belonged to those who believed that the new rulers could be influenced in the direction which he preferred.

In 1933 he published a booklet entitled *Staatsidee und Wirtschaftsordnung im neuen Reich* (*The Idea of the State and Economic Order in the New Reich*).[24] Here, he described the "new nationalism" as "historical activism"[25] and expected "political leadership" to develop from it, which he understood as the task of the "historical shaping"[26] of the economic future. In the sense of the dialectic employed by Marx, he believed that the new national-socialist state would overcome the defects of the interventionist government policies during the twenties and that it would be able to choose

---

24 MÜLLER-ARMACK, A.: *Staatsidee und Wirtschaftsordnung im neuen Reich*, Berlin 1933.
25 *Ibid.*, p. 19.
26 *Ibid.*, p. 34.

a "third way" between the two antagonistic philosophies of socialism and liberalism. He described the "third way" as a synthesis between individualism and collectivism, between "traditionalism and radicalism". Despite the rejection of the separation (fundamental to liberal thinking) between the State (as possessor of monopoly power) on the one hand and society (as the area of individual freedom) on the other by the new rulers, he was of the illusory opinion that the totalitarian state lacked "a reason for basic hostility vis-à-vis individual work and personal initiative". Consequently, it was also out of the question to proceed "without the energies of the individual employers, to whom we owe, without doubt, a large part of the powerful production successes of previous centuries".[27] The new activist economic policy shaped by State decree, should lead to "the State consciously taking over responsibility for the development of the economy".[28]

After the end of the Nazi-regime and especially during the seventies and eighties, the booklet mentioned earned Müller-Armack severe political and moral criticism above all from authors, who were accorded the grace of being born after the 'twelve dark years'. The reasons, which motivated him to put forward the views given above and to turn away from the concept of the democratic constitutional order in the early period of the Third Reich, can only be the subject of speculation today. Much could be explained by his disappointment with Brüning's policy for combating the Great Depression starting in Germany in 1929 and causing massive unemployment as a result of the deflationary policy of the government in 1932, thereby triggering a deepening of the depression[29]. Advice from academic economists to combat the severe crisis with expansionary measures went unheeded at that time. Equally disappointing, then as now, was the growing involvement of political parties with special interest groups. The inability and unwillingness of the politicians in office to defend the general interest against lobbyists and cartels caused many to reject the Weimar Republic. The grave

---

27 *Ibid.*, pp. 47 seq.
28 *Ibid.*, p. 60. Positions such as this, which emerged from the accelerating growth of the government, were frequently represented in the twenties and thirties. A source that is beyond suspicion is J. M. KEYNES: *The End Of Laissez Faire.* [In German under the title, *Ideen zur Verbindung von Privat- und Gemeinwirtschaft,* München and Leipzig 1926.]
29 See BOMBACH, G. among others (Ed.): *Der Keynesianismus,* Vol. 3, Berlin, Heidelberg and New York 1891 and the positions presented there.

mistakes of this anti-Weimarian mood, to which Müller-Armack also succumbed for a while, consisted of the fact that they expected salvation by submitting to the "total State", instead of turning to those, who before the National Socialist seizure of power were giving warning reminders of the foreseeable outcome of a totalitarian movement in power. [30]

How long Müller-Armack maintained his opinion that in 1933 a movement to a better society was underway, is no longer ascertainable today. In all probability, the booklet referred to above can hardly have fostered his academic career. It took six years before he received the appointment in Münster. Later in 1948 he stated that a reprint of the above-mentioned text was banned in 1935 by the NS Reich's Chamber of Literature. This is plausible, since Müller-Armack repeatedly stressed the historical merits of liberalism.

Müller-Armack's catalogue of writings contains nothing published between 1933 and 1940. Had he been a supporter of National Socialism, then it would have been advisable for him to participate actively in the political-economic transformation of the German economy into the Nazi-command system. Instead, Müller-Armack devoted himself to economic-sociological and economic-historical studies. He intended to distance himself from politically dangerous topics, by emphasising sociological-historical aspects referring to dimensions, which found no place in the official racial ideology.

In 1940, he published the first edition of his *Genealogie der Wirtschaftsstile: Die geistesgeschichtlichen Ursprünge der Staats- und Wirtschaftsformen bis hin zum Ausgang des 18. Jahrhunderts* (*Genealogy of Types of the Economies: A History of the Intellectual Roots of State Forms*

---

[30] Among these in particular were economists such as W. Röpke or A. Rüstow, who were exiled by the National Socialists shortly after their ceizing of power. See, among others, in RÖPKE's book *Wider die Brandung* (Erlenbach-Zürich 1962, pp. 84ff.), reprinted articles W. RÖPKE, "Wirrnis und Wahrheit", "Gesammelte Aufsätze", Zürich and Erlenbach 1962, pp. 105-124), in which the new rulers were pitilessly unmasked on the 8th of February 1933, eight days after their "Seizure of Power". Röpke's speech was published once more, thirty years later, by the *Frankfurter Allgemeine Zeitung* on the 30th of January 1963. - RÜSTOW, A.: "Freie Wirtschaft - starker Staat", *Schriften des Vereins für Socialpolitik*, Berlin 1932.

and Economic Reforms up to the End of the 18th Century)[31]. This book had nothing in common with the "national-socialist concept of the economy" and the "anti-capitalism" of the Nazi Party. Taking Max Weber's famous essay "The Protestant Ethic and the Spirit of Capitalism" as a starting point, he expressed the view (as he similarly did in a socio-religious study appearing in March 1945[32]) that European culture was characterised decisively by religious attitudes, a thesis which escaped the censors of those days, intentionally or not, and stood in direct contradiction to the biological racism of National Socialism. The subject of the book - its concern with the intellectual and spiritual foundations of the economy - was in those days unusual for an economist and corresponded in no way with the intentions and aims of the Hitler-regime.

By emphasising the "General Market Economy" (*Allgemeine Marktwistschaft*), the name of the research institute Müller-Armack founded together with Ernst Hellmut Vits in 1941, he contradicted the National Socialist concept of a centrally directed economy, divided into industries and cartels and controlled from above. Within the framework of this research institute, Müller-Armack published work reports over the three following years, the themes of which gave the impression that they correspond to the dry presentations, which are normally produced in such institutions.

Finally, it is to be recalled that, after the end of the war, Müller-Armack was quickly received into scholarly circles and working groups, which were engaged in the reconstruction of the economy in the three Western occupation zones of Germany and were intended to gain influence rapidly. Had he been a fellow-traveller of the Nazi-regime, his contemporaries would have known how to prevent that.

3. The Program of the Social Market Economy

Shortly after W.W.II, Müller-Armack appeared before the West-German public with proposals for the reconstruction of the war-shaken

---

31 MÜLLER-ARMACK A.: *Genealogie der Wirtschaftsstile. Die geistesgeschichtlichen Ursprünge der Staats- und Wirtschaftsformen bis hin zum Ausgang des 18. Jahrhunderts*, Stuttgart 3d edition 1944.
32 See the remarks in Chapter III in the section below.

ALFRED MÜLLER-ARMACK - ECONOMIC POLICY MAKER

German economy.[33] Faced with a catastrophic economic situation he did not see the central problem of the economy as contriving relief through aid from outside or through a reorganisation of the remains of the central planning apparatus left over from the National Socialist era or through isolated day-to-day measures. According to his diagnosis, it was very much more a matter of "understanding the economic decline as a crisis of the existing economic system".[34] The problem of the day - such was his argument - did not lie primarily in the far-reaching destruction wreaked by war and in the manifest shortages that had come about in all sectors, as well as the shortage of goods, but in the shortcomings of the central planning system, which, already during the war, had led to a repressed inflation, rationing of consumer goods, rationing of raw materials, compulsory labour, price-freezes, regulation of the markets and price controls and which led, by way of "disruption and paralysis of each and every personal interest among employers and employees to a stagnation of the whole economic process".[35] This state of affairs had become even more severe after the ending of the war, so that the decline in the economy had continued further. Hence, production was only to be set into motion "by the refashioning of a deliberate and clear economic order"[36], i.e. by a return to the rules of a market economy.

In a situation as it then was, market-oriented recommendations for rebuilding the economic order - in spite of prior experiences with the "total State" - were in large measure exposed to the verdict of recommending a return to nineteenth century Laissez-faire-Liberalism, which was seen by

---

33 MÜLLER-ARMACK, A.: "Zur Frage der vordringlichen wirtschaftspolitischen Maßnahmen", *Forschungsstelle für Allgemeine und Textile Marktwirtschaft an der Universität Münster*, 1945; MÜLLER-ARMACK, A.: *Konjunkturpolitik als Voraussetzung der Währungsreform*, 1945; MÜLLER-ARMACK, A.: "Zur Frage der vordringlichen wirtschaftlichen Maßnahmen", in: *Mitteilungen der IHK Köln vom 15. Oktober 1945*; MÜLLER- ARMACK, A.: "Das Grundproblem unserer Wirtschaftspolitik: Rückkehr zur Marktwirtschaft", in: *Mitteilungen der IHK Köln vom 15. Juli 1946*, and in: *Finanzarchiv*, N.F. Vol. 11, 1948/49; MÜLLER-ARMACK, A.: *Wirtschaftslenkung und Marktwirtschaft*, 1947.
34 MÜLLER-ARMACK, A.: *Zur Diagnose unserer wirtschaftlichen Lage*, Bielefeld 1947, p. 10.
35 *Ibid.*, p. 11.
36 *Ibid.*, p. 22.

wide circles as long outdated[37]. Furthermore, the market order was advocated only by a comparatively small group of academic economists[38], opposite whom a general public was standing, which believed that the question of transforming the economy from central planning to the market was at best of scholarly interest in the face of the pressing needs and the shortages of the day. Therefore, it was necessary to convince the general public of the importance of the economic order for overcoming the neediness[39] and that the market-economic order was not in the least a system discredited by history.

The history of the intellectual debates about the economic order and of the influence of market-economy ideas on the currency and economic reforms of 1948 has not yet been written.[40] Müller-Armack's contribution to this lay in the formulation and explanation of a program, which he named

---

37 For details see the harsh critique of British and American economists of the idea that "the classical medicine" (Keynes) could work in West-Germany quoted by T. W. HUTCHINSON in his book *The Politics and Philosophy of Economies. Marxians, Keynesians and Austrians*, New York (New York University Press) 1981, pp. 166 seq. Hutchinson contrasts their prophesies and analyses with the great success of the Social Market Economy program in the three decades after its introduction.

38 On this, see: BLUMENBERG-LAMPE, CHR.: "Das wirtschaftspolitische Programm der 'Freiburger Kreise'", *Volkswirtschaftliche Schriften*, Heft 261, Berlin (1973).

39 For a view opposing the contrary thesis of W. ABELSHAUSER (*Wirtschaft in Westdeutschland 1945 -1948, Rekonstruktion und Wachstumsbedingungen in der amerikanischen und britischen Zone*, Stuttgart 1975), who claims that the German economy entered a new phase of recovery already in 1946/47 and that the economic order did not matter, see the critique of KLUMP, R.: "Wirtschaftsgeschichte der Bundesrepublik Deutschland. Zur Kritik neuerer wirtschaftshistorischer Interpretationen aus ordnungspolitischer Sicht", *Beiträge zur Wirtschafts-und Sozialgeschichte*, Vol. 29, Stuttgart 1985; WÜNSCHE, H. F.: "Diskussionsbeitrag", in: LUDWIG-ERHARD-STIFTUNG (Ed.): *Die Korea-Krise als ordnungspolitische Herausforderung der deutsche Wirtschaftspolitik. Texte und Dokumente*, Stuttgart and New York 1986, pp. 126 seq. and 140 seq.

40 Important presentations are to be found in the two special issues of the *Zeitschrift für die gesamte Staatswissenschaft*, Vol. 135 (1979) and Vol. 138 (1982), and in the book by GIERSCH, H., PAGUÉ, K.-H. and SCHMIEDING, H.: *The Fading Miracle. Four Decades of Market Economy in Germany*, Cambridge (Cambridge University Press) 2nd edition 1994, pp. 26ff.

ALFRED MÜLLER-ARMACK - ECONOMIC POLICY MAKER

"social market economy", in the elaboration of the details of that programme and in his numerous contributions to the debate with the prevailing socialist ideology.

In later discussions it has often been said that the market economy as such can never be "social"[41] - a statement that can be interpreted very differently in view of the ubiquitous application of the key concept "social" and its opposite "unsocial", for example in the sense of "unjust", "destructive of solidarity", "eliminating social security" "fostering materialism" "furthering 'consumerism'", or "creating social inequality". Müller-Armack always countered the accusation that the market economy is "unsocial" with two arguments. First, with the evidence that a market economy system - under certain institutional conditions - is superior to all other known organisatorial alternatives as far as production and general welfare is concerned, and that a market order in view of its high productivity permits to produce social security on a high level. The social market economy, consequently, was for him an attempt "to find a synthesis between the rules of the market on the one hand and the social necessities of modern industrial mass society" on the other.[42]

In the discussion of those days, to speak up for the market also meant the repudiation of the claim of proponents of a state run economy that their

---

41 On this, see, for instance, the sources cited by ERNST HEUß in his essay "Gerechtigkeit und Marktwirtschaft", in: *ORDO-Jahrbuch für die Ordnung von Wirtschaft und Gesellschaft*, Vol. 38 (1987), p. 3. Further WATRIN, CHR.: "Zur sozialen Dimension marktwirtschaftlicher Ordnungen", in: STREIßLER, E., WATRIN, CHR. (Eds.): *Zur Theorie marktwirtschaftlicher Ordnungen*, Tübingen 1980, pp. 476ff.; GUTKOWSKI, A., MERKLEIN, R.: "Arbeit und Soziales im Rahmen einer marktwirtschaftlichen Ordnung", in: *Hamburger Jahrbuch für Wirtschafts- und Gesellschaftspolitik*, (1985), pp. 49-67; furthermore, LAMPERT, H., BOSSERT, A.: "Die Soziale Marktwirtschaft - eine theoretisch unzulängliche ordnungspolitische Konzeption?" in: *Hamburger Jahrbuch für Wirtschafts- und Gesellschaftspolitik*, pp. 109-130. WILLGERODT, H.: "Soziale Wertvorstellungen und theoretische Grundlagen des Konzeptes der Sozialen-Marktwirtschaft", *Schriften des Vereins für Socialpolitik*, N.F. Vol. 190, Berlin. WILLGERODT, H.: "Soziale Marktwirtschaft - ein unbestimmter Begriff?", in: IMMENGA, W., MÖSCHEL, W., REUTER, D. (Eds.): *Festschrift für E. J. Mestmäcker*, Baden-Baden 1996, pp. 329 -344.
42 MÜLLER-ARMACK, A: *Auf dem Weg nach Europa. Erinnerungen und Ausblicke*, Tübingen and Stuttgart 1971, p. 51.

system was superior to a market economy in social matters. In addition, it had to be explained to the general public that a turn towards the rules of the market did not mean a revival of the much criticised Laissez-faire Capitalism and its accompanying shortcomings[43], but that it concerned a new concept built, admittedly, on market economy principles and the wants of the citizens to enjoy social security.

An important contribution to these problems is Müller-Armack's essay on "Wirtschaftslenkung und Marktwirtschaft" ("Economic Steering and Market Economy") which first appeared in 1947.[44] It contains, alongside a subtle critique of the previous national-socialist economic planning system, a draft for a "socially directed market economy". Against the background drop of the post-war situation, Müller-Armack argued that the particular advantages of such a rule-based system are (1) the energising of the individual propensity to achieve, (2) a variable value and price system, which adapts itself to the constantly changing evaluations of consumers and producers, (3) an effective co-ordination of the economic plans of all participants via the price signals, the working of the market and the promoting of economic progress through competition.

In raising the common prosperity - and not just the standard of living of a few groups - Müller-Armack saw the first argument to justify the concept of a social market economy. He was not of the opinion that every type of market economy should be described as "social" in the sense of the objectives developed by him and others. For instance, he would not have described as "social" a highly monopolised market economy or an economy without accompanying measures in the social field.[45] And as a result, he

---

[43] The critique of the 19th century Laissez-faire Liberalism played a decisive role in the programmatic endeavours of Neo- or Ordo-liberals in the late forties and early fifties. For details see the monumental three volume opus of ALEXANDER RÜSTOW, *Ortsbestimmung der Gegenwart*, which has been published in a shortened version in English under the title *Freedom and Domination*. Further W. RÖPKE's war-time trilogy *The Societal Crisis of our Time*, *Civitas humana* and *International Order*, in which he discusses the social problems causes by an economy on the basis of a market order.

[44] MÜLLER-ARMACK, A.: *Wirtschaftslenkung und Marktwirtschaft*, Hamburg 1947, 2nd ed. 1948.

[45] On this, see the remarks in MÜLLER-ARMACK, A.: *Wirtschaftslenkung und Marktwirtschaft*, pp. 79 seq.

described a market order as an "artificial order"[46], which had to be designed deliberately under the social aims, dominating during the relevant historical situation. Later, certainly under the growth of an all-encompassing welfare state in West Germany, he modified this view by putting stress on the idea that there were economic boundaries for any social policy, which should not be trespassed.

Müller-Armack's conception presupposed that a market economy was sufficiently subject to be influenced through political measures and that, over and above this, economic and social intervention have to be designed in a way which did not destroy the working of the price mechanism and the competitive process. Müller-Armack assessed the finding of a solution to both tasks optimistically. He was convinced that an order, created in accordance with the rules of a market economy, way beyond the boundaries drawn by the liberal 19th century authors, could be set up in the sense wished for. Keeping their experiences with absolutist economic policy and its innumerable regulations controlling economic life in mind, the older Liberals were of the view, that the State's role in a liberal market economy should not go beyond ensuring freedom of trade, of monitoring law, penalising for fraud, granting public security and providing the infrastructure, in short, that a minimal state according to the views held by the social philosophers during the liberal 19th century was the answer. Opposing this, Müller-Armack held the view that further interventions, as long as they satisfied the criterion of being "compatible with the market rules", were still in line with the concept of a liberal order.[47] He knew himself to be at odds in this important view with leading representatives of German ordoliberalism such as Alexander Rüstow and Wilhelm Röpke[48], and that his ideas, insofar as they concerned measures of income redistribution, went beyond the views of these groups.

---

46 *Ibid.*, p. 86.
47 *Ibid.*, p. 93.
48 For details of the discussion of the question of whether and how one can develop political-economic interventions, i.e. State interventions into the market process in a way that conforms to the market order, see RÜSTOW, A.: "Deutschland und die Weltkrise", in: *Schriften des Vereins für Socialpolitik*, E. BOESE, Vol. 187, München and Leipzig, 1932, pp. 62, 65 and 69; RÖPKE, W.: *Die Gesellschaftskrise der Gegenwart*, Erlenbach and Zürich, 5th ed. 1948, p. 259.

Did Müller-Armack represent a constructivist position, i.e. an attitude, which Friedrich A. von Hayek[49] saw as inappropriate to a liberal system and in the end self-destructive? Some formulations in Müller-Armack's writings suggest such an interpretation, such as his frequently used indication that the market economy is "a technical device of data processing"[50], that one has to "to become aware of the technical and partial character of the market system"[51], that the market economy "like every machine, even the best has need of rational human control and steering"[52] and, finally, that a social market economy is something "*toto coelo* different in contrast to the liberal market economy"[53]. On the other hand, it should be noted that he adopted a strictly negative attitude in the discussions during the sixties about national economic programming, and the public control and direction of investments. He described such a "double control" of the economic process, as he called it, by means of the market and by state decree, as not capable of functioning.[54] And for a multiplicity of practical questions he took the view that a market solution was always possible.

Müller-Armack stressed the "instrumental character of the market economy" and the "need for amplifying the rules of the market" by adequate institutions.[55] This raises the question, as to how a market economy may be brought into harmony with the social objectives of a society i.e. how far economic freedom and social security can be linked together. One in his opinion widespread error was the conviction that social or social political aims were only to be achieved by switching off the rules of the market, perhaps via rent-fixing, state or cartelised setting of wages, or the countless price and quantity restrictions which were en vogue during the thirties and

---

49 HAYEK, F. A. v.: *Die Irrtümer des Konstruktivismus und die Grundlage legitimer Kritik gesellschaftlicher Gebilde*, München and Salzburg 1970, p. 4.
50 MÜLLER-ARMACK, A.: *Wirtschaftslenkung und Marktwirtschaft*, p. 93.
51 *Ibid.*, p. 85.
52 *Ibid.*, p. 58.
53 *Ibid.*, p. 58.
54 MÜLLER-ARMACK, A.: "Langfristige Programmierung innerhalb der Marktwirtschaft", *Beihefte der Konjunkturpolitik, Zeitschrift für angewandte Konjunkturforschung*, Heft 10, Berlin 1963; MÜLLER-ARMACK, A.: "Unser Jahrhundert der Ordnungsexperimente", in: *Wirtschaftspolitische Chronik*, Heft 1 (1972).
55 MÜLLER-ARMACK, A.: *Wirtschaftslenkung und Marktwirtschaft*, p. 93.

forties.[56] Such measures, as Müller-Armack noted, caused economic losses precisely for those, whom they were supposed to protect. He considered, that, for instance, minimum wages to be economically unproblematic and socially justified, only if they were at or below the level of equilibrium wages, i.e. that they were appropriate only for preventing arbitrary reductions of individual wages.[57] Other kinds of intervention in the price mechanism were, however, problematic. He writes: "Against social-political interventions, which touch on the process of price building, it seems to be more correct, to prefer a direct balancing of incomes between high and low wages through a direct redistribution of incomes. If, by taxing, higher incomes were reduced and the proceeds that flowed in were redistributed in the form of children's benefit, rent or housing allowances, then a perfectly ideal case of an intervention compatible with the market would exist."[58] A little later, he wrote, "Direct subsidies of this kind have the advantage of greater clarity and make it possible to check that social security is granted only to the really needy".[59]

When Müller-Armack was formulating these sentences in the late forties, he had before his eyes the familiar alternatives to open subsidies, for example hidden subsidies, price regulations, barriers to market entry or state-guaranteed purchases. He could not yet suspect that the social policy in the decades to come would expand in a manner such as has been the case, and that the distribution of transfers would become one of the preferred means of the welfare state. In the meantime, a system has arisen, in which the income redistributing effects, on the one hand, and the repercussions on individual readiness to achieve on the other, can no longer be reliably recorded. In the seventies Müller-Armack followed this development with great concern and emphatically warned against the economic consequences of a redistribution policy that had become uncontrollable.[60]

Independently of that though, he occupied himself with the further *social development of the market economy* - taking as a starting point that "it is a

---

56 *Ibid.*, pp. 107 seq.
57 *Ibid.*, p. 109.
58 *Ibid.*, p. 109.
59 *Ibid.*, p. 109.
60 MÜLLER-ARMACK, A.: *Die fünf großen Themen der künftigen Wirtschaftspolitik. Sonderdruck des Instituts für Wirtschaftspolitik.* Additionally in: *Wirtschaftspolitische Chronik*, Year 27, Heft 1 (1978), pp. 9ff.

disastrous mistake to expect that the mechanism of the market itself will create the ultimately worthwhile social order".[61] From early on he was interested in questions of the position of employees within the firm.[62] Hence, he was, *inter alia,* a co-founder with Franz Greiß of a study group, "Der neue Betrieb" (The new firm), whose Secretary Walter Scheel later became President of the Federal Republic. The main aim of that group was to study the management worker relations aiming at finding an answer of how to organise them at the same time humanely and efficiently.

Long before questions, about the quality of life and the safe-guarding of survival on "Spaceship Earth" claimed the attention of the public, Müller-Armack claimed a social market economy[63] should encompass also cultural policy, education and science policy. According to him these fields should not be separated from each other. Besides the fact that each had its own responsibilities and ideas as to objectives and methods of action, but at the same time each also had to correspond to the rules of a market economy. In the words of W. Eucken, the leading figure of the ordo-liberals, this meant, that there is an "interdependence" between all fields of social activities, which has to be taken into account in a liberal society. For Eucken a competitive market economy comprehends also the political order and the legal foundations of a free society - a view with which Müller-Armack agreed emphatically.

According to Müller-Armack's view such a broad social policy - and, in 1960, this was fresh and unusual - required the constant increase of investment in intellectual capital, the safe-guarding of personal independence, not only for those, which were traditionally counted among the independent, but also for those, whose social positions are usually described as "dependent"; in addition, he included environmental protection and city planning as yardsticks of a humane economy. Müller-Armack believed that these aims could be pursued in the first place through an appropriate design of the social framework by state activities.

---

61 MÜLLER-ARMACK, A.: *Wirtschaftslenkung und Marktwirtschaft,* p. 85.
62 Here - in respect of what follows - see WATRIN, CHR.: *Gedenkrede auf Alfred Müller-Armack on the occasion of the academic memorial ceremony on the 25th of June 1979,* Krefeld 1980, pp. 7f.
63 MÜLLER-ARMACK, A.: "Das gesellschaftliche Leitbild der Sozialen Marktwirtschaft", in: *Wirtschaftspolitisch Chronik,* Heft 3 (1962) and in: *Evangelische Verantwortung,* Heft 12 (1962).

From a methodological point of view, Müller-Armack's position can be described as "Smithian". Starting from a realistic view of man and recognising the all-pervasiveness of ignorance in human affairs[64] he looked for institutions with the help of which economic policy-making could be based on "Ordnungspolitik", that is the design of carefully considered rules which fit together and which minimise conflict among the participants of the economic game. Peaceful co-operation among men - instead of conflict - would increase the welfare of all. In such an irenic world human progress could be achieved on the long road to a free world society.

This view differs substantially from the Ricardian methodology which led to modern neoclassical economics with its world of highly sophisticated models striving for some kind of a Utopian social 'maximum' or 'optimum'[65]. Unlike this dominating orthodoxy the Müller-Armackian approach is much more apt to handle real-world problems. This might have been one reason, why German Ordnungspolitik after WW II had considerable influence on West-German public policy. Whether this impact is still important at the turn to the 21st century is a question which cannot be discussed here[66].

III. Müller-Armack's Religious and Socio-cultural Work

Müller-Armack's works on the sociology of religion, culture and economy were published in the forties and early fifties. His view of the market economy as an instrument, steered by economic politicians, could suggest that he might be labelled a technocrat or social engineer, who strives for efficient solutions. Actually, Müller-Armack, prompted by his religious and sociological studies of cultures, concerned himself intensively with the in-

---

64 HUTCHINSON (1981, p. 162).
65 HUTCHINSON (1981, p. 162).
66 For details see the book of HERBERT GIERSCH, KARL-HEINZ PAQUE and HOLGER SCHMIEDING: *The Fading Miracle. Four Decades of Market Economy in Germany*, Cambridge 2nd ed. 1992, pp. 26 seq., 273 seq. - Further CHRISTIAN WATRIN: "The Social Market Economy: The Main Ideas and Their Influence on Economic Policy", in: PETER KOSLOWSKI (Ed.): *The Social Market Economy: Theory and Ethics of the Economic Order*, Berlin (Springer) 1998, pp. 13-28.

tellectual and social roots of the market economy and of liberal society. His publications on political economy were permeated by social-philosophical reflections, which, unlike comparable writings, were not in the tradition of Anglo-Saxon Utilitarianism or Scottish Moral Philosophy. His works were much more moulded by his critical analysis of Marxism on the one hand and on the other by the reception of philosophical anthropology as it was represented by Max Scheler, Helmut Plessner and many others during the twenties and after the collapse of the Third Reich. Numerous shorter works are evidence for this.[67] His writings are concerned with analysis of various intellectual currents, such as the comparison of the world of economics with the world of faith, attempts to develop a Protestant economic ethic as a counterpart to Catholic social teaching, of rebuttals of various critiques of the market economy from church circles and of draft outlines of a position

---

67 MÜLLER-ARMACK, A.: "Wachstumsringe unserer Kulturform", in: L. H. AD JECK, J. V. KEMPSKI, H. MEUTER (Eds.): *Studien zur Soziologie. Festgabe für Leopold von Wiese*, Vol. 1, Mainz 1948; MÜLLER-ARMACK, A.: "Über die Macht des Glaubens in der Geschichte. Stufen religions-soziologischer Forschung", in: G. Howe (Ed.): *Glaube und Forschung*, Gütersloh 1949; MÜLLER-ARMACK, A.: "Stil und Ordnung der Sozialen Marktwirtschaft", in: LAGLER-MESSNER (Ed.): *Wirtschaftliche Entwicklung und soziale Ordnung. Festschrift für Ferdinand Degenfeld-Schonburg*, Wien 1952; MÜLLER-ARMACK, A.: "Mensch, Geist und Geschichte. Gedanken zu einer anthropologischen Geschichtswissenschaft", in: *Gestalt und Glaube. Festschrift für Vizepräsident D. Dr. Oskar Söhngen zum 60. Geburtstag am 5. Dezember 1960*, published by a circle of his friends, Witten and Berlin (undated) 1960; MÜLLER-ARMACK, A.: "Gedanken zu einer sozialwissenschaftlichen Anthropologie", in: F. KERRENBERG, H. ALBERT (Eds.): *Sozialwissenschaft und Gesellschaftsgestaltung. Festschrift für Gerhard Weisser*, Berlin 1963; MÜLLER-ARMACK, A.: "Der Moralist und der Ökonom. Zur Frage der Humanisierung der Wirtschaft", in: *ORDO Jahrbuch für die Ordnung von Wirtschaft und Gesellschaft*, Vol. 21 (1970), and in: *Kirche und Wirtschaft*, Düsseldorf (1971); MÜLLER-ARMACK, A.: "Soziale Irenik", in: *Weltwirtschaftliches Archiv*, Vol. 64 (1950); MÜLLER-ARMACK, A.: "Holzwege der Universitätsreform", in: *Frankfurter Allgemeine Zeitung*, No. 105 (May 6, 1977), as well as in: *Wirtschaftspolitische Chronik*, Vol. 29 Jg., Heft 2, 1980.

as mediator between the social concepts of different philosophies and religious orientations.[68]

Two of his pieces of research that have been mentioned above are, however, of great significance for the intellectual position taken up by him. These are his "Genealogy of Types of Economy"[69] and his essay "A Sociology of Religion of Eastern Europe"[70] The former starts from the methodological idea that general structures are to be made out through scientific analysis of a wide variety of historical occurrences and phenomena. Nowadays, one is quickly inclined to dismiss such an approach as "inductivistic" without posing to oneself the question as to whether it leads to rewarding hypotheses, which for their part can be empirically tested regardless of their origin. Even today, Müller-Armack's contribution here is still worthy of note. His initial hypothesis was the supposition that a particular conception of the world or "Weltanschauung" generates basic economic convictions, which correlate with it and subsequently steer the behaviour of men in their cultural and economic environment in the same direction. Müller-Armack, as a result, presents a position, which both stands, first, in a diametrical opposition to economic determinism, and the Marxian theory of superstructure-substructure, and, second, is in disagreement with theories of race, the mediocre intellectual status of which admits of no really serious scientific engagement, but which, in view of the political circumstances of the early forties, could be criticised only indirectly.

In detail Müller-Armack explained in his *Genealogie* that not only the economic behaviour but also social and political institutions are shaped by religious convictions.[71] Thus, the Roman Catholic Church's conception of the world created right up to the High Middle Ages a uniform European culture, the national elements of which were not particularly strongly marked.[72] The Reformation dissolved this uniformity and allowed three

---

68 MÜLLER-ARMACK, A.: *Religion und Wirtschaft. Geistesgeschichtliche Hinterründe unserer europäischen Lebensform*, Stuttgart 1959, 2nd ed. 1968, pp. 559-578. (In this book some earlier writings of Müller-Armack are reprinted).
69 MÜLLER-ARMACK, A.: *Genealogie der Wirtschaftsstile*. See footnote 32 above.
70 MÜLLER-ARMACK, A.: "Zur Religionssoziologie des europäischen Ostens", in: *Weltwirtschaftliches Archiv*, Vol. 61 (March 1945).
71 *Genealogie der Wirtschaftsstile*, pp. 110ff.
72 Regarding this and what follows see MÜLLER-ARMACK, A.: *Genealogie der Wirtschaftsstile*, pp. 70f.

doctrinal zones to emerge, the Calvinistic, the Lutheran and the Catholic, each of which passed through their own stages of development in the 17th and 18th Centuries. In Catholic countries the feudal corporative system and the rural and craft type of economy survived to a large extent. For countries and regions coming under the influence of Calvinism, it was typical that democratic institutions and a liberal economic system developed. Finally, the influence of Lutheranism was reflected not just in the system of State Churches, but also in the strengthening of state bureaucracies and in a type of economy largely subject to public control.

Müller-Armack applied the initial assumption that religious convictions have a distinctive influence on the development of economic orders not only in West European cultures but also in those of Eastern Europe. Here the attempt was made, undertaken in his days but nowadays forgotten, to attribute the economic stagnation to racial biological peculiarities or to national characteristics.[73] Müller-Armack considered neither to be convincing. He developed the hypothesis, that the economic backwardness of Eastern Europe, reaching as well as to the organisation of everyday economic life and to the political constitution, could be derived from metaphysical positions of the East, especially the Greek Orthodox Church.

The distinctive feature of Eastern religiosity in comparison with the more rationally oriented Catholicism and Protestantism, lay in the mysticism of religious life, which lacked any speculative theological dogmatics. "The essential thing of this religious world is the devoted self-affection to a radiant celestial world that the believer participates in".[74] This mystical attitude has three significant consequences. Firstly, it brings about a far reaching indifference towards a mediation of the transcendental contact through reason, such as each dogmatically fixed theology aspires to. Following from this is, secondly, that the priesthood does not claim to be the mediating authority between the transcendental world and the earthly vale of

---

73 Regarding this and what follows see also HOFFMANN, H. and WATRIN, CHR.: "Wirtschaft, Gesellschaft und Kultur. Bemerkungen zum Werk Alfred Müller-Armack", in: GREIß, F. and MEYER, F. W. (Eds.): *Wirtschaft, Gesellschaft und Kultur. Festgabe für Alfred Müller-Armack*, Berlin, pp. 643f.
74 MÜLLER-ARMACK, A.: "Zur Religionssoziologie des europäischen Ostens", p. 173.

tears. Finally, the immanent transcendence leads to viewing worldly life as relatively unimportant.[75]

Sociologically speaking, the lack of cultivated dogmatics in Eastern Europe means that the Western churches claim to give guidance to secular life, that is characteristic of the Roman Catholic Church, virtually does not exist. Consequently an authority challenging the emperors power could not grow up. It was this bi-polar tension, that in Western Europe led to liberal developments. For Müller-Armack, this anchoring of the Eastern Church in the transcendental world had the consequence that no intellectual countervailing power could evolve; on the contrary, the Greek Orthodox Church became part of the state power. The lack of an institutionally substantiated rivalry between secular and clerical forces, that is characteristic of much of the church history in western Europe, barred the way to progress in the East, despite the common origins in Christianity. Therefore, the form of theological speculation to empirical science, out of which, with the progressive secularisation of Europe, the foundations of a new economic system emerged could not develop under the influence of Greek Orthodoxy.

Müller-Armack summarised the sociological significance of the dogmatic features of the Eastern European Church as follows[76]: "By renouncing certain demands on the secular life of the faithful, which led to a well disciplined life-style, to an ascetic work ethic and directly to the religious honouring of entrepreneurial economic success as in the West, the Eastern Church created an atmosphere of life, in which the strength of the religious element remains, as it were, captured inside the church walls, without being able to influence in a stimulating way and authoritatively to the wordly affairs". It follows from this that it is misleading to see in the backwardness of the East merely a failure or a lagging behind. "This is to interpret the different attitude to economic life in the East simply as 'a not being able to', but it is based more fundamentally on 'a not wanting to', in the sense of a turning towards other metaphysical values."[77]

A study that appeared in 1948, *Das Jahrhundert ohne Gott* (*The Century Without God*)[78] is to be understood as a continuation of the *Genealogy of*

---

75 *Ibid.*, p. 178.
76 *Ibid.*, p. 181.
77 *Ibid.*, p. 181.
78 MÜLLER-ARMACK, A.: *Das Jahrhundert ohne Gott. Zur Kultursoziologie unserer Zeit*, Münster 1948.

Types of Economy, on this occasion not from the perspective of the influence of religious attitudes towards economic behaviour, but from the effects of the Enlightenment on religious beliefs. Müller-Armack concerned himself with the intellectual consequences of secularisation. It had, in his view, led not only to an enlightened rational attitude but also to the emergence of philosophical movements, which favoured the emergence of totalitarian political philosophies, especially in the Europe of the 20th century. Furthermore, Müller-Armack believed that he was able to show how the dissolution of faith in Lutheran, Calvinist and Catholic areas had not only occurred in different ways, but had also brought about varying styles in the form of different economic ways of living, the traces of which could be followed right up into the recent past.

The religious and socio-cultural works of Müller-Armack found their culmination in the work *A Diagnosis of our Present: On the Determination of our Intellectual Historical Position*[79]. Anyone attempting to achieve a rational form of economic and social life and having to choose between economic systems and not wishing to succumb to a political Utopia, must determine his own position in practical actions through a continuing process, that has no pre-programmed direction, but is to be understood as being "open" in the sense of not being pre-determined. Therefore, the questions such as "Where do we stand?", "What alternatives do we have?" and "Where are we going to?" have to be answered.

In the years directly following WW II, in which the future was viewed as being completely uncertain and German society stood under the impression of experiencing a total breakdown not only in material wealth, but also in a spiritual sense, serious answers could not be given by using models of new communal living (such as the "alternative movement" attempted to bring about later), of new life philosophies or new sects. First of all, the question arose of finding out which intellectual currents had caused political totalitarianism and the catastrophe of the Second World War, and of how restructuring German society, not just in a material, but more precisely in a spiritual sense, could be carried out on top of the post-war ruin.

Müller-Armack's contribution to this debate was at first a richly knowledgeable analysis of intellectual positions held during the closing years of

---

79 MÜLLER-ARMACK, A.: *Diagnose unserer Gegenwart. Zur Bestimmung unseres geistesgeschichtlichen Standorts*, Gütersloh 1949, 2nd revised edition Bern and Stuttgart 1981.

the 19th century and the first half of the 20th century. His view extended to religious changes, to the emergence of surrogates for religion such as culture, art, science and to efforts at finding answers to the questions (posed from secularised positions) as to the meaning of human existence. Using the parallel of growth rings in a tree trunk with circles concentric to one another, he tried to interpret the intellectual situation emerging in Germany after the Second World War.[80] According to his conception, it was characterised by the following six circles:

(1) Western Europe is shaped by its Christian Western tradition. (2) Decisive religious and cultural differences between Christianity in Eastern and Western Europe exist. (3) The differentiations and divergences of cultural awareness, (brought about by confessional splits) are a heavy burden even for those attempting to rid themselves of it.[81] (4) All of the religious and secular currents in Europe collided in Germany and shaped the destiny of that country. (5) The movement towards modernism, which led to the destruction of the unity in religious beliefs and permitted the rise of a secular culture, encouraged the emergence of new idols and unleashed chaotic forces. (6) And, finally, the dissolution of the aristocratic culture of previous centuries and its replacement by a new mass culture set completely new tasks.

Müller-Armack's understanding of the situation after the end of the Second World War was largely based on the idea that a process of dissolution had taken place, which had destroyed everything and was essential to overcome. Hence, the time for a new beginning after the total breakdown presented itself to him as a point in time, in which society's members should stand up for a renaissance of Christian-orientated attitudes to life.

A concluding remark: In his life's work Müller-Armack united in an unusual way the theoretical reflection of the scholar with the practical work of the policy maker. First and foremost, during his period at the Federal Economics Ministry his daily work was accompanied by a mass of writings on central questions of economic policy and on themes of European and national economic integration. Much of it is available only in unpublished memoranda, other pieces were published. The main themes during his time as a Civil Servant were taken up again by him in articles and position papers after he finished his service at the Ministry and were dealt with in

---

80 *Ibid.*, pp. 78-124.
81 *Ibid.*, pp. 107 seq.

greater depth, ultimately in five articles, written during the last year of his life. For him, it had to do with the safeguarding of the market economy order and the foundations of a free society in the anxiety that what had been achieved in the first three decades after the war could be carelessly squandered in the years to come.

Discussion Summary

KRZYSZTOF KLINCEWICZ

Paper discussed:
CHRISTIAN WATRIN: Alfred Müller-Armack - Economic Policy Maker and Sociologist of Religion

At the beginning of the discussion, the question was raised about the connections between Müller-Armack's concept of style and Walter Eucken's concept of social interdependence - as in both cases, all signals of life such as culture, economy and law, should build together a harmonious unity (NÖRR). Eucken's concept is a legal theory, and Müller-Armack's concept of style presents a much broader approach to the question. Besides, Eucken started from the theory of general equilibrium, whereas Müller-Armack's predecessors were Scheler and Plessner, and he represented a more sociological approach focused on social questions and opposed both the classical economy and the German historical school.

The idea of Müller-Armack underwent a long development in accordance with different economic and political factors (NÖRR). Müller-Armack was one of the first economists discussing environmental problems in his essay «The Second Face of Social Market Economy» written in 1967 (WATRIN). However, environment was regarded in terms of Plessner's philosophical anthropology as not only ecology but all factors outside the human being - also culture, civilisation (NÖRR).

Müller-Armack stated that markets do not integrate the society - therefore, it needs another integrating factor. This sociological idea was crucial for Müller-Armack writings as he still was looking for a source of society's integration. In 1932 ("The Laws of Development of Capitalism") his answer was the idea of the nation, then in 1933 ("The Idea of State and the Economic Order") he was mistaken about the character of Nazism, and finally, in 1945, he found the integrative force in religion. This strive for source of integration came from Plessner's philosophical anthropology. There are many similarities between Plessner's idea of self-realised social structures and Müller-Armack's idea of style (HASELBACH). However, the idea of self-realisation cannot be translated into economic thinking - therefore the idea of style remained only a sociological concept (WATRIN).

Müller-Armack used a metaphor of a market economy as a car - very similar to Saint-Simon's metaphor of a market economy as machinery of competition. The question remains: Who should choose the drivers and which way should the drivers choose in order to prevent the car from breaking down? A serious drawback of Müller-Armack's economic ideas was lack of any theory of politics. Directions such as freedom and social justice are not precise guidelines for politicians. There is a difference between Müller-Armack and Eucken, who suggested at least more precise principles of economic policy (WOHLGEMUTH).

The theory of the social market economy was a normative proposal combined with an idealistic view on how politics functions - without an applicable theory of politics, or explanations as to how democracy functions (STREIT). However, a similar social market economy approach helped e.g. Erhard to win elections. Müller-Armack did not discuss the problems of political sociology in a systematic manner. The theories of politics developed in America cannot explain the ways European politics works because of cultural differences. European politics is more ideological than the American one, differences come also from the history and experience with totalitarian regimes in Europe (WATRIN). Purely economic rules are insufficient for solving political problems and the idea of social peace (*irenics*) could be helpful in solving current economic problems - e.g. in Russia, where the introduction of a free market economy without a social basis causes still many social and economic difficulties (KOSLOWSKI).

Müller-Armack was influenced by the post-Marxist theory of capitalism. The topics how capitalism works and what makes it not work were essential for the German historical school as well as for Müller-Armack - even the title "Laws of Development of Capitalism" (1932) sounds Marxist. Common problems were e.g. business cycles and the question of class struggle. Müller-Armack's theory of the social market economy was an answer to Marxist views on economics and politics. Instead of classes, he first stressed the role of a nation. He answered the question asked once by Marx: Where do the basic human orientations and norms come from? Marx's answer was the economic conditions, the basis - but the idea of class-consciousness determined by economic position was wrong, as Max Scheler

DISCUSSION SUMMARY

proved it in his sociology of knowledge. Müller-Armack presented the opinion that religion and culture were the factors in question (KOSLOWSKI).

The book *Laws of Development of Capitalism* was strongly influenced by Schumpeter and presented an alternative to the Marxist description of capitalism. But Müller-Armack was also very pessimistic about the future of liberalism. Liberal societies ended up in imperialism and colonialism in the 19th century. Müller-Armack proposed the idea of social peace (*irenics*), partnership and co-operation instead of class struggles, wars, strikes which destroy wealth. Important is the innovative role Müller-Armack played in the 1930s. In times of the big economic crisis, people thought that only the planned economy could provide social security. Müller-Armack, on the contrary, stated that just the market order and the consensus society are the guarantees for security and wealth (WATRIN).

The theory of the social market economy was not only developed as a theory of reconstructing the German economy after the Second World War. Müller-Armack started it before the war, and it is a general theory of the market economy relevant for different countries, not only for Germany, and for different conditions, not only the post-war ones (KOSLOWSKI).

Chapter 7

The Market Economy and the State
Hayekian and Ordoliberal Conceptions

MANFRED E. STREIT AND MICHAEL WOHLGEMUTH

I. Introduction
II. Hayek and the Freiburg School: Some Historical Notes
III. The Ordoliberal Conception of the State and the Market Economy
    1. The Two-Sided Problem of Power
    2. Power and the Market: the Ordoliberal Conception of the "Wettbewerbsordnung"
    3. Power and the State: the Ordoliberal Conception of "Rechtsstaat"
IV. The Hayekian Conception of the State and the Market Economy
    1. The Two-Sided Problem of Knowledge
    2. Knowledge and the Market: Hayek's Conception of "Catallaxy"
    3. Knowledge and the State: Hayek's Conception of Nomocracy"
V. Common Grounds and Major Differences
    1. Common Grounds
    2. Major Differences
    3. The Meaning of Competition: Austrian and Freiburgian Views
    4. The Emergence of Institutions: Spontaneous Order and Intentional Rule-Setting
    5. The "Social Question": Hayekian and Ordoliberal Views
VI. The Political Economy of Liberalism: A Constitutional Economics Perspective
    1. A Note on Political Economy and Economics of Politics
    2. Constitutional Reforms
    3. Spontaneous Correcting Forces
VII. Conclusion

THE MARKET ECONOMY AND THE STATE

I. Introduction

There is not and has never been *one* liberal conception of the market economy and the state. In fact, the term "liberal" has received connotations that, especially in the United States but also, for example, in France, still support the old dictum of Schumpeter (1954, p. 394): "as a supreme, if unintended, compliment, the enemies of the system of private enterprise have thought it wise to appropriate its label."

We shun the discussing of labels. We will simply identify one particular liberal position with the rich body of social philosophy of Friedrich A. Hayek which one may call "retro-liberal", since basically it represents a rediscovery and reformulation of classical liberalism. Hayek's conception of the market economy and the state will be compared with what is commonly called "ordoliberalism". The term "ordoliberal" already implies some specification since it represents a specific German tradition of this century. Still, there is not *one* ordoliberal conception of the market economy and its politics. For example, there are good reasons to distinguish between a Freiburg and a Cologne mode of (ordo-) liberal thought (e.g. Sally 1996, pp. 248f; Vanberg 1988, pp. 20ff). Even if both "schools" have mostly unofficial and overlapping memberships, the former can be said to be more sceptical towards attempts to combine individual freedom on markets and social balance through government intervention, as highlighted in the politically effective term of a "social market economy" (see Müller-Armack 1956). At any rate it would be wrong to equate any ordoliberal conception with the *practice* of the so-called "social market economy" - which gradually developed into its actual dismal state (see, e.g. Streit 1998a). We will concentrate our analysis of ordoliberalism on Walter Eucken and Franz Böhm, two founding fathers of the "Freiburg School of Law and Economics" (Streit 1994; 1992a). As will be shown, the work of these eminent ordoliberals is mostly complementary and can thus be combined to allow a comparison with Hayek's elaborate system of social philosophy.

Our paper is organised as follows: First, we assess the mutual intellectual influence between Hayek and scholars of the Freiburg School, giving a short account of the respective historical and intellectual backgrounds (II). Next, we present the ordoliberal conception of the state and the market economy. As a main common theme of Eucken and Böhm we identify the problem of social power. This theme underlies the analytic and normative conception of the competitive order ("Wettbewerbsordnung") in the economic context and the rule of law ("Rechtsstaat") in the political context (III). Hayek's views of the market and the state also have one dominant, common theme: the problem of individuals' lack of knowledge. Obviously, this problem dominates Hayek's view of the market as a spontaneous order of actions, or "catallaxy". But also his social philosophy of the law and the state, his theory of the spontaneous order of rules, and his political ideal of "nomocracy" is intrinsically related to the knowledge problem (IV). Having thus established a somewhat parallel plot of our presentation, we next try to establish common grounds and fundamental differences between both conceptions. The points of departure are located mainly in three areas: the appropriate meaning and politics of competition, the emergence and political shapeability of social institutions, and the meaning of the "social question" (V). Finally, the lasting relevance of both liberal conceptions is briefly discussed from the perspective of Constitutional Economics. It is asked if the legacy of Eucken, Böhm, or Hayek contains not only basic insights into the malaise of modern welfare states, but also proposals for feasible constitutional reforms (VI).

II. Hayek and the Freiburg School: Some Historical Notes

The relation between Hayek and the first generation of the Freiburg group around Eucken and Böhm[1] seems to be one of mutual benign neglect. At least, there is a distinct lack of *explicit* references to their respective works. This is surprising because Hayek and the ordoliberals started with a common basic value judgement (individual liberty), focused on similar subject matters (like competition and the social order) and, in principle, arrived at similar policy implications (like limited government). Let us

---

1 Hans Grossmann-Doerth, a professor of law, was the third among those who composed the "ordo manifesto of 1936" (BÖHM et. al., 1936). He died in the war. For the authors' assessments of the Freiburg School, see STREIT (1992a; 1994), KASPER/STREIT (1993) or WOHLGEMUTH (1996). See also SALLY (1996), PEACOCK/WILLGERODT (1989), GROSSEKETTLER (1989), HUTCHISON (1979) or OLIVER (1960).

briefly review the literature in question and look for first explanations in the respective intellectual and historical backgrounds.

At least in his most prominent works, Hayek hardly makes any explicit reference to German ordoliberalism. This holds even for the growing body of his work written after he met Eucken (before 1947) or came to live and work at Freiburg (in 1961)[2]. On the other side, on ceremonial occasions he openly declared his "friendship of many years' standing, based on the closest agreement on scientific as well as on political questions, with the unforgettable Walter Eucken" (Hayek 1962, p. 252).[3] Still, this agreement left virtually no explicit and concrete trace in Hayek's work.

But the reverse is also true. Böhm and Eucken hardly ever explicitly referred to those works of Hayek which early enough became academically challenging (e.g. Hayek 1937 and 1945), widely discussed (e.g. Hayek 1935a, 1935b and 1940) and even notoriously famous (Hayek 1944). Perhaps most surprisingly, Hayek's contributions to the calculation debate went totally unnoticed.[4] As we will see, this observation might be telling, since it

---

2 In the trilogy on Law, Legislation and Liberty (HAYEK 1973; 1976; 1979) Eucken is not mentioned. Böhm is given only one small note referring to his notion of "private law society". In the "Constitution of Liberty" (HAYEK 1960) only two articles of Böhm are mentioned in footnotes.

3 Eucken was invited to come to the first international conference of liberals that Hayek called to the Swiss Mont Pélerin in 1947 (see HAYEK 1983, pp. 191f.). Hayek also invited him to give a series of lectures at the London School of Economics in 1950 (see EUCKEN 1951), during which Eucken unexpectedly died. HAYEK (1951, p. 199) stated that this "sudden death ... robbed the liberal revival of one of its really great men"; later HAYEK (1983, p. 189) even calls Eucken "probably the most serious thinker in the realm of social philosophy produced by Germany in the last hundred years".

4 The debate on the feasibility of socialist calculation and of central emulations of market processes is referred to in only one longer footnote in EUCKEN (1940, pp. 333f) - even though he devotes half of the book to a comparison of centrally administered and exchange economies. Later, EUCKEN (1952, pp. 76f; 99ff, 136ff) fills several pages discussing the ideas of Lange and Barone without mentioning Hayek's contribution. Even Mises is mentioned only once in an editor's note to the posthumously published book. Some negligence may be due to the fact that foreign literature was just not available during the Nazi reign and in the difficult after-war-period (Hayek's "Road to Serfdom" remained censured even in the American Sector). However, Hayek's early contributions to the cal-

reflects the theoretical shortcomings of Eucken's analysis. The problem of dispersed knowledge which cannot be acquired by a central authority, the role of incentives for speculative and innovative entrepreneurship and hence the fundamental importance of capital markets for evolutionary market processes remain mostly unnoticed. While these arguments acted as catalysts for a second generation of Austrian economics (see Vaughn 1994, ch.3, Wohlgemuth 1997), they did not reach the Freiburg School as early. On the other side, Hayek's early work on the "Decline of the Rule of Law" (Hayek 1953) is very friendly received and extensively used by Böhm.[5] And indeed, we will see that the legal and political philosophy of Hayek is very similar to that of Böhm. In some cases the work of Böhm can serve as a bridge connecting to Hayek's conceptions of the institutional order, where Eucken's views seem to be somewhat incomplete or inconsistent.

Hayek's comparative disregard of the literature by German ordoliberals also might not be totally accidental. As it were, his intellectual background seems always to have been predominantly British, Austrian and, to a lesser degree, American. This is not only reflected in his selection of ideas, but also in his choice of empirical background and subject-matters. For example, Hayek's treating of institutional questions - especially his theory of the spontaneous order of the law - is intrinsically linked to the English system of common law. The intellectual Austrian background includes the first generation of Austrian economists (Menger, Böhm-Bawerk) and later Ludwig von Mises as his most important mentor. The influence of the Scottish moral philosophers (Hume, Smith, Ferguson), but also Mill, Mandeville, Locke and Dicey or Lord Acton is visible in all his social philosophy. Even politically, Hayek positioned himself within the history of the British party system, calling himself "an old Whig".[6] The fact that Hayek's ideas were

---

culation debate (HAYEK 1935a; 1935b) are part of a collection of essays (edited by Hayek) which Eucken himself refers to - dealing, however, only with the contributions of Barone.

5   See BÖHM (1953, p. 99 [fn.2]). BÖHM (1957, p. 174) even explicitly names Hayek's work on the rule of law as an example of the general interdisciplinary character of the Freiburg School.

6   Hayek, in his biographical sketch, notes that "the real root" of his ideas lays "with Ferguson and these peoples" (HAYEK 1994, p. 140). Concerning his political affinities, he reports a meeting with the British Prime Minister: "The last time I met her she used the phrase, 'I know you want me to become a Whig; no, I am a Tory'. So she has felt this very clearly." (*ibid.*, p. 141).

deeply rooted in classical liberalism and its conception of a spontaneous development (evolution) of civilisation is essential in understanding his social philosophy. As we will see, this also helps to explain why Hayek on one occasion arrived at the judgement that "the Ordo circle ... was, shall we say, a restrained liberalism." (Hayek 1983, p. 190).

Concerning the Freiburg School, it can be argued, as Hayek (1951, p. 199) once did, that it differed from other schools of liberal thinking "in that its origin cannot be traced back directly to any great figure of the preceding generation." Its philosophical origin perhaps is most aptly described as Kantian[7]. As far as economics is concerned, the works of Eucken and Böhm can hardly be understood without accounting for the intellectual and political climate in Germany. Intellectually, especially Eucken was struggling to find an acceptable position overcoming the "great antinomy" between the "individual-historical approach" of the Historical School and the "general-theoretical" approach of the Marginalist School (e.g. Eucken 1940, pp. 34ff.) that found its expression in the acrimonious *"Methodenstreit"* between Carl Menger and Gustav Schmoller. Eucken's solution lead to his method of "isolating abstraction" (ibid., p. 107), borrowing from the phenomenologist philosophy of Husserl and others[8]. The ordoliberal conception of Eucken and Böhm is also marked by idiosyncrasies of German history. The traumatic experience with both interventionism and collectivism motivated the ordoliberals' declared programmatic interest in active economic policy. The task to reorganise the institutional structure and relationship of state and society - the mutual interpenetrating of which has been a recurrent cause of German "roads to serfdom" - was deeply felt by German ordoliberals. As we will see, this experience might help to explain the

---

7 See also MÖSCHEL (1989, p. 149); ALBERT (1985, p. 54), SALLY (1996, p. 238). References to Kantian conceptions of liberty and the law can be found in EUCKEN (e.g. 1952, pp. 52, 126, 176).

8 Husserl developed the principle of "phenomenological reduction" which influenced Eucken's "abstraction of significant salient features" (EUCKEN 1940, p. 332, note 28). Instead of "generalising abstraction" which seeks to identify common traits of different phenomena, Eucken was convinced that it should be possible to identify certain recurrent elementary forms in economic life. This is how he went to isolate the centrally directed and the exchange economy as conceptual answers to the following question: "Does one central authority direct everyday life, or do countless single individuals make their own decisions?" (*ibid.*, p. 81).

scepticism towards invisible-hand-explanations of institutional change as they were to be taken up by Hayek.

III. The Ordoliberal Conception of the State and the Market Economy

1. The Two-Sided Problem of Power

The theoretical and political programme of the Freiburg School can be described in the words of Böhm (1957, p. 162) as follows:

> The question that preoccupied us all, was ... the question of private power in a free society. This leads by necessity to the further question of what an order of a free economy is made of. From there one arrives at the question, what kinds and possibilities of an economic order are at all feasible, what role is played by power in each, in fact the power of government as well as the power of private persons and groups, and what obstructions of order arise if a distribution of power emerges within state and society which differs from that which conforms to the respective economic system.

Note that these questions referring to "power" and "order" as the key-notions of ordoliberalism differ from typical economic concepts as well as typical legal concepts. For the Freiburg School, they define the fields of common theoretical interest and political concern which centres around the basic concept of the competitive order ("Wettbewerbsordnung"). The central and defining concern of ordoliberalism was to establish "order" as a set of legal rules for a society of essentially self-reliant decision makers whose actions are controlled and co-ordinated by market competition. "The lawyer knows what private law is. The economist knows what the market economy is" (Böhm 1966, p. 46). In order to know what the competitive order is and how it can be achieved in practice, the knowledge of the lawyer and of the economist must be brought together. They combine in a characteristic ordo-view of the economic and political problem of power. It is a key message of the Freiburg tradition that private (market-) power not only reduces the freedom of the many in favour of the domination by the few in the economic system, but that it also penetrates and impairs the political system.

THE MARKET ECONOMY AND THE STATE

We now turn to the first, and, according to ordoliberalism, original, aspect of the problem of social power.

2. Power and the Market: the Ordoliberal Conception of the "Wettbewerbsordnung"

The above question of "how an order of a free economy is constituted" was understood by Böhm as a problem of an adequate legal order. Free market exchange above all requires a system of rules, defining a protected domain (property rights) and allowing co-operation of equals (private contracts) where they seek it and settlement of conflicts (arbitration) where they need it. A society that builds on these principles is justly called a private law society ("Privatrechtsgesellschaft", see Böhm 1966). However, the basic provisions of private law still provide no complete answer to the question of private power. This was a central lesson drawn from German economic and legal history: Private attempts to close markets (e.g. by formation of cartels) were considered legitimate uses of the freedom of contract, and boycotts or collective discrimination applied against outsiders received support from the courts. Thus, the freedom to compete of third parties was reduced to the effect that economic power became vested in the formalism of private law. Therefore, ordoliberals insisted in supplementing the private law society with an institutional guarantee of open markets in order to ensure that market competition can display its central function as "the most genial instrument of emasculating power" (Böhm 1961, p. 22).

This is the most important and original contribution of the Freiburg School to a political economy of the market: competition is not only (and not even primarily) regarded as a means to achieve "economic" goals like growth and efficiency. It is mainly advocated as a procedure to curb the power of economic agents and organisations. Economic power, in turn, is regarded as evil not only because it cripples the price mechanism and its allocative potential, but also, and primarily, because it allows infringements on the liberty of others which is regarded the fundamental precondition of moral behaviour[9]. In accordance with this broader view of competition,

---

9 See e.g. EUCKEN (1952, p. 126) referring to Kant's fundamental moral principle that individuals must be regarded ends in and of themselves, not means towards the achievement of others' ends. Böhm's conception of private autonomy (e.g. BÖHM 1980, pp. 202f) is an expression of the same principle.

ordoliberals developed a broader and more articulate assessment of the preconditions of competition than the neo-classical marginalists. Whereas the latter employed simple "rules" of decision logic to deduce abstract results, ordoliberals emphasised legal rules and principles that structure real market processes.[10]

The institutional framework of the competitive order is most prominently described by the famous "principles" laid down by Eucken (1952, pp. 254ff). As "fundamental principle" the creation of a workable price system is postulated. As "constituent principles", conducive to a well-functioning price system, he enumerates the stability of the monetary system, open markets, private property, freedom to contract, liability for one's commitments and actions, and steadiness of economic policy. Necessities for political interventions that might still arise should be accounted for along "regulating principles" like monopoly control, income policies and the correction of technological external effects (ibid., pp. 291ff). These principles, of course, have no other addressee than government. Now arises another central and, as we will see, somewhat distinguishing trait of ordoliberalism. It is based on the view that "a private law society cannot function without authority ... it requires a support, which it cannot produce from within its own resources, in order to function at all." (Böhm 1966, p. 51). By conferring such an authority to the state and hence to politicians, a second problem of power necessarily emerges: political power.

3. Power and the State: the Ordoliberal Conception of "Rechtsstaat"

As we have seen, ordoliberals assigned to competition a rôle which went beyond its economic importance. Because of its capacity to curb economic as well as ensuing political power it deserved protection by the law. Competition policy was considered a genuine task of the state. This implied also that the state had to refrain from any activities which could restrain competition. Considered from this point of view, it seems rather straightforward that ordoliberals advocate a strong but limited government. It must be

---

10 Regarding the economic properties of his ideal type of "complete competition", Eucken (much more than Böhm) at least terminologically remained in the vicinity of the neo-classical paradigm as he found it. As we will discuss later, the main thrust of the Hayek-critique remained unrecognised.

strong in order to be able to hold out against monopolies and pressure groups, thus safeguarding the "economic constitution"[11]. At the same time, it must be limited to the pursuit of only this genuine task and the use of only liberty- and market compatible means. Hence, it was required that activities of the state should conform to the functioning of the markets. First of all, it was the task of the state to protect the private autonomy of the individual agents against infringements due to restraints of competition resulting in economic power. At the same time this would prevent that private power could impair the political decision making process. This process was supposed to be structured by a political constitution which displayed features corresponding to the economic constitution: It had the double task (1) to grant independence those who are entrusted and legitimised to make laws and to govern, thus allowing for political neutrality or "strength" against economic power groups and (2) to provide a sophisticated combination of checks and balances, thus preventing and limiting an arbitrary use of political coercive power. Such a structure displays the salient features of the ordoliberal conception of the rule of law.

It should be evident that this conception of the "*Rechtsstaat*" is a far cry from an image of the "benevolent dictator" that still looms large in welfare economics.[12] Eucken (1952, p. 338) made this unmistakably clear: "It is wrong to see the existing state as an all-knowing, all-powerful guardian of all economic activity. But it is also incorrect to accept the existing state which is corrupted by interest groups as irreversibly given and consequently to despair of mastering the problem of building a proper political-economic order." Eucken and no less Böhm evidently opposed unlimited government; they clearly exposed the institutional framework of what later became

---

11 A modern interpretation and application of the conception of "economic constitution" is provided by STREIT/MUSSLER (1994, pp. 319ff). It has been developed mainly by one of Böhm's collaborators, ERNST-JOACHIM MESTMÄCKER (e.g. 1973, 1996).

12 It reveals a biased and very selective reading, when KIRCHGÄSSNER (1988) claims that (a) ordoliberals restricted their analysis to the realm of production and consumption of goods and services (ibid., p. 55), when he insinuates that (b) they did not perceive the problem of political power exercised by economic power groups (ibid., p. 57) and when, finally, he is led to argue that (c) ordoliberals "take the image of the benevolent dictator for granted, whose action contradicts the social welfare only if he is either uninformed or malicious." (*ibid.*, p. 60).

known as the "rent-seeking society" (e.g. Tollison 1982); and they proposed institutional precautions to prevent the "wild refeudalisation of society" (Böhm 1958, p. 258) they have witnessed in German history (see already Eucken 1932 and Böhm 1933).[13] At best, therefore, they can be "criticised" for not having produced an "economic theory of politics" which was only later to become a theory of public choice (see section VI).

That a strong and limited state is no contradiction in terms, that political authority, and constitutional limitations actually complement each other, became a central tenet of ordoliberalism. That an unlimited state is always in danger of being weakened and corrupted by economic power groups was a central conclusion that ordoliberals drew from German history, especially from the period of "experimental economic policies". Eucken (1932, p. 307) observed that the "expansion of government activities ... not at all meant a strengthening, but to the contrary, a weakening of the state".[14] The corruption of the political order and unreliability of economic institutions combined with politicians' subsequent dependence upon economic power groups is a prominent example of the general idea of an "interdependence" of the legal, political, and economic order (e.g. Eucken 1952, pp. 332ff). The analysis of the collusion of public and private power in cartel-like, corporativistic arrangements, or the "capturing" of the state by vested interests (Böhm 1950, p. xxxvi) can still serve as very apt descriptions of the weakness of modern welfare states. We will come back to this part of the ordoliberal analysis.

---

13 We do, however, agree with KIRCHGÄSSNER (1988, p. 67) that EUCKEN's (1952, p. 334) principle that politics ought to be "directed at the dissolution of economic power groups or limit their functions" is rather crude and difficult to reconcile with liberal rights to association (see below, VI).

14 This is exactly what HAYEK (1979, p. 99) pointed out, namely that "democratic government, if nominally omnipotent, becomes as a result of unlimited powers exceedingly weak, the playball of all the separate interests it has to satisfy to secure majority support."

IV. The Hayekian Conception of the State and the Market Economy

1. The Two-Sided Problem of Knowledge

Like the ordoliberals, Hayek developed and sharpened his conception of the market and the proper role of the state through the confrontation with practical and theoretical attempts of central planning during the 1930s. However, the perception and reaction to this challenge differ. Eucken and Böhm looked upon Germany's history of political experiments including the later command economy and upon the theory of economic systems focusing on economic and political power. Hayek, in turn, discussed the unfeasibility of socialist planning and the major merits of capitalism focusing on the ability to make use of subjective, non-centralisable knowledge and skills. This is how he discovered the "division of knowledge" which he regarded "the really central problem of economics as a social science" (1937, p. 50).[15] The problem of the division of knowledge and its underlying fact of a constitutional lack of knowledge was to become the starting point of almost all of Hayek's ensuing work, as he repeatedly emphasised:

> The fundamental condition from which any intelligent discussion of the order of all social activities should start is the constitutional and irremediable ignorance both of the acting persons and of the scientist observing this order, of the multiplicity of particular, concrete facts which enter this order of human activities because they are known by *some* of its members. (1967b, p. 71).

This view underlies Hayek's approach to the spontaneous order of economic actions, the "catallaxy", as well as to the rule of law, the "nomocracy".

---

[15] Hayek's basic ideas on the "use of knowledge in society" (HAYEK 1945) have much of their "micro-foundation" in his early studies in cognitive psychology. There he analyses the mental process by which sensory experience of an individual is structured, leading to subjective images of the world as patterns of perception or cognition. Links between the "Sensory Order" (published in 1952 - some 30 years after Hayek wrote the book) and Hayek's later views on the spontaneous order of interactions and social rules are shown by STREIT (1993).

2. Knowledge and the Market: Hayek's Conception of "Catallaxy"

The problem of the division of knowledge concerns the following questions which need to be answered in every economic order (Streit 1998b, p. 40): (a) How are individuals induced to procure knowledge that may turn out to be useful for their own purposes? (b) How is subjective knowledge about economic circumstances disseminated, which may also be useful to others for their own dispositions? (c) How is the utilisation of knowledge controlled in order to reveal possible errors? (d) How are errors counteracted and thus limited in their overall economic consequences? Hayek's (1968) answer was: through "competition as a discovery procedure" and as the driving force of a system of voluntary exchange that he called "catallaxy" (e.g. 1967b, pp. 90ff). In a catallaxy, every individual is free to use his or her unique knowledge of particular opportunities and skills for his or her own purposes. In addition, competitive market processes provide incentives to procure knowledge and use personal skills as means of economic survival. Unfettered markets also convey information to others through changes in the structure of prices, if only "in a coded form" (1976, p. 117). Prices induce promising transactions on the part of those actors who incur (transaction-) costs and command enough skill and good luck in interpreting the signals in view of their personal economic circumstances. Such transactions can counteract errors of others, who in turn are exposed to price effects which provide pressures to adjust. In this way the system allows to discover and use the dispersed knowledge and skills which as a whole are not accessible to anyone[16]. In addition, it tends to be restabilised in the sense that cumulative errors are made unlikely.

Like the price mechanism, abstract rules of just conduct allow individuals to adjust to events and circumstances which are not known to anyone in their entirety. In the market as well as in other complex and anonymous

---

16 This property has far-reaching consequences. It means no less than a renunciation of conventional price theory. Thus, it is no longer appropriate to assume "given" and "homogenous" goods, because "which goods are scarce goods, and how scarce or valuable they are - these are precisely the things which competition has to discover." (HAYEK 1968, p. 181). But also the benchmark of traditional economics - efficiency - becomes irrelevant if applied beyond a pure individual logic of choice: "If we do not know the facts we hope to discover by means of competition, we can never ascertain how effective it has been in discovering those facts that might be discovered" (ibid., p. 180).

interactions, actors who try to co-ordinate their behaviour would be lost if they could not perceive and rely on regularities in the conduct of others, which enable them to form corresponding expectations. In order to act as mutual stabilisers of expectations, or as "successful adaptations to the irremediable limitations of our knowledge" (Hayek 1967b, p. 72), the rules of conduct (institutions) have to conform to certain principles, most notably to the principle of universalisability. This principle is at the heart of Hayek' notion of the rule of law which will now be considered.

3. Knowledge and the State: Hayek's Conception of "Nomocracy"

Eucken (1940, p. 81) once asked: "If many individual economic units, though they make their plans independently, are dependent on and exchange with one another, ..., then the question arises to the form of the system of exchange relationships. What are the rules of the game?". Hayek's answer was that these rules of the game must (a) allow individuals to pursue their own objectives by making use of their own knowledge and skills, and (b) enable them to form reliable expectations about the conduct of others. Such rules would have to (c) define a protected sphere of individuals' autonomy to act, thus preventing interpersonal conflicts while (d) at the same time keeping the system open for the discovery and realisation of actions that have not been thought of before.

Hayek (e.g. 1967b, p. 77) identifies such rules as "nomos", that is abstract or universal "rules of just conduct".[17] Such rules can be found within the formal body of private law, but also as customs and conventions which may even be more important in daily economic affairs (e.g. Hayek 1970, pp. 8f). They conform to the meaning of universalisability in the tradition of Hume or Kant, requiring that the rules be (a) general, i.e. "applicable to an unknown and indeterminable number of persons and instances" (Hayek 1973, p. 50), (b) open, i.e. they merely describe those actions which are not allowed and thus leave it to the individuals to discover innovative modes of action (e.g. Hayek 1976, pp. 36ff) and (c) certain and distinct, i.e. they

---

17 See e.g. HAYEK (1976, p. 31), explicitly pointing at the complementary conceptions of Böhm (and Popper) when he states that the rules of just conduct "are the *nomos* which is at the basis of a 'private law society' and makes an Open Society possible."

can be relied upon, allowing actors to identify in practice those actions which are not allowed (Hayek 1960, pp. 208f).[18]

These abstract rules of just conduct not only contribute to a spontaneous order of co-ordination and control of interactions. For Hayek, most of them are themselves the result of spontaneous development (evolution). Hence, most abstract rules of just conduct are described by Hayek as purpose-free not only in terms of their content but also in view of their creation. Since they have to be appropriate to purposes and circumstances which no one can know in their entirety, the rules can not have been designed to bring about concrete pre-known results. Rather, in a process of learning to cope with many exigencies they were discovered as behavioural guides which proved to be also valuable in unforeseen circumstances. Hayek argues in the tradition of Scottish moral philosophy that civilisations in which abstract rules could prevail prospered because they favoured the "process of adaptation and learning" (Hayek 1960, p. 40) that is necessary for cultural evolution.[19]

Hayek's concept of the Rule of Law is foremost the reformulation of the above-described notion of "nomos" as a political principle. In opposition to a "teleocracy" where citizens' actions are deliberately directed towards particular political ends, Hayek's political ideal of the rule of law is that of a "nomocracy" - the "empire of laws and not of men" (Hayek 1967b, p. 98). Here "the 'public good' or 'general welfare' consists solely in the

---

18 As a main indicator of the "certainty of the law" Hayek (ibid.) names the amount of "disputes which do not lead to litigation because the outcome is practically certain as soon as the legal position is examined." In line with the tradition of the common law, he insists that the rules need not be explicitly known or written down. It is rather an implicit "sense of justice" that in the end guides the judges' application of the rules of just conduct and that, if traditionally transmitted and shared within a community, determines the certainty of the law (e.g. HAYEK 1973, pp. 155ff.).

19 Hayek's theory of cultural evolution (see HAYEK 1988, ch.1 and 8 or 1979, pp. 153ff), based on the principle of group selection in an environment of unconscious learning and adaptation of rules by group members cannot be discussed here in detail. His idea that groups which found and followed certain abstract rules could outgrow the organisational limitations of small groups and reach prosperity in the extended order of catallaxy may be a telling "conjectural history". Its applicability to institutional change of modern legal rules and constitutions is rather dubious, however. Many critics have identified similar weaknesses in Hayek's reasoning (e.g. VANBERG 1986, WITT 1994).

preservation of that abstract and end-independent order which is secured by obedience to abstract rules of just conduct" (ibid.). This means in view of the necessary and legitimate task of the state, that it should conform to "the basic principle of the limitation of the coercive powers of government to the enforcement of general rules of just conduct" (Hayek 1978a, p. 132). As we will see in part VI, this view of the rule of law as "nomocracy" lead Hayek to develop a particular proposal on how the separation of powers in a democracy should be (re-) organised in order to keep the legislative body within the limits of "real" legislation (the setting or "finding" of *nomos*) and separate it from the administration of government which should be controlled through another representative body.

V. Common Grounds and Major Differences

1. Common Grounds

Even if Eucken, Böhm, and Hayek, as we have shown, started from different traditions and chose different approaches, in many respects they met on common grounds. What they basically share is, first of all, a normative position in favour of individual liberty, which created an equally deep interest in problems of the economic and political order, the analysis of which followed a common, basic *Leitmotiv* that "institutions matter". To the question "What matters *most* about institutions?" their answers differ - not in substance, but in emphasis. Hayek would stress the co-ordination properties of institutions regarding the knowledge problem; Eucken or Böhm would stress the controlling properties regarding the problem of power. Neither, however, would have denied or even belittled the importance of *both* fundamental functions of social institutions. Ordoliberals and Hayek evidently share the general position that individual freedom and social order are no opposites and that the observance of social rules of conduct and hence general restraints on behaviour are prerequisite for the attainment of an economic and political order of a free people.[20] They also agree on the princi-

---

20 One must bear in mind, however, that the different perspectives also produced different meanings of "order". For Eucken, "order" has two possible meanings: that of any realised form of a social system within which the ordinary economic process occurs and the normative ideal type of *Ordo*, the order that

ple that public policies should not only be committed to the task of maintaining the legal order, but also more (Hayek) or less (Eucken) strictly limited to do just that. Both are equally strict in rejecting political activism in pursuit of specific market outcomes which they regard as arbitrary (and hence a threat to individual liberty), disorienting and destabilising.[21] Within these common grounds one also finds some rather similar methodological roots. Two aspects may shortly be mentioned:

(1) Ordoliberals and Hayek not only shared normative basic positions. They also held similar views as to how to deal with values. Eucken and Hayek explicitly rejected the common misinterpretation of Weber's dictum on inadmissible value judgements in the social sciences.[22] Hayek (1962, p. 253) argues that this "unfortunately has often produced a fear of expressing any value judgement and even an avoidance of the most important problems which the economist ought frankly to face in his teaching." His own work shows that since the object of analysis, the spontaneous order, is the result

---

"corresponds to reason or the nature of men" (EUCKEN 1952, p. 372). Hayek uses a theoretically more meaningful individualistic definition of "order" which directly relates to the problem of the division of knowledge: "The achievement of human purposes is possible only because we recognise the world we live in as orderly. This order manifests itself in our ability to learn, from the (spatial or temporal) parts of the world we know, rules which enable us to form expectations about other parts." (HAYEK 1967b, p. 72).

21 Consequently, Hayek and the ordoliberals rejected Keynesianism both as a theoretical system and as a political tool-kit. Hayek already during the 1930s was regarded the principal rival of (his personal friend) Keynes in the field of monetary and business cycles theory (see, e.g., HICKS 1967). He repeatedly blamed himself for not returning to the attack when Keynes published his "General Theory" (e.g. HAYEK 1966, p. 284). Later, he could only deplore the Keynesian legacy of inflationary politics (e.g. HAYEK 1972). EUCKEN (e.g. 1948b, p. 44) early pointed at disrupting effects of demand manipulations on the "scarcity gauge" of relative prices.

22 See ALBERT (1972) for a comprehensive recapitulation of Weber's position and its misapprehensions within the social sciences. He argues that one has to distinguish between (a) unavoidable basic value judgements in the process of identifying problems and selecting subject matters, (b) values that prevail within the social and institutional objects under observation and (c) value judgements that express an opinion based on a normative principle and aimed at prescribing a certain behaviour of the addressees. A "*Werturteilsproblem*" is only implied in the latter case.

of complying with rules of just conduct, it would be an inappropriate abstraction to refrain from dealing with norms. These formal and informal rules also reflect and are supported by a basic value, namely individual liberty. Eucken (1952, pp. 340ff) explicitly goes even one step further, claiming it a duty for social scientists to propose what they regard the right and just social order. One has to accept that basic value judgements guiding the interpretation and selection of problems for examination are unavoidable, as e.g. Böhm (1957, p. 159) stated. More importantly, values and norms are an essential part of the institutional structure and hence of the subject matter under analysis.[23] To be sure, ordoliberals and Hayek also did not shun outright value-judgements in politics and morals. However, these were not hidden (or: "*crypto*-normative") but clearly identifiable.[24] At any rate, both strands of liberalism obviously shared the view that social sciences cannot usefully be separated from moral philosophy.

(2) Ordoliberals and Hayek also shared a common uneasiness with the dominant mainstream of economic modelling. While this is most obvious in the case of Hayek, in the case of Eucken the distance to contemporary neoclassical modes of thought is, as we will see, less evident. Still, we may note that Eucken (1948a, p. 197) cites approvingly the following dictum of Lord Robbins: "in the excitement of perfecting our instruments of analysis, we have tended to neglect a study of the framework which they assume." The basic message of "Ordnungstheorie", that depending on the institutional order economic processes have different meanings and take different developments (e.g. Eucken 1952: 24), has only recently been rediscovered by more than just a few economists. At least, this holds true for the "New Institutional Economics", beginning with studies on the effects of different arrangements of property rights (e.g. Furubotn/Pejovich 1972) and con-

---

23 On the "ethics of rules" or the normativity of market institutions, see STREIT (1992c, p. 147ff).
24 See KIRCHGÄSSNER (1988, pp. 62ff) who blames a "crypto-normative content" in ordoliberal and Hayekian statements. What seems to make it worse - according to an implicit value judgement of Kirchgässner - is that some ordoliberal opinions are not in line with what he believes to be a majority opinion. From that it is inferred that such ideas are not "democratic" (ibid., pp. 65ff). We will have to come back to this latter allegation.

tinuing, among others, in the field of economic history and the theory of growth (e.g. North 1990).[25]

2. Major Differences

The different approaches - Hayek's predominant view based on the problem of the division of knowledge and the ordoliberals' preoccupation with the problem of private economic power - led to major differences in the theory and politics of (1) competition, (2) institutional change and (3) social justice.

(1) Hayek's view of competition as a "discovery procedure" forced him to abandon conventional equilibrium theory[26], whereas the ordo-conception of competition as an "emasculating instrument" might have allowed to stick to an ideal type not unlike, for that matter, perfect competition. These differences have consequences in competition policy.

(2) Hayek's concept of institutions as "an adaptation to our ignorance" (1976, p. 39) led most naturally to an evolutionary concept of social institutions and scepticism regarding conscious institutional changes, whereas the ordo-view of institutions as instruments to reduce private power produced the task of "fashioning the legal instruments for an economic constitution", which has to be "understood as a general political decision as to how the economic life of the nation is to be structured." (Böhm et al. 1936, p. 24).

(3) Hayek's concept of catallaxy leaves no room in a meaningful way to pose "the social question" aiming at redistributive justice; his concept of "nomocracy" precludes political attempts to answer this question by employing any discriminatory means. Ordoliberals, in turn, cannot simply discard the social question once they define economic power also in material terms requiring to pass judgements on market results and take a comparatively instrumentalist approach towards the economic constitution.

---

25 See SCHMIDTCHEN (1984) or TIETZEL (1991) for a detailed discussion of relations between ordo conceptions and parts of the New Institutional Economics. Relations to Constitutional Economics will be shortly discussed in section VI.

26 It is not clear if Hayek has completely abandoned the concept of equilibrium. For example, some of his presentations of market processes seem to imply the idea of a "tendency towards equilibrium" not unlike the one used, e.g. by KIRZNER (1973). For an analysis of these questions, see LOY (1988).

All three differences could be stylised to create an outright opposition between Hayekian and ordoliberal views. A more cautious and sympathetic reading of textual and historical contexts, however, should help to explain and qualify some of the differences. It will sometimes even allow for an integrative perspective.

3. The Meaning of Competition: Austrian and Freiburgian Views

Eucken's lifetime struggle with the "great antinomy" led him to produce compromises some of which today appear rather outdated. This particularly holds for his attempt to distance himself from the Historical School by adopting, at least to some extent, concepts of contemporary neo-classical economics. It has often been noted that Eucken's concept of "complete competition" (*"vollständiger Wettbewerb"*, e.g. 1952, pp. 244ff) resembles the static concept of "perfect competition" which, as Hayek (1937, 1945) was amongst the first to show, is totally inappropriate to account for the primary functions and achievements of competitive processes. To take an equilibrium state of an economy at rest, deduced from assumptions of perfect information and foresight, as an objective for political action not only amounts to a conceptually dubious "Nirvana approach" (see Demsetz 1969). It also means taking a constructivist view on the market economy which is treated like a purposeful organisation or "teleocracy" (see Streit 1993, p. 237).

At least in Eucken's writings the presence of both, "Nirvana"- and constructivist fallacies cannot be totally denied.[27] However, it should be remembered that his ideal type of "complete" competition was not in the first instance used as an indicator of efficiency. It was rather circumscribing the ideal of a consumer-oriented economy in which the social and political problem of economic power is solved. Still, the old ordo- view of competition was far from integrating entrepreneurship and innovation in a theory of

---

27 To be sure, deviations from the model of perfect competition can be found. EUCKEN (1952, p. 24) rejected the condition of "perfect competition" that goods be homogenous, as unrealistic. Hayek did so too, but his objection was more substantial: "because of the ever changing character of our needs and our knowledge, or the infinite variety of human skills and capacities, the ideal state cannot be one requiring an identical character of large numbers of products and services." (HAYEK 1946, p. 104).

market processes - processes which necessarily disturb equilibria and create instability (not absence) of economic power. Schumpeter's (1912 and 1942) early attempts in the field of economic development and entrepreneurship were noticed by Eucken - which is about all one can say.[28] Hayek's (1937 and 1945) fundamental critique of any theory of market competition that presupposes given or complete information, went totally unnoticed - so one must say.

The consequences of taking either the knowledge problem or the power problem as basic points of departure become most clear in the field of competition policy. The emerging difference is most striking when it comes to the question of monopoly regulation. For Hayek (e.g. 1979, pp. 70f) any attempt to make a firm act "as if" competition existed is simply absurd, since a discovery procedure's results cannot be anticipated and hence not dictated. In addition, "discretionary power given to authorities for the purpose of merely preventing 'abuses'" would rather lead to the agency protecting the monopoly against newcomers (ibid., p. 86). Thus Hayek's views have led to the political concept of "freedom to compete"[29], which centres around the strict application of "nomos" and can be expressed with a single legal principle: "to declare invalid and legally unenforceable all agreement in restraint of trade, without any exceptions, and to prevent all attempts to enforce them ...by aimed discrimination or the like by giving those upon whom such pressures were brought a claim for multiple damages" (ibid.). Eucken, in turn, did neither seem to be aware of the knowledge problems nor of the risks of "captured" agencies when he explicitly declares it an aim of a governmental monopoly agency to urge monopolists to act "as if there

---

28 EUCKEN (1940) deals with Schumpeter in some footnotes; but there he is mainly concerned with attaching labels like "positivist" or "relativist" on Schumpeter and his social philosophy.

29 This concept was established primarily by Erich HOPPMANN (e.g. 1988, part II), successor of Hayek at Freiburg. It is mainly inspired by Hayekian competition theory. But also the fundamental principles of Böhm's elaborate ideas on competition policy are mostly in line with the concept of "Wettbewerbsfreiheit" or "freedom to compete". Eucken's concept, in turn, bears much more resemblance to the "structure-conduct-performance" paradigm of the Harvard School, in opposition to which Hoppmann developed his concept of a purpose-free order of free competition.

was complete competition" (Eucken 1952, p. 295 or 1949, p. 68).[30] He goes on to state that "the price has to be fixed such that supply and demand reach their equilibrium and at the same time equals marginal costs" (Eucken 1952, p. 297; 1949, p. 69). This is exactly the view that Hayek (1940) challenged in another context, namely when he assessed Lange's proposal of market socialism, attacking "an excessive preoccupation with problems of the pure theory of stationary equilibrium." (ibid., p. 240).

Considering Hayek's view of competition and taking into account new insights of property rights analysis and transaction cost economics, the following central tenets of a modern "neo-ordoliberal" concept of market competition can be formulated: Competition is a process during which (1) knowledge about possibilities of substitution (i.e. opportunity costs) is discovered and disseminated, (2) control of the use of property rights is exerted through actual and potential substitution of partners to (and objects of) transaction and (3) incentives to reassess the individual portfolio of property rights are provided through the price effects of transactions. For competitive processes to sufficiently fulfil these functions, it is necessary that individuals incur transaction costs, the level of which, in turn, depends on the quality of the institutional order that underlies market co-ordination and competitive control. Given this, the intensity of competition is related to the propensity of market participants to incur transaction costs (Streit/Wegner 1992). Along these lines, and setting aside the differences in conceptualising competition and competition policy, the Hayekian knowledge problem and the ordoliberal occupation with the competitive order of rules can be brought together to form one integrated body of thinking in terms of the market-process and the market order.[31]

---

30 Eucken seems to have come under the influence of his disciple Leonhard MIKSCH (e.g. 1949) when he adopted the idea of regulation according to preconceptions of an "as-if competition".
31 The work of Möschel, Mestmäcker and Hoppmann stands for this integration of Hayekian insights into a new ordoliberal assessment; see also the contributions of STREIT (1992a, p. 685; 1992b).

4. The Emergence of Institutions: Spontaneous Order and Intentional Rule-Setting

As we have once again seen in the above context, Hayek emphasised the threat to the free market system emanating above all from the state's attempt to steer a purpose-free, self-organising, and complex order of actions, or from politicians' "presumption of knowledge", whereas ordoliberals stressed that the economic freedom is mainly endangered from within, by economic power groups facing a "weak" state that is unable to maintain the competitive order. This difference in emphasis is also reflected in the respective positive and normative theories of institutional change.

Eucken and, to a lesser degree, Böhm[32] criticised the idea that the rules for a free, competitive order would ever emerge and be maintained spontaneously. For them, "it is not enough to realise certain principles of law and for the rest leave the development of the economic order to itself ... " (Eucken 1952, p. 373). This, at first glance, seems to be in open opposition to (the later) Hayek[33]. And indeed, on a continuum of positions between purely "evolutionist" and purely "constructivist", while none covers the extreme positions, Hayek is closer to the evolutionist position, and the ordoliberals are somewhere in the middle, but tending to the constructivist stance if the institutional framework of the competitive order is concerned.

---

32 Böhm's account of the origins of the private law society is quite in line with Hayek's philosophy of the law; see e.g. BÖHM (1966, p. 46). BÖHM (1957, p. 97) also joins Hayek when he argues that at least the elementary principles of the law are not "made", but "found". Hence it is justified to argue that Böhm "strikes a different, evolutionary note" (SALLY 1996, p. 243).

33 In his "'Free Enterprise and Competitive Order" HAYEK (1948) still argued very similar to the ordoliberals' critique of classical liberalism, and proposed a "policy which deliberately adopts competition, the market, and prices as its ordering principle and uses the legal framework enforced by the state in order to make competition as effective and beneficial as possible - and to supplement it where, and only where, it cannot be effective" (ibid., p. 110). He goes on to discuss unemployment insurance, town planning, patents, trade-marks, cartel building contracts, limited liability corporations and what today are called "incomplete contracts" opting for special legal provisions. Further indications of a somewhat "constructivist" Hayek are found by VANBERG (1986). The fact that Hayek constructed a model constitution is discussed in part VI.

THE MARKET ECONOMY AND THE STATE

Concerning the economic order of actions, ordoliberals and Hayek similarly describe and propagate the image of market co-ordination as spontaneous interactions within rules. Both deplore the effects of the state's intervening in the precarious price-signalling and controlling mechanisms of competitive market processes. When it comes to the institutional order, however, ordoliberals attempt to make a sharp distinction: while the day-to-day economic processes - the market "game" - are not to be planned, the economic constitution should not be left to a similar kind of spontaneity. The adequate rules of the "game" are assumed to be clearly established, they must only be set up and maintained with the help of one organisation - the state[34]. "Laissez-faire" towards the order of rules, ordoliberals argue, cannot work, it would lead to a "fettering of the state by private interests" (Eucken 1932, p. 307) which means that the rules' consistency and neutrality would have to give way to political activism and favouritism and that monopolies would soon reign over both the market and the legal order of society.

The ordoliberals developed this view not only in contrast with what they regarded as "laissez-faire" liberalism, but also in opposition to a then dominant stream of historic determinism. It must be remembered that during the 30s and 40s, historicism was at its height. Not only orthodox Marxists, but also most economists of the German Historical School and even Schumpeter (1942) adopted the idea that economic power in the end necessarily determined political actions and that the monopolisation of the industry was just as unavoidable as the ensuing breakdown of capitalism and advent of socialism. Considering this intellectual background, it is quite understandable that Eucken (1951, ch. II) devotes one of his five London lectures to fight the thesis of the "inevitability of development" arguing that "an intelligent co-ordination of all economic and legal policy" could solve the problem of economic power (ibid., p. 54). In addition, the historical situation in Germany after 1945 has to be taken into account. The need to create a new political, but also economic order of rules was just given. To be sure, lib-

---

34 In a peculiar way Eucken occasionally seems to regard the state as necessary and active and at the same time passively obedient to some laws of nature. Thus, he (EUCKEN 1952, p. 374) argues that "the state does not dictate an economic order, it merely brings to bear what otherwise would be driven back by other tendencies." Such statements indeed remind one of a benevolent dictator-view of the state.

eral ideas were not prevalent within the German democratic parties which after the war all favoured different forms of a socialist organisation of the economy. Ordoliberals, however, took advantage of several unique historical opportunities, thus justifying the importance of what Eucken (e.g. 1952) labelled the "historical moment with its particular power-constellations and imponderabilia". Among these constellations one certainly cannot dismiss the courageous rôle that Ludwig Erhard played as a political entrepreneur or the strategic interests of the western allies that supported the introduction of a capitalist order in Germany (see, e.g. Grossekettler 1989, pp. 67ff)[35].

Hayek (e.g. 1952b, ch.7) condemned historicism as fiercely as Eucken or Böhm. However, the opponent intellectual mood that provoked his evolutionism is not historical fatalism, but rather what he called "rationalistic constructivism". The idea "that man 'created' his civilisation and its institutions" and that, therefore "he must also be able to alter them at will so as to satisfy his desires or wishes" (Hayek 1970, p. 3), which was held by proponents of the French or Continental tradition of liberalism, to Hayek was an expression of a most dangerous hubris and an "abuse of reason" (e.g. 1952b). In the British tradition of evolutionary liberalism, he took the opposite view that modern civilisation with its fine-structured layers of customs, conventions and legal principles can only have grown as the unplanned result of human action and not of human design or political will. For Hayek, the extended order has not been created "at will", and it can only be destroyed by attempts to redesign it with holistic blueprints.

Even if he did not explicitly comment on the matter, we believe that Hayek would not have strictly opposed the ordoliberal attempt to provide guiding principles of an economic constitution for the German institutional reconstruction after the war (also: Vanberg 1989, p. 179). However, a Hayekian evolutionist must frown at parts of the underlying ordoliberal *Weltanschauung*, with its amount of faith in human intelligence and knowledge to design a new order. At any rate, he would protest a constructivistic and naturalistic creed which took an extreme expression in one statement of

---

35 HAYEK (1983, pp. 193f) states that he early became an admirer of Erhard who "deserves far greater credit for the restoration of a free society in Germany than he is given for either inside or outside Germany." He adds: "Erhard could never have accomplished what he did under bureaucratic or democratic constraints. It was a lucky moment when the right person in the right spot was free to do what he thought right, although he could never have convinced anybody else that it was the right thing."

Eucken (1948b, p. 34), according to which "economic policy ought to bring about the free, natural order that God intended." This really is asking too much of politics.

The lasting relevance of these diverging views is illustrated by current debates on the ongoing Eastern European economies in transition (see Streit 1998b, pp. 49ff). In some societies (like the Czech or Polish) a "constructivist" switch of the basic rules of the game was at least partly possible, provoking a comparatively prompt and successful "game of catallaxy" (Hayek 1976, p. 115) to have its way. This was mainly due to the fact that in those cases the state was at least comparatively strong and its population in principle willing to accomplish such a switch. In addition, the Czech and Polish were able to pick up the threads of a longer tradition of a private law system. In other societies, like especially the Russian, exactly these preconditions which can not be created by fiat were not given. Here, even presidential decrees which would entail Eucken's principles in their purest form can not be expected to bring the country nearer to a competitive order. Here, the market economy will probably have to grow much more from "below", as the result of practices within subgroups of merchants and on grey or black markets with their rules based on custom and private conventions much more than on a private law society in its legalistic western form.[36]

5. The "Social Question": Hayekian and Ordoliberal Views

Böhm (1957, p. 160) once described the major pre-scientific interest and raison d'être of the Freiburg School to be a "political concern", which led "all scientific works and aspirations ..." be "... dedicated to the attempt to remove the social question from the dogma of Karl Marx and his historical-dialectic philosophy." In so doing, ordoliberals attempted to integrate the question of social justice into their own concept of the competitive order. To them, the "social question" was not, as Marx and most members of the historical school believed, the result of excessive but rather of insufficient competition, reflecting the failure of the state to set and preserve the

---

[36] A stimulating exchange of views on whether to impose a market economy as a strong state's design "from above" or to rely on the unplanned emergence of market economies as a result of human action "from below" took place between GRAY (1994) and DE JASAY (1994). See also VOIGT (1994).

framework of a competitive order. For this failure, in turn, ordoliberals more or less openly blamed the ideas of classical, or, as they preferred to call them, "laissez-faire" liberals. Adherents of "laissez-faire" are accused for ignoring that - in a monopolistic setting - private citizens exercise power over other private citizens and that - in a corporativistic setting - the state can be "captured" by those who wield economic power (e.g. Böhm 1950, lii; Eucken 1952, pp. 358f). Eucken (1951, p. 56) claimed that "social security and social justice are the great questions of the hour". For him, the "dependence of income levels on market conditions can ... lead to grave injustice and certainly poses a considerable problem" (ibid., p. 63). Not so for Hayek.

Hayek, in his later social philosophical works, comes to the conclusion that "the social question" cannot meaningfully be asked at all since it has no responsible addressee and that "social justice" as such is an almost empty word which definitely looses meaning if applied to the results of the unplanned and purpose-free order of "catallaxy" (e.g. Hayek 1976, chs. 9-11). Hayek's strictly monistic reference to individual liberty as the sole foundation of justice and hence the rules of just conduct does not mean that he ignored the *analytical question* of social justice. Especially in his later work, he tries to identify the origins of what he calls the "atavism of social justice" (e.g. Hayek 1978b). He explains individuals' instinctive demand for social cohesion and warmth that can no longer be satisfied by the abstract "extended order" itself (e.g. 1988, ch. 4), but creates what already Popper (1945, p. 172) described as the "strain of civilisation". The extended order is different from the household economy or tribal society exactly in that it makes no use of purposeful "income distribution". Unequal positions of wealth are the unplanned and temporary results of individual skill and luck in using one's personal knowledge and abilities. Such results can neither be considered just nor unjust according to recognised general principles. Only the rules of the game can be found to be just (fair) or unjust (unfair), which again would depend on the "test of universalizability" (Hayek 1976, pp. 27ff) and thus be a question of procedural justice and not one of material justice (Hayek 1976, pp. 28f). Consequently, the "struggle for formal equality, i.e. against all discrimination based on social origin, nationality, race, creed, sex, etc." finds full support by Hayek (1978a, p. 142) - as long as it aims at general, abstract rules of conduct (and not their "affirmative" manipulation). In addition - and with a certain amount of *ad hoc* reasoning - Hayek granted that there may be reasons to assure "outside of and supplementary to the market" a protection against severe deprivation in the form of guaranteed minimum income to all (e.g. 1976, p. 87).[37]

The latter policy objective is shared by ordoliberals. Most of them, however, would also include progressive taxation and other variants of Eucken's regulatory principle of "income policy" (1952, pp. 300f), which is aimed at correcting the spontaneous income distribution and covering "urgent needs" (ibid.) of the population. But these normative conclusions, again, reflect only differences in degree and not in substance. The difference in substance is at the theoretical stage. Hayek did not follow the enchanting ordoliberal slogan that a well-functioning competitive market order would in itself be the most eminent "social" device or even a major precondition for the solution of the "social question" (ibid., p. 314).[38] He would certainly not follow Eucken in arguing that "the realisation of social justice ... depends on the realisation of the general principle of a competitive economy" (ibid., p. 315) if this implied a concept of material justice. In this case Hayek would argue that the realisation of social justice required "a kind of order of society altogether different from that spontaneous order which will form itself if individuals are restrained only by general rules of just conduct." (Hayek 1978a, p. 140).

---

37 Hayek fails to give the necessary clarifications on the modalities of such a protection and, especially, on how to prevent social insurance schemes from exceeding limits of reasonable "minimalness", as historically they did soon after their introduction in all major welfare states.

38 Hayek's rejection of the German term and concept of "social market economy" as "most confusing and harmful" (HAYEK 1965, p. 83) or as "a real danger" and "camouflage for aspirations that certainly have nothing to do with the common interest" (HAYEK 1957, pp. 238f) is probably intended to be a critique of German politics rather than of ordoliberal concepts. Still, even if only in a more modest form, the critique also applies to the latter.

VI. The Political Economy of Liberalism: A Constitutional Economics Perspective

1. A Note on Political Economy and Economics of Politics

In terms of pre-scientific interests (basic value judgements) and normative conclusions, the ordoliberal concept of an economic constitution and Hayek's "constitution of liberty" (1960) do not differ dramatically from modern constitutional economics as represented, especially, by James M. Buchanan.[39] However, in terms of the analytical structure or "economics" employed, the approaches differ considerably. Obviously, neither Eucken and Böhm nor Hayek would claim "rational choice" or stylised maximising behaviour as used within mainstream economics (including most of constitutional economics) as belonging to the "hard core" of their research programmes.[40] Also "contractarianism" or the "exchange paradigm" are not part of their view of politics and the state. In short, ordoliberals and Hayek are political economists in a traditional sense; they command no "economics of politics" if economics is defined by the above elements.[41]

Regarding the research programme of the ordoliberals and their principles of public policy, the lack of a (positive) theory of politics may pose a serious problem of theoretical incompleteness.[42] Since ordoliberals strictly rely on the state, and hence on elected politicians, to enact the very com-

---

[39] For a programmatic overview and delimitation of the domain of constitutional economics, see BUCHANAN (1990); for an instructive survey, see VOIGT (1997). The relation between ordoliberalism and constitutional economics is discussed e.g. by VANBERG (1988) and LEIPOLD (1990). The relation between Hayek and constitutional economics is analysed e.g. by VANBERG (1983 and 1989) or BUCHANAN (1989) and - in an interesting attempt to build a synthesis - by LESCHKE (1993).

[40] See, e.g. BUCHANAN (1990, pp. 12ff). A vigorous defence of homo oeconomicus can also be found in BRENNAN/BUCHANAN (1985, ch. 4).

[41] See TIETZEL (1991) for a critique from the perspective of mainstream economics of politics.

[42] This is one of KIRCHGÄSSNER's (1988, pp. 55ff) more convincing points of critique. In fact, EUCKEN (1940, pp. 213ff) states that the emergence and changes (but not the effects) of "the social and legal organization" and hence politics themselves ought to be treated as "data" to the analysis. It is here, he argues, that he proposed that "the theoretical explanation has to break off" (*ibid.*).

prehensive institutional reforms advocated by them, the incentive structures of politicians, voters, and interest groups do become empirically important and theoretically worthy of the most sober analysis. To be sure, Eucken and Böhm were not ignorant optimists who disregarded the workings of the real political processes. As we have seen, their historical observations and political demands were rich in considerations of vested interests, of their institutionally determined influence on the political process and of the ensuing effects on the economic order. Thus, Eucken and Böhm to some degree anticipated the "rent-seeking" insight that was later to emerge within the Public Choice movement (e.g. Krueger 1974, Olson 1982). However, they kept on regarding politicians mainly as addressees of programmatic demands rather than as objects for a behavioural analysis.

Hayek's approach to politics can be similarly qualified. Especially his trilogy on Law, Legislation and Liberty is full of accounts of the unromantic side of legislation within the prevailing form of democracy. But the contemporary Public Choice literature is ignored - with the sole exception of Olson (1965). Hayek's political economy hence basically remains tied to political philosophy in the tradition of the Scottish classics; it does not become an economics of politics or of the constitution in the modern meaning. Hayek's remaining a traditional political economist without turning into a protagonist of the economics of politics is certainly not accidental. The kind of market analogy used predominantly within much of Public Choice reflects exactly those elements of neo-classical reasoning that Hayek rejected already for economic theory (see Wohlgemuth 1995a). Hayek reserves the concept of "catallaxy" for the spontaneous order of the market, with its private law institutions and price signals. Politics, according to Hayek, is mainly part of a fundamentally different kind of order, namely that of an organisation or "teleocracy" (e.g. Hayek 1967b, p. 89). Concerning the relationship between the two kinds of order, the basic relation between politicians and citizens, there certainly is no "exchange paradigm" (e.g. Buchanan 1990, p. 9) in the political theory of Hayek. This does not mean that Hayek's analysis becomes in any way inconsistent. He does not use different "models of man" for politicians and for ordinary market actors. Both are assumed to be pursuing their own ends, to be exposed to the constitutional lack of knowledge, and to have to rely on rules of conduct. The rules, however, differ. And it is from here that Hayek's political philosophy starts.

We have seen that ordoliberals and Hayek, even if they tend to disagree on the conceptual role of social justice within a constitution of liberty, have provided similar insights into the political economy of the welfare state, its mutually reinforcing disruptive effects on the economic and the political constitution. For them, the welfare state is "captured" by economic interest groups and forced to supersede the autonomy of the individual and the rule of private law by corporativism and the rule of public law.[43] This process, in ordoliberal terms, leads to the destruction of the competitive order as a means to emasculate economic power, in Hayekian terms it means the abandonment of equality before the rules of just conduct as a precondition of a spontaneous order of free actions. Let us now see what ordoliberals and Hayek have to offer in terms of political reforms or "institutional choice".

2. Constitutional Reforms

As Vanberg (1988, p. 24) observed, ordoliberals have "devoted astoundingly little explicit argument to the issue of what constitutional provisions might be required to make the 'strong government' perform its proper task and not to use its power in an undesired way". Because they believed the main disturbance of the competitive order to originate from *private* agglomerations of power, the economic constitution with its aim of taming economic power seems to prevail over (at least: conceptual work on) the political constitution's traditional task of "taming Leviathan". Hence the ordoliberals' understanding of the rule of law as an institutional arrangement that protects the state from being captured by private power groups. Beyond stating general principles, however, the Freiburg School has little advice to offer by ways of practical antidotes. If it comes to concrete reforms of political institutions, only the following "political principle" (*"staatspolitischer Grundsatz"*) is provided by Eucken (1952, p. 334): "The policy of the state should be directed at the dissolution of economic power groups or limit their functions." The particular elements of a corresponding feasible political reform remain rather obscure and dubious. Efforts to make the activities of interest groups more transparent, to set public hearings or the advice of experts against their pressure, and to reveal their financial support for politicians and parties would be hardly more than cosmetic op-

---

[43] An elaborate and very Hayekian critique of the social welfare state is provided by BÖHM (1953).

erations on the body politic. Stronger measures, like provisions of public law in order to restrict their activities would soon violate the civil liberties of expression, association and assembly besides suppressing useful functions which some interest groups might actually serve. The involved conflict between political equality on the one hand, which becomes distorted because not all interests of the electorate have equal access to the legislature, and the aforementioned civil liberties on the other hand has to be solved in a different way. One way would be to bind the legislature.

Two types of constitutional constraints on parliament are mainly discussed (Streit 1987, pp. 12ff): (1) to reduce the authority of parliament or render its use more difficult, (2) to break up the legislative authority by ways of a strict separation of powers.

The first types are in the tradition of Knut Wicksell (1896, part 2: "A new principle of just taxation") who proposed highly qualified majorities for parliament's fiscal decisions. Building on this tradition, constitutional economics later developed "unanimity- rules" as political translations of the Pareto-principle to serve as ultimate normative benchmarks for the appraisal of collective action (e.g. Buchanan/Tullock 1962). Mainly by using contractarian and hence unanimity- based thought-experiments, they also proposed constitutional constraints on taxation (e.g. Brennan/ Buchanan 1980) and on deficit spending (e.g. Buchanan/Wagner 1977, pp. 180f). Within the context of basic political decision rules and procedures, direct democracy is also proposed as a means for the taming of Leviathan (e.g. Frey 1994). These proposals cannot be discussed here. They are advocated neither by early ordoliberals nor by Hayek.[44]

---

[44] This is not to mean that they would be contradictory to the ordoliberal or Hayekian views. For example, the use of referenda and, especially, of popular initiatives can in principle be recommended on Hayekian grounds. As e.g. BOHNET/FREY (1994) show, such procedures are apt at lowering entry barriers in politics, breaking protective belts of the "classe politique" and fostering political discussion and communication. They can thus bring the political competition of ideas at least somewhat closer to an economic discovery procedure (WOHLGEMUTH 1995a, pp. 83ff). More discursive methods of political decision making can be compatible with the "central belief from which all liberal postulates may be said to spring ... that more successful solutions of the problems of society are to be expected if we do not rely on the application of anyone's given knowledge, but encourage the interpersonal process of the exchange of opinion from which better knowledge can be expected to emerge." (HAYEK 1978a, p.

The second type of reform is in the tradition of John Stuart Mill (1861, ch. 13 "Of a second chamber") idea. Hayek reintroduced the basic concept in the form of "a model constitution" (1979, ch. 17).[45] He (ibid., 3) identified the fact that parliament is "not only highest but also an unlimited authority" as "the fatal defect of the prevailing form of democracy". He argued that "the possession of unlimited power makes it impossible for a representative body to make the general principles prevail on which it agrees, because under such a system the majority of the representative assembly, in order to remain a majority, must do what it can to buy the support of the several interests by granting them special benefits" (ibid.). In order to save the rule of nomos (nomocracy), political decision makers must be put in the position to be able to point at democratically legitimised rules and procedures which simply would not allow themselves to give way to the pressures of special interest groups (ibid., 15ff). Hayek claims that this can only be accomplished if the task to lay down abstract rules of just conduct and the task to govern by ways of regulations and public law are organisationally separated. He proposes to establish two representative bodies with distinct functions and - correspondingly - distinct democratic procedures to recruit their members. As a third institution, the constitutional court would have the task to control that each chamber acts within the boundaries of its authority (ibid., pp. 120ff). The separation of powers would hence be such

---

148). However, the rules of direct democratic legislation would have to be equally strict as those Hayek proposes for representative democracies. Above all, the "universalisability test" would have to be applied.

45 We cannot here go into the details of the model. A thorough analysis has been provided by NIENHAUS (1982). A remarkable evaluation from the point of view of German constitutional law can be found in RUPP (1979). Critical remarks are added by BARRY (1979, pp. 190ff) and VOIGT (1992). The fact that Hayek proposed a "model constitution" has often been observed to be in contradiction with his evolutionary bias in favour of spontaneously grown orders of rules. HAYEK (1979, pp. 107f) of course remarked this possible inconsistency. He makes clear: "I certainly do not wish to suggest that any country with a firmly established constitutional tradition should replace its constitution by a new one drawn up on the lines suggested." His purpose in presenting his constitutional "sketch" was (a) to illustrate the general principles of nomocracy, (b) to advise countries that have no tradition of the rule of law and wish to introduce democratic bodies and (c) to propose organisational rules for supra-national governments.

that the first chamber (the "legislative assembly", ibid., pp. 112ff) would be limited to the "production", or better: "finding" and careful adaptation of the abstract rules which are needed to form and preserve the order of society. A second chamber (or "governmental assembly", ibid., pp. 119f) would be in the position to control government and decide upon the legislation which is still needed for the provision of public services. The latter chamber, however, would itself be controlled by the former; it would be strictly bound by the nomos laid down by the legislative assembly. In this way, Hayek hoped to safeguard his political ideal of nomocracy from the onslaught of politicians and interest groups. Thus, he also wanted to save democracy from deteriorating into a "bargaining democracy" which is unable to reflect common opinion on what is just and fair but would become the "playball of group interests", a pure reflection of the power of organisations[46]

Still, propositions which aim at a change in the institutional structure of prevailing democracies hardly have a fair chance to be realised under normal political conditions. Eucken's demand to displace vested interests, the various contractarian attempts to tame Leviathan and also Hayek's "model constitution" would require a binding decision of self-restraint by those who neither have a vested interest nor are very likely to face a massive electoral pressure to do so.[47] As has often been noted (e.g. Streit 1987, pp. 4ff), political reforms in this direction, but also most framework activities of "Ordnungspolitik" or "nomocracy" are rather unattractive under the prevailing forms of democracy. For political entrepreneurs trying to attract and preserve particular groups of clients (supporters and voters), the political value of the constitution and legislation depends upon the extent to which

---

46 KIRCHGÄSSNER's (1988, p. 66) verdict that Hayek "wants to abolish democracy" is thus totally mistaken. It simply fails to grasp the main idea that to put democratic government under the law means not to abolish, but to strengthen democracy as a method of legitimising collective action and expressing public opinion.

47 On the manifold theoretical and practical problems of self-restraint in the sense of "constitutional commitments" there has grown a respectable body of literature from which we recommend KLIEMT (1993). In the tradition of Hume (and much like Hayek), Kliemt (ibid., p. 146) comes to the conclusion that "the model of opportunistically rational behavior will not work as a *universal* basis of economic or jurisprudential constitutional theory." A comprehensive account of precommitment devices used in history is given by ELSTER (1984).

they promise to provide economic results to particular individuals and groups. The competitive order and nomocracy exactly preclude to assign specific results to anybody. Therefore, reforms in their direction would under every-day political conditions be politically hazardous. They would mean to take away group-specific privileges, thus creating identifiable (private) losses on the one hand and widely dispersed and hardly identifiable (public) gains on the other. Because of this perception problem political entrepreneurs can hardly expect to win the support of the beneficiaries - even if these built a very qualified majority. However, even if the prospects for political self-treatment according to ordoliberal or Hayekian blueprints must be sceptically considered, one must not despair. There still are (and become more and more vigorous) spontaneous market forces at work which can make themselves felt also in the realm of politics, by means of breaking social and political rigidities or acting as additional pressures for politicians to adjust the institutional structures. This leads to a second way of coping with Leviathan.

3. Spontaneous Correcting Forces

Among those spontaneous correcting forces which may at least signal, but perhaps also help to overcome the economic and political malaise of welfare states, the shadow economy and interjurisdictional factor movements (or: "globalised markets") have received special attention. Let us close with a brief assessment of the latter from the perspective of ordoliberal and Hayekian conceptions[48]:

While neither Hayek nor the ordoliberals have done much work on the meaning of open markets between jurisdictions and the potential repercussions of spontaneous processes of exit on incentives within the political process, this general idea of institutional competition can be very well analysed using both Hayekian and ordoliberal *Leitmotive*. In principle these are

---

[48] An analysis of the shadow economy at large - comprising not only black or grey market activities, but also basically marketable household production and voluntary non-profit social services - and its relation to the welfare state is provided by STREIT (1984). There, it is argued that the growth of the shadow economy signals the shadow price of maintaining inefficient welfare-state arrangements and that it might ultimately act as a brake upon the process of institutional sclerosis.

the same as in our above presentation of the respective ideas on economic competition: the problem of knowledge and the problem of power. As we have shown in more detail elsewhere (e.g. Wohlgemuth 1995b and Streit 1996), institutional competition can be regarded a partial solution to the political knowledge problem, being a political "discovery procedure" in Hayekian terms. This means that "exit" of mobile resources (be it the shifting of financial portfolios, foreign direct investment or outright migration of citizens) allows citizens an individual "choice of rules", testing the expediency of available institutional arrangements. At the same time it induces political agents to adapt to signalled preferences about existing alternatives, but also to develop innovative policies in the sense of potentially new institutional solutions to societal problems. Consequently, a competitive order of spontaneous "exit" can serve as a procedure for the discovery of such institutional infrastructure "as, without resort to it, would not be known to anyone, or at least would not be utilised." (Hayek 1968, p. 179).

Furthermore, institutional competition can serve as a non-constructivistic answer to the ordoliberal problem of power. Here, of course, competition in the first instance would act as a device for "taming Leviathan", that is, for reducing the power of politics over citizens. Institutional competition, however, does not necessarily lead to what ordoliberals would have to suspect as a "weak" state, as many reports on the alleged consequences of "globalisation" seem to suggest. We would not so much expect the single states in an increasingly common world market to loose the authority and ability to perform their proper functions. We would rather expect institutional competition to force more and more governments to return to and concentrate on exactly these proper functions which lie mainly within the realm of the "protective state" in the sense of Buchanan (1975, pp. 68ff) or of its proper "coercive function" in the sense of Hayek (1979, p. 135), referring to "the enforcement of general rules of conduct equally applicable to all."[49] However, we have to admit that institutional competition has to be tolerated if not supported by the rules of the game to which political actors

---

49 To be sure, one cannot expect institutional competition to bring about a total erosion of discriminatory welfare state arrangements. This is clearly prevented when taking into account exogenous limits, representing the rules of interjurisdictional competition (like, e.g. many provisions of the EU- treaties), but also endogenous limits which can be traced to the competitive process itself (like limits on the actors' knowledge and mobility, on the institutions' flexibility and changeablity), see STREIT (1996, pp. 241ff).

have to subscribe. Hence the problem of self-restraint comes up again. But it may well be that - on a world-wide scale - political actors are not likely to form a lasting cartel which would make institutional competition ineffective.

VII. Conclusion

Summarising our main findings, we can state that Hayek, Eucken and Böhm developed conceptions of the market economy and of the state that have much more in common than may be indicated by the amount of explicit references. Although they started from different angles and with different intellectual backgrounds, we found our protagonists very often to meet on common grounds and to arrive at rather similar policy conclusions.

To be sure, we also found some plain differences - most of which we attribute to the ordoliberals' predominant occupation with the problem of private (economic) power and Hayek's preoccupation with the problem of private (subjective) knowledge. While concerning the problem of power, the differences are rather of emphasis than of substance, it is concerning the knowledge problem that a fundamental difference can be identified. Whereas for Hayek the problem of the division of knowledge permeates all his theory of the spontaneous order, it remains largely neglected by the early ordoliberals. Even if Hayek could subscribe to most of the liberal principles defining the *"Wettbewerbsordnung"*, his conception of "catallaxy" has much more to offer. It yields a theory of market processes that the early ordoliberals had to do without. Nevertheless, the ordoliberal programme still contains insights and warnings that deserve being rediscovered and refurbished - the problem of power within interventionist and corporatist welfare states is far from being solved.

To close with a personal value judgement we hold that the Hayekian legacy remains more demanding and more promising to exploit and develop. At any rate, there is not and will never be one liberal conception of the market economy and the state.

THE MARKET ECONOMY AND THE STATE

References

ALBERT, HANS: "Theorie und Praxis. Max Weber und das Problem der Wertfreiheit und der Rationalität", in: ALBERT, HANS: *Konstruktion und Kritik*, Hamburg (Hoffmann und Campe) 1972, pp. 41-73.

ALBERT, HANS: "Grundprobleme rationaler Ordnungspolitik. Vom wohlfahrtsökonomischen Kalkül zur Analyse institutioneller Alternativen", in: H. MILDE / H. G. MONISSEN (Eds.): *Rationale Wirtschaftspolitik in komplexen Gesellschaften - Gérard Gäfgen zum 60. Geburtstag,* Stuttgart et al. (Kohlhammer) 1985, pp. 53-63.

BARRY, NORMAN P.: *Hayek's Social and Economic Philosophy*, London (Macmillan) 1979.

BOHNET, IRIS / BRUNO S. FREY: "Direct-Democratic Rules: The Role of Discussion", *Kyklos*, 47 (1994), pp. 341-354.

BÖHM, FRANZ: *Wettbewerb und Monopolkampf - Eine Untersuchung zur Frage des wirtschaftlichen Kampfrechts und zur Frage der rechtlichen Struktur der geltenden Wirtschaftsordnung*, Berlin (Heymann) 1933.

BÖHM, FRANZ: "Die Idee des ORDO im Denken Walter Euckens - Dem Freunde und Mitherausgeber zum Gedächtnis", *Ordo*, 3 (1950), pp. xv-lxiv.

BÖHM, FRANZ: "Der Rechtsstaat und der soziale Wohlfahrtsstaat", in: BÖHM, FRANZ: *Reden und Schriften*, Karlsruhe (Müller) 1960, pp. 82-156 (first publication 1953).

BÖHM, FRANZ: "Die Forschungs- und Lehrgemeinschaft zwischen Juristen und Vokswirten an der Universität Freiburg in den dreißiger und vierziger Jahren des 20. Jahrhunderts", in: BÖHM, FRANZ: *Reden und Schriften*, Karlsruhe (Müller) 1960, pp. 158-175 (first publication 1957).

BÖHM, FRANZ: "Wettbewerbsfreiheit und Kartellfreiheit", in: BÖHM, FRANZ: *Freiheit und Ordnung in der Marktwirtschaft* (ed. by E.-J. Mestmäcker), Baden-Baden (Nomos) 1980, pp. 233-262 (first publication 1958).

BÖHM, FRANZ: "Demokratie und ökonomische Macht", in: INSTITUT FÜR AUSLÄNDISCHES UND INTERNATIONALES WIRTSCHAFTSRECHT (Ed.): *Kartelle und Monopole im modernen Recht*, Karlsruhe: (Müller) 1961, 1-24.

BÖHM, FRANZ: «Rule of Law in a Market Economy», in: A. PEACOCK / H. WILLGERODT (Eds.): *Germany's Social Market Economy: Origins and Evolution*, London (MacMillan) 1989, pp. 46-67 (German publication 1966).

BÖHM, FRANZ: "Freiheit und Ordnung in der Marktwirtschaft", in: BÖHM, FRANZ: *Freiheit und Ordnung in der Marktwirtschaft* (ed. by E.-J. Mestmäcker), Baden-Baden (Nomos) 1980, pp. 195-212.

BÖHM, FRANZ / WALTER EUCKEN / HANS GROSSMANN-DOERTH: "The Ordo Manifesto of 1936", in: A. PEACOCK / H. WILLGERODT (Eds.): *Germany's Social Market Economy: Origins and Evolution*, London (MacMillan) 1989, pp. 15-26 (first German publication 1936).

BRENNAN, GEOFFREY / JAMES M. BUCHANAN: *The Power to Tax*, Cambridge (Cambridge University Press) 1980.

BRENNAN, GEOFFREY / JAMES M. BUCHANAN: *The Reason of Rules - Constitutional Political Economy*, Cambridge (Cambridge University Press) 1985.

BUCHANAN, JAMES M.: *The Limits of Liberty - Between Anarchy and Leviathan*, Chicago (University of Chicago Press) 1975.

BUCHANAN, JAMES M.: "Constitutional Constraints on Governmental Taxing Power", *Wirtschaftspolitische Blätter*, 36 (1989), pp. 183-193.

BUCHANAN, JAMES M.: "The Domain of Constitutional Economics", *Constitutional Political Economy*, 1 (1990), pp. 1-18.

BUCHANAN, JAMES M. / GORDON TULLOCK: *The Calculus of Consent - Logical Foundations of Constitutional Democracy*, Ann Arbor (University of Michigan Press) 1962.

BUCHANAN, JAMES M. / RICHARD E. WAGNER: *Democracy in Deficit - The Political Legacy of Lord Keynes*, New York et al. (Academic Press) 1977.

DEMSETZ, HAROLD: "Information and Efficiency: Another Viewpoint", *The Journal of Law and Economics*, 12 (1969), pp. 1-22.

ELSTER, JON: *Ulysses and the Sirens*, revised edition, Cambridge (Cambridge University Press) 1984.

EUCKEN, WALTER: "Staatliche Strukturwandlungen und die Krisis des Kapitalismus", *Weltwirtschaftliches Archiv*, 84 (1932), pp. 297-331.

EUCKEN, WALTER: *The Foundations of Economics - History and Theory in the Analysis of Economic Reality*, Berlin et al. (Springer) 1992 (first German edition 1940).

EUCKEN, WALTER (1948a): "On the Theory of the Centrally Administered Economy: An Analysis of the German Experiment", in: M. BORNSTEIN (Ed.), *Comparative Economic Systems - Models and Cases*, Homewood, Ill. (Irwin) 1965, pp. 157-197 (German publication 1948).

EUCKEN, WALTER (1948b): "What Kind of Economic and Social System?", in: A. PEACOCK / H. WILLGERODT (Eds.): *Germany's Social Market Economy: Origins and Evolution*, London (Macmillan) 1989, pp. 27-45 (German publication 1948).

EUCKEN, WALTER: "Die Wettbewerbsordnung und ihre Verwirklichung", *Ordo*, 2 (1949), pp. 1-99.

EUCKEN, WALTER: *This Unsucessful Age - or The Pains of Economic Progress*. With an Introduction by J. JEWKES, New York (Oxford University Press) 1952 (first German publication 1951).

THE MARKET ECONOMY AND THE STATE

EUCKEN, WALTER (1952): *Grundsätze der Wirtschaftspolitik*, 6th revised edition, Tübingen (J.C.B. Mohr [Paul Siebeck]) 1992 (first edition 1952).

FREY, BRUNO S.: "Direct Democracy: Politico-Economic Lessons from Swiss Experience", *American Economic Review*, 84 (1994), pp. 338-342.

FURUBOTN, EIRIK G. / SVETOZAR PEJOVICH: "Propertry Rights and Economic Theory: A Survey of Recent Literature", *Journal of Economic Literature*, 10 (1972), pp. 1137-1162.

GRAY, JOHN: Hayek, Spontaneous Order and the Post-Communist Societies in Transition, in: CH. FREI AND R. NEF (Eds.): *Contending with Hayek. On Liberalism, Spontaneous Order and the Post-Communist Societies in Transition*, Bern (Peter Lang) 1994, pp. 29-48.

GROSSEKETTLER, HEINZ G.: "On Designing an Economic Order. The Contributions of the Freiburg School", in: D. A. WALKER (Ed.): *Twentieth Century Economic Thought*, Vol. 2. Aldershot (Elgar) 1989, pp.38-84.

HAYEK, FRIEDRICH A. (1935a): "Socialist Calculation: The Nature and History of the Problem", in: HAYEK, FRIEDRICH A. (Ed.): *Collectivist Economic Planning - Critical Studies on the Possibilities of Socialism*, London (Routledge) 1935 (reprinted 1938 and 1948), pp. 1-40.

HAYEK, FRIEDRICH A. (1935b): "The Present State of the Debate", in: HAYEK, FRIEDRICH A. (Ed.): *Collectivist Economic Planning - Critical Studies on the Possibilities of Socialism*, London (Routledge) 1935 (reprinted 1938 and 1948), pp. 201-243.

HAYEK, FRIEDRICH A.: "Economics and Knowledge", in: HAYEK, FRIEDRICH A.: *Individualism and Economic Order*, Chicago (University of Chicago Press) 1948, pp. 33-58 (first publication 1937).

HAYEK, FRIEDRICH A.: "Socialist Calculation III: The Competitive 'Solution'", in: I. M. KIRZNER (Ed.): *Classics in Austrian Economics - A Sampling in the History of a Tradition, Vol. III: The Age of Mises and Hayek*, London (William Pickering) 1994, 235-257 (first publication 1940)

HAYEK, FRIEDRICH A.: *The Road to Serfdom*, Chicago (University of Chicago Press) 1944.

HAYEK, FRIEDRICH A.: "The Use of Knowledge in Society", *American Economic Review*, 35 (1945), pp. 519-530.

HAYEK, FRIEDRICH A.: "The Meaning of Competition", in: HAYEK, FRIEDRICH A.: *Individualism and Economic Order*, Chicago (University of Chicago Press) 1948, pp. 92-106 (first publication 1946).

HAYEK, FRIEDRICH A.: "'Free' Enterprise and Competitive Order", in: HAYEK, FRIEDRICH A.: *Individualism and Economic Order*, Chicago: University of Chicago Press, 1948, pp.107-118.

HAYEK, FRIEDRICH A.: "The Transmission of the Ideals of Economic Freedom", in: HAYEK, FRIEDRICH A.: *Studies in Philosophy, Politics and Economics*, Chicago (University of Chicago Press) 1967, pp. 195-200 (first publication 1951).

HAYEK, FRIEDRICH A. (1952a): *The Sensory Order - An Inquiry into the Foundations of Theoretical Psychology*, London and Henley (Routledge) 1976 (first publication 1952).

HAYEK, FRIEDRICH A. (1952b): *The Counterrevolution of Science - Studies on the Abuse of Reason*, Indianapolis (The Free Press) 1979 (first publication 1952).

HAYEK, FRIEDRICH A.: "Entstehung und Verfall des Rechtsstaatsideales", in: A. HUNOLD (ed.), *Wirtschaft ohne Wunder*, Erlenbach-Zürich (Rentsch) 1953.

HAYEK, FRIEDRICH A.: "What is 'Social' - What Does it Mean?", in: HAYEK, FRIEDRICH A.: *Studies in Philosophy, Politics and Economics*, Chicago (University of Chicago Press) 1967, pp. 237-247 (first publication 1957).

HAYEK, FRIEDRICH A.: *The Constitution of Liberty*, Chicago (University of Chicago Press) 1960.

HAYEK, FRIEDRICH A.: "The Economy, Science, and Politics", in: HAYEK, FRIEDRICH A.: *Studies in Philosophy, Politics and Economics*, Chicago (University of Chicago Press) 1967, pp. 251-269 (first publication 1962).

HAYEK, FRIEDRICH A.: "Kinds of Rationalism", in: HAYEK, FRIEDRICH A.: *Studies in Philosophy, Politics and Economics*, Chicago (University of Chicago Press) 1967, pp. 82-95 (first publication 1965).

HAYEK, FRIEDRICH A: "Personal Recollections of Keynes and the 'Keynesian Revolution'", in: HAYEK, FRIEDRICH A.: *New Studies in Philosophy, Politics, Economics and the History of Ideas*, London (Routledge) 1978, pp. 283-289 (first publication 1966).

HAYEK, FRIEDRICH A. (1967a): "The Results of Human Action but not of Human Design", in: HAYEK, FRIEDRICH A.: *Studies in Philosophy, Politics and Economics*, Chicago (University of Chicago Press) 1967, pp. 96-105.

HAYEK, FRIEDRICH A. (1967b): "The Confusion of Language in Political Thought", in: HAYEK, FRIEDRICH A.: *New Studies in Philosophy, Politics, Economics and the History of Ideas*, London Routledge (1978), pp. 71-104 (first publication 1967).

HAYEK, FRIEDRICH A.: "Competition as a Discovery Procedure", in: HAYEK, FRIEDRICH A.: *New Studies in Philosophy, Politics, Economics and the History of Ideas*, London (Routledge) 1978, pp. 179-190 (first publication 1968).

HAYEK, FRIEDRICH A.: "The Errors of Constructivism", in: HAYEK, FRIEDRICH A.: *New Studies in Philosophy, Politics, Economics and the History of Ideas*, London (Routledge) 1978, pp. 3-22 (first publication 1970).

HAYEK, FRIEDRICH A.: *A Tiger by the Tail - The Keynesian Legacy of Inflation*, essays complied and introduced by S.R. Shenoy, London (Institute of Economic Affairs) 1972.

HAYEK, FRIEDRICH, A.: *Law, Legislation and Liberty, Vol. I: Rules and Order*, Chicago (University of Chicago Press) 1973.
HAYEK, FRIEDRICH, A.: *Law, Legislation and Liberty, Vol. II: The Mirage of Social Justice*, Chicago (University of Chicago Press) 1976.
HAYEK, FRIEDRICH A. (1978a): "Liberalism", in: HAYEK, FRIEDRICH A.: *New Studies in Philosophy, Politics, Economics and the History of Ideas*, London (Routledge) 1978, pp. 119-151.
HAYEK, FRIEDRICH A. (1978b): "The Atavism of Social Justice", in: HAYEK, FRIEDRICH A.: *New Studies in Philosophy, Politics, Economics and the History of Ideas*, London (Routledge) 1978, pp. 57-68.
HAYEK, FRIEDRICH A.: *Law, Legislation and Liberty, Vol. III: The Political Order of a Free People*, Chicago (University of Chicago Press) 1979.
HAYEK, FRIEDRICH A.: "The Rediscovery of Freedom: Personal Recollections", in: P. G. KLEIN (Ed.): *The Collected Works of F.A. Hayek, Vol. IV - The Fortunes of Liberalism - Essays on Austrian Economics and the Ideal of Freedom*, Chicago (University of Chicago Press) 1992, pp. 185-200 (first publication 1983).
HAYEK, FRIEDRICH A.: *The Fatal Conceit - The Errors of Socialism*, London (Routledge) 1988.
HAYEK, FRIEDRICH A.: *Hayek on Hayek - An Autobiographical Dialogue*, edited by S. KRESGE AND L. WENAR, London (Routledge) 1994.
HICKS, SIR JOHN: The Hayek Story, in: HICKS, SIR JOHN: *Critical Essays in Monetary Theory*, Oxford (Oxford University Press) 1967, pp. 203-215.
HOPPMANN, ERICH: *Wirtschaftsordnung und Wettbewerb*, Baden-Baden (Nomos) 1988.
HUTCHISON, TERENCE W. (1979): "Notes on the Effects of Economic Ideas on Policy: The Example of the German Social Market Economy", *Zeitschrift für die gesamte Staatswissenschaft (Journal of Institutional and Theoretical Economics)*, 135 (1979), pp. 426-441.
DE JASAY, ANTHONY: "The Cart Before the Horse - On Emergent and Constructed Orders, and Their Wherewithal", in: CH. FREI AND R. NEF (Eds.): *Contending with Hayek. On Liberalism, Spontaneous Order and the Post-Communist Societies in Transition*, Bern (Peter Lang) 1994, pp. 49-64.
KASPER, WOLFGANG / STREIT, MANFRED E.: *Lessons from the Freiburg School - The Institutional Foundations of Freedom and Prosperity*, Syndey (Centre for Independent Studies) 1993.
KIRCHGÄSSNER, GEBHART: "Wirtschaftspolitik und Politiksystem: Zur Kritik der traditionellen Ordnungstheorie aus der Sicht der Neuen Politischen Ökonomie", in: D. CASSEL, B.-TH. RAMB, H. J. THIEME (Eds.): *Ordnungspolitik*, München (Vahlen) 1988, pp. 53-75.
KIRZNER, ISRAEL M.: *Competition and Entrepreneurship*, Chicago (University of Chicago Press) 1973.

KLIEMT, HARTMUT: "Constitutional Commitments. On the Economic and Legal Philosophy of Rules", *Jahrbuch für Neue Politische Ökonomie*, 12 (1993), pp. 145-173.
KRUEGER, ANNE O.: "The Political Economy of the Rent-Seeking Society", *American Economic Review*, 64 (1974), pp. 291-203.
LEIPOLD, HELMUT: "Neoliberal Ordnungstheorie and Constitutional Economics - A Comparison Between Eucken and Buchanan", *Constitutional Political Economy*, 1 (1990), pp. 47-65.
LESCHKE, MARTIN: *Ökonomische Verfassungstheorie und Demokratie*, Berlin (Duncker & Humblot) 1993.
LOY, CLAUDIA: *Marktsystem und Gleichgewichtstendenz*, Tübingen (J.C.B. Mohr [Paul Siebeck]) 1988.
MESTMÄCKER, ERNST-JOACHIM: "Power, Law and Economic Constitution", *Law and State*, 10 (1974), pp. 117-132 (German publication 1973).
MESTMÄCKER, ERNST-JOACHIM: «Bausteine einer Wirtschaftsverfassung - Franz Böhm in Jena», *Max-Planck-Institut zur Erforschung von Wirtschaftssystemen - Lectiones Jenenses*, Vol. 4, 1996.
MIKSCH, LEONHARD: "Die Wirtschaftspolitik des Als-Ob", *Zeitschrift für die gesamte Staatswissenschaft (Journal of Institutional and Theoretical Economics)*, 105 (1949), pp. 310-338.
MILL, JOHN ST.: "Considerations on Representative Government", in: G. WILLIAMS (Ed.): *John Stewart Mill - Utilitarianism, On Liberty, Considerations on Representative Government*, London (Everyman Library), Reprint 1993, pp. 187-428 (first edition 1861).
MÖSCHEL, WERNHARD: "Competition Policy from an Ordo Point of View", in: A. PEACOCK, H. WILLGERODT (Eds.): *Germany's Social Market Economy: Origins and Evolution*, London (MacMillan) 1989, pp. 142-159.
MÜLLER-ARMACK, ALFRED: "The Meaning of the Social Market Economy", in: A. PEACOCK / H. WILLGERODT (Eds.): *Germany's Social Market Economy: Origins and Evolution*, London (MacMillan) 1989, pp. 82-86 (first publication 1956).
NIENHAUS, VOLKER: *Persönliche Freiheit und moderne Demokratie - F.A. Hayeks Demokratiekritik und sein Reformvorschlag eines Zweikammersystems*, Tübingen (J.C.B. Mohr [Paul Siebeck]) 1982.
NORTH, DOUGLASS C.: *Institutions, Institutional Change and Economic Performance*, Cambridge (Cambridge University Press) 1990.
OLIVER, HENRY M.: "German Neo-Liberalism", *Quarterly Journal of Economics*, 74 (1960), pp. 117-149.
OLSON, MANCUR: *The Logic of Collective Action*, Cambridge (Harvard University Press) 1965.
OLSON, MANCUR: *The Rise and Decline of Nations. Economic Growth, Stagflation, and Social Rigidities*, New Haven (Yale University Press) 1982.

THE MARKET ECONOMY AND THE STATE

PEACOCK, ALAN, HANS WILLGERODT (Eds.): *German Neo-Liberals and the Social Market Economy*, London (MacMillan) 1989.

POPPER, KARL R.: *The Open Society and its Enemies*, Princeton (Princeton University Press) 1950 (first publication 1945).

RUPP, HANS H.: "Zweikammersystem und Bundesverfassungsgericht - Bemerkungen zu einem Reformvorschlag F.A.v. Hayeks", *Ordo*, 30 (1979), pp. 95-104.

SALLY, RAZEEN: "Ordoliberalism and the Social Market: Classical Political Economy from Germany", *New Political Economy*, 1 (1996), pp. 233-257.

SCHMIDTCHEN, DIETER: "German 'Ordnungspolitik' as Institutional Choice", *Zeitschrift für die gesamte Staatswissenschaft (Journal of Institutional and Theoretical Economics)*, 140 (1984), pp. 55-70.

SCHUMPETER, JOSEPH A.: *The Theory of Economic Development - An Inquiry into Profits, Capital, Credit, Interest, and the Business Cycle*, Cambridge, Mass (Harvard University Press) 1934 (first publication 1912).

SCHUMPETER, JOSEPH A.: *Capitalism, Socialism and Democracy*, London (Unwin Paperbacks) 1987 (first publication 1942).

SCHUMPETER, JOSEPH A.: *History of Economic Analysis*, reprint of the first edition, London (Allen & Unwin) 1982 (first publication 1954).

STREIT, MANFRED E.: "The Shadow Economy - A Challenge to the Welfare State?", *Ordo*, 35 (1984), pp. 109-119.

STREIT, MANFRED E.: "Economic Order and Public Policy - Market, Constitution and the Welfare State", in: R. PETHIG, U. SCHLIEPER (Eds.): *Efficiency, Institutions, and Economic Policy*, Berlin et al.(Springer) 1987, pp. 1-21.

STREIT, MANFRED E. (1992a): "Economic Order, Private Law, and Public Policy - The Freiburg School of Law and Economics in Perspective", *Journal of Institutional and Theoretical Economics (JITE)*, 148 (1992), pp. 675-704.

STREIT, MANFRED E. (1992b): "Das Wettbewerbskonzept der Ordnungstheorie, in: E. GÖRGENS, E. TUCHTFELDT (Eds.): *Die Zukunft der wirtschaftlichen Entwicklung - Perspektiven und Probleme*, Bern et. al (Haupt) 1992, pp. 83-108.

STREIT, MANFRED E. (1992c): "Die Interdependenz der Ordnungen - Eine Botschaft und ihre aktuelle Bedeutung", in: STREIT, MANFRED E.: *Freiburger Beiträge zur Ordnungsökonomik*, Tübingen (J.C.B. Mohr [Paul Siebeck]) 1995, pp. 135-158 (first publication 1992).

STREIT, MANFRED E.: "Cognition, Competition, and Catallaxy - In Memory of Friedrich August von Hayek", *Constitutional Political Economy*, 4 (1993), pp. 223-262.

STREIT, MANFRED E.: "The Freiburg School of Law and Economics", in: P. J. BOETTKE (Ed.): *The Elgar Companion to Austrian Economics*, Aldershot (Edward Elgar) 1994.

STREIT, MANFRED E.: "Competition Among Systems as a Defence of Liberty", in: H. BOUILLON (Ed.): *Libertarians and Liberalism - Essays in Honour of Gerard Radnitzky*, Aldershot (Avebury) 1996, pp. 236-252.

STREIT, MANFRED E. (1998a): "Soziale Marktwirtschaft im europäischen Integrationsprozeß: Befund und Perspektiven", in: D. CASSEL (Ed.): *50 Jahre Soziale Marktwirtschaft - Ordnungstheoretische Grundlagen, Realisierungsprobleme und Zukunftsperspektiven einer wirtschaftspolitischen Konzeption*, Stuttgart (Lucius & Lucius) 1998, pp. 177-199.

STREIT, MANFRED E. (1998b): "Constitutional Ignorance, Sponataneous Order and Rule-Orientation: Hayekian Paradigms from a Policy Perspective", in: ST. F. FROWEN (Ed.): *Hayek: Economist and Social Philosopher - A Critical Retrospect*, London (Macmillan) 1998, pp. 37-58.

STREIT, MANFRED E., MUSSLER, WERNER: "The Economic Constitution of the European Community: From Rome to Maastricht", *Constitutional Political Economy*, 5 (1994), pp. 319-353.

STREIT, MANFRED E., WEGNER, GERHARD: "Information, Transactions and Catallaxy: Reflections on some Key Concepts of Evolutionary Market Theory", in: U. WITT (Ed.): *Explaining Process and Change - Approaches to Evolutionary Economics*, Ann Arbor (University of Michigan Press) 1992, pp. 125-149.

TIETZEL, MANFRED: "Der Neue Institutionalismus auf dem Hintergrund der alten Ordnungsdebatte", *Jahrbuch für Neue Politische Ökonomie*, 10 (1991), pp. 3-37.

TOLLISON, ROBERT D.: "Rent Seeking: A Survey", *Kyklos*, 35 (1982), pp. 575-602.

VANBERG, VIKTOR: "Libertarian Evolutionism and Contractarian Constitutionalism", in: S. PEJOVICH (Ed.): *Philosophical and Economic Foundations of Capitalism*, Lexington, Mass., 1983, pp. 71-87.

VANBERG, VIKTOR: "Spontaneous Market Order and Social Rules: A Critical Examination of F.A. Hayek's Theory of Cultural Evolution", *Economics and Philosophy*, 2 (1986), pp. 75-100.

VANBERG, VIKTOR: "'Ordnungstheorie' as Constitutional Economics - The German Conception of a 'Social Market Economy'", *ORDO*, 39 (1988), pp. 17-31.

VANBERG, VIKTOR: "Hayek as Constitutional Political Economist", *Wirtschaftspolitische Blätter*, 36 (1989), pp. 170-182.

VAUGHN, KAREN E.: *Austrian Economics in America - The Migration of a Tradition*, Cambridge (Cambridge University Press) 1994.

VOIGT, STEFAN: "On the Internal Consistency of Hayek's Evolutionary-Oriented Constitutional Economics - Some General Remarks", *Journal des Economistes et des Etudes Humaines*, 3 (1992), pp. 223-252.

VOIGT, STEFAN (1994): "Der Weg zur Freiheit. Mögliche Implikationen Hayekscher Hypothesen für die Transformation der Wirtschaftssysteme Mittel- und Osteuropas", in: J. HÖLSCHER et al. (Eds.): *Bedingungen ökonomischer Entwicklung in Zentralosteuropa*, Marburg (Metropolis) 1994, pp. 63-105.

VOIGT, STEFAN: "Positive Constitutional Economics: A Survey", *Public Choice*, 90 (1997), pp. 11-53.
WICKSELL, KNUT: *Finanztheoretische Untersuchungen - nebst Darstellung und Kritik des Steuerwesens Schwedens*, Düsseldorf (Verlag Wirtschaft und Finanzen) 1988 (first publication 1896).
WITT, ULRICH: "The Theory of Social Evolution: Hayek's Unfinished Legacy", in: J. BIRNER, R. VAN ZIJP (Eds.): *Hayek, Coordination, and Evolution - His Legacy in Philosophy, Politics, and the History of Ideas*, London (Routledge) 1994, pp. 178-189.
WOHLGEMUTH, MICHAEL (1995a): "Economic and Political Competition in Neoclassical and Evolutionary Perspective", *Constitutional Political Economy*, 6 (1995), pp. 71-96.
WOHLGEMUTH, MICHAEL (1995b): "Institutional Competition - Notes on an Unfinished Agenda", *Journal des Economistes et des Etudes Humaines*, 6 (1995), pp. 277-299.
WOHLGEMUTH, MICHAEL: "Freiburger Schule, Ordo-Liberalismus", in: *Gabler Volkswirtschaftslexikon*, Bd.2, Wiesbaden (Gabler) 1996, pp. 913-917.
WOHLGEMUTH, MICHAEL: "Has John Roemer Resurrected Market Socialism?", *The Independent Review*, 2 (1997), pp. 201-224.

Discussion Summary

TORBEN VESTDAM

Paper discussed:
MANFRED E. STREIT and MICHAEL WOHLGEMUTH: The Market Economy and the State. Hayekian and Ordoliberal Conceptions

The authors investigate shared and differing understanding underlying the ordo-liberalism of 'the Freiburg School of Law and Economics' (Eucken & Böhm) and the evolutionary rationalistic-constructivist' position of Hayek. What is shared by the two position is proposed to be (a) an attitude of individual liberalism, (b) a reflection of normative rules as a dimension of scientific practice, (c) the significance of the order that guide institutional practice and (d) limited framework of government functions under law (conservation/innovation of an order of healthy competition in an accessible market). However, where the ordo-liberals emphasise the need of ordering the terms of market practices for the purpose of protecting the general public against the threats of unlimited competition and capital accumulation, Hayek introduces the idea of a free society emerging according to a process of unplanned evolution and market participation as a creative process of discovery and learning, *catallaxy*, (Greek for 'making friends') which he relates to - for one - a double-chamber parliamentary system of which the first chamber, the governmental assembly - under supervision of a constitutional court - enjoys a position of autonomy in relation to the parliament of constituency representatives, the second chamber, in the interest of both constitutional and minority interests. The authors suggest in response to the question 'who controls the controllers' (ZONINSEIN) that the evolutionary processes generated by institutional competition could serve as control and legitimisation of the government practices of the second chamber, although the authors admit that Hayek's notion of the second chamber only with difficulty coheres with the modern concept of democracy as suggested by CHMIELEWSKI. Secondly, a set of rules for just conduct generated by the second chamber institution, *nomocracy*, being of distinctively negative for-

DISCUSSION SUMMARY

mulation, will allow participants to form expectations as to the behaviour of other participants and identify the dimensions and scope for justified action; CHMIELEWSKI questions not so much the autonomy as impartiality of the participants in the process of generating the rule foundation for *nomocracy*. Hayek emphasises in context of his political-economy reflections 'lack of knowledge' as a significant precondition for both market ordering- and participation practices. KOSLOWSKI remarks that Eucken in his application of a concept of system seems to relate to the liberal tradition of philosophical idealism, including the adaptive concept of human reason. KOSLOWSKI criticises as well Hayek for not considering the issue of asymmetrical distribution of wealth and he suggests instead a concept of evolving networks which allows for an understanding of a seemingly ongoing process whereby nation states are directed as quasi business corporations that interact in a global economy, where nation states and global business corporations act creatively according to adaptive- and strategic thinking, the latter distinguished by its ability to generate innovation. In response the authors remark that Hayek's theory of dynamic market economy implies an idea of a self-organising system which is capable of generating innovation. The authors furthermore remark that the issue of asymmetrical distribution of wealth requires empirical research.

The authors consider in light of these investigations the contributions of Hayek to the understanding of the market process as a precursor of an orientation of 'public choice' and a concept of a 'rent-seeking society' to be of particular contemporary value.

Part Three

The Critique of Capitalism in Hilferding and in the Frankfurt School

Chapter 8

Rudolf Hilferding's Theory of Finance Capitalism and Today's World Financial Markets

JONAS ZONINSEIN

I. Introduction
II. Hilferding and Monopoly Capitalism
III. Finance Capitalism in Late Industrialisation
IV. Financial Globalisation and the Second *Pax Americana*
V. Conclusion and Policy Alternatives to Financial Globalisation

I. Introduction

The theory of finance capitalism developed by Rudolf Hilferding (1981, originally published in 1910) provides a unique approach for interpreting and evaluating the evolution of world financial markets and the world economy since the collapse of the Bretton Woods system of fixed exchange rates in the early 1970s. The contemporary relevance of Hilferding's *Finance Capital* is suggested, for instance, by Sweezy (1994) who argues that the final triumph as well as the political and economic dominance of finance capitalism--only briefly identified a hundred years ago--is a key feature of the contemporary world economy. The analytic power of Hilferding's contributions to an analysis of present day capitalism is also echoed in Arrighi (1994) who discusses the circumstances under which waves of financial accumulation, such as the one the world economy is currently experiencing, can drive the process of global capital formation.

For most of the twentieth century, the accepted view among social scientists has been that the most enduring contribution to political economy of Rudolf Hilferding's *Finance Capital* was his understanding of the monopolistic phase of capitalism. This widespread perception about the scope of Hilferding's work has been disseminated thanks to the influence of such well-known Western authors as Paul M. Sweezy, Paul A. Baran, Ernest Mandel, Michal Kalecki, Josef Steindl, and John K. Galbraith. Hilferding's theory of finance capitalism also has served as the key theoretical foundation for the model of state capitalism adopted by socialist countries since 1917. A critique of the foundations of his theory of monopoly capitalism is the objective of the second section of this paper. This critique provides a theoretical perspective for an historical appraisal of the socialist experiments of the twentieth century.

Two additional dimensions of Hilferding's work on finance capitalism offer original perspectives on the evolution of the world economy in the twentieth century and its current tensions. *Finance Capital* first unveiled a crucial link in the interpretation of *late* industrialisation (such as that experienced in the United States, Germany, Japan, Russia, and other Western economies which followed the path of early British industrialisation) and *late late* industrialisation (such as that of the newly industrialised economies of Asia and Latin America since World War II). The credit system and the financial innovations analysed by Hilferding have played privileged roles in accelerating the process of capital formation in these national development experiments. In the third section of this essay, I focus on Hilferding's contribution to the theory of financial development as a component of late and late late industrialisation. I also briefly introduce the constraints imposed by global financial integration on the dynamism of newly industrialised economies during the 1980s and 1990s.

It is in connection with the process of global financial integration taking place since the late 1960s that another of Hilferding's contributions is crucial for the understanding of present day capitalism. In the last part of *Finance Capital*, Hilferding offered a seminal interpretation of the factors determining the conflicts and co-operation among nation-states. He is one of the most creative authors on the theory of capitalist imperialism, a theory in which economic variables fully explain the most powerful nations' processes of foreign policy making. In Hilferding's theory, imperialism is the economic policy of finance capitalism. On the basis of this theory, section four analyses the role of financial globalisation as a key component of the hegemonic economic regime implemented by the United States since the collapse of the Bretton Woods system in the early 1970s.

The final section evaluates Hilferding's contribution to the socialist project, discusses the perverse implications of an excessive reliance on international capital markets for financing capital formation, and suggests some alternative strategies for confronting the current bias toward market-driven globalisation.

II. Hilferding and Monopoly Capitalism

According to Hilferding, a twofold transformation in markets and institutions gives capitalism the form of finance capital. This transformation is interpreted as the outcome of processes that tend, on the one hand, to abolish competition through the formation of cartels and trusts, and on the other, to promote increasing intimate connections between banks and industrial undertakings with the former becoming the dominant partner. Hilferding's *Finance Capital* is the seminal work which inspired an influential current of political economists that distinguishes two different stages in capitalist development: the stage of free competition and the stage of monopoly capitalism. (see, among others, Baran and Sweezy 1966, Mandel 1970, Itoh 1988)

Capital concentration and centralisation processes, in Hilferding's view, tend to eliminate competition among capitals. The diffusion of cartels and trusts is said to enhance price rises in sectors affected by such monopolistic-oriented combinations, thereby originating differential profit rates among industries. As a result of the elimination of competition, Hilferding asserts that prices cease to be objectively determined; therefore, an arbitrary and incidental component progressively prevails in their determination, the law of value being gradually weakened.

A decisive aspect in the monopolisation process is the influence exercised by banks. By absorbing the different modalities of credit--commercial credit, capital credit, and corporation promotion--bank capital would come to control the reproduction of industrial capital and guide its monopolisation process toward more advanced stages, through the formation of a general cartel.

Hilferding's sources were the institutional and historical characteristics of Germany's late industrialisation. However, his analytical effort is chiefly oriented toward formulating general theoretical principles about the workings of capitalism as of the late nineteenth century and early twentieth century, thereby updating the incomplete work by Marx (1967). Hilferding's treatment of the concepts of competition and credit, however, are cursory and confused. In the following paragraphs, I present a brief summary of an extensive critique of Hilferding's theoretical treatment of competition and credit. (see Zoninsein 1990)

Hilferding's analysis of the processes of capital concentration and centralisation is based on a poor understanding of Marx's theory. At the root of Hilferding's procedure is an identification of Marx's concept of competition with the orthodox and simplistic concept of pure or perfect competition, which in turn, is viewed as an adequate interpretation of the reality of competition among capitals until the late nineteenth century (the imaginary "competitive capitalism"). As a corollary, the concepts of cartel and finance capital (or of imperfect competition and monopoly capital, as suggested by later economists who share ideas resembling Hilferding's) become a signpost to characterise the new modalities of interaction among individual capitals.

In Hilferding's concept of competition, emphasis is laid on the existence of a large number of small firms, the absence of collusion, and the free mobility of capital among the various industrial activities. No thought is given to the time required to make this mobility feasible. Each individual industrial firm plays a passive role (as a price taker) in the process of price determination. As a consequence, Hilferding abandons the notion of competition as a struggle in which individual capitals act offensively.

Once this trivial conception of competition is mistaken for a Marxian interpretation, a number of phenomena of competition--which are necessary in light of Marx's theory - begin to be viewed by Hilferding as part of a process of generalised monopolisation. This is particularly clear in the case of the differentiation of profit rates. Marx's conception regards this differentiation as a necessary element in the process of the equalisation of the profit rates on capital in different industrial activities, as well as necessary within each industry, given the coexistence of several production methods and several levels of efficiency in the use of each method. Yet, since this differentiation contradicts the concept of pure or perfect competition, this same differentiation is turned into evidence of expanding monopolistic power.

RUDOLF HILFERDING'S THEORY OF FINANCE CAPITALISM

The notion of competition in Marx does not imply that monopolies may not occur. Modern monopolies imply the existence of competition, that is, they are part of it and produce, as a result, a renewal of competition, not its progressive and total elimination through a general monopoly as Hilferding would have it. In Marx's conception, the general nature of competition is established by the fact that it constitutes a struggle between capitals in their process of self-expansion.

This conception distinguishes two aspects of competition. (Marx 1967, vol. 3, part 2; Shaikh 1981, 1982) First, there are the struggles between capitalists in the same industry which result in the stipulation of a uniform market price for each use value and presuppose a regulating value as a centre of gravity around which market prices fluctuate. The confrontation between capitalists within the same industry is thus equivalent to a war within the same field or to a war for the occupation of that field. From this perspective, the development of new means of production is equivalent to an arms race, and the development of new weapons consists chiefly of the ability to reduce cost and subjugate competitors.

Second, there are the struggles among capital from different industries. Different industrial activities imply different fields or terrains of war. This confrontation occurs in both the inflow and outflow of capital in different industries, whereby a tendency toward the equalisation of profit rates in the various spheres of production is created. This process of equalisation of the profit rates depends on the faster or slower speed with which new capital, new firms, and new plants and equipment are added; alternatively, it depends on the withdrawal of capital. This speed is basically determined by the production process and, in particular, by the time required to reproduce fixed capital in the different industries. As a result, the concept of a centre of gravity can be now translated into the form of production prices. The equalisation of profit rates in the different industries occurs only in the course of several years. This implies that, at any given point in time, the profit rates of different industries are not equal, and if we consider a short period of time, they may not even be moving toward that equalisation with the average rate.

Competition in Marx's view is a tendency-regulated process; hence, it cannot be analysed as a process of equilibrium even if the long term is taken into consideration. Its primary field of action is the circulation of individual capitals, which must be understood as a sphere of forcible articulation of such capitals in their search for self-expansion within the same space of accumulation.

Both these aspects of competition--intra-industry and inter-industry--cause the existence of differential rates of profit at each point in time. First, however, Hilferding disregards the aspect of competition within the same industry, and therefore, the inevitability of differential profit rates resulting from distinct levels of productivity of the labour being absorbed by different capitals within each industry. Second, Hilferding conceives of competition among different industries as a process in which production prices are real equilibrium prices and not an average of past movements.

Marx's conception of the tendency toward the equalisation of profit rates implies that there is no equality between rates of profit at every moment; this implies, therefore, the existence of differential rates within and among industries. However, from the point of view of the conception adopted by Hilferding, this would be unmistakable evidence for the absence of competition as well as evidence of the expanding monopolistic power.

This concept of an expanding monopolistic power is reinforced by Hilferding's notion of bank domination over industry. Hilferding defines finance capital as the interest-bearing capital that is controlled by the banks and invested in industry. According to him, the process of capital concentration and centralisation stimulates an ever closer relationship between bank capital and industrial capital. In this relationship, industry would be increasingly controlled by the banks, through which financial capitalists would exercise progressive control over social capital.

In Hilferding's view, there is a long-term tendency inherent in capitalism toward the establishment of a private central bank geared to financing capital accumulation and promoting a general cartel in industry. Through the co-ordination of these two central agencies, financial capitalists would then exercise a unitary and centralised power over the remaining functions and forms of capital, thereby consciously regulating production and distribution. As a result, monopoly capitalism in its most developed form would suppress the social division of labour and render superfluous both the law of value and the circulation of money, as well as the very existence of the labour force as a commodity. Private ownership of the means of production, concentrated and centralised in a few large groups of capitalists, would emerge in direct opposition to the mass of those who own no capital.

The notions of bank domination over industry and the tendency toward conscious regulation of capitalist production stand as a watershed, separating the theories of Marx and Hilferding on interest-bearing capital, the system of credit, and finance capital. For Hilferding, the domination of productive enterprise by the banks and the progressive suppression of competition are articulated and complementary phenomena representing the central aspects of the processes of capital concentration and centralisation.

The process of differentiation between the forms of application of bank loan capital--from commercial credit to money-capital credit to long-term loans for financing fixed investment, and finally, to the underwriting of stock capital--is accompanied by an ever larger volume of credit supplied by the banks. This offers the banks certain advantages on the basis of which their domination over industry takes shape. First, industrial firms' capacity to honour their commercial debts begins to depend increasingly on bankers' decisions. Second, the institutionalisation of credit through the banking system changes its eventual utilisation by industrial capital into a need imposed by competition, since it allows: (a) an increase in the profit rate for each individual capitalist as a result of the difference between interest rates and profit rates; (b) an increase in the production scale of an enterprise and a reduction in the cost per unit, which may generate extra profits; and (c) sales below production prices within certain limits, while not implying any sacrifice of the industrial enterprise's own capital.

As long as banking activity consists chiefly of mediating commercial credit, their concern lies basically in checking the solvency of enterprises at any given time. This situation changes when the banks supply loan capital for investment in the production process, particularly, in fixed capital. Then, the industrial enterprises become tied to the banks, and the banks' influence over the industrial firms increases. These loans are usually larger and require a longer period of time to be liquidated. On the other hand, the banks always have liquid capital. As a consequence of developments in the credit system, the industrial firms tend to reduce their liquid capital to a minimum. Under these conditions, any unexpected demand for additional funds involves the need for credit. If it does not materialise, the industrial enterprises will incur losses with bankruptcy as a possible outcome.

A crucial stage in the control of banks over industry is reached with the diffusion of corporations. In the early stages of industrial capitalism, the promotion of corporations rests upon the acquisition of funds directly from individual capitalists who are interested in purchasing shares. With the diffusion of corporations, the bank comes to mediate industrial enterprises' access to the capital market. The bank will advance the resources needed to buy the shares to be resold later on, and/or will take charge of their distribution in the stock market.

According to Hilferding, the monopolisation of banking activity tends to move faster than the monopolisation of industrial activity, thereby leading to the control of banks over industry. First of all, the technical characteristics of bank operations--the various forms of intermediation of financial resources--require that the processes of concentration and centralisation in banking and industrial activities be mutually reinforcing. Hilferding, however, argues that after a certain point in the development of the credit functions, it becomes rather difficult for new banks to be formed for the interest-bearing capital available at any given time is continuously gathered by the banks already in existence. Moreover, he argues that as concentration and centralisation in industry advance, the share of external financing provided via the banks grows faster than its own self-financing. These factors provoke an acceleration in the process of monopolisation in the banking sector, which then becomes the decisive force in the more advanced stages of concentration and centralisation in the industrial sector. The trend toward the formation of a general cartel and a central bank, from which a conscious regulation of production and distribution could be exercised, is, therefore, associated with the domination of banks over industry.

The foregoing theory about bank domination over industry fails, however, to differentiate between the relationship of the functions of industrial capital and credit from the relationship between the forms of industrial capital and bank capital. The first type of relationship is established as a requirement of the reproduction of capital as a whole; hence, it is subject to general laws. Continuity in the processes of concentration and centralisation of capital demands a growing subordination of interest-bearing to the dynamic of industrial capital and the production of economic surplus.

Interest-bearing capital and commercial capital have secondary and dependent functions that are restricted to the circulation process. Industrial capital encounters these older forms in the period of its formation and development, and it transforms them into special or derived functions of itself. However, even in the most developed instances of the credit system, where capital has adopted the form of a corporation, the process of production and distribution of the economic surplus continues to maintain the relevance of the functional differentiation between industrial capital and interest-bearing capital. Profits - dividends in the case of the corporations - continue to be generated in distinct spheres of economic activity and are appropriated by distinct groups of capitalists. In other words, in the path covered from its generation to its final appropriation by corporation shareholders, the economic surplus necessarily continues to cross the differentiated circuits of industrial, commercial, and interest-bearing capital.

The second type of relationship, that is, the relationship between forms of industrial capital and bank capital, on the other hand, derives from competition. These forms express the historical conditions of the process of capital accumulation and the different national attitudes and regulations in the operation of the financial system. Therefore, no general laws can be formulated about the hierarchies among the different forms of capital. Hilferding, however, has confused the two types of relationships and attempted to establish for the relationship between the forms of industrial capital and banking capital an unwarranted general law based on a particular configuration found in the pattern of Germany's late industrialisation.

In short, Hilferding's theory of bank domination over industry rests upon the liquidity of money-capital mediated by the banks and the resulting ease of its concentration and centralisation. These factors would assure the domination of banks over industrial enterprises in the competitive struggle, in the fight over distribution of economic surplus, and in the ownership and control of productive capital. Finally, given the need to reduce risks in their operation and maximise their profits, banks would progressively reduce competition both in the productive sphere and within banking itself, leading to the creation of a general cartel and a private central bank in charge of industrial financing.

However, there is no theoretical or empirical support for the notion that the liquid form of money-capital would provoke bank domination. Industrial enterprises must subject themselves to bankers' conditions only in times of deceleration of capital accumulation and crisis, when these enterprises are faced with the inability to honour their debts. However, even in these conditions, the crucial element in the power relationship involved in credit is still the relative size of individual capitals.

Moreover, the very liquidity and divisibility of interest-bearing capital implies that its sphere of activity must always be subject to the strong pressure exercised by the entry of new capitals and the formation of new banks, which compete with the existing banks and thereby slow down the process of centralisation in banking.

The hypothesis that the processes of capital concentration and centralisation progress faster within the banking system than in the industrial sector also does not correspond to the requirements of capital accumulation as a whole. The main characteristic of banking concentration is it reflexive character, that is, banking concentration accompanies the process of concentration on productive activities. On the other hand, the widely acknowledged existence of economies of scale that occurs in banking - whether they are associated with technical factors involved in the use of inputs or in the reduction of risks in asset and liability operations - is not enough to demonstrate the more rapid progress of banking concentration as compared with industrial concentration where economies of scale are also found.

A more general approach to the relationship between the forms of industrial and bank capital would place Germany's experience as one among various possible outcomes of the competitive process. A distinctive feature of the German banking system that allowed it to play an active role in promoting industrial accumulation was its financial innovations as represented by multiple or universal banks. In those banks, the different functions of credit (circulation credit, capital credit, and investment banking) were articulated between themselves; hence, they could contribute to the banks' greater relative power vis-á-vis industrial capital. Sweezy (1968), for instance, argues that the notion of bank domination over industrial corporations also applies to the United States, but only in regards to the transitional period of monopolisation observed between 1890 and 1910. Once the large corporations were established, they reasserted themselves on the basis of faster self-financing. Also, in the case of Japan's late industrialisation, it is not plausible to argue that banks alone had the control of the *zaibatsu*.

The community of interests notion captures much better the variable hierarchies created with the emergence of economic groups whose major cohesion element is the financial variable. In these economic groups, corporate ownership and control come to be exercised through different coalitions of individual capitalists. Property is formally partitioned into rights represented by share titles which permits the promotion of conglomerates that articulate different corporative interests more or less cohesively and involve distinct activities in the process of capital reproduction, whether in the banking, industrial, or commercial spheres. The variable organisational hierarchies created in this process reflect, above all, the conditions of competition and are, therefore, dependent upon multiples factors of an historical, national, and institutional order.

III. Finance Capitalism in Late Industrialisation

Mainstream economics has failed, so far, to provide a straightforward explanation for the active role of finance in economic growth. This role is seen as a permissive and passive one.[1] In contrast with mainstream economics, Hilferding's approach to the functioning of a capitalist economy assumes an active and supply-leading role for money-capital and finance.

Gurley and Shaw's (1955, 1960, 1967) study of the evolution of national financial systems provides a useful framework to define Hilferding's theoretical contribution to the study of finance in economic development. Gurley and Shaw argue that financial accumulation and national financial structures at given levels of income and wealth differ mainly due to societal choices regarding the combination of alternative techniques for mobilising the economic surplus. They initially compress what it is a longer list of alternative techniques or institutional channels for putting economic surplus to the service of investment into two major groups: processes of internal finance and processes of external finance.[2]

Among the internal processes, Gurley and Shaw identify, in the first place, the self-financing of spending units. Continuous adjustments in relative prices in commodity and factor markets and in foreign exchange allocate the monetary resources required by spending units to internally fund their investment activities. Secondly, the taxation technique employs taxes and other non-market processes to mobilise monetary resources for governmental investments and subsidies to private capital formation.

Within external finance, the credit system is a technique for mobilising the domestic and international economic surplus. Both domestic and international credit are mobilised via direct debt-asset relationships between surplus and deficit spending units and debt-asset relationships involving financial intermediaries, including commercial banks. In the case of international credit, it is also relevant to differentiate loans from portfolio in-

---

[1] GIOVANNINI (1993) illustrates the current state of the art in the field of finance and development.

[2] That is, these processes are internal and external *to the spending units*. My own list of finance techniques expands the original one presented by GURLEY and SHAW (1967). In the 1960s, international credit was a secondary mechanism for mobilising investment funds and was not mentioned by them.

vestment. Two additional external finance techniques which involve spending units from different nations are foreign direct investment and economic aid.

According to Gurley and Shaw, these finance techniques are combined in different ways for each national economy in each phase of its development, but they also are, to a certain point, substitutes for each other. For example, in a centralised economy, taxation and transfers within the state-owned sector would significantly restrict private credit and financial accumulation. In addition, the predominance of self-finance via inflation would shrink the real flow of funds through financial markets and real financial accumulation. On the other hand, a combination of finance techniques which privileges private international credit within a regime of minimum controls in the capital account of the balance-of-payments is likely to crowd out domestic credit, since a high and variable ratio M2/international reserves increases the vulnerability of individual nations to currency attacks.

Based on this taxonomy, Hilferding's financial model can be defined as a specific combination of finance techniques which arose out of a societal motivation to accelerate private capital formation in Germany's late industrialisation in the last quarter of the nineteenth century. In *Finance Capital*, self-finance and domestic credit are not only a macroeconomic combination of finance techniques, but also a mix at the level of individual spending units, thereby giving birth to centralised capitalist finance.

In Marx's *Capital*, competition and credit are levers in the process of the centralisation of capital. For Marx, concentration of capital is identical with accumulation, and expresses the expanding control by individual firms over the means of production and the command over labour on the basis of the average rate of profit. Centralisation, on the other hand, "is the concentration of capitals already formed, destruction of their individual independence, expropriation of capitalist by capitalist, transformation of many small into few large capitals... [With centralisation] capital grows in one place to a huge mass in a single hand, because it has in another place been lost by many." (Marx 1967, Vol. 1, p. 625) Individual industrial firms can then grow over various production periods at rates larger than the average growth of the economy, thereby selectively accelerating capital formation and the introduction of technical progress.

Hilferding expands Marx's theory by arguing that finance capital spending units combine the increased self-finance power resulting from monopolistic rents with a privileged access to the credit provided by universal banks and the stock exchange. For Hilferding, centralised capitalist finance provided the essential mechanism necessary to unfold the cluster of innovations connected to the second industrial revolution in Germany.[3]

Implicit in Hilferding's argument is a point emphasised by modern economic theory regarding the allocative efficiency impact of imperfect information in financial markets. In addition to increasing the aggregate supply of investment funds over the long term, finance capital positively influences dynamic allocative efficiency by facilitating the sharing of information about investment projects and the flow of funds from surplus to deficit spending units. As a general outcome, therefore, finance capital introduces a crucial feedback mechanism in the development process. Firms with lower production costs due to economies of scale and scope can generate higher profit margins, attract external funds, and invest more. Due to the larger resources they manage, they can take more risks and do more research. With greater research and larger productive units, their costs decrease and their market shares expand, enhancing their ability to sustain growth.

The general applicability of Hilferding's finance model can be established in light of a significant number of studies on the active role of finance in the catching-up development processes during the expansive cycles of the world economy before World War I and after World War II.

Gerschenkron (1962), in his analysis of European development in the second half of the nineteenth century, contends that successful industrialisation processes in backward countries show systematic differences with regard to the productive and organisational structures of industry relative to the more advanced countries. Among the relevant differences, Gerschenkron emphasises the creation of special institutional devices for the provision of long-term capital to industry in backward countries, where there is social pressure for industrialisation and *ex-ante* capital/output ratios are high, but where capital funds are scarce and money-capital is diffused. In the case of various European countries (but more visibly in Germany where the property, supervisory, and interlocking directorship ties between banks and heavy industry also became extensive), these institutions were the universal

---

[3] See LANDES (1972) for the scope of the second industrial revolution. CHANDLER, JR. (1991) discusses the creation of the modern industrial enterprise in Germany from the 1870s to World War I.

banks, leading to what Landes (1969) had referred to as the financial revolution of the nineteenth century.[4]

In the development experiences of the newly industrialised countries (NICs) after World War II, centralised capitalist finance is found again, but with an important difference. In the NICs, the ensemble of finance techniques utilised to mobilise the funds required for capital accumulation had at its core the direct intervention and co-ordination of the state over the multiple dimensions of the flow of funds in the economy and system of prices. This complex ensemble included the following elements:

i) the administration of the monopolistic rents of the private industrial sector via barriers to entry; direct administration of key industrial prices; and protection from foreign competition through tariffs, quantitative barriers, and the manipulation of the exchange rate;

ii) the use of fiscal techniques and para-fiscal funds (based on compulsory contributions of salaried individuals in the formal sector) to invest in the production of public goods required by industrialisation; to mobilise funds for state development banks; and to capitalise state-owned enterprises producing the inputs required by the industrial sector (private and public);

---

[4] Universal banks combine the commercial, investment, and portfolio functions of financial institutions. The historical evidence on the specific role of banks, monopolies, and cartels in the late industrialisation of Germany is vast (see, among others, TILLY (1967), CLAPHAM (1968), KEMP (1969), MILWARD and SAUL (1973), NEWBURGER and STOKES (1974), FREMDLING and TILLY (1976), GILLE (1977)). The continuity of the close relationship between banks and industrial enterprises in the German economy before and after World War II is discussed by BRADY (1933), FELDMAN (1977), and ZYSMAN (1983). The specific Japanese institutional arrangements were somewhat different from the German case. Japanese late industrialisation witnessed a more direct presence of the state in the financing of industrial investment and a stronger solidarity of interests and co-ordination within each *zaibatsu* (substituted by a similar sort of business group, the *keiretsu*, after World War II). (see LOCKWOOD 1954) In the case of the United States, where industrialisation started earlier and capital accumulation acquired a more gradual character than that in the European continent and Japan, finance capitalism translated into more loosely structured and less lasting connections between banks and industrial corporations. (SWEEZY 1968, 1972; ZYSMAN 1983)

iii) the use of the central bank, state development banks, and state-owned enterprises to absorb foreign credit or/and to guarantee foreign loans to the private sector;

iv) the mobilisation of funds (domestic and international) via securities issued by the treasury, state development banks, and state-owned enterprises;

v) the allocation of credit and credit subsidies directly by the central bank and state development banks, and indirectly by the private financial sector with resources transferred by the state financial system;

vi) the allocation of foreign exchange for the acquisition of capital goods, technical assistance, and raw materials;

vii) price subsidies provided by state-owned enterprises and fiscal incentives provided by the treasury;

viii) procurement and technological guidance for providers of inputs to state owned enterprises;

ix) self-finance of the state-owned enterprises.[5]

The rationale for the role of the state as a catalyst for capitalist finance in late industrialisation had been suggested by Gerschenkron (1962) in his insights on the Russian case. According to Gerschenkron, the relative scarcity of capital funds in the Russia of the 1890s as compared to the Germany of the 1850s was much larger. As a consequence, no private banking system could conceivably succeed in mobilisng long-term credit to finance large-scale industrialisation. I suggest that an even more acute financial gap existed among the NICs of the 1950s and 1960s, when some of these post WW II late late-comers were initiating the second stage of their own industrialisation. This second stage required moving from light and labour-intensive industries to those industrial activities that initially were developed during the second industrial revolution in the late nineteenth century, such

---

5 The specific articulation of these components varied in different countries and different industrial activities. This summary of finance techniques is, however, a close approximation to the mix of finance techniques adopted by the most industrially advanced NICs such as South Korea, Taiwan, Brazil, and Mexico, but does not strictly apply to any of these countries. It corresponds to what AMSDEN (1997) has called the "fiscalization of industrial finance." On the characteristics of centralised finance capitalism in the NICs, see also WADE (1990), WOO (1991), ZONINSEIN (1993, 1994) STIGLITZ and UY (1996), VITTAS and CHO (1996).

as chemical processes, transportation equipment, electrical and non-electrical machinery. This larger financial gap derives from the plausible assumption that in the 1950s and 1960s, the volume of capital required to embark on these industrial activities was significantly higher than at the end of the nineteenth century.

The success of state-centred finance capital in promoting sustained development and a path of convergence to the income and productivity levels of the industrially advanced countries varied significantly among the NICs. In addition, with few exceptions, the 1980s and 1990s witnessed a radical dismantling of the various mechanisms used by the state to promote industrial accumulation. Some of the factors that explain this variance in results can be identified by referring to the policies pursued in the success stories of South Korea and Taiwan.

From examining these successful cases, my general conclusions are that state-centred finance capital provided the key ingredients for the rapid accumulation of capital and the opportunities for creating a significant group of national firms (a national industrial bourgeoisie) capable of providing a strong and innovative performance when entering into successive new lines of business and mastering progressively more complex technologies. (see Amsden 1997; Nelson and Pack 1997) Adequate incentives provided by government policies pressed for efficient allocation of resources over the long term by entrepreneurs, leading to sustainable increases in capital formation and productivity.

Among the incentives and controls supporting the creation of an environment conducive to sustaining the profitability of national groups and the incentives for entrepreneurship were: i) a continuous effort to create and complement markets rather than replacing them, and to introduce a certain measure of competition among the firms supported by government programs; ii) the adoption of performance standards (linked mainly to gains in production and exports) and phasing-out provisions regarding government support for investment and profitability; iii) strong government investment in human capital; and iv) an anti-inflationary bias as well as a hands-on adaptive approach regarding the financing of the fiscal budget and the broader ensemble of finance techniques co-ordinated by the state with a goal to provide macro-economic stability and avoid excessive vulnerability regarding foreign sources of finance.(see Amsden 1989; Zoninsein 1993; Stiglitz 1993, 1996)

Less successful experiences of state-centred finance capitalism took place in semi-industrialised countries such as Brazil, Argentina, Mexico and India, among others. Government policies oriented to promote national entrepreneurship were less consistent in these countries than in the successful cases of East Asia. Shallow entrepreneurial capabilities together with the inability of state policies to sustain the expansion of domestic sources of finance led to increasing vulnerability to external financial shocks. Policy failure, therefore, opened the door to hyper-inflationary trends, financial crises, and economic stagnation, thereby creating the political space for economic and financial liberalisation under terms dictated by world financial markets.

According to Evans (1995), the key explanation for this differential outcome resides in the internal organisation of developmental states. Successful developmental states possess a meritocratic bureaucracy with long-term career rewards and goals, and a strong sense of corporate coherence which provide for their relative autonomy vis- -vis private business. On the other hand, this autonomous bureaucracy maintains its vision, motivation and flexibility by becoming embedded in "a concrete set of social ties that binds the state to society and provides institutionalised channels for the continual negotiation and renegotiation of goals and policies." (Evans 1995, p. 12)[6]

The lack of this "embedded autonomy" and corporate coherence of the state bureaucracy leads to the progressive capture of different parts of the state by specific groups of private interests; loss of consistency in the goals of industrial development; and wasteful commitment of funds to undertakings without creating a competitive advantage in international markets. As a consequence, the development process is periodically interrupted by successive balance-of-payment crises.

---

6   BARDHAN (1997) argues that the "embedded autonomy" of the state elite in Japan, South Korea, and Taiwan is dependent on the ethnic and cultural homogeneity of these countries, and is, therefore, more difficult to occur in ethnically diverse countries such as India. His argument, however, does not apply to the cases of the late late-comers of Latin America. The explanation for the presence of embedded autonomy and the mechanisms of its development remains to be further studied on the basis of historical and comparative research. Within this line of inquiry, one possible explanation for differential performance of national development policies are their previous ties of dependence and their motivations and societal skills absorbed from previous hegemonic or colonial powers.

Confronted by external and internal financial constraints, the economic elites of individual countries tend to opt for hands-off policy alternatives, leading to the dismantling of state finance capital while appearing to eliminate the external constraints, at least, in the short run. The pressures and conditionalities imposed on individual governments by world financial markets to facilitate their access to external credit, together with the increasing cost of the technologies required to deepen industrial development in the long run, plus the progressive decay of the state run economic sector and policies, restrict the range of strategic choices. Fiscal consolidation and adjustment, trade and financial liberalisation, and the privatisation of state-owned enterprises become the only short run alternative to governments anxious to overcome their balance-of-payments constraints.

This path of economic liberalisation seems to have reinforced, however, a tendency to the excessive utilisation of foreign finance without a corresponding increase in the mobilisation of domestic saving and a recovery in the coefficient of investment. The economic performance of countries which accepted to dismantle state finance capital since the early 1980s has been so far below the standards observed in the four decades previous to the 1982 debt crisis, both in terms of efficiency and equity. This outcome does not mean that a return to past modalities of development strategies is desirable or possible. It requires, instead, a clear understanding of the current constraints on economic policy resulting from the operation of world financial markets. This understanding is a prerequisite for charting feasible alternatives to financial globalisation. The final section of this paper presents some preliminary suggestions regarding the directions that this understanding could lead us.

IV. Financial Globalisation and the Second *Pax Americana*

In Hilferding's theory, the export of capital and imperialism becomes the economic policy of finance capital in its unbounded search for expanding its economic territory. In the historical circumstances of the formation of finance capital observed by Hilferding, the competition of the most advanced industrial nations for the control of the world market intensified to a saturation point which provoked two world wars. This version of Hilferding's theory of imperialism are the most noted, in part due to Lenin's pamphlet (1968) on imperialism, which draws heavily on Hilferding's work.

There is, however, a more general aspect of Hilferding's theory which is useful to interpret the international competition of capital after World War II, including the more recent post-Cold War years. For Hilferding, there are countervailing forces at work which militate against violent outcomes in international competition. The unevenness in the industrial development of individual nations and broader economic territories plus the hierarchies of political and military power produce a differentiation in the forms of capital export. From this differentiation arises the possibility of contradictions, coupled with co-operation and solidarity among international capitalist interests. (Hilferding 1981, pp. 331-332)

This notion of the solidarity of international capitalist interests is necessary for explaining the current degree of integration in the world financial markets.[7] Although Hilferding never discussed in detail imperialistic finance,[8] a logical next step following from the direction of his argument is to ask the extent to which the current process of financial globalisation is

---

7   WADE (1996) argues that multinationalisation in finance has been even more dramatic than in trade, foreign direct investment, and technology. The stock of international bank lending (cross-border lending plus domestic lending denominated by foreign currency) rose from 4 percent of OECD GDP in 1980 to 44 percent in 1990. The world turnover of foreign exchange or currency trading has grown even faster, and runs currently at more than $1 trillion each day. The world market for currencies, government bonds and commodity, currency, and interest futures has become highly integrated over the 1980s and 1990s. Although stock markets are much less integrated than those of standardised financial assets, the portfolios of large financial institutions are being increasingly internationally diversified. Domestic saving and investment rates remain highly correlated in most countries, but the percentage of the variance in investment rates accounted for the variation in domestic saving has been declining in OECD countries. The differences in the price of borrowed funds among national markets remains substantial, but these differences are significant less than those observed in other economic variables such as real wages.

8   The role of finance in British imperialism is briefly discussed in HOBSON's *Imperialism: A Study* (1954, originally published in 1902). For a comparison of Hobson's and Hilferding's approaches see ARRIGHI (1994).

the result of the international economic policy of the country(ies) which held a hegemonic position in world affairs after World War II.

The Bretton Woods system of fixed exchange rates which lasted from 1944 to 1973 can best be described as "embedded liberalism." (Ruggie 1982) It constituted an attempt to balance an increasingly liberal international economy (both in trade and financial relations among countries) and the domestic responsibilities of nation-states in advanced industrial as well as developing economies in promoting economic growth and full employment.

The following lessons from the interwar period regarding the setting of exchange rates summarises the goals of the Bretton Woods international financial regime implemented under the leadership of the United States. Freely fluctuating exchange rates constituted a source of risk and discouraged international trade. Exchange rates as a means of continuous adjustment in the balance-of-payments involved disruptive changes in relative prices and in the allocation of resources which led to uncertainty in investment decisions. Freely fluctuating exchange rates did not constitute a reliable instrument for adjusting the balance-of-payments, since they also generated the anticipation of additional changes in the same direction, giving rise to additional speculative movements of financial capital. Based on these lessons, the designers of the Bretton Woods system determined that exchange rates ought not to be left to market forces, in particular, to the influence of short-term international capital movements, and that national controls on the international movement of capital should be maintained in the post World War II era.

Helleiner (1994) in his political history of the globalisation of financial markets, identifies three main reasons for the widespread use of capital controls during the first two decades of the Bretton Woods system. Policy makers believed that capital controls were necessary, in the first place, to prevent currency attacks. Capital controls created some degree of freedom for national policies prioritising full employment, the welfare state, and the subsidisation of capital accumulation. Second, the free movement of short-term loan and portfolio capital was considered incompatible with stable exchange rates and an increasingly liberal multilateral trading system. Third, financial interventionism and government allocation of foreign financial resources were considered necessary aspects of economic policies in countries searching to accelerate economic growth.

RUDOLF HILFERDING'S THEORY OF FINANCE CAPITALISM

In contrast to the nationalism and isolationism prevailing in the 1930s, the embedded liberal compromise also involved a dimension of international institutional co-ordination. In spite of significant market-based expansion in the flows of international trade and direct foreign investment, the setting of exchange rates, the supply of short-term reserve credit, the co-ordination of trade liberalisation, and the allocation of long-term finance were not left in the hands of individual nation-states or bilateral arrangements. Under the Bretton Woods agreement, national governments became accountable to multilateral agencies--the International Monetary Fund, the General Agreement on Tariffs and Trade, and the World Bank.

This international financial framework was compatible with the combination of finance techniques put in place by individual countries. Until the mid 1960s, international private credit truly was kept as a secondary channel for the mobilisation of the economic surplus. The preferences of the international financial community's investors neither occupied places of honour in macroeconomic policy nor in the allocation of resources in individual countries. Self-finance, taxation, official domestic and international credit, foreign direct investment, and economic aid predominated.

The collapse of the Bretton Woods system during 1967-1973 parallels the rise of economic and financial liberalisation as the new hegemonic ideology for formulating national economic policy. The diffusion of this ideology and the implementation of liberalisation reforms are the result of a long process which accelerated after 1979 when the Federal Reserve Bank of the United States decided to return to a policy of a strong dollar, whose goal was to reaffirm its dominant role in the international monetary system.

Technological and market developments are important parts of the story of the transition to flexible exchange rates, capital account liberalisation and the integration of world financial markets. Global telecommunications have significantly reduced the costs and time of moving capital funds around the world. On the market side, the growth of international trade and the multiplication of the operation sites of multinational corporations have dramatically increased the demands for international financial services. In addition, the recycling of petrodollars and the increase in the volume of external resources needed to finance ever growing and fluctuating current account deficits, as well as the drive by investors to diversify portfolios, have placed additional pressures on financial institutions to expand their operations internationally.

Market forces and telecommunication innovations, however, account for only part of the systemic international changes. As Helleiner (1994) stresses, the governments of advanced industrial countries played a major role since the late 1950s in the process of financial liberalisation and globalisation. The United States and Great Britain, in particular, gave financial institutions ever greater room for their operations in international markets through their support for the Euromarket, and by aggressive promoting liberalisation of capital controls after the late 1960s. This drive towards international financial liberalisation was supplemented by an approach that minimised the losses of speculative capital during financial crises. By intervening through lender-of-last resort operations to control the contagion effects of international financial crises, advanced industrial nations and the multilateral institutions they also contributed to strengthening the process of financial globalisation.

International competition explained why nation-states supported the process of financial globalisation. Competitive deregulation meant that individual states, by attracting foreign financial institutions and resources, encouraged liberalisation at the international level, making the use of comprehensive exchange controls extremely costly for any individual government. Competition among nation-states also meant that the implementation of co-operative controls (minilateral or multilateral) became extremely difficult to implement.[9]

An important factor in the widespread political support of financial liberalisation has been the increasing co-operation among central banks in promoting the norms and procedures adopted by financial institutions operating in global markets. The co-operation among central banks sought to co-ordinate the formulation of these norms and procedures, to supervise their implementation by international financial institutions, to exchange information to reduce international financial instability, and to prevent that financial crises became widespread.

A crucial element in the process of financial liberalisation was the redefinition of the international economic priorities of the United States. This

---

[9] Governments' support for financial liberalisation was also reinforced by the increasing acceptance and enthusiasm of influential academic and policy-maker circles for the tenets of neoliberalism. The predominance of the financial liberalisation ideology in such multilateral institutions as the IMF, the World Bank, and the OECD was most decisive in producing this intellectual climate.

country was the anchor of embedded liberalism, but in the late 1960s and early 1970s, the United States refused to introduce the domestic economic adjustments necessary to limit the outflow of dollars and save the Bretton Woods system from collapse. Various factors account for the United States' role as the gravedigger of the Bretton Woods system and its new function as the decisive promoter of financial globalisation and floating exchange rates. During the crucial years of 1967-1973, a series of connected factors encouraged the U.S. government to seek increasing amounts of foreign credit to support its growing fiscal and current account deficits and maintain a policy of full-employment: the decline in the profitability of the U.S. industrial sector; the economic and political constraints to expanding tax revenues; the increasing requirements of social programs and defence expenditures; the increase in competitive pressures from European and Japanese producers. (see Gilpin 1987, Nau 1990; Shaikh 1992; Duménil and Lévy 1993)

With the refusal to introduce domestic adjustment, the transition to floating exchange rates and financial liberalisation were initially *ad hoc* policies simply oriented to maintaining the autonomy of U.S. macroeconomic policy and to finance U.S. deficits. These did not constitute components of a strategy oriented to establish a second *Pax Americana*. Since the late 1970s, but more clearly in the early 1980s, however, the United States began to view the renewal of its hegemonic position as depending less on its trading performance and more on its military superiority and its large and stable consumer and financial markets, as well as global economic and financial liberalisation.

After a decade or so in which policentric forces prevailed in the world economy, the United States reasserted its economic hegemony. (Tavares 1985) Its monetary policy reinforced a world-wide recession by coupling the second oil price shock to a sustained three-fold increase in nominal interest rates, which after 1982, provoked an international debt crisis and the contraction of international credit and monetary markets. The Reagan administration then added to the policy of high interest rates a spectacular increase in the fiscal deficit oriented to cut taxes to the wealthier groups and to significantly expand defense expenditures. The recovery pulled by these extravagant Keynesian policies put the United States back at the centre stage of the international financial system. Most countries adopted contractionary policies and economic reforms to cope with the recession, to receive foreign investment and to expand their exports, mainly to the United States. The resulting trade surpluses were used to service large external debts or to generate international investment flows which, for lack of alternatives, were mostly put at the service of the United States' current account and fiscal deficits.

This new strategy for a second *Pax Americana* imposed a world-wide subordination of monetary, fiscal and exchange rate policies to the performance of the United States' economy. Economic liberalisation reforms became the *sine qua non* condition for the (limited) success that this new international financial regime allowed for less powerful individual countries from the late 1980s on. Currency attacks, financial crises, and recessive adjustments leading to further economic openings were the prices that these countries paid whenever they dared to push their growth rates beyond the levels permitted by an increasing competitive and volatile world economy.

The limits of this predatory approach to economic hegemony are given by the ability of the United States to maintain a path of sustained growth, with low inflation and financial stability. The confidence of international investors on this performance is the crucial variable of the current international financial regime. In this specific sense, the weakest link in the international financial regime put in place since 1979 seems to be the increasing deficit in the investment income account of the United States' balance of payment since 1994. This deficit and its growing impact on an already sizable current account deficit might eventually reach a critical level in a few years time that could provoke a major increase in United States import restrictions and/or a recessive macroeconomic adjustment which could lead to a major international crisis.

Macro-regionalisation on the basis of trade, investment, and currency areas seems to be, under the present conditions, the only alternative path open for individual countries trying to forge a way out from the grip of hegemonic globalisation. More than that, the economic success of these macro-regionalisation efforts - particularly the European Union - might be the only condition for moving beyond the current global trend towards low and volatile growth rates and/or the prospects of a crash of the world economy.

V. Conclusion and Policy Alternatives to Financial Globalisation

Hilferding's work offers a privileged standpoint from which to interpret the evolution of the world economy in the twentieth century. His analysis of finance capital and his notion of "organised capitalism" (Hilferding 1983) were instrumental for all models of socialist economies implemented in the last eighty years. His emphasis on the potentialities of bureaucratic control of the "commanding heights" of the financial and industrial sector as a mechanism to manage an advanced industrial economy reinforced the economicist (and self-defeating in the long-term) approach to policy making in socialist societies already present in Marx's arguments about the dictatorship of the proletariat. Although Marx never predicted that communism would take hold in pre-industrial societies like Russia and China, rather than in Germany, Britain, or the United States, where the processes Marx described as the "preconditions for communism" were far more advanced, it is doubtful that the centralised management model suggested by Hilferding could have produced the necessary social incentives and co-ordination rules to sustain a communist society in the long run. On the other hand, the experiences of successful centralised capitalism in East Asia after World War II suggest that competition (at the national and international levels) is a crucial element for sustaining technological progress and productivity increase.

Hilferding's contributions to the theories of financial development and economic imperialism also provide relevant insights into the dilemmas created by the current stage of the world financial markets. As the process of financial integration advances, foreign sources of finance tend to crowd out domestic sources, making the investment rate increasingly dependent on decisions taken abroad. This is due, in first place, to the asymmetry between foreign and domestic financial institutions. Foreign financial institutions have a greater ability to mobilise finance - given their relatively larger size, their access to deeper and more dynamic capital markets, their superior technology, as well as the intense competition for market shares at the global level. In addition, competition among countries searching for higher volumes of foreign investment further constrains their ability to increase their tax revenues, to limit the public debt growth, and to generate the public sector investment required to support a sustained increase in private investment. Moreover, the increasing convertibility of national currencies and the risks associated with currency attacks, limit the expansion of domestic credit. A higher ratio of domestic liquid resources/international reserves increases the risks of these attacks for given ratios of current account deficits/GDP.

When the reversal of cyclical phases in the world economy takes place and the interest rates in hegemonic economies increase, the drying up of capital inflow in weaker economies is reinforced by the outflow of previous foreign investment and the capital flight of domestically mobilised funds. In these conditions, financial crises of different magnitudes occur, leading to the decline in capital formation, depreciation of currencies, intense inflationary pressures, and depression in the level of economic activity in the economic territories affected by the contagion effects of these crises. The governments in these countries, then, are left with the task of bailing out the shallow domestic financial system which grew by mediating foreign credit during the previous phase of financial opening.

Supporters of financial liberalisation recommend the expansion of domestic saving, based on a poor understanding of the sources of financial development. Contrary to their views, foreign finance only complements domestic finance when an autonomous strategy of economic growth and financial development is simultaneously in place, as indicated by the East Asian development experience after World War II.

However, creating an international financial regime which is supportive of national autonomy in the implementation of economic policies is also necessary. The proposal of prime minister Mahathir Mohamad of Malaysia, during the IMF-World Bank meeting in Hong Kong in September 1997, to ban currency trading was considered extreme by the world financial community. However, it fully expressed the original intention of the designers of the Bretton Woods system in 1944 who recommended that finance should be kept under national control and, therefore, be politically regulated at the multilateral level, but should never be left to the vagaries of the market. Tobin's proposal (Tobin 1978; Haq, Kaul, Grunberg 1996) for an international tax on foreign exchange transactions that would automatically penalise short-term round trips of speculative investments is an attempt to recover some ground for national financial autonomy.

A more recent proposal with objectives parallel to the Tobin tax was the creation of a regional Asia-only bailout fund backed by Japan to assist countries that run into financial trouble due to currency speculation. (Wall Street Journal 9/24/97) The approach of this fund was to help individual countries to maintain their growth oriented polices while adjustment is introduced, rather than proposing short-term adjustment without any consideration of its impact on the prospects for growth, employment and equity, as currently imposed by the conditionalities of the IMF and World Bank. Similar regional efforts in other parts of the world could, eventually, lead to a multilateral effort of "throwing sand in the wheels" of the global process of financial liberalisation, thereby, contributing to the dampening or elimination of the present world-wide trend toward economic deceleration and increasing inequality.

References

AMSDEN, A. H.: *Asia's Next Giant: South Korea and Late Industrialisation*, Oxford/New York (Oxford University Press) 1989.
AMSDEN, A. H.: "Bringing Production Back in - Understanding Government's Economic Role in Late Industrialisation", *World Development* 25 (1997), pp. 469-480.
ARRIGHI, G.: *The Long Twentieth Century: Money, Power, and the Origins of Our Times*, London (Verso) 1994.
BARAN, P.A., SWEEZY, P.M.: *Monopoly Capital: An Essay on the American Economic and Social Order*, New York (Monthly Review Press) 1966.
BARDHAN, P.: "The Nature of Institutional Impediments to Economic Development", *Workshop on Emerging Issues in Economic Development, The World Bank*, Washington, DC (The World Bank) 1997.
BRADY, R. A.: *The Rationalization Movement in German Industry: A Study in the Evolution of Economic Planning*, Berkeley (University of California Press) 1973.
CHANDLER, JR. A. D.: "Creating Competitive Capability: Innovation and Investment in the United States, Great Britain, and Germany from the 1870s to World War I", in: P. HIGONET, D. S. LANDES and H. ROSOVSKY (Eds.): *Favorites of Fortune: Technology, Growth, and Economic Development since the Industrial Revolution*, Cambridge, MA (Harvard University Press) 1991.
CLAPHAM, J. H.: *The Economic Development of France and Germany, 1815-1914*, Cambridge (Cambridge University Press) 1968.

DUMÉNIL, G., LÈVY, D.: *The Economics of the Profit Rate: Competition, Crises, and Historic Tendencies in Capitalism*, Brookfield (Edward Elgar) 1993.

EVANS, P.: *Embedded Autonomy: States and Industrial Transformation*, Princeton (Princeton University Press) 1995.

FELDMAN, G. D.: *Iron and Steel in the German Inflation*, Princeton (Princeton University Press) 1977.

FREMDLING, R., TILLY, R.: "German Banks, German Growth and Econometric History", *The Journal of Economic History* 36 (1976), pp. 416-424.

GERSCHENKRON, A.: *Economic Backwardness in Historical Perspective*, Cambridge, MA (Harvard University Press) 1962.

GILLE, B.: "Banking and Industrialisation in Europe, 1730-1914", in: C. M. CIPOLLA (Ed.): *The Fontana Economic History of Europe: The Industrial Revolution*, Glascow (Fontana/Collins) 1977.

GILPIN, R.: *The Political Economy of International Relations*, Princeton (Princeton University Press) 1987.

GIOVANNINI, A. (Ed.): *Finance and Development: Issues and Experience*, Cambridge (Cambridge University Press) 1993.

GURLEY, J. G., SHAW, E. S.: "Financial Aspects of Economic Development", *American Economic Review*, 45 (1955), pp. 515-538.

GURLEY, J. G., SHAW, E. S.: *Money in a Theory of Finance*, Washington, DC (The Brookings Institution) 1960.

GURLEY, J. G., SHAW, E. S.: "Financial Structure and Economic Development", *Economic Development and Cultural Change* 15 (1967), pp. 257-268.

HAQ, M., KAUL, I., GRUNBERG, I. (Eds.): *The Tobin Tax: Coping with Financial Volatility*, Oxford/New York (Oxford University Press) 1996.

HELLEINER, E.: *States and the Reemergence of Global Finance: From Bretton Woods to the 1990s*, Ithaca (Cornell University Press) 1994.

HILFERDING, R.: *Finance Capital: A Study of the Latest Phase of Capitalist Development*, London (Routledge & Kegan Paul) 1981.

HILFERDING, R.: "The Organized Economy", in: T. BOTTOMORE, P. GOODE (Eds.): *Readings in Marxist Sociology*, Oxford (Clarendon Press) 1983.

HOBSON, J. A.: *Imperialism: A Study*, London (George Allen & Unwin Ltd) 1954.

ITOH, M.: *The Basic Theory of Capitalism*, New York (Monthly Review Press) 1988.

KEMP, T.: *Industrialisation in Nineteenth-Century Europe*, London (Longman) 1969.

LANDES, D. S.: "The Old Bank and the New: The Financial Revolution of the Nineteenth Century", in: F. CROUZET, F., W. R. CHALONER, and W. M. STERN, (Eds.): *Essays in European Economic History, 1789-1914*. New York (St. Martin's Press) 1969.

LANDES, D. S.: *The Unbound Prometheus: Technological Change and Industrial Development in Western Europe from 1750 to the Present*, Cambridge (Cambridge University Press) 1972.

LENIN, V. I.: *Imperialism, the Highest Stage of Capitalism*, Moscow (Progress Publishers) 1968.

LOCKWOOD, W. W.: *The Economic Development of Japan: Growth and Structural Change, 1868-1938*, Princeton (Princeton University Press) 1954.

MANDEL, E.: *Marxist Economic Theory*, New York (Monthly Review Press) 1970. (2 vols.)

MARX, K.: *Capital. A Critique of Political Economy*, New York (International Publishers) 1967 (3 Vols.).

MILWARD, A., SAUL, S. B.: *The Economic Development of Continental Europe, 1870-1914*, London (George Allen & Unwin) 1973.

NAU, H.: *The Myth of America's Decline: Leading the World Economy into the 1990s*, Oxford/New York (Oxford University Press) 1990.

NELSON, R. R., PACK, H.: "The Asian Miracle and Modern Growth Theory", *Workshop on Emerging Issues in Development Economics, The World Bank*, Washington, DC (The World Bank) 1997.

NEWBURGER H., STOKES, H. H.: "German Banks and German Growth, 1883-1913: An Empirical View", *The Journal of Economic History*, 34 (1974), pp. 710-731.

RUGGIE, J. G.: "International Regimes, Transactions and Change: Embedded Liberalism in the Postwar Economic Order", *International Organisation*, 36 (1982), pp. 379-415.

SHAIKH, A.: "Notes on Advanced Political Economy", unpublished manuscript, 1981.

SHAIKH, A.: "Neo-Ricardian Economics: A Wealth of Algebra, a Poverty of Theory", *Review of Radical Political Economics*, 14 (1982), pp. 67-83.

SHAIKH, A.: "The Falling Rate of Profit as the Cause of Long Waves: Theory and Empirical Evidence", in: A. KLEINKNECHT, E. MANDEL, I. WALLERSTEIN (Eds.): *New Findings in Long-Wave Research*, New York (St. Martin's Press) 1992.

STIGLITZ, J.: "Overview", in: A. GIOVANNINI, (Ed.): *Finance and Development: Issues and Experiences*, Cambridge (Cambridge University Press) 1993.

STIGLITZ, J.: "Some Lessons from the East Asian Miracle", *The World Bank Research Observer*, 1 (1996), pp. 151-178.

STIGLITZ, J. and M. UY.: "Financial Markets, Public Policy, and the East Asian Miracle", *The World Bank Research Observer*, 11 (1996), pp. 249-276.

SWEEZY, P. M.: *The Theory of Capitalist Development*, New York (Monthly Review Press) 1968.

SWEEZY, P. M.: "The Resurgence of Financial Control: Fact or Fancy?" *Socialist Revolution*, 2 (1972), pp. 235-283.

SWEEZY, P. M.: "The Triumph of Financial Capital", *Monthly Review*, 46, 2 (1994), pp. 1-11.

TAVARES, M. C.: "A Retomada da Hegemonia Norte-Americana", *Revista de Economia Política*, 5, 2 (1985), pp. 7-15.

TILLY, R.: "Germany 1815-1870", in: R. CAMERON (Ed.): *Banking in the Early Stages of Industrialisation*, Oxford/New York (Oxford University Press) 1967.

TOBIN, J.: "A Proposal for International Monetary Reform", *Eastern Economic Journal*, 4 (1978), pp. 153-159.

VITTAS, D. and YOON JE CHO: "Credit Policies: Lessons from Japan and Korea", *The World Bank Research Observer*, 11 (1996), pp. 277-298.

WADE, R.: *Governing the Market: Economic Theory and the Role of Government in East Asian Industrialisation*, Princeton (Princeton University Press) 1990.

WADE, R.: "Globalisation and Its Limits: Reports of the Death of the National Economy are Greatly Exaggerated", in: S. BERGER, R. DORE (Eds.): *National Diversity and Global Capitalism*, Ithaca (Cornell University Press) 1996.

WOO, JUNG-EN.: *Race to the Swift: State and Finance in Korean Industrialisation*, New York (Columbia University Press) 1991.

ZONINSEIN, J.: *Monopoly Capital Theory: Hilferding and Twentieth Century Capitalism*, New York (Greenwood Press) 1990.

ZONINSEIN, J.: "Policy Reform and Macroeconomic Performance in Newly Industrialised Countries: The Experiences of Brazil and Korea", in: GILL-CHIN LIM and MAN-HYUNG LEE (Eds.): *Dynamic Transformation of Societies*, Seoul (Nanam Publishing House for the Consortium on Development Studies) 1993.

ZONINSEIN, J.: "Financial Reform, Control of Inflation, and State Intervention: Lessons from the Brazilian Experience", *The Developing Economies*, 32 (1994), pp. 331-349.

ZYSMAN, J.: *Governments, Markets, and Growth: Financial Systems and the Politics of Industrial Change*, Ithaca (Cornell University Press) 1983.

Discussion Summary

ELKE SCHWINGER

Paper discussed:
JONAS ZONINSEIN: Rudolf Hilferding's Theory of Finance Capitalism and Today's World Financial Markets

The main part of the debate dealt with the dynamics of the international financial market and especially with the position of the United States of America in the structure of international political and economic relationships. In this process of capital concentration and centralisation, where - in the view of Hilferding's work - banks are the central agents in the international financial market, the USA came out on the top in the international hierarchy. The link from Hilferdings investigations to the time after World War II is an imperialistic theory of international finance. Questions came up about the relations of the agents in this development and about the importance of the current account deficit of the USA as the dominant state in the system of currency. For the inner-logic of the financial market there must be individual agents. In the case of help-missing China for example the relevant factor is, according to this methodological assumptions, how the Chinese people themselves are behaving in the national financial market (WATRIN). But in an external view, a theoretical approach to the dynamics of the international financial market, like Hilferding's approach as a Marxist, with Marxist methodology, there are collective agents: banks are helping banks (ZONINSEIN). The positive or negative value of the US-account-deficit depends also on this basic perspectives. So WATRIN said that the USA has an account deficit for decades and there is no sign of capital-flight in the USA. This would be a special sensitive reaction of the international financial market to a collapsing national economy. The important problem in this financial system is not the fact of borrowing itself, but the problem of a successful investigation of the money which the country is borrowing. According to the function of international financial system, no system with an autonomous thinking centre, with plans and ideas, investing in growing countries or innovation of countries is valued as productive in contrast to the one spending money in consumer goods. (WATRIN). But for ZONINSEIN, the USA today seems not to use the money very productively on the national level of finance market: for example a lot of money for the consumption of the upper and the middle class ("Supply excess is clear") (ZONINSEIN). On the level of the international financial market: Politics plays the game. Political interventions are necessary in these financial relationships. The main actors are the nation states, collective actors with a certain rationality: the view of interest of the nations, especially of the national governments. But for Hilferding, the national governments are part of the national economy. With this little, but important difference ZONINSEIN agreed with STREIT's explanations about the causes of speculation. The whole history of speculation defines speculations as caused by political decisions (examples: Hong Kong, Great Depression). Besides coping with uncertainty, they try to find out potential or actual political moves. The next interesting question to the US-account-deficit was a question of economic ethics which KOSLOWSKI asked: "Should a nation be allowed to borrow more money than it lends to the rest of the world?" This is a question which stands in the correct opposite to the scholastic question: Whether you are allowed to lend money or interest at all. It is a problem which has ethical relevance and a problem without a solution till today. The subject is the inequality of taking more money by the US from developing countries like Africa than they are investing there. The US does not engage any risk-taking in spite of lending so much money. KOSLOWSKI agrees with ZONINSEIN in the argument of imperialism with a remark, that there are much more forms of imperialism in these international financial relationships than we are used to. So Germany and Japan paid billions of marks more to the USA than the Golf-war had cost. This can be named making profit from warfare (KOSLOWSKI). The other problematic aspect is the ideology of "moral double standard". The USA for example criticised Switzerland 50 years after World War II in the debates about Jewish accounts for the fact that it had had no right to remain neutral and for the fact that it did not understand that the war against Germany was not a war but a crusade. At the same time, the USA never attacked the Czech Republic, which has not returned any Jewish property at all, because the political leadership argued that it did not want to do so, otherwise it would have to return the German property too. Under this broader political aspects of discussion which goes beyond the economic perspective, the American strategy in the world system has to be contrasted.

DISCUSSION SUMMARY

ZONINSEIN extended this picture of the international situation radically to the comparison of the Hobbesian picture of a world of permanent warfare. The situation for him today is a situation of "non-system" with the dominance of the USA. The USA has enough military power and still residual economic power to impose on the rest of the world the decisions of the US-government and ministries. The answer to the question how to overcome this international situation, is to talk about the global civil society, about the possibility of an international regime, which would be able to take in account in a democratic way public goods issues, for example environmental issues. The question is, how to expand this approach, how it is possible to democratise the Bretton Wood institutions and the international finance community (ZONINSEIN). For WATRIN the picture of international economic competition as of warfare must be corrected. Competition is a process which depends on destruction and institutions under which it takes place. It is a game where you can lose in one act and win in the next. And this picture is leading to the next interesting point of the discussion - the practical consequences of Hilferding's theory. There is a weak point in the classical Marxist impacts of Hilferding's approach, which became of practical relevance in 1929 when Hilferding was the finance minister of Germany and the Great Depression broke out: His whole theory has tremendous implications to his behaviour, especially his inactivity in face of the mass unemployment at this time (HAGEMANN): the link between his theoretical implications and his "non-intervention attitude" (PEUKERT) was the central Marxist assumption of this crisis according to the theory of organised capitalism that this was the final crisis of capitalism. Hilferding became famous for his statement: "You should not act as "the doctor at the bed of the patient Capitalism" (HAGEMANN). For Hilferding, there was no theoretical clarity in face of this dramatic historical situation. He was ambiguous because there was only a Marxist projection of the future in the materialistic theory which was a very mechanistic view of the development of society and it did not work. There is no political theory in the Marxist materialistic conception of history, only the liberal idea of a democracy producing a civil society. It is a gap in this theoretical approach, ZONINSEIN agreed. Kautsky was criticising Hilferding's approach because in Hilferding's theory there is room for a quantitative theory of money (YAGI). Hilferding was the only one, who declared the transition from an economic system based on real money to a system based on symbolic money (ZONINSEIN).

DISCUSSION SUMMARY

After discussing this theoretical impacts of Hilferding's theory, the debate came to the question about the vision of Hilferding's approach (PEUKERT). The answer is that this approach is not something you can simply apply to reality. It was very important for the German experiment and for the questions of the political concepts of the Social Democratic party. Hilferding's theory of organised capitalism is not correct, but it is useful to formulate policies. It is important for raising relevant questions of the international finance system we have to discuss (ZONINSEIN).

Chapter 9

The Early Frankfurt School Critique of Capitalism: Critical Theory Between Pollock's "State Capitalism" and the Critique of Instrumental Reason

HARRY F. DAHMS

I. Introduction: The Frankfurt School and the German Historical School
II. From Marx and Weber to "Weberian Marxism": Georg Lukàcs and Rudolf Hilferding Prepare the Critical Social Theory of the Frankfurt School
III. Dividing the Labour of Criticising Postliberal Capitalism: Friedrich Pollock at the Institute of Social Research
IV. Pollock's Concept of "State Capitalism"
V. The Dialectic of Enlightenment and the Critique of Instrumental Reason
VI. Antinomies of "Traditional Marxism" in the Early Frankfurt School Critique of Capitalism
VII. Conclusion

I. Introduction: The Frankfurt School and the German Historical School

Despite profound differences, both the German Historical School and the Critical Theory of the Frankfurt School share a common theoretical and cultural heritage in Central European traditions of social thought and philosophy. Although both schools often are perceived as quintessentially German traditions of economic and social research, their methodological presuppositions and critical intent diverge strongly. Since the objective of the Frankfurt School was to carry the theoretical critique initiated by Marx into the twentieth century, and since its members did so on a highly abstract level of theoretical criticism, the suggestion may be surprising that in terms of their respective research agendas, there was a common denominator between the German Historical School and Frankfurt School Critical Theory. To be sure, as will become apparent, the common ground was rather tenuous and indirect. We must ask, then: in what respects did their theoretical and analytical foundations and orientations overlap? How did the German Historical School, as a nineteenth-century tradition of economic thinking, influence the development of the Frankfurt School?

During its early phase, the German Historical School distinguished itself as a compelling alternative to the conflicting modes of analysing the modern economy and the capitalist production process put forth by classical and neo-classical economic theory, on the one hand, and Karl Marx's critique of political economy, on the other. As a tradition with theoretical intent, the German Historical School was concerned with the actual inner workings of the capitalist market economy, and its embeddedness in social, political, religious and cultural traditions and structures. Accordingly, this tradition emphasised on data collection and historical accuracy rather than theoretical abstractness. It was not oriented toward designing a highly formalistic model for determining the nature of the relationships between different factors and dimensions of economic production and distribution, as in neo-classical economic theory. Neither was the German Historical School concerned with assessing the effects of the capitalist market economy on politics, culture and society in bourgeois societies, as had been the motive force behind Marx's critique of political economy.

By contrast, Frankfurt School Critical Theory emerged as the project of reconstructing Marx's critique of bourgeois society and the liberal-capitalist mode of production, as applied to the socio-economic formation that emerged during the early decades of the twentieth century.[1] Toward this

---

1 For general introductions and overviews, see M. JAY: *Dialectical Imagination. A History of the Frankfurt School and the Institute of Social Research 1923-1950*, Boston (Little, Brown and Co.) 1973; H. DUBIEL: *Wissenschaftsorganisation und politische Erfahrung. Studien zur frühen kritischen Theorie*, Frankfurt/M. (Suhrkamp) 1978. The most comprehensive study of the Frankfurt

end, the members of the Frankfurt School - Max Horkheimer, Herbert Marcuse, Friedrich Pollock and Leo Löwenthal from the beginning, later to be joined by Theodor W. Adorno - combined Hegel's dialectical philosophy, Marx's critique of political economy, Weber's theory of rationalisation, Lukàcs's critique of reification, and Freud's psychoanalysis, to formulate a systematically critical theory of capitalist society. In fact, the Frankfurt theorists were determined to establish the foundations for the *most* theoretically *sophisticated and complex critique* of the advanced capitalist society that emerged during the early twentieth century.

To assess the specific nature of the influence the German Historical School exerted on the Frankfurt School Critical Theorists, we must first recognise the most distinctive feature of the latter as their attempt to reformulate and apply Marx's critique to a *qualitatively later stage* of capitalist development. To do so, the members of the Frankfurt School rendered a reconstruction of Marx's critique of political economy that drew on the emerging social sciences, especially sociology, and on advances in the analysis of the capitalist process made since Marx. In this critical-theoretical reconstruction of Marx's critique for purposes of analysing the advanced capitalist mode of production in relation to its social organisation since the late nineteenth century, the works of one member of the German Historical School featured especially prominently: the analyses of Max Weber. Among Weber's various scholarly contributions, his attempt to determine why modern capitalism emerged only in the West was especially important, along with his answer to this question on the basis of the "Protestant Ethic" thesis.[2] It is Weber's related theory of rationalisation as the underlying principle of the rise of capitalism, and his concurrent critique of bureaucracy that constitute the link between the German Historical School and the Frankfurt School.

The Frankfurt School critical theory of society is mostly known for its culturalist critique of capitalist society, in terms of a *critique of instrumental reason*. This critique was generalised to theorise the patterns of human civilisation as a whole, as they culminated in the contradictions of modern society. Yet, like Marx's own critical theory of capitalist society, including

---

School is R. WIGGERSHAUS: *The Frankfurt School. Its History, Theories, and Political Significance* [1986], Cambridge, Mass. (MIT Press) 1994.

2 M. WEBER: *The Protestant Ethic and the Spirit of Capitalism*, New York (Charles Scribner's Sons) 1930.

all Marxist theories centring around the concepts of alienation and commodity fetishism, the Frankfurt School culturalist critique of capitalist society must rest on the foundations of the critique of political economy. And indeed, the Frankfurt's culturalist critique of capitalism is based on its own critique of political economy. Yet while the Critical Theorists placed themselves squarely in the tradition of Marx's radical critique of capitalism, their analysis of capitalism was not focused on a comparable critique of political economy modulated to discern the specifics of the mode of production in postliberal capitalism. Instead, they contended, the importance of the critique of political economy had been superseded by the need for a critique of the cultural manifestations and forms of coexistence that emerged in postliberal capitalism, in terms of a radical critique of ideology. We must ask, then: How did the Frankfurt School theorists revise and update Marx's critique of political economy to apply to conditions of *postliberal* capitalism?

As will become apparent, it is both in relation to the Frankfurt School's *political-economic* analysis of advanced capitalism and the *culturalist* critique of modern society (with the former serving as the foundation for the latter) that the influence of the German Historical School is most important. In relation to the critique of political economy, it is the newly emerging centrality of bureaucracy to advanced capitalist organisation (drawing on Weber's theory of bureaucratisation); in relation to the culturalist critique of capitalism, it is the "reifying" effects of organised capitalist production on all aspects of society (drawing on Weber's theory of rationalisation).

The political-economic analysis of advanced capitalism is the far less well-known aspect of Critical Theory, and the more neglected in the recent revival of interest in this theoretical tradition, as it centres around the critique of the pernicious effects of the capitalist mode of production on politics, culture and society.[3] Incidentally, the scholars at the Institute who were responsible for the analysis of concrete economic and political organisations and institutions, including political economy and constitutional issues, also remain less well-known, most notably Pollock, Franz Neumann and Otto Kirchheimer. Yet the Frankfurt School's cultural critique of capitalism

---

3   In fact, the only systematic discussion of this aspect of the Frankfurt School was within the context of M. POSTONE: *Time, Labour, and Social Domination. A Reinterpretation of Marx's Critical Theory*, Cambridge (Cambridge University Press) 1993, pp. 84-120.

neither can be fully appreciated without familiarity with the underlying political-economic analysis, nor would the former have been possible without the latter.

In concentrating on this *political-economic* dimension, I will frame the Frankfurt School project in relation to both Marx and Weber, whose respective works were the two most important sources for the development of critical theory, as far as its *economic* analysis of capitalism is concerned. To situate this project among the social sciences of the time, I will introduce the Frankfurt agenda as a step in the development of the tradition of "Weberian Marxism," pointing toward a social-scientifically sophisticated critical theory of postliberal capitalism.[4] Within the Institute's division of labour, the task of analysing the concrete forms of capitalist organisation was delegated to one of its members: Friedrich Pollock was responsible for "updating" Marx's critique of political economy for the new stage of capitalist production and organisation reached during the 1930s. Based on his research, the Institute's members started out from the assumption that during the 1930s, large corporations became the dominant form of economic organisation in advanced capitalism, setting the stage for close co-operation between economic corporations and the state, in "state capitalism", pointing toward what the theorists later would call a "totally administered world". With this emerging co-operation, the stage of liberal capitalism had passed its climax - for all practical purposes.

---

4   See M. LÖWY: "Figures of Weberian Marxism", *Theory and Society*, 25 (1996), pp. 431-46; and H. F. DAHMS: "Theory in Weberian Marxism: Critical Social Theory in Luk cs and Habermas", *Sociological Theory*, 15 (1997), pp. 181-214, where I have described the thrust of Weberian Marxism "as a critique of capitalism that employed elements of both Marxist and non-Marxist social theories ... to facilitate the most sophisticated, critical understanding of the nature of capitalist society in the early twentieth century. Weberian Marxism in this sense emerged as a combination of three related theoretical and practical projects: first, to identify reification as the defining feature of advanced capitalist society within the context of large-scale social, economic, political, and cultural transformations; second, to expound the nature of reification as the dominant principle of processes 'mediating' social, economic, political, and cultural production, reproduction, and exchange; and third, to formulate a strategy for proletarian practice geared toward overcoming the reifying capitalist order" (p. 183).

Once Max Horkheimer, the Institute's director, had arrived at this conclusion, the Frankfurt theorists all but abandoned concern with the specificity and "inner logic" of the economic process in advanced capitalism, rudimentary as it had been to begin with. They turned their attention toward the nature of the effects of capitalist production under conditions of postliberalism on all aspects of society, in terms of the critique of instrumental reason. As will become apparent, however, in the end the *specific* political-economic analysis that informed the development and orientation of the Frankfurt School critical theory of society during the 1930s and 1940s, which was integral to its general critique of capitalism as the culmination of human civilisation, rested on a flawed diagnosis. Yet, since all theories are likely to be in need of revision and flawed in one way or other, my purpose here is not to show *that* the early Frankfurt School critique of capitalism was deficient, but how its deficiencies reverberate both in the general perspective and in the details of the early critical theory of society, and how it warped the culturalist critique of western civilisation for which the Frankfurt School is best known.

Finally, why is it that the Frankfurt School's critique of political economy has remained so relatively unknown, while their culturalist critique continues to attract attention? How compelling is Pollock's conclusion today, that the new arrangement between the economy and the state taking shape during the 1930s was best described in terms of "state capitalism"? How did he characterise this new arrangement, and how did his analysis influence the Institute's research agenda? To address these questions, I shall first provide a brief depiction of the two major early-twentieth century analyses that combined motives of Marx's critique of political economy and of Weber's theory of rationalisation and which prepared the Frankfurt School: Rudolf Hilferding's *Finance Capital*[5] and Georg Lukàcs's *History and Class Consciousness*.[6] These works were attempts to apply Marx's critique to a later stage in the development of capitalist society, considering transformations Weber tried to grasp in terms of his theory of rationalisation. Situating the specific agenda of the Institute of Social Research in

---

5   R. HILFERDING: *Finance Capital. A Study of the Latest Phase of Capitalist Development* [1910], London (Routledge & Kegan Paul) 1981.
6   G. LUKÁCS: *History and Class Consciousness. Studies in Marxist Dialectics* [1923] (translated by Rodney Livingstone), Cambridge, Mass. (MIT Press) 1971.

THE EARLY FRANKFURT SCHOOL CRITIQUE OF CAPITALISM

Frankfurt among related attempts to revise Marx's critique of capitalist society by employing Weber, I then sketch Pollock's version of the critique of political economy as it culminated in the concept of "state capitalism". How did it compare to Neumann's authoritarian capitalism, developed in the context of his comprehensive analysis of National Socialism, as an alternative to Pollock's concept? How did Pollock's writings influence the development of critical theory during the 1940s, in particular Horkheimer's concept of the "authoritarian state" and the critique of instrumental reason developed by Horkheimer and Adorno in *Dialectic of Enlightenment*?

II. From Marx and Weber to "Weberian Marxism": Lukàcs and Hilferding Prepare the Critical Social Theory of the Frankfurt School

The critique of capitalism developed during the 1930s and 1940s by the Frankfurt School critical theorists constitutes the third wave of attempts during the early decades of this century to develop a critical theory of advanced capitalism. In 1910, the economist Rudolf Hilferding had published *Finance Capital*, a work Karl Kautsky regarded as the fourth volume of Marx's *Das Kapital*.[7] Though Hilferding had concentrated on developing the analysis of the latest stage of capitalist development, imperialism, his work was the first sustained analysis of the emerging stage of the organised capitalism. During the years following World War I, the philosophers Georg Lukàcs and Karl Korsch published works - *History and Class Consciousness* and *Marxism and Philosophy*, respectively - that today are regarded as the founding texts of Western Marxism (along with Antonio Gramsci's more politically oriented writings).[8] The works of this second

---

7 E. GLASER: *Im Umfeld des Austromarxismus. Ein Beitrag zur Geistesgeschichte des österreichischen Sozialismus*, Wien (Europaverlag) 1981, p. 214.
8 G. LUKÀCS: *History and Class Consciousness, op.cit.*; K. KORSCH: *Marxism and Philosophy* [1923], London (Verso) 1970. On the beginnings of Western Marxism, see B. AGGER: *Western Marxism: An Introduction. Classical and Contemporary Sources*, Santa Monica, Calif. (Goodyear) 1979; and P. ANDERSON: *Considerations of Western Marxism*, London (NLB) 1976.

wave explicitly reflected on the fact that the proletarian revolution had occurred not in one of the advanced capitalist societies, as according to Marx's theory, but in economically and politically backward Russia. Independently of each other, Lukàcs and Korsch responded by working toward a reformulation of Marx's critique designed to facilitate the socialist transformation of advanced western capitalism. The objective was to formulate an updated critique of political economy which, by taking into consideration advances made in the social sciences since Marx, would analyse and reflect on changes that had occurred in the most developed capitalist economies and their social organisation during the decades following Marx's death in 1883. Like their predecessors, the Frankfurt School theorists during the 1930s tried to meet this challenge by developing an analysis of advanced capitalism that combined Karl Marx's critique of political economy with motives Max Weber systematised in his theory of rationalisation.

The purpose of Marx's critique of political economy had been to discern the general relationship between the mode of production characteristic of a specific stage of societal evolution, and the corresponding relations of production - the structure of inequality in society, especially as far as the ownership of the means of production was concerned, and conditions of political, social and cultural life. Before we can elucidate the nature of the relationship between the cultural and the economic-structural critiques of capitalism in the Frankfurt School's critique of capitalism, we need to recall Marx's approach to the problem.

Marx did not start out as the critic of political economy. Indeed, the vanishing point of his early writings was a critique of alienation. Yet he soon realised that his "culturalist," philosophical critique of bourgeois society (centred around the concept of "alienation," and applied first to political philosophy as represented by Hegel, and then to classical political economy as represented by Adam Smith) was not sufficient. On the basis of a critique of alienation, it would not be possible to lay the critical-theoretical foundation for an effective practice of societal transformation. The critique of political economy became necessary to remedy this problem. The centrality of political economy to Marx's theory is expressive of the fact that the underpinning of all things social, political and cultural, is economic. But Marx did not claim that the nature of the former can be grasped fully on the basis of an understanding of the economy. Rather, without an understanding of how the organisation of society represents a response to the economic challenge of material production and reproduction, there cannot be any critical and systematic understanding of politics, culture and society. Accordingly, before we can conceive of a truly socially transformative practice, we need to understand the economic foundations of the social and political order. Marx wanted to determine the necessary conditions for identifying, and seizing upon, the potential for emancipatory social transformation in capitalist society. As he developed his critique of political economy, Marx realised that neither alienation nor political economy as such were sufficient. Instead, the concept of "commodity fetishism" replaced the former "alienation": commodity fetishism is the "basic" economic mode of mediation that determined the nature of the superstructure - patterns of political, social and cultural reproduction - in capitalism.[9]

By contrast, Max Weber had set out to analyse the underlying dynamic of the development of capitalism, to discern whether the logic of capitalist development described by Marx was the source of social transformations in modern society, or instead the manifestation of a more fundamental process shaping all the spheres in western capitalist societies. The most important structural change that is related to the most significant analytical change, as far as the role of Marx's theory in the social sciences is concerned, was the rise of modern bureaucracy within the economy, and its theoretisation by Max Weber in terms of his theory of rationalisation. On the basis of his studies of the religious foundations of the spirit of capitalism in *The Protestant Ethic and the Spirit of Capitalism*, "The Social Psychology of World Religions"[10], and his various contributions to the comparative sociology of religion in general, Weber concluded that in the rise of the modern economy, in the emergence of the administrative nation state, and in other spheres of society, including religion itself, a more fundamental process of rationalisation was at play that determined the path of modernisation in western societies, and increasingly, of every individual social value sphere as well. As a result, large, rationally organised bureaucratic structures replaced traditional power relations across society.

While Marx had described and critiqued capitalism at the competitive stage, though arguing already at the time that large-scale production would be the necessary outcome of industrial capitalism, Weber developed his

---

9   K. MARX: *Capital*, New York (Vintage Books) 1977, pp. 163-177.
10 M. WEBER: "The Social Psychology of World Religions," in: H. H. GERTH and C. W. MILLS (Eds.): *From Max Weber: Essays in Sociology*, New York (Oxford University Press) 1946, pp. 267-301.

theory of rationalisation during the period when big businesses, large corporations, and trusts and concerns emerged as the predominant form of economic organisation. When he visited the United States at the beginning of the century, Weber was able to observe the beginnings of what was to transform the organisation of the capitalist production process: the managerial revolution.

Following the example of Marx, Hilferding was most concerned with how to reformulate Marx's critique of political economy in a manner which grasped the nature of organised, "finance capitalism," as an important dimension of nineteenth-century liberal capitalism. He did not conceive of his analysis of finance capitalism as an application of Marx's categories and critique to a *qualitatively* later stage of capitalism.[11] In the preface to *Finance Capital*, Hilferding had written:

> In the following pages an attempt will be made to arrive at a scientific understanding of the economic characteristics of the latest phase of capitalist development. ... The most characteristic features of 'modern' capitalism are those processes of concentration which, on the one hand, 'eliminate free competition' through the formation of cartels and trusts, and on the other, bring bank and industrial capital into an ever more intimate relationship. Through this relationship ... capital-

---

11 As Marx had written, in "all forms of society there is one specific kind of production which predominates over the rest, whose relations thus assign rank and influence to the others. It is a general illumination which bathes all the other colours and modifies their particularity. It is a particular ether which determines the specific gravity of every being which has materialized within it. ... Agriculture more and more becomes merely a branch of industry, and is entirely dominated by capital. Ground rent likewise. ... Capital is the all-dominating economic power of bourgeois society. ...

It would therefore be unfeasible and wrong to let the economic categories follow one another in the same sequence as that in which they were historically decisive. Their sequence is determined, rather, by their relation to one another in bourgeois society, which is precisely the opposite of that which seems to be their natural order or which corresponds to historical development. The point is not the historic position of the economic relations in the succession of different forms of society. ... Rather, their order within modern bourgeois society." K. MARX: *Grundrisse. Foundations of the Critique of Political Economy (Rough Draft)* [1857-58], trans. by M. Nicolaus, London (Penguin Books) 1973, pp. 106-107.

ism assumes the form of finance capital, its supreme and most abstract expression.[12]

Instead, *Finance Capital* was an attempt to complete the final step in the critique of political economy Marx had identified as essential in the *Grundrisse*, but had not been able to engage himself.[13] To achieve this objective, Hilferding applied a perspective that is highly compatible with Weber's analyses of the increasing bureaucratization of the world, including the economy, though Hilferding did not acknowledge that Weber influenced his own analysis. Whether Weber's studies on rationalisation enabled Hilferding to analyse monopoly capitalism as a more differentiated and rationalised organisation of the capitalist process or not, there is a fundamental affinity in their motives: that the capitalist process is becoming ever more complex, integrated, and large-scale.[14]

It was only during the years immediately following after World War I that the next systematic attempt to "update" Marx was undertaken. In this case, Max Weber's writings on rationalisation set the stage for reformulating Marx's philosophically sophisticated critique of capitalism. Georg Lukàcs combined Marx's critique of commodity fetishism and Max Weber's theory of rationalisation to reconstruct Marx's early, philosophical critique of alienation, as a critical theory of reification. "Reification" expresses the effects of the capitalist mode of production on human beings and society as *second nature* - at a later stage of capitalist development: advanced, monopolistic capitalism.

Lukàcs did not engage in a critique of political economy à la Marx himself, however, nor did he rely on any sources that would have provided him with a thorough Marxian analysis of the advanced capitalist mode of pro-

---

12   R. HILFERDING: *Finance Capital, op.cit.*, p. 22.
13   BARAN and SWEEZY wrote that the "first to [incorporate monopoly into the body of Marxian economic theory] was ... Rudolf Hilferding... But for all his emphasis on monopoly, [he] did not treat it as a qualitatively new element in the capitalist economy; rather, he saw it as effecting essentially quantitative modifications of the basic Marxian laws of capitalism." P. A. BARAN, P. SWEEZY: *Monopoly Capitalism. An Essay on the American Economic and Social Order*, New York (Monthly Review Press) 1966, p. 5.
14   On some similarities between Hilferding's and Weber's analyses, see H. JACOBY: *The Bureaucratization of the World*, Berkeley (University of California Press) 1973, pp. 79-80, 82.

duction. In his attempt to reconstruct the core of Marx's critique of political economy, Lukàcs did not explicitly take into consideration changes that had occurred in the organisation of capitalism. In fact, Lukàcs arrived at his critique of reification as the defining *effect* of capitalist production at the beginning of the early twentieth century, *by default*. Still, the foundations for the Hegelian brand of Weberian Marxism were laid.

Lukàcs combined Marx the critic of alienation and of commodity fetishism, with Weber the theorist of rationalisation and the critic of bureaucracy. Lukàcs's *History and Class Consciousness* was one of the main inspirations for the founders of the Institute of Social Research. Though Lukàcs was not explicitly concerned with the challenge of analysing specifically early twentieth-century capitalism, he considered Weber's theory of rationalisation essential to complete the Marxian critique of alienation and commodity fetishism. By combining these elements, Lukàcs could formulate his own critique of capitalism in terms of a critique of reification as the defining effect of the capitalist mode of production of all aspects of social life.

As a result, Lukàcs theorised the early-twentieth century mode of capitalist production *without* explicitly setting out to do so, since at the time when Marx worked out his critique of political economy the state of affairs in Britain and Germany, the two societies with which Marx had extensive primary experience, had not reached the point where it was possible to discern the bureaucratizing tendency overtaking capitalism--yet. In the 1880s, the managerial revolution that would fundamentally change the face of modern capitalism, and whose theoretical and analytical implications social scientists only began to recognise around the beginning of the second quarter of this century, was just about to begin in the United States.

One year after the Russian Revolution, during the months following the German Revolution at the end of World War I, Lukàcs "decided" to become a communist, as he was driven by the determination to reformulate Marx's critique of capitalism so as to enable the proletariat in the West to engage what had happened in the East, but should have happened in the advanced West: a socialist revolution. In "Reification and the Consciousness of the Proletariat," the main essay in *History and Class Consciousness*, Lukàcs took Weber's analysis of the increasing entwinement of state and economy at the stage of large-scale capitalist enterprises, along with their need for highly organised bureaucracies, as a given:

> [C]apitalism has created a form of the state and a system of law corresponding to its needs and harmonizing with its own structure. The structural similarity is so great that no truly perceptive historian of modern capitalism could fail to notice it. Max Weber, for instance, gives this description of the basic lines of this development: Both are, rather, quite similar in their fundamental nature. Viewed sociologically, a "business-concern" is the modern state; the same holds good for a factory: and this, precisely, is what is specific to it historically.[15]

While Lukàcs was familiar with Hilferding's writings, in *History and Class Consciousness* he barely acknowledged any influence. Clearly, in his critical analysis of the consequences of the advanced mode of capitalist production, he did not follow Marx's critique of political economy. The concrete forms of economic organisation remain in the background. Lukàcs formulated his critique of reification, drawing on his reading of Marx's critique of commodity fetishism, on Weber's theory of rationalisation, and on Simmel's *Philosophy of Money* - in the process *reconstructing* Marx's early critique of alienation, since the *Economic-Philosophical Manuscripts* had not been rediscovered at the time.[16] Indeed, Lukàcs did not systematically consider the level of economic organisation.[17] Yet his reinterpretation

---

15 G. LUKÁCS: *History and Class Consciousness*, op.cit., p. 95.
16 G. SIMMEL: *The Philosophy of Money* [1907], ed. by D. Frisby, transl. by T. Bottomore and D. Frisby, London (Routledge) 1990.
17 For perhaps the best example for such a linking of forms of theorising to prevailing forms of organisation at different stages of social development, see Schumpeter's early theory of the entrepreneur, and his later thesis of entrepreneurial decline: J. A. SCHUMPETER: *Theorie der wirtschaftlichen Entwicklung*, Leipzig (Duncker & Humblot) 1912; *The Theory of Economic Development. An Inquiry into Profits, Capital, Credit, Interest, and the Business Cycle* [1926], transl. by Redvers Opie, Cambridge, Mass. (Harvard University Press) 1934; and *Capitalism, Socialism, and Democracy*, New York (Harper & Brothers) 1942. For an initial systematic examination of this shift from Schumpeter's "positive" theory of entrepreneur to its "negative" reformulation, see H. F. DAHMS: "From Creative Action to the Social Rationalisation of the Economy: Joseph A. Schumpeter's Social Theory", *Sociological Theory*, 13 (1995), pp. 1-13.

indirectly reflected the changes that had occurred in the organisation of capitalism.[18]

Between Hilferding's and Lukàcs's respective reformulations of Marx's critique of political economy, we can see for the first time, and to the fullest extent, the separation of the analysis of the concrete organisational forms of the capitalist mode of production, and the analysis of its implications for forms of social life. As we will see, following Hillferding the Frankfurt School Critical Theorists regarded monopoly capitalism as the *most decisive developmental tendency* of advanced capitalism. It inspired their attempt to further refine Lukàcs's theory of reification, one decade after its initial formulation, with reification as the category for analysing the *most consequential effect* of the capitalist mode of production on society.

Though Hilferding's *Finance Capital* and Lukàcs's critique of reification are important examples for analyses inspired by the theories of Marx and Weber, however, they constitute rather *implicit* attempts to reformulate and apply Marx's critique to a later stage in the development of capitalism, by considering Weber's theory of rationalisation. In Hilferding, it is more the spirit of Weber's theory of rationalisation, emphasising the growing importance of bureaucracies and expanding control of organisations over every aspect of society, that is combined with Marx's critique; in Lukàcs (and the

---

[18] It has been stated repeatedly that Hilferding's *Finance Capital*, *op. cit.*, is of greater descriptive value for Germany and Austria in the early twentieth century than perhaps for any other advanced capitalist society. Accordingly, the organisational scales reached in Germany were considered "normal". Yet when Marx had written his main works from the second half of the 1840s to the 1860s, the managerial revolution had not occurred anywhere. England, the most developed industrial-capitalist society of the time, was very much organised on the basis of individual ownership. Germany had barely entered industrialization. Accordingly, whether it was because of their primary experience of the organisational levels of capitalist enterprise on the continent, or as a result of the influence of Weber's studies describing and reflecting these developments in theoretical terms, both Hilferding and Lukács effectively theorised capitalism at the brink to corporate capitalism. Along these lines, Lukács's critique of the effects of the prevailing capitalist mode of production on politics, culture and society in terms of reification as second-order commodity fetishism, was already a critique of political economy at a later stage than Marx's writings had theorised.

Frankfurt School), the simultaneous presence of Marx and Weber is more central, though barely acknowledged.

Still, there can be no doubt that Weber's critical analyses of Marxian issues, particularly the origins of capitalism in terms of a process of continually expanding rationalisation, had a profound impact on Central European social scientists during the first decades of this century.[19] While Lukàcs has long been recognised as a "founder" of the tradition of Western Marxism, more specifically in the sense of Weberian Marxism, Hilferding is usually not considered a contributor to Western Marxism. Instead, Hilferding is counted among the *Austro-Marxists*, who, as Ben Agger put it, "divided Marxian science and Marxian ethics", adhering to "a Weberian type of Marxism [that] split between empirical causality and ethical optimism and values, ... avoid[ing Rosa] Luxemburg's activism while remaining faithful to Marx, combining socialist 'values' and Marxian 'science.'"[20] Though both the contributions of Hilferding and Lukàcs were influenced more or less directly by the works of both Marx and Weber, there are important differences in their respective readings of these classics.

During the 1920s, Lukàcs and Hilferding went in opposite directions. Hilferding, who had belonged to the more radical Independent Social Democrats during the First World War, played an important role in their reconciliation with the Majority Social Democrats. He was finance secretary twice during the Weimar Republic. By contrast, Lukàcs recanted his analyses and conclusions in *History and Class Consciousness* after being forced to do so at the Fifth Comintern in 1925. The further the decade progressed, the more ardently communist Lukàcs became. The pattern of their differences is most conspicuous with regard their respective attitudes toward the subject of history: to Lukàcs, it had to be the proletariat, while to Hilferding the rise of socialism had to entail a transformation of society as a whole, before the socialist revolution. As Lukàcs put it in his essay on "What is Orthodox Marxism?":

---

19 An excellent case in point is Weber's influence on Joseph A. Schumpeter, which is barely acknowledged in the latter's writings; see J. A. SCHUMPETER: "Max Weber's Work" [1920], in: R. SWEDBERG (Ed.): *The Economics and Sociology of Capitalism*, Princeton (Princeton University Press) 1991, pp. 220-227; ELIZABETH BOODY SCHUMPETER (Ed.): *History of Economic Analysis*, New York (Oxford University Press) 1954.

20 B. AGGER: *Western Marxism*, op. cit., p. 83.

> [T]he essence of the method of historical materialism is inseparable from the "practical and critical" activity of the proletariat: both are aspects of the same process of social evolution. So, too, the knowledge of reality provided by the dialectical method is likewise inseparable from the class standpoint of the proletariat.[21]

With implicit reference to Hilferding's *Finance Capital*[22], he continued:

> The question raised by the Austrian Marxists of the methodological separation of the "pure" science of Marxism from socialism is a pseudo-problem. For, the Marxist method, the dialectical materialist knowledge of reality, can arise only from the point of view of a class, from the point of view of the struggle of the proletariat. To abandon this point of view is to move away from historical materialism, just as to adopt it leads directly into the thick of the struggle of the proletariat.

In terms of the high standards characteristic of Marx's philosophical-theoretical foundations of his critique of political economy, his contributions were not followed by any prominent attempts to apply his perspective to the stage of capitalist production emerging in the late 1800s in the United States and - with some delay - in Germany. Developments in the political economy of Germany, foreordained during the first two decades of the century, came to full bearing in the Weimar Republic, during the 1920s. These developments were analysed by social scientists like Hilferding, Lederer, Heimann, Schumpeter, and others.

Yet Hilferding's *Finance Capital* and Lukács's *History of Class Consciousness* foreshadowed the two dimensions of Weberian Marxism as a social-theoretical research programme designed to trace the changing relationship between the evolving capitalist mode of production and its effects in society. In the German-speaking world, Weber's theoretical contributions on rationalisation and bureaucratization greatly influenced early-twentieth century reinterpretations and applications of Marx's theory both in Austro-Marxism and in Hegelian Marxism, engendering a major qualitative and theoretical transformation of Marxian theory. This transformation was related, more or less visibly, to Weber's idea of the "inner logic of value

---

21 G. LUKÁCS: *History of Class Consciousness*, op. cit., p. 21.
22 In a footnote, Lukács singled out chapters VIII and IX of that work as examples for such a perspective (p. 26).

spheres" - his insight that we must carefully identify the developmental logic of all the different spheres in society and their empirical constellation, before we can consider the feasibility of changing that constellation.[23] These value spheres are centred around the diverse values that are being generated and regenerated in order for an advanced capitalistic society to function. To grasp the nature and unique features of modern societies, we must be willing to concede that each value sphere - the economy, the administrative state, the legal system, the education system, etc. - is related to a function that is essential to these societies' survival. Further each value sphere must be demarcated, at least to some degree, by a developmental "inner logic" of most rationally solving the type of problems specific to the value sphere at hand. Along these lines, and for the purpose of this chapter, Weberian Marxism is oriented toward the development of a "critical theory of the inner logic of value spheres". Though the Frankfurt School did not succeed, as will become apparent, it represents an important step in the right direction.[24]

---

23 In the German original of M. WEBER: *Economy and Society. An Outline of Interpretive Sociology* [1922], translated by E. Fischoff et al.; edited by Guenther Roth and Claus Wittich, Berkeley (University of California Press) 1980, the term *Eigengesetzlichkeit*, as one of the basic concepts of his theory of rationalisation, is applied above all to the market process and the development of law, but is also includes artistic production. In *Economy and Society*, *Eigengesetzlichkeit* was not translated consistently, but as "independence" (p. 650), "their own laws" (p. 1309), and "own autonomous tendencies" (p. 636). The latter expression is instructive regarding the concept's substance: "Where the market is allowed to follow its own autonomous tendencies, its participants do not look toward the persons of each other but only toward the commodity; there are no obligations of brotherliness or reverence, and none of those spontaneous human relations that are sustained by personal unions. They all would just obstruct the free development of the bare market relationship, and its specific interests serve, in their turn, to weaken the sentiments on which these obstructions rest."

24 See H. F. Dahms: "Toward a Critical Theory of the Inner Logic of Value Spheres: The Early Frankfurt School", *Current Perspectives in Social Theory*, 19 (1999).

HARRY F. DAHMS

III. Dividing the Labour of Criticising Postliberal Capitalism: Friedrich Pollock at the Institute of Social Research

In 1924, the Institute of Social Research was founded under the leadership of Carl Grünberg, a German "socialist of the chair" (*Kathedersozialist*). The Institute, with an explicit orientation toward the systematic analysis of society, was designed to revise Marx's critique of capitalism and bourgeois society, and to utilise social research toward that end in the process. When the Institute opened in 1924, the general sense that led to its establishment was that Marxian theory was in need of rejuvenation; during the preceding year, Lukàcs's *History and Class Consciousness* as well as Karl Korsch's *Marxism and Philosophy* had appeared, giving the desire for a reconstruction of Marx's theory, using social-scientific theories and techniques, a strong impetus. During the early years, before the formulation of the project of a critical theory of society and the programme of the Frankfurt School, the research conducted at the Institute was geared toward providing a theoretical alternative to both Social Democracy with its realpolitical orientation, and a western alternative to the theory that informed the Soviet experiment. The objective was to create the context for developing a systematic analysis oriented toward identifying the necessary social, political and cultural preconditions for a successful proletarian revolution.

Under the leadership of its first director, Carl Grünberg, the research conducted at the Institute was directed toward the condition of the working class and the labour movement. It was not the Institute's purpose to develop a distinct critique of capitalism within the tradition of Marx's critique of political economy. While during its early years, the activities and successes at the Institute were not especially noteworthy, the circumstances changed profoundly when Max Horkheimer, a professional philosopher, was chosen as the new director of the Institute in early 1931.

With Max Horkheimer at the helm, the definition of the Institute's purpose underwent a major transformation. Horkheimer brought a new impulse to the work conducted at the Institute, and pursued a new programme that shaped the research agenda for decades to come. To Horkheimer, the research objective was *precisely* to update Marx's critique to considerably altered socio-historical conditions: the issue was no longer the critique of political *economy* in the sense of the accumulation process and its intricacies, but the critique of *political* economy - the relationship between state and economy. To develop a sophisticated and systematic critical theory of advanced capitalism as postliberal capitalism, two necessary steps had to be taken. First, the problems and promise of this socio-economic formation needed to be examined in terms of how the underlying contradictions of capitalism had changed, and how new opportunities for societal transformation had arisen since Marx had developed his theory. And second, in the process of analysing post-liberal capitalism, the question had to be answered: does the critical analysis of this new formation, on the basis of Marx's critique of political economy, reveal flaws in Marx's theory itself? To analyse this new social formation in the most rigorous fashion, Horkheimer regarded it as essential to draw on advances that had been made since Marx's death, in the theoretical and social-scientific understanding of capitalist society. To be as social-scientific as possible, and, heeding the increasing division of labour, to integrate Marx's unsurpassed critique, directed at overcoming capitalism's contradictions, needed to be intergrated with contributions made by the social sciences - as an explicitly collaborative effort.

This critique of *political* economy was to be the foundation for the more important cultural critique of capitalism: a social-scientifically more refined version of Lukács's critique of reification that would consider the actual socio-historical circumstances, and the potential for social transformation it entailed. In other words, what appeared in Marx as critiques of alienation, political economy, commodity fetishism - and what had been intrinsically entwined in Marx's own theoretical work - reappears in the Frankfurt School in a different constellation, to be understood in terms of the division of labour. In a sense, the Frankfurt School Critical Theorists followed the pattern of Hilferding and Lukács, where the critique of political economy and of alienation/commodity fetishism had fallen apart: different members of the Institute where responsible for analysing different dimensions of postliberal capitalism. At the next stage, the pieces were to be recombined by Horkheimer and his colleagues.

> One question ... is not just of current relevance, but ... indeed the contemporary version of the oldest and most important set of philosophical problems: namely, the question of the connection between the economic life of society, the psychical development of individuals, and the changes in the realm of culture in the narrower sense (to which belong not only the so-called intellectual elements, such as

science, art, and religion, but also law, customs, fashion, public opinion, sports, leisure activities, lifestyle, etc.). The project of investigating the relations between these three processes is nothing but a reformulation - on the basis of the new problem constellation, consistent with the methods at our disposal and with the level of our knowledge - of the old question concerning the connection of particular existence and universal Reason, of reality and Idea, of life and Spirit (pp. 11-12).

In terms of the objective of developing a systematic critique of advanced capitalism - not one comprehensive systematic theory, though, but to engage in a collaborative project, working towards an *open-ended* critique of capitalist society - the main theoretical impulses came from the works of Marx and Weber. Although the contributions of other predecessors, especially Hegel and Freud, played important roles as well, for the trajectory of Frankfurt School critical theory, Marx and Weber were most central. Despite basic similarities between Hilferding's analyses, the Lukács of *History and Class Consciousness*, and an array of works attempting to grasp the transformation of capitalism underway during the 1920s and 1930s, the specific critique put forth and developed further by the Frankfurt theorists is unique. Though they saw their theoretical project in the tradition of Western Marxism, their simultaneous embrace of social-scientific standards in general, and their rejection of some specific standards in particular, constitutes this critique's most distinguishing feature.

The theories of capitalism presented by Hilferding, Lukács and the Frankfurt School theorists can all be compared in terms of their relationship to the theories of Marx and Weber. The appeal of Hilferding's structural analysis, and even more so, of Lukács's critique of reification, was expressive of the promise derived from linking Marx's theory of historical materialism, emphasising the challenge of analysing the changing mode of capitalist production, with Weber's writings on rationalisation.

While the Frankfurt School theorists' interest in Hilferding's analysis of finance capitalism remained rudimentary, Lukács's reformulation of Marx's critique of alienation and commodity fetishism in terms of reification, which corresponded to conditions of advanced capitalism fostering commodity fetishism as "second nature," provided a major impetus for their own development of a critical theory of capitalism during the Great Depression. Hilferding's economically oriented analysis of finance capitalism seemed to have fewer implications for the kind of cultural criticism that guided most

THE EARLY FRANKFURT SCHOOL CRITIQUE OF CAPITALISM

Western Marxists, including the Frankfurt School theorists. While recognising, in principle, Hilferding's importance for a Marxist analysis of early twentieth-century capitalism, they did not regard his approach as central to their analyses.

In addition, Horkheimer and his colleagues started out from the assumption that since our understanding *of* society is itself shaped *by* society, there is a special need for a critical theory that does not reproduce the patterns of the social formation it is designed to elucidate. To achieve this objective, critical theorists must first identify the conditions that would have to be fulfilled for discerning an understanding of advanced capitalism that opens up, rather than closes off, future possibilities of qualitative social transformation. The vanishing point for such a critical theory would have to be a qualitatively different critique of political economy - because the state-economy relationship had changed, because the analytical and research tools had become more varied and more refined, and because the historical goal may have changed.

Along the lines of this strong emphasis on an Institute organised on the basis of social-scientific principles, Horkheimer posed his agenda in terms of an overall division of labour. For Marx, the critique of political economy was, and had to be, central to an integrated endeavour, where one element attained primary significance in relation to all the other elements; and where analysis and critique, theory and practice were parts of an integrated whole. By contrast, in Horkheimer's vision of the Frankfurt Institute of Social Research, the analysis of different dimensions of modern capitalist society was to be the responsibility of individual researchers, within the Institute's division of labour, while it was the responsibility of the entire staff to facilitate the most powerful understanding of advanced capitalism.

The members of the Institute of Social Research engaged in the critique of capitalism on two levels. On the first level, they saw the need to revitalise the later Marx's critique of political economy, to be applied to the stage of capitalist development reached at the end of the first third of the twentieth century. Heeding the continuous division of labour in the social sciences, Horkheimer determined that the members and affiliates of the Institute be responsible for specific tasks (e.g. for sociology, psychology, economics, or law). Since each of the social sciences pursues a specific analytical and theoretical agenda, Horkheimer argued, the Critical Theorists had to presume the relative autonomy ("inner logic" in Weber) of the social sciences' respective tasks, and of the dimensions of social life ("value spheres" in Weber) these sciences are designed to analyse. Only on this basis would it be possible, in a later step, to critically relate the different inner logic to the prevailing patterns of how these tasks are fulfilled in actually existing societies. Along these lines, the task of providing an updated diagnosis of the state of political-economic affairs along Marxian lines fell to Friedrich Pollock, while the overall purpose of the Institute was to generate a highly sophisticated, systematic critique of post-liberal capitalism and its effects on political, social and cultural dimensions of life.

As Seyla Benhabib has pointed out, the research programme at the Institute of Social Research evolved in three phases from the 1930s to the mid-1940s, from the explicitly collaborative beginnings oriented toward the integration of philosophy and science, via a "philosophical critique of the epistemological bases of the sciences,"[25] to the culturalist critique of western civilisation. The initial phase of "interdisciplinary materialism" (1932-1937) was followed by the phase of "critical theory" proper (1937-1940), to culminate in the "critique of instrumental reason" (1940-1945).[26] The middle phase of "critical theory" in the more narrow sense began with the publication of Horkheimer's essay, "Traditional and Critical Theory".[27] As Benhabib put it, Horkheimer argued in this article that

> the findings of the specialized sciences cannot be integrated with philosophy without the latter exercising a critique of the foundations upon which the sciences are based. Both the specialized sciences and those philosophical theories which consider their achievements to be the only valid model of knowledge perpetuate an epistemological illusion: the object of cognition is presented as a ready-made, ahistori-

---

25 S. BENHABIB: *Critique, Norm, and Utopia*, New York (Columbia University Press) 1986, p. 152.
26 *Ibid.*, pp. 149-50. To be sure, Frankfurt School Critical Theory never was a unified body of thought: there are more or less profound differences between the orientations, interests, and specific contributions of all the members of the Institute of Social Research. However, in their self-understanding, they were engaged in the common project of developing a highly complex theory of advanced capitalism, a theory of the kind that only can be achieved in an explicitly interdisciplinary research environment with continuous exchange and critical debate.
27 M. HORKHEIMER: "Traditional and Critical Theory" [1937], in: *Critical Theory. Selected Essays*, transl. by M. J. O'Connell and others, New York (Continuum) 1986, pp. 188-243.

cal reality, and the relationship of the knowing subject to this object is presented as one of passive cognition or limited experimentation. ... Traditional theories question neither the historical constitution of their own object, nor the purposes to which the knowledge they produce is put in society.[28]

This distinction between traditional and critical theory is especially pertinent with respect to economic theory. The critique of political economy in the Marxian sense entails a "philosophical" dimension facilitating three types of insights: first, the core concepts of economic theory are self-contradictory (in terms of their logical implication, they are not capable of explaining the capitalist mode of production); secondly, the critique of political economy emphasises the fact that capitalist society is not "an objective, law-governed, nature-like sphere," but "socially constituted"; and thirdly, the critique of political economy "exposes the internal contradictions and dysfunctionalities of the system in order to show how and why these give rise to oppositional demands and struggles which cannot be satisfied by the present."[29]

To put it differently, the logic of the social sciences in capitalism is itself a manifestation of the effects of capitalism: the theories of capitalism are epiphenomena of capitalism, not theories of it; they are reflections of capitalism, not reflections on it. The "traditional" theories of capitalism from Smith to twentieth-century neo-classical economics are not also critiques of it - capitalism shapes the way we think to such a degree that we cannot help but reproduce its defining features and core patterns even in our theories of it.

In this context, Weberian Marxism is the project of analysing the logic of capitalist production and development, which leads from liberal capitalism to various forms of postliberal capitalism: bureaucratic capitalism, managerial capitalism, finance capitalism, and beyond - to a totally administered world. In the process, the contingencies of an increasingly complex socio-historical reality are reduced to means-ends relations. Critical theorists were interested in the relationship between the inner logic of capitalist production at the stage of postliberal capitalism reached during the 1920s and early 1930s - and the different logics of other spheres of life in society, which become increasingly oppressed, enslaved, or altogether eliminated -

---

28 S. BENHABIB: *Critique, Norm, and Utopia*, op. cit., p. 152.
29 *Ibid.*, pp. 154-55.

by increasingly sophisticated capitalist organisations, for which there is no match in society. Under such circumstances, the need for a systematic critical theory (as opposed to "traditional" neo-classical economic theory) of economic organisations as well as their relationship to the state in postliberal capitalist society became all the more urgent, since anything *but* a systematic critique was bound to merely reflect, rather than reflect on, this society and its corresponding mode of capitalist production.

In essence, Pollock's task was to accomplish for the 1930s what Hilferding had achieved in 1910, namely to provide "a study of the latest phase of capitalist development," as Hilferding had subtitled *Finance Capital*. However, while the latter had not claimed to have presented the analysis of a later stage of capitalist development that constituted a qualitatively different politico-economic and socio-economic arrangement, Horkheimer and Pollock started out from the assumption that the political economy that emerged during the 1920s, and especially during the 1930s, called for a different type of critique.

On the second level, which turned out to become the core concern of the critical theorists, the critique of capitalism took the shape of a social-philosophical critique of western civilisation in the spirit of Marx's critiques of alienation and commodity fetishism. Lukács's reconstruction of Marx's critique of alienation within the framework of Marx's later critique commodity fetishism, in terms of *reification*, prepared the Frankfurt theorists' critique of capitalism, in terms of their critique of *instrumental reason*.

IV. Pollock's Concept of "State Capitalism"

In 1930, at the very end of the final volume of the so-called *Grünberg Archive*, Pollock published an extended review of five books on socialism, progress, competition and the end of capitalism.[30] In this review, Pollock

---

30 F. POLLOCK: «Book Review of Gustav Cassel», *Sozialismus oder Fortschritt*, etc., *Archiv für die Geschichte des Sozialismus und der Arbeiterbewegung*, 15 (1930), pp. 464-473. The *Grünberg Archive* was the precursor of the *Zeitschrift für Sozialforschung*, the journal the Frankfurt Institute of Social Research started to publish in 1931, under Horkheimer's editorship.

raised an issue that was novel at the time, but whose importance has become increasingly apparent as the century progressed: Can we adequately analyse the logic of economic decision-making processes in society, if we employ theoretical and analytical categories as the basis for the analysis that derive from, and are designed for, micro-economic problems and conditions? How realistic are such micro-based analyses once the predominant form of economic organisation shaping economic decision-making processes are no longer based on individual utility considerations and the reference frame of small to medium-sized firms, but are shaped by large-scale, complex, and monopolistic corporations?

Pollock raised this issue in his discussion of two of the books, Gustav Cassel's *Sozialismus oder Fortschritt*[31] and Georg Halm's *Die Konkurrenz*.[32] Cassel had praised the model of free competition as remaining the prime mechanism by which to solve the economic problems of the early twentieth century, a view whose validity Pollock questioned. In his discussion of Halm's book, Pollock returned to this issue. Halm had claimed that "despite all weaknesses, the free, capitalist economy of competition [is] the best of all possible constitutions of the economy."[33] Implying that the industrialized economies of Continental Europe had ceased to be free-market economies (if they ever had been "free" to begin with), Pollock formulated the challenge for a systematic analysis of the economic affairs of the time: "the question of whether a system of monopoly capitalism has replaced the competitive system today [1930] ... can only be resolved ... by means of an unprejudiced analysis of the economic facts from the second half of the previous century to the present."[34]

Given Pollock's contention, he himself might have taken up the challenge of engaging in such a systematic study. Since the members of the Frankfurt School placed themselves squarely in the tradition initiated by Marx's critique of political economy, the rigorous analysis of the developmental stage of the capitalist economy reached at the time might have been of central importance to the Institute's agenda. However, as it turned out,

---

31 G. CASSEL: *Sozialismus oder Fortschritt*, Berlin (R. Hobbing) 1929.
32 G. HALM: *Die Konkurrenz. Untersuchungen über die Ordnungsprinzipien und Entwicklungstendenzen der kapitalistischen Verkehrswirtschaft*, München (Duncker & Humblot) 1929.
33 F. POLLOCK: "Book review...", op. cit., p. 468; my translation.
34 *Ibid.*.

neither did Pollock pursue this line of research, nor was the emerging research orientation at the Institute conducive to a critically systematic analysis of yet another "latest" stage of capitalist development (in Hilferding's sense). Instead, such the focus on the economy as most central aspect of modern western societies, following Marx, was replaced by an interest in the emerging relationship between the economy and the administrative state. After Horkheimer became the director of the Institute of Social Research in 1931, Pollock continued to function as co-director. Since 1927, as the deputy of Horkheimer's predecessor, Carl Grünberg, Pollock had been the chief administrator and in charge of day-to-day operations. With Horkheimer as the Institute's leading theorist, and Pollock in charge of administrative matters, his academic work remained secondary to his administrative responsibilities. In concrete terms, this meant that as the only person explicitly in charge of engaging a structural analysis of advanced capitalism within the Institute's overall division of labour, Pollock was not in the position to make a full-time commitment to that task.[35]

It is not surprising, then, that compared to the research and publications produced by the Institute's other core members during the 1930s, Pollock's output was rather scarce. According to Wiggershaus,[36] Pollock published altogether three books and nine articles. The first book addressed Sombart's purported repudiation of Marxism; the second examined the attempts in the Soviet Union to establish a planned economy during the decade following the Russian Revolution; both books appeared as publications of the Institute of Social Research.[37] He published six articles during the time period covered in this chapter, all in the Institute's official outlets.[38]

---

35 "Horkheimer was the more talented and ambitious of the two, while Pollock was submissive, satisfied with his role as an administrator and economist. It was this which led to Horkheimer's becoming director of the Institute instead of Pollock, although Pollock was Grünberg's deputy ... and had been a member of the Institute's staff from the start. Pollock's publications and administrative abilities, which were anything but inspiring, meant that there were no protests against this development, or at least none worth mentioning. By the beginning of the 1930s Pollock was thus firmly established in his role as an administrative director and financial officer of the Institute, and as chairman of the Society for Social Research." WIGGERSHAUS: *The Frankfurt School*, op. cit., p. 64.

36 *Ibid.*, pp. 750-51.

37 F. POLLOCK: «Sombarts "Widerlegung" des Marxismus», *Beihefte zum Archiv für die Geschichte des Sozialismus und der Arbeiterbewegung*, 3, ed. by Carl

THE EARLY FRANKFURT SCHOOL CRITIQUE OF CAPITALISM

During the 1920s, Pollock had placed high hopes in the success of the Soviet experiment. He had visited the Soviet Union in 1927, and returned with a most favourable assessment of the "particularly unfavourable conditions which the Russian revolutionaries had faced at the outset, their tremendous, continuing difficulties, the often glaring mistakes they had made, and their constant changes of direction and frequent reorganisations," as Wiggershaus put it.[39] In Pollock's related book[40] based on his experiences, he expressed his confidence that he had proven that a socialist planned economy could work. As he was mostly concerned with whether a planned economy in general could work, rather than a *socialist* economy in particular, he left open the possibility that a non-socialist, authoritarian-type of planned economy might work as well. He did not assert, however, that the Soviet experiment as such led to any necessary conclusions about the viability of a planned economy since, according to Marx's theory, a successful socialist takeover of the economy by the state was contingent on a high level

---

Grünberg, Leipzig (Hirschfeld) 1926; «Die planwirtschaftlichen Versuche in der Sowjetunion 1917-1927», *Schriften des Instituts für Sozialforschung*, 2 Leipzig (Hirschfeld) 1929. His third book, on automation, appeared in 1956, as a publication of the rebuilt Institute, and was published in English translation the following year: «Automation. Materialien zur Beurteilung der ökonomischen und sozialen Folgen» [1956], *Frankfurter Beiträge zur Soziologie*, 5 Frankfurt/M. (EVA) 1964; *The Economic and Social Consequences of Automation*, transl. by W.O. Henderson and W.H. Chaloner, Oxford (Basil Blackwell) 1957.

38 Chronologically, they include four articles in German in Institute publications, and two articles in English, in the last issue of the Institute's journal: "Zur Marxschen Geldtheorie", *Archiv für die Geschichte des Sozialismus und der Arbeiterbewegung*, 13 (1927), pp. 193-209; "Sozialismus und Landwirtschaft", in: *Festschrift für Carl Grünberg zum 70. Geburtstag*, Stuttgart (Kohlhammer) 1932; "Die gegenwärtige Situation des Kapitalismus und die Aussichten einer planwirtschaftlichen Neordnung", *Zeitschrift für Sozialforschung*, 1 (1932), pp. 8-27; "Bermerkungen zur Wirtschaftskrise", *Zeitschrift für Sozialforschung*, 2 (1933), pp. 321-54; "State Capitalism: Its Possibilities and Limitations", *Studies in Philosophy and Social Science*, 9 (1941), pp. 200-25; "Is National Socialism a New Order?", *Studies in Philosophy and Social Science*, 9 (1941), pp. 440-455.
39 R. WIGGERSHAUS: *The Frankfurt School*, op. cit., p. 61.
40 F. POLLOCK: *Die planwirtschaftlichen Versuche in der Sowjetunion 1917-1927*, op. cit.

of development, which had not been reached in Russia in 1917. For this reason, as far as Pollock was concerned, the Soviet case had no bearing on the possibility of a socialist planned economy as projected by Marx.

Pollock's perspective on capitalism in the 1930s and 1940s is laid out best in the articles, "Die gegewärtige Lage des Kapitalismus" and "State Capitalism," published in 1932 and 1941, respectively. Pollock's theory of advanced capitalism was clearly influenced by Hilferding's writings, and developed in its early version under the impression of the Great Depression and before the rise of National Socialism in Germany. His study on "the present state of capitalism," published in the *Zeitschrift* in 1932,[41] the year *before* Hitler's ascension to power, circumscribed the condition of capitalism as *monopoly* capitalism, a view that was immediately embraced by the Institute; at this time, his interpretation of capitalism was not exposed to further critical scrutiny. Pollock posited as fact the overall tendency of capitalism to facilitate the formation of ever larger units of economic organisation, and to force an ever greater role for the state in economic matters. In his view, this entailed the progressive suspension of markets. Important economic decisions were being made at ever higher levels of economic and administrative organisation, ranging from "monopolistic" corporations to the administrative state. Under such circumstances, planning increasingly subverted markets, and brought about the end of liberal-competitive capitalism, and the advent of "state capitalism."

The urgency of developing a theory of advanced capitalism was heightened when Hitler and the National Socialists took control of the German government in early 1933, inducing the members of the Institute to leave Germany; they arrived in New York in 1934, after "stop-overs" in Geneva and Paris. The Institute's analysis of the specific meaning of the capitalist mode of production thus continued under exceptionally pressing circumstances that called for research oriented toward analysing the transformations of the economy underway at the time. As the 1930s progressed, the political and economic success of the National Socialist regime became ever more apparent. Pollock's immediate response was that developments in Italy under Mussolini, in Germany under Hitler, and in the U.S. under Roosevelt were indicative of a qualitatively new stage of political economy

---

41 F. POLLOCK: "Die gegenwärtige Lage des Kapitalismus und die Aussichten einer planwirtschaftlichen Neordnung", *op. cit.*

in capitalism, to which he referred as "state capitalist intervention."[42] He assessed the prospects of capitalist planning as viable and promising. Horkheimer initially had considered this new development a temporary return to an authoritarian form of government. By 1940, however, Horkheimer agreed that the rise of authoritarian regimes like National Socialism was not an aberration in the logic of capitalist development, but a necessary consequence under conditions where capitalist production had created its own potential nemesis, the Great Depression. Accordingly, the rise of authoritarian regimes had to be theorised in terms of capitalist categories. As Wiggershaus put it, "Horkheimer held that the epoch of liberal capitalism must be conceived as a process which made a spiral of lasting despotism possible by atomizing human beings and producing large-scale companies and gigantic organisations."[43]

In a controversial article Pollock published in 1941, entitled "State Capitalism: Its Possibilities and Limitations," he drew out the implications of this analysis. Theoretically speaking, Pollock identified as the Archimedean point for analysing capitalism the ideal-typical concept of "state capitalism". He asserted that state capitalism had constituted the vanishing point for analysing advanced capitalism for some time, reaching its peak in National Socialism,[44] though a trend in this direction could be observed elsewhere as well. The most central feature of state capitalism was the suspension of the market mechanism in economies dominated by large corporations: in state capitalist societies, the primacy of the economy characteristic of liberal capitalism had been replaced by the primacy of the state. Pollock introduced a set of crucial distinctions. First, there are four aspects of the new economy that are better explained in terms of "state capitalism" than of designations that presume the primacy and relative autonomy of the economic sphere, such as "'[s]tate organised private property monopoly capitalism', 'managerial society', 'administrative capitalism', 'bureaucratic collectivism'," and others. The four aspects are: "state capitalism is the successor of private capitalism, ... the state assumes important functions of the private capitalist, ... profit interests still play a significant role, and ... it is not socialism."[45] The main features of Pollock's article thus are related to

---

42 F. POLLOCK: "Bemerkungen zur Wirtschaftskrise", *op. cit.*.
43 R. WIGGERSHAUS: *The Frankfurt School*, op. cit., p. 280.
44 F. POLLOCK: "Is National Socialism a New Order?", *op. cit.*.
45 F. POLLOCK: "State Capitalism", *op. cit.*, p. 201.

the question of how private capitalism had been succeeded by a non-private, "public" form of capitalism. Since the medium-sized businesses that had dominated the industrial economies of the later nineteenth century had been replaced by "monopolistic" enterprises during the early decades of the twentieth century, the categories developed for analysing nineteenth-century political economy, as well as its Marxian critique, had become outdated for the political economy emergent during the early twentieth century. As a result, the very pertinence of such core categories and distinctions of economic theory as market vs. planning, private vs. public, itself had to be questioned. Pollock did not provide a clear economic argument as to why the larger size of businesses mattered independently of its implications for the market/planning and private/public distinction; but he did argue that with the rise of "monopolistic" economic organisations, the administrative state had become a central *economic* player.

State capitalism can appear in two forms: totalitarian or democratic.[46] Depending on which form of government is in place and which social groups control it, the nature of state capitalism can vary greatly. Since the economic process has become fully manageable, the important question is, toward what end will it be put, what is the capitalist economy being admin-

---

[46] Pollock wrote, "We define 'state capitalism' in its two most typical varieties, its totalitarian and its democratic form, as a social order differing on the following points from 'private capitalism' from which it stems historically:

(1) The market is deposed from its controlling function to coordinate production and distribution. This function has been taken over by a system of direct controls. Freedom of trade, enterprise and labour are subject to governmental interference to such a degree that they are practically abolished. With the autonomous market the so-called economic laws disappear.

(2) These controls are vested in the state which uses a combination of old and new devices, including a 'pseudo-market', for regulating and expanding production and coordinating it with consumption. Full employment of all resources is claimed as the main achievement in the economic field. The state transgresses all the limits drawn for peacetime state activities.

(3) Under a totalitarian form of state capitalism the state is the power instrument of a new ruling group, which has resulted from the merger of the most powerful vested interests, the top ranking personnel in industrial and business management, the higher strata of the state bureaucracy (including the military) and the leading figures of the victorious party's bureaucracy. Everybody who does not belong to this group is a mere object of domination." *Ibid.*

istered for, and who administers it and distributes its product - for what end. Since Pollock's and Horkheimer's emphasis was on the politics of advanced capitalism, they did not directly address how exactly it is that managerial capitalism produces economic growth and development, nor how it mediates people's conceptions and perceptions of the world. Though the inner-organisational dimension of the economy is touched upon, it is only peripherally addressed in its relationship to culture. After all, reaching a new stage of capitalism, if it was indeed the case, would have important implications for the theory of capitalism, and modern society, for the possibility and direction of social change, and for our understanding of society and the basic concepts we employ to organise society meaningfully, such as freedom, self, individual, and emancipation.

In the context of his depiction of the "new set of rules", Pollock did draw a definite distinction between market capitalism as an economy where "men meet ... as agents of the exchange process, as buyers or sellers," as opposed to state capitalism as a system where "men meet ... as commander or commanded,"[47] as will apply in particular to the working population in general. But again he skirts the issue of the inner logic of economic production as well as distribution, by asserting that in state capitalism, the profit motive is replaced by the power motive. Though Pollock should have considered whether and under what circumstances the levels of productivity achieved during the early twentieth century in the most advanced industrial societies could be maintained once large corporations were subject to state supervision and regulation in state capitalism, he did not do so. Instead, he presumed that once those high levels of industrial production had been reached, they would not be negatively effected by a shift of society's economic planning function from monopolistic corporations to the state. The above mentioned, five new rules are: (1) "a general plan gives the direction for production, consumption, saving, and investment"; (2) "[p]rices are no longer allowed to behave as masters of the economic process but are administered in all important sections of it"; (3) "the profit interests of both individuals and groups as well as all other special interests are to be strictly subordinated to the general plan or whatever stands in its place"; (4) "[i]n all spheres of state activity (and under state capitalism that means in all spheres of social life as a whole) guesswork and improvisation give place to the principles of scientific management"; and finally, (5) "[p]erformance of

---

47 *Ibid.*, p. 207.

the plan is enforced by state power so that nothing is left to the functioning of laws of the market or other economic 'laws'."[48]

Pollock further elaborated the implications of these new rules in sections on the control of production and distribution, respectively. Again he asserted that in state capitalism, there no longer will be a need to heed the inner logic of the economic process: the entrepreneurial and capitalist functions are being "interfered with or taken over" by management and the government.[49] Though production and distribution facilities will continue to be privately owned, control of the cartellized industries and its enterprises will be with the government. Pollock also presented arguments for why there can be an adequate incentive structure for a state capitalist system; why the separation of price and production will not hurt the latter; why the state capitalist system does not need to suffer from the kind of wastefulness and inefficiency characteristic of market capitalism; and why economics as a social science will lose its object.[50]

Who will control the state in state capitalism? There will be a new ruling class of "key bureaucrats in the business, state and party allied with the remaining vested interests."[51] The "capitalists" of old will lose any necessary social function. Instead, the free professions and those owning small and medium-sized businesses will play a role. The majority, salaried employees, "are subject to the leader principle of command and obedience."[52] The new state will appear as what it is: the embodiment of power and the instrument of the ruling class.

Finally, Pollock asked whether a non-totalitarian, democratic form of state capitalism can function. "If our thesis [about state capitalism] proves to be correct," he wrote, "society on its present level can overcome the handicaps of the market system by economic planning. Some of the best brains of this country [United States] are studying the problem how such planning can be done in a democratic way, but a great amount of theoretical work will have to be performed before answers to every question will be forthcoming."[53] Economics as a social science becomes superfluous. Pol-

---

48 *Ibid.*, pp. 204-207.
49 *Ibid.*, p. 210.
50 *Ibid.*, pp. 210; 215; 203; 217.
51 *Ibid.*, p. 221.
52 *Ibid.*, p. 222.
53 *Ibid.*, p. 225.

THE EARLY FRANKFURT SCHOOL CRITIQUE OF CAPITALISM

lock was so convinced of the empirical superiority of his "model" over market capitalism that he did not contemplate viable or desirable alternatives, nor the relationship between the existing contradictions in capitalism and the potential for qualitative social transformation. Since state capitalism was capable of covering up and domesticating class conflict and social inequality by means of full employment, this non-progressive forms of social, political and economic organisation even was capable of managing the danger of social and political eruptions resulting from its underlying economic contradictions. For this reason, as well as its economic superiority, Pollock regarded state capitalism as a social formation that, once in place, could continue to exist for a long period of time.

While the earlier article[54] had been an example for the kind of work conducted at the Institute during the initial, "interdisciplinary materialist" phase, the latter article was published at the turn from the "critical theory" phase to the period that brought about the more pessimistic critique of instrumental reason. It is important to note that during the intermediary phase, when the Frankfurt School spelled out the differences between "critical theory" and "traditional theory", they did not consider the implications of their new perspective for the conflict within mainstream economics waged during the second half of the 1930s. The "traditional" neo-classical economic theory based on the marginal utility paradigm that had been prevalent up until then, experienced its first major challenge from the new paradigm for economic theory proposed by John Maynard Keynes in his *General Theory of Employment, Interest and Money*.[55] Keynes called for an explicit and direct role for the state in economic policy toward sustaining (or generating) the conditions for continued economic growth, especially under the conditions of world-wide economic crisis, the Great Depression.

Though Pollock's analysis was closely related to the analyses of the stage of capitalist development characteristic of what has been referred to in the literature variously as managerial capitalism, corporate capitalism, organised capitalism, monopoly capitalism and, more generally, *post-liberal* capitalism, he did not expend much energy on the rigorous critical analysis of political economy in the sense of an analysis of the intricacies of corpo-

---

54 F. POLLOCK: "Die gegenwärtige Lage des Kapitalismus", *op. cit.*.
55 J. M. KEYNES: *The General Theory of Employment, Interest and Money*, New York (Harcourt, Brace) 1936.

rate capitalism.[56] In his view, the logic of capital accumulation of the latter followed closely the patterns characteristic of liberal capitalism, and thus did not call for a thorough revision of the mode of analysis in Marx's critique of political economy - nor whether and to what degree the categories of classical economic theory Marx had criticised still were viable. As a result, Pollock's analysis was not a critique of political economy in the Marxian sense.

On the one hand, Marx's critique of political economy was presumed to continue to apply (despite the fundamental transformation of entrepreneurial capitalism into managerial capitalism that had occurred since the late nineteenth century), even though Marx's theory did not provide the means for the systematic analysis of the latter. On the other hand, as the Frankfurt School theorists, *including* Pollock, were not in the position to systematically analyse managerial capitalism on the basis of a radical revision of Marx's critique of liberal capitalism designed for post-liberal conditions, they were concerned rather with the indirect manifestations *deriving* from the shift from one organisation of the capitalist production process to another.

Since for the Frankfurt theorists, the "traditional" classical economic theory had been proven wrong by Marx, they did not see any need to relate its 1930s version to the challenge of developing a *critical* economic theory of managerial capitalism. Nor did they consider the implications deriving from the historical coincidence of the "managerial revolution" that began during the early century and the Great Depression of the 1930s for the development of a critical economic theory, and how it had eroded the empirical adequacy of classical economic theory regarding the inner logic of the functioning of the market mechanism under conditions of organised capitalist production. Further, they did not consider how Keynes' statist response bore on the theoretical understanding necessary for grasping the inner logic of managerial capitalism, and for political, social and cultural forms of life in modern society. Instead, the critical economic theory of capitalism developed by Pollock and appropriated by his colleagues abandoned the notion that the inner logic of the economic process needed to be theorised posi-

---

56 For the type of analyses I am referring to, see the collection of articles and book chapters by political economists and economic sociologists: H. F. DAHMS (Ed.): *Transformations of Capitalism: Economy, Society and State in Modern Times*, New York (New York University Press) 1999.

tively in order for the *specific* nature of its negative consequences (and their historical situatedness and significance) to be identified adequately. The theoretical critique they developed moved beyond the challenge of systematic economic analysis altogether, and posited that in postliberal capitalism, it was not the inner logic of the capitalist production process that warranted attention, but the relationship between the economy and the state - hence the need to develop a critical theory specifically designed for identifying the nature of this relationship and its effects on all aspects of society. In the experience of the Frankfurt theorists, with the entrenchment of National Socialism in Germany and of the New Deal in the United States, the urgency of analysing emerging "state capitalism" as a qualitatively different system of political economy no longer could be ignored.

To be sure, given the relative lack of an infrastructure conducive for focused economic analysis at the Institute, Pollock was in a poor position to take on the challenge of updating Marx's critique of political economy for post-liberal capitalism on his own. Yet already when Pollock's manuscript on state capitalism circulated at the Institute, one of the other members examining macro-institutional change, Franz Neumann, a reformist theorist of monopoly capitalism, entered the fray on whether, and in what sense, National Socialism could indeed be regarded as the closest approximation of state capitalism, as Pollock had claimed. In his major work, *Behemoth*, the first comprehensive study of National Socialism, Neumann rejected Pollock's analysis, and proposed instead the concept of "Totalitarian Monopoly Capitalism."[57] Despite significant similarities between their respective diagnoses pertaining to increasing bureaucratization and organisation, there were profound differences as well. In particular, Neumann insisted that the market process had not been suspended in National Socialism; that instead, the market process exposed the Nazi government to tremendous economic and financial pressure. Neumann argued that the capitalist mode of production continued unabated, albeit in a highly organised, integrated and state-coordinated fashion. He wrote that

> the antagonisms of capitalism are operating in Germany on a higher and, therefore, a more dangerous level, even if these antagonisms

---

57 F. NEUMANN: *Behemoth. The Structure and Practice of National Socialism*, New York (Oxford University Press) 1942, p. 261; for his critique of "state capitalism", see pp. 221-234.

are covered up by a bureaucratic apparatus and by the ideology of the people's community. ...
Does the economic theory of National Socialism coincide with the ... 'state-capitalistic' doctrines? The answer is no. There is no National Socialist economic theory except the slogan that general welfare is more important than self-interest, a slogan ... used to cloak almost every economic decision. ... [W]e can find as many economic theories as there are groups within the National Socialist society. ... [T]he National Socialist economic system does not follow any blueprint, is not based on any consistent doctrine, be it neo-mercantilism, any guild or `Estate' theory, or liberal or socialist dogma. The organisation of the economic system is pragmatic. It is directed entirely by the need of the highest possible efficiency and productivity required for the conducting of war.[58]

At the time, in a letter to Horkheimer, Neumann wrote, "For a whole year I have been doing nothing but studying economic processes in Germany, and I have up till now not found a shred of evidence to show that Germany is in a situation remotely resembling state capitalism."[59] Similar concerns were voiced by Adorno, who rejected the affirmative tone of Pollock's depiction of state capitalism.[60] Even Horkheimer himself had reservations, despite his decision to support the publication of Pollock's article on state capitalism.[61]

The difference between "state capitalism" and "totalitarian monopoly capitalism" (which, for the argument's sake, I will refer to as "authoritarian capitalism," even though Neumann does not seem to have used the term) is more than nomenclature. Pollock's term places greater emphasis on the state than Neumann, as far as the inner logic of the economy is concerned.

---

58 *Ibid.*, pp. 227-228.
59 R. WIGGERSHAUS: *The Frankfurt School*, op. cit., p. 285.
60 In a letter to Horkheimer, Adorno expressed his reaction to Pollock's article as follows: "I can best sum up my views on this article by saying that it represents a reversal of Kafka. Kafka represented the bureaucratic hierarchy as a hell. In this article, hell is transformed into a bureaucratic hierarchy. In addition, it is all formulated so axiomatically and condescendingly ... that it lacks all urgency, quite part from the undialectical assumption that a non-antagonistic economy might be possible in an antagonistic society." Cited in R. WIGGERSHAUS: *The Frankfurt School*, op. cit., p. 282.
61 *Ibid.*, pp. 280-291.

To the former, state capitalism signifies a qualitative transformation expressing the shift of society's economic planning function from the economy to the state. In Neumann, by contrast, the economic planning function continues to be held by large corporations in Germany during the Nazi period, many of which actively supported the Nazi regime, e.g., using politics to secure favourable business conditions. Moreover, he asserted that Pollock's vision entailed nothing less than the end of history, and the destruction of any prospect for future qualitative societal transformation.

State capitalism and authoritarian capitalism both constitute more openly co-operative forms of business-government relations. In this respect, the difference is mainly one of emphasis, especially if we consider that Pollock's concept of state capitalism had to be understood as an ideal-typical model: state capitalism places greater emphasis on the state, authoritarian capitalism on the economy. The more important difference, however, relates to the theoretisation of the inner logic of the economic process itself. According to Pollock, the inner logic of capitalist production is secondary to understanding the politics of state capitalism. According to Neumann, the inner logic of capitalist production and its understanding remain central. The nature of authoritarian capitalism cannot be discerned without a sophisticated grip on the inner logic of the economic process under changing conditions, and its relative independence from the state.

Yet the Institute members, most of all Horkheimer, were more interested in the general similarities between Pollock's and Neumann's respective diagnoses. In the end, Pollock's analysis carried more weight than Neumann's, and in terms of its theoretical implications, largely was accepted by Horkheimer and his colleagues. As a result, the foundations were laid for the reformulation of Marx's critique of political economy, into the critique of instrumental reason. The specifics of capitalism's presumably inherent tendency toward ever greater organisational units controlling production and distribution, and toward the suspension of the market mechanism in favour of the allegedly less wasteful and more efficient planned allocation of resources and the means of production--pointing toward the state as the ultimate capitalist working in concert with large, "monopolistic" corporations - was no longer of any concern. State capitalism would be far more stable, and even in economic terms, far superior to private capitalism. What Pollock theorised in Marxian terms as the rise of *state* capitalism needed to be carefully examined, in terms of whether the organisational foundations of the economic dynamics of *corporate* capitalism indeed prepare the inauguration of the all-powerful state. As we shall see, however, in the final analysis, the problem with Pollock's analysis was not that it was flawed, but that it provided the Frankfurt School from the 1940s on with a reference frame that tilted all their subsequent analyses, especially as far as economic matters were concerned. By deciding the Weberian question of how the inner logics of the economy and the administrative state relate to each other, in favour of the latter, Pollock engendered a major misunderstanding of the nature of economic processes in large-scale capitalism, its relationship to the administrative state, and the corresponding limitations of and possibilities for social, political, and cultural transformation.

V. The Dialectic of Enlightenment and the Critique of Instrumental Reason

During the 1930s the need for developing a forceful yet constructive critique of capitalist society with concrete practical implications continually had been heightened by the National Socialists' consolidation of power in Germany, the perversion of the Soviet experiment with socialism into Stalinism, and the proliferation of corporate planning in the United States. For all practical purposes, by the early 1940s Horkheimer and the other non-economists at the Institute regarded it as of minor consequence whether the "latest stage" of capitalist development in Germany and elsewhere in the Western world was described more aptly in terms of state capitalism or in terms of authoritarian capitalism. It was more important to accept that the category "liberal" no longer sufficed to describe the nature of twentieth-century capitalism, and that the realms of politics, administration and economy grew ever closer together. Although the attempt to diagnose the nature and logic of advanced capitalism by applying the critique of political economy to the specific mode of capitalist production reached in the 1920s, prepared the way for the critique of instrumental reason, significantly more energy went toward the development of a systematic critique of the *effects* of the latest mode of capitalist production.

Despite reservations, Horkheimer had accepted Pollock's concept of "state capitalism" well before the article was published in 1941. In 1940, in his own essay, entitled "The Authoritarian State," Horkheimer had written that "state capitalism is the authoritarian state of the present," and that "state capitalism does away with the market and hypostatises the crisis for the duration of eternal Germany."[62] Ironically, it appears as if in substance (though not literally in form), Horkheimer tried to reconcile the insights and respective analyses of Pollock and Neumann, by combining the qualifiers of Pollock's and Neumann's respective concepts, omitting their common noun: state capitalism and authoritarian capitalism (i.e., "totalitarian monopoly capitalism") turned into the "authoritarian state". To Horkheimer, this concept more clearly signified the primacy of the political than either Pollock's or Neumann's. In the early Frankfurt School critique of capitalism, this shift from Pollock's and Neumann's respective analyses of the "latest stage" of capitalism, whether with regard to industrial society, as in Pollock, or in National Socialist Germany, as in Neumann, constituted nothing less than the submergence of economic concerns altogether. Considering that the Frankfurt School Critical Theory had begun by claiming to continue the Marxian project under qualitatively changed socio-historical circumstances, this shift away from economic matters was particularly remarkable. What had been the primacy of the economy in Marx, had turned into the primacy of the political. As a result, the focused economic analysis of capitalism had lost its significance, and was no longer essential to the systematic critique of twentieth-century society. Instead, the analysis of capitalism was replaced by a critical analysis of the various mediations of the economic basis in politics, culture and society. In other words, Horkheimer combined Pollock's and Neumann's analyses in a manner that eliminated, rather than emphasised, the economic dimension. For critical-theoretical purposes, the inner logic of the economic process in the "latest stage" of capitalism had become irrelevant, and inconsequential for purposes of critiquing the nature of twentieth-century capitalism.

Paradoxically, the vanishing point of the early Frankfurt School's Critical Theory had been a post-liberal society in the post-capitalist, socialist sense. Yet in National Socialism, and in their experience, to a lesser degree even in the United States, the rise of "post-capitalist" society as a "post-liberal" society constituted the inversion of the former, as it was based on a kind of planning that enabled the new ruling classes to manage society more

---

62 M. HORKHEIMER: "The Authoritarian State" [1940], in: A. ARATO and E. GEBHARDT (Eds.): *The Essential Frankfurt School Reader*, New York (Urizen Books) 1978, pp. 96-97.

effectively in their own interest, rather than enhancing society's capacity to more rationally solve its problems.[63] The planning of post-liberal capitalist society utilises and manipulates the multi-facetted interests of society for private political and economic purposes.

Considering the ensuing neglect of economic matters, it would have been consequential for the Frankfurt theorists to shift their attention to the nature of politics in the twentieth century; however, this did not occur. Within the Institute, the systematic analyses of political institutions, as those conducted by reformists such as Neumann, Otto Kirchheimer and others, remained peripheral because their critique of post-liberal society was not considered sufficiently radical. This neglect by the Institute's core members of the political dimension of modern society constituted yet another move away from institutional analysis of the structural conditions of capitalism, toward a preoccupation with culture.[64]

In the most important work of the early Frankfurt School, *Dialectic of Enlightenment*, written by Horkheimer and Adorno during the first half of the 1940s, the concept of critique is driven far beyond its scope in Marx's theory.[65] In very broad terms, Horkheimer and Adorno investigated whether the focus on economics in Critical Theory constituted a deflection from more fundamental categories and issues, i.e., whether the Marxian focus on the critique of political economy was directed at an epiphenomenon rather than at the final cause of the defining problems of modern society. This orientation resembles the more narrow interest Weber pursued in his work, why modern capitalism only emerged in the West, as well as his

---

[63] Referring to the type of critique characteristic of the early critical theory, Albrecht Wellmer characterized their central motif and basic theoretical reference frame as follows: "Critical social theory lives by the anticipation of a 'total social subject'; only on the basis of this anticipation is it able to conceive the apparent forms of a social disorder or `unnatural essence' of society; the validity of its findings is bound up with the efficacy of a liberating *interest* in cognition--in knowing." A. WELLMER: *Critical Theory of Society* [1969], translated by John Cumming, New York (Continuum) 1971, p. 135.

[64] See the section on "Franz Neumann and Otto Kirchheimer: unexploited opportunities for intensive interdisciplinary research", in: R. WIGGERSHAUS: *The Frankfurt School*, op. cit., pp. 223-236.

[65] M. HORKHEIMER, TH. W. ADORNO: *Dialectic of Enlightenment* [1944], New York (Continuum) 1995. Incidentally, the book was dedicated to Friedrich Pollock.

answer: that we cannot explain the rise of modern capitalism solely in economic terms, but as the result of the more fundamental process of rationalisation. As Ben Agger aptly formulated,

> Horkheimer and Adorno contended that positivism, when generalised from a metatheoretic principle of scientific investigation into a lived principle of culture and ideology, becomes a powerful force of domination. The dialectic of enlightenment refers to the recurring alternation between preindustrial mythology and "rational" science. In this regard, the Frankfurt critics were concerned to confront the problem of enlightenment and rationalisation in a more dialectical way than Weber had done... They suggest that, under the rule of positivism, we fetishize immediacy and factuality and thus reinforce a false consciousness that prevents us from recognising dialectical possibilities of liberation concealed in the present.[66]

To address the question of whether post-liberal capitalism can be analysed properly in terms of the critique of political economy, however refined, the authors developed the concept of instrumental reason, to theorise the central thesis of the contradictory nature of the Enlightenment, and all enlightenment processes. As Seyla Benhabib put it,

> the history of humanity's relation to nature does not unfold an emancipatory dynamic, as Marx would have us believe. The development of the forces of production, humanity's increased mastery over nature, is not accompanied by a diminishing of interpersonal domination; to the contrary, the more rationalized the domination of nature, the more sophisticated and hard to recognise does societal domination become. Labouring activity, the act in which man uses nature for his ends by acting as a force of nature (Marx), is indeed an instance of human cunning. ...[the] effort to master nature by becoming like it is paid for by the internalization of sacrifice. Labour is indeed the sublimation of desire; but the act of objectification in which desire is transformed into a product is not an act of self-actualization, but an act of fear which leads to control over nature within oneself. Objectification is not self-actualization but self-denial disguised as self-affirmation.[67]

---

66 B. AGGER: *Western Marxism*, op. cit., pp. 135-36.
67 S. BENHABIB: *Critique, Norm, and Utopia*, op. cit., p. 167.

On the basis of this insight, Horkheimer and Adorno formulate the critique of instrumental reason as a radical critique of western civilisation. All of human history is marred by countless attempts to achieve the impossible: control over nature and self, without assimilating the self to that which is being controlled and dominated. With the transformation of Marx's critique of political economy, the Frankfurt School's "interdisciplinary materialist" critique of post-liberal capitalism, followed by the critique of traditional theories as reflections of social reality that do not self-critically reflect upon the larger context of their production and application, into the critique of instrumental reason - there is no basis left for assuming that positive attempts at bettering society are at all likely to be successful. Though *Dialectic of Enlightenment* is far too intricate a work to provide an adequate portrayal here, as far as the critique of economic reason is concerned, the work's main point is immediately apparent: capitalism is but the culmination of an essential feature of human co-existence, and a trend in human civilisation that can be traced to the beginning of intelligent life, shaping all forms of economic life rather than being shaped by the latter. Once Horkheimer and Adorno had arrived at this conclusion, that capitalism is but the highest form to date of the imperative to confront and utilise nature in the interest of self-preservation, the centrality of any focused critique of political economy beyond Marx had become inadequate. Once Horkheimer and Adorno understood the history of human civilisation as the continual refinement of techniques to subjugate the world ever more effectively, their presumption that a good society was possible on the basis of the vast productive powers achieved in industrial society, had lost its ground. The radically modernist, Marxist optimism of the 1930s turned into its opposite: a deeply rooted, culturally oriented pessimism about the prospects of advanced western civilisation as a whole.[68]

---

68 Horkheimer and Adorno completed the manuscript of *Dialectic of Enlightenment* in Spring 1944, during the darkest period of the twentieth century. As Jürgen Habermas wrote, "In the blackest book, *Dialectic of Enlightenment*, Horkheimer and Adorno ... conceptualize[d] the Enlightenment's process of self-destruction. On their analysis, it is no longer possible to place hope in the liberating force of enlightenment. Inspired by [Walter] Benjamin's now ironic hope of the hopeless, they still did not want to relinquish the now paradoxical labour of conceptualization." J. HABERMAS: "The Entwinement of Myth and Enlightenment: Max Horkheimer and Theodor

Since on the basis of their critique of instrumental reason, Horkheimer and Adorno could no longer conceive of any social movement or any other kind of collective agent that would be able to step into the void left by the increasingly ineffective and accommodating labour movements in industrial societies, the concern with practice that had inspired the first two phases of Frankfurt School Critical Theory during the 1930s - the interdisciplinary-materialist and critique-of-traditional-theory phases - all but vanished. The Frankfurt School's loss of the "subject of history" as represented by the industrial proletariat, induced Horkheimer and Adorno to turn more directly toward philosophical matters, the project of a culturalist critique of post-World War II society, and toward social research in a more narrow sense. Peculiarly, however, they were not concerned with questions that related directly to the link between analysing society philosophically, sociologically, and culturally and the growing importance of economic, political, and social organisations as the context where politics, culture and society are shaped and modelled. After all, how powerful is an analysis of the culture of capitalism that abstains from a sophisticated, careful analysis of the structural and organisational foundations of cultural production and reproduction in mass society? Ironically, one of the essays included in *Dialectic of Enlightenment*, "The Culture Industry: Enlightenment as Mass Deception," could have provided a strong foundation for such an analysis for the constellation of social structure, economic organisation, and culture.[69]

Consequently, the Frankfurt theorists diminished their ability to develop practically viable, constructive responses to concrete economic conditions. At a time when capitalism's productive capacities were employed at an accelerating pace for the creation of destructive powers, the Frankfurt School theorists perceived the progressive integration of state and economy as an overwhelming and inescapable system of power in emergence. The more differentiated the economic system became, and the more economic functions the state fulfilled, the fewer opportunities they saw for modifying

---

Adorno", in: *The Philosophical Discourse of Modernity. Twelve Lectures* [1985], translated by Frederick Lawrence, Cambridge, Mass. (MIT Press) 1987, p. 106. On the Frankfurt School's pessimism, see also M. POSTONE: *Time, Labour, and Social Domination*, op. cit., pp. 84-120; and M. POSTONE, B. BRICK: "Critical Pessimism and the Limits of Traditional Marxism", *Theory and Society*, 11 (1982), pp. 617-58.

69 HORKHEIMER and ADORNO: *Dialectic of Enlightenment*, ibid., pp. 120-167.

its organisation; instead, the political-economic system forced *all* value spheres in society to assimilate to the logic of organised capitalist production and reproduction. Still, by radically thinking through the price Western societies had to pay for continuous productivity and increasing economic wealth, the Frankfurt School theorists provided the means for rigorously examining how conditions in post-liberal capitalist society, oriented toward sustaining profit opportunities, made the move towards a society governed by the emancipatory Enlightenment principles of liberty, equality, and solidarity ever more doubtful.

VI. Antinomies of "Traditional Marxism" in the Early Frankfurt School Critique of Capitalism

During the early 1930s, Frankfurt School Critical Theory emerged as an programmatically interdisciplinary project to reconstruct Marx's materialist critique of political economy under changed historical conditions, with the support of the emerging social sciences, and with clear practical intent. By the time it reconstituted itself as the critique of instrumental reason during the early 1940s, it had lost virtually all practical relevance. In light of the preceding analysis, the early Frankfurt theorists' presupposition that political-economic analysis no longer could serve as the foundation for the systematic critique of capitalism, was highly problematic. Since the critique of political economy became one of several research projects - without being central - the Frankfurt theorists were able to turn their attention away from the organisational foundations upon which politics, culture and society in capitalism are built. In addition, the shift of the focus of the critique from political *economy* to *political* economy suggested by Pollock provided Horkheimer and the others with a rationale for concentrating on the critical analysis of the *cultural* dimensions of advanced capitalism, more conducive to their interests to begin with, while abstaining from applying a similarly critical attitude to analysing the economy, the production process, and its form of organisation.

At this point, we should ask how the early Frankfurt School's critiques of capitalism, in its "state capitalist", "authoritarian capitalist", and "critique of instrumental reason" variants, appear in light of developments that have occurred since the 1940s, in the constellation between economy, state and society. Since I cannot answer this question in due detail here, I will address it by introducing the most compelling recent "reinterpretation of Marx's critical theory," Moishe Postone's *Time, Labour, and Social Domination*.[70] Though much broader in scope, this work contains the most systematic re-evaluation of Pollock's contribution, in relation to the evolution of Frankfurt School Critical Theory. While the latter is among the more sophisticated and theoretically ambitious traditions of Marxist thinking, Postone points out that it carried with it, from the start, some of the baggage of the less refined variants of Marxist theory. The purpose of Postone's work is to show how the initial intent of Marx's theory, the "spirit" in which it must be read, got lost over the course of the century that followed his death. Before we can reconstruct this initial intent, in light of more recent theoretical developments that pertain to the specific types of challenges for which the multiplicity of social theories as well as critical theories were designed and formulated, we must carefully and systematically identify the specific reasons responsible for the supposed practical as well as the analytical failure of Marx's theory, inferred so frequently in recent years. Toward this end, Postone pursues above all a *theoretical* objective: how do we need to read Marx's critical theory today, considering that he devised it for a capitalist society at an earlier stage of socio-economic and industrial development, for purposes that cannot be conceived of without a clear sense of the basic features and orientations of his theory, within the context of liberal capitalism in nineteenth-century Europe.

Accordingly, Postone's purpose is twofold: "to provide as coherent and powerful a reinterpretation of the categorical foundations of the Marxian theory as possible, distinguishing it from traditional Marxism, and suggesting that it may be able to provide the foundation for an adequate critical analysis of the contemporary world."[71] In the closing section of this chapter, it is not the subtleties of Postone's brilliant reinterpretation of Marx's theory that are of primary interest here, but his critique of the basic patterns of "traditional Marxism". How does this critique apply to Pollock's analysis of state capitalism and - to the extent that it carried through to the more culturalist studies of the other members of the Frankfurt School - especially Horkheimer and Adorno? In the process, Postone also provides an explana-

---

70 M. POSTONE: *Time, Labour, and Social Domination*, op. cit.
71 *Ibid.*, p. 394.

tion of the above mentioned pessimism of the Frankfurt School, as it derived from Pollock's economic analysis.

Postone draws mostly on *Grundrisse der Kritik der politischen Ökonomie*, "since [Marx's] analysis there of the essential core of capitalism and of the nature of its historical overcoming has contemporary significance; it casts doubt on interpretations of his theory that centre on considerations of the market and class domination and exploitation."[72] His reinterpretation leads Postone to three major insights about how Marx's theory must be read to do it justice with regard to his own intentions, as well as to his theory's current relevance.

As social theories, most versions of traditional Marxism do not distinguish between elements of Marx's theory that he designed to analyse the mode of capitalist production in force at the time when he developed his critiques of political economy, and components that are intended as suprahistorical categories with universal validity. More specifically, during the twentieth century, many theorists and political actors attempting to interpret or apply Marx's perspective to a variety of social, political, economic and cultural issues, chose a specific element of his theory as the Archimedean point for their analysis. Marx's theories of exploitation, surplus value, immiseration, social class, class struggle, or of bourgeois society - to name just a few - frequently served this purpose. As a result, both Marx's theory and the social reality or phenomenon to be analysed, criticised, or overcome, were being interpreted in terms of the specific theory serving as the supposed core of Marx's concerns. Yet determining the "core" of Marx's concerns and theory constitutes a far more daunting challenge than most Marxist theorists and practitioners were aware of. When viewed from a historically sensitive vantage point, Postone argues convincingly, even the most comprehensive of Marx's individual theories, the theory of surplus value, appears to have been designed specifically for purposes of critically analysing liberal capitalism during the nineteenth century. Once we become aware of this distinction between elements of his theory that are historically specific, and components that carry a greater claim for universality - such as Marx's theories of alienation, species-being, mode of production, relations of production, forces of production - however, we need to confront the challenge of determining what an updated version of Marx's critical theory

---

72 *Ibid.*, p. 21.

for the present stage of the capitalist mode of production would have to look like.

Postone describes the core of Marx's theoretical concern as follows:

> Marx's theory of the centrality of labour to social life in capitalism ... is a theory of the specific nature of the form of social mediation in this society - one that is constituted by labour and has a quasi-objective character - rather than a theory of the necessary social primacy of the labour-mediated interactions of humans with nature. This focus on social mediation, rather than on "labour" (or class), means that Marx's social theory of knowledge, relating labour and consciousness, should be understood as one that grasps forms of social mediation (constituted by structured forms of practice) and forms of subjectivity as intrinsically related. Such a theory has nothing in common with a reflection theory of knowledge or with the notion that thought is "superstructural." It also contravenes the common identification of a "materialist" theory of subjectivity with a theory of interests alone.[73]

Within the context of this reinterpretation of Marx's theory, as a theory of the socially constituted nature of economic reality, Postone introduces two categorical distinctions that played a key role in the self-inflicted derailment of Marx's theory in traditional Marxism. First, while traditional Marxists understood Marx's theory as arguing the need to critique capitalist society from the point of view of labour, Postone argues that in fact, Marx provided a theory that criticises the specific organisation of the labour process in capitalism. Secondly, traditional Marxists criticised capitalism from the point of view of distributing the wealth produced in the economic process, presuming the productivity and efficient organisation of the capitalist mode of production and process as given; they were concerned with how to distribute the wealth generated, not how to produce it. To put it differently, traditional Marxists were not concerned with the imperatives of the economic process in the sense of grasping its inner logic; they were not concerned about the possibility that once a socialist state would be in control of the means of production, an economy that had been reliably efficient up to the point of take-over, might not continue to produce at the same level, speed, and quality. By contrast, Postone argues that the vantage point of Marx's theory is not the distribution process, but eminently the production

---

73 *Ibid.*, p. 386.

process: how can the achievements of a highly efficient capitalist industrial economy be secured beyond the point (or period, depending on whether one applies a short-term or a long-term perspective to Marx's related writings) of revolutionary transformation. Marx's argument, that the socialist transformation of capitalism can only occur when the time is ripe, i.e., when the forces of production can no longer develop any further without a transformation of the relations of production (i.e., the social structure, especially with regard to the ownership of the means of production), presumes the existence of a highly productive and efficient industrial economy.

In the chapter on the "limits of traditional Marxism and the pessimistic turn of Critical Theory", Postone shows that contrary to the presumption that Frankfurt School Critical Theory with its high level of theoretical refinement, was better positioned to fend off the temptations of reducing Marx's theory to a caricature of itself. Postone singles out Pollock as having played a key role in preventing the other Critical Theorists from moving beyond the traditional understanding of Marx's theory. Because Pollock's analysis suffers from both the above mentioned flaws of traditional Marxism--criticising capitalism from the point of view of labour, and especially concentrating on the distribution side of the economic equation while ignoring the production side altogether - the Frankfurt School's adoption of his analysis had a profound effect on its further development, partly explaining its pessimism.

Postone points out that contrary to his intentions, Pollock's line of reasoning indicated that the very basic categories of economics, such as market and private property, must be reconsidered. Yet despite the thrust of his analysis, Pollock remained tied to these very categories shared by both traditional economic theory, and traditional Marxism. Though Pollock's analysis of state capitalism showed that a planned economy is not necessarily emancipatory, his critique thereof remains inadequate: "Pollock's break with the traditional theory does not really overcome its basic assumptions regarding the nature of labour in capitalism."[74] As a result, critical theory loses as it referent the possibility of qualitative transformation: the contradiction of capitalism remain in state capitalism, but they are too shackled to engender any kind of revolutionary change.

Postone concludes that

---

74 *Ibid.*, p. 103.

> The frequently described shift of Critical Theory from the analysis of political economy to a critique of instrumental reason does not ... signify that the theorists of the Frankfurt School simply abandoned the former in favour of the latter. Rather, that shift followed from, and was based upon, a particular analysis of political economy, more specifically, a traditional understanding of Marx's critique of political economy.
> Pollock's and Horkheimer's analysis of the social totality as both non-contradictory - that is, one-dimensional - and antagonistic and repressive implies that history has come to a standstill. ...[I]t indicates, instead, the limits of any critical theory resting on the notion of "labour". The critical pessimism, so strongly expressed in *Dialectic of Enlightenment* ... cannot be understood only with reference to its historical context. It also must be seen as expressing awareness of the limits of traditional Marxism in the absence of a fundamental reconstitution of the dialectical critique of what, despite significant transformations, remains a dialectical social totality.[75]

VII. Conclusion

It is one of the many ironies of the process of theoretical production that flawed foundations can lead to profound insights with far-reaching implications. In the case of the early Frankfurt School, the choice in favour of Pollock's "uncritical theory" of state capitalism precluded the possibility to consider an array of observations and questions relating to the nature and logic of capitalism in the twentieth century. The Institute of Social Research might have provided an excellent context for contrasting implications to be derived from Pollock's state capitalism and Neumann's authoritarian capitalism (in the sense of "totalitarian monopoly capitalism"), provoking a highly productive debate about the specific nature of postliberal capitalism in relation to its cultural manifestations. Yet on the other hand, it appears that precisely because they favoured Pollock's highly problematic analysis, the Frankfurt School Critical Theorists were in the position to formulate one of the most powerful theories of the nature of the effects of the twentieth-

---

75　*Ibid.*, pp. 119-120.

century mode of capitalist production on all aspects of social life: the critique of instrumental reason.

At this historical juncture, however, as advanced capitalism is undergoing yet another major transformation with unforeseeable social, political and cultural consequences, critical theorists once again must turn their attention to the challenge of developing a sophisticated critique of political economy. The lack of theoretical sophistication characteristic of many attempts to examine processes of globalization, the rise of network-based, decentralized transnational corporations, and the dissipating autonomy of the administrative nation state in all advanced societies, are causes for great concern. There can be no doubt that Pollock's concept of state capitalism in the narrow sense was proven wrong by subsequent developments and the evolution of capitalism in the West. Yet today, in the face of increasing international competition, individual nation states have no choice but to ally themselves ever more closely with the economic interests of national and transnational corporations, in order to survive. In the end, critical theorists may be well-advised to take a closer look at Neumann's analysis of authoritarian capitalism, even though his framework was geared towards analysing National Socialism.[76] Clearly, the flaws of traditional Marxism identified by Postone are far less manifest in Neumann's thinking and work than in Pollock's. Neumann did, after all, analyse capitalism from both the distribution *and* the production side. His reformist perspective on the critique of political economy was also more complex than the critique of capitalism "from the point of view of labour" would have allowed for. In this sense, too, Neumann was more of a Weberian Marxist than Pollock. Since Neumann insisted that critical theorists must confront the nature of the relationship between the economy and the state as an empirical question, instead of precluding is scrupulous examination on the basis of theoretical prejudice, his perspective may be of great value for the development of a critical theory of the inner logic of social value spheres.

---

76 Surprisingly, in Postone's work, Neumann is not mentioned, nor any of this works cited.

THE EARLY FRANKFURT SCHOOL CRITIQUE OF CAPITALISM

References

AGGER, B.: *Western Marxism: An Introduction. Classical and Contemporary Sources*, Santa Monica, Calif. (Goodyear) 1979.
ANDERSON, P.: *Considerations of Western Marxism*, London (NLB) 1976.
BARAN, P. A., SWEEZY, P.: *Monopoly Capitalism. An Essay on the American Economic and Social Order*, New York (Monthly Review Press) 1966.
BENHABIB, S.: *Critique, Norm, and Utopia*, New York (Columbia University Press) 1986.
CASSEL, G.: *Sozialismus oder Fortschritt*, Berlin (R. Hobbing) 1929.
DAHMS, H. F.: "From Creative Action to the Social Rationalisation of the Economy: Joseph A. Schumpeter's Social Theory", *Sociological Theory*, 13 (1995), pp. 1-13.
DAHMS, H. F.: "Theory in Weberian Marxism: Critical Social Theory in Lukács and Habermas", *Sociological Theory*, 15 (1997), pp. 181-214.
DAHMS, H. F.: "Beyond the Carousel of Reification: Critical Social Theory After Lukács, Adorno, and Habermas", *Current Perspectives in Social Theory*, 18 (1998), pp. 3-62.
DAHMS, H. F. (Ed.): *Transformations of Capitalism: Economy, Society and State in Modern Times*, New York (New York University Press) 1999.
DUBIEL, H.: *Wissenschaftsorganisation und politische Erfahrung. Studien zur fruehen kritischen Theorie*, Frankfurt/M. (Suhrkamp) 1978.
GLASER, E.: *Im Umfeld des Austromarxismus. Ein Beitrag zur Geistesgeschichte des österreichischen Sozialismus*, Wien (Europaverlag) 1981, p. 214.
HABERMAS, J.: "The Entwinement of Myth and Enlightenment: Max Horkheimer and Theodor Adorno", in: *The Philosophical Discourse of Modernity. Twelve Lectures* [1985], translated by Frederick Lawrence, Cambridge, Mass. (MIT Press) 1987, pp. 106-130.
HALM, G.: *Die Konkurrenz. Untersuchungen über die Ordnungsprinzipien und Entwicklungstendenzen der kapitalistischen Verkehrswirtschaft*, München (Duncker & Humblot) 1929.
HILFERDING, R.: *Finance Capital. A study of the latest phase of capitalist development* [1910], London (Routledge & Kegan Paul) 1981.
HORKHEIMER, M.: "The Authoritarian State", in: A. ARATO, E. GEBHARDT (Eds.): *The Essential Frankfurt School Reader*, New York (Urizen Books) 1978, pp. 95-117.
HORKHEIMER, M.: "Traditional and Critical Theory" [1937], in: *Critical Theory. Selected Essays*, transl. by M. J. O'Connell and others, New York (Continuum) 1986, pp. 188-243.

HORKHEIMER, M., ADORNO, TH. W.: *Dialectic of Enlightenment* [1944], translated by John Cummings, New York (Continuum) 1995.
JACOBY, H.: *The Bureaucratization of the World*, Berkeley (University of Caifornia Press) 1973.
JAY, M.: *Dialectical Imagination. A History of the Frankfurt School and the Institute of Social Research 1923-1950*, Boston (Little, Brown and Co.) 1973.
KEYNES, J. M.: *The General Theory of Employment, Interest and Money*, New York (Harcourt, Brace) 1936.
KORSCH, K.: *Marxism and Philosophy* [1923], translated by Fred Halliday, London (Verso) 1970.
LUKÁCS, G.: *History and Class Consciousness. Studies in Marxist Dialectics* [1923], translated by R. Livingstone, Cambridge, Mass. (MIT Press) 1971.
LÖWY, M.: "Figures of Weberian Marxism", *Theory and Society*, 25 (1996), pp. 431-446.
MARX, K.: *Grundrisse. Foundations of the Critique of Political Economy (Rough Draft)* [1857-58], trans. by M. Nicolaus, London (Penguin Books) 1973.
MARX, K.: *Capital. A Critique of Political Economy* [1867], translated by Ben Fowkes, New York (Vintage Books) 1977.
NEUMANN, F.: *Behemoth. The Structure and Practice of National Socialism*, New York (Oxford University Press) 1942.
POLLOCK, F.: "Sombarts 'Widerlegung' des Marxismus", *Beihefte zum Archiv für die Geschichte des Sozialismus und der Arbeiterbewegung*, 3, ed. by C. Grünberg, Leipzig (Hirschfeld) 1926.
POLLOCK, F.: "Zur marxschen Geldtheorie", *Archiv für die Geschichte des Sozialismus und der Arbeiterbewegung*, 13 (1927), pp. 193-209.
POLLOCK, F.: "Die planwirtschaftlichen Versuche in der Sowjetunion 1917-1927", *Schriften des Instituts für Sozialforschung*, 2, Leipzig (Hirschfeld) 1929.
POLLOCK, F.: "Book Review of Gustav Cassel, Sozialismus oder Fortschritt, etc. ", *Archiv für die Geschichte des Sozialismus und der Arbeiterbewegung*, 15 (1930), pp. 464-473.
POLLOCK, F. (1932a): "Die gegenwärtige Lage des Kapitalismus und die Aussichten einer planwirtschaftlichen Neordnung", *Zeitschrift für Sozialforschung*, 1 (1932), pp. 8-27.
POLLOCK, F. (1932b): "Sozialismus und Landwirtschaft", in: *Festschrift für Carl Grünberg zum 70. Geburtstag*, Stuttgart (Kohlhammer) 1932.
POLLOCK, F.: "Bermerkungen zur Wirtschaftskrise", *Zeitschrift für Sozialforschung*, 2 (1933), pp. 321-54.
POLLOCK, F. (1941a): "State Capitalism: Its Possibilities and Limitations", *Studies in Philosophy and Social Science*, 9 (1941), pp. 200-25.
POLLOCK, F. (1941b): "Is National Socialism a New Order?" *Studies in Philosophy and Social Science*, 9 (1941), pp. 440-55.

THE EARLY FRANKFURT SCHOOL CRITIQUE OF CAPITALISM

POLLOCK, F.: "Automation. Materialien zur Beurteilung der ökonomischen und sozialen Folgen" [1956], *Frankfurter Beiträge zur Soziologie*, 5, Frankfurt/M. (EVA) 1964.

POLLOCK, F.: *The Economic and Social Consequences of Automation*, transl. by W. O. Henderson and W. H. Chaloner, Oxford (Basil Blackwell) 1957.

POSTONE, M.: *Time, Labour, and Social Domination. A reinterpretation of Marx's critical theory*, Cambridge (Cambridge University Press) 1993.

POSTONE, M., BRICK, B.: "Critical Pessimism and the Limits of Traditional Marxism", *Theory and Society*, 11 (1982), pp. 617-58.

SCHUMPETER, J. A.: *Theorie der wirtschaftlichen Entwicklung*, Leipzig (Duncker & Humblot) 1912.

SCHUMPETER, J. A.: "Max Weber's Work" [1920], in: R. SWEDBERG (Ed.): *The Economics and Sociology of Capitalism*, Princeton (Princeton University Press) 1991, pp. 220-227.

SCHUMPETER, J. A.: *The Theory of Economic Development. An Inquiry into Profits, Capital, Credit, Interest, and the Business Cycle* [1926], transl. by R. Opie, Cambridge, Mass. (Harvard University Press) 1934.

SCHUMPETER, J. A.: *Capitalism, Socialism, and Democracy*, New York (Harper & Brothers) 1942.

SCHUMPETER, J. A.: *History of Economic Analysis*, ed. by E. Boody Schumpeter, New York (Oxford University Press) 1954.

SIMMEL, G.: *The Philosophy of Money* [1907], ed. by D. Frisby, transl. by T. Bottomore and D. Frisby, London (Routledge) 1990.

WEBER, M.: *The Protestant Ethic and the Spirit of Capitalism*, New York (Charles Scribner's Sons) 1930.

WEBER, M.: "The Social Psychology of the World Religions," in: H. H. GERTH, C. WRIGHT MILLS (Eds.): *From Max Weber: Essays in Sociology*, New York (Oxford University Press) 1946, pp. 267-301.

WEBER, M.: *Economy and Society. An Outline of Interpretive Sociology* [1922], translated by E. Fischoff et al.; edited by G. Roth and C. Wittich. Berkeley (University of California Press) 1978.

WELLMER, A.: *Critical Theory of Society* [1969], translated by J. Cumming, New York (Continuum) 1971.

WIGGERSHAUS, R.: *The Frankfurt School. Its History, Theories, and Political Significance* [1986], Cambridge, Mass. (MIT Press) 1994.

Discussion Summary

ELKE SCHWINGER

Paper discussed:
HARRY F. DAHMS: The Early Frankfurt School Critique of Capitalism: Critical Theory Between Pollock's "State Capitalism" and the Critique of Instrumental Reason

Whereas the paper of DAHMS is focused more on the special work and history of Pollock who was a member of the earlier Frankfurt School, the discussion was concentrated on the philosophical basis of the work of Adorno and Horkheimer, especially of the "Dialectic of Enlightenment". For the current discussion of the tradition of the Critical Theory the theoretical differences to the approach of Jügen Habermas, the most prominent present disciple of the Frankfurt School, are interesting. It is important to understand the theoretical development of the earlier Frankfurt School, the reception of Marxian theory of capitalism, and the personal destinies of the Frankfurt theorists during the Nazi-time.

First of all the category of "instrumental reason", the central category in the "Dialectic of Enlightenment", was the subject of the debate. The concept "instrumental reason" can be seen as the theoretical key to the critical world view of the earlier Frankfurt School and its special reception of the Marxian critique of capitalism. KOSLOWSKI said about its radical critique of the capitalistic system and of the human civilisation-process itself that the dichotomy of instrumental and social reason as strictly bad and good elements of the social development cannot be seen so clear-cut as Horkheimer and Adorno did. KOSLOWSKI agreed with Leo Löwenthal, who argued in his essay "Zugtier und Sklaverei" that the instrumental reason enabled human beings to move from slavery to free labour: Technical inventions have in this sense a clearly socially liberating effect. Habermas as one of the present theorists in the tradition of the Frankfurt School also remains in his "Theory of Communicative Action" in this dichotomic worldview. In the social reality Habermas' "Lebenswelt", so he names the sphere of society with liberation power against the destructive aggression of instrumental reason, is clearly the smaller part of everyday life in contrast to its theoretical function: Habermas neglects the importance of the economic world for the people. The remark of PEUKERT showed that the sceptical position of Löwenthal has to be related to the historical fact that Löwenthal was already a renegade of the Frankfurt School when he wrote this essay.

For DAHMS the understanding of the critical concept of instrumental reason depends on methodological aspects of the critique: One has to examine the specific arguments of the authors in their approach. Obviously the earlier Frankfurt School was quite Marxian in a very orthodox way. It's important to know that the Frankfurt theorists adopted in the concept of the "instrumental reason" the Marxian position without questioning it essentially. The basic assumption of their analysis was that the way in which a society organises and reproduces itself has direct effects on the way in which human beings are related to themselves and to each other (so-called "Junktim-These", remark of PEUKERT). If a society for example organises itself in a direct exploitative manner in respect to nature one can assume that a similar relationship exists between the owners of the co-operations and the employees. That assumption was almost a dogma for the first generation of the Frankfurt School. In the case of Habermas' work "Theory of Communicative Action" the situation is different. Habermas' theory doesn't give simple answers in a manner the "Dialectic of Enlightenment" does. With an extension of the "lifeworld" and of the concret circumstances Habermas tries to find potential sources of new forms of solidarity (DAHMS). As PEUKERT argued the substantial point here is that the "Dialectic of Enlightenment" and the "Theory of Communicative Action" are two different types of theory. The reception of Marxian theory is only one part of the problem, much more it concerns the philosophical question of the development of knowledge and of human consciousness. The "Dialectic of Enlightenment" is a critique of civilisation as such, concerning a problem of human beings which can never be solved: It is a tragic world view. Horkheimer was mostly influenced by Schopenhauer's pessimistic philosophy. He became a politician because the Nazis came to power. Adorno was influenced by Hegel, Kant, and Kierkegaard, combined with the Weberian pessimism. The "Dialectic of Enlightenment" is a much deeper theoretical approach to the society than the politically orientated theory of Habermas'

DISCUSSION SUMMARY

"Theory of Communicative Action". The linguistic turn of Habermas has another goal.

DAHMS agreed with PEUKERT in all the explications about the differences between the approaches of the earlier Frankfurt School and of the most prominent present disciple, Jürgen Habermas. DAHMS complemented the discussion again with methodological aspects for the reception of social theories, especially for the reception of the Marxist theory by Critical Theory. DAHMS is in line with Moishe Postones' critique of traditional marxism in his book *Time, Labour and Social Domination* (Cambridge University Press 1993): The central argument of this methodological critique is that in the reception of all social theories it is necessary that we have to make a distinction between statements of the authors which are intended to be universally valid and those which are historically specific. In this sense most of the parts of Marx' theory, which have been applied, were designed to analyse liberal capitalism only and for the finance capitalism they were not supposed to be used in the same manner. In the case of the Marx-reception of the earlier Frankfurt School DAHMS reported Postones' argumentation that there are four causes which are responsible for putting the Frankfurt School in a situation, where the first generation of this theoretical tradition could not help but be pessimistic. There is at first for example the importance of immanent critique, which means that we have to recognise that any theory is just a beginning attempt to grasp the complexity of reality and the only adequate critique is to check it in its immanent structure. Marx argued that it is important in an immanent critique of capitalism to show that there is an immanent tendency in the capitalistic social system that leads to different stages of development which can not only be understood formally in terms of its organisation, but also in terms of social organisation. With respect to Pollock's analysis of state capitalism there is no point from which to start in any kind of immanent critique, because in his perspective state and economy are integrated, and the state can bear the conflicts that used to be produced in capitalism. The second point of Postones argumentation is that the Marxist theory was primarily not only distribution-orientated, but production- and distribution-orientated. So we cannot presume that productivity-levels of the economy can be retained by taken politically measures. The challenging question is, how we can change the social structure without endangering the productivity-levels we have achieved. Pollock was not interested in that at all, he was interested in questions about distribution. The third point is that the Marxist critique has been interpreted as a critique of capitalism from the point of view of labour and as a critique of the specific form of labour in capitalism. If we take that point of view then we recognise that the division of labour in its specific forms is the main problem. For the "Dialectic of Enlightenment" of Adorno and Horkheimer the rationality and consciousness of men seems to be the main problem, which can not be solved practically with alternative forms of labour-division. As TRALAU remarked, it is the same kind of instrumental reason that we can see in present times in the modern atomic energy. That means: As long as we try to increase our control over the natural world we will not be able to escape this dialectic-process of enlightenment. The critique of the dominance of instrumental reason in the capitalistic society of the earlier Frankfurt School shows the theoretical connection to Max Weber and the explanation for this theoretical tradition is also called "Weber-Marxism".

The discussion of this topic led to the question about the difference between the reception of Weber's arguments on the one hand by Habermas and on the other hand by the earlier Frankfurt School (SCHWINGER). For DAHMS the important issue of Weber's work about the cultural problem of capitalism is the law of "Eigengesetzlichkeit" of social value spheres. In this perspective we can not analyse a society unless we admit and recognise that there are different value spheres in a society and that each of them has its own inner logic. If we presume for example, as Pollock did, that the capitalistic state is able to control the economy, than we can infer that the inner logic of the state and administration supersedes the inner logic of the economic sphere. The important question in a critical perspective is, how this spheres are related to each other. It need not necessarily be the Marxist perspective, but the Marxist perspective is useful with respect to the economy. In the year 1997 we have to understand that the most productive way of reading the Frankfurt School over the course of the century is that it was always a continuous attempt to get to this core of Weberian Marxism. In the first generation of the Frankfurt School it was still rudimentary because for this generation the organisation of the state and of the economy is identical. They assume that the inner logic of the capitalistic productive process supersedes the inner logic of the other spheres. Habermas now recognises for the first time the importance of the inner logic with full force. For DAHMS the "Theory of Communicative Action" does not only represent a major qualitative leap with respect to its answers in terms of the linguistic turn, but also with respect to its recognising the need to differentiate different value spheres in society and to analyse how they evolve. The other point is that this perspective enables us to recognise different forms of capitalism, a variety of capitalisms - especially since 1989, when the fall of the wall occurred. The German Historical School is very sensitive with respect to the fact, that any notion like "capitalism" is obviously an analytical notion. In the Weber-Marxist perspective it is possible to ask how this different capitalistic societies solve the economic problems.

For the members of the earlier Frankfurt School the USA did not belong to the solution, but to the problem, because the cultural industry of the US seems clearly to be part of the fatal process of civiliszation. With respect to the Nazi-regime, a question asked of RAUSCHER, their opinion in that historical situation was that national socialism in Germany would not survive. Neumann, Marcuse and Kirchheimer worked for the US State Department within the Organisation for Strategic Studies against the Nazi-regime. Pollock's relationship to the national socialism was ambivalent, because he assumed that a state-capitalistic system was unavoidable and the Nazi-regime was an example of state-capitalism. But also for him a democratic system would have been preferable. Everyone of them returned in 1948. They never became familiar with the US-style of empirical studies. The leading ideology about research programs in the USA was pragmatically orientated and was therefore opposed to their own program.

These notes should end with a few remarks about the personal destinies of the members of the earlier Frankfurt School and a little anecdote. All the members of the first generation of the Frankfurt School were Jewish or of Jewish origin and therefore they moved out of the country. They got out very early because, as a result of an empirical study of their institute among German workers, they knew about the authoritarian atmosphere in Germany and about the coming totalitarian danger (KOSLOWSKI). As soon as the Nazi-Party came to power the whole institute was transferred to New York and later to Los Angeles where Horkheimer and Adorno wrote the *Dialectic of Enlightenment*. For more information about the historical details the book *Die Frankfurter Schule* of Rolf Wiggershaus (München 1989) was recommended by DAHMS. YAGI closed the session with a little anecdote about a biographical work of Felix Weil, who wrote about the foundation and the history of the Frankfurt School in his memories. Weil finished this book just before he died, but it was never published by the German publishers specialised in the works of the Frankfurt School. The correspondence of YAGI with the son of Weil ended without any answer to the question about the content of this memories: So it can obviously be assumed that there are

DISCUSSION SUMMARY

many secrets in the history of the earlier Frankfurt School which had better not to be published today.

Part Four

The Theory and Critique of Capitalism and Economic Ethics in Solidarism (Christian Social Thought): Heinrich Pesch and Gustav Gundlach

Chapter 10

Solidarism, Capitalism, and Economic Ethics in Heinrich Pesch

PETER KOSLOWSKI

I.   Solidarism Between Individualism and Collectivism
II. Capitalism and the Principle of Satisfying the Needs of Subsistence in the Economy
III. The Legitimacy of Taking Interest
     1. The Equivalence Principle and the Justification of Interest
     2. Improvements in the Theory of Interest
     3. Consequences of the Theory of Interest for a Theory of Capitalism
IV. Ethics and Economics
V.   Heinrich Pesch and the Historical School of Economics
VI. The Relationship of Solidarism with Catholic Thinking

Solidarism[1] as a social philosophy was founded by Heinrich Pesch S.J. (1854-1926), and further developed by Gustav Gundlach S.J. (1892-1963) and Oswald von Nell-Breuning S.J. (1890-1991). It is usually also interpreted as a short description of Catholic social teaching in Germany. Pesch, Gundlach, and Nell-Breuning chose the term solidarism consciously to avoid denominational and religious limitations to the claim to universal validity of their theory. In their view solidarism is the social philosophy

---

1   Solidarism has its beginnings in France and the French philosophical social ethics by L. Bourgeois, Y. Guyot and Ch. Gide. - Cf. GUSTAV GUNDLACH: Article "Solidarismus", in: *Staatslexikon* (ed. by Hermann Sacher), Freiburg i. Br. (Herder) 1931, 5th ed. 1931, col. 1613-1621. - It was then developed as a social philosophy and economic ethics and given a systematic foundation by Heinrich Pesch, Gustav Gundlach, and Oswald von Nell-Breuning.

derived from the natural right tradition and is therefore not only dependent of its religious foundations. As a theory of natural right it claims to be the adequate interpretation of human nature and the social philosophical and economic conclusions to be drawn from it.

I. Solidarism Between Individualism and Collectivism

Pesch's main work is his textbook of economics which comprises the essence of his work. It starts, however, not with a pure theory of exchange and price formation but with a treatise on anthropology and the foundations of human nature. This renders it also understandable why Pesch's main contribution is not a theory of economics but the theory of solidarism. Pesch is convinced that the model of man is prior to the model of the economy and that social philosophy is the founding discipline for economics. Therefore, the general social theory forms the foundation of the theory of economic systems. Liberalism, solidarism and socialism are founded on metaphysical and anthropological presuppositions which determine their approach to the economy and to economic policy. This does, however, not mean that economics can be replaced by social philosophy. In the contrary, Pesch's main interest has been the theory of economics.

By their nature, principle answers to questions of the economic order are founded in the principles of the social order which in turn are founded on answers to the question of the essence of the human or anthropology. The relationship of mutual foundations exists between personalism as the anthropology and basic model of the human, solidarism as the social philosophy, and the idea of a social market economy or market economy temperated by economic and social policies. The same holds true for liberalism where liberalism as the social philosophy, individualism as liberalism's concept of the human, and capitalism as its model of the economy condition each other. Accordingly, socialism as a social philosophy is founded on a collectivist anthropology or theory of the human being, and both, the socialist social philosophy and the collectivist theory of the human justify the economic order of the planned economy.

Solidarism together with personalism and a theory of the social market economy considers itself to be a social theory that is located between liberalism which embraces the capitalist economic order and the individualist conception of the human and socialism which comprises the collectivist theory of the human and the theory of the planned economy. Solidarism may, however, not be considered just as a mean or *juste milieu* between two extremes which keeps equal distance to these extremes. Gustav Gundlach takes pains to make clear that it is not a matter of "et - et" or "as well - as" and not the question of constructing a mean between two extremes that characterises solidarism.[2] It is not the equal distance of solidarism to individualism and to collectivism that distinguishes it from both but the different principle of the centre, *Prinzip der Mitte*, that distinguishes it from individualism and collectivism.

The human self is seen in solidarism as an individual being in relation with others, not as a individual entering into relationships like in liberalism nor as a part of a primordial collectivist entity divided only secondarily and accidentally into individuals like in socialism. Pesch states that the human is neither only the generic humankind nor the individual only.

The human is able to be complemented and it is in need of being complemented by others (*Selbstdarstellung*, p. 200). It is this synthesis in the nature of the human individual between individuality and sociability and the human ability of being complemented by others that is at the centre of solidarism. This synthesis distinguishes it from individualism which emphasises only the ability of the human to complement him- or herself by exchange and trade. It also distinguishes it from the socialist idea that the human can realise its nature only in the collective since the individual is so much in need of the others that it cannot enter relationships of exchange as an individual standing in itself.

The duality of being able to be complemented and of being in need of being complemented causes the duality that exists in humankind's ability to realise the division of labour and the association of labour. The division of labour and the association or union in labour belong together and cannot be separated. In contrast to this complementarity of the division and association of labour in solidarism, liberalism and its model of the economy, capitalism, emphasise the need for the division of labour only whereas socialism and its economic theory of the planned economy are centred on the need for associations of labour and labour unions only. Solidarism maintains the dual need for a division and an association of labour. The human individual is

---

2 GUNDLACH: Article "Solidarismus", *loc. cit.*.

capable of realising the division of labour because the human is an individual standing in herself that receives her ontological status not only from the collective. The human individual is in need of associating in labour, and it is in need of forming co-operations of labour in firms and industries since it is in need for being complemented. Solidarity as a basic trait of humankind describes this duality of the individual and the societal nature of the human. It is founded in the personalist model of the human which neither falls in the one-sidedness of individualism restricting the model of the human to the individual's ability of self-control and self-managing nor falls into the collectivist idea that the human individual realises herself in the generic "humankind".

The human is fundamentally dependent on the solidarity of her individual existence with the existence of the social community into which she is embedded. Pesch distinguishes three levels of solidarity:

1. The general human solidarity of all humankind
2. The solidarity of the citizens of a state or nation

Since each human is born into a state or nation the state has the task to secure public welfare and the common good in subsidiarity with the larger group of the human race and the smaller groups like the association of professions, families and so on.

3. The solidarity of one's associates in one's profession.

Pesch puts strong emphasis on the solidarity of the members of a profession. Since the economy as a national economy forms a social unity that is teleologically ordered towards guaranteeing the means of subsistence of a nation or a people it relies on the performance in solidarity of the professions and on the co-operation of all the professions within an economy. The reliance of the economy on the performance of the professions in turn requires the organisation in solidarity of these professions and the synergy in solidarity of the different professions.

On an even higher level, the economy forms a body in solidarity that in turn is part of the total welfare of society and serves the purpose of furthering the total welfare or common good of the society.

That the economy is an institution being at the service of the society implies that the economy is only *relatively* autonomous and independent of the totality of the culture and society in which it works. The economy stands in manifold relationships with the other systems of culture in society. (*Selbstdarstellung*, p. 201) Solidarity of the parts of a whole means that the parts of a whole can only realise their individual teleology or self-realisation if the whole of which they are parts also flourishes and reaches its teleology. Humanity as a whole can only flourish when the single peoples or nations forming it flourish. The national economy can only flourish when the professions constituting the economy flourish, and the individual can only flourish when the profession of which it is a part is prospering.

The idea of solidarity has great impact for the concept of the organisation of an economy. Individualism starts from the idea of the individual and his or her goals. The economy appears to individualism as the sum of absolutely free private economic units that indulge in the unlimited pursuit of wealth. Socialism in turn renders the state or the society to be the subject and basic unit of the economic process. The national economy appears to socialism to be one single economic household with socialised property in the means of production.

Solidarism does not start in a one-sided way from the individual or the society only. It rather takes its starting point from both at the same time by integrating the individuals, the professions, the industries into a moral-organic unity of the economy. The individuals and the collective together realise the economic task.

The economy is not only a process of exchange or a catallaxy but it is a teleological unity serving a material purpose. The purpose of the economy is the material welfare of the nation, but the national wealth must be realised in such a way that the economic purpose remains in harmony with the postulates of higher culture. To realise this purpose, the order of the economy must first be created, it does not exist by itself. (*Selbstdarstellung*, p. 202) Economics cannot satisfy itself by only stating what is the case as it is possible in the natural sciences. Economics must also take into account that order that is demanded by reason. In the causality of economics, the economist must not omit the final causes to the benefit of the mechanic causes.

According to the two elements of human nature, its ability to complement itself by others and its need of being complemented by others, the duality of the division and the association of labour means that labour is the cause of the wealth of nations as Adam Smith and the other classical economists stated it. Human labour is, however, not only one of the main causes for the wealth of nations, it is also the means of association. It associates nations and individuals, entrepreneurs and workers if the market economy is in the state in which it ought to be. (*Selbstdarstellung*, p. 203)

Pesch remarks that his insistence on the teleological nature of the economy caused the divergence of his approach from that of Max Weber and the other proponents of a value-free, non-teleological economic science. His insistence that the economy has the purpose to serve the wealth of a nation separated him from Weber and the other economists who denied a material purpose of the economy, only acknowledged the subjective purposes of the individuals in the economy, and took the economy only for a catallaxy. (*Selbstdarstellung*, p. 204).

II. Capitalism and the Principle of Satisfying the Needs of Subsistence in the Economy

Pesch states clearly that solidarism is a critique of capitalism if capitalism is understood as the system in which the totality of the economy is controlled by the money interests of the capital owners. The theory of pure capitalism must reject the idea that the economy has a material purpose and inherent teleology. If the interest in the accumulation of capital gains and the increase of capital only is the single purpose of the economy the economy is a catallaxy only, a system of exchanges for the maximum gain or profit. Pesch emphasises that this is a wrong conception of the purposes of the economic process. The economic process is teleologically ordered not only to the ever increasing production of material goods or the ever increasing formation of capital but to the national welfare.

"Therefore, the ruling principle of the economy cannot be the capitalist principle of accumulation and profit maximisation, but the principle of satisfying the needs of subsistence".[3]

Pesch also rejects the Manchester individualism of a completely free economic order. He admits that freedom is an element of national welfare. All kinds of freedom that are reconcilable with national welfare must be preserved. Freedom is however, according to Pesch, never the principle of the order since it needs itself order and regulation unless it becomes the

---

[3] "*Darum kann auch nicht das kapitalistische Erwerbs-Gewinnprinzip leitendes Prinzip sein, sondern das Bedarfdeckungsprinzip.*" (PESCH: *Selbstdarstellung*, p. 205)

pure exercise of decision making at random (*Willkür*). The principle ruling and inspiring the economic order is the economic task, the task of satisfying needs. The regulating factors for the fulfilment of this task are the individual morality, the organisations of the professional associations, and the state. It is particularly the organisations of the professions in their self-regulating ability that are necessary for a healthy economic order (*Selbstdarstellung*, p. 205). Pesch emphasises that moral norms of conduct and an economic ethics are to be preferred to state measures and state intervention (*Selbstdarstellung*, p. 191).

Pesch makes clear that he rejects communist socialism in principle as well as for practical reasons. In 1931 he writes that the first great attempt to realise this system failed completely. The Russian Bolshevism of his time is not total or partial communism but state socialism. This state socialism can only last and has only prospects for a longer duration since it is realised in a nation that has been used to absolutism for a long time. (*Selbstdarstellung*, p. 205)

Solidarism is also distinguished from capitalism by its defending an extensive economic policy of the state. Solidarism argues for an extensive state economic policy but only exceptionally for economic activity of the state: "Ausgedehnte Wirtschaftspolitik, aber nur ausnahmsweise Staatswirtschaft!" (*Ethik und Volkswirtschaft*, p. 225)

Solidarism is furthermore distinguished from capitalism by its insistence that in the exchange relationships of the people acting in the economy not only the principle of mutually beneficial exchange and non-coercion must be obeyed but also the principle of equivalence. The condition that exchange relationships should not only be consensual and be no negative sum- or zero-sum games is not sufficient. Exchange relationships rather also should make sure that both parties in an exchange get back in return the equivalent of what they give away to the other exchange partner. The recompensation for what one gets must correspond to the value of the commodity, and the commodity must correspond in value to what one gets in money for it. No partner of the exchange should undergo a loss in wealth by the exchange. His net wealth must not be lower after the exchange than before it. (*Ethik und Volkswirtschaft*, p. 52)

This principle of equivalence or of the recompensation according to the value of the commodity is also the deeper reason for the prohibition of usury and, since in the Medieval social teaching of the church taking interest was considered to be usury, for the prohibition of taking interest.

PETER KOSLOWSKI

One of the most interesting papers by Pesch analyses the problem of interest under the title "The Legitimation of Interest and the Limitations of the Interest Rate" (*"Zinsgrund und Zinsgrenze"* [ZuZ])[4]

III. The Legitimacy of Taking Interest

In his paper, Pesch as scholar of Christian social thought intends to prove the continuity of the ethical and legal rules on interest propagated by the Catholic church. He argues that there has been no revolutionary change in the ethical and legal code of the church concerning interest. There has been only the adjustment of the same ethical and legal code to changing conditions and circumstances of economic history. Pesch's reasoning is of interest as well for economic history as for the understanding of modernity. If he is right the change to modernity in the economy and in the laws concerning interest is not as revolutionary as it is often assumed. Rather, this change is evolutionary and gradual. Modernity is not separated from the Middle Ages by an insurmountable gap and by a revolution of emancipation and growing autonomy - in the economy of the emancipation from legal and ethical restrictions of the right to take interest, to lend and to borrow. The transition to modernity is rather a gradual modification of the ethical and legal rules of the economy.

According to the teaching of the church, interest is usury, and usury is a violation of the rights of one's neighbour and therefore a crime. (ZuZ, p. 38) Usury is the unlawful appropriation of the other's property. If interest is usury it is the unlawful appropriation of a part of the debtor's property. The laws against usury are strict laws. Any justification of interest must therefore demonstrate that taking interest is not usury and therefore no unlawful appropriation of the other's property.

---

4 HEINRICH PESCH: "Zinsgrund und Zinsgrenze", *Zeitschrift für Katholische Theologie*, 12 (1888), part I, pp. 36-74, part II, pp. 393-418.

SOLIDARISM AND CAPITALISM IN HEINRICH PESCH

1. The Equivalence Principle and the Justification of Interest

A lender can claim compensation if he undergoes a sacrifice or loss. Interest payments would be justified if they were the compensation payment for a sacrifice the lender has made or a loss he suffered. But in order to justify interest in general it must be proven that the lender makes a sacrifice in lending. It must be shown that every lender makes a sacrifice he is compensated for by paying interest in addition to returning the loan. (ZuZ, p. 41)

According to Pesch, the theory that interprets interest as the payment for a sacrifice the lender makes and as a reward for abstinence is, however, ridiculous since there are now whole classes who live on lending. The great capitalists lend money without undergoing any sacrifice or abstinence from consumption. (ZuZ, p. 42) The generality of sacrifice on the side of the lenders is not given and cannot serve as a justification for a general admissibility of interest.

Although the teaching of the church was clear in the laws against usury the church expressed only a conditioned prohibition of interest, never an absolute one. (ZuZ, p. 42) The conditions for the prohibition and the allowance of interest were the following:

1. A loan as such does not give justification to take interest.

2. There are, however, titles or entitlements beside the loan that may justify interest where they are applicable.

3. There are contracts that allow taking profit from transferring capital. But these contracts are fundamentally different from the lending contract. It is legitimate to make a contract of transferring capital and of including a profit for the investment in another person's firm. The shareholder relationship is not a lending relationship but a form of investment and co-ownership sharing in the risk of the enterprise.

4. In cases of need, an individual is obliged under certain circumstances by the law of love or *caritas* to help out his neighbour with a simple loan that bears no interest. (ZuZ, p. 42)

A contradiction in the ethical and legal rules on interest in the past and present teaching of the church would only exist if today's business ethics of the church accepted an unconditioned right to take interest although it almost unconditionally condemned taking interest before modernity (ZuZ, p. 43)

In such a situation, Catholic business ethics and solidarism have two tasks according to Pesch: They must - at the same time - defend the older teaching and the present practice, and they must still offer protection against usury for the poor and the weak. A defence of the church's position in the question of taking interest must demonstrate that there is no alteration of principle in this question. This implies the demonstration that the change of the church's actual position in this question "is exclusively induced by objective alterations in the economic conditions and that there is no contradiction in principle between the old ecclesiastical norms and the present ecclesiastical practice". (ZuZ, 43)

The unchanged fundamental law underlying all questions of economic ethics is the equivalence principle. Each contract that formulates a mutual obligation to deliver a service or a commodity for an agreed price presupposes the common principle of the equality of value between giving and taking, the principle of *equalitas permutationis*. The principle of equivalence applies to all contracts of exchange. (ZuZ, 44) The contributions of both sides must be equal in value. The contribution of the lender gives the measure for the contribution of the borrower. The problem of interest is a special case of the law of equivalence. "Every right theory of interest must be a theory of equivalence." (ZuZ, 44) From the law of equivalence follows that, prima facie, the borrower is not obliged to return more than he received: the loan. (ZuZ, 45) He is not obliged to return more than the full and undiminished amount of the loan. He does not seem to be obliged to return the loan augmented by the rate of interest.

Interest is neither *fructus*, usufruct, nor share in profit, nor rent. So what is it? Already the medieval theory of interest justified certain exceptions from the prohibition to take interest. It discussed the question whether interest is justified as the compensation for an "*interesse*", for a profit forsaken during the period of credit. (ZuZ, 46) Interest seems to be a payment for the opportunity forsaken to use the money while it is lent. It seems to be a compensation for the opportunity cost of money. This justification of interest by the idea that it is a general opportunity cost of money or for a general profit forsaken is, however, unacceptable as a *general* justification since the occurrence and the amount of the profit forsaken is uncertain and therefore not general.

The economic ethics of the natural right tradition has only accepted the theory of *interesse* where in individual cases the profit forsaken by giving the loan can be proven. Interest as the compensation for an opportunity forsaken to make profit, as *lucrum cessans*, was accepted under the conditions that it could be proven in the individual case.

How were these conditions further specified that justified interest in certain cases? By giving a loan, the lender needed to be hindered to use an actually given - not only a fictitious - intention and opportunity to use his or her money. A general, uncertain, and unspecified opportunity was not sufficient to give an entitlement for taking interest on the money given for a certain period of time. (ZuZ, 47) The opportunity forsaken was also not imputed to the payment of a general interest rate in its totality. The opportunity forsaken justified the payment of an "interesse" only after the precise calculation of the probability and risk of the realisation of the opportunity. The probability and risk of the realisation of the opportunity and the time and effort the lender saved by not undergoing the effort of making a productive use of his money but borrowing it to someone else needed to be deducted. The *titulus lucri cessantis*, the title for a profit forsaken, also required a real and given intention, not a fictitious general will of the lender, to use the money of his loan profitably in production.

The modern, new theory of interest, however, yields the right to take interest to "whole classes of capitalists who have said good bye for ever to production." (ZuZ, 47) The justification of interest, particularly of taking interest by the class of capitalists, cannot be derived from their opportunity forsaken to make productive use of their money since it is characteristic of their profession not to live on production but on lending. The old theory of interest demanded a *subjective and objective* opportunity of an alternative profitable investment of the sum lent. (ZuZ, 48) The conditions of lending do not give a general justification of taking interest on the ground of the arguments of the theory of *interesse* or of the opportunity costs of money. The theory of *interesse* is only justifiable on the basis that the lender fulfils the individual and subjective reasons and specifications that an *interesse* for profit forsaken is effective. The possibility and probability to make profit in the meantime while the money is lent must not be an abstract possibility or probability but an in every respect concrete one. (ZuZ, 51)

A general justification for taking interest would be viable if the concrete opportunity to make alternative use in production of the money lent is given for *all*. Only under the condition that all have a concrete opportunity to use the money lent "in the mean time", an *interesse* theory of interest makes sense. (ZuZ, 52)

When the concrete opportunity to make alternative productive uses of credit and money is general money has the same importance and effective value for the lender and the borrower. Under conditions of a general opportunity of money to make profit in production, the lending of money is the rendering of a service of a specified value by the lender to the borrower the value of which is independent of the individual circumstances of the borrower and the lender. When everyone can make use of the opportunity to use money productively in a loan money is not a purely individualised asset anymore but capital that has an objective and general real value.

If the good or service the lender renders to the borrower has an objective value under the given circumstances of an economic order the borrower is obliged to offer and to return an equivalent for this value of the service rendered. Such an equivalent for a commodity or a service is usually called a price. Interest is therefore the price for a service: "Pure interest is, therefore, nor *fructus*, nor dividend, nor rent, nor compensation for *interesse* or a subjective and individual opportunity forsaken but it is the price for the real value given besides the capital transferred in yielding the credit sum." (ZuZ, 53)

Pesch's theory of interest does not imply that each lender could and will make the same rate of profit in the alternative productive use in production of the money lent. Since the opportunities to use money productively and to make profit have been extended extremely it is untenable that all lenders have the same opportunity cost of lending and deserve the same rate of *interesse*. The condition that every lender will be productive in the mean time does not apply to every lender since not every lender can and intends to become active in production successfully. Pesch gives the example of the university professor who has been able to build up a certain capital, who lends money from this capital but who will never be able to become immediately productive in the production of commodities. (ZuZ, 53)

The basis of the justification of interest is not the assumption that every individual can make - subjectively as a person and objectively under the given objective economic circumstances - productive use of the capital. Not the idea that every lender undergoes opportunity costs of profit by lending money justifies taking interest, but the observation and fact that under the present conditions of the economy the loan for productive purposes and not for the needs of subsistence is the normal case. The normal use and value of money is its value-in-use in its function as capital. Since the credit given for productive purposes is the normal case in lending, credit must normally be paid for by a normal price, the rate of interest. (ZuZ, 53)

The economy is changed under conditions of modernity in such a way that it turns the unlikely and highly subjective profit or *lucrum cessans* that is forsaken due to the loan given into a likely and objective general phenomenon that applies to all lenders. All lenders undergo the opportunity costs of lending. The principle of equivalence requires, therefore, that the lender must receive, if he gives the capital loan *and* the productive capacity of his capital to the borrower, the sum of the loan unchanged in return and a price for the use of the productive capacity of the capital borrowed. The loan must be returned unchanged as far as the amount and value is concerned together with a price for the use of the productive capacity of the capital borrowed, the interest payment.

Paying a reasonable rate of interest has become under the conditions of modernity even a norm derived from the principle of equivalence. The sphere of capital and money lending must be protected against the loss of wealth like any other sphere of wealth. The entire sphere of wealth is protected, according to Pesch, by the firm and unchanging norms of morality. The moral norms protect against every unjustified tort or intrusion violating the ontological status of the sphere of wealth, be it that this tort is theft, robbery, or blackmailing. "These are all judged and condemned by the cutting sword of justice sentencing these torts by the strict obligation to give restitution." (ZuZ, 61)

Interest is the compensation and restitution of the lender for letting the borrower not only use the amount of money given to buy goods or services but also to make use of the productive capacity of money as capital "in the time that passes between receiving and returning the credit", to make use of "*id quod interest*". Interest is justified as the payment of the price for the use of this productive capacity of money for a certain time.

From the changes in the function of credit and interest the following conclusion can be drawn according to Pesch: "The ecclesiastical theory of interest did not change, only the circumstances did so." (ZuZ, 64) The circumstances changed in as far as, in the Middle Ages, only consumptive credit or credit for consumption purposes was usually given and no general opportunity existed to make profit from capital. There existed only subjective conditions and opportunities dependent on the persons that could justify interest as a subjective, individual compensation for an *interesse* in the special case. *Interesse* did, however, not apply to all participants in the market and in the borrowing-lending relationships. In modern times, these credit conditions changed fundamentally. Credit for production or productive credit becomes dominant, and a general opportunity exists to increase wealth by using capital. This opportunity is not anymore a subjective and unique, and therefore highly specified chance to increase one's wealth with the money lent in the meantime, but it is a concrete and immediate possibility for everyone. (ZuZ, 65) *Interesse* is not subjective anymore but objective and must therefore be compensated by paying a price, the amount of interest given by the interest rate. (ZuZ, 66)

Looking back at economic history it is visible that the church intended to prevent the abuse of giving credits to the poor for consumptive purposes and at high rates like 30 per cent interest and more. (ZuZ, 71)

2. Improvements in the Theory of Interest

Pesch claims that his new theory of interest is better than the older ones existing in the Catholic tradition for the following reasons:

1. The loan is still considered to bear no interest but to be returned as such and at the original value. Interest as the price for rendering the service of credit, i.e. for the opportunity given by the credit to create value by production, is based on a legal title that is external to the relationship of lending and to the title of the loan. The entitlement for taking interest is not based on the lending relationship but on acknowledging that the opportunity given by the credit to make productive use of money is a general reality under the economic conditions of modernity and yields an economic value-in-exchange which requires the payment of a price. (ZuZ, 72)

2. This theory does not give everyone the entitlement for *interesse* or for a recompensation by interest for the opportunities forsaken during the period of the credit since even under the present conditions not everyone can become a producing entrepreneur "in the meantime". The modern theory of interest is not an *interesse* -theory in the medieval sense. (ZuZ, 73)

Pesch's theory of interest explains why everyone may take interest at a modest rate with the general permission of the church even if he or she does not want to become a producing entrepreneur with her capital for her own person in the time of the credit given. On the contrary, the theory of *interesse* and the justification of interest by the unspecified and unspecifyable *interesse* as the opportunity forsaken by the lender cannot offer an adequate justification of interest. (ZuZ, 74)

3. Consequences of the Theory of Interest for a Theory of Capitalism

Pesch describes and defends the continuity of natural law and its norms concerning taking interest. The underlying norm is unchanging: No loss of wealth on any side of the contract relationship may occur. Paying interest for a loan for consumptive purposes would mean a loss of wealth on the side of the borrower. Under the changing conditions of modernity, the borrower is, however, able to make and actually makes profit by taking the loan and the lender really forsakes the general opportunity to make profit with the money he borrows during the time of credit. The lender undergoes a loss of wealth unless he is compensated by the borrower. This just compensation is the interest payment.

Capitalism, capitalist calculation and the taking of interest are justified as long as the principle of just compensation or equivalence and the principle of avoiding losses in wealth are applied and followed. Capitalism is the adequate economic system as long as it works within the norms of solidarity and the framework of solidarism: Exchange relationships should be equivalent in the contributions of both contract partners, and all commercial relationships should be so that there is no loss of wealth on any side. Since the contract partners form a community of solidarity they cannot accept that one of them suffers a loss in an exchange relationship. (*Ethik und Volkswirtschaft* [EuV], 52)

Capitalism, capitalist calculation, and the taking of interest are unjustified where this principle of a solidarist economy and the principle of satisfying the needs of its members as the final purpose of the economy are not adhered to. The market economy becomes an illegitimate order if the conditions of the pursuit of the economic goal in solidarity are not fulfilled. This is the case if a market economy gives up this principle for the pursuit of unlimited capital accumulation, for allowing contracts that do not realise the principle of equivalence and that imply losses in wealth on one side of the contract. The conditions of a market economy are furthermore violated if the concept of the economy is changed into one that assumes that the economy is only a catallaxy that has no material purpose but is only a formal sphere of exchange. Equally, the solidarist interdependence of the members of the community of an economy is not observed but violated if the economy is seen as an exchange relationship only in which the repercussions of the actual exchanges on the needs of the population or nation are not taken into account

IV. Ethics and Economics

The principle of mutually beneficial exchange is not sufficient as a basis for the sphere of exchange of the market. The idea of mutually beneficial exchange is not sufficient from the point of an economic ethics if it is considered to imply only exchange as a non-negative-sum- or zero-sum-game. Prices must not only follow the conditions of market price formation but they must also follow the ethical principle of the recompensation according to the value. (EuV 52) Since justice and just legal relationships are the basis of a society of solidarity justice must also be applied in the formation of prices. No one wants to suffer a loss in his or her wealth by an exchange, no one wants to pay a too high price, a price that exceeds the value of the commodity or service exchanged. (EuV 53) A theory that bases price formation on convention only is insufficient since consensus cannot be the only criterion for a just price since consensus is also reached where a fake commodity is at stake or a mutual deceit or misapprehension of reality prevail.

In general, the price is found by the mere convention of the two contract partners. There are, however, quite a few situations where this is not a sufficient condition for price formation. Pesch quotes Wilhelm Roscher, one of the main theoreticians of the Historical School of Economics, that there are quite a few kinds of commerce which are profitable for the private person but are completely unproductive for humanity, that are even detrimental for it since they detract at least as much or even more wealth from the others than they yield profit to the one engaging in this kinds of commerce. Roscher mentions not only the formal crimes against property but also gambling, usurious speculations, and measures to detract competitors from their clients. (EuV 60) The principle of the recompensation according to the value of the services rendered is also necessary according to Pesch for the preservation of certain professions that could not be preserved otherwise since market demand does not secure their ongoing existence.

Pesch is well aware that economics is not the same as ethics. Economics has a different formal object but it shares the same material object with ethics, the human action aiming at satisfying human needs. He emphasises that the causal analysis of economics remains incomplete unless it takes into consideration the enormous importance of ethical motives and rules. The political and the economic order of a society require that their rules are founded in the morals and conscience of its citizens. "If the political and societal order is not founded in the conscience of the citizens, the economic order also lacks every secure fundament." (EuV 123)

Ethics and economics are also connected since for economics the "principle of the unity of culture" holds true as well as for ethics. Welfare or national wealth is not measured in economic terms only but is formed by the totality of the cultural and religious flourishing of a nation. (EuV 124) The conception of economics as an autonomous science being independent of ethics, aesthetics and politics is in danger of losing sight of the interrelations of economics with the other human sciences.

Pesch remarks that the rise of economics as an autonomous science coincides with the rise of the large philosophical systems and the system-building of philosophy. Economics as a system of thought and the ideas of the economic order as an autonomous system are in danger to fall victim to a fallacy characteristic of all kinds of "system building": The construction of the system and the freedom to construct it or not are mistaken to be the autonomy and self-sufficiency of the object itself of the system. The autonomy and self-sufficiency of the system-building is taken to apply also to the reality, the description and analysis of which the system is developed for. (EuV 126)

A free economy should not be mistaken for a libertarian economy. Pesch agrees that a freer economy is to be preferred to a closed and unfree one. The free economy should, however, not be misunderstood as a libertarian economy: "Not liberty but order is the highest principle and best guarantee for the rightly conceived freedom." (EuV 132)

Capitalism is the model of the economy which conceptualises the individuals working and exchanging in this economy as atomised individuals that are co-ordinated by the great mechanism of the market. Socialism on the other hand conceptualises the economy as a physical organism like the body of an animal: The human is then only a limb of this organism. (EuV

151) Solidarism avoids this misconceptions of society. Society is neither only a mechanistic general equilibrium of atomised individuals nor a physical organism of a collective of which the human members are only limbs. Rather the economy is a moral organism in which the members retain their status as free and freely acting parts or members. The individuals are neither atoms of an economic mechanism nor mere parts of a societal organism, but members who have the origin of their actions in themselves.

The economic principle or principle of economic rationality can only be adequately grasped if its relationship and interactions with the other principles of the orientations of human action are considered, the aesthetic and the ethical principle. The economist has not the task to find out what is aesthetically adequate and what is ethically correct. But he must acknowledge that the postulates of ethics and aesthetics are economically relevant, influence the object of his theory and that they must be observed in the right way if the task of the national economy and the task of economics are adequately fulfilled. (EuV 158)

The consequence of this consideration of the complementarity of the economic and the ethical principle is that the ethical as well as the economic principle of recompensation according to the value of a service rendered replaces the individualist principle of an absolutely free pursuit of profit. (EuV 162) The aim is a free economy with the self-reliance (*Selbständigkeit*) and self-responsibility (*Selbstverantwortlichkeit*) of the people acting in the economy. "This free economy will, however, not be the individualist, capitalist economy of economic libertinism but a social and regulated economy which will become a social economy (*Gemeinwirtschaft*) by the ordering of the private economic units into the unity of the national economy and by their subordination under the task of the national economy."[5]

---

[5] "*Freie Volkswirtschaft, mit Selbständigkeit und Selbstverantwortlichkeit der wirtschaftenden Subjekte ... Es wird aber nicht mehr die individualistische, kapitalistische Volkswirtschaft des wirtschaftlichen Libertinismus sein, sondern eine sozialisierte und geregelte Volkswirtschaft, die zur Gemeinwirtschaft wird durch die Einordnung der Einzelwirtschaften in die volkswirtschaftliche Einheit und durch ihre Unterordnung unter die volkswirtschaftliche Aufgabe.*" (EuV 163)

SOLIDARISM AND CAPITALISM IN HEINRICH PESCH

V. Heinrich Pesch and the Historical School of Economics

Pesch's relationships with the Historical School are manifold. He studied with Schmoller, Adolf Wagner and Max Sering in Berlin. About Schmoller he writes that he was not very satisfied by Schmoller's theoretical insights but that he was impressed by his analysis of morality and ethos, *Sitte und Sittlichkeit*. He remarks however that Schmoller did not clarify the relationship between morality and ethos in a more specific way (*Selbst-darstellung*, p. 197) - a striking analysis of one of the crucial weaknesses of Schmoller and his concept of an "ethical approach to economics".[6]

That Pesch does not belong to the Historical School is obvious when one takes into account his foundations in the natural right tradition and the tradition of scholasticism. There are, however, many important theoretical agreements between Pesch and the Historical School. The first concerns the emphasis on the ethical causes in the economy and on the need for an inclusion of ethical analysis into economics.

The second is the emphasis on the national character of an economy and of the solidarity of a people in economic terms that influences all economic actions. For Pesch, the solidarity of the members of a nation and a people is, however, only taken in subsidiarity with the solidarity of all humankind. The solidarity of humankind complements the nation and is in subsidiarity with the solidarity of the other communities below the level of the nation, the professions and the family. The nation is, according to Pesch, only one community within the structure of subsidiarity of the communities whereas for some authors of the Historical School, the nation assumes a higher and intrinsic value. Both, solidarism and the Historical School, emphasise, however, the economic meaning of the nation. In this they are in contrast to the free trade tradition for which the nation is not an economically relevant entity. This is already visible in the emphasis the Historical School and

---

6 Cf. P. KOSLOWSKI: *The Theory of Ethical Economy in the Historical School. Wilhelm Roscher, Lorenz von Stein, Gustav Schmoller, Wilhelm Dilthey and Contemporary Theory*, Berlin, Heidelberg, New York, Tokyo (Springer) 1995 (= Studies in Economic Ethics and Philosophy Vol. 7), and P. KOSLOWSKI: "Ethical Economy as Synthesis of Economic and Ethical Theory", in: P. KOSLOWSKI (Ed.): *Ethics in Economics, Business, and Economic Policy*, Berlin, Heidelberg, New York (Springer) 1992, pp. 15-56 (= Studies in Economic Ethics and Philosophy Vol. 1).

Pesch put on the term "Volkswirtschaft" which is only insufficiently translated as "national economy".

For the present globalised economy, it is an important question whether the nation or the people as the kind of natural subdivision of the world market that Pesch assumes it to be is still the relevant subject of solidarity and can fulfil the functions of creating and organising solidarity, e.g. of funding the welfare state.

The nation is also relevant for the second organisational unit of solidarity, the professional associations. Pesch assumes that the professional associations also follow the limits of nations. There is a development of the global economy perceivable in which the professions will organise themselves in international professions that create a solidarity between the "colleagues" or members of a profession well above the national level. The allegiance to a profession may become more important for an individual than the allegiance to a nation.

Gustav Gundlach emphasised the close relationship of solidarism with the Historical School by saying that the principle of solidarity and the principles of solidarism are intrinsically connected with the concrete-living conditions and the historical reality and that they are, therefore, distinguished from rationalist sociology which denies the forces of history and historical reality.[7] Gundlach makes however at the same time qualifications to this proximity of solidarism to historism: Solidarism cannot follow the mere empiricism and historism of the Historical School. It maintains that, within the historicity of society, the idea of natural right that there are unchanging norms of society and of the economy must be present. "Society in its dynamics or, what is the same, the essence of history as the network of the actions of the human that takes place in space and time, realises the objective norms of culture." (*ibid.*, 1617.) These norms of culture are the object of solidarism. Within the process and stream of history there are objective norms of culture that must be realised in the network of the actions of humankind.

Pesch and Gundlach emphasise the role of law in the formation and life of the institutions and norms of the society and the economy.[8] Solidarity is

---

7   GUNDLACH: article "Solidarismus", p. 1617.
8   Cf. PESCH: *Selbstdarstellung*, p. 191; GUNDLACH: article "Solidarismus", p. 1615.

for both, Pesch and Gundlach, a fact *and* an ethical principle.[9] Solidarism tries to secure the right in two directions. It tries to defend the rights of the individual towards society and its collectives in contrast to socialism, and it secures the rights of society and of the communities of solidarity towards the individual and towards individualism in contrast to liberalism.

In contrast to historism, solidarism also secures the unity of humankind as a community of solidarity against the historist tendency to dissolve the unity of humanity into a final, non-unified plurality of peoples and nations that the Historical School is tempted to assume due to its affection for the particular.

VI. The Relationship of Solidarism with Catholic Thinking

Gundlach emphasises that the social theory of solidarism offers a bridge between the facts of revelation and dogma and the natural organisation of society to the Catholic interpretation of existence and society.[10] Solidarism is in this respect an expression of the natural right tradition and of its attempt to bridge the religious revelation with the autonomy of reason. Solidarism is not a theological system but can be proven by the means of natural cognition. It is however in a relationship of correspondence with Catholic thinking. The emphasis on the freedom and self-responsibility of the individuals in solidarism corresponds to the idea of the person given in revelation. It overcomes the holistic models of society that stem from Plato and Aristotle. The critique of the holistic theories of society that exaggerate the idea of unity and of organism in social theory started already with the medieval philosophy of the great scholastics. The idea of personality in the biblical tradition is taken up in solidarism in its emphasis on individual freedom.

On the other hand the idea of community in solidarism has its parallel in the religious idea of community that relates to the dogmatic facts of original sin and redemption. The idea that humankind is generally affected by sin and is generally in need of redemption emphasises the origin of the feeling

---

9   Cf. PESCH: *Selbstdarstellung*, p. 201; GUNDLACH: article "Solidarismus", p. 1615.
10 GUNDLACH: article "Solidarismus", p. 1619.

and of the idea of solidarity in the shared nature of the humans being all affected by original sin and the strive for redemption. Gundlach emphasises however that the Christian idea of a community of love is taken up in solidarism as a principle of law. The structure of human society requires a principle of law which is not identical with the principle of love but should be supplemented by it.

From the point of view of the history of ideas, solidarism also gave Catholicism the possibility for a intellectually fruitful debate with and reassessment of the lines of thought of liberal individualism and of socialist collectivism. In the debate with liberalism, solidarism was able to give a positive assessment to the liberal idea of individual initiative and of the incentives for performance that economic competition creates in society. The idea of the community of solidarity, however, limits the rights of individual freedom.

In its debate with socialism, solidarism found itself in agreement in the critique of certain features of the liberal capitalist economy. It recognised like socialism the tendencies for a cleavage in society into classes stemming from the capitalist labour market. In contrast to socialism, solidarism interpreted the conflicts between the classes as a fight for the restauration of a union and unity of solidarity in the national economy.[11]

Major works by Heinrich Pesch

"Zinsgrund und Zinsgrenze", *Zeitschrift für Katholische Theologie*, 12 (1888), part I, pp. 36-74, part II, pp. 393-418.
Liberalismus, Sozialismus und christliche Gesellschaftsordnung (Liberalism, Socialism, and Christian Social Order), 2 vols, 1896, 2nd ed. 1900.
Die soziale Befähigung der Kirche (The Social Ability of the Church), 3rd ed. 1898.
Lehrbuch der Nationalökonomie (A Textbook of Economics), 5 vols., Freiburg im Breisgau (Herder):
 Vol. 1: *Grundlegung* (Foundations), 1905, 3rd and 4th ed. 1924;
 Vol. 2: *Allgemeine Volkswirtschaftslehre I*

---

11 Cf. GUNDLACH: article "Solidarismus", p. 1619f.

SOLIDARISM AND CAPITALISM IN HEINRICH PESCH

Volkswirtschaftliche Systeme. Wesen und disponierende Ursachen des Volkswohlstandes (General Economics I Economic Systems. The Essence and Preparative Causes of the Wealth of Nations), 1908, 4th and 5th ed. 1925;
Vol. 3: *Allgemeine Volkswirtschaftslehre II*
Die aktiven Ursachen im volkswirtschaftlichen Lebensprozesse (General Economics II The Active Causes in the Economic Process) 1913, 2nd to 4th ed. 1926;
Vol. 4: *Allgemeine Volkswirtschaftslehre III*
Der volkswirtschaftliche Prozeß 1. Deckung des Volksbedarfs als volkswirtschaftliche Aufgabe; 2. *Produktion* (General Economics: The Economic Process 1. Satisfying the Needs of Subsistence of a Nation as the Task of National Economics; 2. Production), 1st and 2nd ed. 1922;
Vol. 5: *Allgemeine Volkswirtschaftslehre IV*
Der volkswirtschaftliche Prozeß 3. Tauschverkehr; 4. Einkommens- und Vermögensbildung; 5. Störungen des volkswirtschaftlichen Prozesses (General Economics: The Economic Process, 3. The Relations of Exchange; 4. The Creation of Income and Wealth; 5. Frictions in the Economic Process), 1st and 2nd ed. 1923.
Ethik und Volkswirtschaft (Ethics and Economics) Freiburg i. Br. (Herder) 1918.
"Heinrich Pesch S. J. Selbstdarstellung" (Autobiography), in: *Die Volkswirtschaftslehre der Gegenwart in Selbstdarstellungen,* edited by Felix Meiner, Leipzig (F. Meiner) 1924, pp. 191-208.

Literature About Pesch

BRIEFS, G.: "Pesch and His Contemporaries", *Social Order* (St. Louis), 1 (1951), pp. 153ff.
GUNDLACH, GUSTAV: Article "Heinrich Pesch", in: *Handwörterbuch der Sozialwissenschaften,* Stuttgart (G. Fischer), Tübingen (Mohr Siebeck), Göttingen (Vandenhoeck & Ruprecht) 1964, Bd. 8, pp. 280-281.
HARRIS, A. L.: "The Scholastic Revival: the Economics of H. Pesch", *Journal of Political Economy,* 54 (1946), pp. 38ff.
HÄTTICH, M.: *Wirtschaftsordnung und katholische Soziallehre. Die subsidiäre und berufsständische Gliederung der Gesellschaft in ihrem Verhältnis zu den wirtschaftlichen Lenkungssystemen,* Stuttgart (Fischer) 1957.

JENNI, J.: "Pesch's Goal of the Economy", *Social Order* (St. Louis), 1 (1951), pp. 169ff.

LECHTAPE, H.: *Der christliche Solidarismus - nach H. Pesch dargestellt*, Freiburg i. Br. (Herder) 1919, 2nd ed. 1922.

MOREAU, H.: *De la Solidarité*, Paris (Librairie des Juris-classeurs – Editions Godde) 1930.

MUELLER, FRANZ H.: *Heinrich Pesch and His Theory of Christian Solidarism*, St. Paul, Minnesota (The College of St. Thomas) 1941.

MUELLER, FRANZ H.: *Heinrich Pesch. Sein Leben und seine Lehre*, Köln (J. P. Bachem) 1980.

MULCAHY, R. E.: *The Economics of Heinrich Pesch*, New York (Holt) 1952 (with bibliography).

NELL-BREUNING, O. VON: "The Peschian Interest Theory", *Social Order* (St. Louis), 1 (1951), pp. 177ff.

REDER, F.: "Die Grundlagen der Wirtschaftstheorie Heinrich Peschs", *Jahrbücher für Nationalökonomie und Statistik*, 74 (1928), pp. 747ff.

WEINBERGER, O.: "Heinrich Pesch", *Zeitschrift für die gesammte Staatswissenschaft*, 82 (1927), pp. 512ff.

Discussion Summary

TORBEN VESTDAM

Paper discussed:
PETER KOSLOWSKI: Solidarism, Capitalism, and Economic Ethics in Heinrich Pesch

The author distinguishes Pesch's philosophy of solidarism from Hayek's philosophy of catallaxy by adding to its system of exchange, which serves the purpose of generating material wealth, the purpose of cultural integration, which requires modification of the market process according to principles of (a) non-coercion, (b) equivalence of exchange and (c) interest taking on financial transaction to the extend that it can be justified as a fee for profit forsaken. The author adds that Aquinas introduced a clear concept of credit, that is to say time, which per ethical definition have to be exempted from the market process. However, Pesch's philosophy implies that under conditions of financial capitalism, the exchange of credit for a fee of interest is a justified practice. The author adds in response to ZONINSEIN that scholastic philosophy does not until the 19th century consider the issue of social justice, as the distribution of the factors of production is taken as given according to a philosophy of natural right. The idea of social justice is introduced by Luigi Taparelli d'Azeglio (1793-1862) as an extension of the question of justice from merely justice in exchange to justice in terms of distribution of wealth. WOHLGEMUTH remarks that Hayek's concept of catallexy implies beyond merely material exchange the ethical dimension of friendship and appeasement, and in response the author remarks that his treatment implies acceptance of Hayek's concept in so far as issues of social justice are taken into account. NÖRR remarks that Pesch's attempt to substantiate a claim that a concept of usury emerges in references to an ethical dilemma associated with economic circumstances of poverty exploitation, but he does not consider that it actually emerges during the 13th and 14th centuries in references to practices of shipping finance transaction. Furthermore NÖRR remarks that Pesch is not aware that the concept of money

DISCUSSION SUMMARY

has changed completely, and that this requires a reconsideration of the scholastic concept of usury and natural law, that can allow for not only partnership but as well shared ownership (financial capitalism). ZONINSEIN remarks that investment in shares of corporate capital is investment in perceived capacity of a corporation to generate future profits, and that speculation in this capacity generates a surplus profit which he refers to as 'social profits'. ZONINSEIN remarks that a philosophy of solidarism has to consider this dimension of the market process. In response to SCHWINGER the author remarks treatment of the issue of natural law in relation to the values that educational institutions can promote always commences from a choice of one among several images of man. In response to SHIONOYA the author remarks that Pesch criticises welfare economics for its reliance on mathematical methodology that never reaches the sphere of actual market processes.

Another distinction is set between Pesch's philosophy of solidarism, which implies a normative set of values and the value-relativism of historism. Pesch's philosophy of solidarism implies a conception of the individual being in relation according to principles of division of labour, professionalism (associations of professions) and Christian theology (original sin / salvation).

Chapter 11

Theory and Critique of Capitalism in Gustav Gundlach

ANTON RAUSCHER

I. The Historical Situation
II. What Is Capitalism?
III. The Crisis of Society and State
IV. Classes, Class Struggle, Class Society
V. The Renewal of Society

Gustav Gundlach (1892-1963) was one of the leading catholic scientists, who greatly influenced the social teaching of the Church.[1] Many of his ideas have been taken up by Pope Pius XI in the social encyclica *Quadragesimo Anno* (1931), especially the formulation of the principle of subsidiarity.[2] Even much closer was the co-operation with Pope Pius XII (1939-1958). He was preparing for the pope the vast number of allocutions, documents, and statements on a great variety of social questions. He also proposed the main lines for the famous Christmas allocutions of Pius XII. There is no doubt that Gundlach's work was most important at a time, when the social teaching of the Church was just developing and the orientation was bitterly needed.

Gundlach was professor for social philosophy and social ethics at the Pontifical University Gregoriana from 1934 to 1962. At the age of seventy he left Rome and on behalf of the German bishop he took over the task of building up the "Katholische Sozialwissenschaftliche Zentralstelle" (Center

---

1 A. RAUSCHER (1975), J. SCHWARTE (1975).
2 VON NELL-BREUNING (1972).

for Catholic Social Sciences) in Mönchengladbach. But he died after a few months in office.

I. The Historical Situation

To understand Gundlach's contribution to the social teaching of the Church we have to reflect the historical situation of the modern society. With the French Revolution of 1789 the Church had lost its traditional place in policy, but for a great deal also in society. It became more and more isolated. Familiar with the economic, social, cultural and political structures of the old system, the Church found it difficult to understand the very different nature and structures of industrial economy, of pluralistic society and of democratic policy. In former times the Church stood for ethical values and norms of people in living and working together. What about the new economy and society? Did the "market economy", as the liberals put it, function without ethical orientation? It did not. In the centres of industrial economy rose the so-called "social question": Labour was just a factor of production and no one asked about the human and social requirements.

With regard to the "social question" there was no answer at hand. The liberals dominating the political scenery in most of the European countries during the 19th century had an individualistic view of society. To solve all the problems it was sufficient to follow the market rules and to have competition. The liberals saw in the "social question" a problem of the single worker who was not able to use the market rules for his own advantage or who was not working hard enough. Since society was thought of as a mere conglomeration of individuals, there was no further question of just wages, of human conditions of work, of integration of the workers into the industrial society.

On the opposite the social question led to the socialist revolution. Karl Marx developed his ideology on the grounds of historic and dialectic materialism and his analysis of the capitalist society. According to him the original sin was the private property destroying the collective unity of human beings and dividing society into classes: here the capitalists, there the proletarians. In Russia the communist revolution took place in 1917; in many western European countries the communist and the socialist parties became a major and even a decisive power in policy.

In the new industrial centres the Church in its pastoral work has been confronted with the "social question". In Germany, in France, in Italy, in Austria and in Switzerland there were priests and lay people considering the situation and working conditions in the fabrics. They were shocked by the misery of many workers and their families. In many ways they criticised sharply the capitalist society. The famous bishop of Mainz, Wilhelm Ketteler, and Pope Leo XIII - he published the first social enzyclica *Rerum novarum* (1891) - revived the thinking of Thomas Aquinas on private property and its social obligations. They were convinced that neither the liberals nor the revolutionary socialists were able to solve the social question. They insisted on just wages and on social policy of the state to change the capitalist system.

As for all others, for Christians as well it was not easy to understand and to analyse the new industrial system, to detect the faults, to adapt the ethical orientations to the modern conditions of work and to find out new ways to organise the economy in a just way. The social teaching of the Church is not a mere pastoral endeavour, but it has to provide guidelines of orientation. Its "authority" depends on rational arguing so that all, who are interested in, also scientists and politicians can follow the argumentation or can argue against it. Therefore the scientific reflection on the issues and problems is very essential. In preparing the social teaching of the Church the German Jesuit Heinrich Pesch played a major role. He advocated "solidarism" in contrast to individualistic liberalism and collectivist socialism. Man is not an individuum; from his very nature he has a social dimension and only within society he can develop his abilities and possibilities. Pesch used the expression: "Der Mensch inmitten der Gesellschaft" (man in the midst of society). Society is not a mere conglomeration, but a unity; the single ones are united in pursuing the common aims and purposes.

After his philosophical and theological studies G. Gundlach, who had joined the Society of Jesus, was asked to continue the work of Heinrich Pesch.[3] For a better understanding of the industrial economy he studied at Humboldt University in Berlin and gained his doctorate in 1927 under

---

3   GUNDLACH: (1961, 1931).

Werner Sombart, the noted economist and researcher into capitalism.[4] He became well acquainted with the elements and methods of economical sciences and equally with the massive criticism of the capitalist system, as it was practised by the historical and ethical schools but, above all, by the "welfare policy" of Adolph Wagner, whose lectures Heinrich Pesch already had listened to. The end of the period of high capitalism had come with the crash of the New York Stock Exchange (1929) and the world economic crisis unleashed by it.

Social Catholicism in Germany and Austria was in a difficult situation after the First World War. The social encyclical *"Rerum novarum"* had worked as a guide, but the different positions in practice and in theory sharpened. A fundamental clarification became necessary as to whether or not the capitalist economic system was compatible with the social ethical orientations of the Christian understanding of man and society. Gundlach very soon was given the opportunity to clear up the differences and uncertainties.

With regard to the social teaching of the Church Gundlach belonged to the small group of priests and catholic scientists preparing papers for the social encyclical *"Quadragesimo Anno"* (1931). The contribution of Gundlach was of particular significance. Especially he was responsible for the formulation of the principle of subsidiarity.[5] After the Second World War this principle has been recognised throughout the world.

The principle of subsidiarity arises from the reflection on the human person as the origin, the basis and the aim of all social life ("Die menschliche Person ist Ursprung, Träger und Ziel allen gesellschaftlichen Lebens"). In this way Gundlach deepened the concept of Solidarism and the Christian understanding of man and society. All social life is based on the human person. Also the social structures have to correspond to this. Already H. Pesch pointed out, that the family, the private property and the state are the necessary institutions of social life. Gundlach followed these lines and insisted in many articles on the importance of the personal foundation of social life. Gundlach's strength lay in the social-philosophical consideration of life, to which a practical ethical and political sense was added.

---

4 SOMBART (1902), cf. the instructive observation by KUMPMANN (1929, pp. 3f.).
5 VON NELL-BREUNING (1972).

II. What is Capitalism?

Anyone who is concerned with Gundlach's writings - they were collected following his death by the "Katholische Sozialwissenschaftliche Zentralstelle" and published in two volumes in 1964[6] - must be surprised at first glance by the fact that in their nearly 1400 pages there is no article dealing with "Capitalism".[7] That admittedly does not mean that Gundlach had not concerned himself intensively with the elements of Capitalism and come back to them again and again in many of his articles.

A lecture, which Gundlach gave in 1945 in the "Istituto Cattolico di Attivitá Sociale" on "Socialism and Communism" is illuminating. In it he stated that he regarded these social systems as belonging to the "Capitalist century" or, as the case may be, to the "Epoch of Capitalism" just as he regarded the system of individualistic Liberalism as belonging to them.[8] The "capitalist system" had developed gradually since the end of the 17th Century. Gundlach named three preconditions, which should usher in a completely new development in the economy and society. As far as the political level was concerned, the old political system, local and corporate barriers had fallen. The old social classes and the corporations had had their day. From now on the way was free for the individual, who managed his own private wealth. At the same time - and this is the second precondition - modern technology had begun to celebrate its triumph over inorganic nature with the invention of the steam engine and electricity and had placed itself at the disposition of the economy. Thirdly, reference was made to the great increase of population in the new industrial regions, that provided a growing pool of labour force for free work contracts during the first decades of the new era.

With this, the time for the "capitalist entrepreneur" had dawned. The "Capitalist" is a man, who with the help of "Capital", i.e. with his own saved and unconsumed income or that of others invests, in a free contract, the means of production (land, buildings, machines, raw materials) and personnel (workers and staff employees) to produce goods that have a cash

---

6 GUNDLACH (1964).
7 Cf. with this: BRIEFS (1925), BAUER (1959), KAUFHOLD (1987), KOSLOWSKI (1987).
8 GUNDLACH (1964, Vol. 2, p. 65).

value, which he brings to the market in order, once again, to obtain from the corresponding profit the capital which had been invested. He then repeats the same process with increased and improved means of production, i.e. with the greatest possible investment of capital in the shortest possible time.

In this article, which was published in 1945, the results of research into Capitalism were included as well as elements of the Marxist analysis of the economy and society. New, to be sure, was the central role, which according to Gundlach devolved upon the entrepreneur. In this respect the discovery of the entrepreneur by Joseph A. Schumpeter[9] was reflected, whereas there was no place in the classical economic sciences for the entrepreneur in the course of supply and demand workings of the market. Even Karl Marx had no knowledge of the entrepreneur, but only of the capitalist exploiter.

Let us follow for a moment the way Gundlach's thinking went. The entrepreneur believed himself to be absolutely free in the investment of the capital (where, when, why) - free in his contracts in regard to the material means of production and in respect of the human work-force; free in the profit margins, that is in the greatest possible increase of his capital. "Whoever observes the great development of the human economy in the 19th Century can see what was achieved objectively by this economic system. There is a growing volume of production in ever greater choice and quality and this is the case not just in Europe but also in America."[10]

He went on to say that the entrepreneur was the "much abused bourgeois", from whom the capitalist era received its first and fundamental stamp. In this way of looking at Capitalism there was no swing towards a hidden yearning for the old order, such as it has been frequently attributed to the Catholic view of the world. Neither did it contain that radical critique which became for Karl Marx the occasion for the outline for his materialistic conception of history and for his analysis of the capitalist system, which no longer seemed capable of reform and curable, but which could only break out into a revolution for Socialism. With Grundlach emerged a fundamentally positive attitude to the new ways of the economy, which is in the position to provide the greatly increased population with goods and services at low cost and also to create the necessary work places. In this regard Gundlach finds himself along the lines of both Bishop Ketteler and Pope

---

9   SCHUMPETER (1928).
10 GUNDLACH (1964, Vol. 2, p. 66).

Leo XIII in *Rerum novarum*, who did not condemn the capitalist system and held it to be capable of being reformed.

On the other hand Gundlach was not, like the Liberals and the "Progressives" blind to the disastrous consequences, almost unimaginable today, which the capitalist economic system brought about in the social structure of society. It was no less of a characteristic that the bourgeoisie formed on the one side and the proletariat on the other. These were the people, whom the capitalist with capital at his disposal took into his service with the help of contracts for work. The workers possessed no capital and had no means of production at their disposal. In order to earn a livelihood for themselves and their families, they were forced to offer their labour to the owner of the means of production. They did this voluntarily and were therefore not slaves in a legal sense; but the state of necessity out of which they offered their labour robbed them of their independence and liberty as well as of all that affects labour contract from start to finish and the conditions of the same, particularly wages and working hours. "It is the constant lack of freedom, caused by the non-ownership of the means of production, that is the characteristic feature of the proletariat. The concept of a proletariat does not depend on the question of low wage."[11]

What Gundlach was getting at was not primarily the wage level, neither was it the formal liberty of the labour contract but a real freedom, which is only understood by the worker when the need to have to offer his labour is done away with at least at its core. To overcome the conditions of being a proletarian can finally only happen through the acquisition and creation of property, since it removes the coercion, which is a burden to the workers. This charge regarding the lack of freedom stands in radical opposition to the Marxist analysis.

III. The Crisis of Society and State

The collapse of the feudal and craft-guild social order, which had become powerless and meaningless, made possible the rise of the liberal burgess class with its watchword of "free" property, "free" competition and

---

11 *Op. cit.*

"free" development of self-interest.[12] From a sociological viewpoint, Gundlach remarked that liberal-bourgeois theory saw the ideal of society in the greatest possible number of independent individuals not too much at variance in their economic and social power. Part and parcel of this ideal was the conception of a wide, where possible an unlimited, economic area, where the competition of the individuals could develop fully. In this system "property and education" were the maxims of the liberal bourgeoisie. The state, which had sought to incorporate the economy and society in the period of princely absolutism, was forced politically out of these areas, so that one may plainly say of it that the state, in its Hegelian sense, had been "set aside" in bourgeois society.

In reality, however, the alleged dissolution of the relationships of state and society in the liberal sense of the "bourgeois society" was a fiction, as Gundlach stressed in a 1932 lecture.[13] Into the place of the free economic society based on the competition of many independent individuals stepped the growing concentration and domination of power in the whole economy. One year previously Pope Pius XI had likewise spoken in *Quadragesimo Anno* (No. 105 ff.) of the "domination of power in the economy", of which the final phase of high capitalism bore the stamp. Gundlach reached the conclusion that the hoped for self-control of the competing individuals did not function. In the case of Pius XI, it read thus, - that competition left to itself could not establish any order in society (No.88) but led to domination by whoever happened to be the more powerful.[14]

The reverse side of the liberal-individualistic approach was the increasing exploitation and impoverishment of many workers. Socialism unmasked the ideal of the bourgeois society as a fiction. It destroyed the liberal-bourgeois notion of the supposed and never attained regulatory function of the ownership of capital left to its own devices, of free competition and of unrestrained self-interest. Socialism believed in the power of the institutional and in the magic effect of social centralisation and control. "In the place of the myth of the individual without any social responsibilities it sets

---

12 GUNDLACH (1964, Vol. 2, p. 66).
13 *Op. cit.*, p. 106.
14 It is noteworthy that the founder of the Neoliberalism too, W. Eucken, recognised the danger that the tendency to its own self-annulment is inherent in free competition, if it is not embedded in an order framework to be set up by the state.

the myth of 'society' and its regulatory function.»[15] Gundlach spoke of a "collective individualism" at the foundations of Socialism and qualified it as a child of the capitalist era.

How does Catholicism stand in relation to the capitalist economic system and to the changes and developments in society? In Catholicism in Germany and Austria for a long time there were very diverse reactions and trends, but there were these in Switzerland, Belgium, France and Italy too. This was related to the fact that Catholicism was quite familiar with the traditional forms of life in the economy, in society, in culture and politics and to the fact that the Church had propagated the basic values of the Gospel and of the Christian view of man and society, but that the new groupings in society and politics and, above all, the new capitalist economic system had not been looked into for a long time. Church and Catholicism were not alone in such a helpless situation. Even the economic and social sciences found it a difficult task - in spite of the efforts of Adam Smith and so-called classic economists - to analyse the new ways of production (capital, division of labour, questions of wages), to identify the causes of the "social question" and to look for ways to resolve it. The analyses of the causes were often contradictory as were the positions of the political parties, which ranged from the prevailing Liberal movement to the decidedly conservative Agrarians; and it took a long time before Socialism was able to reach and organise the workers, a fact that is still today hardly reflected in most of the history books.

Within Catholicism, it was agreed that the exploitation of the working class and the impoverishment of many workers and their families could not be tolerated. They were not consonant with the orientation of Christian values and with church traditions in Europe. But there was no agreement as to opinion regarding the capitalist economic system. On the one side there was a marked "anti-capitalism", which was to be found early on among the so-called romantics such as Adam Müller and later, first and foremost, in the Viennese School around Karl von Vogelsang.[16] The division of labour

---

15 GUNDLACH (1964, Vol. 2, p. 108).
16 The question became acute once again following the encyclical of Paul VI *Populorum progressio* (26th March 1967) and the Offenburg Declaration of the Social Committee of the CDU of the 9th of July, 1967: see RAUSCHER (1968), (with contributions, among others, from G. BRIEFS, J. MESSNER, O. VON NELL-BREUNING, W. WEBER).

and the functional separation of labour and capital, the idea of competition and individualism were all rejected; the contract-wage was held to be incompatible with the dignity of man and there was a desire to return to pre-industrial conditions. On the other side stood the "realists", who did not condemn the capitalist economic system bag and baggage but regarded it as being capable of social reform. For more than one century social Catholicism concentrated on this theme: the reform of society (Franz von Buß, Bishop Ketteler, Franz Hitze, the "Volksverein für das katholische Deutschland" (The Peoples' Union for the Catholic Germany"), Heinrich Pesch, Gustav Gundlach und Oswald von Nell-Breuning). The great goal was to bring into the capitalist economic system social structures and to build a society of justice and solidarity.

Gundlach did not stand on the side of the "eternally retrogressives", who were unable to loose themselves from the feudal and craft-guildsman forms.[17] He was open-minded in respect of freedom for the individual and for the development of self-interest, also in regard to the importance of competition and of the market. This realistic basic attitude affected his perception of the changes that had occurred in society. The separation of labour and capital in the production process had led to new groupings around the labour market: the organised "classes" of the owners of the means of production and of the workers. With regard to their position in the economic process and to the distribution of the economic yield, the class struggle became violent.

IV. Classes, Class Struggle, Class Society

Since the earlier deep gulf between the classes in the socially advanced industrial states has been overcome, one can scarcely realise today how difficult it was for socially engaged Catholicism to understand and acknowledge the reality of the classes and of the class struggle. In his analysis Karl Marx had uncovered this state of affairs and incorporated it into his ideology. For many Catholics that was reason enough to avoid this terminology and, in its place, to speak of the "Stand" and "Standwerdung" of the work-

---

17 GUNDLACH (1964, Vol. 2, p. 109).

ers.[18] Above all, Catholic workers wanted nothing to do with the atheistic and materialist philosophy of revolutionary Socialism. When, in 1929/31, Gundlach wrote the articles "Class", "Class Struggle" and the "Proletariat" in the new edition of the State Lexicon and reclaimed these matters of fact for the Christian-realistic way of looking at things too, it came to protests within social Catholicism, precisely even from the Catholic workers' movement.[19]

For Gundlach classes and "Stände" were social differentiations within the one social unity. It is worthwhile to cite the central parts in his own words:

> Social group ranking, therefore, is on a basis of being drawn from a large grouping of the same or similar professional organisation organised and working in co-operation with the other professional associations of a similar type in the same State and from among the same people with the aim of putting the 'welfare of the public' - this is the aim of the state - into practice in a specified and lasting manner. If, however, a concrete state of affairs of the bonum commune, is no longer recognised by one section of the members of the State as meaningful, i.e. as an appropriate means to make possible the welfare of all members of the State and it is defended by another section as an appropriate means against the first, then the individuals joining together to a common purpose either for or against the actual state of affairs of the 'public welfare' form classes. The class is therefore a large group organised within a State with the purpose, through debate with another large group of a similar type, of combating as contrary to or, as the case may be, of defending as sensible a specific form of the 'public welfare', of the bonum commune.[20]

Whereas die "Stände" in the old social order had been related to the unity of society as having vital functional and professional cohesion, the class structure in society was related to the contrast between ownership and

---

18 This terminology was to be found also among socialist writers: MEYER (1874), RODBERTUS JAGETZOW (1875).

19 JOS. PETERS had turned against Gundlach in the *Germania* - the Catholic national newspaper - under the title "Christian Class Struggle?", because his articles on "Class" and "Class Struggle" were being taken up by the so-called Catholic Socialists. GUNDLACH defended his position against this blame (1964, pp. 217-223).

20 GUNDLACH (1964, Vol. 2, p. 207).

non-ownership - with here owners of the means of production and there wage-slaves. The functional split between labour and capital in the production process becomes the occasion for the organisation of the society into classes, which fight against each other to push through their own interests. For Gundlach, the class struggle is, under these circumstances, an appropriate means, possibly even a necessary means, whereby society overcomes the class split and the organic purpose of the State, namely the 'public welfare' will again be achieved.[21]

Does the application of the concept of class and class struggle mean that the analytical matrix of the capitalist economic system revealed by Karl Marx has been taken over? On the one hand, Gundlach has not shrunk back from including these concepts in the Christian-social viewpoint, since they expressed the real conditions then dominating the labour market and society. On the other hand, he was intent on thrashing out the essential differences from Marxism, in order not to allow misunderstandings to arise either among the Christian workers or in the Church to whose mission the social teaching also belongs.[22] For Marxism, the classes and the class struggle are a product of "the" economy, because it is not man who determines the economy but the economy that determines man and his social development. For Gundlach the splitting of society into classes is a sign of the grave disease in the economic society and the class struggle has the recuperation of society, i.e. the overcoming of the class society as its aim. Marxism, which denies the moral foundation of the State and of its being ordered for the benefit of the people, for whom also the classes are not directed at the renewal of society, - this Marxism aspires to the "socialised" stateless and classless man as the ultimate condition. The Christian view of class and the class struggle is on the contrary directed at the reform of society and the restoration of public welfare.

Here too the contrast once again becomes clear with the liberal economic conception, which derives from a juxtaposition of atomised individuals, who have been abandoned to the free play of forces.[23] The social living together and the unity of the people in the realisation of the joint aims and purposes ensues in this viewpoint all but automatically, following a "natural law" that is supposed to bring about the "harmony of interests" as a conse-

---

21 *Op. cit.*, pp. 208 f.
22 *Op. cit.*, pp. 214 f.
23 *Op. cit.*, pp. 215 f.

quence of everybody's competition. Social power, even the organisation of the interests can only upset this process. Man's social dimension, his ties in society are denied. In the same way there is no understanding of the social power and the shaping of the public order and law in the sense of the bonum commune. Even the formation of the classes in society is not identified as a reaction to the fiction of an economy free of the State. The individualistic view of economy and society opens up no access to the perception of the tensions and dislocations within society, not even to the mission of the State to intervene for the benefit of the working class. On this account the bourgeoisie has for a long time defended itself against every type of association, against the formation of organisations with common interests among the workers and trade unions and against the idea of regulation of the labour and wages conditions and, not last in the queue, against the State's welfare policy, which finds their intrinsic explanation in the service to "public welfare" that is to be granted by the State.

V. The Renewal of Society

In many aspects Gundlach influenced by his ideas and arguments the social encyclical *Quadragesimo Anno*. As already mentioned this held true primarily for the principle of subsidiarity (Nos. 79 and 80). This principle stands not only against collectivist ideologies and a wrong dominance of the centralised political power, but also against concentration of economic and social power. This held true as well for the realistic study of the situation in the labour-market, the grouping of the participants in "two classes, so to speak on two battlefronts" and the class struggle, who made the labour-market into a "battlefield" (No. 83), whereas in truth capital and labour are in need of another (No. 53). Without strong regulations free competition cannot avoid the dominance of economic power (Nos. 105-108). The question of whether the wage contract and the wage system were at all acceptable as a central part of the capitalist economic system was particularly a matter of dispute among Catholics. The encyclical laid down that the wage contract could not "of itself be characterised as unjust and its substitution by the feudal contract be demanded" (No. 64). One would have to distinguish the capitalist organisation of economy, which stood in need of an arrangement that was just and could not be fashioned without regard to the human dignity of the worker, without regard to the social character of the economy, without regard to the common good and the social justice (No. 101) - between all that and the "abominable class warfare" in the viewpoint of Communism and Socialism (No. 112 and No.114). The thought that the proletariat could be overcome, in the final analysis, only by enabling the workers to become also proprietors is likewise a concern of Gundlach, even if, in the encyclical, it is mentioned not the absence of freedom but the insecurity of the workers. Gundlach's thinking is traceable in a special way in the analysis of the individualistic spirit as the prime cause of disorder in society and of absence of responsibility by the State for the welfare of the public (Nos. 78, 99, 88).

If the capitalist system is not of itself bad and the "social question" is to be traced back to the incompetence of economic liberalism to build up effective and in time social structures, then the question comes back to the title, which is named at the beginning of *Quadragesimo Anno*: "The social order, its restoration and its building according to the message of the Gospel". The reform of society had been the main aim of social Catholicism since the 19th Century. Gundlach too made it his own with the analysis that a class society is sick and in need of restoration. The answer that the encyclical gave was the recommendation to build up an "order based on professional groupings".

With the article "Stand; Ständewesen" (Professional Grouping) Gundlach had certainly furnished preparatory studies. Of course he did not want a return to the old craft-guilds arrangement.[24] His positive evaluation of the capitalist economic system with its extraordinarily high productivity was already speaking quite another language. Moreover, in comparison with contemporary essays on order based on professional groupings, the cautious reserve with which Gundlach expressed himself on this question of society is remarkable. In the article on "Berufsständische Ordnung" from the year of 1957 he raised the question of why Leo XIII in *Rerum novarum* did not seize on the enthusiasm for the Middle Ages passed on by the Romantics and take up the idea of professional order.[25] Although Catholic circles in Vienna (Karl von Vogelsang) and Fribourg/Schweiz (Bishop Mermillod) were exerting pressure in Rome together with the later Cardinal Jacobini,

---

24 *Op. cit.*, pp. 237-247.
25 *Op. cit.*, pp. 236-288.

the Pope held back. Gundlach surmised that the American Cardinal Gibbons, to whom the idea of professional order was wholly unknown, had made an intervention. Ludwig von Hertling alludes to this in his book on the history of the Catholic Church in America. The revival of this idea in *Quadragesimo Anno* was connected, for Gundlach, with the development of the economy to a machine absolutely dominated by the great powers instead of social structures, with continuing class antagonisms between the employers and the employed and with the incapacity of the State to utilise its power of regulation yet more strongly in favour of public welfare for the working masses.

Even after the break through of "Social Market Economy" in Germany Gundlach was of the opinion that the idea of professional order was suitable as a regulating framework for economy and also for organising the social life between individual people and the State. Perhaps he was still under the influence of the fateful class structures in Europe, so that he did not sufficiently value the new social structures, which were arising with the reconstruction of Germany and also in the countries of western and southern Europe. This is true, above all, for the system of tariff autonomy that, really only since 1945, has become part of the economic and social regulating power. It is also true for the Welfare State, which sought to fashion public welfare comprehensively and of which the integration into modern society of employees is to be seen as the core part. Had Gundlach who was teaching in Rome experienced close-up the deep transformation which happened with the establishment of the Social Market Economy and had he the opportunity of intensive talks and discussions with economists and social scientists, then he would probably have perceived that the main concern of the regulating power in society determines for a good deal the scope of the aims of the tariff-partners and of social policy, even if a healthy scepticism were to remain in respect of the dangers of individualism, such as are being discussed today by the communitarists.

In the whole, one should not overlook the fact that to Gundlach's way of thinking three institutions are necessary for the canalisation of power in society: the family, private property, which makes the necessary freedom possible for workers too, and the State. The many questions, which are posed today in all three areas and which indicate the major and minor deficiencies in the social relationships in Germany and in many countries of Europe, show the considerable need for reforms, which we have to care for also in the advanced societies.

References

BOER, C.: "Kapitalismus", in: *Staatslexikon*, 4 Vol., 6th ed. (1959), pp. 813-833.
BRIEFS, G.: "Die Wirtschafts- und sozialpolitiscen Ideen des Katholizismus", in: *Die Wirtschaftswissenschaft nach dem Kriege*, (München und Leipzig) 1925.
DIE KATHOLISCH-SOZIALE TAGUNG IN WIEN, Wien (Volksbund-Verlag) 1929.
GUNDLACH, G., S. J.: "Solidarismus", in: *Staatslexikon*, Vol. IV, 5th ed. (1931), pp. 1613-1621.
GUNDLACH, G., S. J.: "Sombart", in: *Staatslexikon*, Vol. VII 6th ed. (1962), pp. 122-125.
GUNDLACH, G., S.J.: *Die Ordnung der menschlichen Gesellschaft*, Vol. 1 and 2, Köln 1964.
GUNDLACH, G., S. J.: "Pesch, Heinrich", in: *Staatslexikon*, Vol. VI, 6th ed. (1961), pp. 226-229.
KAUFHOLD, K. H., KOSLOWSKI, P.: "Kapitalismus", in: *Staatslexikon*, Vol. 3, 7th ed. (1987), pp. 294-308.
KUMPMANN, K.: *Kapitalismus und Sozialismus*, Essen 1929.
MEYER, R.: *Der Emanzipationskampf des vierten Standes*, Berlin 1874.
NELL-BREUNING, O. V.: *Wie sozial ist die Kirche? Leistung und Versagen der katholischen Soziallehre*, Düsseldorf 1972, pp. 97-136.
PESCH, H., S. J.: *Lehrbuch der Nationalökonomie*, Vol. 1: Grundlegung, Freiburg I. Br., 3d and 4th eds. 1924.
RAUSCHER, A. (Ed.): *Ist die katholische Soziallehre antikapitalistisch?*, Köln 1968.
RAUSCHER, A.: "Gustav Gundlach (1892 - 1965)", in: MORSEY, R. (Ed.): *Zeitgeschichte in Lebensbildern*, Vol. 2, Mainz (1975) pp. 159-176.
RODBERTUS-JAGETZOW, K.: *Zur Beleuchtung der sozialen Frage*, Berlin 1875.
SCHWARTE, J.: *Gustav Gundlach S. J., (1892 - 1963). Maßgeblicher Repräsentant der katholischen Soziallehre während der Pontifikate Pius' XI und Pius' XII*, Paderborn 1975.
SCHUMPETER, J. A.: "Unternehmer", *Handwörterbuch der Sozialwissenschaften*, Jena 4th ed. (1928), pp. 476-487.
SOMBART, W.: *Der moderne Kapitalismus*, Vol. 1/2, Leipzig 1902.
SOMBART, W.: *Der moderne Kapitalismus. Historisch-systematische Darstellung des gesamteurop ischen Wirtschaftslebens von seinen Anfängen bis zur Gegenwart*, Vol 1, München and Leipzig 1928.
STRIEDER, J.: *Zur Genesis des modernen Kapitalismus*, Leipzig 1904.

Discussion Summary

ELKE SCHWINGER

Paper discussed:
ANTON RAUSCHER: Theory and Critique of Capitalism in Gustav Gundlach

The discussion of the contribution about Gundlach was concentrated in its first part to the question about the special meaning of the central category of Gundlach's work, the "Berufsständische Ordnung" ("Order of the Professions' Associations"). In the second part of the discussion there dominated the question about the important influence of the Catholics to the German debate as to how to deal with the problems of capitalism.

To understand the meaning of "Berufständische Ordnung", at first it is necessary to give a theoretical definition. The differentiation of the theological background of the social mission led certainly to the thomistic idea of the "bonum commune" (NÖRR), but the most important influence has to be seen in the tradition of the Spanish late scholasticism especially concerning the problems of economic justice. In the 19th century these theoretical impacts were awakened by Franz Baader and they found their culmination in the works of Gundlach and Nell-Breuning (RAUSCHER). To understand the central ideas in the Catholic tradition is only possible by considering the Catholic conception of human beings as persons, in contrast to the conception of human beings as mere individuals (NÖRR): Every single man is regarded as gifted with free will and responsibility, but he also needs the society for his personal development. In this conception of human nature the social dimension is already ontologically included and does not depend on the free will, the needs or the opportunities as individualistic approaches maintain. To say it with Pesch: "Der Mensch steht inmitten der Gesellschaft". The social dimension in the Christian social doctrine does not only mean a number of interpersonal relationships, but the whole social structures of the community the human is living in (RAUSCHER). It is possible to compare this idea of the social dimension with the institutionalistic ap-

DISCUSSION SUMMARY

proaches, but there is one little difference: In the Christian belief there is an inalienable self (PEUKERT) and not only single persons but also the institutions are included in the social responsibility to serve all members of the social community (RAUSCHER).

For the idea of the "Berufsständische Ordnung" the following theoretical consequences in the economic field emerge: First, there are no class-differences: Entrepreneurs and employees should both be jointly organised at the branch-level without the possibility of state interference, which has characterised the difference to the totalitarian forms of corporatism under the NS-Regime. And second, the employees should be shareholders in the firms to overcome the status of wage earners only. Nell-Breuning has written about this special basic element in the "Wörterbuch der Politik" (1949), as well as Johannes Messner in his publication about the "Berufsständische Ordnung" (1945). But for Messner the idea disappeared in his classical work "Die Soziale Frage" (RAUSCHER). The theoretical definition of "Berufsständische Ordnung" was supplemented in the debate with comments of Gundlach and Nell-Breuning to the existing forms of corporatism after World War I. So after 1920 Italy had been organised pretty much in the "berufsständische" or corporatist form of order (HASELBACH). But the main difference of the concept of "Berufsständische Ordnung" and the Italian system and the NS-time also was that in Italy and Germany the state practically organised the corporations. In Germany during the NS-time there were no classes, no professional associations, because the workers were organised together with the entrepreneurs and these corporations were directed by the state government, especially the NS-party. In *Quadrogesimo Anno* these structures were criticised. In the Weimar Republic there was a continuous class struggle and no possibility to regulate this conflicting interests by a tariff-system. For that reason Gundlach and Nell-Breuning reminded us of the idea of professional associations. There has been only one attempt to realise this social construction in Austria. But it failed, because the state had a greater impact on these professional associations. After 1945 the system of the social market economy was also accepted by the workers, and therefore the idea of "Berufsständische Ordnung" was no longer interesting. Nell-Breuning himself was convinced in this concept as practical advice, but he thought that it was a too demanding concept to be practically relevant.

The second part of the discussion was centred around the historical phenomenon that the Catholic teaching became very important for the German debate about capitalism and its social problems. For KOSLOWSKI this phe-

DISCUSSION SUMMARY

nomenon can be explained by sociological reasons. Looking at the history of Germany you can see that the social policy of the "Zentrumspartei" and the Catholic church has been very influential in spite of the smaller number of Catholics in the country. On the one hand, the Catholic position was the position of a minority, but on the other hand, this minority had a very special impact on the German social politics, which it had in no other European country except Belgium. But in contrast to the Protestant social reformers the Catholics were able to unify their members during the time of the "Kaiserreich". The sociological explanation to this could be a very high degree of organisation of the Catholic reformers in contrast to the Protestants. In this way a third stream of teaching and of discussion concerning the problems of capitalism developed. A stream, which is situated between liberalism and socialism and which is still quite powerful (KOSLOWSKI). RAUSCHER's reply to this sociological deliberations about the influential role of the Catholic teaching in social politics was that this development of the leading position of the Catholic church depended on two factors: special persons, personalities and special historical occasions. One of such historical occasions, which could also explain the higher degree of organisation of the Catholic reformers, was the "Kulturkampf". Wilhelm von Ketteler, Bishop of Mayence in the 19th century, can serve as an example of a person with a great influence. He had a tremendous impact on this development. He was very well informed and he continuously tried to extend his know-how about economics and social politics. For example, through contacts with socialist leaders and thinkers like Lasalle. In practice Ketteler initiated two examples of productive associations in his diocese, but they did not work. As a consequence, Ketteler changed his position in social politics and came to the conclusion that only the state can act in favour of the workers. This idea, named "Soziale Monarchie", was also created by thinkers like Lasalle or Lorenz von Stein. Another example of the importance of personal influence in the Catholic church is Hitze. Hitze was a priest and a representative in the parliament. He was the founder of the "Arbeiterschutzpolitik". Last but not least, as a reply to the question about the idea of "subsidiarity" (WOHLGEMUTH), it became clear that Gundlach's work gave an important and decisive impulse for the realisation of this idea as a principle of German social politics. In a matter of dialectic process there are special persons and historical occasions working together to form the great influence of Catholic teaching. (RAUSCHER).

Part Five

Historism in Other Schools of Economics

Chapter 12

Intensive and Extensive Mobilisation in the Japanese Economy: An Interpretation of Japanese Capitalism in Historical Perspective

KIICHIRO YAGI

I.	Developmentalism Debate
II.	Efficient Bureaucracy or Civil Society
III.	Developmentalism After 1945
IV.	Mobilisation Under a Dual-structured Society
V.	Totalitarian Mobilisation
VI.	From the Extensive Mobilisation to the Intensive Mobilisation
VII.	Present Crisis of the Japanese Mobilisation System

> "The independence of the nation is the purpose. In this situation our civilisation is the art to attain this purpose." Yukichi Fukuzawa (1875)[1]

I. Developmentalism Debate

Giving a glance to the collapse of the etatist socialist economies, the late Professor Murakami predicted the emergence of the "developmentalism

---

1 YUKICHI FUKUZAWA: "Bunmei Ron no Gairyaku" (A Summary of Civilisation), 1875, in: KEIO GIJUKU (Ed.): *Fukuzawa Yukichi Zenshu* (Collected Works), Tokyo (Iwanami) 1959, vol. 4, p. 209. I quoted Fukuzawa to show that the developmentalist strategy does not collide with the best enlightenment thought in a late starting nation.

debate" in the intellectual world that had been so far occupied by the great debate on "socialism."[2] The term "developmentalism" signifies here a general attitude of developing nations to whom the state-lead industrialisation has priority in the shaping of the society with liberal democratic ideals.[3] Based on the experience of Japan and other newly industrialised economies in Asia, Murakami concluded that "developmentalism" retained its attractiveness to the nations who felt themselves challenged by mighty advanced competitors.

"Developmentalism" does not deny modern ideals such as individualism, liberalism and democracy whose theory comes basically from the Western world. It even counts them as main causes of its legitimacy, particularly when it is confronted by such enemies as communism or reactionary fundamentalism. In this sense, "developmentalism" is a version of modernisation theory that does not make a radical break with the course of Western nations. Leaders in this camp could be considered as modernists or Westernisers.[4] However, developmentalists' praise for modern ideals is restricted in the sense that it does not believe the effectiveness of those ideals in the very process through which the advanced stage is to be attained. Therefore, it propagates a modification of those ideals according to which such elements as state and community take a significant role in guiding free actions of individuals.

---

2 YASUSUKE MURAKAMI: *Han-Koten no Keizaigaku*, 2 vols., Tokyo (Chuo-Koronsha) 1992 (English edition: *An Anti-classical Political-Economic Analysis: A Vision for the Next Century*, (Stanford University Press) 1996, vol. 1, p. 50, translated by Kozo Yamamura).

3 "Developmentalism is such an economic system whose basic frame consists of private property and market economy (i.e. capitalism) but permits government intervention to the market with a long-run perspective so long as it serves for the goal of industrialisation (i.e., continuous per capita growth of production). Clearly developmentalism is a politico-economical system that is established on the state (or similar political community) as its unit. In many cases, certain limitations (monarchy, one-party system, military dictatorship etc.) are added to the parliament democracy." MURAKAMI: *ibid.*, vol. 2, pp. 5-6.

4 Some sympathetic observers even conclude that a paradoxical tendency to produce the basis for the transformation to a new stage of society which fits more to the modern liberal democratic ideals is inherent in this type of economic development.

MOBILISATION IN THE JAPANESE ECONOMY

The modern history of Japan apparently offers us evidence for this general attitude of "developmentalism." "Developmentalism" in Japan formed itself as a reaction of nationalist leaders as well as intellectuals who recognised the significance of the newly founded Meiji state in the catching-up process to the advanced Western nations. The Meiji state was to them a project for the future, not the outcome of the existing social structure. Of course, a state could not be maintained without the firm support of a mighty base in the society. The existence of the state (government-people relations) promoted the formation of interest groups out of the existing or emerging social structure. The real modern Japanese state was, therefore, the mixture of the project for the future (industrialisation/modernisation) and existing/emerging social interests.

In establishing this developmentalist project, Japanese politicians looked for a model of modernisation. At last they found Germany,[5] which had accomplished its national unification led by Prussia just a few years after the Meiji Restoration. Not only the monarchical structure of the new-born German state but also its effective control system over the people attracted Japanese politicians who had been annoyed by the demand of parliamentary constitution. After the split of the government in 1881, the dominance of the German model in Japan became apparent year by year. Young scholars and ambitious bureaucrats who returned from Germany introduced German ways of learning as well as administration. Also in economics, German influence gradually surpassed the economic liberalism of British or French economists; and the first Japanese academic society was organised in 1897 as a Japanese miniature of the German Verein für Sozialpolitik.[6] However, the influence of the German Historical School over Japanese academicians was only a part of the total concept of developmentalism in Japan. The position of developmentalism and the choice of the German model existed before the influence of particular theories or of individual scholars. In this chapter, therefore, instead of dealing with German influences in economics, I will concentrate on the problem of developmentalism in the modern history of Japan.

---

5 See B. MARTIN (Ed.): *Japans Weg in die Moderne. Ein Sonderweg nach Deutschem Vorbild?*, Frankfurt a. M. (Campus Verlag) 1987.
6 For German readers: cf. YAGI: "Wirtschaftswissenschaften und Modernisierung Japans," *The Kyoto University Economic Review*, LX, no. 1-2 (April-October 1990).

Socialism or communism, too, was often considered as an ideology of industrialisation. It had also affinity to the "developmentalism" in its ambiguous praise of modern ideals. However, socialism was itself a clear break with Western way of industrialisation in the sense that it propagated totally different institutions and denied private property and free exchange at least in the core part of the economy. Compared with the socialist/communist alternative, the "developmentalism" was still a modification of the capitalist pattern of industrialisation. It retained basic elements of the market economy and encouraged the self-interest of individuals as far as it was in accordance with the overall national course of development. If one can count the Meiji state in the series of developmentalist states, developmentalism has a longer history than the centralised socialist economy that first emerged after the Russian revolution. However, the practice of the planned economy of socialists impressed policy makers of developmentalist states so heavily that its influence brought developmentalist states such as Japan to a higher stage of mobilisation.

II. Efficient Bureaucracy or Civil Society

As many economists argue, there is no "rationale" for state intervention as far as it is considered statically. Murakami's argument is based on his view of the general tendency of diminishing cost (increasing return) in the process of industrialisation. As A. Marshall taught, one century ago, competitive equilibrium is impossible and monopoly is the only stable state in the industry where marginal cost diminishes as production increases. This reasoning has some affinity with socialists' argument for an etatist monopolised economy based on the economy of scale. However, this tendency is not clear to anyone at the beginning. The process of the finding and carrying out of this tendency is dynamic, or historical, in the sense that innovation and learning are significant factors. In such a dynamic process, state intervention by patronising those entrepreneurs who dare to operate in that industry might be effective.

In Murakami's developmentalist scheme, the government selects promising industries to give its support but as well restricts the number of operating firms so as to avoid detrimental price competition. The function of a guide as well as a judge of competition is assigned to the government. Apart from an ideological (anti-socialist) one, the reason developmentalist government itself will not operate in those sectors is twofold; first, developmentalists consider the profit motive of private businessmen mightier than the neutral loyalty of bureaucrats especially in pursuing cost reduction; second, the selection of supported industry changes as time goes by and in an ideal case the government should retreat from industries when they reach a stable stage where the possibility of dynamic increasing return is exhausted. In other words, the patronised industries are, in principle, changeable in each stage of the developmentalist economies.

Therefore, industrialisation in developmentalist economies should be supplemented by industrial policy formulated by competent bureaucrats. Indeed, the success of developmentalist strategy depends on the sensitive control of the degree of competition (in the phase of diminishing cost) as well as on the definite decision in switching of the supported industry. This implies the delicate relations between government and business in a developmentalist state. To Murakami, the decisive factor for successful developmentalist policy is whether the nation concerned has a modern effective bureaucracy that can make decisions impartially from the existing interest structures. The bureaucrat as the administrator[7] of a developmentalist state should even be harsh to the welfare of the people today for the sake of tomorrow's welfare. Japanese bureaucrats before 1945 were not civil servants but "servants of the Tenno (Emperor)" who was the symbol of the project of the developmentalist state.

However, this reliance on the impartial and competent bureaucracy seems ridiculous. The reason is not limited to the personal concerns of individual bureaucrats. Murakami seemed to ignore the inherent political and ideological tension of developmentalism that cannot cope with by mere cleanness or ability of the bureaucracy. One of the dangers is aggressive nationalism that sometimes takes on the form of invasive expansionism. It is one of the conventional tactics of developmentalist states to leading fan patriotism among people by focusing on trivial conflicts in their foreign relations. But since developmentalism is in itself born as a nationalistic

---

7   The term "administrators" is used by a Dutch journalist, KAREL VAN WOLFREN: *The Enigma of Japanese Power*, 1989, to signify the small circle behind government and large organisations in contemporary Japan.

response to the crisis, it has no effective control over the wave of aggressive nationalism it has ignited.

Another danger is reactionary fundamentalism that is rooted in the traditional culture or mentality. It is negligible as far as the promise of the developmentalist project seems to becoming truth. However, in the years of the crisis when a reactionary fundamentalism emerges as an ideological reaction to the negative social consequences of the developmentalist strategy, it has an overwhelming power to expel any pragmatic rationalism of bureaucrats. In the last two decades we have observed the long and severe battle between developmentalist governments and religious fundamentalism in lots of developing countries. Developmentalists have not always been winners in this battle. Mao's Cultural Revolution, too, might be interpreted as a fundamentalist-type reaction to the Russian type industrialisation, though this institutional structure is different from the capitalist pattern of industrialisation.

In Japan's case, the ambiguous fundamentalism exemplified by the term of "Kokutai" (National Polity)[8] dominated the political discourse during 1930-45. Top bureaucrats were rationalists who had generally no sympathy to such ideology. Their function was basically that of the co-ordinator/administrator within the existing state structure. Their resistance to fundamentalism was limited on the level of the procedures of their service. Most of them followed the new track in policy matters as well as in ideology, after it was once fixed by the political situation. Even the mighty alliance of the military and "new bureaucrats" had to make concessions when ideological fundamentalists accused them of the offence of violating the sacred "Kokutai."

The vulnerability of developmentalist bureaucracy to aggressive nationalism and ideological fundamentalism consists in their half-hearted modernism. Indeed it is not their job to put the modern ideals into practice. The establishing of the modern bureaucracy is not an isolated phenomenon in the process of industrialisation/modernisation. It encourages also the formation of political parties on the one hand, and the growth of modern journalism

---

8   "Kokutai" was originally the translation of "nation" or "nationality" as is seen in writings of Fukuzawa. However, the ideological institutionalisation of Tenno worship in cultural system and the preventive intent against "dangerous thought" (anarchism, socialism, and communism) moulded this term by an ideological combination of the both.

on the other hand. There is some truth in saying that the Fifteen Years' War (1931-1945) of Japan could have been, at least in some of its parts, avoided, if party politicians as well as journalists had definitely rejected the temptation of aggressive nationalism and ideological fundamentalism and had kept a rational idea of world economic/political order in the 1920s and 1930s. In other words, the weakness of public discourse and civilian politics allowed the disastrous course of a developmentalist state.

Public discourse is linked with the world of learning and education, and politics stemming from several kinds of social movements. The weakness or dependency on the state in both spheres was related to the ineffectiveness in the functioning of the public sphere.

I would like to call it the problematic of the formation of civil society under developmentalist states. The civil society that can convey modern ideals does not exist at the outset. Though the diffusion of modern ideals encourages political consciousness of the gentry class, the early democratic movements will be absorbed by the developmentalist state so long as their basis is the traditional one. This corresponds to the opposition of the democratic movements in the 1880s. The task of the formation of civil society under the developmentalist state cannot be understood with the cannon of the classical liberalism that corresponds to the living conditions of the wealthy middle class. A new civil society[9] should be constructed on the economic situation where employment relations are prevalent and the public service in the consumption process of the people is indispensable. This task coincides rather with the "new liberal reform" which became the foci in British politics at beginning years of this century.

In Japan's case, conditions for the formation of a new civil society matured around the years of the First World War. In 1914 Tanzan Ishibashi, the chief editor of the *Toyo Keizai Shimpo* (Oriental Economist) declared the end of etatism and bureaucratism since the Meiji Restoration and concluded that the new economic philosophy of modern Japanese should be a liberal and pacifistic one based on individualism and democracy.[10] Ishibashi

---

9 This term is used by Yongho Kim in his observation of contemporary North-Eastern Asian nations. See YONGHO KIM: "Tohoku Ajia no Saihen to Kan-nichi Kankei no Saikochiku" (Reorganisation of the Northeast Asia and the Task of Reconstruction of Korea-Japan Relations), *Sekai*, 612 (August 1995).
10 TANZAN ISHIBASHI: "Gendai Nihonjin no Keizai Shiso" (Economic Philosophy of Contemporary Japanese), in: ISHIBASHI TANZAN: *Chosaku-shu*, vol. 1, Toyo

extended his position of new liberalism by organising a detailed policy research on economic, social and international problems. His activity is one of the most consequent efforts to establish a new civil society out of the conditions that the developmentalist state of Japan had so far attained.

Ishibashi remained as an exceptional figure in the pre-1945 history of Japan, though he had some friends among top elite administrators in banking, industry, and bureaucracy. As for the question why new liberals like Ishibashi could not lead the politics of the inter-war years, two explanations occur to my mind:

First, the attraction of a new totalitarian vision of developmentalism was mightier than Ishibashi's new liberalism, since it was supported energetically by the military. While Ishibashi worked out a view of the new international order after the war as a pacifist one, the military learned it was urgent to prepare for the next war that would surely surpass in scale the Russo-Japan War of 1904. The military anticipated the conflict with the United States already during the war years, and in the 1920s the menace of Soviet Russia was added. The staff officers who were obsessed by the "total war" allied with the new bureaucrats who wished to introduce control over industry in order to modernise facilities and to establish new industries. They sought intellectuals and politicians who might support their position. The loyalty to the Tenno state was amalgamated with the interventionist measures that sometimes resembles a sort of state socialism.

The claim of domestic reforms from this front attracted most intellectuals after the disappearance of communist/socialist activities under harsh repression. The flourishing of Marxism in the 1920s is another reason for the relative unpopularity of the new liberalism. Of course, Marxism still has merits as a social theory as well as a political ideology. However, I confine myself here just to mentioning a peculiar pattern of the adoption of Marxism by Japanese intellectuals. The problem is that the devotion to Marxism

---

Keizai Shimpo-sha, 1995. Ishibashi wished to integrate the element of fairness in distribution as well as public service into his liberalism. He later found himself very neat to Keynse and made criticism to economic policies from similar perspective. After 1945 he joined the conservative Liberal Party, though he was invited by his friends in the Socialist Party. He became the finance minister of the Yoshida Cabinet 1946-47, but he was purged due to his resistance to the financing of luxury expenditure of the occupation army as well as his misunderstood reputation as an "inflationist".

was performed in most cases as a heroic deed of self-sacrifice and thus maintained no stable relations with individualism in daily life. In particular, to the youth, it was the rejection of the hypocritical fusion of the self-interest and the "interest of the nation", which was typical under a developmentalist state. This primacy of "Gesinnungsethik" was shown typically by Hajime Kawakami who was deprived of his chair at Kyoto Imperial University to join an illegal communist activity. The new liberalism of Ishibashi who propagated sound utilitarianism was remote from the vogue of Marxism in the 1920s and those youth would not come back to liberalism even after their forced conversion. Very ironically, the theory and knowledge of Marxism were applied by the totalitarianist camp so as to mobilise resources for the wartime economy.

III. Developmentalism After 1945

However, Murakami's system of the developmentalist policy is conceived not on the basis of the pre-1945 Japan, but from Japanese experience after 1945.[11] To conclude the retrospective part of this paper, a brief dis-

---

11 MURAKAMI (*ibid.*, vol. 2, p. 98) listed the following eight points as the set of policies of developmentalism:
1) Competition in the market based on the institution of private property is the basic principle.
2) Government executes industrial policy (i.e., it leads prices in the promotion of the growth of promising new industries with diminishing cost tendency as the arbitrator as well as the judge. This is valid in the import and development of technology.)
3) Export-oriented industries should be included in the promising industries concerned above.
4) It promotes the growth of small- and medium-sized firms.
5) It equalises the distribution and supports the growth of the domestic demand whose main part is the consumption of the mass.
6) It executes an egalitarian distribution of agricultural land holdings with the intention of the equalisation of income.
7) It establishes a solid educational system at least up to the middle level education.

cussion on the meaning of Japan's defeat and the occupation by the United States will be necessary.

My criticism of Murakami is that the existence of an impartial and competent bureaucracy is not a sufficient condition for the success of developmentalist strategy. Bureaucracy is by its nature vulnerable to politics and it has no means to control the aggressive nationalism as well as reactionary fundamentalism. Japan's pre-1945 experience provides us a typical failure in this respect. The conceit of the military and "new bureaucrats" in their capability was punished by plunging into a hopeless war under the pressure of irrational fundamentalism.[12]

The defeat and the successful occupation of Japan eliminated that element (expansionism and fundamentalism) from Japanese politics. The military dissolved, Shinto shrines were separated from public patronage and Tenno (the Emperor) himself denied his sacredness.[13] A radical land reform was executed and mighty business groups were dissolved. It is not to be overlooked that the massive purge of wartime leaders forced the Japanese to start rather anew than returning to pre-war normalcy. Through the expropriation of the Zaibatsu families together with the purge of the top managers who were loyal to the owners, separation of management from ownership in Japanese large companies became irreversible.

Most Japanese accepted the American ideals, of course, on the basis of their own experience and understanding. The only relatively untouched power-group was the bureaucracy. As the series of prime ministers after 1945, Yoshida, Kishi, Ikeda, Sato, Ohira, Nakasone clearly shows, the ex-

---

8) It establishes an impartial and capable modern bureaucracy that is alien to nepotism.

12 Though I regard Japan's experience in the nineteen thirties and forties as failure of developmentalism, I do not deny its impact of breaking the hierarchical mould by the totalitarian mobilisation then. Apparently, the development of Japanese economic system shows the feature of path-dependency from that experience. See important study of TETSUJI OKAZAKI: "The Japanese Firm Under the Wartime Planned Economy", in: MASAHIKO AOKI and RONALD P. DORE (Eds.): *The Japanese Firm: Sources of Competitive Strength*, Oxford (Oxford University Press) 1994.

13 To the eyes of an American advisor for the reform of personnel management of Japanese public administration, Dr. Carl Hoover, Tenno is just the first of the new born civil servants. His list which placed Tenno among "servants to the whole" astonished Japanese administrators.

bureaucrats formed the main stream of the ruling party. As it was not the power of civil society that eliminated reactionary elements, Japanese developmentalism survived under the bureaucratic control particularly in its economic aspect.

Under the substitute national goal of the "Recovery", the administrators continued their job using the know-how they had learned from the controlled economy of wartime. However, three points of reorientation related to the characteristics of the post-war developmentalism should not be overlooked:

1) The first is the turn to the market economy in which not extensive mobilisation but efficiency is the decisive factor. By the time of stabilisation program of 1948-49 most of the subsidies were cut and a drastic rationalisation began in every Japanese industry. Most firms experienced severe labour disputes and the final compromise became the base on which industrial relations in the high growth period developed. Japanese developmentalism separated its state socialistic heritage from the wartime economy and transformed itself into a market-oriented one.

2) Another reorientation consists in the setting of the goals in the world market competition. The Dodge mission of 1949 fixed the exchange rate of $1 = ¥360 that was valid up to 1971. As the poor endowment of natural resources was evident, the autarchy concept was discarded and the promotion of the exports became the main concern of the elite administrators. On the side of imports, too, the most effective cost reduction was done by the switch to the materials and energy provided by foreign suppliers.

3) Although the developmentalist policy on the national level was practised by the ministerial bureaucracy, the key element lay in the managerial entrepreneurship of the private sector. Entrepreneurship means here the foreseeing the promising technological tendencies of the dynamically increasing return and mobilising every available resource to attain this goal. This kind of entrepreneurship was sustained by several conditions in the corporate governance structure. The firm (or the company) became the core of post-1945 Japanese developmentalism.

Thus, the post-1945 developmentalism consists of the bureaucracy and business managers. This alliance is now decaying and the possibility of the formation of a new civil society is emerging again (for the third time).

IV. Mobilisation Under a Dual-structured Society

C. Lévi-Strauss once proposed a societal dichotomy of the society by using a dual concept of "hot societies" and "cold societies."[14] According to this thermo-dynamic analogy, the distinction lies in the degree of random movement of molecules (men and women) in their societies. The order of a modern society (a hot society) emerges out of the anonymous synthetic result of the movements and collisions of particles, while the order of a traditional society is dominated by repetitive patterns. Allow me to use this crude dichotomy to draw an image of the transformation of the society under a developmentalist state.

As I pointed out in the preceding chapter, developmentalism is a project that has its axis directed to the future. The model taken from advanced nations is the target that is placed on the axis. However, the social base is traditional at least at the beginning. At first it is only a small elite circle that have made some progress along this time axis. However, the developmentalist government promotes the movement from the traditional base by offering business chances, cultural curiosity, education, and career chances. Together with the middle structure, which emerges out of such a movement, the society under the developmentalist state makes a cone-shaped structure.

In this dual-structured society, the top and the middle of the cone are supported by the movement coming from the traditional base. If I repeat it in terms of political economy, industrialisation by the developmentalist state is in this historical context maintained by the mobilisation of resources from traditional industry. In Japan's case, though it is difficult to say how much economic surplus of the traditional sector was directly transferred to the modern sector, traditional agriculture supported the enormous expenditures of the new government by the high rated land tax and traditional industries. They were stimulated and improved by contact with overseas customers financed the import necessary to the establishing of modern Western industries in the middle structure.

Mobilisation in the developmentalist nations with a dual-structured society has social and economic aspects that are related each other. Looking

---

14 CLAUDE LÉVI-STRAUSS: *The Scope of Anthropology*, London (Jonathan Cape) 1968, p. 53 (translated from French by S. O. Paul and R. A. Paul).

from the social aspect, mobilisation means the liberation of individuals from the traditional constraints. Kunio Yanagita vividly describes the development and the growth of the mobility and housing after the fall of strict regulations vividly in his *Meiji-Taishoshi Seso-hen* (1931) (Secular History of the Meiji-Taisho Era). Not only the second and third sons or widows in the provinces went to towns but ambitious youth also left home aiming for success in the centre. The developmentalist state shares its time axis with these people and canalises their movement. Not the mere maintenance of the family holdings in the traditional industry but the foundation of new business or making careers on the basis of education became the dream of the youth. They invested in their dream in longer perspective as they felt that they were participating in the modernisation project of the nation. The happy accord of direction between the developmentalist state and the self-interest of ambitious youth is the characteristic of the exploration age of developmentalism.

This movement of individuals from the base to the middle or to the centre brings economic resources such as labour forces, entrepreneurship, small capitals, fresh brains from the base to the middle or to the centre with them. Of course, the transfer of resources through banks, capital markets, and state is important, particularly in the financing of the investment fund. However, the significance of the transfer of resources that goes together with the mobilisation of individuals should not be overlooked.

V. Totalitarian Mobilisation

Wartime mobilisation[15] is different from individualistic mobilisation as is stated above. Wartime mobilisation that removes economic resources

---

15 In Japan Yasushi Yamanouchi considers the totalitarian mobilisation during wartime as an epoch-making transition from a modern society to a system society. YASUSHI YAMANOUCHI: *Sisutemu Shakai no Gendai-teki Iso* (Modern Aspect of the System Society), Tokyo (Iwanami) 1996. In my view, Yamanouchi seems to grasp the development of mobilisation too linear. The application of the concept of "mobilisation" to the Japanese economy was made by HIDEHARU SAITO in his *Nomado no Jidai* (The Age of Nomad), (Omura-Shoten) 1994. He

from one place to another even against their owner's will is the opposite to the order of normal civil life. Economic life keeps the form of a market economy, except for the coercive military or working draft, but the content is changed heavily by the control of production as well as prices. It does not deny the normal order, but suspends its validity for the time of emergency. The legitimacy of such radical measures is given by the principle of the common fate of the total nation.

In Japan it was the enforcement of the Law of the Total National Mobilisation of 1938 that marked the founding of the regime of the wartime economy. However, already from the breakout of the Sino-Japanese War in 1937, the economy of Japan was under the pressure of massive operation in the Mainland China. The military who maintained the concept of "total war" since the late 1920s and experimented with a planned economy in alliance with new bureaucrats (Shinsuke Kishi) in Manchuria (Japan's puppet state founded in 1931) pushed the Diet to approve this law. New bureaucrats of the Planning Board (Kikaku-in: established in 1937), which had been conceived originally as a consultation organ clearly switched their policy to the enforcement of the direct control of resources and propagated the "new order" in which firms operate for public interest (in this case wartime production) without the limitation of the profit-motive. Shareholders were isolated from daily management. In the planning, the method of material balance with an iterative modification process clearly resembled the Soviet type planning was introduced.[16]

In accordance with the planning of material resources, personnel resources, fund financing, and trade, organisations for rationing and supporting were organised in each industry, in each workshop. The massive reorientation in the flow of resources to warfare production changed the structure of the Japanese economy from a market-oriented one to a control-oriented one together with corresponding policy measures and the introduction of controlling organisations. The fund for investment was supplied now by registered banks according to the priorities in the fund plan. Collabora-

---

characterises Fordism also as a "mode of mobilisation of social aspiration of the people".

16 In the years of the financial crisis, the new German cartel theory that maintained productive functions of the cartel was introduced. This provided "new bureaucrats" with the general consensus on which they constructed their planning.

tive societies for war time production that integrated blue collar workers as well as administrative personnel were organised in most factories and the status of workers in firms was elevated. Firms were considered now as an "organic whole of capital, management, and labour".[17] Whether these changes are properly considered as the origin of the post-1945 regime of Japanese economy is now an issue of hot discussion in Japan.

In contrast to the individualistic mobilisation in the developing dual-structured economy, the wartime mobilisation can be described as totalitarian. However, Japanese wartime mobilisation retained certain communal feature that is apparent when one compares it with the German case or with the Russian case. Though some activists claimed a radical revolution that should surpass the Meiji Restoration (the "Showa Restoration"), no radical break was made in politics. Most politicians joined the official patriotic movement and its name, "Movement for the Total Mobilisation of the Spirit of Nation", spoke literally its communal nature. At the local level the same community leaders as before propagated patriotic services to the nation. It was not the "Gleichschaltung" of the individuals under some mighty ideology but the heated conformity to the general direction of the community that realised the wartime mobilisation in Japan. Every Japanese family enthusiastically responded to the appeal by sending its youth to the front or to factories, but private-interest survived behind the official principle of the public first.

Contrary to the ideals of some progressive "new bureaucrats," the real Keizai Shin-Taisei (New Economic Order) could not function without the profit motive. Firms under Japanese wartime economy were more than production units as was supposed by the planners of socialist economies. The controlling societies that were organised in each industry, too, were not purely centralistic. Since the military always worried about the reduction of production capacity, price competition was avoided within each industry.

---

17 Originally, the "new bureaucrats" in the Planning Board desired to introduce the removal of the capital's domination over management in the concept of "New Economic Order". The expression of the "organic whole" of three factors was the product of the roll-back of liberal business men. As for the origin of the idea of "New Economic Order" and its legitimisation by economists, see KIICHIRO YAGI: "Economic Reform Plans under Japanese Wartime Economy - The case of Shintaro Ryu and Kei Shibata", in: AIKO IKEO (Ed.): *Economic Development in Twentieth Century East Asia*, London (Routledge), 1997.

Instead, the privileged fund and rationing tickets for important materials were sought for by private firms that were involved in the warfare production. The officials of the controlling society had to co-ordinate this kind of hidden competition among rent-seekers.

Looking into the image of Japanese firms under the wartime mobilisation, the following will be suggested as characteristics of the firms in a mobilising environment:

1) Production volumes are determined from outside. In the wartime economy, the necessary amounts of military goods that are dependent on the aim as well as the current war situations are imposed on the economy. The forerunner of this type of exogenous determination was the Hindenburg Plan of Germany that intended to sustain massive military consumption in the two fronts during the First World War. Not only military staffs of the whole world but also socialists were strongly impressed by this mobilisation experiment of the whole economy. While the former nourished the idea of total mobilisation in the modern war, the latter shaped their image of a planned economy as the successor to the preceding "wartime economy". Of course, the volume that is determined from the needs of the front will not be automatically transmitted to the economy as the goal. In most cases, the original volume will be modified by the realistic estimate of the production capacity (including convertible capacity) and is by some intermediary process divided and assigned to each firm as obligatory production volume. Clearly this will not coincide with the optimum production volume from the viewpoint of the cost condition of the firm. The primacy lies in the aim that depends on each peculiar situation that is out of the control of the firm.

2) The resources necessary to production are procured from outside. Under the wartime economy privileges given to munitions industry are not confined to the access to funds, fuel and materials. It even extends to the use of production equipment as well as personnel that belong to other industries under normal situation. Precious information and technology that are held by the military or by the government is provided nearly gratis to them. Academic research resources are not exempted from the mobilisation. As for labour forces when a wide range mobility over trades, firms, and industries does not satisfy the needs of the munitions industry, working

service of students as well as women will be introduced.[18] Some of these procurements retain the form of a market economy, but the level of the remuneration (prices, wages, and interest etc.) is controlled in most cases to avoid inflation. Therefore, in spite of its market form, seen from the determination of its distribution, this procurement is essentially the mobilisation of resources for certain production goals.

3) The nature of the firm's profit will change. In the pricing of the munition goods, the market mechanism is not used, though some allowance for the negotiation exists in most cases. On the other hand, firms are not allowed to adjust their production volume in order to maximise profits. Consequently, as far as private firms are concerned, reasonable profits should be distributed to them. This kind of profit is no longer the profit acquired by true entrepreneurial activity such as developing a cost-reducing production method, developing a new product, or opening a new market. It is, in essence, remuneration for collaboration. However, in determining the level of reasonable profit, it might be rational in most cases to take the level of profit in the non-controlled industry into consideration.

4) The enormous fund that is necessary for large-scale investments and founding new firms is beyond the capacity of individual firms or investors. Investment is performed in a mixed form under deep participation of financial institutions (and the state). In case of large-scale investment a consortium of big banks is organised under the guidance of one that has close relations with the firm concerned.[19] Sometimes a joint investment is preferred by firms and banks. The military also, usually, desires a co-operative investment of related firms and institutions because of its interest in secur-

---

18 In Japan the Ordinance for National Service Draft (Kokumin Choyo-rei) was proclaimed in 1939. By this ordinance 1,610 thousand people were drafted and 4,550 thousand people were reclassified for the wartime production. In addition 3,430 thousand students and 470 thousand housewives were mobilised. The coercive transportation of Korean workers amounted 120 thousand in 1942, 130 thousand in 1943, and 290 thousand in 1944. About 40 thousand Chinese workers were also transported up to 1945. MINORU SAWAI: "Senjiki" (Wartime), in: YASUSHI KOSAI et al. (Eds.): *Nihon Keizai Jiten* (Encyclopaedia on Japanese Economy) (Nihon Keizai Shinbunsha) 1996.

19 In Japan the close network of banks was introduced under the name of Financial New Order (Kinyu Shin-Taisei) in the wartime. It is argued that the so-called "main bank" system in post-war Japan originated in this joint financing system under the wartime financial system.

ing of a stable provision of munition goods. In a tight financial situation, firms have to rely on public funds or financial institutions under direct control of government particularly in case of such risky large-scale investment. In addition to the daily reliance on bank credit, the joint investment alters the nature of the firm. Firms under a mobilisation economy have a kind of mixed nature in this context of firm-bank-state relations.[20]

5) Strategic behaviour of firms becomes more significant. Firms under a controlled economy are not always passive actors, because they also have chances to intervene into the process of concretisation and implementation of the aims that come originally from the non-economic situation. The firm that is more talented in this intervention is able to occupy the controlling heights of the industry concerned and to choose the most promising part of the production scheme. Even in the midst of an ongoing process which is totally beyond control of individual firms, an experienced leading firm might use its advantage in forecasting and providing for future development. A controlled economy may offer such a firm the chance to establish its dominance and to domicile challengers. On the other hand, other of firms that cannot enjoy such advantages would urge a co-operative order in the industry in order to ensure their survival. This order is often supported by the government and constrains the arbitrary behaviour of leading firms. Consequently, prices or rationing of resources and products would be fixed so as to allow the survival of marginal producers.

6) The typical behaviour of firms under a mobilisation economy described above can be considered from its effects. The effect of strategic behaviour in such situations ranges from a secured share in rationing, privileged access to resources including fund and information, the chance of joining a new promising branch of industry, to the presiding prestige of controlling organ. Sapir[21] referred to this with precise term, "authority

---

20 The nature of business concerns (Zaibatsu) alters accordingly. The exclusive relation of the bank and firm under the common family ownership was weakened by the joint financing and by the forced retreat of the Zaibatsu families from the management. In this respect the transformation of new business groups (Nissan, Riken, etc.) were faster than such old business groups as Mitsui, Mitsubishi, etc.
21 In conceiving this characteristics as well as drawing the table I received several hints from Japanese translation of JACQUES SAPIR: "Transformation de la societe

effect". Another side of this effect is the extra-profit that is generated as rent due to the non-existence of competition. Not only the top firm but also most firms receive extra-profit, because prices are fixed by the production costs of the weakest. This aspect of the effect is to be called the "rent effect". Distribution of both effects will play an important role in the real implementation of the mobilisation economy.

Table 1. Mobilised Type of Firm

CHARACTERISTICS	IMPLICATIONS
Production volume is imposed from outside (rationing)	Primacy of situation and goals
Procurement of resources from outside	Control over prices (wages)
Distribution of reasonable profit	Profit as the compensation of collaboration
Joint investment	Mixed nature of firms
Strategic behaviour	Co-operative business order
Authority effect	Rent effect

VI. From the Extensive Mobilisation to the Intensive Mobilisation

In the preceding part of this chapter, I drew the picture of the mobilised economy that is placed under the heavy demand coming from non-economic situation. Of course, it is incorrect to say that no attention is paid in the mobilised economy to the problems of efficiency, cost-reduction, or technological innovation. But filling the emergent needs by coercive conversion of existing resources has the dominating priority and this mobilisation itself is sometimes considered to accompany the promotion of productivity. In essence, it is an "extensive mobilisation."

---

et modes de regulation", "Regulation et transition", in: R. BOYER and T. YAMADA: *La Grande Transformation du Socialisme* (Fujiwara-Shoten) 1993.

However, the most important implication in using the term "mobilisation" lies in its motivational aspect. Since most economic resources have their owners, "mobilisation" must have some mechanism to persuade them to provide their resources to goals set by other persons (or the state). Sharing the recognition of the situation and aims has (at least formally) great significance in moulding the conduct of persons in a mobilised economy. It is the sense of the common fate that legitimates the implementation of direct mobilisation which is not admitted in a normal situation. If this sense is lost, the mobilised economy is just a command economy controlled by unlimited authority. The personnel mobilisation in wartime contains coercive labour service of those deprived such as prisoners, captives and foreigners. Their status corresponds to their belonging to the cause or common fate of the political community (the nation).

In case wartime mobilisation does not abolish the basic institutions of private property, the return to normalcy means the revival of the market economy. If the mobilised type of production should be continued in peace time, in order to adapt itself to the market economy, three conditions are to be satisfied. The first is the maintenance of the common recognition of the situation and goals especially on the side of providers of resources without the excitement of wartime (or under a coercion of formal common fate convictions). The second is the necessity of the mechanism to procure sufficient resources under the reduced range of the mobilisation system that is compatible with a market economy. The last but not the least is the formation of the mechanism by which continuous increase in efficiency and innovation are promoted in a long-term process. In contrast to the extensive mobilisation which is not concerned with efficiency in market economy, I would like to call the features of an economy that fulfils the above three conditions of "intensive mobilisation."[22]

The Japanese economy just after the defeat still remained as an economy of extensive mobilisation. Systems of price control and rationing of important materials remained at this time under the new cause of maintenance of the nation's survival. Through loans from the Reconstruction Finance Bank

---

[22] It is now the prevalent view that the residue goes to the owner of property. (PAUL MILGLOM, JOHN ROBERTS: *Economics, Organisation and Management*, (Prentice-Hall International) 1992, chap. 9.) The specific feature of the mobilisation phenomenon lies indeed in the opposite result. The residue (profit) appears on the side of the agent who called for the mobilisation.

enormous money was poured into key industries such as coal mining and steel production. Though lots of labour disputes occurred, workers together with clerks and engineers maintained the production ethics that had been implanted in them during war years. Against the labour's offensive, managers attempted to establish their own functions and responsibilities for the maintenance and development of firms, but the interest of shareholders was neglected. Paradoxically enough, economic reforms under the guidance of American advisors turned out to produce a peculiar Japanese pair of enterprise union and in-firm-breeding of managers. However, the Japanese firms then contained enormous personnel redundancy. The serious adaptation to the market economy began at the end of the occupation, 1949 and 1950, when the government switched to the austerity programme and dissolved the Reconstruction Finance Bank. After the massive reduction of personnel in most heavy industry, the phase of consolidation began by managers and employees who learned from their experience of serious labour disputes the vital role of steady growth of the firm for their own interest.[23]

However, the Annual Economic Reports of the Economic Planning Agency in the 1950s often complained[24] about the high cost structure of the Japanese economy. The Japanese economy was then in a vicious circle of small market size - low productivity - high costs and high prices. The government helped several industries to get out of this vicious circle by direct intervention together with the supply of preferential funding.[25] Shipbuilding and steel production are the most successful industries under this sort of "rationalisation plans". The main factors for the reduction of cost consist of the introduction of modern mass production technology and the switch to cheap foreign materials. Under the conditions of a labour-surplus economy

---

[23] For example, Toyota MC experienced a serious labour dispute when it announced a voluntary retirement of 1600 in number in March 1950. At this time 2,146 retired and 5,994 remained. TOYOTA MOTOR COMPANY: *Toyota: A History of the First 50 Years*, 1988, pp. 109-110.

[24] See KEIZAI KIKAKU-CHO CHOSA-KYOKU (Ed.): *Siryou Keizai-hakusho 50 nen* (50 Years of Annual Economic Reports), Nihon Keizai Shimbun-sha, 1972, pp. 64f., 70f., 182f., 232f.

[25] TETSUJI OKAZAKI: "Sengo Shijou Keizai Ikouki no Seifu-Kigyou kan Kankei" (Government-Firms relations in the years of the Post-war Transition to the Market Economy), in: HIDESHI ITOH (Ed.): *Nihon no Kigyou Sisutemu* (Corporate System in Japan), Tokyo (University of Tokyo Press) 1996.

up to the beginning of the nineteen-sixties the rise in wages lagged behind productivity growth and thus reduced the real unit labour cost. Lack of confidence was erased by the inter-industrial consensus that was arranged by the Ministry of Trade and Industry. MITI and several policy-oriented banks supported both large scale investment, such as construction of new production sites and the exports by special preferential loans. As the mechanism of the increasing return sets in, the MITI intervened as the controller of fierce share competition of ambitious firms.

This is the age when the intensive mobilisation system of the Japanese economy gradually formed. The most apparent difference with the extensive mobilisation lies in the relative slim structure of the core firm. From the side of capital the rate of own capital was clearly underscored compared with both international standards as well as that of pre-war Japan. Though it is questionable whether Japanese firms then enjoyed cheap growth money, the banks financed the ambitious projects of managers whose position was secured against the claims of investors so long as it squared with their interest in the growth of deposit.[26]

Also on the side of personnel composition, the regular employee occupies only a part of the total working force that consists of provisional workers, workers in supplier-firms or many sorts of subcontracting firms. The close relation of the firms under the core firm originated in the controlled economy of war years. However, to attain efficiency and flexibility by this complicated system, Japanese firms had to develop special skill to keep suppliers and subcontractors under competitive pressure but at the same time to support their growth. The most co-operative and most successful supplier would be remunerated by the assignment of the most promising order and acquiring relative independence from the core firm. On the other hand, there are many small subcontractors who are totally dependent on the order of the core firm or major subcontractors and are forced to produce without acquiring profit. This is a sort of competition that is administered

---

26 See SHIGEO TERANISHI: "Mein Banku Sisutemu" (Main Bank System), in: TETSUJI OKAZAKI, MASAHIRO OKUNO (Eds.): *Gendai Nihon Keizai Sisutemu no Genryu* (Origins of the Contemporary Economic System of Japan), (Nihon Keizai Shimbun-sha) 1993. See also MASAHIKO AOKI, HUGH PATRICK (Eds.): *The Japanese Main Bank System*, Oxford (Oxford Univ. Press) 1994. Whether the policy of low rate interest contributed to the growth of the Japanese economy is a topic of hot discussion.

by core firms in which ranking[27] and distribution of rent played important roles.

The same logic of administered competition is valid in the personnel of the core firm. In principle Japanese personnel administration is egalitarian. However, not only productivity but also general attitudes in working life is evaluated regularly. The result determines the promotion speed of workers in the wage table and in their function. Under the peculiar Japanese mentality which is very sensitive to age or entry-year groups, even a small lead or lag within one's peer group has considerable significance. However, the Japanese wage system has so far assured most personnel an increase of income in accordance with the increasing expenditure and the dominant consumption norms in each stage in the life cycle. Some argue that the relative high wage of senior employees is the remuneration of the donation or "hidden investment" which they made in their youth to the firm.[28] It is highly problematic, because workers themselves have no guarantee that they can acquire the remuneration for their services in future. However, it is reasonable to assume that workers also expect the relative high wage in future from the steady growth of the firm.

The strength of intensive mobilisation lies in the coincidence of incentives of partners in their long run expectation. All of the managers, workers, subcontractors, banks, and bureaucrats share a consensus in economic growth. Extraordinary service which is beyond the written obligation of the contract would be compensated in the long run with the growth profit. Since it would be wrong to assume there the growth of such a substantial entity as "invisible capital", the compensation should be considered as a sort of distribution of rent. This exchange of services and rent do not always take the form of economic exchange in which both are clearly discerned and influenced by general market conditions. The range of the administered competition corresponds with the range of mobilisation of services as well as that

---

27 The significant role of the ranking in the incentive mechanism of the Japanese type firm is one of the main theses of MASAHIKO AOKI: *Information, Incentives, and Bargaining in the Japanese Economy*, Cambridge (Cambridge University Press) 1988.

28 See Kobayashi's part in TAKAYUKI ITAMI/TADAO KAGONO/TAKAO KOBAYASHI/KIYONORI SAKAKIBARA/MOTOSHIGE ITOH: *Kyousou to Kakushin - Jidousha Sangyou no Kigyou Seichou* (Competition and Innovation: Growth of Firms in Automobile Industry), (Toyo Keizai Shimpo-sha) 1988.

of distribution of rent. As Murakami proposed, an application of social exchange theory might be revealing in understanding this relation.[29] However, this exchange is imaginary, depending on lots of unpredictable factors in the future. What exists is the range of mobilisation of resources/distribution of rent and the delicate mechanism to channelise the conduct of actors into certain purposes.

It is easy for a senior Japanese to find in this sphere of mobilisation/distribution a reflection of the pattern of social structure in rural communities (Mura). The basic entity of the community is the family household (Ie) which has its own long time perspective. Among the members of the community, a fierce competition that might ruin others is avoided, though ranking in wealth and prestige is always sought for. Various sorts of social exchange are performed in the daily life of the community. The sense of the common fate of the community has its historical origin in the taxation system in the Edo period in which the community as a whole assumed the responsibility of the completion of payment. As Samurais lived in the city, it was the function of community leaders to persuade and monitor their neighbours. The demand from outside is mediated at the community level and supported unanimously. But in the process of implementation, various sort of strategic action as well as hidden negotiation would be performed. This pattern was already reflected even in totalitarian mobilisation in wartime and seems to be transplanted to social conduct within the mobilisation network around Japanese firms in the high-growth period.[30]

Looking back at the starting point of the story, the mobilisation first began with the individuals' movement from the basis (periphery) to the top (centre). Then the totalitarian mobilisation grasped the whole nation with the help of bureaucracy and community leaders. The dual structure was

---

29 YASUSUKE MURAKAMI and THOMAS P. ROHLEN: "Social-Exchange Aspects of the Japanese Political Economy: Culture, efficiency, and Change," in: S. KUMON and H. ROSOVSKY (Eds.): *The Political Economy of Japan, (vol.3): Cultural and Social Dynamics*, (Stanford University Press) 1992.

30 Cf. my short memorandum added as an appendix to my paper on Yanagita Kunio. KIICHIRO YAGI: "Japan Model?", in: KIICHIRO YAGI and TAKASHI MATSUGI (Eds.): *Shakai Keizaigaku no Shiya to Hoho* (Method and Perspective of Social Economics), (Mineruva Publ.) 1996. See also RESEARCH PROJECT TEAM FOR JAPANESE SYSTEM/MASUDA FOUNDATION: *Japanese Systems - An Alternative Civilisation?*, Yokohama (Sekotac) 1992 (English and Japanese).

eliminated by the levelling of Japanese society by a shared totalitarian view of the nation. But it remained only an extensive mobilisation that could not attain the efficiency that was required for the immediate needs of wartime production. Its significance lay in the break with previous pattern of economic co-ordination and in the introduction of various controlling measures and organisations. At last an intensive pattern of mobilisation that combined individual interest with a mild pattern of communal service/distribution emerged on the basis of the experiences during wartime mobilisation and the occupation years. The intensive mobilisation was far more sustainable than totalitarian mobilisation because it could solicit voluntary commitment to the common aim of economic growth.

It would be a mistake to attribute its success totally to this motivational aspect of mobilisation. In this chapter, I put the problematic of the Japanese economy in the historical perspective of economic development. The rationale of the developmentalist strategy lay in the deliberate selection of strategic industries that promised increasing return and in the mobilisation of economic resources for the growth of these industries. Post-war Japanese firms practised this developmentalist strategy within their relations with suppliers/subcontractors, employees, banks, and distributors. Combined with supplementary industrial policy this entrepreneurial developmentalism opened the leap of Japanese industry.

VII. Present Crisis of the Japanese Mobilisation System

Over thirty years have lapsed since Japan was declared to pass the turning point in the labour market. In accordance with the rapid increase of real per capita national income, Japan reached the stage of high consumption in the nineteen-sixties. The world-wide stagnation caused by the oil shock stopped the growth of heavy industry such as shipbuilding and steel production; and the drastic change of the cost structure made several kinds of material production in Japan unprofitable. Apart from the construction industry that owes much to public spending, it was the automobile and electronics industry which could continue steady growth for the two decades after the first oil crisis.

In the automobile industry, we can see the well-developed intensive mobilisation system that does not need any patronising intervention of the state. At the working place, mobilisation is transformed into steady work dealing with continuous flow of mixed sort of product or operation with several machines at once. The network of production is synchronised from the final assembly line up to the production of parts in suppliers' factories by a pull-down information system. In the field of product design, engineers of both the core firms and suppliers work under a high pressure of short term rotation of a model change. At least in the field of personnel management as well as of the administration of suppliers' networks, the automobile industry represents one of the finest images of the intensive mobilisation.[31]

However, the mobilisation system of the Japanese industry now faces several irrefutable difficulties that might dissolve the system itself:

1) First, while the productionism that was shared by every actor in the Japanese economy has lost its validity, the Japanese industrial system so far cannot present a new convincing aim that can be shared by all of the partners concerned. The sense of common fate is vanishing with the entry of new generations who are mostly more individualistic than their seniors. The decay of the common recognition of the situation and purposes brought the original and fatal defect in the legitimacy of the mobilisation to light. In the beginning of the nineties many Japanese firms established new corporate principles which contain social participation and environmental criteria. But the continuing recession seems to have been enough to let them refrain from any further steps that is to combine new principles with the active conduct of individuals.

2) Second, due to the drastic reduction of personnel in the work place after the oil crisis the communal character of the working organisation is decaying. This was once the basis on which the range of flexible services as well as distribution of rent was extended along with the line of employees as a whole and the managers. The rapid change in technology undermines the long-term perspective of the skill-formation by the employees. In order to

---

[31] Jean-Pierre Durand considers the "mobilisation of internal ability of wage workers" as the central element of the Japanese type production system. See ROBERT BOYER and JEAN-PIERRE DURAND: *L'apres-fordisme*, Paris (Sylos) 1993.

keep the flexible mobilisation/distribution networks around the core firm, a new concept of space-time structure would be necessary.

3) Third, as an extensive waste of visible resources accompanies to the extensive mobilisation, the dangerous waste of invisible resources is accompanied by intensive mobilisation. One main reason that Toyota built his new production site in Kyushu is the drying up of the supply of a young work force in Toyota's main production area, namely east Aichi prefecture. Toyota's personnel management consists of absorption of young work force, filtering those who can endure the intense labour, and then taking care of the total life cycle of a loyal Toyota man. This system presupposes a rich supply of a young and obedient labour force which is not expected in a metropolitan area. In the new Kyushu production site, Toyota avoided the midnight work-sift and admitted a modest size for buffers.[32] The incredible hard work is more common in the middle structure in which completion of normative or other responsibilities are concentrated. This is the group in which the notorious "karoshi" (work to death)[33] or "burn out" symptom appears. It is understood that short-sighted productionism accompanies various forms of the destructive waste of external resources (environmental destruction, congestion etc.).

4) Fourth, the maintenance of the mobilisation network is not costless. Japanese firms have so far given guarantees of employment and possibility of promotion in wages and position to the core personnel. But most Japanese firms could not continue sufficient growth especially after the oil crisis to fulfil their implicit promise to those senior employees who entered at the high growth period and who had now reached in their fifties. Several measures to relax the guarantee and to introduce selection in this age group have already been taken. This naturally undermines the long-term loyalty to the firm among personnel.

On the other hand, the maintenance cost of the fixed network of suppliers as well as distributors/customers is now felt severely. In the domestic market, new kinds of distributors (independent chain stores, discounters,

---

32 See KOITCHI SHIMIZU: "Kaizen et gestion du travail chez Toyota Motor et Toyota Kyushu" (Gerpisa paper presented at the Deuxieme Rencontre Internationale "Le nouveaux modeles industriels des firms automobiles"), Paris, June 16-18, 1994.
33 See KAROSHI-BENGODAN ZENKOKU-RENRAKU-KAIGI (National Association of the Lawyers against Karoshi) (Ed.): *Karoshi*, Tokyo (Mado Publisher) 1990.

etc.) have grown out of the control of manufacturers. On the world market, in accordance with the growth of machine industries in NIEs/ASEAN, the flexible combination of the location of the production site or purchasing of parts on the market level has become possible. Though there still remains the possibility for the Japanese industrial system to extend its mobilisation network to East Asian and Pacific Rim countries, it is clear that the fixed mobilisation system in the present form is going to lose its advantage in cost competition.[34]

Table 2. Extensive and Intensive Mobilisation

	Extensive Mobilisation	Intensive Mobilisation
1. Environment	Controlled economy (planning)	Market economy (competition)
2. Range of mobilisation	(Block)/National/Regional/Industrial/	Groups of private firms (sometimes international)
3. Communal legitimacy	National or political community	Community of economic interest
4. Way of enforcement	Formal and compulsory approval	Voluntary (but de facto compulsory) approval
5. Distribution within industry	Rationing	Share competition
6. Nature of firms	Fat (reserve keeper)	Lean (slack eliminator)
7. Equipment	Maximum utilisation of existing equipment	Replacement by modernised equipment
8. Attitude of employee	Ambivalence (formal obedience)	Commitment (supply beyond written contract)

---

34 In this last section, I could not deal with the financial difficulties that the Japanese economy experienced since the mid 1990s. The routinised behaviour pattern of financial institutions that was moulded by the developmentalist-type financial system lay behind this difficulty.

Discussion Summary

Torben Vestdam

Paper discussed:
Kiichiro Yagi: Intensive and Extensive Mobilisation in the Japanese Economy: An Interpretation of Japanese Capitalism in Historical Perspective

The author adopts a historical approach as he interprets the evolution of the Japanese economy during the 20th century as a transformation from liberal developmentalism (nation state-lead industrialisation through administered competition) in response to a state of feudalism over extensive mobilisation motivated by an ideology of fundamentalist nationalism towards a post-war stage of intensive mobilisation, which currently have reached a stage, where the Japanese national economy can be characterised by symptoms of crisis.

The author outlines an interpretation which allows us to see the stage of successful intensive mobilisation as a synthesis of the preceding stages of evolution as the idea of central, long-range planning, which is taken over from the Russian communist movement, according to an ethics of productionism is applied in a context of a capitalist economy which maintains principles of private property and commercial, yet politicised enterprise as the Japanese government extensively intervenes and co-ordinates interests of government/military, finance and enterprise; referred to by Shionoya as 'the iron triangle'. An ideology of fundamental nationalism that refers to the feudal institution of communities of rural families, which trade taxes for war-lord protection, motivates the economic participation of the Japanese population in the interest of the nation state.

The outcome of the World War II required constitutional and administrative reorientation which made it appropriate to introduce an adapted version of developmentalism (intensive mobilisation) with a new emphasis on enterprise, efficiency and export that allows the central administration to

DISCUSSION SUMMARY

maintain a function of temporary promoter of industries of strategic, national interest. The substantial change is the shift in location of decision-making and co-ordination from the offices of the central political administration (the civil servant) to the offices of the industrial conglomerates (the corporate manager) which emerges during the stage of internalised mobilisation. During this stage the existential treats to the 'rural-national family' change from physical risks of security to economic risks of welfare experienced during the transition from state- to corporate economic co-ordination, and the large corporation adopts a welfare strategy as motivational glue which can stabilise its relations with financial institutions, suppliers/subcontractors and employees on the basis of voluntary participation. This history of Japanese political economy allows the author to position post-war Japanese developmentalism as a decentralised, 'third way' approach characterised by liberalism, pacifism, individualism and democracy compared to (a) fundamentalism/communism and (b) liberal capitalism. KOSLOWSKI remarks that Germany and Japan share the 20th century experience that individually motivated mobilisation seems to be more successful compared to collectively motivated approaches.

The contemporary tendency towards a weakening of positions of the Japanese economy is interpreted by the author as a consequence of the process of globalisation. A process which reduces the significance of nationality as core value of corporate identity and the economic pressures exerted upon the Japanese corporations force them to let go of welfare benefits which used to be considered as employees rights according to the corporate contract resulting in diminishing employee loyalty and organisational cohesion. A significant dimension of these processes which influence the preconditions for the corporate contract is the rapidity of technological innovation, which diminishes returns on investment in employee training, internal recruitment and maintenance. Also increasing investment requirements for development of sources and distribution networks that support the production-conglomerates constitute a significant cost-generating factor. Such an interpretation of the evolution of the Japanese economy during the 20th century suggests that it appears to lose competitive strength both in terms of effectiveness and innovation.

Chapter 13

The Historical School in Sweden: A Sketch

HANS DE GEER

I. The Historical School Defined
II. The Leading Scholars: A Sceptical Response
III. The Exceptions: Important, but not Leading Scholars
IV. *Verein für Socialpolitik* - The Swedish Version
V. The Winning Paradigm? The Emergence of the Stockholm School
VI. The 1980s: New Institutionalism
VII. Conclusion

What was the influence of the German Historical School on Swedish economists and, in a wider sense, its impact on the emerging élite that formed the political discourse in Sweden in the early decades of the 20th century? In this paper I will try to formulate an answer, though it must be quite preliminary. This aspect of Swedish intellectual history remains to be written in a broader scope; here I will just indicate some lines along which the answers might be found. My view differs from those previously presented in that it takes into account not only the impact on Economics as a science but also in a wider societal context, an interpretation by the way that is quite in tune with the understanding of the Historical School as such.

I. The Historical School Defined

The Historical School can be defined by four criteria:

1. Inductionism: new knowledge is obtained by means of an inductive rather than a deductive process, focusing on empirical data of an economical/historical character.

2. Historicism: there are no general "economical laws"; economical regularities must be analysed in their historical settings and as results of unique combinations of circumstances.

3. Wholism: the relation between economy and other fields of research; economy must be regarded as an integrated part of a more comprehensive whole of human and social sciences. Also, the debate over the Historical School within the economical sciences was not an isolated process; it goes parallel to the "Methodenstreiten" in the humanities.

4. State interventionism: the State has the right and the duty to interfere with the working of the economy, not least to ensure social conditions that are acceptable.

II. The Leading Scholars: A Sceptical Response

Let me now first turn to the question, whether Swedish economists of the first generation were influenced by the German Historical School. That would have been quite normal, given the general cultural climate in Sweden at the end of the 19th century. Before, the main influences came from France, but after 1870 Germany came more and more into focus and Germanic and nationalist sentiments paved the way for German influence, as well as a more sober reception of German philosophy and theory of science. However, looking at the evidence we will find quite another situation.

The leading Swedish Economists before the emergence of the "Stockholm School" in the interwar years all studied for a shorter or longer period in Germany. The result was ironical. The seminars in Berlin or Göttingen did not turn the then young students into advocates for the Historical School. Instead, it seems to have had the opposite effect. Their experience in Germany made them utterly critical.

David Davidson, 1854-1942, the eldest son of German Jewish parents, who immigrated to Sweden in the 1840s. He became Doctor of Economics in 1878 and his dissertation treated the economic laws of capital accumulation. Between 1889 and 1919 he was full professor of Economics at Uppsala

University. In 1899, he was the founder of *Economisk tidskrift* (Journal of Economics) in 1919, the first of its kind in Sweden.

In 1879, Davidson got a scholarship for studies abroad, and he went to Heidelberg, where he followed Karl Knies' lectures on monetary theory. Later, in the mid 1880s, he visited Hamburg, Bremen and Lübeck for research on income tax legislation. These two were also his main fields of scholarly interest, monetary theory and taxation. In the first, his contributions never did have much impact, while in the other field the arguments that he developed resulted in both theoretical attention and practical reforms in Sweden. A major change in the fiscal legislation in 1910 was mainly inspired by his thinking on the progression of taxes and the need and justice of a capital tax.[1] In his preferences for progressive taxes, the influence from the German Historical School can be traced.

Due to his background, Davidson was originally oriented towards Germany. His immediate impressions from Karl Knies' seminar in Heidelberg were rather positive, and the young man became more and more inclined towards a broader, social perspective on his discipline than he had adopted in Uppsala. Also, from Knies he learned a more critical attitude towards the epistemological basis for economic theory. His paper from 1880 on ground rent shows a definite influence from the Historical School, as represented by Rodbertus and, first and foremost, Knies. At the same time, that research made him look closer at the works of David Ricardo and in the Briton he found his main source of theoretical inspiration for the time to come. Ricardo, in his deductive, analytic approach, was of course the prominent figure of the English classicism that the German Historical School opposed.

There is a third field of scholarly interest in which Davidson shows inspiration from the German Historical School, namely in his sceptical view of the necessity of free competition and his acceptance of cartels in economic life. The overall impression, however, is that Davidson's position more and more became that of a classical economist; the main references in

---

1 UHR, C. G.: *Economic Doctrines of David Davidson*, Uppsala 1975; UHR, C. G.: "David Davidson", in: JONUNG and STÅHLBERG (Eds.): *Ekonomiporträtt. Svenska ekonomer under 300 år*, Stockholm (SNS Förlag) 1990.

his later lectures were made to Ricardo, Wicksell, Böhm-Bawerk and Marshall.[2]

Knut Wicksell, 1851-1926, has been called the greatest Swedish economist of all times. He had a broad academic basic education, stretching from mathematics and astronomy to history, and it was quite late in his intellectual life that he specialised in economics. He spent most of the 1880s participating in the cultural and political debates of the time, writing numerous articles on a great variety of topics. He became famous as a radical man, a friend of the author August Strindberg and the socialist leader Hjalmar Branting. Wicksell was already a man of 44 when in Uppsala he defended his doctoral thesis with David Davidson as the opponent.

His oevre covers a great deal of economic theory of his time; one of his skills was his eminent talent for synthesising and summarising the state of the art in different fields of the economic sciences. He published important works on fiscal policy, finance, capital rent, production theory, and a number of other topics. His most influential works cover monetary and price theories, which directly influenced political action in the wake of the First World War when European governments strived to get back to normalcy. Wicksell, who was appointed professor of Economics at the university of Lund in 1901, spent the last ten years of his life as an emeritus at the Stockholm School of Economics, where he became a source of inspiration for the young generation of economists, later to become known as the Stockholm School.[3]

In his wide scope of interests, and his combination of radicalism in social affairs and his criticism of Marxism, one might think that he should have been sympathetic to the Historical School. However, that was definitely not the case, rather the contrary. 1887/88 Wicksell studied in Strassbourg and attended lectures by Knapp and Brentano, but he thoroughly disliked the German nationalist and militarist spirit that he met and he had no interest whatsoever for the historical investigation of mediaeval economic life that seemed to be la mode. In the spring of 1888 he left for Austria, where he attended the lectures of Carl Menger and applauded his

---

2 CARLSSON, BENNY: *De institutionalistiska idéernas spridning*, Stockholm (SNS Förlag) 1995.
3 JONUNG, LARS: "Knut Wicksell", in: JONUNG and STÅHLBERG (Eds.): *Ekonomiporträtt. Svenska ekonomer under 300 år*, Stockholm (SNS Förlag) 1990. See also GÅRDLUND, TORSTEN: *The Life of Knut Wicksell*.

intellectual assault on Schmoller. In 1888-89 he went to Berlin and the lectures of Adolph Wagner, which he found too elementary and too historic. The stay in the German capital made him even more critical to everything German. There seem to have been an emotional aversion in addition to his intellectual dislike of the empiricist spirit of the Historical School. Wicksell was first and foremost a theorist and a classical/neo-classical economist. In some investigations he appears as an economic historian, but that never became his trade. In his works on fiscal policy, he relates to work by Wagner, but he does not share his position. Also, Wicksell was in all important aspects a liberal thinker, always keen on dissociating himself from both conservatives and socialists, the two intellectual traditions that met and sometimes merged in the German Historical School.

Gustaf Cassel, 1866-1945, started as a mathematician, passed his PhD degree in 1895 and moved to Germany where he took on economics in Berlin under Schmoller and Wagner. Later he moved to Göttingen, to Lexis and Cohn. These studies, however, did not turn him into an admirer of the German professors.[4]

From start he reacted firmly against the lack of theory in the German tradition, and devoted himself to the establishment of an economic science using a purely deductive logic of economics expressed in quantitative data. In fact, during the decades to come he developed an idea of the total functions of the market which was walrasian, though Cassel never admitted it but claimed the originality of his own thinking.

The differences in epistemological sense did not prevent him, however, from developing some ideas in the fields of economic and social policy, that were quite close to and presumably inspired by German thinking, especially by Wagner. The young Cassel was no liberal thinker; on the contrary he was willing to accept a far-reaching State intervention in the function of the market, close to a planned economy. The main instrument would be the use of customs tariffs. Moreover, the efficient use of the human factor in production, he said, would require an ambitious social policy. As he grew older, Cassel moved along the ideological scale and developed in the late 1910s into the full-fledged liberal economist that the world came to know during the 1920s. Soon, however, he was left behind when Keynesianism and the Stockholm School took the lead in the economists' race for influence and power.

---

4 CARLSSON, BENNY: "Gustaf Cassel", in: JONUNG and STÅHLBERG, *op. cit.*

HANS DE GEER

III. The Exceptions: Important, but not Leading Scholars

The majority of the first generation of modern Swedish economists opposed the Historical School. There are however the exceptions, the figures who were influential, but not, at least not by posterity, regarded as the greatest. Johan Leffler, senior lecturer in economics and member of the Riksdag, became a pioneer and advocate for the Historical School in Sweden, but was never really invited to the inner circles of Academia.

Nor was **Gustaf Steffen**, 1864-1929, though he was the first holder of the chair of economics in Gothenburg.[5] As many economists of his generation he started his academic studies in the natural sciences. In 1885 he moved to Berlin in order to work at a geological institute, and aside from that he took up studies in political economy under Schmoller and Wagner. At about the same time he became a socialist and started fraternalizing in radical circles. He made a remarkable journey to France in the company of August Strindberg in 1886. The two became enemies for life, and Strindberg gives a very mean portrait of Steffen in one of his plays. In 1887, Steffen moved to London, where he worked as a journalist and correspondent for several Swedish newspapers. He also approached the Fabian Society and reported back on a diverse of radical ideas, including those of William Morris, John Ruskin and the American, Henry George. During the 1890s, Steffen's thinking moved from left to right and from Marxism in the direction of the Historical School. He found himself more and more uncomfortable in England and moved for a five-year period to Italy. In 1902 he was appointed to the newly established chair in economics and sociology at the University of Gothenburg.

Steffen is by far the economist in Sweden with the broadest scholarly interests. At the same time he has been accused of being shallow in his analysis, and his ambition to cover a wide range of topics in economics and politics was definitely not in step with the development in the discipline. Even less so in 1903, when he declared that economics had to be not only theoretical, but historical and nationalist: "the economic man ... is a fiction", and he recommended students to study psychology, history, and ethnology parallel to economics. It was, says Steffen's biographer, the influ-

---

5   LILLIESTAM, ÅKE: *Gustaf Steffen, samhällsteoretiker och idépolitiker*, diss Götabor 1960.

ences from Fabianism during his stay in London that worked as a catalyst and made him recall and view his German lessons in a new light.

During the 1890s Steffen turned more towards sociology, a field of interest that he regarded as more comprehensive than economics. But his main sources of inspiration were not sociologists, but philosophers, mainly Nietzsche and, later, Bergson, as well as psychologist like Wilhelm Wundt. As he more and more recognised the importance of the èlite personalities in historical change, he distanced himself from his Marxist/socialist thoughts from the 1880s. But he did not give up the ambitions to find a pattern of regularity in history and in fact he constructed his own version of a theory of evolution, much in the spirit of the positivist August Comte and the biologist Herbert Spencer.

Steffen made no success as an academic teacher. Clearly he demonstrated that he looked for other options within journalism or politics. In 1910 he was elected member of the parliament (the First Chamber) for the social democrats and he found his ideological position at the party's right wing. He never acknowledged the importance of the party whip, and in a number of important issues he rebelled against the party policy. That, in combination with his academic superciliousness, made him not very popular in the Social Democratic Party and diminished his political influence. Also, his pro-German attitude during the First World War and slightly racist interpretation of the causes of the war, made it impossible for him to remain in the party; together with some other opponents he was expelled in 1915 and was not re-elected to the Riksdag when his period was out.

After the war Steffen re-entered the party, but did not participate in the public debate as he had used to, and as an academic he worked more with private tutoring in his home than giving public lectures. It was increasingly obvious that Steffen had become marginalised within his own discipline: that is not to say that he ever was a central figure. In the broad scope of his interests, in his intellectual and human curiosity, rather than in the very sharpness of his analysis, he was unique among his colleagues and he got no disciples. Academically speaking, he represented a deadlock.

Eli Heckscher, 1879-1952, had, as many of his generation, a thorough, German education. A pupil of Davidson and Cassel, he was introduced to theoretical thinking in economics. He made important contributions to economics in Sweden, and, through Bertil Ohlin and Paul Samuelson, on the theoretical development at the international level. In spite of this, he turned into an economic historian, the most prominent figure of that discipline in Sweden.[6]

Given this scholarly inclination towards history as a source of both inspiration and evidence one might think that the Historical School would have been attractive to the young Heckscher, especially since his co-operation with Cassel started at a time when Cassel was still a "Kathedersozialist". But we have to be careful here. Heckscher was as deductive in his scientific mind as ever Davidson or Cassel, but he combined that with a certain historical interest, that his teachers did not have. He solved the problem by drawing a definite line of demarcation between the two academic disciplines, between economics on one hand, economic history on the other, giving each of them a specific, scientific role and task. Roughly speaking, economics ought to explain the system, the interdependencies in an economy working towards an equilibrium, while economic history should explain the dynamics, the change, the movement through time. That is, instead of pulling history and economy together in one explanatory system, Heckscher tried to separate them into two independent, intellectual fields. In that respect he did not share the suppositions of the Historical School, on the contrary he fiercely opposed it. But, one the other hand, in his quest to mobilise history in order to understand and explain economic phenomena, he belongs to the German tradition, rather than to the more puristic, classical tradition of British economics. In his older days, when he since long had left his chair in economics for a chair in economic history, Heckscher choose to use historical evidence in his argumentation with the proponents of the Stockholm School, whose expansionist and planned-economy approach he most decidedly opposed.

Let us go a bit further from pure economics and look at **Gustaf Sundbärg**, 1857-1914. Sundbärg worked for a long time within the National Statistics Office in Sweden, and his main oevre falls within demography. Sundbärg never studied abroad, but he developed far-reaching professional relations all over Europe. He represents a branch in the growing statistical science that is characterised by its descriptive and historical approach, in contrast to more mathematical methods that were introduced around the turn of the century.

---

6 HENRIKSSON, ROLF: "Eli Heckscher", in: JONUNG and STÅHLBERG: *op. cit.*; SANDELIN, BO: *The History of Swedish Economic Thought*, London (Routledge) 1991.

Since 1903, Sundbärg had combined his work at the Statistics Office with a position as associate professor at Stockholm University (at that time Stockholms Högskola). In 1910, Sundbärg was appointed the first professor of statistics in Sweden, at the University of Uppsala, but he was not able to hold the chair for but a very short time, owing to other public businesses and growing sickness. Just like Steffen, Sundbärg represents something like a deadlock. He never got a number of followers ready to spread his understanding of statistics. Instead, when statistics grew as an academic discipline it was the more theoretical, mathematical branch that was promoted.

But the interesting thing is that Sundbärg's influence, minor as it was in scholarly circles in a longer perspective, was the more important in a shorter perspective, and outside the ivory tower of Academia. Sundbärg was very productive, and his most impressive work was a voluminous investigation into the causes and effects of the emigration from Sweden to the Americas (*Emigrationsutredningen*). It included a number of appendices, often important investigations in itself. Sundbärg was the author of several of them, writing not just on statistical or demographic questions, but also on things like "the Swedish national character". The practical influence of the investigation was important in a variety of political and economical issues, ranging from questions like the compulsory military service, the establishment of a national own-your-own-home movement, local poor-relief schemes, to the introduction of Scientific Management in Swedish industry. In his broad, empirical approach to emigration as a social phenomenon, Sundbärg came across and interpreted a wide range of social problems, and in many cases he indicated solutions that were later implemented in praxis. Sundbärg was not identified as a proselyte of the German Historical School, but his approach and his intellectual fate bring him close. Sundbärgs activity brings a more general perspective to our attention. Let us continue to look outside of the narrow academic circles.

IV. *Verein für Socialpolitik* – The Swedish Version

An association, the CSA, *Centralförbundet für Socialt Arbete*, was founded in 1903 and the inspiration came directly from a similar activity in Berlin, namely the *Verein für Socialpolitik*, and indirectly from the Fabian

Society. In the wake of industrialisation, it combined a wide scope of interest in all kinds of social questions, with an ardent appetite for political debate and patient, practical social work.

In the new association, tiny as it was from start, people joined from all parts of society. They shared an interest in the social question, widely defined. It was a practical work, the CSA arranged exhibitions, lectures and seminars to encourage debate, published a periodical and focused different issues, which all could be covered by the broad concept of social policy. The activity was strictly neutral from a point of party politics and we find within its cadre members of both right- and left wing parties. The most part, however, were liberals, believing in the possibility to use a scientific approach to detect and diagnose social evils, and to use public power to correct them. And science in this respect meant economics in that broader sense of the Historical School. Among the young people working close to CSA we find economists like the young Cassel, Heckscher, Sven Brisman and others.

The CSA worked rather like a task force, focusing the attention on one important question after the other, and over time its scope became quite impressive. The association took initiatives concerning poor relief, children care, housing, land reform, labour market relations and mediation, unemployment, social insurance etc. No field within the concept of social policy was left untoiled and CSA's influence was considerable. Without exaggeration it could be stated that the entire structure of legislation and other kinds of institutionalisation of social policy, like the corporatist patterns at the labour market, was prepared and formed by the CSA think-tank during the period before World War I.

From the late 1930s, with the Social Democrats firmly in the saddle, things changed. For CSA it had in fact changed already in the early 1920s. The association lost some of its momentum and mission when a Ministry for Social Affairs was created in 1920 and a central bureaucracy was built to administer the whole range of social issues (*Socialstyrelsen*). This was not a defeat, it was a victory for the CSA, and its people manned the new structures. But, as it is stated in the association's historical account, the CSA moved into the shadow of its own results. In 1923, the association changed its statutes, and left its more activist period. Later, after World War II, there was no longer room for the kind of private initiative that was CSA's; the organisation of public administration was established and more and more of the ideological initiative was channelled through the established political parties. These arenas were at that time already imbued with "modern" keynesianism; there was no use for the "old-fashioned", welfarist views of the CSA, which was subsequently transformed into merely a fund, sponsoring research on social work.

One of the last initiatives of CSA before its reorganisation brings us back to the impact of the Historical School. Since 1904, Gustaf Cassel had been professor of Economics at the Stockholm University (then: Stockholms högskola). As mentioned, Cassel developed into a more neo-classical position, leaving the broader social questions behind. In 1920, the CSA raised the funds for a second chair in economics, now with the important addition "Economics and Social Policy". To the new chair was appointed Gösta Bagge.[7]

Gösta Bagge, 1882-1951, was of another generation than the previous mentioned economists. He was the first Swedish economist to study in the USA; in 1904 he went to the John Hopkins University in Baltimore. Economics at John Hopkins was once formed by Richard Ely, who had studied in Germany under Wagner and Knies and was determined to establish the Historical School in the New World. His mission was carried forth by his successor Jacob Hollander. Now Bagge was deeply influenced by this institutionalist message and brought it back to Sweden. At the Stockholm University he continued his research on labour market and other aspects of societal institutions. One of his pupils was Gunnar Myrdal, who never abandoned the institutionalist perspective, and thus Myriad's work brings the influence of the Historical School into our time and almost up to the 1980s, when the new institutionalism started to attract the attention.

V. The Winning Paradigm?
The Emergence of the Stockholm School

The "Stockholm School" competes with Keynesianism to claim the honour of exploring demand-side economics. On the basis of works of Wicksell and others, a generation of economists like Erik Lindehl, Bertil Ohlin and Erik Lundberg developed theories on inflation, employment and stabilisation

---

7 *Centralförbundet för Socialt Arbete 1903-1928.* Minneskrift.

policy. All of them located in Stockholm, these young economists dominated their trade, with access to the important scholarly networks and journals, and with more and more intensive contacts with the political leadership of the time. Several of them contributed to forming the theory behind radical political reforms – Sweden had a social democratic government since 1932 – and some of them even took the step from being scholars into being administrators; the most well-known of them was Dag Hammarskiöld. Their theoretical approach reduced the historicist and institutionalist alternative to a minimum. The most creative period of the Stockholm School was the 1930s; later the more straightforward keynesian model offered a better and widely accepted ground for the further theoretical development of economical sciences in Sweden.

VI. The 1980s: New Institutionalism

The overwhelming dominance of Keynesianism in Sweden during the three decades that followed the World War II was challenged during the 1980s. It was in fact part of the crisis of the Swedish model in its more comprehensive understanding. It was obvious that other factors than public demand and spending had to be taken into account in order to cope with the economic crisis. Supply side economics and monetarism attracted attention. Structural problems came into focus and paved the way for new institutionalism. In a new moulding the broader, societal perspective was again accepted in economics in Sweden. The heritage from the Historical School was brought in again, but through the backdoor. It had to come from the US to be fully accepted in the right circles. But that is the start of another story...

VII. Conclusion

The German Historical School has had a rather weak influence on the development of economics as a science in Sweden. In fact, it could be better described as a negative starting-point for the economists who became the most influential. The advocates for the Historical School were scholars more on the margin of economics as an academic discipline, on the verge of statistics, sociology or economical history. The dominance of the Stockholm School made generations of Swedish economists immune to any historicist inspiration. It is only in the last decade that international attention has made Swedish economists more conscious of institutional aspects of the economy.

Let alone that the impact of the Historical School was weak on economics, its impact on practical life, on social policy, on the other hand, was considerable and presumably more important. Within the CSA, with its committedness and typical ideological mix of conservativism, liberalism and socialism, many of the ideas characterising the emerging welfare state were fostered, spanning all over the spectrum of social and economical policy. This private welfarist initiative played an important role in between old paternalism and modern, corporatist and bureaucratic welfare systems.

The intellectual heritage from the German Historical School, through American institutionalism to Myrdal and to late, new institutionalism survived the lean years of Keynesian dominance, and the broader societal perspective is now, more that ever before, a possible theoretical standing.

Discussion Summary

TORBEN VESTDAM

Paper discussed:
HANS DE GEER: The Historical School in Sweden: A Sketch

What is the influence of the German Historical School on Swedish economists and, in a wider sense, its impact on the emerging élite that formed the political discourse in Sweden in the early decades of the 20th century?

The author concludes that the Swedish theorists of political economy of the 1930's whom later assumed positions of administrators and politicians and came to dominate the Swedish economic-political discourse until 1980's and 1990's was only negatively influenced by the German Historical School. The reason for this negative influence stems from their appreciation of negative and deterministic Marxist theory of historical materialism and Keynesian demand-side political economy and disappointment among these Swedish political economist, who did not receive education in the scientific, deductionist methodology at the German universities, they expected. The author emphasises additionally that reference to the Stockholm School implies a disregard for the ethical- and historical dimension of political economy, which the approaches of German Historical School implies. KOSLOWSKI remarks that the German Historical School ought to be considered as an orientation for scientific practices which adopt German language as medium of communication and applies to locations that transcends border lines defining nation states.

The author draws an outline of an intellectual setting where a scientific-deductionist paradigm dominates the scientific discourse of political economy and the discourse of government and political administration, while proponents of historical approaches which actually subscribe to significant dimension of approaches proposed by affiliates of the German Historical

DISCUSSION SUMMARY

School, practice in the wider periphery of the academic centre of the University of Stockholm.

The author furthermore outlines the process which transforms practices of social work from a stage of private, philanthropic enterprise during the first four decades of the 20th century into a stage of public welfare practice, where social security is considered as a social-democratic responsibility and therefore as object for political administration. The author adds that a relation between these philanthropic practices and the scientific practices could be identified by the initiative in 1920 by *Centralföbundet für Socialt Arbete* to fund a new professor chair of 'Economics and Social Policy' at University of Stockholm, which was offered to Gösta Bagge, who during his visit to John Hopkins University was introduced to and positively influenced by contributions of Schmoller in particular and affiliates of the German Historical School in general. This allows the author to introduce a broader definition of the German Historical School by adding a dimension of ideology. However, the influence that Bagge exerts from his position at the University of Stockholm is more in the capacity of fund-raiser and recruiter of the 'would be' members of the Stockholm School rather than as affiliate of the German Historical School.

Part Six

Historism in Economic Law

Chapter 14

Jurisprudence, History, National Economics After 1850[1]

SIBYLLE HOFER

I. Introduction
II. Links Between Civil Law Dogmatics and National Economics
   1. Heinrich Dankwardt
      a) Jurisprudence and National Economics
      b) The Reason of Legal Clauses
      c) National Economics as a Standard of Evaluation Concerning Legal Regulations
      d) Relationship to the Historical School of Law
   2. Burkard Wilhelm Leist
   3. Result: An Evaluation of the Roman Law with the Aid of an Economic Viewpoint - a Trend in the Jurisprudence in the Middle of the 19th Century
      a) Wilhelm Arnold
      b) The Importance of the New Direction
   4. Otto von Gierke
      a) 'Living' Law as the Basic Foundation of Legislation
      b) Jurisprudence in Parallel to National Economics
      c) The Problematic Nature of 'Social' Private Law
III. Result

---

[1] I would like to thank Bryan Black who translated the first draft, and Gabriela A. Eakin who revised it.

SIBYLLE HOFER

I. Introduction

When one speaks of 'historism', in regard to jurisprudence, one usually associates this notion with the historical school of law and especially with the name Friedrich Carl von Savigny. Indeed it was Savigny who founded a journal entitled "*Zeitschrift für geschichtliche Rechtswissenschaft*" in 1815 and spoke in the foreword to this publication of a "historical school". Later in 1888, Rudolf Stammler used the term 'historism' to characterise the method of the historical school of law. He was, however, critical of this method.[2] Both the establishment of the historical school as well as the criticism of method at the end of the 1880s have parallels in the field of national economics. The subject matter of the following investigation, however, is neither the historism of the historical school of law nor analogies between this and the historical school of national economics. Nor should it be seen as an analysis of Stammler's critique of historism or a comparison of this with the discussion of method in national economics. Instead, the following contribution deals with a subject lying between these points in both time and content. With regard to time, the generation of jurists after Savigny interests. This generation is rather neglected in current legal-historical investigations. But it is of considerable interest to examine how Savigny's concept of historical jurisprudence was treated later. It is immediately noticeable that a 'turning point' in jurisprudence in the middle of the 1850s is spoken about.[3] This formulation lets it be known that the jurists of this time obviously had the feeling that they had to reach a new level of civil law dogmatics in relation to the historical school of law and also that they felt able to attain such a level. When the headword 'nature' is used repeatedly in the texts, it does

---

2 See WITTKAU (1994, pp. 80ff.).
3 See the title of KUNTZE (1856): "Der Wendepunkt der Rechtswissenschaft". And JHERING (1857): "That something new is preparing itself within jurisprudence, this realisation, I believe, can even not be overlooked by someone who does not consider the new to be something good." ("(...) *daß sich innerhalb der Jurisprudenz in der Tat etwas Neues vorbereitet, dieser Wahrnehmung, meine ich, wird sich selbst der nicht verschließen können, der dies Neue keineswegs für etwas Gutes hält.*"). LEIST (1859) p. xi, speaks of a "whirlwind of a peculiar type" ("*Wirbelwind eigentümlicher Art*") which had risen up in civil law jurisprudence.

JURISPRUDENCE, HISTORY, NATIONAL ECONOMICS AFTER 1850

not solely mean a reference to scientific research.[4] Moreover, very differing concepts are hidden in the notion of 'nature'.[5] One of these concepts is the subject of the following investigation. This concept is characterised by the inclusion of contemporary national economic research in civil law jurisprudence which on the other hand is based on a historical investigation of the law.

The subject "Law and Economics" is still today of relevance in both the area of legal-historical research[6] as well as in the dogmatics of private law[7]. For those works involved here from the middle of the 19th century it must be remembered that the history of law and the civil law dogmatics cannot be separated in the same way as today. This is determined by the situation concerning the sources of law. There existed no uniform civil law for Germany (*Deutscher Bund*, later *Norddeutscher Bund*, since 1871 *Kaiserreich*).[8] Before the coming into force of the German Civil Code (*Bürgerliches Gesetzbuch, BGB*) on 1.1.1900, there was a pluralism of sources of law. Apart from codifications which were only valid in certain parts of Germany, the legal foundation for civil law was the so-called *'gemeines*

---

4   In many books of this time the work of the jurist is compared with that of the natural scientist. Cf. L. GOLDSCHMIDT's comment (1898, p. 149): "Two of our most outstanding jurists are considerably influenced in this way by natural scientists: The first, Jhering in Gießen, applies the principles of chemistry to the analysis of legal institutes - the other, Leist in Jena, construes the organism of legal life according to Schleiden's elementary concepts." (*"Zwei unserer bedeutendsten Rechtsgelehrten sind in dieser Weise von Naturforschern wesentlich influiert: der eine, Jhering in Gießen, wendet mit Glück die Grundsätze der Chemie vergleichsweise auf die Analyse der Rechtsinstitute an, - der andere, Leist in Jena, konstruiert den Organismus des Rechtslebens nach Schleiden's Elementarbegriffen."*).
5   It is inaccurate if, as often happens, one only thinks of Jhering in this context.
6   Cf. the method discussion within legal history in the 1970s (see SENN: 1982, pp. 153ff.) and as an example of co-operation between economic and legal historians HORN/KOCKA: *Recht und Entwicklung der Großunternehmen im 19. und frühen 20. Jahrhundert*, 1979.
7   See the economic analysis of law.
8   Somewhat different was the situation regarding commercial law. The general German Code of Commercial Law came into effect in 1869 within the area of the *Norddeutscher Bund*. But already since 1861 it was introduced in most of the individual *Bundesstaaten* through parallel legislation.

Recht' (common law).[9] To a considerable extent this contained Roman private law in the form of the codification from the time of the emperor Justinian (530-534; *Corpus Juris Civilis)*. The consequence was: The Roman law was at the same time both a historical law and the basis of the prevailing law. So for the jurisprudence of civil law of the 19th century every consideration of the Roman law meant simultaneously a consideration of the law in effect at the time. The topical question for the jurisprudence was: Which of the Roman rules should be considered as effective law? Representative of the importance of the Roman law at this time is the title of Savigny's book *System des heutigen römischen Rechts* (published between 1840 and 1849).

In the following investigation of a historical jurisprudence of civil law in the second half of the 19th century, which is characterised by the inclusion of economic research, four jurists are of central importance: H. Dankwardt, W. B. Leist, W. Arnold, and O. Gierke. The works of these jurists - except that of Gierke - are little known today.[10] In their time, the books of Leist, Arnold, and especially of Dankwardt were, however, carefully observed. It will be shown that the works of these jurists and also those of Gierke have something fundamental in common: In fact they all judge on prevailing law. Thereby Savigny's idea of necessary elements of law was linked in a particular way with the results of national economic research.

The selection of texts ensues from explicit references to a link between jurisprudence and national economics.[11] Here also is the reason why Jhering's name is missing. Jhering was indeed a member of the *Verein für Sozialpolitik* and he once contributed to *Schmollers Jahrbuch*.[12] This article, however, is made up of extracts from a chapter of the second volume of Jhering's book *Der Zweck im Recht*. An explicit reference to national economics does not appear in this essay.

---

9   Still the most exact overview of this situation before the coming into effect of the BGB can be found in F. ENDEMANN (1903 § 2 footnote 13). On the previous codification in the Länder cf. DÖLEMEYER and BUCHHOLZ in COING (1982, pp. 1440ff.).

10 Only KROESCHELL (1975, pp. 253ff.) devotes himself to the life and work of W. Arnold.

11 See below the quotations at the beginning of each section.

12 "Die geschichtlich-gesellschaftliche Grundlage der Ethik", *Schmollers Jahrbuch*, 6 (1882), pp. 2ff.

On the other hand, the selection remains limited to private law academics. Due to space limitation, an analysis of the works of commercial lawyers (e.g. Goldschmidt, H. Thöl, W. Endemann) is not included.

II. Links Between Civil Law Dogmatics and National Economics

1. Heinrich Dankwardt

The first link: In 1862 a book entitled *Nationalökonomisch-civilistische Studien* was published in Germany. Its author, Heinrich Dankwardt,[13] a lawyer from Rostock, had written already four papers on the topic "Nationalökonomie und Jurisprudenz" (1857-1859). W. Roscher drew up the foreword for the 1862 publication in which he wrote: "Like the earlier writings (...) this one is also destined to establish a reciprocal fertilising link between economics and jurisprudence."[14]

a) Jurisprudence and National Economics

The titles themselves show that Dankwardt strives to establish a link between jurisprudence and national economics (*Nationalökonomie und Jurisprudenz*, *Nationalökonomisch-civilistische Studien*). Dankwardt achieves the inclusion of national economic research into jurisprudence by means of the following train of thought: All law is the product of actual circumstances. In order to understand the law, therefore, it is at first necessary to know the actual conditions involved. And this knowledge is provided by

---

13 Apart from the fact that Dankwardt was active as a lawyer in Rostock, little is known about this jurist. LANDSBERG does not give dates of birth or death for him (1910, pp. 762ff., notes p. 328). In *Allgemeine/Neue Deutsche Biographie, Deutscher biographischer Index* Dankwardt is not mentioned. Besides the works mentioned here, Dankwardt wrote a book about the *negotiorum gestio* as well as several essays published in *Jherings Jahrbücher*.

14 ROSCHER: in: DANKWARDT (1862, p. III): "*Wie die früheren Schriften, womit der geistvolle Verfasser einen neuen Schacht in das Bergwerk der Wissenschaft getrieben hat, so ist auch die vorliegende bestimmt, zwischen der Volkswirtschaftslehre und Jurisprudenz eine gegenseitig befruchtende Verbindung einzuleiten.*"

national economics.[15] Dankwardt bases this argumentation on Roscher's assertion that the main task of national economics should be "the simple portrayal of the economic nature and needs of the people, of the laws and institutions which exist for the satisfaction of the population and finally of their success obtained to a greater or lesser degree as though it were the anatomy or physiology of the national economy."[16]

The assertion that the law is a product of actual conditions - with the result that national economics are therefore meaningful for legal research - is supported by Dankwardt through the explanation of the reasons for legal clauses. Thereby he differentiates two main categories. Firstly, according to his view, there are those clauses which the legislator is compelled to draft with almost "dictatorial power". The society as an "organism" creates laws which have effects working with "the same iron necessity as natural laws".[17] Dankwardt assumes that the practical needs and economic conditions can force a certain legal regulation. In such cases the legal clause, according to Dankwardt, can be seen as a "necessary" result of actual conditions[18], the legal clauses then have "national-economical reasons". With the idea of an 'organism', Dankwardt succeeds in drawing an arc to national economics exactly in the sense of Roscher's definition: "These causes (of legal rules) are taught by national economics, which one can then characterise as the physiology of the social organism."[19] Herewith, Dankwardt emphasises the fact that concerning this category of legal clauses changes in legal regulations may be ascertained - by the aid of national economics - with "absolute certainty".[20]

Results of the same level of certainty are also attainable by the effort of national economics, Dankwardt claims, in his other category of legal clauses. The latter are based on, as he calls them, "ethical grounds". He thinks mainly of laws being enacted to remedy abuses before a deplorable

---

15 1862, p. 17; 1857a, pp. 3ff.
16 ROSCHER (1857a) § 26, quoted by DANKWARDT (1857a, p. 5 note*): "(...) *die einfache Schilderung der wirtschaftlichen Natur und Bedürfnisse des Volks, der Gesetze und Anstalten, welche zur Befriedigung der letzteren bestimmt sind, endlich des größeren oder geringeren Erfolgs, den sie gehabt haben, also gleichsam die Anatomie oder Physiologie der Volkswirtschaft.*"
17 (1862, p. 2; compare also p. 20: "*naturnothwendiger Prozeß*".
18 Cf. 1857a, p. 3; 1857b, p. 17; 1862, p. 135.
19 1862, p. 2.
20 1862, p. 4.

state of affairs forces a regulation.[21] The process, whereby the motive of such legal clauses may be determined is described by Dankwardt in the following passage: "I eliminate the legal clause as though it does not even exist and examine then with the aid of economic insight which dire conditions exist in the social organism as a result. Such conditions may be ascertained easily and with absolute certainty in the majority of cases. Then I have found simultaneously the purpose or the *ratio* of the legal clause involved."[22]

b) The Reason of Legal Clauses

Roscher had named the essential difference as being that the jurisprudence researches only the "external how" while national economics concerns itself with the "deeper why".[23] When Dankwardt places decisive importance on the reason of legal clauses in the above quoted passages, he wishes to include the question as to the 'why' in the area of jurisprudence.[24] In his eyes, this starting point offers the medium of solving the current questions of jurisprudence. Dankwardt's ultimate aim is the construction of a system of private law.[25] The first main question to be addressed, however, is the assertion as to what the prevailing law is. Arising from the *Corpus Juris Civilis* as the legal source for a greater part of Germany[26], this question was still up to date in 1860. Which of these jurists' partly contradictory opinions collected in the codification of the East Roman emperor Justinian (530-534) should be valid in Germany in the 19th century? In 1814, Savigny had seen the solution for this in a "strict historical method" whose endeavours should be "to trace every given element back to

---

21 1862 pp. 3, 7.
22 1862, p. 8: "*Ich streiche den Rechtssatz aus, betrachte ihn als nicht vorhanden und untersuche nun mit Hilfe volkswirtschaftlicher Einsicht, welche Übelstände dadurch im gesellschaftlichen Organismus entstehen. Diese ergeben sich in den meisten Fällen leicht und stets mit apodiktischer Gewißheit. Damit habe ich aber gleichzeitig den Zweck oder die ratio des Rechtssatzes gefunden.*" DANKWARDT characterises his procedure as a use of the "baconist experimental-method" on jurisprudence (1862, p. 9 note 10).
23 ROSCHER (1875a, § 16) quoted by DANKWARDT (1857a, p. 11).
24 Cf. 1862, p. 4, note 3.
25 Cf. 1857a, p. 10; 1862, pp. 11ff., 128. DANKWARDT understands his works as "preparatory work" for the drawing up of a system (1862, p. 16).
26 See above I.

its roots and so discover its organic principle through which that which still has life may be separated from that which is defunct and simply belongs to the past."[27] Such optimism soon turned out to be an illusion. The question remained, however, "what still has life"[28]- or as it is called by Dankwardt "what the present day theory considers as effective law"[29]. Interestingly, Dankwardt takes up the key word "history" and applies it to signify his suggested method of solution. However, he sees an important difference between his approach and that of the historical school of law. His way is explicitly an investigation of the "internal history"[30] - in contrast to an explanation of the "external" or "mechanical" history. According to Dankwardt, the historical school of law merely examined the external history, i.e. simply compared different types of legal clauses even though it characterised this mere comparison as 'internal history'.[31] In contrast to this, Dankwardt seeks to uncover the reasons for changes in legal regulations "so that they may appear as the effects of certain causes".[32] That is, he calls for a consideration of history "according to the law of causality".[33] And for Dankwardt these causalities are economic causalities because the legal clauses have economic causes[34]. As a consequence, the question of the (economic) 'why' is then directed by him towards those clauses inherited from Roman law.

An example of how Dankwardt tries to attain results for the prevailing law from the 'internal history' may be seen in his handling of the property rights of produced goods. It was (and still is) a contentious question whether the producer or the deliverer of raw materials retains the property rights to

---

27 SAVIGNY (1814, pp. 117-178): "(...) *jeden gegebenen Stoff bis zu seiner Wurzel zu verfolgen, und so sein organisches Prinzip zu entdecken, wodurch sich von selbst das, was noch Leben hat, von demjenigen absondern muß, was schon abgestorben ist, und nur noch der Geschichte angehört*".
28 See RÜCKERT (1974, pp. 230, 233).
29 DANKWARDT (1857a, p. 27).
30 Cf. (1857a, p. 7).
31 (1862, pp. 19, 133, 138). For the relationship between Dankwardt's method and that of Savigny, see below. "*Innere Geschichte*" is well-known as a head word in HUGO (1832, p. 2).
32 1862, p. 138, see also p. 133.
33 1862, p. 32; cf. also pp. 133, 135.
34 See a).

the finished goods.[35] This point becomes even more important when the property rights of the raw material are not transferred to the manufacturer e.g. because the goods were stolen or because the deliverer has a right to reserve such rights. Dankwardt reaches his judgement by firstly presenting the respective opinions of the Roman jurists dating back to the 3rd century BC until the 6th century AD. As a justification for some of these very much differing decisions as regarding their content, Dankwardt states a practical need without any further explanation. He only substantiates, for instance, with the interest of the industry the decision that the producers retain the property rights.[36] For the prevailing law, Dankwardt first examines the comparability of the present day economic stages and those stages in which the clauses were developed. His scheme for this examination is, however, quite coarse. He only differentiates between a period of "isolation of the individual" and that of a "division of labour".[37] As a result, only a very few of the old Roman clauses are excluded as being unsuitable because they belong to the first economic period. So the examination as to whether the practical need, which was the basis for the Roman view, is comparable with that of the present day, becomes a central one. Here again, Dankwardt does not carry out an exact investigation but simply claims without analysis or justification: "We must keep distant from our law all that which cripples industry in complete or individual areas."[38] That opinion which favours the industry as far as possible is then propagated as the foundation for the prevailing law.[39]

That means: The most suitable provisions are discovered by Dankwardt through the comparison of economic conditions and practical needs in Rome with those of the present. From the various decisions as to a question of law in the course of the development of Roman law, those are chosen which "in

---

35 Cf. todays §§ 950ff. BGB.
36 1857a, p. 30.
37 1857a, p. 28. This differentiation is the only type of marking off the developmental stages used by DANKWARDT. It is found frequently throughout his work; cf. (1862, pp. 2, 135; 1857a, pp. 5, 9, 23). In ROSCHER's work, by contrast, one finds the periodisation nature, work, capital (see 1875a, § 47), taken over by LEIST (1859, p. 29).
38 1857a, p. 40.
39 1857a, pp. 38ff.

their content and as according to our social conditions are most suitable."[40] These legal clauses are then defined by Dankwardt to be the "true" ones (*richtiges Recht*)[41]. This notion is worthy of notice. With the idea of working out correct, true law Dankwardt takes a unique stand between the (older) historical school of national economics and the historical school of law as will be shown in what follows.

c) National Economics as a Standard of Evaluation Concerning Legal Regulations

For Dankwardt's categorisation of legal clauses as "wrong", "false", "incorrect"[42] or "true"[43] parallels can be found in W. Roscher's work. Roscher also evaluates legal regulations. Schmoller accurately observes that Roscher examines "the justification of regulations of economic policy". And Schmoller continues in his essay on W. Roscher: "The most general clauses possible, natural laws as Roscher prefers to name them, are extracted which on the basis of causal relations facilitate the assessment, and should show the way to the practical life much better than any abstract ideals."[44] Roscher's "natural laws" (*Naturgesetze*) have to be separated from the also often mentioned "developmental laws". The idea of "developmental laws" supposes that the nations pass through uniformly determined steps of development.[45] "Natural laws" in the sense of Roscher's definition, however,

---

40 (1857a, p. 39). Cf. also (1862, p. 183): "The work of theory, in solving the question as to the validity of a Roman legal clause, will have to limit itself to the examination whether a legal clause satisfies a practical need or not." ("*Die Arbeit der Theorie wird sich daher bei der Frage, ob ein römischer Rechtssatz gelte, auf die Untersuchung zu beschränken haben: - ob der Satz ein praktisches Bedürfnis befriedigt oder nicht.*").
41 1857a, pp. 39, 9.
42 1857b, p. 36.
43 Cf. (1857a, p. 9).
44 SCHMOLLER (1888, p. 168): "*Es werden möglichst allgemeine Sätze, Naturgesetze nennt Roscher sie mit Vorliebe, gewonnen, die auf Grund von Kausalverhältnissen die Beurteilung erleichtern, dem praktischen Leben besser, als diese oder jene abstrakte Ideale, die Wege weisen sollen.*"
45 Differently HILDEBRAND (1863 pp. 21ff.) who identifies with Roscher's natural laws the idea of self-interest.

describe causalities concerning the satisfaction of material needs.[46] An instructive example for a "natural law" can be found in Roscher's essay of 1849 "Der gegenwärtige Zustand der wissenschaftlichen Natinalökonomie und die nothwendige Reform desselben". In this article Roscher talks about the right of farmers to remove grass and foliage (so-called '*Waldstreu*') from the forest. Such legally regulated entitlements (so-called '*Waldservituten*') were widely spread in the 19th century.[47] Their abolition was, however, also heavily discussed at this time. Roscher now comments on this entitlement by designating the "turning point" in which the *Waldservitut* becomes detrimental for an economy instead of being beneficial. And Roscher is convinced of being able to fix this turning point with "almost mathematical precision"[48]. He determines this point with the aid of the prices of beech wood and straw and defines: If 3 to 7 cubic feet of beech wood are worth more than 24 to 36 pound of straw, an abolition of the *Waldservitut* is favourable.[49] The connection between "relevant circumstances"[50] (here: the prices of straw and beech wood) and their effects on the national wealth is to be understood as belonging to what Roscher understands as natural law. Roscher aims at examining this connection through historical considerations, especially through the comparison of different nations.[51] The given example shows that through the research of natural laws the point in time at which rights are to be protected or abolished for a particular people may be calculated with "certainty". Natural laws thereby serve as a standard for the judgement of legal regulations. And this standard is, in Roscher's eyes, "almost mathematically" certain. In particular, Roscher executes this point of view in his "Nationalökonomie des Acker-

---

46 ROSCHER (1849, pp. 180ff): "The national economics are concerned with the investigation of those natural laws according to which the people satisfy their material needs." ["*Ihr (sc. der Nationalökonomie) kommt es darauf an, die Naturgesetze zu erforschen, wonach die Völker ihre materiellen Bedürfnisse befriedigen (...).*"]
47 See KNÖPPEL (1994, p. 1118).
48 ROSCHER (1849, p. 188).
49 ROSCHER (1849, p. 188): "*Wo 3 bis 7 Cubikfuß Buchenholz weniger werth sind als 24 bis 36 Pfund Stroh, da würde das Volksvermögen durch Abschaffung der Streuservitute im Feld ein größeres Minus erreichen, als im Walde das Plus beträgt, und umgekehrt.*"
50 P. 188.
51 ROSCHER (1849, p. 181; 1861, p. 13ff.).

baus"[52]. In this work, he delivers clues for the "correct time" for the introduction of mobilisation of immovables[53], or judges a regulation as "suitable for the particular time" because it takes into consideration the "law" (i.e. natural law) that the introduction of intensive agriculture on fertile pieces of land is possible much earlier than on infertile land[54]. Roscher maintains rather optimistically that all economic discussions could simply be ended with the recognition of natural laws.[55]

Dankwardt uses these thoughts for the jurisprudence. As we have already seen, he calls for a research of the 'internal history' which he understands as an investigation of causalities of legal regulations. And these causalities should be, according to Dankwardt, regarded from an economic point of view, i.e. the regulations should be compared with the practical needs, the factual conditions. Based upon Roscher's theory of 'natural laws' the supposition that there are true, correct regulations for certain conditions becomes possible. In this sense, Dankwardt judges rules to be a "mistake" on the part of the legislator.[56] Thereby, national economics become a standard by which private law is to be judged.

This has decisive consequences when dealing with Roman law. The opinion that legal clauses may be justifiably criticised from an economic point of view[57] leads to the situation where Dankwardt feels free from all inherited Roman law: "In our opinion, Justinian's will is not relevant for us."[58] And he also remarks: "In what the nature of a legal transaction consists, is a question at which we have a free hand and are not bound by Roman law at all. If we can prove that the Roman view of the nature of a legal transaction is wrong: The Roman concept loses all meaning for us and we are thus entitled to strike out all legal clauses as invalid which appear to us to be pure consequence of this incorrect view."[59] These statements again

---

52 First edition in 1859.
53 1875b, § 148.
54 1875b, § 100, note 1.
55 1849, pp. 186ff.; 1875a, § 27.
56 See (1862, p. 7, note 8).
57 Cf. (1862, p. 139).
58 (1857a, p. 39) The East Roman emperor Justinian (482-565) ordered the drawing up of the Corpus Juris Civilis.
59 (1857b, p. 36-37): "*Worin die Natur eines Rechtsgeschäfts bestehe, dies ist eine Frage, bei welcher wir völlig freie Hand haben und an die Aussprüche des Römischen Rechts, berall nicht gebunden sind. Können wir den Römern nach-*

make it perfectly clear that the investigation of the nature of legal transactions - that is the economic nature - is central for Dankwardt. A suitable clause will then be sought for the obtained result regarding the question of the economic nature. The legal history is therefore used as a type of quarry from which the suitable elements for the construction of current law are taken from. This use of history distances itself from the idea that an examination of the historical development is the basis for the understanding of present conditions.[60] It is closer to the older view of history as a collection of examples.[61]

d) Relationship to the Historical School of Law

As already has been mentioned, Dankwardt sees his methodical approach as being in contrast with the procedure of the historical school of law. Regarding the question with which he begins, this claim is not accurate, however. Indeed Savigny had also incorporated the 'why' in the historical investigation: "(...) much more basic knowledge is necessary than for the usual work of the jurists; one should familiarise himself well with the letters of the historical material that it may be used as an implement for the portrayal of new forms."[62] In no way only the external history of law is being questioned here, but rather much more the investigation as to why certain groups of cases were decided in a certain way in certain times.[63] Thereby Savigny differentiates coincidental and necessary elements of law[64]. At the same time, however, some questions remain, namely concerning the relationship between coincidental and necessary elements and

---

weisen, daß ihre Anschauung von der Natur eines Rechtsgeschäfts falsch ist: so verliert der Römische Begriff für uns alle Bedeutung, und wir sind berechtigt, auch alle Rechtssätze als ungültig zu streichen, welche lediglich als Konsequenzen der von uns als irrig erkannten Anschauung erscheinen." Cf. also (1862, pp. 24ff.).

60 So SAVIGNY (1815, p. 4).
61 Cf. KOSELLECK (1995, pp. 38ff.).
62 SAVIGNY (1814, pp. 124ff.: *"Gerade für diese Anwendung auf eigene, neue Produktion ist noch weit mehr gründliche Kenntnis nötig als für das gewöhnliche Geschäft des Juristen; man muß über den Buchstaben des historischen Materials sehr Herr geworden sein, um dasselbe frei als Werkzeug zur Darstellung neuer Formen gebrauchen zu können."*
63 RÜCKERT (1987, p. 677).
64 RÜCKERT (1984, pp. 309ff.) and also cf. the headword *'notwendig'* in the index.

especially with regard to an empirical provable sign for a distinction between the two.[65]

In comparison with Savigny's scheme, the fact attracts attention that Dankwardt is also speaking of "necessary" provisions in contrast of "historically coincidental"[66] regulations. Where Dankwardt's approach, however, differs from Savigny's is that Dankwardt attempts to determine the type of a regulation with empirical certainty. That which may be seen as 'necessary' is to be determined as according to factual conditions. And the knowledge of these conditions - and the resulting necessary regulations - should be provided by national economics Dankwardt believes. While Savigny attempted to search for the "organic principle" in order to elaborate which law "still has life"[67], Dankwardt wishes to investigate the "economic principle" instead, in order to ascertain the prevailing law.

At this point again the relationship to Roscher is to stress. Roscher's optimism concerning the demonstration of natural laws allows Dankwardt to suppose that certainties for the law are obtainable through economic research. And it should be mentioned that it is also Roscher's aim to "differentiate the done and the ephemeral from the necessary and permanent, the old and the dying from the hopeful and living in public things."[68]

2. Burkard Wilhelm Leist

The second link: Published in the years 1854, 1855, 1859 and 1877, were the investigations of Burkard Wilhelm Leist[69] on the subject of

---

65 RÜCKERT (1984, p. 310).
66 DANKWARDT (1857a, p. 39).
67 See above, note 27.
68 ROSCHER (1849, p. 180): "(...) *durch das historische Studium (...) in öffentlichen Dingen das Gemachte und Ephemere von dem Notwendigen und Dauerhaften, das Altersschwache und Absterbende von dem Lebens- und Hoffnungsvollen zu unterscheiden (...).*"
69 Professor in Basel, Rostock and Jena. E. I. BEKKER (1907) places the Romanist Leist in the same list as the great names Mommsen, Bruns, Jhering, Windscheid and Brinz. Apart from those works which follow, Leist wrote several volumes of *Glück's Kommentar*, which had been established at the end of the 18th century explaining the *Pandekten* (*Digesten*, part of the *Corpus Juris Civilis*). Later, Leist occupied himself with the pre-history of the Roman law (see BEKKER (1907), LANDSBERG (1910, text pp. 835ff.).

Civilistische Studien auf dem Gebiete dogmatischer Analyse. In 1860, Leist completed a supplement to these works in which he wrote: "When the first of my writings of civil studies was published (at the same time as Roscher's economics), the thought had planted itself in my mind that property is to be braced back to work as its source. I saw then (...), as soon as Roscher's book came into my possession, that this idea was by no means a new one. I confess openly, that up to that point I had never concerned myself with national economics, indeed, on my part these thoughts were forced from an entirely different side, namely, through the need to find the leading thread in the labyrinth of the 'nature of the object' (*Natur der Sache*). "On his own methods used after this discovery Leist comments: "I therefore simply quote Roscher (...) and attempt (...) to lead the thought through the individual civil doctrines."[70]

Leist succeeds in obtaining similar results as Dankwardt at the approximately same time.[71] Leist's starting point is the improvement of the methods for the "dogmatic analysis of Roman legal institutions".[72] As the decisive point he works out the investigation of "natural clauses" (*Natursätze*). As well as juristic and ethical elements, legal relations also contain a "natural element", according to Leist.[73] His train of thought is as follows: Legal regulations are based on living conditions. These living conditions bear a

---

70 LEIST (1860, pp. 35-36): "*Als das erste Heft meiner zivilistischen Studien erschien (gleichzeitig mit der Roscher'schen Volkswirtschaft), hatte sich schon längere Zeit bei mir der Gedanke festgestellt, daß das Eigentum auf Arbeit zurückgeführt werden müsse. Ich sah dann (...) sehr bald darauf, indem mir das Roscher'sche Buch in die Hand fiel, daß mein Gedanke gar nicht neu sei. Ich gestehe offen, daß ich mich bis dahin um Nationalökonomie gar nicht gekümmert hatte, ich meinerseits war in diesen Gedanken von ganz anderer Seite her getrieben worden, nämlich durch das Bedürfnis, in dem Labyrinth der 'Natur der Sache' einen leitenden Faden zu finden. (...) Ich zitiere einfach Roscher (...) und versuche, was die eigentlich zivilistische Aufgabe ist, den Gedanken durch die einzelnen zivilistischen Lehren durchzuführen.*"
71 ROSCHER does not mention Leist in his history of the national economics in Germany (1874) but rather names as jurists who were involved with national economic research L. Goldschmidt, W. Arnold and H. Dankwardt (p. 1041). In 1857, however, FITTING (1857, p. 626) remarked that Leist's demand for a study of nature meant a link between jurisprudence and national economics.
72 Cf. the title of the first part of his *Studien* (1854), and there pp. 1ff.
73 (1860, p. 13).

particular nature inherent in themselves, i.e. they are in accordance with natural clauses.[74] Regarding the relationship between these natural clauses and legal clauses, Leist goes on to differentiate two types of legal clauses, namely those which appear as a sanction of natural clauses and those which are not based on such natural clauses.[75] In the first instance, the natural clause is the *ratio* of the positive law with the result that a knowledge of the former is necessary in order to develop the content of the positive law from the *ratio*.[76] On the other hand, Leist does admit that both positive and customary law can prescribe to observe a particular legal clause being inconsistent with a natural clause.[77] However, he restricts this immediately with the comment that if a departure from a natural clause occurs without reason the latter reacts with a resistant force which leads to a change of the legal clause "not simply from the point of view of expedience but rather that of necessity."[78] Thus, Leist reaches a central meaning of natural clauses also for the second group of legal clauses which he views as a smaller part, anyhow. And he can assert that one can only understand a clause fully if it is viewed in light of the "natural principle" (*naturales Prinzip*).[79]

It is to notice that Leist's starting point has similarities to Dankwardt's view. Like Dankwardt, Leist supposes that the law is produced by factual conditions. In this way the factual respectively the living conditions become part of the juristic field of research.[80] Not surprisingly the investigation of the nature is then the point where Leist establishes a parallel to national

---

74 1854, p. 62.
75 1854, p. 71; cf. also pp. 76, 83.
76 1854, p. 71.
77 Cf. (1854, p. 34).
78 1854, p. 90; cf. also p. 86.
79 1859, p. 21.
80 Cf. LEIST (1854, pp. 27ff., 1859, p. 3).

economics after the readings of Roscher's system.[81] As a consequence, Leist sometimes speaks of the "economic nature"[82] of a legal institution.

And also like Dankwardt, Leist seeks to work out "true law"[83] with the research on natural clauses: "The positive law, the will of the legislator, is not the boundary of our research, but has within the living conditions again natural law as its basis which it has not to follow blindly, but which rather continuously has an influence on it. Only when we exactly have separated and shown what natural law is and just how the will of the legislator adopts it or distances itself from it, has scientific research fulfilled its aim. Therefore, we are able to search for principles of objective dogmatic truth and, indeed, are able to find them."[84] The central notions are "true", "objective" or "necessary" as opposed to "coincidental".[85] It has already been mentioned that these are also the headwords which Savigny uses in the description of his historical method.[86] Unlike Dankwardt, Leist now understands his studies as "the necessary continuation of those works begun by the historical school of law".[87] He bases his argument on the fact that the histori-

---

81 See above; (1860, pp. 14ff., 35ff.). There, LEIST also mentions Dankwardt without examining his works and parallels to his own point of view in detail. Cf. also the references in 1865, pp. 49ff. Leist speaks there, perhaps under the influence of Roscher, only of "natural laws" (*Naturgesetze*). The link to Roscher goes far over the thought of work as the basis of property, as Leist in the quotation (see note 70) notices.
82 (1865, pp. 66, 72), cf. also (1860), where LEIST uses the notion "private economic natural laws" (*privatökonomische Naturgesetze*) in the headlines pp. 14, 20.
83 "*Richtige" Rechtssätze*; cf. LEIST (1865, p. 86).
84 (1865, pp. 86-87): "*Die positive Satzung, der Rechtswille, ist hier nicht die Grenze unserer Forschung, er selbst hat in den menschlichen Lebensverhältnissen wieder Naturgesetze zu seinem Grund, denen er nicht blind zu folgen braucht, die aber doch immer auf ihn einwirken. Erst wenn wir genau auseinander gelegt haben, was das Naturgesetz ist und wie der Rechtswille es adoptiert oder sich von ihm entfernt, hat die wissenschaftliche Forschung ihr Ziel erreicht. Darin liegt, daß wird hier Prinzipien von objektiver dogmatischer Wahrheit suchen und finden könne.*" Cf. also (1854, p. 62): "*leicht nachweisbare absolute Wahrheit*", and similarly (1865, p. 3).
85 Cf. also (1854, p. 8): Differentiation of "positive arbitrary" elements and "inner necessity" in Roman law.
86 See above note 64 and RÜCKERT (1984, Index of headwords).
87 1859, p. XXIII.

cal school of law considered the "objective given facts"[88] as the focal point. Leist, however, provides this "objective given facts" with a different content than Savigny. It is not simply made up of the "ethical and legal collective awareness of the population" but, according to Leist, rather and moreover of "non-ethical and non-legal" "organisms" which are necessarily[89] created through the co-habitation of human beings[90]. "The *naturalis ratio* is (...) something objective, which is contained therein in human relations."[91] Accordingly, Leist sees the main task of the jurisprudence as "confronting the nature of relations and the content of positive legal clauses."[92]

And thereby Leist, like Dankwardt, reaches a position free of the Roman law by investigating the 'nature' of legal institutions[93]: "If we have recognised this truth, it can neither confuse us, when we find this truth expressly only in one passage of the *Institutione*[94], nor can it confuse us if we should come across a misjudgement of this truth in our Roman sources."[95] With the help of the "economic nature", it is determined which clauses of Roman law are to be considered "necessary" and thereby, which are deemed to be "correct". In this way, "clauses of general validity stemming from that which is antiquated" can be extracted, according to Leist.[96]

---

88 To "objective" for Savigny, see RÜCKERT (1984, pp. 100ff.).
89 Cf. (1865, p. 231): "Necessities of nature come from the organism of living conditions with all their factual material." ("*Naturnotwendigkeiten sind etwas aus dem Organismus der Lebensverhältnisse mit allem darin liegenden faktischen Material sich Ergebendes.*").
90 (1859, pp. XXIIff.); cf. also (1865, p. 59).
91 1854, p. 96.
92 1859, p. XXIV.
93 (1854, p. 94) LEIST speaks of a possible "correction of the Roman law". He continuously emphasises his aim to attain an "independent" analysis of Roman law, cf. (1854, pp. 5, 20, 26; 1859, p. 4).
94 Part of the *Roman Corpus Juris Civilis*.
95 (1865, p. 87): "*Haben wir diese Wahrheit erkannt, so kann uns dabei weder bedenklich machen, wenn wir (...) diese Wahrheit nur in einer einzigen Institutionenstelle direkt ausgesprochen finden, noch könnte es uns irre machen, wenn wir in unseren römischen Quellen auch einmal einem Verkennen dieser Wahrheit begegnen sollten.*"). Similar (1859, p. 99).
96 1865, p. 4.

3. Result: An Evaluation of the Roman Law with the Aid of an Economic Viewpoint - a Trend in the Jurisprudence in the Middle of the 19th Century

Savigny published his famous work *System des heutigen römischen Rechts* between 1840 and 1849. In this book, he worked out the principles of the present day civil law supported by the Roman law. But already since the middle of the 1850s, the idea arose that the question as to what extent present law is based on Roman law must be explained in a way other than that of Savigny. The above mentioned works of Dankwardt and Leist belong to that circle of works, in which such a new orientation of the civil law was striven for. Indeed, Dankwardt begins his book *Nationalökonomie und Jurisprudenz* with the sentence: "The following work contains the attempt at progress in the treatment of Roman law." Therewith exists an important similarity to Savigny's approach, namely the idea that apart from coincidental and arbitrary elements of the law there also exist some which may be categorised as "necessary". Dankwardt and Leist now try to succeed in securing this extra-positive material empirically and through this, extract a "reliable" basis for the civil law. Both see the solution as lying in the economic nature of legal institutions. As Dankwardt and Leist both start with the assumption that certain factual conditions demand necessarily certain legal rules, they can presume that certainties for the law are obtainable through their method. Here they can rely on Roscher. According to Roscher's historical method, the links between factual conditions and laws are to be recognised and investigated in the history. And thereby it is possible, in Roscher's opinion, to determine the point in time in which a certain legal regulation is correct with regard to the economic circumstances. This thought does not, however, lead in Dankwardt's and Leist's case to a deepened explanation of factual or economic conditions either in the past or in the present, as would naturally be expected as a consequence of their concept.[97] But this task was being taken up at roughly the same time by another jurist who must not be overlooked when speaking about the relationship between national economics and jurisprudence. His name was Wilhelm Arnold.

---

97 Also Roscher undertook no considerable detail examination concerning the economic history; see JAHN (1967, pp. 43f.).

a) Wilhelm Arnold

The third link: In 1865, Wilhelm Arnold[98] published his research entitled "Cultur und Rechtsleben"[99] as well as another book in 1868 under the title *Cultur und Recht der Römer*[100]. In the 1860s, he held a series of lectures on the topic *Recht und Wirtschaft*[101] in which he argued: "Both sciences (jurisprudence and national economics) remain totally independent; each emanates from different motives and standpoints, each has its own particular principle, its own particular method, its particular tasks; the link lies neither in the area of the dogmatics nor in that of the system but in the area of history. It is here the link increases almost to the identity of the objects: The economist develops the conditions and circumstances of life from natural laws and cultural conditions and the jurist derives the instructions and rules for the living conditions from the law. In the historical examination, both disciplines become part of a higher unity. One can infer the law from economic life just as the economic life of the population may be inferred from the law."[102]

---

98 1826-1883; professor for German law and constitutional law in Basel and Marburg. Arnold, who amongst others was a friend of the brothers Grimm, was a student of Leopold von Ranke. Apart form those works mentioned in the text, the following writings should be highlighted: "Verfassungsgeschichte der deutschen Freistädte" (1854), "Zur Geschichte des Eigentums in den deutschen Städten" (1861) and besides the legal historical works, the book *Ansiedlungen und Wanderungen deutscher Stämme, zumeist nach hessischen Ortsnamen* (1875). In 1881, Arnold was voted conservative representative in the *Reichstag* (on the life and work of Arnold see KROESCHELL (1975); LANDSBERG (1910, text pp. 760ff., notes pp. 327ff.).
99 See KROESCHELL (1975, pp. 264ff.).
100 In the foreword Arnold speaks of having worked for 12 years on this book (pp. V, VI) that is he began to consider the issue at approximately the same time as Dankwardt and Leist.
101 Printed in 1863; 3 parts: 1) "Ueber das Wesen des Rechts", 2) "Zur Geschichte der Nationalökonomie", 3) "Die Nationalökonomie der Gegenwart".
102 P. 63: "*Beide Wissenschaften (sc. Jurisprudenz und Nationalökonomie) bleiben also vollkommen selbständig; jede geht von verschiedenen Motiven und Gesichtspunkten aus, jede hat ihr besonderes Prinzip, ihre besondere Methode, ihre besonderen Aufgaben; die Verbindung liegt nicht sowohl auf dem Gebiet der Dogmatik oder des Systems, als auf dem der Geschichte. Hier steigert sie sich auch fast bis zur Identität der Objekte: der Nationalökonom entwickelt aus Naturgesetzen und Kulturzuständen die Bedingungen und Verhältnisse des Le-*

JURISPRUDENCE, HISTORY, NATIONAL ECONOMICS AFTER 1850

Not unlike Leist, Arnold perceives his research as a continuation of the approach of the historical school of law. In particular, he thinks of Savigny's starting point that the law has no separate existence in itself but rather an existence in close connection with the life of the people.[103] For the present day jurisprudence of civil law it is, according to Arnold, important to bear in mind this aforementioned connection and indeed furthermore, to follow it exactly. In his own works, Arnold concerns himself with the complexity of law and culture, and especially with the relationship between law and economic circumstances.[104] But he warns against a subordination of jurisprudence to economics, and against the view that in the law only the economic considerations are to be regarded as decisive.[105] However, the consideration of economic conditions is, according to Arnold, important for the understanding of the historical development of the law[106]: "(...) a completion is also possible concerning the historical treatment, and this completion is to be found in the link between law and economics. This link was far from the historical school of law because it had other issues to direct its attention towards. (...) But correctly understood and brought through to its logical conclusion, this link contains the perfection of the historical method, a mere consequence of Savigny's train of thoughts, and when the present in a feeling of a certain necessity pursues and pushes for this, then it is absolutely correct."[107] Arnold refers to Roscher and Knies without overlooking

---

bens, und der Jurist leitet aus dem Recht die Vorschriften und Regeln dafür ab. Der geschichtlichen Betrachtung gehen beide Disziplinen zu höheren Einheit auf, und man kann eben sowohl aus dem wirtschaftlichen Leben auf das Recht, wie aus dem Recht auf das wirtschaftliche Leben eines Volks schließen (...).".

103 ARNOLD (1865, pp. VIII, Xff. Cf. SAVIGNY (1814, p. 8; 1815, p. 3).
104 Like Roscher, Arnold sees peoples lives defined by 7 factors: language, art, science, morals, economy, law, and state. ARNOLD (1863, pp. 18, 24; 1865, p. 17); ROSCHER (1875a, § 16).
105 1865, pp. XII, 227ff.
106 Cf. (1863, p. 63; 1865, pp. 229ff.).
107 1865, p. 231: "(...) einer Ergänzung ist aber auch die historische Behandlung fähig, und diese findet sie allerdings in der Verbindung des Rechts mit der Nationalökonomie, die nur darum der Schule (sc. historische Rechtsschule) selbst noch fern lag, weil sie ihre Aufmerksamkeit zunächst auf andere Dinge zu richten hatte, vor Allem auf die Lehre von den Rechtsquellen. Aber richtig gefaßt und durchgeführt enthält diese Verbindung erst die Vollendung der geschichtlichen Methode, eine bloße Konsequenz des Savigny'schen Gedankenganges, und*

the fact that a history of the economy of important peoples had not yet been written.[108] Arnold thereby also comes to the conclusion that a co-operation between economics and jurisprudence could lead to supra-positive elements of the law. So he indicates that it could be possible to draw up a "new kind of natural law"[109]: "And likewise there are certain rules in the development of the law which recur among every population (...). From this general part of the law a new natural law (*Naturrecht*) could be created which, unlike the earlier absolute law, would have the bases and conditions of every law and the general rules of the development of the law as its content and which would then fairly exactly correspond to the general part of national economics."[110]

In his work, in which he analyses the relation of Roman law, Arnold identifies relying on Roscher[111] individual stages of development and interests himself in particular in the reasons for the decline of Rome. He describes his aim in the foreword as a desire to show the way which can lead to "a free an unfettered critique of the Roman law."[112] This conception connects Arnold with Dankwardt and Leist. Through the inclusion of economic viewpoints, all three jurists wish to secure a basis for the assessment of the Roman legal rules. The 'present day Roman law' should be attained through analysis and comparison of economic relations (Dankwardt), or may be gained by examining whether the Romans correctly understood the economic nature in their legal clauses (Leist).

---

wenn die Gegenwart im Gefühl einer gewissen Notwendigkeit danach drängt und treibt, hat sie vollkommen Recht."

108 1865, pp. XIII, 232ff. References to Roscher and Knies are to be found everywhere in Arnold's works.

109 1865, p. 97.

110 1865, p. 106: "*Und ebenso gibt es Gesetze der Rechtsentwicklung, die bei jedem Volk wiederkehren (...). Aus diesem allgemeinen Teil des Rechts ließe sich in der Tat ein neues Naturrecht herstellen, das nicht wie das frühere absolutes Recht, wohl aber die Grundlagen und Bedingungen jedes Rechts und die allgemeinen Gesetze der Rechtsentwicklung zum Inhalt hätte und dann ziemlich genau dem allgemeinen Teil der Nationalökonomie entsprechen würde.*" Arnold takes on Roscher's conception of generally valid development laws; cf. ROSCHER (1861, pp. 13ff., 33) and WEBER (1988, pp. 11ff., 22ff.).

111 See (1863, p. 84).

112 1868, p. VIII.

JURISPRUDENCE, HISTORY, NATIONAL ECONOMICS AFTER 1850

As against the historical school of law, respectively Savigny, a new direction in German jurisprudence of civil law of the 19th century arises. A characteristic feature of this new departure is the fact that the study of the Roman sources is no longer of central importance[113] but instead a critique of Roman law. The free dealings with the Roman sources are grounded in the belief that there is "true" law for the respective economic conditions. This belief is strongly supported by Roscher and his idea of natural laws. To this extent, it can be said that Roscher's historical method, which can be seen as a transfer of the method of the historical school of law into national economics[114], in itself favours a new direction in the jurisprudence regarding the dealing with Roman law.[115]

b) The Importance of the New Direction

The question remains what importance this new direction has with regard to the jurisprudence of its time. An exhaustive answer to this question can not, of course, be given here as that would involve the writing of the history of the late 19th century jurisprudence which has been missing up until now. One aspect should, however, be briefly discussed, namely the impression given by the reviews of the works mentioned so far. Firstly, the large number of reviews of Dankwardt's books must be addressed. In review indices[116] the unusually high figure of 19 critiques can be found. And in these critiques further reports are referred to. Obviously, Dankwardt's writings raise considerable attention. This might be explained by the fact, that a link between national economics and jurisprudence, as reported in one review, "were expressed from different viewpoints, both jurists and economists alike. In spite of this, the attempt to bring these thoughts to completion in a considerable way has not been made up until now, and for the first time it is the (...) writing of Dankwardt which attempts to realise the task in

---

113 Cf. the characteristic observation by DANKWARDT (1862, p. 9): "Luckily I found subsequently (i.e. after working out of economic reasons of legal clauses) my principle in Justinian's *Institutiones* for those who insist on a *Corpus Juris* passage." ("*Glücklicherweise fand ich nachträglich (sc. nach der Herausarbeitung der ökonomischen Gründe eines Rechtssatzes) für Diejenigen, welche sich durchaus an einer Corpus-juris-Stelle erwärmen müssen, mein Prinzip in Justinians Institutionen bestätigt.*")
114 ARNOLD (1863, pp 59ff.), WEBER (1988, p. 9).
115 LANDSBERG (1910) had already commented on this, text p. 761.
116 In: *Jahrbücher für deutsches Recht* and *Zeitschrift für Handelsrecht* 1.

greater measures."[117] This observation is to be read in the second volume of the *Zeitschrift für das gesamte Handelsrecht* founded in 1858. In the introductory article of this journal, L. Goldschmidt had called for an "economic" consideration of commercial law besides the historical and dogmatic approach which he more exactly defined as "the nature of the object" (*Natur der Sache*)[118]. The "sometimes highly praised then deeply criticised nature studies (*Naturstudium*)" are, according to Goldschmidt, to be understood as nothing more than "the clear comprehension of economic laws, according to which the will of the parties is defined, and according to whom this will makes the rules which gradually become part of the positive law in the form of custom or act."[119] Obviously, the idea of the nature of the object in the sense of economic rules was widely spread about 1860. Also, in the reviews of Dankwardt's works in juristic and economic journals the major reaction was to welcome the inclusion of economic ground rules in the jurisprudence.[120] One agreed with the concept of internal natural laws and indispensable development.[121] At the same time, however, Dankwardt's presentation was severely criticised because of the perfunctory nature of its portrayal not only concerning the economic but also the juristic parts.[122]

The works of Leist and Arnold were considered to a lesser degree. With regard to Leist, the problem might lie in the difficulties of his method of presentation.

---

117 FITTING (1859, p. 177).
118 GOLDSCHMIDT (1858, p. 20).
119 P. 19: *Das "bald hoch gepriesene, bald tief geschmähte 'Naturstudium' (sc. sei nichts anderes) als die klare Erfassung der wirtschaftlichen Gesetze, nach denen der Wille der Verkehrtreibenden sich bestimmt, und denen gemäß er die Regeln aufstellt, welche allmählich in Form der Gewohnheit oder des Gesetzes sich zum positiven Recht verdichten."* To the meaning of this observation for the discussion of commercial law, see RÜCKERT (1993, p. 49).
120 See *Archiv für praktische Rechtswissenschaft*, 6 (1859), pp. 184, 185 (A. B.); FITTING (1859, pp. 177ff.), W. ENDEMANN (1863, p. 106).
121 See FITTING (1859).
122 W. ENDEMANN (1863), FITTING (1859). In contrast to the basically positive reviews, KUNTZE rejects the argument that the legal clauses could be necessary results of factual living conditions, claiming that to do so would place jurisprudence in a position as "a complete servant to economics" (1859, pp 303, 305, 308). Opposed to Dankwardt also F. CH. V. ARNOLD (1857, p. 470).

JURISPRUDENCE, HISTORY, NATIONAL ECONOMICS AFTER 1850

4. Otto von Gierke

The fourth link: Otto von Gierke[123] - a friend of the national economists Schmoller, Brentano, and Adolph Wagner and a member of the *Verein für Sozialpolitik*[124] - dealt intensively with the drafts for the German BGB. One of his famous critiques of the first draft appeared for the first time in *Schmollers Jahrbuch* (1888, 1889). Shortly before this, Gierke had published an article with the title "Die Stellung des künftigen bürgerlichen Gesetzbuches zum Erbrecht im ländlichen Grundbesitz" in the same journal. In this article it is written: "The *germanistische Rechtswissenschaft* found support in the modern national economics which also highlighted from the point of view of economy the dissimilarity of immovables and movables, and especially the unique economic nature of rural real property, and thus unveiled the internal untruth and the disadvantageous result of the legal mobilisation of all immovables postulated by the abstract school."[125]

a) 'Living' Law as the Basic Foundation of Legislation

With Gierke both a well-known name and simultaneously a younger generation of researchers in jurisprudence and national economics are reached.[126] In contrast with the 1850's and 1860's, the situation had changed, however, also in respect to the sources of private law. Since 1873, it was decided that a comprehensive German Civil Code should be written and since 1874, a (first) commission was entrusted with the task of formu-

---

123 1841-1921, professor in Breslau, Heidelberg and Berlin. As well as the mentioned discussions about the BGB, important books by Gierke are: *Das deutsche Genossenschaftsrecht*, 4 volumes 1868-1913; *Deutsches Privatrecht*, 3 volumes 1895-1917. On Gierke's life and work see KLEINHEYER/SCHRÖDER (1989, pp. 96ff.).
124 See STUTZ (1922, pp. XXIIIff.).
125 (1888a, p. 413): "*Der germanistischen Rechtswissenschaft aber erwächst hier ein mächtiger Beistand in der modernen Nationalökonomie, welche auch von der wirtschaftlichen Seite her die Ungleichartigkeit von unbeweglichem und beweglichem Vermögen und insbesondere die eigenartige ökonomische Natur des ländlichen Grundbesitzes aufgezeigt und so die innere Unwahrheit und den unausbleiblichen Unsegen der von der abstrakten Schule postulierten rechtlichen Moblisierung alles Grundeigentums enthüllt hat.*"
126 Leist 1819-1906; Arnold 1826-1883, Roscher 1817-1894; Gierke 1841-1921; Schmoller 1838-1917; L. Brentano 1844-1931; A. Wagner 1835-1917.

lating a draft. The main issue for the jurisprudence was now no longer the question of what valid (Roman) law was, but rather, how the legal institutions should be regulated. Of course, the law so far formed the basis of the argumentation. However, it was also quite clear that the law book would mean a deep incision in the German civil law. Gierke, who like many of his colleagues supported the idea of codification, remarked on this: "The planned German Civil Code must in any case appear destructive in the beginning. For the sake of the necessary unity it will destroy a large amount of the law which has been inherited. In many cases it will, however, be only outdated law which will in this way be more quickly discarded".[127] Here, Gierke's conception displays an affinity with the separation scheme which, as already shown, was in use since Savigny: In historical law, living law should be separated from those parts which are dead. This idea has as its premise that "today's" law is developed on principles of (living) historical law. In this sense, Gierke expresses the opinion, prior to the publication of the first draft of the *Bürgerliches Gesetzbuch* (BGB), that the legislator must examine "whether a legal institution is about to die or while appearing to be in decay contains a seed for future growth which deserves of care."[128] In this consideration, whether a rule is to be regarded as living respectively in effect, parallels to Dankwardt and Leist may also be seen. As Dankwardt and Leist achieve a critique of Roman rules by virtue of factual relations respectively of an "economic nature", so Gierke pleads for an assessment of the draft of the BGB which "exceeds the jurisprudence's train of thoughts". According to Gierke, "juristic problems" are "incident points of the large problems of life in our current day society". An examination of the draft has to investigate "in which relationship the planned change of the law is to the spiritual and material total development of the nation, and of ethical and economic elementary questions of our age with regard to our future hopes and fears."[129] Gierke prepares such a critique in his essay "Die Stellung des künftigen bürgerlichen Gesetzbuches zum Erbrecht im ländlichen Grundbe-

---

127 (1888a, p. 403).
128 (1888a, p. 403). Cf. also p. 435 and p. 436.
129 1888a, p. 404 (written shortly before the announcement of the draft which until this point had been kept secret by the commission). Cf. also GIERKE's emphasis on the interaction between law and the remaining parts of social life (e.g. political, religious, economic, and social conditions) (1883, pp. 1097ff., 1113ff.); see JANSSEN (1974, pp. 131ff., 171ff.) who interestingly draws parallels to the argument of W. Arnold.

sitz". Therein, he suggests regulations concerning the succession of rural immovables based on national economic research.[130] As the remark quoted at the beginning of this section[131] shows, Gierke also claims it possible to judge "truth" or "untruth" of provisions with the help of and with regard to the "economic nature".

b) Jurisprudence in Parallel to National Economics

It has already been indicated in the preliminary quotation[132] that the contrast true untrue is identified by Gierke with juristic and national economic research areas. On the one side - that is the one of truth - *"germanistische Rechtswissenschaft"* and "modern national economics" are to be found. On the other side, Gierke places the "abstract school". By this notion, he understands with regard to the juristic area the so-called *'Romanistik'* (as opposed to the *'Germanistik'*). This differentiation (*Romanistik - Germanistik*) is as old as the historical school of law. It was used at first to indicate the various research interests involved - the Romanists concerned themselves with the Roman legal texts, the Germanists with the German legal sources. Then in the 1840s, the Germanists developed an argument against the Roman law as being foreign, not popular and non-national.[133] Later, the discussion took yet another direction for which the writings of C. A. Schmidt from 1853 entitled *Die prinzipielle Unterschied zwischen römischen und germanischen Recht* are the most characteristic.[134] For this differentiation, Schmidt puts forward the argument that the principle of unlimited subjective freedom is the foundation of the Roman law while the German

---

130 It is to Gierke's advantage that individual connections had been investigated in numerous detailed works about the national economy unlike the time of the older historical school; cf. JAHN (1967, p. 44). Gierke relies here especially on the work of Miaskowski which appeared in the writings of the *Verein für Sozialpolitik*, as well as on the discussions in this association and in the *deutscher Landwirtschaftsrat*, see references (1888a, pp. 405ff.).

131 See above in footnote 125.

132 See above in footnote 125.

133 GIERKE describes this very clearly in a lecture in 1903 "Die historische Rechsschule und die Germanisten". There is a lot of literature on this, cf. WIEACKER (1967, pp. 403ff.) and RÜCKERT (1974).

134 As to the meaning of this work for the development of the contrast Roman-liberal and German-social see LUIG (1995, pp. 114ff.). In particular for the concept of property, KROESCHELL (1977, pp. 54ff.).

law, in contrast, is based on the principle of limited freedom of the individual, that is a freedom limited in the interest of the community through objective moral rules.[135] Gierke now bases his argumentation on this division when he characterises the Roman view of the law as an "individualistic" order and the German view as a "social order".[136] Thus, Gierke succeeds in establishing a connection with the "quarrel about principles in national economics"[137], i.e. the division between the economists within the *Verein für Sozialpolitik* and the economists who advocate the principle of *laissez-faire*. It is then possible for Gierke to compare the alleged individualistic conception of the Romanists to the national economic direction which "preaches the absolute blessing of free economic movement as its creed"[138]. The Germanists, however, are linked by Gierke to the "modern national economics", i.e. that direction which was represented in the *Verein für Sozialpolitik*. Herewith, - in relation to Dankwardt, Leist, and Arnold - a new anchoring of national economics in jurisprudence may be seen. The link is grounded now in corresponding principal thoughts regarding the formation of social order. The Germanist Gierke can therefore draw upon national economics to support his elaboration of that law which is living and true, and which therefore has to be the basis for the present day civil law and the future codification. This law for him is German law - the historical German law - but not, as Gierke emphasises, the German law "in its medieval state but the German law in its immortal content".[139] He thus wishes to "discover" the "spirit" of the law through historical research.[140]

c) The Problematic Nature of 'Social' Private Law

Gierke's central key word for the shaping of private law is that of "social". As an opposing concept to an "individualistic" notion, this has the meaning that private legal rules should be formulated with regards to soci-

---

135 Cf. SCHMIDT (1853, especially pp. 29ff., 161ff.).
136 See (1889, p. 36); cf. also LUIG (1995, pp. 95ff.).
137 See title by HELD, *Preußische Jahrbücher* 1872, p. 185 ("Der Prinzipiensreit in der Nationalökonomie").
138 (1888a, p. 410), cf. also (1888b, p. 845).
139 (1988a, p.14).
140 See (1883, pp. 1114ff.). On the importance of the historical research in Gierke's view, see JANSSEN (1974, p. 46).

ety.[141] With the again and again refused individualistic conception, Gierke rejects freedom as a sole principle of civil law. He demands a restriction of the freedom of property, contract, and testamentary freedom.[142] Particular importance he lays on the fact that these limitations should not take place through special legislation but rather should be subsumed in the Civil Code itself. With that he wants to prevent that the law book would be determined by the principle of freedom alone while the "social work will be left to the special laws"[143]. This shows that Gierke is aiming towards the establishment of a principle for the shaping of private law. However, he does not succeed in formulating the content of this principle as enunciated by him. Characteristic of this is what is probably the best known sentence from Gierke's famous lecture "Die soziale Aufgabe des Privatrechts" which he delivered before the Viennese juristic society in 1889: "(...) our private law must contain a drop of socialistic oil"[144]. Just how large this drop should be and how Gierke relates it to the not completely rejected idea of freedom remains unclear. Gierke formulates demands for legal regulations on individual points only. So he postulates protection for the weaker party in contractual law[145], the protection of the family against the selfishness of individual family members in family law and law of succession[146], the preservation of the position of the farmers in the community - "the strongest fortress against outer attack and inner upheaval" - as a thought for property law[147], as well as the strengthening of associations on which the "immunity of the social body against inner and outer dangers" is based[148]. Using the headword 'social', Gierke characterises the aim, the task[149], which in his opinion the private law must fulfil. But such tasks do not constitute a principle. Especially the extent of the limitation of freedom is not principally outlined in detail.

---

141 See NÖRR (1991, p. 46).
142 Cf. (1889, pp. 18, 20, 28ff., 39).
143 (1889, p. 16), similar (1888a, p. 418).
144 (1889, p. 13): "(...) *unser Privatrecht muß ein Tropfen sozialistischen Öles durchsickern.*"
145 (1889, pp. 29, 31).
146 (1888a, p. 434), (1889, pp. 36ff.).
147 (1889, pp. 23ff.).
148 (1889, pp. 43ff.).
149 See title (1889) and cf. the headword '*Aufgabe*' on almost every page.

For this conception of Gierke's *BGB*-critique parallels can be found in Schmoller's opinions.[150] Of special interest is the comparison with one of Schmoller's lectures in 1878 also concerning a legislation plan, namely a reform of trade law (*Gewerbeordnung*)[151] Both Schmoller and Gierke are very involved in the assessment of legislation projects because those have important consequences in the future, for which the present carries a responsibility. Both want to influence the development on the basis of a historical understanding of the current situation.[152]

In 1878, (that is ten years before Gierke's *BGB*-critique), Schmoller declared himself in respect to a new regulation of trade law against unlimited freedoms (here: economic freedom).[153] On the other hand, he stresses that it is not necessary to act against "free competition in private economic dealings in principle": "Only where the examination of general conditions shows very predominant drawbacks, do I wish to introduce certain legal restrictions."[154] These "certain" restrictions are defined by Schmoller through individual points, e.g. the battle against fraud, the consideration of the position of lower classes and that of a normal family life, as well as the preservation of the middle-class.[155] Schmoller generally characterises this as "social reform". He paraphrases the notion "social" with "just", "moral", "ethical": "And this spirit of reforms can and should not be any other than that of a social reform, reform in the sense of justice, the penetration of

---

150 Parallels and links between Gierke's and Schmoller's approach have not been comprehensively analysed up until now. JANSSEN does not address this point more closely (1974, pp. 178, 180); H. SPINDLER indicates similarities without a more precise examination (1982, pp. 92ff., 127ff.).
151 (1878) *Schriften des Vereins für Sozialpolitik*.
152 On Schmoller see Pankoke (1989, pp. 21, 31). On Gierke's emphasis as to the responsibility on the part of the codification cf. (1888a, p. 45), (1888b, pp. 844f., 846, 855). And see (1889, p. 4): "From the deepening in the history sense grows for the future." ["(...) *aus der Vertiefung in die Geschichte (sc. erwächst) Sinn für das Künftige.*"]
153 Pp. 182ff.
154 P. 184: "*nur wo die Prüfung der Gesamtverhältnisse ganz überwiegend Schattenseiten zeigt, will ich die Konkurrenz in gewisse rechtliche Schranken gebannt wissen.*"
155 P. 187.

economic life with moral and ethical thoughts."[156] When Schmoller then does not develop any principles for law regulations this is consistent. In his opinion, the permission or limitation of (economic) freedom is to be decided "as according to the persons, conditions, morals, and times"[157]. He therefore resigns to develop principled statements and limits himself to concrete individual suggestions.

The problems which are caused by the use of this conception for the jurisprudence are apparent in Gierke's work. For the codification of private law, principles for the shaping of the legal rules must be drawn up before the dealing with the law book itself, in order to control the limitations of individual freedom. But Gierke does not come up with evidence here, since the relationship between private autonomy and social considerations is not explained by him. With his imprecise reference to "immanent limits" of laws in terms of "Germanic view"[158], Gierke follows the tradition of C. A. Schmidt who also dubiously saw freedom limited through moral rules.[159] Schmoller's national economics, which also focus central importance on the key words "social" and "moral", strengthen the tendency not to commit oneself to a principle.

III. Result

In summary, it is notable that the contemporary national economic research was not only known to the civil law academics in the second half of the 19th century but, moreover, there were strong attempts to incorporate it into civil law dogmatics.[160] A starting point for this arose from the idea that necessary elements of the law and therewith 'true' law exists. This idealistic

---

156 P. 189: "*Und dieser Geist (sc. von Reformen) kann und soll kein anderer sein, als der der sozialen Reform, der Reform im Sinne der Gerechtigkeit, der Durchtigkeit, der Durchdringung des wirtschaftlichen Lebens mit sittlichem, mit ethischen Gedanken.*"
157 P. 184.
158 1889, p. 20.
159 SCHMIDT (1853, pp. 48, 162).
160 See above II., 3.

basic attitude, typical of its time[161], was formed for jurisprudence by Savigny. In this opinion, the law could be explained through historical investigations (in the sense of developmental investigations). The peculiarity of those works analysed here from Dankwardt, Leist, Arnold, and Gierke - which also justifies their compilation and speaking of 'one direction' - is that the idea of a true law is no longer merely linked to historical developmental considerations alone but rather, above all, to the results of national economic research. A decisive requirement for this was Roscher's optimism that for certain situations there exist unequivocal, accurate regulations. Building on this, it is presumed on the part of the jurists that the economic nature of legal relationships show the way to a 'true' law. The agreement of a legal rule with this economic nature of legal relationships thereby becomes the standard for the assessment of legal clauses.

At this point, it becomes possible to define the position of the direction of civil law jurisprudence examined here to the juristic historism debate[162]. Under the title "Über die Methode der geschichtlichen Rechtstheorie", Rudolf Stammler criticises in 1888 the historical school of law and in particular Ernst Immanuel Bekker as their representative. His central argument asserted that the historical school was lacking a standard for the assessment of law.[163] An answer to the important question of jurisprudence "whether that which is law should also be lawful"[164] has, Stammler believes, not been given by the historical school. Dankwardt, Leist, Arnold, and also Gierke answer that question, however, when they measure historical and effective law with the standard of the economic nature of legal institutions. They were less interested in how the law appeared at particular times than primarily in how the law (at a particular time, under particular circumstances) should be. Here, a considerable difference can be seen as opposed to the historical method which Stammler condemns. His criticism does not affect Dankwardt, Leist, Arnold, and Gierke who, by the way, are not mentioned by Stammler in 1888. Later, however, Stammler does take a stand on Dankwardt in his book *Lehrbuch der Rechtsphilosophie* - and in-

---

161 Cf. Ranke, W. V. Humboldt, see OEXLE (1996, pp. 29f.).
162 See WITTKAU (1994, pp. 80ff.).
163 STAMMLER (1888, pp. 18f.).
164 STAMMLER (1888, pp. 12, 14ff.): "*ob dasjenige, was Recht ist, auch Rechtens sein sollte.*"

deed it is a negative one.[165] Thereby his view is not based on the absence of an answer to the question what law should be, but rather on the type of answer given by Dankwardt. Stammler supposes that a pure apriori knowledge alone shows the way to 'true' law (*richtiges Recht*). In contrast, the direction of jurisprudence as examined here works empirically in comparison. Unlike Savigny, Bekker, and others, however, the historical sources of law here are not - at least not alone - the central point, but rather the economic relationships belonging to them (as conveyed through economic examination).

The orientation of jurists towards national economics means that regulations can only be seen as true under particular pre-conditions. This trueness is relative. This leads to a free position against historical law. Even if a Roman legal clause is categorised as true for its time, its validity as present day effective law may be rejected because it is not suitable to present day living conditions. Another important consequence of the idea of relativity can be seen in Gierke's writings. Here, the idea supports the fact that the thorough elaboration of a principle for the private law is neglected.

References

ARNOLD, FRIEDRICH CHRISTIAN VON: "Rezension zu H. Dankwardt, Nationalökonomie" I, *Der Gerichtsaal*, 9 (1857), p. 470.
ARNOLD, WILHELM: *Recht und Wirtschaft nach geschichtlicher Ansicht. Drei Vorlesungen*, Basel (H. Georg) 1863.
ARNOLD, WILHELM: *Cultur und Rechtsleben*, Berlin (F. Dümmler) 1865.
ARNOLD, WILHELM: *Cultur und Recht der Römer*, Berlin (F. Dümmler) 1868.
BEKKER, ERNST IMMANUEL: "Burkard Wilhelm Leist unter seinen Äqualen", *Zeitschrift der Savigny-Stiftung (Romanistische Abteilung)*, 28 (1907), pp. 129-157.
COING, HELMUT (Ed.): *Handbuch der Quellen und Literatur der neueren europäischen Privatrechtsgeschichte III 2*, Munich (Beck) 1982.

---

165 STAMMLER (1922, p. 302, footnote 5).

DANKWARDT, HEINRICH (1857a): *Nationalökonomie und Jurisprudenz I. Begriff, Production, Umlauf der Güter*, Rostock (Leopold) 1857.
DANKWARDT, HEINRICH (1857b): *Nationalökonomie und Jurisprudenz II. Umlauf der Güter (Forts.)*, Rostock (Leopold) 1857.
DANKWARDT, HEINRICH: *Nationalökonomisch-civilistische Studien I*, Leipzig, Heidelberg (Winter) 1862.
ENDEMANN, FRIEDRICH: *Lehrbuch des Bürgerlichen Rechts I*, Berlin (Carl Heymann) 9th edition 1903.
ENDEMANN, WILHELM: "Rezension zu Dankwardt, Nationalökonomie und Jurisprudenz I", *Jahrbücher für Nationalökonomie und Statistik*, 1 (1863), pp. 106-107.
FITTING, H.: "Rezension zu Dankwardt, Nationalökonomie und Jurisprudenz I", *Germania*, 66 (1857), pp. 625-626, 638-640.
FITTING, H.: "Rezension zu H. Dankwardt, Nationalökonomie und Jurisprudenz I", *Zeitschrift für das gesamte Handelsrecht*, 2 (1859), pp. 177-185.
GIERKE, OTTO VON: "Labands Staatsrecht und die deutsche Rechtswissenschaft", *Schmollers Jahrbuch*, 7 (1883), pp. 1097-1195.
GIERKE, OTTO VON (1888a): "Die Stellung des künftigen bürgerlichen Gesetzbuch zum Erbrecht im ländlichen Grundbesitz", *Schmollers Jahrbuch*, 12 (1888), pp. 401-436.
GIERKE, OTTO VON (1888b): "Der Entwurf eines bürgerlichen Gesetzbuches und das deutsche Reich", part 1, *Schmollers Jahrbuch*, 12 (1888), pp. 843-946.
GIERKE, OTTO VON: *Die soziale Aufgabe des Privatrechts*, Berlin (J. Springer) 1889.
GOLDSCHMIDT, LEVIN: "Über die wissenschaftliche Behandlung des Handelsrechts und den Zweck dieser Zeitschrift", *Zeitschrift für das gesamte Handelsrecht*, 1 (1858), pp. 1-24.
GOLDSCHMIDT, LEVIN: *Ein Lebensbild in Briefen*, Berlin (Emil Goldschmidt) 1898.
HILDEBRAND, BRUNO: "Die gegenwärtige Aufgabe der Wissenschaft der Nationalökonomie", *Jahrbücher für Nationalökonomie und Statistik*, 1 (1863), pp. 5-25, 137-146.
HUGO, GUSTAV: *Geschichte des römischen Rechts bis auf Justinian*, Berlin (Mylius) 1832.
JAHN, GEORG: "Die Historische Schule der Nationalökonomie und ihr Ausklang - von der Wirtschaftsgeschichte zur geschichtlichen Theorie", in: A. MONTANER (Ed.): *Geschichte der Volkswirtschaftslehre*, Köln, Berlin (Kiepenheuer und Witsch) 1967, pp. 41-50.
JANSSEN, ALBERT: *Otto von Gierkes Methode der geschichtlichen Rechtswissenschaft*, Göttingen, Frankfurt, Zürich (Musterschmidt) 1974.
JHERING, RUDOLF: "Unsere Aufgabe", *Jahrbücher für die Dogmatik des heutigen römischen und deutschen Privatrechts*, 1 (1857), pp. 1-52.
KLEINHEYER, GERD/SCHRÖDER, JAN: *Deutsche Juristen aus fünf Jahrhunderten*, Heidelberg (C. F. Müller) 3rd edition 1989.

JURISPRUDENCE, HISTORY, NATIONAL ECONOMICS AFTER 1850

KNÖPPEL, V.: "Waldgerechtsame", in: *Handwörterbuch zur deutschen Rechtsgeschichte*, Berlin (Schmidt) 1994, pp. 1117-1120.

KOSSELLECK, REINHARD: "Historia magistra vitae", in: R. KOSSELLECK: *Vergangene Zukunft*, Frankfurt (Suhrkamp) 3rd ed. 1995, pp. 38-66.

KROESCHELL, KARL: "Ein vergessener Germanist des 19. Jahrhunderts. W. Arnold,» *Festschrift für H. Krause*, 1975, pp. 253-275.

KROESCHELL, KARL: "Zur Lehre vom 'germanischen' Eigentumsbegriff", in: *Festschrift für H. Thieme*, Köln, Wien (Böhlau) 1977, pp. 34-71.

KUNTZE, JOHANNES EMIL: "Rezension zu Dankwardt, Nationalökonomie und Jurisprudenz", *Jahrbücher der deutschen Rechtswissenschaft und Gesetzgebung*, 5 (1859), pp. 301-308.

LANDSBERG, ERNST: *Geschichte der deutschen Rechtswissenschaft*, III 2, Munich, Berlin (R. Oldenbourg) 1910.

LEIST, BURKARD WILHELM: *Civilistische Studien auf dem Gebiete der dogmatischen Analyse I. Ueber die dogmatische Analyse römischer Rechtsinstitute*, Jena (F. Frommann) 1854.

LEIST, BURKARD WILHELM: *Civilistische Studien auf dem Gebiete der dogmatischen Analyse III. Ueber die Natur des Eigenthums*, Jena (F. Frommann) 1859.

LEIST, BURKARD WILHELM: *Naturalis ratio und Natur der Sache*, Jena (F. Frommann) 1860.

LEIST, BURKARD WILHELM: *Mancipation und Eigenthumstradition*, Jena (F. Frommann) 1865.

LUIG, KARL: "Römische und deutsche Rechtsanschuung, individuelle und soziale Ordnung", in: WILLOWEIT RÜCKERT (Ed.): *Die deutsche Rechtsgeschichte in der NS-Zeit*, Tübingen (Siebeck) 1995, pp. 95-137.

NÖRR, KNUT WOLFGANG: *Eher Hegel als Kant*, Paderborn (F. Schöningh) 1991.

OEXLE, OTTO GERHARD: *Geschichtswissenschaft im Zeichen des Historismus*, Göttingen (Vandenhoeck und Ruprecht) 1996.

PANKOKE, ECKART: "Historisches Verstehen und geschichtliche Verantwortung", in: TENBRUCK SCHIERA (Ed.): *Gustav Schmoller in seiner Zeit: die Entstehung der Sozialwissenschaften in Deutschland und Italien*, Berlin (Duncker und Humblot) 1989, pp. 17-53.

ROSCHER, WILHELM: "Der gegenwärtige Zustand der Nationalökonomie und die nothwendige Reform desselben", *Deutsche Vierteljahresschrift*, (1849), pp. 174-190.

ROSCHER, WILHELM: "Über das Verhältnis der Nationalökonomik zum klassischen Alterthume", in: W. ROSCHER: *Ansichten der Volkswirtschaft aus dem geschichtlichen Standpunkt*, Leipzig, Heidelberg (Winter'sche Verlagsbuchhandlung) 1861, pp. 3-46.

ROSCHER, WILHELM: *Geschichte der National-Oekonomik in Deutschland*, Munich, Berlin (Oldenbourg) 1874.

ROSCHER, WILHELM (1875a): *System der Volkswirtschaft I. Grundlagen der Nationalökonomie*, Stuttgart (Cotta) 12th ed. 1875.

ROSCHER, WILHELM (1875b): *System der Volkswirtschaft II. Nationalökonomik des Ackerbaus und der verwandten Urproductionen*, Stuttgart (Cotta) 8th ed. 1875.

RÜCKERT, JOACHIM: *August Ludiwig Reyschers Leben und Rechtstheorie*, Berlin (Schweitzer) 1974.

RÜCKERT, JOACHIM: *Idealismus, Jurisprudenz und Politik bei Friedrich Carl von Savigny*, Ebelsbach (Rudolf Gremer) 1984.

RÜCKERT, JOACHIM: "Dogmengeschichtliches und Dogmengeschichte im Umkreis Savignys, bes. in seiner Kondiktionslehre", *Zeitschrift der Savigny-Stiftung für Rechtsgeschichte (Rom)*, 104 (1987), pp. 666-678.

RÜCKERT, JOACHIM: "Handelsrechtsbildungen und Modernisierung des Handelsrechts", *Zeitschrift für Handelsrecht*, 6 (1993), pp. 19-66.

SAVIGNY, FRIEDRICH CARL VON: *Vom Beruf unsrer Zeit für Gesetzgebung und Rechtswissenschaft*, Heidelberg (Mohr und Zimmer) 1814.

SAVIGNY, FRIEDRICH CARL VON: "Ueber den Zweck dieser Zeitschrift", *Zeitschrift für geschichtliche Rechtswissenschaft*, 1 (1815), pp. 1-12.

SCHMIDT, CARL ADOLF: *Der prinzipielle Unterschied zwischen römischem und germanischem Recht*, Rostock 1853.

SCHMOLLER, GUSTAV: "Referat über die Reform der Gewerbeordnung", *Schriften des Vereins für Sozialpolitik*, 14 (1878), pp. 173-203.

SCHMOLLER, GUSTAV: "Wilhelm Roscher", in: G. SCHMOLLER: *Zur Literaturgeschichte der Staats- und Sozialwissenschaften*, Leipzig (Duncker und Humblot) 1888, pp. 147-171.

SENN, MARCEL: *Rechtshistorisches Selbstverständnis im Wandel*, Zürich (Schulthess) 1982.

SPINDLER, HELGA: *Von der Genossenschaft zur Betriebsgemeinschaft*, Frankfurt a. M., Bern (P. Lang) 1982.

STAMMLER, RUDOLF: "Über die Mothode der geschichtlichen Rechtstheorie", in: *Festgabe zu B. Windscheids fünfzigjährigem Doctorjubiläum*, Halle (M. Niemeyer) 1888, pp. 1-63.

STAMMLER, RUDOLF: *Lehrbuch der Rechtsphilosophie*, Berlin, Leipzig (Walter de Gruyter) 1922.

STUTZ, ULRICH: "Otto Gierke", *Zeitschrift der Savigny-Stiftung (Germanistische Abteilung)*, 43 (1922), pp. VII-LXIII.

WEBER, MAX: "Roscher und Knies und die logischen Probleme der historischen Nationalökonomie", in: M. WEBER: *Gesammelte Aufsätze zur Wissenschaftslehre*, Tübingen (Mohr) 7th ed. 1988, pp. 1-145.

WIEACKER, FRANZ: *Privatrechtsgeschichte der Neuzeit*, Göttingen (Vandenhoeck und Ruprecht) 2nd ed. 1967.

JURISPRUDENCE, HISTORY, NATIONAL ECONOMICS AFTER 1850

WITTKAU, ANNETTE: *Historismus*, Göttingen (Vandenhoeck und Ruprecht) 2nd ed. 1994.

Discussion Summary

JOHAN TRALAU

Paper discussed:
SIBYLLE HOFER: Jurisprudence, History, National Economics After 1850

It is quite impressive that jurists considered the Historical School of Economics to be a critique of the legal historical school. One must not forget that the Historical School was also theoretically oriented; the claim that it had no theory is, as is shown in the text, wrong. Could one say, then, that the Historical School in law was even more historical than the one in economics (KOSLOWSKI)? This is a difficult question, and it is very hard to separate the two branches, since the research conducted was oriented toward both legal and economic issues (HOFER). There is a methodological problem as regards the investigation of possible influences of the Historical School of economics on the juridical research of the time. This, however, one must solve by searching for explicit elements, and not mere structural analogies (RÜCKERT). Could Dankwardt be seen as a precursor of the recent discussion of law and economics (KOSLOWSKI)? To this question different answers were given. On the one hand, similarities were emphasised (HOFER, RÜCKERT), on the other hand, it was claimed that the differences between them are more important. Dankwardt's method was completely different, since it was purely descriptive (NÖRR). At this stage of the discussion, the focus shifted to the concept of natural laws. Firstly, what did Roscher mean by "natural laws"? Secondly, what did "socialism" imply in Gierke's dictum of the "drop of oil of socialism" that must be added to society? It would seem that this is not socialism as we know it, but rather social conservatism (NÖRR). Roscher quite clearly does not differentiate between natural laws and developmental laws (HOFER). Would this mean, then, that natural laws are economic laws (NÖRR)? Here, "law" does not imply simple causality, but rather development. There most certainly is a normative element to it, but it is not clear what Roscher meant (RÜCKERT). Surely, Gierke's "socialism" really was social conservatism. After all, even

DISCUSSION SUMMARY

Bismarck did not mind being called a socialist (HOFER, RÜCKERT, KOSLOWSKI). Moreover, it is worth noting that the conception of developmental laws is associated to neo-classical theory and its emphasis on equilibrium, rather than to the Historical School. Furthermore, one must not forget that there is not *one* economic judgement of the law, but several. The evaluation of the effects of a particular law hence always varies between different economists and different schools of economics (WOHLGEMUTH). The importance of the jurist Ferdinand Walter was emphasised. Walter, unlike neo-classical economics, posed a normative basis for natural law. There is a faculty within man which enables him to distinguish between right and wrong. From this point, the discussion mainly concerned the distinction between the public and private spheres in the Roman right. Did Gierke wish to introduce another distinction? Distinguishing between public and private epitomises in all too limited an extent societal reality, since there is also a social sphere, which is neither completely private nor public. Legal theory must, then, do away with the old Roman distinction altogether and develop a different one (RAUSCHER). This would be quite impossible, since "social" means nothing to a jurist. For the enforcement and interpretation of law one needs principles, and as a jurist one cannot have more than one principle at a time. The abolition of the Roman distinction would lead to arbitrary judgements (HOFER). It might be possible to differentiate in the principles; this was, however, never proposed by Gierke (RÜCKERT). In connection to this, the difference between Germanic and Roman right was discussed, and it was pointed to the fact that the former was more oriented toward the community rather than the individual. This can be demonstrated by the fact that associations, for instance families, in many cases were treated as legal subjects (KOSLOWSKI). The methodological problems of showing a possible influence of the Historical School of economics on the Historical School of law were once again mentioned, and explicit references were considered to be the most reliable evidence (HOFER). At the end of the discussion, the importance of integrating the legal and the economic perspectives was emphasised. This has been done by Dankwardt and others, as well as in the present legal discussion. It is of great importance that one should find out how juridical and economic elements were combined in the Historical School, and how this can be done in our time (RÜCKERT).

Part Seven

Historism, Relativism, and the Critique of Historism

Chapter 15

Karl Popper's Critique of Historicism, the Historical School, and the Contemporary Debate

ADAM J. CHMIELEWSKI

I.   General Assessment of Karl Popper's Philosophy
II. Popper's Concept of Historicism
     1. Antinaturalist Historicism
     2. Pronaturalist Historicism
III. Popper's Critique of Historicism
IV. Criticism of Popper's Critique of Historicism
V.   Open Society or Community?

I. General Assessment of Karl Popper's Philosophy

Popper's name is usually associated with the idea of open society and the deductive hypothetical method. Now, barely three years have passed since Sir Karl's death, it looks as though the memory about both of these concepts, as well as Popper's name itself, are almost equally dead. Popper's philosophy of science as well as his social philosophy are commonly considered things of the past. Such a judgement, though harsh to Popper and his philosophy, does not seem to bother too many Western philosophers, always very sceptical of Popper's philosophy, and of his own robust self, anyway. What is far more interesting is that similar attitude has been adopted by intellectuals in Central and Eastern Europe, who, apparently at least, have had most reasons to follow his teaching.

The wholesale transformation of the Central and Eastern Europe has reached also the sphere of philosophy. Polish philosophers, just as Polish politicians, are being exposed to all sorts of influences suggesting to them adoption of all sorts of replacements for the so-far dominant Marxism. For example in a recent talk given in Warsaw, Jüregain Habermas has encouraged Polish philosophers to adopt the philosophy of historicism. At the same time he had warned that he does not mean historicism as defined by Karl Popper, but something wholly different. He rather meant historicism as understood within the tradition of Wilhelm Dilthey, Hans-Georg Gadamer, and also of the Frankfurt School. Habermas's suggestion created quite a lot of confusion among Polish philosophers since the general feeling there is that it is philosophically wrong to replace one kind of historicism - and Marxism certainly was one - by another one, for, despite all the differences, they both belong to the same species and were vehemently condemned not only by Popper, but are also critically viewed by the analytical movement which is gaining on popularity in Poland. At the same time, however, Popper's own philosophy, widely accepted among dissenting intellectuals before 1989, has recently suffered dramatic setback in its popularity, even in countries like Poland.

Some say that it is quite paradoxical that Popper, who lived long enough to see the opening of the totalitarian societies - something which he always advocated - did not see his philosophy universally accepted in the region by the nations of the newly open societies[1]. The solution to this paradox, however, as in the case of most paradoxes, is quite trivial: Popper's philosophy has not become an official philosophy in the region of Central and Eastern Europe in virtue of the simple fact that even though it contained *some answers* as to why societies become close and why it is wrong, it provided few answers as to how to open them, how to keep them open, and, once they are open, what to do next. It seems, then, that Popperian critical rationalism, as an ideology, seemed quite useful during the more or less energetic propagandist skirmishes of the Cold War, but as soon as the war was won (or lost, as the case may be), its usefulness was radically diminished. No wonder that most of the intellectuals and politicians turned their back on the ideology in the name of which they fought against communist oppression. The phenomenon is quite old and has been keenly observed by Hegel, who remarked that "crack and fall of civilisations" is a result of "a morbid inten-

---

[1] Even George Soros's Open Society Institutes, active throughout the Central and Eastern Europe, are being increasingly criticised for their ways which are in sharp contrast with the idea of openness and democracy.

sification of their own first principles"[2]. In the case of Popper's ideology of the open society, we have a pretty perfect example of an ideology which has been made redundant by its very success.

But there is something more important involved in this attitude toward Popper. His social philosophy, despite its vehemence (or just because of it), is rather meagre and can largely be reduced to the heated (but not always correct) criticism of communism and other totalitarian regimes. It should not come as a surprise, then, that such a doctrine has made itself redundant among the peoples in the Central and Eastern Europe, who were the victims of the totalitarian regimes, for they, having shed - unaided - the constraints of the totalitarianism, did not wish anymore to be insistently reminded about the dreadful time they went through, especially by the boastful critics of communism who personally never knew its atrocities.

Popper has proposed a number of original philosophical theses which were subsequently critically developed and criticised by many authors, among them Lakatos, Watkins, Putnam, Kuhn, Feyerabend, and others. Indeed, many Popper's solutions to numerous philosophical problems seem inadequate, dogmatic, if not quite ideological, and were considered as such from the very moment of their publication. Among these problems the most striking examples are Popper's ontological theses and the fact that they run counter a healthy principle of paucity of entities; his over-optimistic evolutionism and evolutionary theory of knowledge; his inability to address properly the issue of criticisability of critical rationalism; and also his inadequate answer to the relativistic challenge of the so-called relativistic philosophy of science.

Despite the fact that Popper assiduously developed his philosophy throughout his long life, he failed to achieve clear-cut formulation of his position (even though he thought he did, and was even praised by his followers for the clarity of his writings). An another problem, which severely impeded Popper's ability to arrive at proper formulations of his philosophical contentions was the fact that he certainly was very reluctant to accept any criticisms of his position, or even to give up anything he had said[3], and

---

2 Quoted after GEORGE SOROS: "The Capitalist Threat", *The Atlantic Monthly*, February (1997), p. 2.
3 In my conversation with Sir Karl, shortly before his death, he acknowledged that his methodological ideas were widely criticised but he considers all the criticisms wrong.

- as Paul Feyerabend's phrase has it - staunchly defended his philosophy by imposing the yoke of the critical rationalism on his followers.

This matter, quite embarrassing to the family of critical rationalists as a whole, needs to be at least somehow accounted for. A part of the explanation can be found, I believe, in Popper's psychological outfit. There are many historical data which seem to justify a historical hypothesis according to which Popper's most central philosophical views and contentions were almost wholly shaped in the very early period of his development. His subsequent work and achievements in the philosophy of science and methodology suggest strongly that they were formulated with the sole aim in view: to comply with the requirement of coherence with these early beliefs. Many biographical data unmistakably testify to the fact that there were no revolutionary changes in Popper's views, no radical reformulations of his positions, only a continuous and consistent effort towards a formulation, and a staunch defence, of these early acquired central beliefs and convictions, which Popper treated throughout his whole life as if they were a result of intuitions of his inborn genius incapable of error. The fact that such an attitude was abundantly displayed by a man who repeatedly asserted fallibility of human mind put off many people, who, finding a critical discussion with him highly difficult, or sometimes impossible altogether, turned their back on the man and on his philosophy as well.

A very telling example of this "infallibility" is Popper's disrespectful attitude towards the analysis of philosophical concepts, as a result of which he adopted a disrespectful stance towards many philosophical theories, concepts, and problems. Popper's position in this regard is quite similar to Humpty Dumpty's (of Lewis Carroll's *Alice in Wonderland*) conviction that "When I use a word... it means just what I choose it to mean - neither more nor less". A careful reader of Sir Karl's biography will find that this extreme attitude towards language - the very basic philosophical tool - was adopted by him, in a self-conscious opposition to his father's reserved opinion, when Popper was about... fifteen years old! He subsequently saw fit to stick to this prejudice uncritically and spent considerable part of his scholarly life trying to make sense of this vague intuition which he struck upon in his boyhood. His very dubious conception of three worlds is one of outcomes of his determination to show that he was *always* right, even (or rather, especially) in his youthful dispute with his Father, the Big Other.

KARL POPPER'S CRITIQUE OF HISTORICISM

This is, I think, very symbolic behaviour which calls for a psychoanalytic genius of Slavoj Žižek's[4] to fully make sense of. It is, however, a proper place to mention that similar ideas were suggested or implied by many authors, most recently by John Watkins[5]. He writes, for example, very insightfully:

> "I rather suspect that there were extra-philosophical factors behind this [Popper's] deep seated animus toward Carnap's philosophy. Giant slaying was a motif in Popper's intellectual life, and while Carnap was not in the same league as Plato, Hegel, Marx, or Freud, he was w formidable figure in the post-war Anglo-American philosophy. It's even possible that his being over six feet tall and Popper's being short had something to do with it. Or it may have been the contrast in their status back in the early 1930's, when Carnap was a professor and Popper was a schoolteacher. After they emigrated, in 1936-37, Popper found himself virtually isolated in New Zealand while Carnap was hobnobbing with Russell, Tarski and Quine in America".

There are many philosophical problems unsatisfactorily solved by Popper. One of them is related to the fact that in his evolutionary epistemology he identifies ability to (biological) survival with the rationality of the carriers of this ability, and at the same time asserts identity of thus conceived rationality with an ability to discover the true knowledge about the world. However, one cannot have both: ability to survive cannot be equated with ability to discover the truth since, for example, if ability to discover the truth leads to the mastery of the working of the atomic bomb, cockroaches will turn to be more adapted to the world after it is blown up according to this scientific truth, and more rational than humans who discovered this mighty piece of true knowledge.

---

4   In his many brilliant books, a Slovenian psychoanalyst and philosopher, SLAVOJ ŽIŽEK attempts at an explanation of the workings of the philosophical mind, following the vague teachings of JACQUES LACAN, influential French psychologist.

5   Cf. JOHN WATKINS: "Karl Popper. Memoir", *The American Scholar*, Spring (1997), pp. 205-219. Quotation is from p. 213. Ideas very much similar to Watkins's are suggested by a reading of ERNST GOMBRICH's *The Open Society and Its Enemies: Remembering Its Publication Fifty Years Ago*, LSE, London 1995.

Popper also fails to provide conclusive reasons to believe that his critical theory is itself criticisable, from which it follows that Popper's theory of rationality, that made criticisability a condition of rational acceptance of a theory in science, and which denied such a status to Marxism and psychoanalytical theories, turns out to be guilty of the same sin, is not distinguishable from them in this regard, and, as a result, according to its own requirements, has to be - like them - rejected.

One has also to draw attention to the fact that Popper's attempt to answer relativism is inadequate and, as is now common knowledge, Davidson's argument against the idea of untranslatability of languages is in much better position to provide an antirelativistic argument, though it is, too, fundamentally flawed. As Alasdair MacIntyre and others has shown, despite Popper's efforts, relativism - in some of its multiple versions - remains the greatest worry to rationalists. On the other hand relativism, in the area of social philosophy, seems the only rescue for the rational and liberal idea of tolerance. It thus seems that, on the one hand, there are good reasons to believe that it is *not* rational to reject relativism in epistemology, and, on the other hand, to assume it as a means of preserving the principle tolerance in liberal social philosophy.

Finally, Popper's critique of historicism has enticed a number of very critical responses, most of which have drawn attention to many faults in Popper's understanding of historicism. I shall come to this topic presently.

II. Popper's Concept of Historicism

Popper has expounded his views on historicism in a number of publications, the most prominent of which were *The Poverty of Historicism*[6] and *The Open Society and Its Enemies*[7]. Apart from them there are a couple of

---

6 KARL R. POPPER: "The Poverty of Historicism", *Economica* vol. XI, nos 42 & 43, 1944, and vol. XII, no. 46, 1945. The book was published by Routledge and Kegan Paul, London, in 1957.
7 KARL R. POPPER: *The Open Society and Its Enemies*, London (Routledge and Kegan Paul) 1945. The book was published a couple of months before Sir Winston Churchill's Iron Curtain speech in Fulton, Missouri, delivered on March

his papers related to the subject of historicism, collected in the *Conjectures and Refutations*[8]. Jürgen Habermas has not explained why he thinks Popperian concept historicism repugnant. Thus it is worthwhile to dwell upon the issue in a more detailed way and find out what is wrong with it.

Historicism is understood by Popper as a doctrine alleging that history is directed by underlying currents, trends, laws and movements which are independent of human purposes and actions. There are, however, two kinds of historicism, antinaturalist and pro-naturalist. The antinaturalist kind upholds that in their attempts to know, predict, and change the history people must recognise the fact that methods of natural sciences cannot be applied to the subject matter of history.

1. Antinaturalist Historicism

In particular, antinaturalist historicism holds the following views concerning the history and the possibility of its knowing. Physical laws are universal, that is they are valid, and can be applied, throughout the physical universe, since they describe real uniformities existing in the nature itself. Not so with the sociological laws, since they differ in different places and periods. It follows that their validity is strongly context-dependent and their application has to be limited to those contexts[9]. Specifically, historical laws

---

5, 1946. The fact led some Marxist critics of it to assert that it was not Churchill but Popper who started the cold war. The main outline of his views was first presented in the paper "The Poverty of Historicism" in 1936 and published in *Economica* in 1944-1945. It was reissued in a book form in 1957. As Popper himself recounts the story of his work, one of the chapters of *The Poverty of Historicism* was met by doubts and reservations from his friends in New Zealand, so he set to explain his views more elaborately in one of its chapters, which, to his surprise, grew in size out of his expectations. Faced with a barely manageable manuscript, he cut out what is now known as *The Poverty of Historicism* and the remaining manuscript, dealing with the history of the development of the historicism, became later on *The Open Society and Its Enemies*.

8   KARL R. POPPER: *Conjectures and Refutations*, London (Routledge and Kegan Paul) 1963, especially papers "What is Dialectic?"; "Prediction and Prophecy in the Social Sciences"; "Utopia and Violence", and "The History of Our Time: An Optimist View".

9   *The Poverty of Historicism*, pp. 5-6.

cannot be generalised over the all human history, thus there are no long-term and wide-range laws describing persistent historical uniformities. According to Popper a pronaturalist claim that there are everlasting trends in history tend to support fatalistic and pessimistic view of history, whereas the opposite, antinaturalist claim gives its support to the activist view of human role in history. Let us remember, however, that one of the proponents of the beliefs in inevitable laws of history suggested that there *is* a possibility to change it, not only to interpret it.

Antinaturalistic historicism claims that it is not possible to perform any experiments in social life, for it is not possible to isolate particular situations to repeat them at will. It is impossible to perform any experiments in precisely the same conditions since the conditions of the second performance must be influenced by the fact that the experiment has been performed before. This idea rests on a view that society resembles an organism which possesses some kind of memory of what went before. Thus social sciences are always faced with *novelty* which is absent from natural sciences. Situations in social sciences are also characterised by *complexity* arising from impossibility of isolation of experimental situations which is due to the fact that social life presupposes the mental life of conscious individuals. Thus any predictions within social sciences must be inexact and imprecise. In this context Popper puts forward a concept of the *Oedipus effect*, which is meant to designate self-fulfilling, or self-refuting, effect of predictions of particular events on coming to pass (or otherwise) of those events. A special case of such an influence is the fact that social scientists themselves are a part of the domain they investigate, thus one cannot assume that they will strive to truth and nothing but the truth. It is rather that the very fact of their situatedness renders them unable objectively to perceive the truth about social matters. Another obstacle in their seeing the truth is that their systems of values and preferences prevents them from objectivity in their cognition. False consciousness as described by Marx is an example of such an inability. Popper suggests that historicism thus understood leads to extreme form of relativism. Another reason why the methods of natural sciences cannot be applied in social scienccs is holism, that is the idea that social life resembles an organism and has to be viewed as a whole, and not in the atomistic manner typical of natural phenomena. "The social group is more that the mere sum total of its members, and it is more than the mere sum total of the merely personal relationships existing at any moment between any of its members"[10]. Holism thus defined implies biological or organic theory of social structures, which runs counter the concept of the methodological individualism defended by Popper in his writings.

Historicism, according to Popper, claims that the proper method to achieve knowledge of social life is the method of intuitive understanding. This method is to be applied in explaining the behaviour of individuals, social groups or nations, or of the character of historical epochs or periods. There are three variants of intuitive understanding; one of them claims that actions of individuals or groups are to be understood in accordance with their aims; second claims that not only teleological analysis but also understanding of "the meaning" or "significance" of events or actions is necessary; the third variant claims in addition that it is necessary to understand historical trends, tendencies and traditions prevailing in a period. This claim is based, according to Popper, on the inference by analogy from one historical period to another. All the above shows that the methods of social sciences has to have qualitative character, which distinguishes them from quantitative-mathematical methods.

This in turn is based on the assumption of essentialism. The school of methodological essentialism was founded, according to Popper, by Aristotle. "Methodological essentialists are inclined to formulate scientific questions in such terms as 'what is matter?' or 'what is force?' or 'what is justice?', and they believe that a penetrating answer to such questions, revealing the real or essential meaning of these terms and thereby the real or true nature of the essences denoted by them is at least a necessary prerequisite of scientific research"[11]. In opposition to that, methodological nominalists put the following question: "how does this piece of matter behave?". They hold that the task of science is only to describe how things behave, and to "suggest that this is to be done by freely introducing new terms wherever necessary, or by re-defining old terms wherever convenient while cheerfully neglecting their original meaning. For they regard words merely as useful instruments of descriptions"[12].

The idea of essence is closely related to the idea of change, for the essence of things can be known, and makes itself understood, only through change. Essence of things enables us to talk about persistence of things

---

10 *Ibid.*, p. 17.
11 *Ibid.*, p. 29.
12 *Ibid.*

despite the fact that they undergo constant changes. The essence is a sum or source of potentialities inherent in a thing, which are made apparent through the change in time, or rather, the change itself is a result of an inherent activity of the essence.

> Methodological essentialism can accordingly be based on the historicist arguments which actually led Plato to his metaphysical essentialism, the Heraclitean argument that changing things defy rational description. Hence science or knowledge presupposes something that does not change but remains identical with itself - an essence. History, i. e. the description of change, and essence, i. e. that, which remains unchanged during change, appear here as correlative concepts.[13]

2. Pronaturalist Historicism

Popper asserts that historicism is basically of antinaturalist character, but, as he puts it, is by no means opposed to the idea that there is a common element in method of physics and of social sciences. This comes from the fact that social sciences can also be understood as theoretical and empirical sciences. Popper's claims in this respect resemble those of Michael Oakeshott and Friedrich Hayek who, despite many differences between them, formulated arguments against rationalism in social sciences and in politics[14]. General feature of a theoretical discipline is that it aims at explaining and predicting events. Pronaturalistic doctrines of historicism, despite their closeness to the antiscientistic historicism, have this theoretical aspect, which distinguishes them from the former kind. By an analogy to astronomy, pronaturalistic historicist claims that, since it is possible to predict solar eclipses with great exactitude, it must be possible to predict social revolutions, though at the same time will warn that the same level of ex-

---

13 *Ibid.*, p. 33.
14 Cf. especially MICHAEL OAKESHOTT: "Rationalism in Politics", in: *Rationalism in Politics and Other Essays*, Indianapolis (Liberty Fund) 1991, new, expanded edition, and FRIEDRICH VON HAYEK: *Constitution of Liberty*, London (Routledge and Kegan Paul) 1960. The difference between Popper and especially Oakeshott is very great indeed since Oakeshott's essay is in fact a veiled attack of Popper's *Open Society* and the idea of social engineering advocated in it.

actitude cannot be reached. Since pronaturalistic doctrines of historicism wish to remain empirical, they imply that such predictions must be formed on a basis of empirical facts understood as a historical record or chronicle of events. The analogy with astronomy leads this kind of historicism to assert that social events are also characterised by a dynamics which is responsible for the changes occurring in history. Social dynamical forces are operating according to historical laws which determine historical development.

The aim of a pronaturalist sociologist it to predict the future, not so much of individuals, but the one of groups or even human race. Popper introduces here a distinction between historical prophecy, which is based on non-experimental observations, and experimental historical prediction which forms a basis for social engineering.

III. Popper's Critique of Historicism

In his criticism of historicism, Popper distinguishes two kinds of technological approach to social life. One is piecemeal, the second is Utopian engineering.

> "The piecemeal technologist [...] recognises that only a minority of social institutions are consciously designed while the vast majority have just 'grown' as undesigned results of human actions. [H]e will look upon them from a 'functional' or 'instrumental' point of view. He will see them as means to certain ends, or as convertible to the service of certain ends; as machines rather than organisms"[15]. "The characteristic approach of the piecemeal engineer is this. Even though he may perhaps cherish some ideals which concern society 'as a whole' - its general welfare - he does not believe in the method of re-designing it as a whole. Whatever his ends, he tries to achieve them by small adjustments and re-adjustments which can be continually improved upon. His ends may be of diverse kinds, for example the accumulation of wealth or of power by certain individuals, or by certain groups; or the distribution of wealth and power. [...] Thus public or political social engineering may have the most diverse ten-

---

15 *Ibid.*, p. 65.

dencies, totalitarian as well as liberal. The piecemeal engineer knows, like Socrates, how little he knows. He knows that we can learn only from our mistakes. Accordingly, he will make his way, step by step, carefully comparing the results expected with the results achieved, and always on the look-out for the unavoidable unwanted consequences of any reform; he will avoid undertaking reforms of a complexity and scope which make it impossible for him to disentangle causes and effects, and to know what he is really doing"[16].

In contradistinction to this:

"Holistic or Utopian social engineering [...] aims at remodelling the 'whole of society' in accordance with a definite plan or blueprint; it aims at 'seizing the key positions' and at extending 'the power of the State [...] until the State becomes nearly identical with society', and it aims, furthermore, at controlling from these 'key positions' the historical forces that mould the future of the developing society: either by arresting this development, or else by foreseeing its course and adjusting society to it"[17].

Popper claims that the holistic method of changing the society is impossible since the greater the holistic changes are attempted, the greater are their unintended and largely unexpected repercussions, forcing the engineer to improvise according to the piecemeal method. It always leads him to do things he never planned, that is to the unplanned planning.

"Thus the difference between Utopian and piecemeal engineering turns out, in practice, to be a difference not so much in scale and scope as in caution and in preparedness for unavoidable surprises. One could also say that, in practice, the two methods differ in other ways than in scale and scope [...] Of these two doctrines, I hold that one is true, while the other is false and liable to lead to mistakes which are both avoidable and grave"[18].

Popper's main criticism of the historicist holism is that it is difficult enough to be critical of our own mistakes, but is nearly impossible for us to persist in a critical attitude towards those of our actions which involve the

---

16 *Ibid.*, pp. 66-67.
17 *Ibid.*, p. 67.
18 *Ibid.*, p. 69.

lives of many men: in other words, it is very hard to learn from very big mistakes[19].

> "But the difficulty of combining holistic planning with scientific methods is still more fundamental than has so far been indicated. The holistic planner overlooks the fact that it is easy to centralise power but impossible to centralise all that knowledge which is distributed over many individual minds, and whose centralisation would be necessary for the wise wielding of centralised power. But this fact has far-reaching consequences. Unable to ascertain what is in the minds of so many individuals, he must try to simplify his problem by eliminating individual differences: he must try to control and stereotype interests and beliefs by education and propaganda. But this attempt to exercise power over minds must destroy the last possibility of finding out what people really think, for it is clearly incompatible with the free expression of thought, especially of critical thought. Ultimately, it must destroy knowledge; and the greater the gain in power, the greater will be the loss of knowledge"[20].

Criticism of essentialist and intuitive understanding, typical of the antinaturalistic historicism, has been elaborated by Popper in *Objective Knowledge*, where he criticises historicists Dilthey and Collingwood for their claim that in order to understand an action of an individual it is necessary to re-enact in one's own mind the aims, purposes and emotions of a man whose action is being explained. He claims that such a faculty may a help to a historian, but what is essential is a situational analysis of an activity or a person that is being under analysis,'. Indeed Popper claims that we can learn much more about a man's mind from analysis of the ready-made, objective artefact created by him rather than from guessing, by means of empathy, or *Einfühlung*, what was his subjective state of mind while he engaged in the creative process.

> "The historian's analysis of the situation is his historical conjecture which [...] is a metatheory about [someone's] reasoning. Being on a level different from [one's] reasoning, it does not re-enact it, but tries to produce an idealised and reasoned reconstruction of it, omitting inessential elements and perhaps augmenting it. Thus the historian's central metaproblem is: what were the decisive elements in

---

19 *Ibid.*, p. 88.
20 *Ibid.*, pp. 89-90.

[one's] problem situation. To the extent to which the historian succeeds in solving this metaproblem, he understands the historical problem. Thus what he has to do *qua* historian is not to re-enact past experiences, but to marshal objective arguments for and against his conjectural situational analysis"[21].

He also dismisses the idea of hermeneutic circle, according to which in order to understand a whole - a text, a book, a philosopher's work, an individual's life, or a period - it is necessary to understand its constituent parts, whereas in order to understand the parts of a whole, it is necessary to understand a whole they are parts of, he also claims that the idea of the hermeneutic circle has been first formulated by a philosopher of natural science, Francis Bacon (in *De Augmentis*, VI, X, VI).

IV. Criticism of Popper's Critique of Historicism

In his criticism of historicism Popper takes to task writers such as distinct as Hegel, Comte, Marx, Spengler, Croce, Toynbee, Mannheim, and others. His basic criticism is that in their attempts toward understanding history, and possibly changing it, they adopt a false conception of science. Some of them, antinaturalists, as we have seen, reject the idea of making the history an object of scientific study if science is understood on the model of natural sciences. Others are adopting the positivistic view of science, which Popper also rejects and wishes to replace with his of own conception of science as a continuous search for ever better knowledge through bold guesses and their empirical elimination. Popper's explanation of historicism and his criticisms were themselves severely criticised by a number of authors, Marxists, Hegelians and analytical philosophers. Many of them found his definition of historicism essentially vague. Especially it is difficult to understand the connection between antinaturalistic doctrines of historicism with pronaturalistic ones, since the claims of the former one are in a direct contradiction with those of the other, yet Popper asserts, twice in the *Poverty of Historicism*[22], that the doctrines of pronaturalistic historicism

---

21 POPPER: *Objective Knowledge*, Oxford (Oxford University Press) 1972, p. 188.
22 *Ibid.*, pp. 35 & 105.

have much in common with antinaturalistic ones, even though he made the reader to understand that it is otherwise. For example Jerzy Giedymin[23] suggested that it is wholly unclear whether it is necessary to adopt all doctrines of historicism listed by Popper in order to be counted as a historicist, or only some of them, and if so, then which doctrines make one a historicist.

It is difficult, for example, to deny that in social life it is impossible to disregard the necessity of taking into account the teleological aspect of human behaviour. Indeed, human actions cannot be understood without the reference to the aims people set themselves in their social dealings with each other. Popper however seems to take the fact as not as a difficulty in scientific explanation of history, but as a simplification and a help, asserting that it makes it possible to adopt a principle of rationality, that is an assumption that in a similar situation people will behave in a similar way. Most of the authors usually think that this is a difference responsible for the situation of the unbridgeable divorce between science and humanities, and not an argument for the idea of the unity of method in natural and social sciences.

This difference has been noted by very many authors. Even the ancient philosophers were conscious of it. It will suffice to remind here that the Platonic and Aristotelian concepts of scientific explanation were formulated self-consciously against the reductionist and pre-scientific views expounded by Anaxagoras, Democritus and Antisthenes. For example in a dispute with Antisthenes's definition of the house as *a assemblage of bricks and stones covered by a roof*, Aristotle defined the house teleologically as *a shelter for man and his belongings*. It is evident that the Aristotelian essentialist definitions have much wider scope of application in social sciences than the reductionist, atomistic definitions proffered by scientists of all ages. Teleology in its turn leads inevitably to essentialism, which was condemned by Popper, but which seems an unavoidable tool in explaining the social life, or making it teleologically understandable.

Winch, for example, in his *The Idea of A Social Science* cheerfully admits committing the sin of "methodological essentialism" and his guilt against Popper's "methodological individualism". He writes:

---

23 JERZY GIEDYMIN: "Model historycyzmu prof. K. Poppera", *Studia Filozoficzne* 1958, 3, pp. 205-214 (in Polish).

"Popper's statement that social institutions are just explanatory models introduced by the social scientists for his own purposes is palpably untrue. The ways of thinking embodied in institutions govern the way the members of societies studied by social scientist behave. The idea of war, for instance, which is one of Popper's examples, was not simply invented by people who wanted to *explain* what happens when societies come into armed conflict. It is an idea which provides the criteria of what is appropriate in the behaviour of members of the conflicting societies. Because my country is at war there are certain things which I must and certain things I must not do. My behaviour is governed, one could say, by my concept of myself as a member of a belligerent country. The concept of war belongs *essentially* to my behaviour. But the concept of gravity does not belong essentially to behaviour of a falling apple in the same way: it belongs rather to the physicist's explanation of the apple's behaviour. To recognise this has, *pace* Popper, nothing to do with a belief in ghost behind the phenomena. Further, it is impossible to go far in specifying the attitudes, expectations and relations of individuals without referring to concepts which enter into those attitudes, etc., and the meaning of the actions of any individual persons"[24].

In addition to the problem of teleology and essentialism, dismissed by Popper, his principle of rationality seems to violate his prohibition of inductive reasoning from science, since the principle of rationality seems to be based on the assumption of persistent regularity and normality of human behaviour, or a universal, and unchanging human nature - a question which Popper does not seem to notice.

Other authors questioned validity of Popper's attribution of the historicist position even to such thinkers like Hegel, who is considered by Popper one of the most important representative of it - indeed, Popper accuses Hegel of "hysterical historicism". Kaufmann for example claims that from the point of view of Popper's definition of a historicist, Hegel cannot be thought to be one, for he did not claim "to have discovered laws of history which enabled [him] to prophesy the course of historical events". Kaufmann asserts that such a claim is controversial in detail and questionable in principle. A sound critique of Hegel should take into account that Hegel did not

---

24 PETER WINCH: *The Idea of A Social Science and Its Relation to Philosophy*, London (Routledge and Kegan Paul) 1958, pp. 127-128.

attempt to play the prophet and was content to comprehend the past[25]. After all it is Hegel who claimed that the owl of Minerva is flying only at dusk.

In general Popper's attack on Hegel and his historicism has been viewed as biased, prejudiced and outstepping the limits of a civilised, rational scientific dispute. Kaufmann bitterly notices that judging after the way Popper criticised Hegel it is difficult to believe that the criticism has been formulated by an author of an important book in the methodology of science. Very much similar opinion was expressed by Gilbert Ryle, who, in his otherwise enthusiastic review of Popper's *Open Society*, has written:

> "Dr. Popper hates Hegel as much as he hates Hegelianism. His comments, in consequence, have a shrillness which detracts from their force. It is right that he should feel passionately. The survival of liberal ideas and liberal practices has been and still is in jeopardy. But it is a bad tactics in a champion of the freedom of thought to use blackguarding idioms characteristic of its enemies. His verdicts are, I think, just, but they would exert a greater influence if they sounded judicial"[26].

Much more critical of Popper's critical methods is Kaufmann who, in a detailed way shows that Popper doctored many quotations taken from Hegel in order to make him say what Popper wanted him to say, and points out that it is philosophically and morally wrong to support one's judgement of Hegel on Arthur Schopenhauer's vituperations of him.

Inadequacy of Popper's discussion with historicism, and in particular his advocacy of piecemeal of social engineering has been made apparent in the more practical context of contemporary transformation in Eastern Europe. It seems that if the countries which freshly delivered themselves from the constraints of the communist regime were to follow only the piecemeal social engineering in order to avoid the dangers of the Utopian revolutionary changes, they very likely would not achieve as much as they managed to do in a relatively short period of time. Imagine e.g. Mr. B. who has been put in charge of a comprehensive reform of economy in one of the countries of the Central Europe. He is faced with hidden unemployment in the ineffi-

---

25 WALTER KAUFMANN: "The Hegel Myth and Its Method", in: Hegel: *A Collection of Critical Essays*, edited by Alasdair MacIntyre, Notre Dame-London (Notre Dame Press) 1976, pp. 42-43.

26 GILBERT RYLE: "A review of Karl Popper's *Open Society and Its Enemies*", in: *Mind*, vol. 56, No. 222, April 1947, p. 171.

cient and wasteful heavy industry, inefficient agriculture divided between overpopulated small households, nearly universal tax evasion, flourishing black-market economy, demoralisation of the workers, high expectations of the consumers, together with the dramatic drop in the standards of life, and all other afflictions typical of the postcommunist region. My claim is that, however much he would like to follow the precepts of the piecemeal social engineering, the situation itself will make him a holistic planner whose actions will have to have a large scale and he will have to brace himself for dramatic unforeseen consequences, *but, at the same time, he will have no other choice*. It is this fact that makes the transformation in countries so difficult, and it is this very fact that shows inadequacy of Popper's piecemeal engineering. In situations like that one, much more is expected, and, accordingly, much more is necessary than piecemeal patching over of particular bad spots.

Similar criticisms can be levelled against Popper's prohibition of historical prediction or prophecy. For example it seems quite right to say that, other things being more or less equal, the countries of Central and Eastern Europe will increasingly be included into the mechanisms of world-capitalist economy. This is a large-scale prediction or rather a prophesy. It seems evident, however, that such an assumption forms an important element of the decision-scheme of rational agents in Western financial institutions which are venturing into the region. Popper would be right in saying that such a prediction is very shaky, for many things may go wrong; he is also right that such a prediction is to a large extent self-fulfilling. For if many agents would adopt it as a principle of their actions, the result will be that by the very fact of making this assumption and acting on it, the region will be taken over by the capitalist system and included it into the world-economy, thus making the prediction come true. But then it is irrational to act on such a prediction? Very much to the contrary; also it seems highly questionable to forbid people to form their expectations as to the future just because they are not scientific in Popper's sense.

Indeed, it seems that it is good moment to question the very notion of scientificity as defined by Popper. It has been done by many authors in similar contexts.

For example one of the leading British Marxists, Maurice Cornforth, in his response to Popper's *Open Society* attempted to contest the adequacy of Popper's conception of science, attempting at the same time to defend the scientific status Marxism. He asserts that the scrutiny of Marx's fundamental ideas about science reveals that it has a scientific character. He agrees with Popper that science proceeds by making conjectures and devising all possible ways of falsifying them. He adds, however:

> "But yet the body of scientific theory consists of more than just a collection of falsifiable conjectures which are variously revised and replaced by other conjectures as falsification actually overtakes them. Every well-developed science rests on its fundamental theory, and is guided by it in its inquiries. This is a feature of science which Popper never examines - possibly because he distrusts such expressions as 'fundamental theory', which he thinks redolent of pseudo-scientific metaphysics"[27].

Should one think that such a defence of the scientific status of Marxism is biased or flawed, he should be advised to consider the revision of Popper's conception of science put forward by Imre Lakatos who claims that a mature scientific theory consists of a metaphysical hard core which is not directly exposed to falsifications, and is protected from them by a belt of subsidiary hypotheses the aim of which is to face directly the empirical data. And if one is not inclined to trust Lakatos, who has been described by some as a Stalinist holist, one can invoke the authority of two other eminent philosophers of science, those of Pierre Duhem and Villard Van Orman Quine, who, similarly, advocate a holistic concept of science as a field of forces which is exposed to empirical data only at the fringes protecting the inside of the field. It is also worth remembering that Thomas Kuhn's view of science bears analogous features. Despite the essential vagueness of the Kuhnian notion of the paradigm, it can be understood as a "fundamental theory" or "pattern" which is not given up despite its temporary inability to deal with problems and anomalies, and that it is an important scientific discovery if one manages to show compatibility of such a "pattern" with phenomena so far unexplained by it. Cornforth, in his analysis of Popper's criticism of Marxism, draws the following conclusion:

> "What Dr. Popper seems to have overlooked in his pronouncements about prohibitions and falsifications is the work of abstraction and generalisation in scientific theory. The task of "fundamental" theory is to abstract the necessary or universal condition of existence of the phenomena studied, and to put forward corresponding generalisa-

---

[27] MAURICE CORNFORTH: *The Open Philosophy and the Open Society*, London (Lawrence and Wishart) 1968, p. 29.

tions. Such fundamental theory, very abstract and very general, does not, and cannot satisfy Dr. Popper's principle that 'the more a theory forbids the better it is'. It is, indeed, difficult to imagine why on earth Dr. Popper should ever have enunciated such a principle - except that it gives him a stick to beat Marxism with. But it is not a 'good' stick, and in wielding it Dr. Popper joins the very numerous and very distinguished company of those who have allowed anti-communism to cloud their judgement"[28].

Having in mind numerous personal experiences that Popper recounts in his autobiographical remarks, it is difficult not to agree with Cornforth, even if one is inclined neither to historicism in general, nor to Marxism in particular.

V. Open Society or Community?

Popper's philosophy has been a very fruitful source of inspiration for Polish philosophers and intellectuals for more than forty years, despite the fact that these years have been one of the most difficult periods in Polish intellectual history, when nearly all liberties, including freedom of speech, have been taken away from the people, and together with them all hope for regaining freedom. This dreadful time has been successfully and peacefully put to an end. It is fair to say that it has been made possible by many diverse factors, and that one of the most important of them was the vigorous *spiritual presence* of Karl Popper's philosophical thought among the Polish intellectuals, politicians and the people.

We have changed our world, and we believe that it is going for the better now. We have been changing our world according to our understanding of ideals for which Karl Popper stood for throughout his whole life. But we also believe that not all work has been done yet, for we cannot be certain that society, once opened, will remain open, and that we do not need to worry about it ever after. The future course of the society cannot be predicted, and its problems are equally unpredictable.

---

28 *Ibid.*, p. 30.

KARL POPPER'S CRITIQUE OF HISTORICISM

In his *Conjectures and Refutations* late Sir Karl Popper said - optimistically, if somewhat bluntly - that in his opinion the world of Western liberal democracies is perhaps not the best of all possible worlds, yet it certainly is the best of all existing worlds[29]. The phrase parallels Winston Churchill saying that democracy is the worst of all political systems, but that a better one has not been found. Popper also rejoiced in the fact that the peaceful revolution took place and that he lived long enough to see it happening. For he spent most of his life fighting the enemies of the open society and, I do not hesitate to say, if the peaceful revolution of the 1989 had its own theoretician, it was Karl Popper.

Yet, until quite recently intellectuals in Central and Eastern Europe lived in a great comfort. The comfort came from the *uncritical* acceptance of the convictions like the one just quoted from Sir Karl; namely that all our problems, if they will ever get solved, will be done away with for ever by the theory and practice of liberalism. The prevalent intention was to achieve the state of affairs which Sir Karl so luringly described. So it was only natural to wish to join this heaven on earth as soon as possible. Yet even Sir Karl, one of the staunchest defenders of the 20th century liberalism, said that it is nonsense to make a godhead of the dogma of the free market and of its principle[30].

Towards the very end of the 20th century, we are now facing a widely debated dilemma: whether we should concentrate our efforts on building an *open and just society of free and autonomous individuals*, or rather a *coherent communities striving to achieve some common good*, uniting its members in their practices. Many nations which, following the collapse of communism, have regained their independence, and are now urgently seeking to rebuild the structure of their societies and states, having precious few examples to follow in that painful, difficult and costly process. Conflicts dividing the reality of social life, particularly in the East (but also, though in a less acute way, in the West as well), find their philosophical spokesmen in thinkers who formulate rival conceptions of social life. Within the sphere of philosophy, the opposition seem to have come about as a result of the advocacy, or rejection (as the case may be) of the Platonic and Enlightenment's rationalism, according to which, in our social life, we are supposed to fol-

---

29 In the last conversation we had Sir Karl assured me that, even though he had a temptation to do it, he did not change his opinion.
30 *Ibid.*.

low the principles of reason possessed of final truth. With the failure of the communist experiment, which is widely considered by the advocates of the open society a failure of all constructivist attempts to create heaven on earth according to the inexorable laws discovered by the "dialectical science" of Marxism (itself an offspring of the Enlightenment), the so-called *Enlightenment project* came under a renewed fire. Many thinkers seem to be (to invoke Edmund Burke's dictum) "afraid to put men to live and trade each on his own stock of reason; because [they] suspect that this stock in each men is small and that individuals would do better to avail themselves of the general bank and capital of natures and of ages".

Liberalism is now being met with an important challenge. First of all, it is claimed that if trade unions work only for the immediate betterment of the working conditions within the confines of the capitalist system and parliamentary democracy, they are in danger of losing most of their social power and effectiveness. That is exactly what is currently taking place in many liberal societies: the liberties of the open society are sacrificed for wealth and the effectiveness of power. Secondly, liberalism increasingly becomes a politics for a political elite in charge of the media influencing the democratic vote. The membership in those elites is being limited almost exclusively to the people of wealth, and the positive influence of the voting public is an object of increasingly effective manipulations via mass media. An individual voice and preference is being lost and neglected, and the individuals in their needs and thinking are increasingly stereotypical products of the media serving the interests of the capital. Such a society is not a place of achieving common good, but rather a place of pursuit of atomistically conceived interests of particular groups and individuals.

Thus, together with the notion of *community*, the concept of *tradition* is receiving tremendous attention within the so-called communitarian critique of liberalism. For many communitarian critics of liberalism, the Aristotelian idea of πολις seem to be a model for (to quote MacIntyre) "the construction of new forms of community within which the moral life could be sustained so that both morality and civility might survive the coming ages of barbarism and darkness", the barbarism being usually identified with the permissive, irreligious, individualistic and aesthetically oriented culture of the Western civilisation.

A crucial and novel consequence of this debate seems to be nearly universal agreement in *rejection of the traditional priority of epistemology over social philosophy*, expressing itself in a conviction that (to rephrase Richard

Rorty's formulation) *solidarity* is more important than *objectivity*, or that *democracy, in order to function, does not need epistemological justification or metaphysical grounding*. Instead, the principles currently sought are the principles of *practical*, not *theoretical* reason, and the justification for social action is being sought within the sphere of *morals and values*, not the theory of knowledge.

The two above-mentioned notions: that of the *Open Society* and of *Community*, are symbolising two distinct and opposed trends in the current moral, social and political philosophy, which strive to formulate rival and competing visions of possible ways of shaping and transforming social life. They are also symbols of the problem we have to solve if we are to deal with successfully the tensions of the current historical epoch.

Discussion Summary

Krzysztof Klincewicz

Paper discussed:
Adam J. Chmielewski: Karl Popper's Critique of Historicism, the Historical School, and the Contemporary Debate

The discussion focused mainly on the issue of social engineering. Some situations may require more than piecemeal social engineering - e.g. the change of the economic system in post-socialist countries. The process is violent and uncontrolled, therefore the application of piecemeal solutions is impossible. That kind of social engineering represents a pragmatic approach, and was designed to cope with other problems (Kettner). Piecemeal social engineering did not prove in Central European countries to be successful - it may be useful under certain conditions, but in the situation of transition a holistic approach is necessary. For example, in Poland, the transition programme, called Balcerowicz plan, was a set of procedures aiming at a holistic change. Actually, it did not really address all the problems that had been involved in the economic process - and in these areas piecemeal social engineering should have been applied (Chmielewski). The Russian experience was similar - political and economic reforms were strongly influenced by disagreement about tactics: holistic or piecemeal change (Hamlin).

The pragmatist approach can be described as the suggestion not to put more into question than is necessary in the specific situation as opposed to the concept of total planning. This is also the case of corporate strategy designing (Steinmann). Piecemeal social engineering is reductionist, it involves criticism and reduces problems to details, opposed to the whole (De Geer).

The distinction between the piecemeal and holistic social engineering is wrong as based on a false opposition between an open society and a community-based society. In fact, modern companies apply both kinds of engineering. An example is IBM, where the process of changes consisted not

DISCUSSION SUMMARY

only of structural replacement, but also of benchmarking-analysis of factors contributing to the company's success - a holistic, but at the same time also piecemeal approach (SOLOMON).

A deeper analysis of differences between holistic and piecemeal approach reveals common ways of thinking based on technical rationality. However, there is a third way: avoidance of coping with the problem in a technical way, but looking at it as a question of practical reasoning: How to design a modern society. Popper's theory is old fashioned and the nature of the social world requires a change of epistemology, recognition of the primacy of practical reason over theoretical reason (ULRICH). The theory of action provides solutions similar to social engineering, but well aware of this practical reason: a kind of case-based reflective engineering involving no instrumental treatment of human beings (KETTNER). Nevertheless, under time pressure and efficiency requirements, managers sometimes must handle people as objects, and ethical principles of designing cannot be applied then (STEIMANN).

Other important topics of the "*Open Society*" concern problems of Hegelian and Marxian theory. Revolution was presented as an experiment with the whole nation, and its outcomes would only be known after some time. A society subjected to such a risk is in a different situation than a business company: when the changes are destructive, a firm cannot simply go bankrupt. The concept of holistic social engineering is mistaken as it presupposes that outside of the society there is someone who knows what to do with the society - that cannot be true (KOSLOWSKI).

Chapter 16

Does Historism Mean Relativism? Remarks on the Debate on Historism in the German Political Economy of the Late 19th Century

ANNETTE WITTKAU-HORGBY

I. Introduction
II. The Background of the Economic Debate About Historism and Relativism
III. Schmoller's Concept of Political Economy
IV. Menger's Concept of Political Economy
V. Historism and Relativism

I. Introduction

The two topics 'historism'[1] and 'relativism' were in 19th century Germany largely controversial themes. The discussion about the relationship

---

[1] The German term 'Historismus' has several meanings. This ambiguity can be traced back to specific historical roots, and it is still typical for the present discussion in history. See further O. G. OEXLE, J. RÜSEN (Eds.): *Historismus in den Kulturwissenschaften*, Köln (Böhlau-Verlag) 1996 and W. BIALAS, G. RAULET (Eds.): *Die Historismusdebatte in der Weimarer Republik*, Frankfurt a. M. (Peter Lang) 1996. The historical development of this term has been investigated by K. HEUSSI: *Die Krisis des Historismus*, Tübingen (J.C.B. Mohr/Paul Siebeck) 1932; E. ROTHACKER: *Das Wort Historismus*, Zeitschrift für deutsche Wortforschung, Vol. 16 (1960), pp. 3-6; O. G. OEXLE: *Geschichtswissenschaft im Zeichen des Historismus. Studien zu Problemgeschichten der Moderne*, Göt-

DOES HISTORISM MEAN RELATIVISM?

between them slowly started at the beginning of the 19th century.[2] The debate became intensive during the second half of the 19th century, and it continued until the beginning of the Nazi-regime in 1933.[3] During this period there were fierce debates about historism and relativism within all German humanities.[4] The central topic in this discussion was the question, 'Was it historism that had caused relativism, specifically the relativisation of values (Relativierung der Werte)?'

In this paper, I will try to analyse the relationship between historism and relativism by focusing on the debate about historism in the German political economy of the late 19th century. The background of this discussion in economics, however, was the process of the "historisation[5] of thought"

---

tingen (Vandenhoeck & Ruprecht) 1996, pp. 41; and A. WITTKAU: *Historismus. Zur Geschichte des Begriffs und des Problems*, 2nd Edition, Göttingen (Vandenhoeck & Ruprecht) 1994. An English translation of the term 'Historismus' is difficult for several reasons. 'Historismus' lacks a clear definition in the German language in the first place. This does not make it easier to translate into English. The common way to translate it has been 'historicism'. However, since Popper's famous book *The Poverty of Historicism* (1944), the English word 'historicism' has specific connotations which do not fit for the German discussion. Therefore, I will use the term 'Historism' which is not so popular in the English language but which enables us to have a better understanding of the specific problems the scholars dealt with in Germany at the end of the 19th and the beginning of the 20th century. In respect to the understanding of the terms historism and historicism in ethical economy see P. KOSLOWSKI: "Is Postmodernism a Neohistorism? On the Absoluteness and the Historicity of History", in: P. KOSLOWSKI (Ed.): *The Theory of Ethical Economy in the Historical School*, Berlin (Springer-Verlag) 1995, pp. 286.

2 See G. SCHOLTZ: *'Historismus' als spekulative Geschichtsphilosophie: Chr. J. Braniß*, Frankfurt a. M. 1973.
3 See K. LICHTBLAU: *Kulturkrise und Soziologie um die Jahrhundertwende. Zur Genealogie der Kultursoziologie in Deutschland*, Frankfurt a. M. (Suhrkamp) 1996.
4 See A. WITTKAU: *Historismus. Zur Geschichte des Begriffs und des Problems*, 2nd Edition, Göttingen (Vandenhoech & Ruprecht) 1994.
5 I have translated the German word 'Historisierung' with the English term 'historisation'. This translation was made in analogy to the term 'relativisation'. As relativism is the outcome of the process of the relativisation of thought, historism is the outcome of the process of the historisation of thought.

(Troeltsch)[6] which is typical of the 19th century in general. This process formed the frame of the economic discussion. The term 'Historisation of thought' aims thereby at the phenomenon of an increasing consciousness of the historical dimension of reality, which was developed during the 19th century and had been enforced by social and political changes on the one hand, and by the establishment of the historical empirical method within the social sciences, the so-called «Geisteswissenschaften», on the other hand.

In the late 19th century, the consequences of this historisation of thought were discussed not only in political economy but in other disciplines like law and theology as well.[7] At the beginning of the eighties the historical empirical method was so well established in the field of political economy that the process of the 'historisation of economy' could be regarded as finished. Then a counter movement arose that questioned the use of history for political economy. The catchword, however, which was introduced by these critics of the historical method in order to sum up their programme was 'historism'.

In political economy, the term 'historism' thus obtained clearly negative connotations. It became a catchword for the reproach: 'too much history!' and it implied the accusation of an exaggeration of history in two respects. On the one hand, the historians were accused of accumulating a historical knowledge which was without any relevance for the present. On the other hand, the term 'historism' implied the reproach that this exaggeration of history was responsible for the phenomenon of the relativisation of values.[8] In this second respect 'historism' became a synonym for 'relativism'.

This use of the term 'historism' was established in political economy during and after the debate between Carl Menger and Gustav Schmoller in the late 19th century,[9] and Menger established in this way not only his understanding of the term but his special attitude towards history as well.

---

6   See E. TROELTSCH: *Der Historismus und seine Probleme*, Tübingen (J.C.B. Mohr/Paul Siebeck) 1922, p. 102.
7   See A. WITTKAU: *Historismus. Zur Geschichte des Begriffs und des Problems*, 2nd Edition, Göttingen (Vandenhoeck & Ruprecht) 1994, pp. 80.
8   See P. KOSLWOSKI: "Ethical Economy as Synthesis of Economic and Ethical Theory", in: P. KOSLWOSKI (Ed.): *Ethics in Economics, Business, and Economic Policy,* Berlin (Springer-Verlag) 1992, pp. 31.
9   See A. WITTKAU: *Historismus. Zur Geschichte des Begriffs und des Problems*, 2nd Edition, Göttingen (Vandenhoeck & Ruprecht) 1994, pp. 108.

DOES HISTORISM MEAN RELATIVISM?

Schmoller's attitude towards history was a different one. His concept had been to establish the new, historical way of thinking in the field of economics.[10] He was among those scholars who enforced the process of the 'historisation' of economy by supplementing the classical interpretation of economic institutions through a historical one.[11] These different understandings of the function of history and historical perception within economics formed the core of the debate about historism in the German political economy of the late 19th century.

In the following, I will begin with a brief sketch of the background of this debate in order to show the general problem that formed the basis of the discussion between Schmoller and Menger (II). Thereafter, I will concentrate on Gustav Schmoller's and Carl Menger's conceptions, and, although others have emphasised the similarities between Schmoller and Menger,[12] I will especially point out the differences between these conceptions. In order to do this, both positions will be presented in two separate passages. I will begin with Schmoller's concept of political economy (III) because his position was the one which was attacked. Then, I will present Menger's position (IV) and his critique on Schmoller. Finally (V), I will try to answer the question, 'Was it actually *historism* that had caused *relativism*?' by pointing out in which respects Menger's critique was right and in which respects he was wrong.

---

10 See R. RICHTER: "Bridging Old and New Institutional Economics: Gustav Schmoller the Leader of the Younger German Historical School, Seen with Neoinstitutionalists' Eyes", *Journal of Institutional and Theoretical Economy*, Vol. 152, No. 4 (1996), pp. 567-592, p. 587. See also G. SCHMÖLDERS: "Statt Wirtschaftstheorie Staatswirtschaftslehre: Erinnerungen an Gustav Schmoller", in: J. G. BACKHAUS (Ed.): *Gustav von Schmoller und die Probleme von heute*, Berlin (Duncker und Humblot) 1993, pp. 99-103, p. 101.

11 See C. NARDINELLI and R. E. MEINERS: "Schmoller, the Methodenstreit, and the Development of Economic History", *Journal of Institutional and Theoretical Economics*, Vol. 144 (1988), pp. 543-551, p. 543.

12 See K. HÄUSER, "Historical School and 'Methodenstreit'", *Journal of Institutional and Theoretical Economics*, Vol. 144 (1988), pp. 532-542.

ANNETTE WITTKAU-HORGBY

II. The Background of the Economic Debate About Historism and Relativism

Since the end of the 18th century and especially in the 19th century, the historical dimension of reality had attracted more and more attention of the European scholars. The increased interest in history had been caused by the practical experience of a fundamental change of almost every sphere in life. The French Revolution, the Napoleoneon Wars, and the following period of Restoration were some of the reasons why waves of changes occurred in several European societies during this time. Especially in Germany, the political life, the social structure, the legal system and the economic order were openly discussed and changed in several fields.[13] Within the population, these changes caused feelings of a big crisis. And Jacob Burckhardt[14] and Friedrich Nietzsche[15] were among the first who contemplated the relationship between the practical experience of a crisis and the increasing interest in history.[16] In his famous book *On the Studies of History*, which became popular under the title *Weltgeschichtliche Betrachtungen*, Jacob Burckhardt wrote in 1868:

> The continuous change of times carries unceasingly off the forms which shape the outer garment of life. The enormous changes since the 18th century contain something which forces us strongly to deal with the past and to investigate older fashions [...] A troubled period like these eighty-three years of the age of revolution must create itself such a counterweight in order not to loose all consciousness.[17]

---

13 See T. NIPPERDEY: *Deutsche Geschichte 1800-1866*, München (C. H. Beck) 1983, p. 11.
14 See W. HARDTWIG: "Jakob Burckhardt. Trieb und Geist - Die neue Konzeption von Kultur", in: N. HAMMERSTEIN (Ed.): *Deutsche Geschichtswissenschaft um 1900*, Wiesbaden (Steiner-Verlag) 1988, pp. 97-112.
15 See O. G. OEXLE, *Geschichtswissenschaft im Zeichen des Historismus,* Göttingen (Vandenhoeck & Ruprecht) 1996, p. 75.
16 See W. BIALAS, G. RAULET (Eds.): *Die Historismusdebatte in der Weimarer Republik*, Frankfurt a. M. (Peter Lang) 1996, Introduction by G. RAULET, p. 29.
17 J. BURCKHARDT: *Gesamtausgabe*, 14 Volumes edited by E. DÜRR et. al., Stuttgart 1929-1934, Vol. 7, p. 11. Translation A.W.-H.

DOES HISTORISM MEAN RELATIVISM?

This historical interest was satisfied by a new form of historical perception. Since the end of the 18th century and the beginning of the 19th century people had started to investigate the past *scientifically*. Questions in respect to the past were now answered by looking at the sources and other historical materials. The empirical proof for a hypothesis became the decisive criterion for a scientific answer to a historical question. These early approaches to scientific answers within the field of humanities were based essentially on an inductive understanding of science. Scientific answers within the field of history were regarded to be 'provable' with the help of historical materials. The modern assumption that scientific answers are not 'provable' but only 'falsifyable' did not yet exist.[18]

With the help of this new empirical method the historical genesis and development of cultural phenomena such as economics or law, music or art or even moral and religion was investigated. In the disciplines of law and economics, the big so-called 'Historical Schools' emerged in Germany within this movement.[19] The outcome of these historical investigations, however, was double-sided. On the one hand, it became clear that cultural institutions were generally in a process of development. In this respect, the historical investigations showed that as soon as cultural institutions came into being, a continuous change of these institutions began as well; different institutional forms replaced one another in the historical development. This was a fascinating observation. On the other hand, this insight began to change the attitude of people towards their own culture. The discovery that the development of cultural institutions was path-dependent and that they only existed for a relatively short time made it clear that social acceptance of values was relative. This, however, weakened the respect for present forms of cultural institutions to a large degree. As historians convincingly showed that cultural phenomena in general were only of relative worth and durability, the contemporary cultural institutions were put under the same suspicion of relative worth and contingent durability. Thus, any form of absolute demand of cultural phenomena became doubtful. In his final con-

---

18 See K. R. POPPER: *Logik der Forschung*, Tübingen (J.C.B. Mohr/Paul Siebeck) 10th edition 1994, p. 47.
19 See K. HEUSER: "Historical School and 'Methodenstreit'", *Journal of Institutional and Theoretical Economics*, Vol. 144 (1988), pp. 532-542, p. 537.

clusion, Burckhardt showed that the process of the historisation of thought led unavoidably to "the collapse of moral and religion".[20]

The core of Burckhardt's argumentation was that the scientific investigation of the historical development of cultural phenomena had led to a relativisation of present values. As a logical consequence, Burckhardt answered the question 'Was it historism that had caused relativism?' with a clear and categorical 'Yes!'

Friedrich Nietzsche who had become professor in Basel in 1869 attended Burckhardt's lecture "On the Studies of History" as a young professor in 1870/71 or 1872/73.[21] He admired Burckhardt,[22] and he certainly got important inspirations from this lecture for his own reflections on history and historical perception. In 1874, Nietzsche published his famous treatise "On the Use and Abuse of History", and like Burckhardt, he accused historism of being responsible for the phenomenon of relativism. Nietzsche argued that historical knowledge was dangerous for two reasons. On the one hand, he pointed out that the historians were in danger of accumulating knowledge which was of no use for their everyday life. Therefore, Nietzsche argued that they wasted their lifetimes. On the other hand, Nietzsche showed that the accumulated historical knowledge had led to a relativisation of all present values because this historical knowledge had deprived man "of the base of his security and rest: of the belief in perseverance and eternity".[23] The consequence of this loss of "the belief in perseverance and eternity", however, was a loss of orientation in respect to the question of how to act. Nietzsche argued that the historians were able to explain the values people had acted upon in previous times, but when asked according to which values one should act upon now, they were helpless. Thus history was *investigated*

---

20 J. BURCKHARDT: *Über das Studium der Geschichte* (1868), edited by P. GANZ, München (C. H. Beck) 1982, p. 229.
21 See J. BURCKHARDT: *Über das Studium der Geschichte* (1868), edited by P. GANZ, München (C. H. Beck) 1982, Introduction by P. GANZ, p. 54.
22 See J. BURCKHARDT: *Über das Studium der Geschichte* (1868), edited by P. GANZ, München (C. H. Beck) 1982, Introduction by P. GANZ, p. 54.
23 F. NIETZSCHE: *Werke*. Critics Gesamtausgabe edited by G. COLLIE and M. MONTINARI, Dritte Abteilung, 1. Band, *Unzeitgemäße Betrachtungen* I-III (1872-1874), Berlin 1972, p. 326.

by people who were, as Nietzsche put it, "completely unable to *make* history themselves."[24]

The result of Nietzsche's reflections was the same as Burckhardt's. Nietzsche accused historism of being responsible for the relativisation of values. According to him as well, it was historism that had caused relativism.

But in spite of the fact that Burckhardt and Nietzsche described this phenomenon precisely, they, as far as I know, neither used the term 'historism' nor 'relativism'. It was not before the beginning of the eighties of the last century that these specific terms became popular catchwords in the German discourse. In 1883, the Austrian Carl Menger, the most violent critic of historism in economics, accused the Historical School of being responsible for a lack of economic theories according to which one could act in the practical political process. In order to get a more differentiated understanding of Menger's critique, we have to compare the function of historical knowledge in Schmoller's and Menger's conceptions.

III. Schmoller's Concept of Political Economy

During the second half of the 19th century, the economists Wilhelm Roscher, Bruno Hildebrandt, and Karl Knies had applied the historical empirical method to the field of economics.[25] They had concentrated on the investigation of economic history and had in this way started to enforce the process of the historisation of economics.[26] "Schmoller, without being a

---

24 F. NIETZSCHE: *Werke*. Kritische Gesamtausgabe edited by G. COLLI and M. MONTINARI, Dritte Abteilung, 1. Band, *Unzeitgemäße Betrachtungen* I-III (1872-1874), Berlin 1972, p. 280.

25 See C. NARDINELLI and R. E. MEINERS: "Schmoller, the Methodenstreit, and the Development of Economic History", *Journal of Institutional and Theoretical Economics*, Vol. 144 (1988), pp. 543-551, p. 543.

26 Hutchison has shown that the historical approach has already been essential for the Scottish founders of political economy. It was used by Hume, Smith, and Steuart but was excluded shortly afterwards by Ricardo and his successors; see T. W. HUTCHISON: "Gustav Schmoller and the Problems of Today", *Journal of Institutional and Theoretical Economics,* Vol. 144 (1988), pp. 527-531, p. 528.

historian by training, was apparently fascinated by the research technique of historians."[27] During his studies, he had read Roscher[28] and had adopted the historical understanding of science. This understanding was based on the Kantian idea that only those statements which could be proved empirically could be regarded as 'scientific statements'.[29] Sensual experience and rational reflections, so argues Schmoller following Kant, are the basic elements that form 'scientific knowledge'. Both elements are thereby of equal importance. And although "in the great historical development of all human understanding the two elements of empiricism and rationalism have been fighting for priority,"[30] it is the *acting in unison* of both elements that leads to scientific knowledge. The only field, however, in which economic sentences can be proved empirically is history.

«If we ask for the use of history ... (for) political economy, the fundamental answer to this question is easy: History provides an unequalled material of experience in respect to the knowledge of reality. And this material of historical experiences serves the purpose to illustrate and verify theoretical sentences. Especially in complicated fields of political economy progress can only be achieved with the help of historical investigations.»[31] Therefore, Schmoller argues that scientific knowledge in the field of economy can

---

27 R. RICHTER: "Bridging Old and New Institutional Economics: Gustav Schmoller the Leader of the Younger German Historical School, Seen with Neoinstitutionalists' Eyes", *Journal of Institutional and Theoretical Economy*, Vol. 152, No. 4 (1996), pp. 567-592, p. 569.
28 See R. RICHTER: "Bridging Old and New Institutional Economics: Gustav Schmoller the Leader of the Younger German Historical School, Seen with Neoinstitutionalists' Eyes", *Journal of Institutional and Theoretical Economy*, Vol. 152, No. 4 (1996), pp. 567-592, p. 568.
29 See K. HÄUSER: "Historical School and 'Methodenstreit'", *Journal of Institutional and Theoretical Economics*, Vol. 144 (1988), pp. 532-542, p. 537.
30 G. SCHMOLLER: "Die Volkswirtschaft, die Volkswirtschaftslehre und ihre Methode", (1893), in: G. SCHMOLLER: *Über einige Grundfragen der Sozialpolitik und der Volkswirtschaftslehre,* Leipzig (Duncker & Humblot) 1898, p. 230. Translation A.W.-H.
31 G. SCHMOLLER: "Die Volkswirtschaft, die Volkswirtschaftslehre und ihre Methode", (1893), in: G. SCHMOLLER: *Über einige Grundfragen der Sozialpolitik und der Volkswirtschaftslehre*, Leipzig (Duncker & Humblot) 1898, p. 264. Translation A. W.-H.

only be achieved with the help of history. It is the investigation of economic history that forms essentially the scientific part of political economy.

The presupposition in respect to economics, which was implied in this understanding, was that economic institutions generally undergo a historical development. "Economic institutions ... slowly develop through the centuries ... (and) establish themselves, only after long struggles, in the practical life of a people (*im praktischen Volksleben*) ... Eventually, again in the course of several centuries, they make room for other institutions as a consequence of slow successive changes in economic demands, feelings, customs and legal convictions."[32]

Schmoller was of the opinion that in respect to the historical development there was no difference between economic institutions and other cultural institutions as well.[33] They all had to be regarded as subjects to a general historical change, and, therefore, had to be understood as historical entities. From Schmoller's point of view, economic institutions appeared to be part of the culture of a people, and they were not only part of this culture but depended on the cultural context as well.[34] A proper *understanding* of economic phenomena as well as a *further development* of economic institutions was, therefore, only possible with the help of a historical analysis of their cultural context.[35] Schmoller argues, "Only he who knows the forma-

---

32 G. SCHMOLLER: "Die Strassburger Tucher- und Weberzunft. Urkunden und Darstellung nebst Regesten und Glossar", - *Ein Beitrag zur Geschichte der deutschen Weberei und des deutschen Gewerberechts vom XIII. - XVII. Jahrhundert*, Strassburg (Karl J. Trøbner) 1879, p. XI. The English translation was taken from R. RICHTER: "Bridging Old and New Institutional Economics: Gustav Schmoller the Leader of the Younger German Historical School, Seen with Neoinstitutionalists' Eyes", *Journal of Institutional and Theoretical Economy*, Vol. 152, No. 4 (1996), pp. 567-592, p. 570.

33 See P. KOSLOWSKI: "Economics as Ethical Economy in the Tradition of the Historical School", Introduction, in: P. KOSLOWSKI (Ed.): *The Theory of Ethical Economy in the Historical School*, Berlin (Springer-Verlag) 1995, pp. 1, 6.

34 See P. KOSLOWSKI: "Ethical Economy as Synthesis of Economic and Ethical Theory", in: P. KOSLOWSKI (Ed.): *Ethics in Economics, Business, and Economic Policy*, Berlin (Springer-Verlag) 1992, pp. 15-56, p. 18.

35 A similar understanding in respect to the origins of law was at the same time presented by the German Ernst Immanuel Bekker, the leading figure of the so-called «Younger Historical School» in law. See M. KRIECHBAUM: *Dogmatik und Rechtsgeschichte bei Ernst Immanuel Bekker*, Ebelsbach (Verlag Rolf Germer)

tion of the present day's state and today's economic circumstances is able to judge them correctly and to help in developing them further."[36]

With this conception, Schmoller deviated from the classical economists, especially - as Hutchison has shown[37] - from Ricardo and his successors in two important respects. The later English classicals had "followed the narrow, deductive abstractions of Senior and Ricardo"[38] and had regarded economic institutions to be essentially an outcome of the 'invisible hand',[39] of self-interest and rationalisation. From their point of view, the rational, deductive analysis of the aims and interests of people was the appropriate approach to a proper understanding of economic phenomena, and the *deductive method* was regarded to be the one that provides *scientific knowledge*. Schmoller, however, did not only stress the *historicity* of economic phenomena. He, in consequence of this, established as well a different understanding of *science* within economics. By regarding the *historical proof* for a hypothesis to be the constitutive element of any scientific sentence the

---

1984. A comparison of both positions is presented in A. WITTKAU: *Historismus. Zur Geschichte des Begriffs und des Problems*, 2nd ed. Göttingen (Vandenhoeck & Ruprecht) 1994 and A. WITTKAU-HORGBY: "Vom Nutzen und Nachteil der Historie für Nationalökonomie und Jurisprudenz", in: W. BIALAS, G. RAULET (Eds.): *Die Historismusdebatte in der Weimarer Republik*, Frankfurt a. M. (Peter Lang) 1996, pp. 71-89.

36 G. SCHMOLLER: *Umrisse und Untersuchungen zur Verfassungs-, Verwaltungs- und Wirtschaftsgeschichte, besonders des Preussischen Staates im 17. und 18. Jahrhundert*, Leipzig (Duncker & Humblot) 1898, p. VIII. The translation was taken from R. RICHTER: "Bridging Old and New Institutional Economics: Gustav Schmoller the Leader of the Younger German Historical School, Seen with Neoinstitutionalists' Eyes", *Journal of Institutional and Theoretical Economy*, Vol. 152, No. 4 (1996), pp. 567-592, p. 571.

37 See T. W. HUTCHISON: "Gustav Schmoller and the Problems of Today", *Journal of Institutional and Theoretical Economy,* Vol. 144 (1988), pp. 527-531, p. 528.

38 See T. W. HUTCHISON: "Gustav Schmoller and the Problems of Today", *Journal of Institutional and Theoretical Economy,* Vol. 144 (1988), pp. 527-531, p. 528.

39 See A. SMITH: *Der Wohlstand der Nationen* (1776), München (Deutscher Taschenbuch Verlag) 1996, p. 371, and earlier B. MANDEVILLE: *Die Bienenfabel,* Frankfurt a. M. (Suhrkamp) 1980. Compare also F. A. HAYEK: *Freiburger Studien* (1969), Tübingen (J.C.B. Mohr/Paul Siebeck) 1994, p. 126.

inductive method[40] was established as the one which truly provided scientific knowledge.

In methodological contrast to the later English classicals who had supported the consideration of general cases, Schmoller thus «demanded the consideration of the special case, (and) this in turn demanded a primarily descriptive method which could do justice to each individual characteristic.»[41]

But what was the use of this scientific knowledge about economic history for political economy in general, and which purposes did this knowledge fulfil in respect to economic policy and practical economic action? Schmoller argues that the knowledge about economic history forms the basis of prognoses and decision making.[42] He points out that the economist has to start with the investigation of economic history when he tries to find regularities in the economic process. In a second step, he abstracts general rules from these historical regularities, and these abstractions can finally be used for the development of economic theories.

The economist discovers, for example, "repetitions of the movement of prices, the same effects of good and bad money, of rich and poor harvests, the same regularities in the number of births, deaths and marriages" in history.[43] The experience that a fact A has usually led to an effect B in

---

40 See K. DOPFER: "How Historical is Schmoller's Economic Theory?", *Journal of Institutional and Theoretical Economy*, Vol. 144 (1988), pp. 552-569, p. 563.
41 K. HÄUSER: "Historical School and 'Methodenstreit'", *Journal of Institutional and Theoretical Economics*, Vol. 144 (1988), pp. 532-542, p. 537.
42 See G. SCHMOLLER: "Die Volkswirtschaft, die Volkswirtschaftslehre und ihre Methode", (1893), in: G. SCHMOLLER: *Über einige Grundfragen der Sozialpolitik und der Volkswirtschaftslehre*, Leipzig (Duncker & Humblot) 1898, p. VIII. "Only he who knows the formation of the present day's state and today's economic circumstances is able to judge them correctly and to help in developing them further". The English translation was taken from R. RICHTER: "Bridging Old and New Institutional Economics: Gustav Schmoller the Leader of the Younger German Historical School, Seen with Neoinstitutionalists' Eyes", *Journal of Institutional and Theoretical Economy*, Vol. 152, No. 4 (1996), pp. 567-592, p. 571.
43 G. SCHMOLLER: "Volkswirtschaft, Volkswirtschaftslehre und -methode", *Handwörterbuch der Sozialwissenschaften*, Vol. 8, 3rd ed. (1906), pp. 426-501, p. 481. Translation A.W.-H.

history leads to the abstraction, when A, then B. This abstraction becomes the basis of the prognosis. However, this abstraction is only *likely* to come true. Although historically A has always been followed by B, this does not necessarily mean that A will be followed by B in any case. It is possible that A might unexpectedly be followed by C in the future, although it has been followed by B in all observed cases in the past. Therefore, Schmoller claims a sharp distinction between historical observations which have epistemologically the quality of *scientific knowledge* and economic prognoses and theories which have epistemologically only the quality of *probability*. "Economic history as well as history in general that tells us about economic events are not economic theory, but only building stones to theories."[44]

According to Schmoller, the *function of historical knowledge* is to provide a *scientific basis of economic theories*. But scientific knowledge itself does not give clear directions for practical action. The theories which guide practical action in economic policy have only the epistemological quality of probability, and they are more or less arbitrary. The core of Schmoller's understanding of the relationship between science and practical action in the field of political economy is that scientific knowledge cannot guide economic policy directly. The scientific historical observation of economic phenomena only gives hints in respect to general structures. However, it does not lead to scientific theories which are certain in the sense that they give an unequivocal direction of how to act.

In his concept, Schmoller concentrates on this aspect. But when addressing the relationship between historical knowledge and economic theories, he stresses the importance of historical knowledge without describing in detail the way in which economic theories have to be developed out of it.[45] On the contrary, he supports the position that, at the present state, the

---

44 G. SCHMOLLER: *Zur Methodologie der Staats- und Sozialwissenschaften*, Jahrbuch für Gesetzgebung, Verwaltung und Volkswirtschaft im Deutschen Reich, 7. Jahrgang, 3. Heft, Leipzig 1883, p. 267.

45 As Richter convincingly has shown, the Neoinstitutionalists have chosen a fruitful different approach in precisely this respect. "The different attitude of old German institutionalists and modern institutionalists towards theorizing or model building is striking. What made New Institutional Economics so interesting was not alone the critique of neo-classical assumptions but the introduction of new and more realistic hypotheses plus their use in making deductions". R. RICHTER: "Bridging Old and New Institutional Economics: Gustav Schmoller the Leader of the Younger German Historical School, Seen with Neoinstitu-

economists should *wait* with the development of further theoretical conclusions until the historical investigations were completed. "Schmoller ... was against any kind of theorising as long as the set of behavioural assumptions were not completed. Before one starts to draw general conclusions, the assumptions must pass the test that they truly are the crucial causes of the economic phenomena in question."[46] "Schmoller does not question the need of deductive reasoning. Yet before one starts deducing, one has to know all the relevant causes of the economic phenomena at hand ... Schmoller assumes an extreme position by demanding that *all* relevant causes have to be known before one may 'risk' making deductions."[47]

This demand that *all relevant data* have to be collected before one can build a theory does not only appear to be impossible from Popper's point of view, but it also over stressed the importance of history for political economy in Schmoller's time. It was an exaggeration that was rooted in Schmoller's methodological inductionism. However, Schmoller was epistemologically correct all the same when he stressed the point that economic theory only has the quality of probability. Schmoller's assumptions in respect to the relationship between science and practical action have, therefore, to be regarded as basically correct, although the development of theories appeared to be of minor importance within his methodological approach.

---

tionalists' Eyes", *Journal of Institutional and Theoretical Economy*, Vol. 152, No. 4 (1996), pp. 567-592, p. 582.
46 R. RICHTER: "Bridging Old and New Institutional Economics: Gustav Schmoller the Leader of the Younger German Historical School, Seen with Neoinstitutionalists' Eyes", *Journal of Institutional and Theoretical Economy*, Vol. 152, No. 4 (1996), pp. 567-592, p. 582.
47 R. RICHTER: "Bridging Old and New Institutional Economics: Gustav Schmoller the Leader of the Younger German Historical School, Seen with Neoinstitutionalists' Eyes", *Journal of Institutional and Theoretical Economy*, Vol. 152, No. 4 (1996), pp. 567-592, p. 585.

ANNETTE WITTKAU-HORGBY

IV. Menger's Concept of Political Economy

In opposite to Schmoller, Menger exposes the decisive importance of the development of theories for political economy.[48] He argues that building theories is the essential part of economy, and in explicit contradiction to Schmoller, he points out that *abstraction and theoretical thinking* are the tools to achieve economic theories while historical knowledge is of minor importance in this respect.[49]

So far the differences between Schmoller and Menger appear to be only differences in respect to the *weight* they put behind the importance of history for political economy. However, on a second glance it becomes obvious that behind these different understandings of the function and importance of history, Schmoller and Menger actually have different understandings of 'science' and 'scientific knowledge' as well. Menger expects from science clear and unequivocal directions for economic policy. In order to gain such directions, he develops an understanding of science which is fundamentally different from that of the Historical School.

Menger differentiates between two basic types of human understanding. On the one hand, he introduces a knowledge that focuses on the individual (*'Erkenntnis des Individuellen'*), and, on the other hand, defines a form of perception that concentrates on general laws. Menger calls this form 'knowledge of the general' (*'Erkenntnis des Generellen'*). These two types of knowledge exist according to Menger in all spheres of human understanding; and they exist in the field of political economy as well.

"In the field of political economy as well, we find forms of knowledge of the individual and those of knowledge of the general, and conform to this, sciences of the individual and sciences of the general. The first type includes history and statistics of political economy. The second type consists

---

48 See in respect to Menger's approach in general I. M. KIRZNER: "Menger, classical liberalism, and the Austrian school of economics", in: B. J. CALDWELL (Ed.): *Carl Menger and his legacy in economics*, Durham and London (Duke University Press) 1990, pp. 93-106.

49 This did not mean that Menger was against the historical approach in general. On the contrary, he had dedicated his famous "Grundsätze der Volkswirtschaftslehre" to Wilhelm Roscher, the head of the so-called Older Historical School. Compare also K. HÄUSER: "Historical School and 'Methodenstreit'", *Journal of Institutional and Theoretical Economics*, Vol. 144 (1988), pp. 532-542, p. 535.

of the theoretical science of political economy ('die theoretische Nationalökonomie'). History and statistics investigate individual phenomena in the field of political economy. The theoretical science, however, focuses on the investigation of general laws and tries to find out the general essence («das Wesen») and the general connections of economic phenomena. History and statistics of political economy are thus historical sciences; while political economy itself is a theoretical science."[50]

This stress on the fact that political economy was a *theoretical science* can in respect to methodology be interpreted as a new establishment of relations to the late English classicals. And I would like to interpret the differences between Menger and Schmoller by looking at their controversy from this point of view.[51] In respect to the general understanding of the political economy, the German-Austrian tradition in the 19th century had strongly supported the importance of the roll of the state[52] while the English tradition had emphasised the roll of the individual and, therefore, the German economists were only partly prepared to take over the English approach.[53] However, in respect to methodology, Menger's position can be

---

50 C. MENGER: *Untersuchungen Über die Methode der Sozialwissenschaften und der politischen Ökonomie insbesondere* (1883), in: C. MENGER: *Gesammelte Werke*, edited by F. A. HAYEK, Vol. 2, Tübingen (J. C. B. Mohr/Paul Siebeck) 2nd edition 1969, p. 6. Translation A. W.-H.

51 Streissler has shown that Menger's ideas in respect to economic policy can also be regarded as in continuity with the classical school. "Evidently the subject of the economic policy of the classical school touched Menger deeply: he made Richard Schüller write the last thesis of habilitation completed under his supervision on this topic." E. W. STREISSLER: "Carl Menger on economic policy: the lectures to Crownprince Rudolf", in: B. J. CALDWELL (Ed.): *Carl Menger and His Legacy in Economics*, Durham and London (Duke University Press) 1990, pp. 107-130, p. 109. Streissler goes in respect to political economy so far as to say (p. 111), "In fact Menger was the rediscoverer of Adam Smith in Austria."

52 See I. M. KIRZNER: "Menger, Classical Liberalism, and the Austrian School of Economics", in: B. J. CALDWELL (Ed.): *Carl Menger and His Legacy in Economics*, Durham and London (Duke University Press) 1990, pp. 93-106, p. 100.

53 See E. W. STREISSLER: "Carl Menger on Economic Policy: The Lectures to Crownprince Rudolf", in: B. J. CALDWELL (Ed.): *Carl Menger and His Legacy in Economics*, Durham and London (Duke University Press) 1990, pp. 107-130, pp. 128. See further K. HÄUSER: "Historical School and 'Methodenstreit'",

interpreted as in continuity to the late English classicals.[54] By claiming the existence of a form of 'deductive science' which could provide knowledge about the general laws of economic action, Menger held a view which was at least much more in continuity with classical economy than Schmoller's.

Menger claimed to concentrate on the perception of the general structures of economic phenomena again. He thus turned away from the inductive approach of the Younger Historical School as represented by Schmoller. While Schmoller had *deviated* from the classical approach in respect to the interpretation of institutions as well as to the understanding of science, Menger was of the opinion that *continuity* to the classical understanding in both respects was necessary and fruitful.

In agreement with the classicals, he argues that the general laws which determine the economic process can only be realised "through deduction from a priori axioms."[55] The method of the theoretical science is, therefore, to transcend the sphere of sensual perception with the help of pure reason and abstraction. Menger claims that it is possible to gain knowledge about the laws and general structures which actually determine the economic process over time. This implies the expectation that *science* - in the shape of the theoretical science - is able to provide concepts of action.

While the historical sciences, history and statistics provide knowledge about facts, theoretical economy provides knowledge about general laws and thus scientific knowledge in respect to concepts of action. "It is the task of theoretical science to inform us about the types, the typical relations and the laws of (economic) phenomena and to give us the theoretical understanding,

---

Journal of Institutional and Theoretical Economics, Vol. 144, (1988) pp. 532-542, p. 536.

[54] See E. W. STREISSLER: "Carl Menger on Economic Policy: The Lectures to Crownprince Rudolf", in: B. J. CALDWELL (Ed.): *Carl Menger and His Legacy in Economics*, Durham and London (Duke University Press) 1990, pp. 107-130, p. 129. «The notebooks of Crown Prince Rudolf present us Carl Menger, both politically and also theoretically, as a very neo-classical economist - in fact hardly 'neo' at all, but nearly a pure classicist.»

[55] C. MENGER: «Untersuchungen Über die Methode der Sozialwissenschaften und der politischen Ökonomie insbesondere» (1883), in: C. MENGER: *Gesammelte Werke*, edited by F. A. HAYEK, Vol. 2, Tübingen (J. C. B. Mohr/Paul Siebeck) 2nd edition 1969, p. 53. Translation A. W.-H.

a form of knowledge which transcends our direct experience and provides us with power over these phenomena."[56]

Menger was of the opinion that theoretical science provided clear and unequivocal directions for *economic policy* and practical economic action.[57] Practical action could, according to him, *be guided by science directly*. As theoretical science makes clear the laws which guide the economic process over time, it would be absurd not to act according to them. Thus science does not only *inform* us about facts, but it is a *normative institution* as well. Within Menger's conception, this conclusion is logically necessary and consistent.

Undoubtedly, it would be of the highest value to get to know such laws as described by Menger. However, the laws one gets with the help of Menger's theoretical science cannot at all be proved empirically. Those 'exact laws', as Menger calls them, are constructions of pure reason, and they *may not* be compared with history.[58] Menger stresses this point explicitly.[59]

---

56 C. MENGER: «Untersuchungen Über die Methode der Sozialwissenschaften und der politischen Ökonomie insbesondere» (1883), in: C. MENGER: *Gesammelte Werke*, edited by F. A. HAYEK, Vol. 2, Tübingen (J. C. B. Mohr/Paul Siebeck) 2nd edition 1969, p. 34. Translation A. W.-H.

57 We do not have many hints in respect to the contents of this direction of economic policy. Streissler has explained this fact with the circumstance that there existed separated professorial chairs for economic theory and economic policy. As Menger held a chair for economic theory, he did not deal much with economic policy. "Menger held the chair of economic theory in Vienna ... Thus economic policy was none of his academic 'business' ... So it is not surprising that we have practically no published accounts by him of what he thought about the principles that should guide economic policy." See E. W. STREISSLER: "Carl Menger on Economic Policy: The Lectures to Crownprince Rudolf", in: B. J. CALDWELL (Ed.): *Carl Menger and his legacy in economics*, Durham and London (Duke University Press) 1990, pp. 107-130, p. 107.

58 C. MENGER: «Untersuchungen über die Methode der Sozialwissenschaften und der politischen Ökonomie insbesondere» (1883), in: C. MENGER: *Gesammelte Werke*, edited by F. A. HAYEK, Vol. 2, Tübingen (J. C. B. Mohr/Paul Siebeck) 2nd edition 1969, p. 52.

59 C. MENGER: «Untersuchungen über die Methode der Sozialwissenschaften und der politischen Ökonomie insbesondere» (1883), in: C. MENGER: *Gesammelte Werke*, edited by F. A. HAYEK, Vol. 2, Tübingen (J. C. B. Mohr/Paul Siebeck) 2nd edition 1969, p. 53.

Theoretical perception is purely a priori, and its results have no empirical correspondence. Nevertheless, Menger claims that this knowledge has the epistemological quality of *'scientific knowledge'*. And precisely here lies the fundamental difference in the understandings of science between Schmoller and Menger. According to Schmoller, no statement can be regarded as 'scientific' which cannot be proved empirically. From Schmoller's point of view, Menger's «exact laws» may be interesting hypotheses, but they have only the quality of probability and have, therefore, to be regarded as non-scientific statements.

So it was basically not only the understanding of *science* but also the understanding of the *relationship between science and practical action* which formed the decisive difference in the conceptions of Schmoller and Menger.[60] These fundamental differences were connected more or less directly with the question of the *function of historical knowledge* within political economy and, therefore, this question became the focal point in the debate between Menger and Schmoller.

V. Historism and Relativism

Menger started to fight 'Historism in Economy' at the beginning of the 1880s, and in his famous publications from the years 1883 ("Investigations on the Method of the Social Sciences and Particularly of Political Economy") and 1884 («The Errors of Historism in the German Political Economy»), the two main arguments Menger was using against the Historical School were precisely the ones Burckhardt and Nietzsche had already used earlier. First, it was the argument that the historians were wasting their lifetimes with historical investigations without addressing their relevance for the present. Second, it was the argument that these historical investigations had led to an unfruitful relativisation of values.

---

60 See R. RICHTER: "Bridging Old and New Institutional Economics: Gustav Schmoller the Leader of the Younger German Historical School, Seen with Neoinstitutionalists' Eyes", *Journal of Institutional and Theoretical Economy*, Vol. 152, No. 4 (1996), pp. 567-592, p. 585. «Seen from a safe distance the central issue of the debate (between Menger and Schmoller) seems to have been the problem of the realism of assumptions.»

DOES HISTORISM MEAN RELATIVISM?

Historism, which was Menger's reproach, had completely led the interest of the economists into a wrong direction.[61] They had begun to occupy themselves with the historical investigation of economic problems. However, the outcome of these investigations was not a consistent theory.[62] On the contrary, the historians investigated the past following Schmoller's attitude towards economic theory.[63]

"If the economists waited with the development of economic theories until the historians were ready with their investigations - remember only the prices for meat in Elberfeld! in Mühlheim! in Hildesheim! in Gersheim! in Zwickau! and so on - they would have to get used to the idea that this will take an enormous amount of time. Similar to the astronomers who were forced to introduce the term of light-years in order to calculate their enormous distances, we economists would at least have to calculate with the lifetimes of sun systems in order to get only to some extent an approximate idea of the amount of time that would be necessary in order to get a sufficient historical-statistical basis for economic theory according to Schmoller."[64]

Schmoller had claimed that the economists should wait with the development of further theories until the historical basis for these theories was completed. Menger correctly opposed that this was an exaggerated demand and an inadequate approach to economic problems. He accused the historians of wasting their intellectual capacities by applying all their strength to an object which was of no concrete use for practical economic action. On the contrary, from the historical perspective all economic phenomena ap-

---

61 See J. NIEHANS: *A History of Economic Theory*, Baltimore (Johns Hopkins University Press) 1990, pp. 220.
62 See C. MENGER: «Die Irrtümer des Historismus in der deutschen Nationalökonomie» (1884), in: C. MENGER: *Gesammelte Werke*, edited by F. A. HAYEK, Vol. 3, 2nd Edition Tübingen (J. C. B. Mohr/Paul Siebeck) 1970, p. 18.
63 See R. RICHTER: "Bridging Old and New Institutional Economics: Gustav Schmoller the Leader of the Younger German Historical School, Seen with Neoinstitutionalists' Eyes", *Journal of Institutional and Theoretical Economy*, Vol. 152, No. 4 (1996), pp. 567-592, p. 582.
64 See C. MENGER: «Die Irrtümer des Historismus in der deutschen Nationalökonomie» (1884), in: C. MENGER: *Gesammelte Werke*, edited by F. A. HAYEK, Vol. 3, Tübingen (J. C. B. Mohr/Paul Siebeck) 2nd edition 1970, p. 38. Translation A. W.-H.

peared to be of equal importance and only relative value.[65] This perspective, so Menger argued, led to a general relativisation of values. The historians became uneasy when they were asked in which direction normative theories should be developed, and the immediate consequence of this was that normative theories were no longer produced. In Menger's view, economic theory should support efficient decision making in the practical political process.[66] This was the main task of economics. The historians did not contribute to the development of normative theories and, thus, failed to accomplish the task of an efficient decision making.[67]

At a first glance, this argumentation sounds convincing. But, when one looks further, it turns out to be correct only in some respects. We have to remember Menger's understanding of science and of the relationship between science and practical action in order to understand the core of his critique.

When Menger coined the term 'Historism' and started to use this expression in his fight against the Historical School, it appeared that he was mainly fighting the dominance of history in political economy. In this respect his critique was justified. Actually, he was fighting for a different understanding of science and its functions in political economy. Although he correctly criticised the exaggeration of history which was connected with Schmoller's inductive methodological approach his own demand that scientific knowledge could and should guide economic action and policy *directly* was without any sufficient epistemological basis. This fundamental problem of Menger's approach was not realised in political economy to its full extent. Menger's critique was on the contrary regarded to be appropriate by many economists, because the methodological approach which Menger

---

65 See C. MENGER: «Die Irrtümer des Historismus in der deutschen Nationalökonomie» (1884), in: C. MENGER: *Gesammelte Werke*, edited by F. A. HAYEK, Vol. 3, Tübingen (J. C. B. Mohr/Paul Siebeck) 2nd edition 1970, p. 38.

66 See C. MENGER: «Untersuchungen über die Methode der Sozialwissenschaften und der politischen Ökonomie insbesondere» (1883), in: C. MENGER: *Gesammelte Werke*, edited by F. A. HAYEK, Vol. 2, Tübingen (J. C. B. Mohr/Paul Siebeck) 2nd edition 1969, especially p. 6 and p. 34.

67 See C. MENGER: «Die Irrtümer des Historismus in der deutschen Nationalökonomie» (1884), in: C. MENGER: *Gesammelte Werke*, edited by F. A. HAYEK, Vol. 3, Tübingen (J. C. B. Mohr/Paul Siebeck) 2nd edition 1970, p. 18 and 38.

suggested was in the well-established tradition of Ricardo and his successors and, therefore, regarded to be basically fruitful.

From the epistemological point of view, Menger's reproach that *historism*, specifically Schmoller's understanding of science, had led to *relativism* turns out to be inappropriate. This critique was rooted in Menger's own different - and in this respect deficient - understanding of science and scientific methodology. When compared with the assumption that science should guide practical action directly, Schmoller's claim, that science could and should not do that, could easily be interpreted as an uneasiness in respect to normative questions. However, if we take into consideration that this claim of Menger's was without sufficient epistemological basis the situation turns out to be completely different. As Menger's understanding of the relationship between science and practical action was deficient, his critique was actually inappropriate as well.

His reproaches did neither meet Schmoller's understanding of science, nor did it meet Schmoller's personal attitude towards economic policy.[68] Schmoller's political action and his commitment to social policy clearly show that he was actually not at all uneasy in respect to the values he was acting upon.[69] Menger's critique has to be regarded as inappropriate in this respect. The reproach that historism had led to relativism was based on his misunderstanding of the abilities of science in the field of political economy.

But Burckhardt's and Nietzsche's critique in respect to the use and abuse of history shows that Menger's critique was quite common in his time. The phenomenon of the historisation of thought was accused of being responsible for the relativisation of values in the German Geisteswissenschaften until the time of Max Weber.[70] Weber, however, showed that this reproach de-

---

68 In this respect Menger appreciated - as Kirzner has shown - Schmoller's activities. "In fact, the only thing that he appreciated in Schmoller was his passionate concern for the poor and weak." I. M. KIRZNER: "Menger, Classical Liberalism, and the Austrian School of Economics", in: B. J. CALDWELL (Ed.): *Carl Menger and His Legacy in Economics*, Durham and London (Duke University Press) 1990, pp. 93-106, p. 94.

69 See C. H. POWERS and K.- H. SCHMIDT: "Justice, Social Welfare, and the State in the Eyes of Gustav Schmoller", in: J. BACKHAUS: *Essays on Social Security and Taxation. Gustav von Schmoller und Adolph Wagner Reconsidered*, Marburg (Metropolis-Verlag) 1997, pp. 239-257.

70 See A. WITTKAU: *Historismus. Zur Geschichte des Begriffs und des Problems*, Göttingen (Vandenhoeck & Ruprecht) 2nd edition 1994.

pended on a wrong understanding of the abilities of science. He argued that historical knowledge and normative questions were of completely different epistemological quality and pointed out that historical knowledge could, therefore, neither do damage to ethics nor could it provide ethical concepts.[71] Weber's clear distinction between science and values deprived the reproach that historism had caused relativism of its basis.

Weber made it clear that in the debate between Menger and Schmoller each of the contradicting parties held some truth. The historians were right when they claimed that scientific knowledge had to be empirically based knowledge.[72] Menger, on the other hand, was right when he claimed that the main task of political economy was to provide concepts of action. Weber pointed out that empirical science did not deal with the question 'what shall we do?'[73] and he argued that it was inappropriate to expect scientific concepts of action. Nevertheless, he showed as well that the question 'What shall we do?' was of essential importance for political economy although it was a non-scientific one. By making a clear distinction between historical and normative knowledge, Weber was able to show the different spheres of competence of both types of knowledge,[74] and he could thus do justice to each of them.

In the light of Weber's epistemological approach the question 'Was it actually historism that had caused relativism?' gains a more differentiated profile. If we take into consideration Weber's arguments, the answer to this question has - according to my opinion - to be: No. The process of the historisation of thought did not cause the relativisation of values but it sharp-

---

[71] See M. WEBER: "Wissenschaft als Beruf" (1919), in: M. WEBER: *Gesammelte Aufsätze zur Wissenschaftslehre*, edited by J. Winckelmann, Tübingen (J. C. B. Mohr/Paul Siebeck) 6th edition 1985, pp. 582-613.

[72] See especially M. WEBER: "Roscher und Knies und die logischen Probleme der historischen Nationalökonomie", in: M. WEBER: *Gesammelte Aufsätze zur Wissenschaftslehre*, edited by J. Winckelmann, Tübingen (J. C. B. Mohr/Paul Siebeck) 6th edition 1985, pp. 1-145.

[73] See M. WEBER: "Wissenschaft als Beruf" (1919), in: M. WEBER: *Gesammelte Aufsätze zur Wissenschaftslehre*, edited by J. Winckelmann, Tübingen (J. C. B. Mohr/Paul Siebeck) 6th edition 1985, pp. 582-613, p. 609.

[74] See M. WEBER: "Die 'Objektivität' sozialwissenschaftlicher und sozialpolitischer Erkenntnis", in: M. WEBER: *Gesammelte Aufsätze zur Wissenschaftslehre*, edited by J. Winckelmann, Tübingen (J. C. B. Mohr/Paul Siebeck) 6th edition 1985, pp. 146-214.

ened the consciousness for the fact that normative concepts cannot be derived from science directly.

Discussion Summary

ANNETTE KLEINFELD

Paper discussed:
ANNETTE WITTKAU-HORGBY: Does Historism Mean Relativism? Remarks on the Debate on Historism in the German Political Economy of the Late 19th Century

The discussion started with an example of the Jewish religion, based on the historical development of values. Surprisingly, history in this case was not a source of relativism (SOLOMON). The idea of relativism was formulated not only by representatives of historism, but also by the sophists, whereas the ancient Greeks did not take into consideration the idea of history. Pindar presented the opinion that not the history (regarded as a flow of time or a change), but also different communities were sources of various relative values. Alasdair MacIntyre tried to find in history values which could give us a direction without becoming absolute. Different communities and points of view constitute criteria common for all of them - and this is a successful way of overcoming relativism. It shows that Troeltsch was not completely mistaken (CHMIELEWSKI).

It was not only historism that caused relativism - relativism had existed long before historism appeared. A possible factor causing relativism can be history itself. A question arises whether the philosophy of history can provide any solution to the problem of relativism. Troeltsch's theory was not the only one - let alone previously mentioned MacIntyre: many historians in the 20th century tried to overcome relativism (DE GEER). However, no successful steps were taken by modern philosophers of history towards solving the problem of values and historical development, and authors like Fukuyama cannot be compared with Troeltsch (WITTKAU-HORGBY).

The problem of materialism was discussed with reference to historism. The concept of values derived from history cannot be acceptable for a materialist - but it does not mean that Troeltsch was wrong. The fact that a particular group of people refuse general obligations does not imply they do not exist (TRALAU). Materialists describe themselves as value-blind - that is why they cannot really consider any value-based theory (KETTNER).

Suggestions appeared that the Darwin's theory mentioned is not incompatible with Troeltsch's ideas. Both theories are value-based - Darwin presented the opinion that the evolution was based on one absolute value: the enhancement of fitness (KETTNER). Nevertheless, Darwin regarded it only as a material outcome of the evolution process - his materialistic approach excluded values at all (WITTKAU-HORGBY).

The presenter's own epistemological position was regarded as a critical factor in assessing Troeltsch's ideas (STEINMANN). It was the Kantian epistemological approach, based on a distinction between empirical and metaphysical spheres of life (whereas the metaphysical assumptions are not brought in question), but at the same time objections to Kantian ethics, especially to the concept of general obligations (relativism) (WITTKAU-HORGBY). The actual epistemological approach can be called intuitionism as well (KETTNER).

The presented critique of Troeltsch's ideas was based on the argument that he committed an epistemological mistake - but his theory was simply unfinished. A real source of Troeltsch's failure was his statement concerning the fact that a derivation of values from history can only be possible in a specific cultural context - in which he presupposed a kind of relativism, which he could not overcome later (KETTNER). Another mistake was also the presupposition that values are metaphysical realities in the historical process, which led Troeltsch to the point that it was possible to derive values from the history (WITTKAU-HORGBY).

The paper presented attempts to overcome the problem of historism by its own means, but maybe another interesting approach would be looking at the chances of historism. The historism appeared in the 19th century, when values and cultures were changing rapidly - we can observe the same phenomenon nowadays, as even values of our own societies change in the course of time. This fact is liberating, as accepted values do not have to remain the same all the time. Somehow it leads to postmodernism which can be regarded as a kind of neohistorism. But an important question is: Why should a society have stable, unchanging values? It should be rather taken into consideration, which values can change and which ones ought to be unchangeable (KOSLOWSKI).

DISCUSSION SUMMARY

Finally, prospects for future value development were discussed. A utopian view of the economy was presented which will set the values for the society (FRENCH). Nevertheless, economic values cannot be stable from the ethical point of view. It is important to achieve stability for different sorts of values - but at the same time it is impossible to achieve absolute values as they are still changing. The critique is focusing on law, which results from the tradition, and is a means that helps to overcome the changes of values (WITTKAU-HORGBY). The question was discussed whether Troeltsch was wrong. But a more challenging issue is finding out why he was wrong - to what extent scientific theories can cause relativism, and to what extent the social development is responsible for it (DAHMS).

List of Authors and Discussants

ADAM J. CHMIELEWSKI is Professor at the Institute of Philosophy, University of Wroclaw, Poland.

HARRY F. DAHMS is Assistant Professor of the Department of Sociology at Florida State University, Tallahassee, USA.

HANS DE GEER is Historian and Professor of Business History and Ethics at the Centre for Ethics and Economics, Stockholm School of Economics, Sweden.

HARALD HAGEMANN is Professor of Economic Theory at the Department of Economics, University of Hohenheim, Stuttgart, Germany, and Theodor Heuss Professor (1999-2000) at the Graduate Faculty, New School for Social Research, New York.

DIETER HASELBACH is Professor at the Languages and European Studies Department, Head of Politics and Modern History Department, Aston University, Birmingham, United Kingdom.

SIBYLLE HOFER is Assistant Professor at the Faculty of Law, Institute of the History of Law, University of Frankfurt am Main, Germany.

KRZYSZTOF KLINCEWICZ is Assistant Professor at the Collegium Invisibile, Warsaw, Poland.

PETER KOSLOWSKI is Director of the Centre for Ethical Economy and Business Culture, The Hannover Institute of Philosophical Research, Hannover, and Professor of Philosophy and Political Economy at the University of Witten/Herdecke, Germany.

KNUT WOLFGANG NÖRR is Professor of Private Law and History of Private Law at the University of Tübingen, Germany.

HELGE PEUKERT is Professor at the University of Riga, Latvia.

ANTON RAUSCHER is Professor of Social Ethics at the University of Augsburg.

ELKE SCHWINGER is Assistant Professor at the Faculty of Social Sciences, Institute of Theology and Society, the University of Bundeswehr München, Germany.

LIST OF AUTHORS AND DISCUSSANTS

YUICHI SHIONOYA is Professor Emeritus at Hitotsubashi University and President of the National Institute of Population and Social Security Research, Tokyo, Japan.

MANFRED E. STREIT is Director of the Max-Planck-Institut zur Erforschung von Wirtschaftssystemen - Max-Planck-Institute for Research into Economic Systems, Jena, Germany.

JOHAN TRALAU is Ph.D Student at the University of Stockholm, Sweden.

TORBEN VESTDAM is Assistant Professor at the Art and Cultural Sciences Department, Faculty of History and Art Sciences, Erasmus-University, Rotterdam, The Netherlands.

CHRISTIAN WATRIN is Professor of Economic Policy at the University of Cologne, Germany.

ANNETTE WITTKAU-HORGBY is Assistant Professor for the History of Science at the University of Hannover, Department of History, Germany.

MICHAEL WOHLGEMUTH is Research Expert at the Max-Planck-Institut zur Erforschung von Wirtschafssystemen - Max-Planck-Institute for Research into Economic Systems, Jena, Germany.

KIICHIRO YAGI is Professor of Economics at the Faculty of Economics, Kyoto University, Japan.

JONAS ZONINSEIN is Associate Professor at James Madison College, Michigan State University, USA.

Index of Names

Page numbers in italics refer to quotations in footnotes or references

Abelshauser, W. *206*
Abendroth, W. *79*
Acton, Lord 228
Ad Jeck, L. H. *214*
Adorno, Th. W. 311, 315, 344, 348-351, 353, 362f., 365f.
Agger, B. *315, 323,* 349, *359*
Albert, H. 106, *133, 214, 229, 240,* 261
Albrecht 118
Alsmöller, H. 126, *133*
Alter, A. 104, *133*
Amsden, A. H. 290, *301*
Anaxagoras 523
Anderson, P. *315, 359*
Antisthenes 523
Aoki, M. *428, 440, 441*
Aquinas, Th. 395, 399
Arato, A. *347*
Arendt, H. 47
Arisawa 52
Aristotle 101, 107, 391, 517, 523, 530
Arndt, H. 130, *133*
Arnold, F. Ch. von *490, 499*
Arnold, W. 470, *481,* 485-492, *498, 499*
Arrighi, G. 275, *293, 301*
Atkins, B. 94, 128, *133,*
Azeglio, L. T. 395

Baade, F. 37, 41
Baader, F. 414
Baader, R. *138*
Backhaus, J. G. *143,* 537, 555
Bacon, F. 104, 522
Baeck, L. *60*
Bagge, G. 459
Baran, P. A. 42, 276f., *301, 319, 359*
Bardhan, P. *291, 301*
Barkai, H. 60, 84
Barnes, H. E. *64, 84*
Barry, N. P. 124, *133,* 255, 261
Barth, P. 62
Bartling, H. 126, *133*
Bauer, O. 26, *401*
Baum, G. 127, *133*
Becker, G. S. 111
Becker, H. P. *84,* 129, *133*
Beckerath, E. 127, *133,* 137, *144f.*
Bekker, E. I. *480,* 498, *499*
Benda, J. 102
Benhabib, S. 330, *331,* 349, *359*
Benjamin, W. *350*
Berger, S. *304*
Berle 124
Bernstein, E. 64, 69
Bertrand 116
Beveridge 16

INDEX OF NAMES

Bialas, W. *534, 538, 543*
Binswanger, H. C. *133*
Bismarck, O. von 101, 146, 151, 505
Blainville, H. de 6
Blomert, R. *28*
Blum, R. 129, *133*
Blumenberg-Lampe, Chr. 108, *133, 206*
Böckenförde, E.-W. 191, *200*
Boer, C. *412*
Boettke, P. J. 114, *133, 267*
Böhm, F. 102, 122, 130, *133*, 148-191, 225-235, *237*, 239, 241f., *244*, 246, 248ff., 252ff., *254*, 260, *261*, 269
Böhm-Bawerk, E. von 4, 26, 42, 47, 109, 124, *133*, 228, 442
Bohnet, I. *255, 261*
Bombach, G. *37, 48*, 125, *134, 202*
Bonn, M. J. 99, *143*, 155
Borchardt, K. 11, *134*
Borgese 45
Bortkiewicz, L. von 43
Bourgeois, L. *371*
Bowley 116
Boyd, R. 97, *134*
Boyer, R. 121, *134, 437*
Brady, R. A. *288, 301*
Brandt, K. 115, *134*
Branting, H. 452
Braun, H. 42
Brennan, G. *252*, 255, *262*
Brentano, L. 27, 452, 491
Brick, B. *351, 361*
Briefs, G. 156, *393, 401, 405, 412*

Brisman, S. 458
Brocker, B. 107
Brüning 36, 39f., 202
Buchanan, J. M. 251ff., 255, 259, *262*
Buchholz *470*
Büchner, R. 102, *134*
Burckhardt, J. 538, *539*, 540ff., 552, 555
Burke, E. 530
Buß, F. von 442

Caldwell, B. J. *547, 549, 551, 555*
Carlsson, B. *452f.*
Carnap, R. 513
Carrol, L. *512*
Carte 104
Caspari, V. *55, 60, 78, 82, 84ff.*
Cassel, D. 99, 113, *265*, 453, 456, 458
Cassel, G. 333, *359*
Chaloner, W. R. *302*
Chamberlan 45, 115
Chandler, A. D. 117, *134*
Chandler Jr. A. D. *287, 301*
Cho, Y. J. *289, 304*
Churchill, W. *514f.*, 529
Cipolla, C. M. *302*
Clapham, J. H. *288, 301*
Cohn 453
Coing, H. *470, 499*
Colli, G. *540*
Collingwood 521
Colm, G. 36ff., 45ff., *48*
Commons, J. R. 110, 118, 128, *134*
Comte, A. 6, 21, 146, 455, 522

INDEX OF NAMES

Cornforth, M. 526ff.
Cournot, A. 111f., 116
Cox, H. *134*
Croce 522
Croner, F. 29
Crouzet, F. *302*

Dahms, H. F. *313, 321, 342, 359*
Dankwardt, H. 470-494, 498, *500*, 504
Darwin, Ch. 103, 559
Davidson, D. 450ff.
Democritus 523
Demsetz, H. 243, *262*
Descartes, R. 104
Dicey 228
Dickler, R. A. 27, *35, 48f.*
Diesing, P. 95, *134*
Dilthey, W. 510, 521
Dölemeyer *470*
Dopfer, K. *544*
Dore, R. P. *304, 428*
Dörge, F.-W. 101, *134*
Dowe, D. *68, 84*
Dubiel, H. *310, 359*
Dugger, W. M. 130, *134*
Duhem, P. 527
Dühring, E. 68-71
Duménil, G. 297, *301*
Durand, J.-P. *444*
Dürr, E.-W. 100, *134, 196*

Edgeworth 116
Ehrlicher, W. 99, *134*
Eichengreen, B. 132, *134*
Elster, J. *257*
Ely, R. 97, 459

Endemann, F. *470, 500*
Endemann, W. 471, *490, 500*
Engels, F. 64, 68f.
Engels, W. 129, 131
Erhard, L. 37, 57, 79, 81f., *84*, 88, 97, 103, *134*, 248
Esslinger, H. U. *28, 32, 40, 42, 49*
Eucken, R. 96
Eucken, W. 82, 93-147, 156, 193, 212, 221f., 225-229, *231*, 232-235, 237, 239-254, 257, 260, *262f.*, 269f., *404*
Evans, P. 291, *301*

Factor, R. A. *49*
Fehl, U. 100, *136*
Feiler, A. 41
Feldman, G. D. *288, 301*
Ferguson 228
Feyerabend, P. 105, 511
Fischer, T. 127, *136*
Fisher, I. 99
Fitting, H. *481, 490, 500*
Folz, W. J. 99, *136*
Frei, Ch. *263, 265*
Fremdling, R. *288, 301*
Freud, S. 328, 513
Frey, B. S. 255, *261, 263*
Friedman, M. 99, 105, 122, *136*
Friedrich, C. J. 120, *136*
Fries, J. F. 79
Fukuyama, F. 15, *200*, 558
Fukuzawa, Y. 419, *424*
Fullarton 99
Furubotn, E. G. 242, *263*
Fuss, F. *60, 84*

INDEX OF NAMES

Gadamer, H.-G. 95, 104, *136*, 510
Ganz, P. *540*
Gårdlung, T. *452*
Garvy, G. 36f., 40, *49*
Gasset, O. Y. 101
Gebhardt, E. *347*
Georg, H. 87
George, H. 59, 63, *71*, 454
Gerken, L. 130, *136*
Gerloff 107
Gerschenkron, A. 287, 289, *302*
Gerth, H. H. *317, 361*
Gestrich 122, 127
Gibbons 411
Gide, Ch. *371*
Giedymin, J. 523
Gierke, O. von 150, 470, 490-499, *500*, 504f.
Giersch, H. 99, *137, 206, 213*
Gijuku, K. *419*
Gille, B. 288, 302
Gilpin, R. 297
Giovannini, N. 28, *285, 302f.*
Gitterman, J. M. *63*
Glaser, E. *315, 359*
Goethe 110
Goldschmidt, L. *469*, 471, *481*, 490, *500*
Gombrich, E. *513*
Görgens, E. *269*
Gossen 109, 111
Gothein, E. 27
Gottl-Ottlinienfeld 97
Götz, H. H. 96
Gourvitch, A. *35, 49*
Graham, B. 122
Gramsci, A. 315

Gray, J. *249, 263*
Greiß, F. 193, *194*, 212, *216*
Greven, M. Th. *58*
Gröner, H. 124, *137*
Grossekettler, H. G. 97, 129, *187, 226*, 248, *263*
Grossmann-Doerth, H. 102, *226*
Grünberg, C. 326, 334
Grunberg, I. 300, *302*
Gumplowicz, L. 70, 75
Gundlach, S.J., G., 52, 371, 373, 390ff., 397-415
Gurley, J. G. 285, *302*
Gustafsson, B. *69, 84*
Gutkowski, A. 207
Gutmann, G. 120, *137*
Guyot, Y. *371*

Haberler 44
Habermas, J. 117, *137*, 191, *313, 350, 359*, 362-365, 510, 515
Hagemann, H. *36f., 41, 44, 49*, 87
Hahn 99
Halasi, A. B. 27
Halm, G. 333, *359*
Hammarskiöld, D. 460
Hansen, K. 129, *137*
Haq, M. U. 132, *137*, 300, *302*
Hardtwig, W. *538*
Harris, A. L. *393*
Haselbach, D. *78, 84*, 97
Hättich, M. *393*
Häuser, K. *537, 539, 542, 545, 548*
Hayek, F. A. von 34, 43f., *49*, 106, 118, 120, 128, 130,

566

INDEX OF NAMES

146, 190, 193, 210, 224-270, 395, 518, *549f., 553f.*
Heckscher, E. 455f., 458
Hegel, G. W. F. 27, 120, 159, 316, 328, 363, 510, 513, 522, 524f.
Heidegger, M. 108
Heilbroner, R. 93, *137*
Heimann, E. *40,* 43, 45, *49, 63,* 77ff., *85, 324*
Held *494*
Helfferich 99
Helleiner, R. 294, *302*
Henriksson, R. *456*
Hensel, K. P.119
Henwood, D. 130, *137*
Herbst, J. 97, *137*
Herkner, H. 28
Herrmann, W. 127, *137*
Herrmann-Pillath, C. 114, *138*
Hertztka, Th. 70ff.
Herzl, T. 59, *60, 85*
Heuss, E. 111, 115, *138, 207*
Heussi, K. 103, *138, 534*
Hicks, Sir John *240, 265*
Higonet, P. *301*
Hildebrandt, B. 94, 107, *476, 501,* 541
Hilferding, R. 26f., 275-308, 314-325, 327ff., 332, 334, 336, *359*
Hitler, A. 46, 147, 336
Hitze, F. 406, 415
Hobson, J. A. *293, 302*
Hoffmann, H. *196, 214*
Hollander, J. 459
Hollingsworth, J. R. *134*
Holzwarth, F. 94, 114, 118, *138*

Hoover, C. *428*
Höpker-Aschoff, H. 193
Hoppmann, E. 127, *138, 244f.*
Horkheimer, M. 311, 314f., 326f., 329f., 332, 334, 337, 339, 344-353, 357, *359f.,* 362f., 365
Horn *469*
Hugo, G. *474, 500*
Hume 228, 237, *257*
Humboldt, W. von *498*
Husserl 104, 114, *229*
Hutchison, T. W. 94, 103, 108, *138, 206, 226, 265, 541, 544*

Ikeda 428
Ikeo, A. *433*
Immenga, W. *207*
Isard, P. 100, *138*
Ishibashi, T. 425ff.
Issing, O. 122, 129, *138*
Itami, T. *441*
Itoh, M. 277, *302, 441*

Jacobini 410,
Jacoby, H. *319, 360*
Jaffé, E. 42
Jahn, G. *485, 493, 500*
Janssen, A. *492, 494, 496, 500*
Jasay, A. de *249, 265*
Jay, M. *310, 360*
Jenni, J. *394*
Jhering, R. von 152, *468,* 470, *480, 500*
Johnson, A. 28
Johnson, D. 108, *138*
Jöhr, W. A. 94, 96f., 106, *138*
Jonung, L. *501f., 456*

INDEX OF NAMES

Justinian 473, 478

Kaehler, A. 34, 45, *48, 50f.*
Kagono, T. *441*
Kaldor, N. *34, 50*
Kalecki, M. 276
Kames 149
Kant, I. 104, 107, *229*, 237, 363, 542
Kaplan, A. 95, *138*
Kapp, K. W. 112, *138*
Kasper, W. *226, 265*
Kaufhold, K. H. *401, 412*
Kaufmann, W. 524f.
Kaul, I. 300, *302*, 558
Kautsky, R. 307, 315
Kawakami, H. 427
Kelly-Holmes, H. *54*
Kelsen, H. 44, *50*
Kemp, T. *288, 302*
Kempski, J. von *214*
Kerrenberg, F. *214*
Ketteler, W. 399, 402, 406, 415
Keynes, J. M. 3f., 8, 16, 37, 65, 119, *202, 441*, 342, 362
Kim, Y. *425*
Kirchgässner, G. *233f., 241, 252, 265*
Kirchheimer, O. 43, 312, *348*, 366
Kirzner, I. M. 114, *138*, 242, *265, 547, 549, 555*
Kishi, S. 428, 432
Klär, K.-H. *79, 85*
Klaus, V. 120, 129, *138*
Kleinewerfers, H. 129, *138*
Kleinheyer, G. *491, 500*
Kleinwächter 98

Kliemt, H. *257, 266*
Kloten, N. 106, 112, 129, *138f.*
Kluke, P. *61, 85*
Klump, R. 103, *139, 206*
Knapp 99, 452
Knies, K. 94, 97, 451, 459, 487, 541
Knight, F. H. 97
Knöppel, V. *477, 500*
Kobayashi, T. *441*
Kocka, J. *134, 469*
Kondratieff, N. 43
Könke, G. *40, 50*
Koopmans, T. C. *139*
Korsch, K. 315f., 326, *360*
Kosai, Y. *435*
Koslowski, P. *213, 389, 401, 535f., 543*
Kosselleck, R *479, 501*
Kotzenberg, K. 61, *62*
Kraft, J. 79
Kriechbaum, M. *543*
Kroeschell, K. *470, 486, 493, 501*
Krohn, C. D. *28, 45, 50*
Kröll, M. 112, 118, *139*
Kruck, W. *78, 83*
Krueger, A. O. 253, *266*
Kühler, P. *58*
Kuhn 105, 511, 527
Kumon, S. *442*
Kumpmann, K. *400, 412*
Kuntze, J. E. *468, 490, 501*
Kurz, H. D. *55, 75, 85*
Lacan, J. *513*
Lachmann, L. M. 97, 114, *138*
Lagler-Messner *214*
Lakatos, I. 105, *139*, 511, 527

INDEX OF NAMES

Lancaster, K. 121, *139*
Landes, D. C. *287,* 288, *301f.*
Landsberg, E. *486, 489, 501*
Lasker, B. *50*
Lasalle 415
Laum, B. 103, *139*
Lautenbach, W. 37
Lechtape, H. *394*
Lederer, E. 26-53
Lederer-Seidler, E. *50*
Lee, R. B. 112
Leffler, J. 454
Leipold, H. 111, *252, 266*
Leist, B. W. *468f., 470, 475,* 480-492, 498, *501*
Lenel, H. O. 94, 96f., 106, 126, 129, *139*
Lenin, V. I. *302*
Leo XIII, Pope 399, 402, 410
Leontief, W. 19, 38, 43, *51*
Lerner, A. P. *198*
Leschke, M. *252, 266*
Lévy, D. 297, *301*
Lévy-Strauss, C. 430
Lexis 453
Lichtblau, K. *535*
Liefmann 98
Lilliestam, . *454*
Lindehl, E. 459
Lindenlaub, D. 102, *139*
Link, W. *79, 85*
Lipsey, R. G. 121, *139*
Locke, J. 190, 228
Lockwood, W. W. *288, 302*
Lowe, A. 34, 36,f., 39, *40, 51, 55, 77, 82, 85*
Löwenthal, L. 311, 362f.
Lowie, R. *64, 85*

Löwy, M. *313, 360*
Loy, C. *242, 266*
Luig, K. *493, 501*
Lukàcs, G. 27, 311, *313,* 315-329, 332, *360*
Lundberg, E. 459
Lundquist, L. 459
Lutz, F. A. 94, 96f., 113, *139,* 146f.
Luxemburg, R. 323

Mach, E. 5, 20, 127
Machlup, F. 106, *139*
MacIntyre, A. 514, *525,* 530, 557f.
Macleod, W. Ch. *64, 85*
Maier, K. F. 109
Mandel, E. 276f., *302*
Mandeville, B. 228, *544*
Mannheim, K. 27, 44, 522
Marcuse, H. 43, 311, 366
Marshak, J. 29f., 33, 36f., 40-44, *47, 51*
Marshall, A. 422, 442
Martin, B. *421*
Martin, H.-P. 131, *139*
Marx, K. 3, 5, 8, 15, 19ff., 26ff., 32, 34, 41, 46f., 104, 120, 196-199, 222, 249, 277-281, 286, *303,* 305, 310-313, 315-336, 342f., 345, 347, 349f., 352-358, *360, 362ff.,* 398, 402, 406, 408, 513, 516, 522, 526
Matsugi, T. *442*
Mayer, H. 116, *140*
Mayer-Iswandy, C. *58*
McCloskey, D. N. 95, *140*

INDEX OF NAMES

Means 124
Meijer, G. 122, *140*
Meiners, R. E. *537, 541*
Menger, C. 5, 10, 26, 43, 94, 99, 104, 106, 228f., *452, 536f., 541,* 547-556
Merklein, R. *207*
Mermillod 410
Messner, J. *405*
Mestmäcker, E.-J. 124, *140, 233, 245, 266*
Meuter, H. *214*
Meyer, F. W. 99, 103, *136, 194, 216*
Meyer, R. *407, 412*
Miaskowski *493*
Michels, R. 44
Mierendorff, C 41.
Miksch, L. 98, 126, *140, 245, 266*
Milberg, W. 93, *137*
Milglom, P. *438*
Mill, J. S. 6, 228, 256, *266*
Mills, C. W. *317*
Milward, A. *288, 303*
Mises, L. von 34, 43, *51,* 97, 99, 120, *227,* 228
Mishkin, F. S. 99, *140*
Mitnitzky, M. 42, 45
Mitscherlich 107
M ller, H. 109, *140*
Molsberger, J. 96, *140*
Montinary, M. *540*
Moreau, H. *394*
Morgenstern, O. *44*
Morris, W. 454
Möschel, W. 129, *140, 207, 229, 245, 266*

Mozetič, G. 70, *85*
Mueller, F. H. *394*
Mulcahy, R. E. *394*
Müller, A. 405
Müller-Armack, A. 24, 97, 129, *140,* 192, 223, 225, *266*
Murakami, Y. 420, 422f., 427f., 442
Musgrave, A. 105
Mussler, W. *233*
Mussolini 147, 336
Myrdal, G. 459, 461

Nakasone 428
Nardinelli, C. *537, 541*
Nau, H. 297, *303*
Nawroth, E. E. *140*
Nef, R. *263, 265*
Neisser, H. 34, 36f., 40, 45, *51*
Nell-Breuning, O. von S.J. 371, *394, 397, 400, 405,* 406, *412,* 414f.
Nelson, L. 79f.
Nelson, R. R. 290, *303*
Neuling, W. 109, *140*
Neumann, F. 312, 315, 343ff., 347f., 357-358, *360,* 366
Neumark, F. 79
Neurath, O. 26
Newburger, H. *288, 303*
Nicholls, A. J. *83, 85*
Niehans, J. *552*
Nienhaus, V. *256, 266*
Nietzsche, F. 455, 538, 540
Nipperdey, T. *538*
Nörr, K. W. *188, 495, 501*
North, D. C. *266*

INDEX OF NAMES

Oakeshott, M. 518
Oberender, P. 103, *140*
Oexle, O. G. *498, 501, 534, 538*
Ohira 428
Ohlin, B. 455, 459
Okazaki, T. *428, 439f.*
Okuno, M. *440*
Oliver, H. *226, 266*
Olson, M. 253, *266*
Oppenheimer, F. 28, 44, 54-89, 97
Oswalt, W. 130, *140*
Oswalt-Eucken, I. 108, 125, *141*
Ott, A. 116, *141*
Ott, C. *141*
Ottel, F. 125, *141*

Pack, H. 290, *303*
Palyi, M. 99, *141, 143*
Pankoke, E. *496, 501*
Paquè, K.-H. *206, 213*
Pareto, V. 21, 106, 127
Patinkin, D. *37, 51*
Patrick, H. *440*
Paul VI, Pope *405*
Peacock, A. 129, *133, 141, 145,* 158, *161, 226f.*
Pejovich, S. 242, *263*
Penz, R. 129, *141*
Pesch, S.J., H. 371-396, 399f., 406, *412,* 414
Peter, H. 79, *141*
Peters, H.-R. 107, *141*
Peters, J. *407*
Peukert, H. 94, 103f., 112f., 116f., 120, 130, *141*
Philippovich, E. von 26
Pigou 44

Pius XI 397, 404
Pius XII, Pope 397
Plato 107, 391, 512, 518, 523
Plessner, H. 214, 221
Pohle 98f.
Polanyi, K. 43, 127, *141*
Pollock, F. 309-367
Popper, K. R. 105, *198, 238,* 250, *267,* 509-533, *539,* 547
Postone, M. *312, 351,* 353-356, *361,* 364
Powers, C. H. *555*
Preiser, E. *80f.,* 87
Priddat, B. P. 129, *141*
Prychitko, D. L. 114, *133*
Putnam 511

Quine, V. V. O. 513, 527

Raab, F. 103, *142*
Ramb, B.-Th. 265
Ramstad, Y. 110, *142*
Ranke, L. von *486, 498*
Rathenau, W. 40, 119
Raulet, G. *534, 538, 543*
Rauscher, A. *397, 407, 412*
Reagan, R. 16
Recktenwald, H. C. *145*
Reder, F. *394*
Reheis, F. 130, *142*
Renner, A. 130, *136*
Reuter, D. *207*
Ricardo, D. 34, 104f., 113, 451f., 544
Richter, R. *142, 537, 541f., 546f., 552f.*
Rittstieg, H. 124, *142*
Robbins, Lord 241

INDEX OF NAMES

Roberts, J. *438*
Roberts, W. F. *71*
Robinson 115
Rodbertus-Jagetzow, K. *407, 412*
Rohlen, T. P. *442*
Roosevelt, Th. 336
Röpke, W. 44, 82, 106, 108, *142,* 193, *203, 208,* 209
Rorty, R. 530
Roscher, W. 94, 96, 101, 104, *142,* 386, 471ff., *475,* 476ff., 480f., 485, 487ff., *491, 501f.,* 504, *548*
Rosovsky, H. 301, *442*
Roth, G. *325*
Rothacker, E. *534*
Rousseau, J. J. 190
Rückert, J. *474, 479, 483, 493, 501f.*
Ruggie, J. G. *303*
Runge, U. 127, *142*
Rupp, H. H. *256, 267*
Rüsen, J. *534*
Ruskin, J. 454
Russel 513
Rüstow, A. *65, 75, 86,* 87, 123, *203, 208,* 209
Rutherford, M. 96, *142*
Ryle, G. 525

Sakakibara, K. *441*
Sally, R. 225, *226,* 229, *246, 267*
Salomon, A. 45, *50*
Salomon-Delatour, G. 76f., *86*
Samuelson, P. A. 19, *21,* 43, *51,* 455
Sandelin, B. *456*

Sapir, J. *436*
Sato 428
Saul, S. B. *288, 303*
Savigny, E. C. von 468, 470, 473, *474,* 479f., 484f., 489, 492, *502*
Sawai, M. *435*
Schachtschabel, H. G. 107, *142*
Scheel, W. 212
Schefold, B. *55, 60, 78, 82, 84ff.,* 129, *142*
Scheler, M. 214, 221
Schellschmidt, H. 129, *142*
Scherer, F. M. 116, 126, *142*
Schiera, T. *501*
Schlecht, O. 129, *142*
Schmidt, C. A. 493, *494,* 497, *502*
Schmidt, K.-H. 97, *142, 555*
Schmidtchen, D. *142, 242, 267*
Schmieding, H. *206, 213*
Schmitt, C. 66, 101, 146, 191
Schmitz, M. *58*
Schmölders, G. *537*
Schmoller, G. von 5, 7, 9-14, 21, *22,* 26, 28, 61, 95, 98, 100, 103f., 106f., 110, 114-118, 123, 125, 127ff., 131, *142f.,* 147, 151, 189, 229, 389, 453f., 463, *476,* 491, 496f., *502,* 536f., 541-550, 552-556
Schneider, D. 118, *143*
Schneider, E. 109, *143*
Scholtz, G. *535*
Schopenhauer, A. 525
Schröder, J. *491, 500*
Schüller, R. 43

572

INDEX OF NAMES

Schumacher, E. F. 97, *130*
Schumann, H. 117, 131, *139*
Schumann, J. *143*
Schumpeter, A. 75
Schumpeter, E. B. *321*
Schumpeter, J. A. 3-26, 28, 32, 42f., 47, *51*, 87, 94, 99, 101, 106, 122, 130, *143*, 196f., 199, 225, 244, 247, *267, 321, 361*, 402, *412*
Schwarte, J. *397, 412*
Seidler, E. 27, 31
Seligman, E. R. A. 97, *143*
Senior 544
Senn, M. *502*
Senn, P. R. 97, *143*
Sering, M. 389
Shackle, G. 114
Shaikh, A. 279, 297, *303*
Shaw, E. S. 285, *302*
Sherman, H. J. 128, *143*
Shimizu, K. *445*
Shionoya, Y. *3, 5f., 8, 10, 12, 22f.*
Simmel, G. *61*, 77, *321, 361*
Simons, H. C. 122, 130, *143*
Smith, A. 105ff., 110, 120, 124, *143*, 149, 228, 316, 375, *542*
Socrates 520
Sohn-Rethel, A. 41
Sombart, W. 37, 42f., 97, 105, 107, 109f., 113, *143*, 400, *412*
Sorel, G. 66,
Sorokin, P. A. *64, 86*
Soros, G. 24, 131, *143, 510f.*
Spann, O. 97, 105
Speier, H. 29, *40,* 45f., *47*

Spencer, H. 103
Spengler, O. 127, 522
Spiethoff, A. 44, 107, 109f.
Spindler, H. *496, 502*
Stackelberg, H. 106f., 109, 115f., *143*
Ståhlberg *451, 456*
Stammler, R. 468, 498f., *502*
Starbatty, J. *195*
Staudinger, H. 31, 40, 46, *50f.*
Steffen, G. 454f., 457
Stein, L. von 191, 413
Steinbrück, K. *143*
Steindl, J. 276
Stern, W. M. *302*
Sternberg, F. 77
Stigler, G. J. 117, *143*
Stiglitz, J. *289,* 290, *303*
Stokes, H. H. *286, 301*
Stolper, G. 98, *144*
Stolper, W. F. *28, 51*
Streissler, E. W. 122, 129, *144, 207, 549, 551*
Streit, M. E. 129, *144,* 225, *226, 233, 235,* 236, *241,* 243, 245, 249, 255, 257, *258,* 259, *265, 267f.*
Strieder, J. *412*
Strindberg, A. 452, 454
Stutz, R. *502*
Strubl, G. 127, *144*
Stützel, W. *144*
Sundbårg, G. 456f.
Sweezy, P. M. 20, 275ff., 284, *288, 301, 303, 317, 359*

Tarnow, F. 41
Tarski 513

INDEX OF NAMES

Tavares, M. C. *303*
Tenbruck, F. H. *144*
Tenfelde, K. *68, 84*
Teranishi, S. *440*
Thatcher, M. 16
Thieme, H. J. *265*
Thöl, H. 471
Thucydides 107
Tiburtius, J. 77
Tietzel, M. *242, 252, 268*
Tilly, R. *288, 301, 303*
Tinbergen, J. *198*
Tobin, J. 132, 300, *303*
Tollison, R. D. 234, *268*
Tönies, F. 44, *61*
Tooke 99
Toynbee, A. 522
Troeltsch, E. 536, 557-560
Tuchtfeldt, E. 120, 129, *144, 196, 267*
Tugan-Baranowsky, M. 42
Tullock, K. 255, *262*
Tumlir, J. *188*

Uhr, C. G. *451*
Ulpianus 157
Uy, M. *289, 303*

Vanberg, V. 224, *238, 246,* 248, *252,* 254, *268*
Varian, H. R. 106, *144*
Vaughn, K. E. 228, *268*
Veblen, Th. 128
Veit, R. 109, *144*
Vittas, D. *289, 304*
Vitts, E. H. 193
Vleugels, W. *144*
Voeller, J. *144*

Vogelsang, K. von 405, 410
Vogt, B. *60, 78, 83, 86*
Voigt, S. *249, 252, 256, 268f.*
Wade, R. *289, 293, 304*
Wagemann, E. 37, 97, 99
Wagner, A. 61, 389, 400, 453f., 459, 491
Wagner, R. E. 255, *262*
Wagner, V. F. 98, 102, *144*
Walker, D. A. *263*
Wallich, H. C. 119, *144*
Walras, L. 3, 5, 104
Walter, F. 505
Watkins, J. 511, *513*
Watrin, Chr. 129, *144, 194, 196, 207, 212, 216*
Webb, B. 42
Webb, S. 42
Weber, A. 27f., 31, 42
Weber, M. 5, 10, 20f., 28, 42f., *51,* 52, 97, 107, 110, 112, 121, 127, 204, 222, 240, 311-325, 328-332, 346, 348, *361,* 365, 375f., *489, 502,* 555f.
Weber, R. L. 121, *144*
Weber, W. *405*
Wegner, G. 126, *144,* 245, *268*
Weil, F. 43, 366
Weinberger, O. *394*
Weippert, G. 105, 117, *144*
Weisser, G. 107, *144,* 193
Wellmer, A. *348, 361*
Welter, E. 96f., *145*
Wendt, S. 97, *145*
Wicksell, K. 99, 255, *269,* 452f.
Wieacker, F. *493, 502*

INDEX OF NAMES

Wieser, F. von 4, 26, 107, *145*
Wiggershaus, R. *311*, 334f., 337, *344, 348, 361*
Wilkop, H. 129
Willgerodt, H. 129, *133, 141, 145*, 158, *161*, 194, *207, 226*, 266f.
Williamson 117
Winch, P. 523
Wiseman, J. 124, *145*
Witt, U. *238, 269*
Wittfogel, K. A. 43
Wittich *325*
Wittkau, A. *468, 498, 503, 535, 536, 543, 555*
Wohlgemuth, M. 131, *144, 226*, 228, 253, *255*, 259, *269*
Wolfren, K. van *423*
Woll, A. 129, *145*
Woo, J.-E. *289, 304*
Woytinsky, W. 37, 41
Wundt, W. 455
Wünsche, H. F. 82, *86*, 103, *145, 206*

Yagi, K. *433, 442*
Yamada, T. *435*
Yamanouchi, Y. *431*
Yanagita, K. 431
Yeager, L. 100, *145*
Yoshida 428

Žižek, S. 513
Zoninsein, J. 278, *289*, 290, *304*
Zweig, K. 129, *145*
Zysman, J. *288, 304*

Studies in Economic Ethics and Philosophy

P. Koslowski (Ed.)
Ethics in Economics, Business,
and Economic Policy
X, 178 pages. 1992
ISBN 3-540-55359-2 (out of print)

P. Koslowski and Y. Shionoya (Eds.)
The Good and the Economical: Ethical Choices
in Economics and Management
X, 202 pages. 1993
ISBN 3-540-57339-9 (out of print)

H. De Geer (Ed.)
Business Ethics in Progress?
IX, 124 pages. 1994
ISBN 3-540-57758-0

P. Koslowski (Ed.)
The Theory of Ethical Economy
in the Historical School
XI, 343 pages. 1995
ISBN 3-540-59070-6

A. Argandoña (Ed.)
The Ethical Dimension
of Financial Institutions and Markets
XI, 263 pages. 1995
ISBN 3-540-59209-1 (out of print)

G. K. Becker (Ed.)
Ethics in Business and Society
Chinese and Western Perspectives
VIII, 233 pages. 1996
ISBN 3-540-60773-0

P. Koslowski (Ed.)
Ethics of Capitalism and Critique
of Sociobiology. Two Essays with
a Comment by James M. Buchanan
IX, 142 pages. 1996
ISBN 3-540-61035-9

F. Neil Brady (Ed.)
Ethical Universals in International Business
X, 246 pages. 1996
ISBN 3-540-61588-1

P. Koslowski and A. Føllesdal (Eds.)
Restructuring the Welfare State
Theory and Reform of Social Policy
VIII, 402 pages. 1997
ISBN 3-540-62035-4 (out of print)

G. Erreygers and T. Vandevelde
Is Inheritance Legitimate?
Ethical and Economic Aspects
of Wealth Transfers
X, 236 pages. 1997
ISBN 3-540-62725-1

P. Koslowski (Ed.)
Business Ethics in East Central Europe
XII, 151 pages. 1997
ISBN 3-540-63367-7

P. Koslowski (Ed.)
Methodology of the Social Sciences, Ethics, and
Economics in the Newer Historical School
From Max Weber and Rickert
to Sombart and Rothacker
XII, 565 pages. 1997
ISBN 3-540-63458-4

A. Føllesdal and P. Koslowski (Eds.)
Democracy and the European Union
X, 309 pages. 1998
ISBN 3-540-63457-6

P. Koslowski (Ed.)
The Social Market Economy
Theory and Ethics of the Economic Order
XII, 360 pages. 1998
ISBN 3-540-64043-6

Amitai Etzioni
Essays in Socio-Economics
XII, 182 pages. 1999
ISBN 3-540-64466-0

P. Koslowski (Ed.)
Sociobiology and Bioeconomics
The Theory of Evolution in Biological
and Economic Theory
X, 341 pages. 1999
ISBN 3-540-65380-5

J. Kuçuradi (Ed.)
The Ethics of the Professions:
Medicine, Business, Media, Law
X, 172 pages. 1999
ISBN 3-540-65726-6

S. K. Chakraborty and S. R. Chatterjee (Eds.)
Applied Ethics in Management
Towards New Perspectives
X, 298 pages. 1999
ISBN 3-540-65726-6

P. Koslowski (Ed.)
Contemporary Economic Ethics and
Business Ethics
X, 267 pages. 2000
ISBN 3-540-66665-6

Printing: Weihert-Druck GmbH, Darmstadt
Binding: Buchbinderei Schäffer, Grünstadt